AM   ,
we i.   alk

AMERICA,
we need to talk

A SELF-HELP BOOK
FOR THE NATION

(Or, Why Americans Should Stop Blaming Politicians and Take
Personal Responsibility for Fixing Our Country)

JOEL BERG

SEVEN STORIES PRESS

New York • Oakland • London

Seven Stories Press
140 Watts Street
New York, NY 10013
www.sevenstories.com

College professors and high school and middle school teachers may
order free examination copies of Seven Stories Press titles. To order,
visit www.sevenstories.com/textbook or send a fax on school letterhead
to (212) 226-1411.

Book design by Jon Gilbert

Library of Congress Cataloging-in-Publication Data

Names: Berg, Joel, author.
Title: America, we need to talk : a self-help book for the nation / Joel Berg.
Description: A Seven Stories Press first edition. | New York : Seven Stories
    Press, 2017.
Identifiers: LCCN 2016050942 | ISBN 9781609807290 (paperback)
Subjects: LCSH: Political participation--United States. | Political
    culture--United States. | Responsibility--Political aspects--United
    States. | BISAC: POLITICAL SCIENCE / Public Policy / General. | POLITICAL
    SCIENCE / Government / National. | SELF-HELP / Motivational &
    Inspirational.
Classification: LCC JK1764 .B464 2017 | DDC 320.60973--dc23
LC record available at https://lccn.loc.gov/2016050942.

Printed in the USA

9 8 7 6 5 4 3 2 1

FOR MY GRANDPARENTS
Pauline, Harry, Ethel, and Louis, who shed the tongues, friends, and customs of their birth countries, and who rewarded their children and grandchildren—and their adopted nation—with the gifts of their sacrifices.

Their advice, both heeded and unheeded, could have filled a Library of Congress-sized warehouse of self-help books.*

---

* My paternal grandfather's original surname was Berkowitz, but he changed it to "Berg" soon after arriving at Ellis Island, because he thought "Berg" sounded more American.

Contents

AMERICA, WE NEED TO TALK.

Yes, *that* kind of talk.

I know it's after midnight, and I know you have to go to work early in the morning, but this just can't wait.

I don't know how to say this, so I'll just say it: I am deeply unhappy with this relationship and I have been for years. I love you, but I'm no longer *in* love with you, America.

This just isn't working for me. I'm hurt and I'm angry. You've betrayed, ignored, and humiliated me. You've lied to me and cheated on me.

My knee-jerk reaction is to leave you. But we have so much shared history. We have children together. I like your taste in music. Plus, it's in our economic and social self-interest to stay together. And besides, I hate hockey and Céline Dion songs, so Canada is out of the question.* ABBA and pickled fish make Sweden unlivable, despite its advanced social programs.

Both you and I know that I won't—I *can't*—leave you. I can't ignore all that you've given me in the past. You and I are destined for each other. I can't live happily without my own country and you can't continue to exist without me as your happy citizen.

And, despite all your flaws, America, you are still one of the most diverse, welcoming, and freest nations on the planet.

So that's why I'm going to stay with you and fight to make this work.

You're asking me what you did wrong? You're kidding, right? You must know. How could you screw up as badly and frequently as you have and think this day would never come? How could you have ignored the signs of my growing unhappiness?

---

* In fairness, though, Canada has a lot going for it, including the best side of Niagara Falls, universal healthcare, stand-in movie locations, poutine, and Second City Television.

(Long pause. Deep silence. America shuffles its feet and glances at the TV.)

Oh come on, you mean to tell me that you haven't noticed that you're seriously broken? You've totally lost your senses. You are so far off-track that you're beyond derailed.

Well, what do you have to say for yourself?

(Another long pause. America turns off the TV and sighs.)

If you don't know, I'm not going to tell you.

(A pause that seems longer than Gone with the Wind. *A silence quieter than a monastery. A nervous cough. An exaggerated sigh.)*

But then again, if I don't tell you, this book won't exist and we have no future together. Are you ready?

(Sheepish nod.)

Okay, here goes. Let's start with this: does the name "government shutdown" mean anything to you? Don't play dumb. Don't act like you don't remember. Don't even make me take out my massive scrapbook of news clips.

Yes, *that* government shutdown. You know, the one in which you allowed a handful of extremists, in a rabid hissy fit, to padlock your entire government, supposedly to protest paying the bills for things that those very same extremists previously voted to fund? Oh, *now* you remember? I thought so. You have a pretty short attention span, so I also hope that you recall that the shutdown closed national parks, shuttered medical research facilities, idled Alaskan fishing fleets, delayed flights, and furloughed nearly a million workers.

Do you remember when a fanatical, right-wing congressman, Randy Neugebauer, who forced all government facilities to close, then went to DC's World War II Memorial to stage a media stunt in front of visiting veterans in which he berated a park ranger for shutting down the very same memorial that he, the fanatical, right-wing congressman, Randy Neugebauer, forced to close?* America, do you remember that Standard & Poor's—not exactly a leftist institution—calculated that the shutdown took $24 billion out of your economy? Yes, it was a $24 billion political temper tantrum. Oh, so it's all

---

* Randy Neugebauer (R-TX) scolding a park ranger by saying, "The Park Service should be ashamed of themselves." Mark Segraves, "Congressman Confronts Park Ranger Over Closed WWII Memorial," NBC TV News4, Washington, DC, October 3, 2013.

coming back to you now, is it? Our political system is now as dysfunctional as Italy's, but with far less tasty food.

And then in the 2014 midterms, you totally lost your mind, America. Even though you were furious at the gridlock and knew deep down that the Republicans caused most of it—you actually voted to give those same Republicans still more power. You went apeshit, angrily tossing your car keys to the same people who just totaled your new car, yelling at them, "You wrecked it, assholes, so now it's yours." Yes, out of a twisted spite, you gave our country to those who harmed it most.

By 2016, America, you let the anger boiling within many of your residents be channeled into an even crazier, even more self-destructive force by handing over the presidential nomination—and complete control over—one of the nation's two great political parties to mega-wealthy and mega-buffoon reality TV star Donald J. Trump, who was more laughably/dangerously unqualified for the job—based on skills, experience, temperament, and every other possible criteria—than any major party nominee in US history. Now get this: tens of millions of working class people were conned into believing that very worst exemplar of the self-serving crony capitalism that shafted them for decades was the very savior needed to "Make America Great Again." You shredded both your soul and your mind at the same time, America. I couldn't recognize you anymore.

Also in 2016, not content to simply shut down the executive branch, the Senate GOP effectively dropped the curtain on the judicial branch as well, refusing to so much as consider any Obama nominee to fill the Supreme Court seat of the late Justice Antonin Scalia, even after the President nominated Merrick Garland, a highly moderate, impeccably credentialed jurist. Fulminating that Obama was a lame duck who didn't deserve to select a justice, conservatives ignored the fact that Democrats had previously unanimously confirmed Reagan appointee Anthony Kennedy to the Supreme Court in an election year. Republicans would surely excoriate any coach who'd quit a game at the start of the fourth quarter, but they openly quit their Constitutional responsibility to review judges at the start of Obama's fourth quarter.

And, while your Republicans are most to blame for the mess in DC and in statehouses, America, your Democrats of the last 15 years have been mostly gutless, soulless, and ineffective. They've even acted like they're embarrassed by their successes. They could give cowardice lessons to George Costanza. While Republicans may cast no shadows, if they did, Democrats would be afraid of them.

In 2010, when Democrats were still in charge of the White House and Congress, they were too timid to pass key budget and debt ceiling bills, so it was their lily-livered refusal to act that created the opening for the Republicans to later slam shut the government.

The Republicans need hearts, but the Democrats need spines.[*]

At the end of 2015, Congressional Democrats, in exchange for a Republican concession to an extension of vital tax credits for low-income working Americans, agreed to extend truly indefensible Republican tax cuts for the wealthy. As part of the same deal, Congress passed a bill to keep the government running for the rest of the year. Both sides had a tacit understanding that most Democrats would vote against the tax cuts for the rich, satisfying their base, while most Republicans would vote against the spending, satisfying *their* base. All in all, the deal exploded the deficit and boosted inequality. The only time the parties seem to agree is when they jointly do something harmful—or cowardly.

It's no shock that your Democratic presidential primary voters finally rose against these sellouts through their support of Senator Bernie Sanders. But Sanders and his supporters too often eschewed realistic discussions of the costs, policy pitfalls, and political difficulties associated with many of his most ambitious proposals, instead pining for a pie-in-the-sky "revolution." Even progressive, Nobel Prize-winning economist Paul Krugman said Sanders's numbers just didn't add up, calling them "fairy dust."[1] I'm all for idealism and thinking big, but unless coupled with a fact-based game plan for making dreams a reality, the end result will be failure, and ultimately, more cynicism and apathy. America, merely venting your rage in scattershot protest votes won't solve our most pressing troubles.

Your problems, America—and those of the world—are deep, struc-

---

* House Democrats showed true backbone in June 2016 in their gun safety sit-down protest, but it was unclear whether that was the start of a long-term trend of increased Democratic assertiveness.

tural, and too often everyone's collective fault. Neither political party seriously questions why, every time there is so much as a security hiccup overseas (even in countries most Americans can't find on a map), the US government feels it has no choice but to spend billions of tax dollars on drones to bomb lots of tents—and even some hospitals— so long as that country's people have darker skin than those of white Americans. Even peacenik candidate Sanders repeatedly spouted vague language about the need to use military force to "crush and destroy ISIS."[2] Democrats occasionally opt for diplomacy, as in Iran, and that's a welcome bit of sanity, but before you can say Raytheon, the US is off bombing some new land again. And, on top of that, because, America, you're so scared witless by foreign threats—even if, statistically, those threats pose very little risk to average Americans—you then also voluntarily place US civil liberties (which everyone around the world used to admire) in hock.

Adding yet another level of national insanity, every mass shooting in the US inexplicably results in some states *relaxing* gun laws. In states with Republican-controlled legislatures, the number of laws passed to loosen gun restrictions rose by 75 percent.[3] Texas actually voted to allow guns in mental institutions and some school districts are arming teachers. Despite all that, too many (not just Trump) still find a way to falsely blame all our mass gun deaths on Muslim terrorists or young black men.

America, mass shootings still happen all the time—including 372 in 2015 alone[4]—so don't even try to claim that I shouldn't keep bringing up "the past." Besides, you keep on bringing up stuff that's, like, 225 years old. You go on and on—and on—about the original Constitutional Convention, although you keep leaving out the part about the document they adopted that declared that each African American counted as only three-fifths of a human being. If you keep bringing up ancient history, albeit selectively, don't you *dare* blame me for bringing up things that continue happening every day.

And, no, I *won't* keep my voice down. Our neighbors *already* know. You already humiliated me before the world. That's right, the very country that enacted the first bill of rights, saved Europe from tyranny, welcomed the masses at Ellis Island, and created jazz—the very country that was the envy of the world for generations—has become the pitiable laughing stock of the globe. Thanks for that, America.

And, no, this isn't just an isolated example of your bad behavior.* This isn't just one drunken slip-up in Vegas. It's a pattern. A sordid, dirty pattern. You're not the country I knew when I was young. You've changed.

Are you actually still denying it? You really want *more* examples? Well, here are some more for you:

America, you obliterated our economy, eviscerated the middle class, exploded the number of people in poverty, and plundered the savings and homes of tens of millions of working people—all the while making the billionaires even billionaire-ier. Apparently, that was all going on behind my back for decades, but I didn't find out about it until the 2008 Wall Street collapse, which left green lipstick stains on your collar.

But did you punish the plutocrats—and their lackeys in elected and appointed offices—who did this to us? Nooo! You didn't even have the guts to stop golfing with them. What did you do? You actually snuck around behind my back and gave them even more money and more power. The massive "Cromnibus" budget bill, which both parties in Congress passed in the dead of the night at the end of 2014**— without any serious debate—eliminated a regulatory restraint on big banks engaging in the same risky trading that tanked the economy in 2008, thereby gutting a key provision of the Dodd-Frank Wall Street regulation bill that passed Congress after the economic collapse. Massachusetts Senator Elizabeth Warren said the cave-in would again let Wall Street "gamble with taxpayer money."[5] Rather than own up to what they had done, key leaders shamefully claimed that the loosened Wall Street regulations were actually meant to help farmers more easily get credit. Yeah sure, history proves that the well-being of American farmers has always been the top concern of massive banks. Wanna buy a bridge? Not only that, the same stealthy Cromnibus deal actually

* We are a nation of Nick Noltes.
** Washington often makes up complicated sounding words, meaningless to the general public, to obfuscate their own actions (and inactions). The so-called "Cromnibus" bill was a case in point. It was a catch-all spending bill, passed in one giant package that probably no one read, because Congress failed to do its job and neglected to pass multiple, department-specific spending bills each year (how the system is supposed to work).

increased the amount of money the mega-rich could give to political parties, raising the amount that individuals could donate to $777,600 from the previous $97,200 limit. Thank goodness for that change— the paltry $97,200 donation limit must have been really cramping the style of uber-donors. On top of that, in a move that benefitted no one except highly-compensated defense contractors, the bill also provided funding for yet another undeclared war (this one against ISIS) in the Middle East, to the tune of another $64 billion, an amount that equaled 128 *years* of funding for free summer meals for low-income American kids.

You're *still* letting the plutocrats push you around, America, and tell you what to do. You're even giving them your votes. When will you figure out those guys are *not* your real friends?

The very mix of power, arrogance, wealth, and incompetence that so grievously harmed you and the global economy in 2008 is still ruining the country and the world today. The system is *still* rigged.

As has been the case since the Reagan era, our kids will likely do *less* well than we did.

So yes, America, it is all *your* fault.

You let them do this to us.

Not only have you and your buddies given us the highest rates of hunger[6] and homelessness in the western industrialized world, but instead of using your vast wealth to fix those and other pressing problems that tear at our civic fabric, you've squandered our inheritance on ever more tax cuts for the rich, on corporate welfare for the super-wealthy, and on countless, endless, pointless wars. You allowed climate change to accelerate, threatening the globe and creating such meteorological extremes that you can't tell the difference between the Weather Channel and your worst nightmares. Yet the Republican chair of the US Senate's Committee on Environment and Public Works claimed that he could prove that climate change is a hoax because he could bring one snowball to the Senate floor.*

(America looks at its watch.)

You *still* don't understand? You want more examples? Are you sure you can handle it?

---

* February 26, 2015, Oklahoma Senator Jim Inhofe, Chair of the Committee on Environment and Public Works, with his pet snowball.

Ok, let me lay it out for you.

Let's start with the money. The net worth of the 400 wealthiest Americans in 2015, according to *Forbes*, was $2.34 trillion (yes, *trillion*). According to the US Department of the Treasury, the entire American budget deficit in 2015 was $424 billion. That means that 400 individuals had nearly six times as much money as the entire federal shortfall for a nation of 319 million people.

Yet 48 million Americans were ravaged by food insecurity and couldn't always afford enough food in 2014, according to the US Department of Agriculture. No, I didn't say 48 million Somalis or 48 million North Koreans. I said 48 million *Americans*—your own people—struggling to feed their families. That equals one in six of our neighbors and

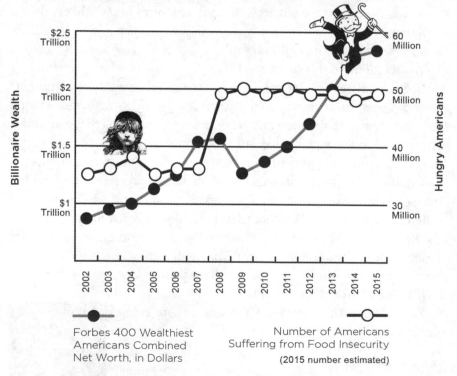

news flash!

THE MEGA-RICH ARE GETTING MEGA-RICHER WHILE THE POOR ARE GETTING HUNGRIER

Forbes 400 Wealthiest Americans Combined Net Worth, in Dollars

Number of Americans Suffering from Food Insecurity
(2015 number estimated)

Source: Forbes and USDA

represents a 55 percent increase overall since 1999. More than 15 million of your children lived in food-insecure homes in 2014, marking a 27 percent increase since 1999. Can you believe that, in the wealthiest nation in the history of the world, one in five of our kids still doesn't always have enough to eat? Yes, your head *should* be hanging in shame.

Our soaring hunger is the most disturbing emblem of our mind-numbing inequality of wealth. As the chart above (yes, I made charts and kept them stashed in our closest to whip out just at this moment) demonstrates, between 2002 and 2013 the combined net worth of the Forbes 400 wealthiest Americans rose by 261 percent, while food insecurity rose by 40 percent. You keep buying yachts instead of paying the child support your children need so they can eat.

Now, America, I know that, as the ultimate foodie nation, you love artisanal pork belly shards nestled in Brooklyn-rooftop-grown mounds of organic baby arugula served with sustainably grown quinoa patties, all for only $20 per ounce. You can't imagine not having enough food and you're clueless to the economic causes of food deprivation within your own borders. So naturally, you think that the answer to hunger is for everyone to grow their own food in their own gardens and then cook it very, very slowly—from scratch—preferably while hosting their own TV cooking shows. That elitist, superficial prescription prevents you from recognizing the deeper structural issues that cause poverty and screw up our agriculture. Why won't you allow yourself to accept that this is about your systemic, societal failings, not about the isolated personal behavior of some of your inhabitants?

In 2014, 46.7 million Americans lived below the meager federal poverty line, which was $19,790 annually for a family of three. Another 14.6 million Americans were "near poor," in families with annual incomes below $24,738.[7] In 2009, five years after economists declared that the recession was officially over, one in five US families lived in—or at the brink of—poverty, making mass destitution the "new normal." No other Western industrialized nation is even close to these high levels of hunger and poverty, even per capita. Those are the facts. Deal with it.

Too many Americans remain unemployed, and many more are under-employed, able to find only part-time work, usually without benefits. The US median family income in 2014 was $53,657, down from

$54,462 in 2013, despite the rising cost of living. Calculating for infla-tion, the median American family in 2014 had $3,700 *less* in income in 2014 than in 2007.[8] Yet according to Gallup, "adults employed full time in the US report working an average of 47 hours per week, almost a full workday longer than what a standard five-day, 9-to-5 schedule entails . . . Nearly four in 10 say they work at least 50 hours."[9] Your inhabitants are working harder and longer and yet they are earning less, on what feels like a backwards treadmill, and you wonder why they are exhausted and angry and tired of you, America?

The key factors that threaten the middle class—too few full-time jobs and low wages, combined with high costs for housing, healthcare, edu-cation, food, and childcare—are the very same factors causing poverty.

America, I *know* you and I'll bet you're *still* going to blame people for their own poverty, despite the facts. You keep listening to that crap from your gym buddy, Paul Ryan. You're going to say that anyone who needs SNAP (formerly known as food stamps) benefits is a lazy bum, so you want to take even that meager help *away* from families. Even though it was you and your pals who enacted the policies that sunk our economic ship, you want to take away life preservers from the drowning. Chutzpah.

I'm sure you assume that most poor American families are impov-erished for long, continuous periods of time, often over multiple generations, but that's just not the case for most people who experi-ence poverty on your shores, America. In the 48 months spanning the years 2009 to 2012, only 2.7 percent of your families were poor for all of those 48 months but more than a third (34.5 percent) of all US families experienced poverty in at least *two* of those months.[10] In other words, while only one in 37 Americans were poor the entire four years, more than one in three Americans were poor sometimes. We have met the poor man and she and he is *us*.

And it's simply false to imply that people who suffer from poverty are mostly nonwhite. As has been the case throughout your history, and is the reality today, the plurality of Americans who are poor, receive SNAP, and/or obtain cash welfare are native-born white people. So, your attempts to convince working-class white people that nonwhites are all "takers," stealing the whites' hard-earned tax dollars, is nothing but crass race-baiting.

HOUSING IS INCREASINGLY UNAFFORDABLE
FOR WORKING PEOPLE

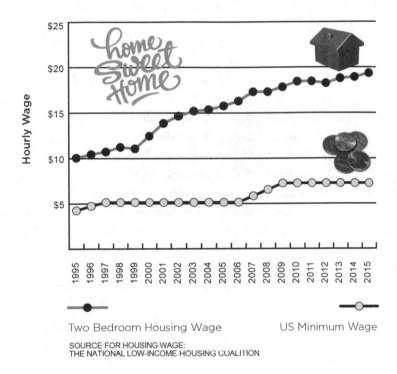

Two Bedroom Housing Wage   US Minimum Wage

SOURCE FOR HOUSING WAGE:
THE NATIONAL LOW-INCOME HOUSING COALITION

(Gets up from the sofa and tries to leave the room.)

Sit the hell down. You asked me for details and I'm giving you details.

The US median income equaled about $26 an hour in 2015. Yet, according to the National Low-Income Housing Coalition, a worker would have needed to earn $19.35 an hour (nearly double the amount of 20 years ago) to pay for an average two-bedroom housing unit nationwide, leaving typical families only seven dollars per hour to pay for every other expense. In no American state could a full-time minimum wage worker afford a one-bedroom or a two-bedroom rental unit at fair market rent.

Yes, I know you don't want to hear so much math this late at night. But tough. This explains why millions of your citizens don't have enough money for the basics. As the chart above demonstrates, the wage needed to afford two-bedroom housing was, in 2015, two-and-a-half times the federal minimum wage. In 1995, a minimum wage salary paid only 42 percent of such average housing costs; by 2015, it paid a paltry 37 percent.

Come on—admit it—if your people are working full time and still can't afford to pay their rent, even you have to agree it's not their fault.

College education—once the best pathway to upward mobility—is now an out-of-reach mirage for most middle-class and poor kids, and even if they can somehow manage it and graduate, they're saddled with a lifetime of debt. For too many, the American dream of going to college, owning a home, and retiring comfortably is now a fiction.

While you always seem to find enough money to build new sports stadiums and arenas, America, you've let your schools, parks, and public housing crumble. Your highways are pothole minefields, and your bridges are on the verge of collapse. Your national railroad—Amtrak—is the little engine that couldn't, breaking down more frequently than other railroads in developing countries but charging princely sums for tickets.

And let me point out that Scandinavia (yes, I *am* bringing up Scandinavia again and holding it over your head, and I will *keep* bringing up Scandinavia again and again until you get the point)—simply doesn't have the inequality, poverty, hunger, and homelessness problems we do. Not only do they have sleek furniture and excellent meatballs, they also have a thriving middle class.* Ditto for many of the rest of our international competitors beyond Scandinavia. Our education is worse than theirs. And our life expectancy is lower. But we've got bigger prison populations and more gun deaths, even per capita. Oh boy! Our public transportation works less well, and is more expensive. Terrific!

Love isn't blind—it's far-sighted. You can't see your lover's imperfections up close. That's why sometimes it takes a trip to parts of Europe and Asia to understand basic social amenities that the US is lacking.

Sadly, though, many of these countries are starting to replicate

---

*

 +  =

(Deliriously happy Scandinavians)

some of our worst mistakes—replacing guaranteed safety nets with underfunded charities and allowing their own inequality of wealth to explode—but that's only because they don't truly understand how bad things are here today.

And yes, this *is* your fault, America. It's not an accident that you fall behind the rest of the developed world on just about every key economic and social indicator. It's not because you are larger or more diverse. It's because your politics and policies stink. It's because, even though history has proven exactly which actions can solve your economic and social problems, you are doing precisely the *reverse*. Insane.

And it's just not your politics that's screwed up, America.

Of course, it would be wrong to blame all these problems on Mexicans and Muslims. Conversely, as culpable as the too-big-to-fail banks and the top 1 percent have been, it's far too facile to pin all the nation's problems on just them.

Every major institution of your society is now corrupt in some way, America. Religious orders and prep schools are havens for pedophiles and cover-ups. Business leaders place personal profit above worker safety and public health. Athletes, coaches, and owners cheat and then cheat some more, at least when they are not busy uttering racist epithets or beating their spouses. Even many so-called nonprofit groups are either outright crooked, or engaged in behaviors, which, while technically legal, are repugnant. Sure, such bad acts have happened in the US (and in every country) for centuries, but the current 24-hour news and social media culture shoves this unscrupulousness in our faces constantly. Of course, many athletes, clergymen, politicians, businesspeople, and nonprofit leaders are honest, model citizens, but the forces of corruption do seem to be seeping into every pore of society.

Take wealthy New York University (NYU), based in the wealthy borough of Manhattan. In order to further boost its income and enhance its status, NYU opened a campus in Abu Dhabi, under the oil-soaked dictatorship of the United Arab Emirates, where stoning and flogging are still legal punishments. After exposés proved that the campus was built by workers paid miserably and housed in absurdly cramped, unsanitary conditions, NYU issued a "statement of labor values" that it said would guarantee fair treatment of workers. Yet even after that, most of the men had to work "11 or 12 hours a day, six or seven days a week, just to earn close to what they had originally been promised . . . Some men lived in squalor, 15 men to a room. The university said there should be no more than four."[12] NYU later apologized to the workers, and promised to compensate them; a year later Human Rights Watch detailed that most of the abuses continued.[13] At the same time, back in New York, NYU gave multimillion-dollar loans to its leaders to finance luxury homes for them in the city. Since all elites apparently need more than one home, NYU even gave eye-poppingly large loans to "executives and star professors for expensive vacation homes in areas like East Hampton, Fire Island, and Litchfield County, Conn., in what educational experts call a bold new frontier for lavish university compensation."[14] In 2015, NYU spent at least $1.1 million to renovate a 4,200-square-foot penthouse duplex for its incoming president with "four bedrooms, four-and-a-half bathrooms, and an expansive rooftop terrace." And other institutions spent far more than NYU: Yale spent $17 million, Vanderbilt spent $6 million, and Columbia University spent more than $20 million to redo their presidential ~~palaces~~ residences.[15] And keep in mind, these are all supposed to be *nonprofit* institutions, which is why they are all exempt from paying taxes. Meanwhile, the full costs to attend each of these four institutions for just *one* year ranged from $61,000 to $75,000 in 2015, compared to the annual American median family income of $52,000.

Is it illegal for university executives to lavish themselves with massive pay and perks while making it nearly impossible for low- and middle-income students to attend their institutions? No, that's all perfectly legal. But it's certainly immoral. Why do they do it? Because they compare themselves economically not to the families of potential students, but to leaders of other universities, who reward themselves similarly, as well as to their ultra-wealthy social peers, some of whom also do unsavory things to get rich and stay rich.

Once one set of societal institutions is corrupt, the decay spreads to others, and we have trickle-down ethical collapse that gives a green light for everyone to declare moral bankruptcy. It's a race to the bottom of the nation's moral sewer. As the movies *The Big Short* and *Spotlight* both demonstrated, society won't allow itself to recognize problems if it is too compromised by self-interest to even look for them.

Yes, this is about national policies, but it is also about national values. Your shallow, narcissistic, selfie culture, America, has made Kim Kardashian far more famous and admired than most Nobel Prize winners, and *Bachelor* contestants better paid than teachers.

Now, let's talk about our sex life.

(America squirms on the couch.)

Yes, sex. Ok, I'm glad you've finally accepted same-sex marriage. That's a start. But I'm not going to let you off the hook until it's actually illegal in all 50 states, Guam, and American Samoa to fire people simply because they are LGBTQ. As of November 2015, employment discrimination against LGBTQ workers remained *legal* in 30 states. And while LGBTQ equality is about far more than sex, it is about sex, too.

Sex. Sex. Sex. It's everywhere you look. Prime time broadcast TV now regularly mentions masturbation, erections, and orgasms. Billboards, magazine covers, and what seems to be about 98 percent of all Internet content are filled with sex, pure sex. America, you are all about S.E.X. You love sex. You hate sex. You are *obsessed* with sex. Sex shames and titillates you. You reward sex (think Paris Hilton) and punish sex (think *Mad Men*'s Peggy Olson). But the punishment is reserved mostly for women.

How else can you explain the US Supreme Court ruling that employers don't have to provide birth control to their female employees? How else can you explain some states making it so difficult to perform abortions that their legislatures have essentially destroyed the guaranteed right to reproductive choice, restrictions that even the right-wing Supreme Court found beyond the pale? How else can you explain that you want women to dress provocatively, but when they do you call them sluts and convince them they deserve the sometimes-terrifying consequences?

Can't you see the obvious? If you love sex and hate sex at the same time, it means that you love yourself and hate yourself at the same time. Talk about a national neurosis. And, no, you can't blame this all on your mother.*

And it's not just money and sex. Can't you see *all* the ways that you've turned against yourself, America,

---

* Although your mother, England, sure does have her own problems with sex. But that's a topic for another book, preferably written by the remaining cast of Monty Python.

tormenting your own heart by failing to live up to your self-professed ideals?

Can't you see how harmful it is that a nation that inspired the world by electing a nonwhite president is now torn apart by racial division and inequality? Can't you see how twisted it is that a nation of immigrants became a nation of immigrant-haters?

Can't you see, America, that since you deluded yourself into believing that you were powerless to go after the bankers who wrecked the nation, you instead went after the only people with less power than you? You joined up with that awful Tea Party crowd to blame middle-class families for losing their own homes, to blame poor people for not working hard enough, and to blame immigrants for trying to better their lives.

Can't you see that the first little blip of progressive pushback—the Occupy movement—capped its own knees by unwittingly adopting the self-defeating position that government couldn't solve our problems? People who considered themselves left-wing anarchists ended up advancing the main contention of conservatism—that government action is virtually always problematic and virtually never a solution to social ills.

America, can't you see that you've been conned into believing that nonprofit groups and state and local governments are always more responsive and effective than the federal government?

Can't you grasp, America, how utterly hypocritical it is that you claim to hate any and all government programs even as your very way of life and well-being depend heavily upon a host of government programs?

Can't you see that your obsession with pouring ice water over your head is distracting you from being outraged that Congress cut funding for medical research?

Can't you see that the way you are yelling lies on cable TV and social media makes you both coarser and dumber?

Can't you see that your fixations with a few, high-profile controversies (often fabricated ones)—which take on great symbolism but are unrepresentative of national trends—prevent you from understanding that your biggest problems are structural and systematic?*

---

* Starbucks, single-handedly killing Christmas, Western civilization, and all that is true and good.

Can't you see, America, that your economic and moral collapse is killing you—and killing us?

Formerly idyllic small New England towns are now heroin pits. In 2014, the overall US suicide rate reached a 30-year high.[16] American soldiers are now more likely to die from suicide than from battle. Our national prison population is as large as the populace of Philadelphia and black men serve as target practice for racist police, while Americans of all races (but particularly young men of color) shoot each other with numbing regularity. Despite major advances in medicine, life expectancy is actually *decreasing* for non-wealthy Americans.

Can't you see, America, that this is all your fault?!?

(Longest pause ever in your life.)

(Heavy sobbing. Reaches for the Kleenex. More heavy sobbing.)

Remember the good old days? We were great together, you and I. We were the Greatest Generation. We really clicked, didn't we? We cared about each other, right? The sex was great, too, but it was more than that.

We beat the Nazis, wore down the Soviets, preserved national parks, raised productive families, elected responsible public officials, and built the awe-inspiring American middle class. Remember how we did it? We took personal responsibility for ourselves, our families, our country, our world.

Americans of all economic backgrounds and races volunteered to serve in the military. Government was a partner, not a perceived enemy. We paid our fair shares of taxes.

We started innovative businesses, worked hard at our companies, and gave back to our communities. Those who became personally wealthy generally did so by bringing greater wealth to the entire society, producing steel, cars, appliances, and medical devices that improved the standard of living for most Americans. Business leaders paid their workers a living wage, either because they voluntarily agreed to pay themselves less and their workers more, or because they were forced to do so by unions and labor laws.

Now, I fully realize, America, that we never had a truly golden age for all. Even when the broad middle class thrived, you were still deeply scarred by hatred, discrimination, and division. But mass movements began to take on bias based on race, gender, and sexual orientation, and while discrimination wasn't vanquished, we made things better.

Our political leaders were at least slightly more likely to place the good of the country ahead of their own personal interests or the advancement of their political parties. The middle class surged and poverty declined, even as our wealthy enjoyed the highest standard of living in the world.

We had a "win-win society."

Now thanks to you, we have a "heads I win, tails you lose, and either way, I'm moving my company to Panama to avoid taxes" society. A few rich white men try to buy our elections and then rig the economy for their sole benefit, becoming even richer, whether the economy thrives or tanks. Many of these same men bust unions, outsource jobs, and slash wages—sometimes just so that they can own seven vacation homes instead of six. Some of them are the biggest cheerleaders for more war, even though they avoided military service themselves and never in a million years would let their *own* children enlist. And the S.O.B.s in charge pay soldiers so little that, out of all the American households that include at least one soldier, reservist, or guardsman, 620,000 of them (a quarter) must rely on charitable aid from food pantries.[17]

And many of the same people in charge scheme to get away with not paying even the minimal taxes required under current law, taxes which pay for those wars and for your highways, public schools, and other vital functions that benefit them, their families, and all of us.

And the worst part is, you let them get away with it.

The only cause you seem willing to fight for now is your right to party hearty. America, you've given up.

Enough! Take some pride in yourself, America! Stop going out to dinner every night in your sweatpants!

(America sinks more deeply into sofa, cowering.)

But now that I truly think about it, *I* am sorry. It *is* at least 50 percent my fault. OK, maybe more than that. It's not you, it's *us*, America.

You're just a country. We are the citizens that *made* you a country. We are supposed to be *better* than you.

We Americans caused this problem by allowing ourselves to be conned by slick campaign ads and, more frequently, by not voting at all. We citizens choose not to exercise the very rights that much of the world still risks their lives to obtain. Sure, in 2008, we voted for a black man on a white horse that we hoped would fix all our problems, but after he didn't solve every challenge in the first year, we slunk back onto our couches to watch reality TV, play video games, view Internet porn, take naps, and passively hope you would address your own issues without us.

When things got worse, we copped out: we blamed unnamed "politicians" and claimed they were all exactly the same and all crooked and all awful—even though they were the very same people that we had put into office by voting, and more frequently, by not voting. In the 2016 presidential race, *we* upped the ante on nuttiness.

Policymaking in Washington is now more detached from the public will than at any time in modern history because we've *allowed it to be.* We rarely marched in protest. We rarely organized our neighbors to fight back. We rarely so much as wrote a letter of complaint.

We took it all for granted. We were lazy. We were gutless. We gave up.

We blamed you—our country and our leaders—but we never blamed ourselves.

Diverting blame was wrong. *We* were wrong.

(America nods off, exhausted.)

Wake the hell up. I am still talking . . . and thinking.

Now that I think about it even more, it's *both* our faults. The interaction that our citizens have with you, America—and vice versa—really *is* a personal relationship. Like virtually all relationships, this one has its ups and downs, and it can be alternatively loving and abusive. But it's also a relationship so vital to our own collective well-being that it absolutely *must* be saved. There's really no point assigning blame unless you're looking to blow up the relationship entirely, which is something we can't do.

We must all move beyond simply lambasting "the politicians" and the "system" and own up to our own individual roles in letting the nation slide, and our joint obligation to save it. If we take personal responsibility for renewing this relationship, maybe you'll agree to join with me to do the hard work we need to do to fix it.

The America I remember is the love of my life and our relationship is worth fighting for. I think we should go for counseling to sort through our problems. We can yell, cry, do whatever we have to do, just as long as we come back together. The rest of this book is that counseling session.

We *can* do better. We can have better lives than our parents did. We can tackle this, just like our grandparents did. They came together, with the help of the government, to climb out of the Depression and then to fight World War II. We're just as good as them, right? We're just as strong. Just as smart. Plus, we have smartphones and computers that they didn't have. That's got to count for something, right?

Don't give me that crap that it's too late for us, or that our challenges are too big. Our ancestors made the ultimate sacrifices for us. They shed oceans of blood to end slavery, spent decades of the 20th century beating back totalitarianism, and risked death at Selma and countless other protests.

Even today, when buffoons pass for legitimate presidential candidates and our attention spans are disappearing faster than polar bears, there *is* a ray of hope. There *is* a way forward for us.

The stunning political success of the marriage equity movement proves that progressive change *can* still happen if we fight back in strategic, smart ways—using both our hearts and our heads. The recent organizing efforts by fast food employees and farmworkers also show us that idealism and courage are still alive and well. Those are the kinds of sparks and the passions that once made us great. Those are the things I loved most about you. That I still love.

Let's do it, America. Let's fix our country.

Hold me. Love me. Caress me. Strategize with me.

I'm getting hot now. If we work this out, imagine how great it will be to have make-up sex.

1.

No We Can't
Getting to No While Giving In

The church, in Pittsburgh's African American Hill District, was packed to the rafters, and then past them. It was three days before the 2008 general election and a black man stood a better-than-good chance of becoming president. The crowd was overwhelmingly African American, with a handful of white Obama campaign volunteers, such as me, sprinkled throughout. The air was vibrating with expectation and excitement—and a smattering of fear.

Multiple local pastors spoke as the organ churned out a slow, simmering accompaniment, punctuated by a few sharp, loud chords played in unison with particularly impassioned points made by each speaker. The event was billed as a generic get-out-the-vote meeting, not a Barack Obama rally, likely in order to protect the tax status of the church. The orators spoke of history, destiny, the exodus of Egyptian slaves, and reaching the Promised Land. Few so much as mentioned Obama by name. They didn't need to.

The final minister summed up the evening with a sermon that began as quietly as a snowfall and slowly as a mid-August baseball game and concluded like a steam locomotive barreling down a track, with hot coals and billowing smoke and bells clanging loud enough to wake neighbors miles away. "Once there was a man," the pastor intoned, "who was sent to us by God to die on a cross for all our sins and redeem all of humankind. Now there is another man, also sent to us by God, who will also redeem humankind."[1] Yes, he *was* essentially likening Obama to Christ. There wasn't a dry eye in the house, or a person left sitting in the pews. Even the people who entered the sanctuary using walkers rose to their feet. Though I'm a secular Jew, by the time that preacher finished bringing us all to church, I was a *believer*, at least as far as his claim that Obama's election would redeem us all.*

I left the meeting more inspired than ever to spend the next few days volunteering to help get out the vote in Pittsburgh's black neighborhoods.** America, you were making history and I wanted to do my small part.

The neighborhood campaign office, housed in a former synagogue,*** was busier and more upbeat than any campaign office I'd worked in my life. Endless streams of African American volunteers, mostly middle-aged or elderly, came through to happily take away massive piles of literature and yard signs and to bring equally copious mountains of homemade food for the campaign workers.

Going door-to-door for Obama in a black neighborhood was the easiest campaign work I'd ever had in my life. It was like selling ice cream in the Sahara. It was the first—and only—time that I've canvassed neighborhoods where people who opened the doors were happier to see me than I was to see them. I have no doubt they would have warmly welcomed any Obama volunteer, but their shock and joy at seeing a white person working for Obama was unmistakable in their laughter and welcome. No, you didn't need to tell them about the upcoming election. Yes, they *would* be voting on Election Day, and so would their aunties and their great-aunties and every single person in their extended families and social circles.

---

* For the record, I didn't convert to Christianity that day, or any day since, but I still felt connected to the other congregants. This may—or may not—be a picture of me dancing to the choir at that church that night. I was so caught up in the moment that I can't recall.

** Also for the record, I was volunteering for the campaign in my free time, as a private citizen, having taken time off from my day job heading a nonpartisan nonprofit group. As long as I work for a 501(c)(3) organization, any time that I volunteer for a political campaign I do so on vacation days, and use neither my work phone nor my work computer. Hey, lawyers and IRS officials: are you satisfied now?

*** The Hill District of Pittsburgh has long been a famous African American neighborhood, which once fostered a world-class jazz scene. The brilliant dramatist August Wilson immortalized black life there in his plays. Many years ago, the area also had a sizable Jewish population.

Still, there were some warning signs that not all was Eden, pre-apple. Relatively few of the neighborhood's resident volunteers were young, so most of the campaign workers who ended up going door-to-door were imported white students, many of whom, I suspect, had spent very little, if any, extended time in an African American neighborhood before. Some were too scared to enter local public housing complexes, so they left their stacks of flyers outside the entrances to large buildings.

Some neighborhood dwellers—usually young people or others who appeared to be drunk or strung-out on drugs—asked to be paid cash to vote. "That's how it is in Pittsburgh," I was told. "Even for the first black president?" I asked. "Even for the first black president," they answered in dead voices. "He's not going to do anything for us," said one inebriated man. While the Obama campaign had prepared literature explaining what he would do as President for a wide variety of groups—including teachers, hunters, union members, small business owners, and veterans—it had patently refused to create materials explaining what Obama would do for the African American community; thus began the trend in which Obama sometimes took that community's support for granted.

On election night, I attended a returns-watching party at a Pittsburgh union hall. The crowd was about 50 percent black and 100 percent nervous. A large number of the attendees was convinced—absolutely convinced—that some massive conspiracy would rig the vote against the future president. (Given that the 2000 election was stolen even from a white guy who won half a million more popular votes than his opponent, such vote tampering was not entirely implausible.)

When Pennsylvania was called for Obama soon after the polls closed, the crowd went wild. A few tense hours later, when Ohio—and thus the presidency—was called for Obama, the crowd went wilder than wild. People screamed and screamed, then screamed some more, way past hoarse. Others danced unrestrainedly. Quite a few combined the past-hoarse screaming and the unrestrained dancing. Others, including burly union activists, turned to jelly. Some African Americans were stunned, simply stunned, with disbelief frozen on their faces. And then everyone screamed and danced some more. People were happy, I tell you.

As for me, I sobbed with joy and relief. As a life-long advocate for racial justice, I was electrified by the thought that our country, which once enslaved four million African Americans at one time, would soon be run by a black man. We were all so damn proud of you, America.

As a longtime progressive activist, I was thrilled that a liberal Democrat beat a conservative Republican for the most powerful office in the land.* Having previously worked for President Bill Clinton's administration for eight years, I knew how high the stakes were for control of the executive branch. As a diehard idealist, I was buoyed by the fact that Obama ran a campaign fueled by unabashed idealism.

But I'm also a hardcore realist, with a mind often clogged with cynicism that has accumulated, like plaque, over decades of hard-fought political and governmental battles.** That's why, despite my glee, doubts about the future of Obama's hope-and-change agenda gnawed at me that night. I knew the future president would have it rough and that there were mighty forces, way beyond his control, that would sink many of his plans. I also recall being warned by a Chicago activist, who knew Obama well, that he was neither as progressive nor as politically brave as his new national supporters were led to believe in the campaign. So I turned to my girlfriend next to me, who was an unabashed optimist, and said, "Tonight, I am marginally less enraptured than everyone else here. But in three years, I will be marginally less disappointed." I was, in effect, emotionally bracing myself for a future letdown, knowing that a picture-perfect candidate can never become a picture-perfect president.

The next morning, despite my exhaustion, I woke at dawn and bought every type of newspaper in sight. Yes, it was *still* true. Obama had *still* won. At every rest stop on the long ride home, every time I saw an African American, I smiled and nodded to them, assuming they were as jubilant as I was. Many were. But tellingly, some—particularly those pumping gas—weren't.***

---

* No, Senator John McCain was *not* a moderate, as I will explain later in the book. And we were also pretty happy that night that Sarah Palin was defeated, and that good ol' Joe Biden finally got a promotion of sorts.

** I am either the world's most idealistic cynic, or the world's most cynical idealist. Or, alternatively, I am just a self-referential jerk. You decide, dear reader.

*** I particularly remember wondering whether the black gas station attendants we saw that day would, eight years into the future, enjoy significant improvements in their lives because of President Obama, and whether other low-income and nonwhite Americans would as well. Spoiler alert: most didn't.

THE 2008 UNITY MYTH

The election results themselves, when more deeply examined, made it clear that a new age of fantastic racial and ethnic unity was *not* at hand. True, Obama won the election by a national landslide, winning Pennsylvania by 10 points and Allegheny County (where Pittsburgh is located) by 15 points. In the Hill District, he practically won a shutout.* Yet Obama lost neighboring Beaver County—a mostly white, working-class area which suffered mightily from the collapse of the local steel industry—by 3 percent that year, even though the county had previously been so reliably Democratic that Walter Mondale won it by 26 points in 1984, even as Mondale was trounced across the nation by 18. Obama also lost neighboring Butler County—a mostly white, growing, and professional-class suburb—by 27 points.

According to exit polls, nationwide in 2008 Barack Obama won the black vote by 95 points, the Latino vote by 36 points, and the Asian American vote by 27 points, but lost the white vote by 13 points. In contrast in 1992, Bill Clinton won the African American vote by 73 points, won the Latino vote by 36 points, and *lost* the Asian American vote by a whopping 23 points.[2] But Clinton lost the white vote by only 1 point. It turned out that the 2008 presidential election, which, conventional wisdom said, overcame the nation's racial divides, had, in actuality, deepened them. The reason Barack Obama won the general election wasn't that he transcended race, but that he succeeded in getting more nonwhite Americans—a growing proportion of the nation—to vote for him. In other words, he won the majority of *all* votes. This was how democracy was *supposed* to work, but that's not how many angry white people saw it.

All the talk that Obama had energized new and different voters to take part in politics in a new and different way was also over-hyped. Even though it was indeed the most historic election of modern times, more than a third of voting-age American citizens still failed to vote. (In contrast, voter turnout has been 87 percent in Belgium, 86 percent in Turkey, and 82 percent in Sweden.[3]) Woody Allen has said

---

* In Obama's 2012 race against Romney, there were actually six African American precincts in the Pittsburgh area in which Romney did not win a single vote.

that "showing up is 80 percent of life." By that standard, a third of voting-age Americans flunk their life's social contract test at election time, regularly abandoning their responsibilities as citizens. While restrictions on, and delays in, voter registration and balloting put in place by Republicans were responsible for some of the low turnout, the truth is that, for most Americans, voting is actually relatively easy, taking just a few minutes. The top reason people don't vote is they simply don't care enough—or don't think their votes matter.

Black's Law Dictionary defines abandonment as the "surrender, relinquishment, disclaimer, or cession of property or of rights. Voluntary relinquishment of all right, title, claim, and possession, with the intention of not reclaiming it." Willful nonvoters are the ultimate political abandoners.

As for the relationship definition of "abandoners," Abandonment. net says (yes, there *is* an Abandonment.net) there are "serial abandoners—abandoners who get secondary gain from inflicting emotional pain on someone who loves them. For them, creating devastation is their way of demonstrating power."[4] While abandoners may want to convince themselves that leaving a spouse or child demonstrates power, everyone else knows that abandonment actually exemplifies the opposite: a weakness of character. Likewise, while nonvoters like to dupe themselves into thinking that they are sending a message that they are rejecting a broken system, the real message they're sending is that they are too lazy to spend five minutes exercising a most basic democratic right, a privilege for which many Americans died, and for which many people worldwide are still giving their lives today. Their true message is: we don't give a damn. Abandonment is the surest way to end a personal relationship; just as nonvoting is the surest way for citizens to sever their relationship with the nation.

The New York Times reported that, in the 2008 election, "More than three times as many whites as blacks said they did not like the candidates or campaign issues. Overall, 18 percent of nonvoters said they were too busy, 15 percent said they were prevented because of an illness or disability, and 13 percent each said they were not interested or did not like the candidates or issues."[5] Some of those white nonvoters were among those who hated Obama the most.

Even though African American turnout reached historic highs in 2008, and equaled white turnout for the first time in history, nearly half of black people aged 18–24, and more than a third of those 25–44, still did not vote.[6] Only 50 percent of eligible Hispanics and 47 percent of eligible Asian-Americans voted. In addition, since people of color are disproportionately entangled in the criminal justice system, they are disproportionately prevented from voting due to ballot restrictions on current felons in 48 states, and voting restrictions on ex-felons in 10 states. In the subsequent, off-year Congressional elections of 2010 and 2014, when Obama was not on the ballot, nonwhite turnout dropped precipitously from its 2008 and 2012 highs—and Democrats took a drubbing. Thus, the President's agenda was hampered not just by whites voting against him in droves, but also by nonwhite voters who supported Democrats but who didn't bother to show up at the polls when he wasn't personally on the ballot.

The 2008 election fostered another counterproductive myth: that Barack Obama financed his campaign mostly from a historic out-pouring of support from small donors, thereby freeing him from the need to kowtow to moneyed interests. While Obama did obtain more money from small donors than his opponents, 23 percent of donations came from people who gave between $201 and $999, and another 42 percent from people who gave $1,000 or more. He raked in about $1 million from employees of Goldman Sachs alone.[7] Because the American people didn't know how beholden Obama was to Wall Street and other special interests as a candidate, they didn't know that he'd be less willing and/or less able to go against those same interests as president.

BOLD TRUTH-TELLERS ARE *LOSERS*

One of the top problems with American political campaigns today is that candidates are rewarded by voters for false promises and punished for unvarnished truths. The rhetoric needed to win is often contrary to the information Americans need to know to help their leaders govern effectively. It's no wonder that candidates generally do and say whatever it takes to achieve victory on Election Day, essentially taking the attitude that "we'll figure out that governing thing after we win." In the classic movie *The Candidate*, just after Senate aspirant Bill McKay (played by Robert Redford) wins an upset victory, he turns to his top advisor with a panicked look and implores, "What do we do now?" But just as any personal relationship built on lies will eventually come to ruin, any presidency built on essential campaign untruths will fail. When angry, podium-thumping, populist candidate George Herbert Walker Bush bellowed at the 1988 Republican National Convention, "Read my lips: no new taxes," his alter-ego—calm, patrician, even-toned, career public servant George Herbert Walker Bush—must have known that was a lie. That false promise, along with Bush's race-baiting on Willie Horton and red-baiting on the Pledge of Allegiance, haunted and then wrecked his presidency.* An untruthful and unethical campaign can't lead to truthful and ethical governing.

In the rare instances in which candidates do accurately explain how much their proposals will cost or how difficult they will be to achieve, they are lambasted by the media and punished by voters. The very honesty that is central to good governance is antithetical to good campaign messaging. To give a specific example, in that same 1988 election cycle in which Bush made his "read my lips" pledge, one candidate for the Democratic nomination, Bruce Babbitt, did deliver uncomfortable truths—and earned my loyalty as a campaign staffer. Babbitt is a brilliant and witty man, who racked up an impressive record of progressive accomplishments as governor of Arizona, a state that was home to both John McCain and Barry Goldwater. Even though Babbitt was unknown to the general public outside Arizona, our strategy at the time was to break through to the American consciousness by finishing near the top in the Iowa caucuses and then doing even better in the independent-minded New Hampshire primary. Throughout his campaign, Babbitt repeatedly explained that the only way to reduce the deficit would be to raise taxes and reduce entitlements. That was true then, and history has proven that it is even truer today. So how did voters in New Hampshire and Iowa—who got to hear Babbitt's message directly through town hall meetings and retail campaigning—react to this

---

* George Herbert Walker Bush's 1998 campaign attacked his opponent, Massachusetts Governor Michael Dukakis, for releasing a black murderer, Willie Horton, from prison, using racially-charged imagery. Bush also repeatedly lambasted Dukakis for vetoing a bill requiring that the Pledge of Allegiance be recited in public schools.

bracing dose of reality? In Iowa, Babbitt finished a distant fifth place, with 6 percent of the vote, 3 points below fourth-place finisher Jesse Jackson and 16 points under third-place candidate Michael Dukakis.* In New Hampshire, Babbitt managed to sink even lower, finishing in sixth place, with 5 percent of the vote. Two days later when he dropped out of the race, Babbitt remarked, "The bible says the truth shall set you free, but it doesn't say it would happen so quickly."

So, America, the next time you blame a politician for breaking a campaign promise, remember that it's largely *your* fault. You keep dating the exciting liars instead of the boring, honest, loyal companions. After enough time, you even start lying to yourself (mentally turning your lover's flaws into strengths) so you can erase your lover's/candidate's misdeeds from your memory. You enable a downward spiral of deception. You embrace change we can deceive in.

That's why there are some issues so challenging that no serious political contender is ever willing to discuss the unvarnished truth about them. For instance, when candidates (including Bill Clinton in 1992 and Barack Obama in 2008) talked about healthcare reform, they always made it seem as if *everyone* would get better, cheaper healthcare. That can *never* be true, given the current US healthcare structure, where the healthcare system is so complex, so overpriced, and so unequal, that even if someone designs a program that provides better coverage to the vast majority of Americans, at least a few will need to get fewer services and/or pay more in taxes, premiums, and/or co-pays.

CAMPAIGN PROMISES, LIKE BABIES, ARE EASY TO MAKE BUT HARD TO DELIVER

While all kept campaign promises are alike, each broken promise is broken in its own way.** Campaign vows that are kept are often politically or administratively easy to fulfill. But failed promises fail for a host of reasons.

---

* When you finish well below Michael Dukakis—whose campaign became a synonym for "worst run campaign . . . ever"—that's a good time to cancel your moving truck contract to haul your furniture to 1600 Pennsylvania Avenue. I should note, though, that Dukakis was an effective two-term governor and dedicated his entire life to principled public service. Fat lot of good that did him in the 1988 campaign. Since then, however, he even lost his record for "worst campaign ever" to "Jeb!" Bush.
** Tolstoy said that. Or maybe it was Pussy Riot. I get my Russians confused.

Sometimes, politicians make pledges they know they can't possibly deliver. (See above listing under: "Lips, Read My.")

Frequently, candidates (and their over-eager, young staffs) are naïve, making huge commitments without fully understanding what it takes to get things done in the current political climate. Working as a presidential campaign staffer in my youth, I can attest that the lightning pace of modern campaigns makes it impossible to fully research the merits and flaws of most proposals.

Yet other times, circumstances beyond a leader's control change so dramatically that the original promise becomes impossible to achieve. Often, a leader *does* take some steps to carry out a pledge but is thwarted by opposing forces.

Almost always, though, the failure to keep a promise is more than the failure of any individual politician. The opposition party, special interests, the media, and yes, even the American people shoulder some of the blame.

PolitiFact tracked Obama's 2008 and 2012 campaign promises and determined that, as of January 2016, he kept 45 percent, compromised on 25 percent, broke 22 percent, stalled on 2 percent, and was still working on another 6 percent.[8] In other words, he either carried out, or tried to carry out, nearly 80 percent of his promises. That's a far higher record than most of his detractors admit, but a far less successful record than his most ardent supporters had hoped for, especially since he failed on some of his most important promises, such as closing the prison at Guantánamo Bay, eliminating child hunger in the US by 2015, bringing bipartisanship back to Washington, and ending all of our wars. "Yes, we can" all-too-often became "no, we can't." The greatest casualty was the loss of hope.

WHAT'S THE MATTER WITH OBAMA?

Americans (and most people on the planet) have always longed for one great leader to rise up and magically solve all their problems. Even in democracies, many voters (consciously or unconsciously) seek all-powerful political saviors, and some American voters thought they found their messiah (either literally or figuratively) in Barack Obama.* Many of his supporters were convinced that, once he became president, Obama could make good on all his campaign promises and solve the nation's most pressing problems virtually overnight, with little help or sacrifice needed from his supporters. They assumed their knight in shining armor would fix everything. Why did the jubilation fade so quickly?

Part of the problem is that the electorate was still more divided than anyone admitted or recognized. Another issue was that too many of Obama's core supporters stayed home in off-year elections, giving power to the Right who could reliably get their voters out in every election.

Another factor: Obama and his staff got away with winning a campaign based mostly on ultra-vague hagiography that created unrealistic expectations. In truth, both the Obama and the McCain campaigns purposely shied away from communicating to the public that the next president would face hard, unpopular choices, so voters were unprepared when, as president, the winner was forced to make them.

The Obama campaign successfully portrayed his broad calls for "hope" and "change" as all things to all people. Progressives assumed he was one of them, partially because he told them so, and partially because many believed the false stereotype that all nonwhite people are naturally progressive. Moderates who preferred bipartisan compromise believed Obama was one of them, partially because he told them so, and partially because they believed the false stereotype that all biracial people are naturally adept at bringing together diverse worlds. Neither Obama nor his campaign directly said either of those things, but they implicitly reinforced those messages to targeted voters. Plus, throughout his life and career, Obama *did* actually demonstrate, at various times, both progressive and moderate tendencies, not to mention

---

*

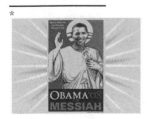

some wishy-washy* attributes. Truly understanding Barack Obama means understanding nuance, and America, you don't do nuance.

Besides, when Obama *did* make specific pledges in the 2008 campaign, voters who supported him tended to ignore, or at least discount, any statement of his that contradicted what they *wanted* their candidate to say. For instance, while Obama called for pulling US troops out of Iraq, he was quite clear that he would double-down on the war in Afghanistan. When, as president, Obama sent more troops to Afghanistan, peaceniks were aghast, but only because they either didn't hear what Obama clearly said during the campaign or because they refused to believe it.**

Moreover, the candidate, his staff, his supporters, and the media alike all bought their own hype over the central narrative of his campaign: that Barack Obama's transcendent personal history and winning personality could triumph over decades of entrenched structural problems in American politics and society. They seemed to seriously believe he could overcome long-term historical trends and massive forces of opposition with a few charismatic smiles, an amazing life trajectory, and triumphant speeches about red states and blue states coming together. Americans learned the hard way that Obama's personal wonderment was enough to win a campaign but not to build a day-to-day governing coalition. Obama consistently delivered some of the most inspirational—and substantive—speeches of any modern president. It is crucial for a president to set an appropriate moral tone for the nation and I'm darn proud he represented the United States to the world. That being said, great speeches rarely change national policy.

Because the reality of the Obama age didn't live up to the hype and because extremist conservatives took control of most US political institutions, America is now royally, colossally ~~fucked~~*** damaged. I hate to start this book with such negativity, but one of my mottos is (and, as

---

* As an Illinois state senator, Obama voted "present" 129 times, avoiding casting a straight "yes" or no" vote. While those votes represented a little less than 3 percent of the roughly 4,000 votes he took as a state senator, those "present" votes were on some of the thorniest issues facing that legislative body.

** Similarly in 1992, candidate Bill Clinton was crystal clear that he would push for welfare reform as a way to lift families out of poverty, but liberals were astonished and horrified when, as president, he did so.

*** I've got to keep this clean so I don't ruin my chances of selling this book as a junior high school civics text.

you'll see, I have many mottos) "Why wait until the bitter end when you can start with a bitter beginning?" Or to put it in a marginally less snarky way: if you don't want to be shocked by how bad things are at the end of a relationship or a presidential administration, pay attention to how bad things are at the beginning.

Cults of personality surrounding presidents are nothing new. We certainly built them around FDR and Reagan, although both had more clearly defined ideological edges than Obama. Perhaps the closest historical antecedent to Obama in this regard was JFK, whose sophisticated charm, wit, and style often superseded specific policy objectives in the public imagination. In fact, Kennedy's inaugural speech didn't even mention domestic issues.* It is no coincidence that JFK also failed to accomplish much of the domestic agenda he sought as president.

President Obama did most things right, and he deserves a lot more credit from both the Right and Left than he's gotten. His economic policies saved the world from depression and his diplomatic skills averted World War III by forging a nuclear deal with Iran. His White House and administration were almost entirely free of scandals, the first time in decades that was the case. There is no question that the main reason so many white Americans think Obama is a horrible stain on the republic is racism, which is also the only plausible explanation for why a white congressman from South Carolina, Joe Wilson, felt both compelled and entitled to heckle the President, yelling out, "you lie"—interrupting a State of the Union address, no less.**

Obama won two nationwide elections with landslides in both the popular vote and the Electoral College, which means, of course, that he was an illegitimate president. Nearly half of all Republicans believed the racist, obviously untrue, claim that Obama was a Muslim born in Kenya, a canard that was, not coincidentally, fervently promoted by Donald Trump for five years to gain popularity within the GOP.[9] Not only did Obama haters unpatriotically discount the legitimacy of a

---

* The only vague reference to domestic issues in JFK's inaugural speech was the phrase "and at home," tacked on to a sentence on protecting human rights abroad. It was included at the last minute at the insistent prompting of JFK aide—and later US senator—Harris Wofford, who was also a key figure in the Civil Rights movement.

** Rep. Wilson claimed that Obama was lying when the President stated that his healthcare plan wouldn't aid illegal immigrants. Obama told the truth. It was Wilson who lied, and did so in a particularly obnoxious way.

leader elected in free elections, they tried to undermine his basic personhood.

No charge against Obama was too extreme or too absurd for the Right to make. Many in the Right believed in 2015 that a routine military training exercise was actually, as *Newsweek* put it, an Obama plan for "a military takeover of Texas using secret tunnels built under closed Wal-Mart stores so troops can move silently about the state." Both Texas Governor Greg Abbott and Texas Senator Ted Cruz (Republicans, of course) made statements implying that such a military takeover could be a serious threat.[10]

A leading GOP congressman, Rep. Peter King, once slammed Obama for wearing a tan suit, implying that it made him seem weak against terrorism.[11] How could I make this up? I am surprised they didn't accuse the President of creating Black Friday as an Afro-Socialist plot or call him "soft on crime" for pardoning Thanksgiving turkeys every year. Maybe they weren't clever enough to think of it.

On most days, on most issues, conservatives wouldn't even go through the motions of pretending to work with the country's leader. In Obama's last year as president, the GOP House and Senate budget committees refused—for the first time in the history of the modern budget process—to allow the President's budget director to so much as testify at a budget hearing. Even more shocking, the Senate GOP said they would not confirm or even have hearings on *any* potential Supreme Court replacement for the late Antonin Scalia, who died early in Obama's final year of office; some refused to take a *courtesy* meeting with Obama's moderate and extraordinarily qualified nominee, Merrick Garland. Yes, they actually admitted they would not extend the courtesy. Seven of the hypocritical Republicans in the Senate had even voted to confirm Garland in 1997 for the US Court of Appeals.

The opposition wouldn't give Obama credit for squat. They even found a way to criticize him for killing Osama bin Laden. If Obama had cured cancer, his opponents would have complained that he put chemotherapy companies out of business.

But even given the harsh, often racist, opposition, and even acknowledging Obama's historic achievements, not only was his presidency still a disappointment for many supporters, it also failed to reverse many of the most pernicious economic and social trends harming the nation.

Yes, Barack Obama did enact a major improvement in America's broken healthcare system and significantly decreased the number of uninsured Americans, but 10 percent of the population, equaling 33 million Americans, were still uninsured in 2014,[12] and many more faced skyrocketing premiums and diminishing healthcare choices.

The 2009 stimulus bill passed by the President and the then-Democratic Congress prevented the US—and arguably the global—economy from collapsing entirely. That was a landmark accomplishment. But because the stimulus package was too small and expired too soon, and because Obama failed to raise the national minimum wage or prevent GOP cuts in social programs, by 2016 American wages were still flat, the middle class was still headed for extinction, and poverty and hunger remained near the same sky-high rates as they were during the height of the recession. Levels of black unemployment, poverty, incarceration, and hunger were still far, far higher than they were for whites.

The entire country, but particularly those areas of the nation populated mostly by nonwhites, remained wrecked in fundamental ways. The water supply in Flint, Michigan was poisoned by a criminally inept state government, with an assist from the federal Environmental Protection Agency. Men and boys were too frequently murdered by police officers for being in the wrong place at the wrong time. Detroit schools were so vermin-infested, crumbling, and unsafe that a "sick-out" protest by teachers closed down most of them.

So, who was responsible for these problems? Choose one:

a) President Obama personally, who managed to garner burning hatred from the opposition without engendering significant Congressional loyalty from his own party;

b) Heartless Republicans and spineless Democrats in Congress, statehouses, and city halls;

c) A broken political system, riven by partisanship and drenched in big money;

d) A petty, partisan, shallow, and fact-adverse media;

e) A public too complacent to fight back;

f) The Kardashians;

g) All of the above.

If you guessed (g), then ding, ding, ding—you're a winner!

The rest of this book will deal with points (b) through (f). But for now, let's address Barack Obama's deficiencies as a leader.

Let's start with the Republican critique of the President: he's a tyrannical dictator; while at the same time he is the weakest leader since Mayor Quimby.* He never compromises with anyone on anything, but too easily gives in. He's a socialist. A Muslim. He's soft on terrorism. He preaches unity but makes no effort to engage personally with Republicans.

Only the most hardcore GOP lemmings and right-wing Kool-Aid drinkers believe all those obviously false and contradictory things about Obama. But how about all the more "serious," "level-headed" purveyors of conventional wisdom who say the problem is that Obama didn't reach out enough to Washington elites, including political opponents, to socialize? They basically allege that his problem is that he won't go to parties. There's a nugget, but only a small nugget, of truth to this argument. Obama worked far fewer holiday party receiving lines at the White House than did George W. Bush. "It's just long and tiring and pretty hard to get through," said Mrs. Obama's chief of staff.[13]

Columnist Ron Fournier, a longtime Washington observer, wrote in the *National Journal*:

> For Obama, learning how to schmooze could mean the difference between a good and great presidency. Franklin Roosevelt, Lyndon Johnson, Ronald Reagan, and Bill Clinton (to name just a few) were masters at building relationships that furthered their political aims. They dined and drank with lawmakers, and they ventured to Capitol Hill out of respect.[14]

---

*

But this critique of Obama ignores key structural changes in American politics in the last 77 years between the times FDR and Obama took office. For most of that time, there were still significant numbers of moderate (and sometimes downright liberal) Republicans in the Northeast and plenty of right-wing Democrats in the South. Democrats largely replaced Northeast Republicans and the reverse happened in the South, where Republicans have replaced many Democrats. Now that the parties are more ideologically pure than at any time in history, it is far harder to get a member of Congress to cross party lines on key votes.

At the same time, it's now more difficult than ever for presidents to discipline errant members of their own parties. It used to be that, as the titular heads of their parties, presidents could more easily keep their own party members in line by threatening to withhold party funds or support. But once candidates could maintain their own computerized voter lists, they no longer needed their political party's ward heelers to keep track of voters. Once candidates could use television, radio, direct mail, e-mail, and websites to communicate directly with the public, they no longer needed rank-and-file party workers to hold torchlight parades or go door-to-door for them. And once air travel enabled individual candidates to fly quickly around the country to meet directly with the wealthiest political donors, and long distance phone rates plummeted so they could afford to call mass numbers of donors at any time of day or night, they no longer needed the political parties to raise most of their money. The two big national party political machines were replaced by the 535 personal political machines owned by each and every member of Congress. The only possible way for the national party to truly discipline a renegade Congressional member these days is to mount a challenge against them in a primary, but most of those challengers lose. And in the Senate, you might have to wait six years to challenge an incumbent, and by then party regulars may have forgotten the senator's apostasy.

Before the advent of mass media and the Internet, it could take generations for the American public to realign their allegiances between the major parties. If you were, let's say, a House Republican in the 1970s, and you knew that your party would not likely retake the

House for decades, you had lots of incentive to compromise in order to advance your legislative priorities and/or your political career. Now massive flips in party allegiances can take place in just one election cycle, in part because ubiquitous electronic media coverage can change public opinion far more rapidly than could old-time newspapers and broadsides. A Bill Clinton landslide in 1992 was followed by a GOP takeover in 1994 and large Obama wins in 2008 and 2012 were followed by Republican surges in 2010 and 2014. The party out of power has all the incentive in the world to sink the governing party's agenda, hoping their opponents' failures will translate into their victory in the next election cycle.

As the movie *Lincoln* demonstrated, even our most distinguished presidents had numerous ways to ~~bribe~~ convince wavering members of Congress to accept the merits of their proposals. Presidents used to have many more lucrative patronage jobs to give out, in places like federal customs houses and post offices. The job of postmaster general used to be so political that the person who held that job under FDR, James Farley, was the head of the Democratic National Committee and was FDR's chief political fixer—while he simultaneously ran the US Postal Service. Now the vast majority of federal jobs are hired through the civil service system, with presidential administrations playing little or no role in the hiring processes. Also, most pork-barrel, district-specific appropriations (budget items) have been eliminated. Presidents have very few new dams or bridges to offer anymore.

So, between the reduction in pork and the disappearance of patronage jobs, presidents today are left with fewer carrots to dangle in front of wavering elected officials. When you combine those changes with the systematic shifts in the nature of our political parties, media coverage, political fundraising, and partisanship, it's doubtful that, even had Obama been much more of a social butterfly, he would have gotten through much more of his agenda.

Jamelle Bouie, writing in the *American Prospect*, noted,

> Forty years ago, bipartisan coalitions were (relatively) easy to assemble . . . It was possible to assemble a legislative majority of, for instance, northern Republicans and Democrats to pass

something like the Civil Rights Act of 1964. And because the Senate operated by ... simple majorities, something controversial like the Social Security Act of 1965 could pass without need of a supermajority. Since then, the parties have become less heterodox and more polarized. ... It takes a favorable political environment for any president to have a shot at greatness.[15]

Elias Isquith made a similar point in *Salon*:

Rather than point to structural explanations, pundits ... would suggest that if President Obama would just spend more time "schmoozing" and glad-handing, he'd be able to get various members of Congress—including some Republicans!—to go against whatever they deem to be in their self-interest and do what he wanted instead. This was always a cockamamie theory ... Tea Party Republican Congress members, worried about a primary challenger from their right, were never going to place those concerns aside in order to work with the hated Obama. He could've invited them to golf every weekend and given them all the Oval Office swag they could carry. It would not matter, because it would not change their rational self-interest.[16]

Yet, even though more fraternizing with Congress wouldn't have been a game changer, Obama should have done more of it anyway. If you Google the phrase "Photos of Obama Socializing with Republicans," you will actually get almost exclusively photos of Obama alone.* Would I personally enjoy golfing with Eric Cantor or playing Twister

---

* These are the actual photos that come up when you search for "Photos of Obama Socializing with Republicans." I left out the one where someone Photoshopped the President to look like he was wearing vampire teeth, horns, and a pitchfork.

with Mitch McConnell in my rec room? No, I would not. But if I had the great privilege to live in the White House and ride Air Force One, and if I got the votes of the majority of the American people, I would make it my job to entertain cranky Republicans once in a while. Heck, if you watch a movie, you don't even have to talk. Everyone in a bad relationship knows that.

As for the charge that Obama (and his wife) are too "arrogant," I have three responses. First, the tone with which that adjective is thrown at the Obamas is uncomfortably similar to the tone used by abject racists when they utter the phrase "uppity Negroes." Second, if you were born with a name, Barack, that sounds "off" to average American ears, but despite that, led the *Harvard Law Review*, became a state senator, a US senator, and then a two-term president—or alternatively, if you were Michelle, and, regardless of the double discrimination you faced as an African American woman, you rose from a working-class family to graduate from Princeton and Harvard Law School and then became a high-powered lawyer—you'd be rightfully proud too. And third, I regretfully conclude that sometimes the Obamas' words and tone could give the impression that they have uncomfortably high self-regard. Too often, they have made the fight about what they personally wanted or felt, not what the American people needed or deserved. Too often they complained about the tough challenges they faced personally and the privacy they gave up to be President and First Lady. While Michelle Obama was courageous and correct to point out at the 2016 Democratic National Convention that the White House was built by slaves, it was problematic when she complained, on another occasion, that the White House had so reduced her privacy that it had "prison elements to it."[17]

The Obamas (like the Clintons) are at their best when they are fighting for a better country and world and at their worst when they are nursing a persecution complex, even a justified one. Once I received a fundraising e-mail, supposedly from Michelle Obama, with the subject line, "Do you have Barack's back?" I respectfully suggest that's an awful question for any First Lady to ask. A much better question would have been, "Will you join with Barack to help the country?"

Too often, President Obama made it seem as though it was him against the world. In a podcast interview with the President, comedian-turned-social-commentator Marc Maron said, "I think left to its own devices, sadly, the government is only going to cede so much to poor people." Maron asked if the President agreed that was true, and this was Obama's response:

> You know when I ran in 2008, you know, there were those posters out there, "HOPE," right, and "CHANGE," and those are capturing aspirations about where we should be going: a society that's more just, a society that's more equal, a society in which the dignity of every individual is respected, a society of tolerance, a society of opportunity. And the question then is, how you operationalize those abstract concepts into something really concrete. You know, how do we get somebody a job? How do we improve a school? How do we make sure that everybody gets decent health care? As soon as you start talking about specifics, then the world's complicated and there are choices that you have to make . . . And you've got these big legacy systems that you have to wrestle with and you have to balance what you want and where you're going with what is and what has been . . . I have [conversations] with supporters who will say to me, you know, we think you're a great guy, you've done some good things but I'm so disappointed with "x" because "x" didn't happen exactly the way I wanted it, and what I have to explain to them is that progress in a democracy is never instantaneous and it's always partial and you can't get cynical or frustrated because you didn't get all the way there immediately.[18]

To me, the central problem with this statement—and indeed, with the whole Obama presidency—is that Obama not only failed to systematically challenge his supporters to join with him to knock down the barriers to change—he and his staff seem to act aggrieved by their own supporters when they tried to hold President Obama accountable for carrying out promises that candidate Obama made in order to win.

After the electorate cast their votes for massive change in 2008, Obama sent the public a message (consciously or not) that essentially

instructed, "I've got this from here, guys."* American political culture is passive by nature, so it takes very little prompting to convince
Americans to again opt out of politics. That's why, absent a big push
from Obama for them to stay involved, the American people essentially
slunk back onto their couches to watch reality TV, play video games,
take naps, and hope the nation would be magically fixed by their new
hero president.

I fault not only the President, but also my fellow progressive activists. Especially in the first few years of the Obama presidency, too few
marched and agitated for change in any particularly organized manner.
Others did speak out, but sometimes lost sight of the forest for the
trees, focusing too much on minor differences with Obama rather
than on colossal differences with conservatives. After eight years of
George W. Bush's administration, it's as if progressives were too shell-
shocked to figure out how to interact effectively with a president who
mostly agreed with them. They often couldn't seem to find the balance
between pushing him when he truly needed to do better on big issues
(like marriage equality, immigration, peace, poverty, or the public
option for healthcare) versus when they needed to defend him and his
agenda against withering right-wing attacks.

That's why, soon after Obama was elected, I wrote a piece for the
Huffington Post urging Obama supporters to forcefully support his proposed stimulus package, even though I thought it should have been
larger, writing, "Now is the time for all good progressives to come to
the aid of country. Now is the time to rally around this forward-thinking
economic plan and work our hearts out to get it passed. This is no time
to continuing carping about some perceived imperfections in the new
President's policies or statements. This is a rare window of opportunity
to enact massive, meaningful change."

While most mainstream liberal groups supported the stimulus
package, few of them mounted major campaigns to mobilize massive

---

* At the 2016 Democratic National Convention, President Obama tried to correct this impression a bit, saying, "America has never been about what one person says he'll do for us. It's about
what can be achieved by us, together, through the hard and slow and sometimes frustrating, but
ultimately enduring, work of self-government." But for most of his presidency, he did little to
actively ask his supporters to do anything other than donate money to Democratic campaigns,
including his own reelection campaign.

grassroots support on its behalf. Neither did Obama try to re-energize his formidable campaign operation to do so. Allowing the GOP to publicly nitpick away some of the least palatable items to be funded by the bill, the Dems never sold the public on the idea that the overall bill, as a complete package, was necessary to revitalize the economy. The President then made the fatal mistake of agreeing to water down the bill significantly to try to get Republican votes, but in the end, all 177 House Republicans and 37 of 41 Republicans in the Senate voted against the bill anyway.

Healthcare reform faced even greater challenges in both messaging and mobilization. Any type of serious healthcare reform was bound to be a historic struggle, but, once again, the Democrats neglected to mobilize the masses who would benefit from reform, and again they let the other side dominate the public discourse. Obama and Congressional Democrats were particularly miserable in their failure to explain how the reform they proposed would be far superior to the broken healthcare status quo, which cost Americans far more money per person than healthcare in other industrialized countries but didn't always ensure better health. When the Right derided the supposedly massive healthcare bureaucracy to be created by Obamacare, the Left should have lambasted the even more bureaucratic processes of major health insurance companies that were causing those with private health coverage to drown in red tape.

At the time Obamacare was first proposed, the number of Americans participating in either the federal Medicaid or Medicare programs was a combined total of about 100 million people, nearly a third of the country's population. The most liberal version of the bill, proposed by House Democrats, would have created a public option for eight million people, but the more moderate version of the bill, proposed by Senate Democrats, would have added only four million people to a public option. In other words, the bills—usually mischaracterized as major new socialist deviations from American capitalism—in actuality would have increased existing government healthcare efforts by only 8 percent and 4 percent, respectively, while mostly aiding private insurance companies.

Part of the reason that our national leaders were unable to explain

health reform to the American people is that few understood it themselves, and their aides and handlers were usually even less informed.
"Most of Washington's professional class arrives as some form of
impostor: 23-year-old legislative aides pretending to understand sug-
ar-cane tariffs, small-town businessmen swept half-wittingly into
House Intelligence Committee seats, campaign speechwriters with
newly minted administration jobs planning the invasion of countries
they've never visited," according to writer Charles Homans. "It is a
city where the social and professional fabric is held together by the
unspoken agreement that nobody look too closely at anyone else's bona
fides."[19]

At least Nancy Pelosi, then Speaker of the House, hung tough on
health reform, saying that, in order to pass a bill, "We'll go through the
gate. If the gate's closed, we'll go over the fence. If the fence is too high,
we'll pole vault in. If that doesn't work, we'll parachute in, but we're
going to get health care reform passed for the America people, for their
own personal health and for their economic security."[20]

But rather than demand even a minimal public option, Obama sent
mixed messages about whether he would fight for one and Senate
Democrats were weak-kneed on fighting for even the tiny one they
proposed. Democrats later lost any remnants of remaining courage
when Republican Scott Brown shockingly won the special election in
Massachusetts to succeed the late Senator Ted Kennedy, a longtime
champion for universal healthcare.* In the end, Obama and the Democratic leadership caved, hoping against hope that dropping the public
option would win Republican votes. Ultimately, not a single Republican in Congress voted for healthcare reform, even though the final
plan was very similar to a program implemented in Massachusetts by
then-Governor—wait for it—Mitt Romney.

---

* This Senate election, which played a huge role in
the debate over whether and what kind of healthcare
tens of millions of Americans would later receive,
was decided in large part because the Democratic
candidate, State Attorney General Martha Coakley,
refused to stand outside Fenway Park shaking hands
with voters in the cold, and because the Republican
candidate, State Representative Scott Brown, proved
his "average man cred" by riding around the state in a
pickup truck, wearing a leather jacket.

The Democrats seemed willing to give away the store. But the Republicans were unwilling to accept even a free store, dropped off on their doorstep and wrapped in a big red ribbon next to a box of chocolates.

Just a year and a half into the Obama presidency, instead of figuring out how to better battle its mortal enemies on the Right, the White House unloaded on what it called the "professional Left." *The Hill* reported,

> The White House is simmering with anger at criticism from liberals who say President Obama is more concerned with deal-making than ideological purity . . . White House press secretary Robert Gibbs blasted liberal naysayers, whom he said would never regard anything the president did as good enough. "I hear these people saying he's like George Bush. Those people ought to be drug tested. I mean, it's crazy." He dismissed the "professional left" in terms very similar to those used by their opponents on the ideological right, saying, "They will be satisfied when we have Canadian healthcare and we've eliminated the Pentagon. That's not reality."[21]

Sure, some liberals did have unrealistic expectations of perfection. But Gibbs's statement was way out of line—and counterproductive to White House goals. It exhibited extraordinarily thin skin—the liberal criticism of Obama was still relatively rare and mild at that time. Plus, one of the most basic axioms of politics is that "you dance with the person who brought you"—meaning that you stick with your allies. Given that Obama won his primaries against Hillary Clinton in 2008 thanks mostly to support from the most liberal voters (promising the perfection his staff now derided), such nasty language against them seemed pretty ungrateful. Many in the progressive movement were fighting harder for the President's healthcare goals than he or Congressional Dems were. This also reinforced the already existing perception of White House arrogance. Besides, most on the Left are hardly "professional."

If the success of a leader is measured by whether he dominates events or events dominate him, then Obama in his first six years holding office was often remarkably unsuccessful. In 2010, having both infuriated right-wing enemies and turned off many liberal allies, the Democrats forfeited control of the House, lost six seats in the Senate, and faced massive defeats in statehouses nationwide. Some blamed the losses on the Democrats seeming too liberal. Other analysts attributed the losses to the Democrats not fighting hard enough for their core beliefs. Paradoxically, both assessments were true, as I will explain later in the book.

Some commentators, most notably Senator Chuck Schumer, a top Democrat from New York, claimed his party made a strategic mistake in pushing healthcare reform when they did. *The Hill* reported that

> Schumer says Democrats "blew the opportunity the American people gave them" in the 2008 elections, a Democratic land-slide, by focusing on healthcare reform instead of legislation to boost the middle class. "Americans were crying out for an end to the recession, for better wages and more jobs; not for changes in their healthcare . . . So when Democrats focused on healthcare, the average middle-class person thought, 'the Dem-ocrats are not paying enough attention to me.'" Schumer's con-cession is a striking change of tone from what he said shortly after the passage of the healthcare law, when he predicted that ObamaCare would turn out to be a strong political issue for his party.[22]

Second-guessing on the politics of healthcare reform is not only wrong, but is also pointless. Given that the US healthcare system was so expensive and dysfunctional, it was a major cost for both employers and employees and thus it was (and still is) a major drag on the US economy; it would have been impossible to create many living-wage jobs without healthcare reform of some kind. But by claiming the bill didn't aid the middle class, Schumer implied that most of the people who lacked healthcare lived in poverty, but 73 percent of those unin-sured in 2014 were above the poverty line, mostly in the lower middle class.[23] Plus, it's pretty insulting to low-income Americans to imply that Democrats shouldn't help them because that will lose them votes.

The fortunes of the poor and the middle class are indelibly interwoven, both economically and politically.

Furthermore, both great nations and great political parties need to do at least two things at once. If a battleship is both on fire and taking on water, the ship's commander doesn't choose between having his sailors put out the fire *or* bail out water; he must have them do both or the ship will sink; likewise, President Obama and Congress needed to both create jobs *and* reform healthcare. The problem wasn't that the Dems tried to do something big—voters generally reward leaders who take firm positions and try to get big stuff done—the problem was the Democrats allowed conservatives to mischaracterize the healthcare bill as some horrible left-wing social experiment that would aid "takers" who didn't want to work. Dems took the hit from the Right while, at the same time, passing a bill so watered down that it would help far fewer people and thus win far fewer votes from their base. Modern Democrats have become experts at bungling negotiations, always seeming to be Getting to No.

HOW TO FAIL AT NEGOTIATIONS WITHOUT REALLY TRYING

After the Republicans took charge of the House, things went from worse to worser.* Obama kept drawing negotiation lines in the sand, then immediately erasing them, as Republicans refused to meet even his most minimal demands.

Again, some of this was connected to the President's temperament, and personal weaknesses of Democratic leaders. But many of the opposing forces were beyond his control. In the seminal book on how to strike deals that work for both sides, *Getting to Yes: Negotiating Agreement Without Giving In*, Roger Fisher and William L. Ury called for "principled negotiations" that allow each side at least some claim to victory.[24] But for negotiations to be *principled*, both sides need to have *principles*, and that's too rare in Washington these days. *Getting to Yes* laid out five pillars of effective negotiations: 1) Separate the people from the problem; 2) focus on interests, not positions; 3) Invent options for mutual gain; 4) Insist on using objective criteria; and 5) Know your best alternative to negotiated agreement—or make sure you have a backup

---

* I know "worser" isn't an actual word, but it *should* be.

plan for when you can't reach agreement. Given the current dysfunction in Washington, it's hard to effectively utilize any of these concepts.

"Separate the people from the problem" means "try to focus on the issues at hand, not the personalities of the individuals conducting the negotiations." But even if Paul Ryan and Mitch McConnell hadn't despised President Obama personally, they couldn't have been seen as sharing common ground with him publicly or they would have risked losing support among their constituents. In fact, New Jersey Governor Chris Christie's career in the Republican Party was derailed primarily because he allowed the President to visit his state to inspect storm damage (gasp!), because he didn't flinch when the President lightly tapped on him the shoulder (oh my!), and then committed the cardinal sin of shaking Obama's hand (which conservatives disparaged as a "hug" . . . ew).

Democrats and Republicans could certainly try to "focus on interests, not positions," but the problem is that many low-income, white Republicans vote against their own economic interests repeatedly, while Democrats often refuse to see that voters have self-interests beyond economics, as I'll demonstrate in future chapters.

The parties could also attempt to "invent options for mutual gain," but since they've defined politics as a zero-sum game—in which one side's loss means the other side's victory—mutual gain is, by definition, impossible.

"Insist on using objective criteria." Now, there's a concept that should be *easy* for both sides to agree upon. Surely they could find common ground by agreeing on basic facts, right? Surely not. When the head of the nonpartisan Congressional Budget Office—the impartial referee of Congressional budget disputes—declared, based on irrefutable economic facts, that tax cuts for the wealthy do not automatically generate more revenue (through economic growth) than they cost the US Treasury, the Republicans running Congress simply booted him from the post. NASA is an agency that, by definition, is full of rocket scientists, but when the department used hard science to prove that the Earth and oceans are warming, the Republicans tried to discount and discredit them. If we can't agree on thermometer readings, how could we come to a consensus on anything else?

The President and Congress thought they had the "know your best alternative to negotiated agreement" principle more than covered. Not only did they have a Plan B to their failed budget negotiations, they had a Plan C for their Plan B. When they couldn't agree on a plan to raise the debt ceiling in 2011, they agreed to create a "Supercommittee" of a handful of negotiators to work out a deal, but if the Supercommittee couldn't agree, onerous across-the-board "sequestration" cuts of military and domestic spending would be automatically imposed. The threat of sequestration was supposed to be so awful that it would force the Supercommittee to reach agreement. Yet the Supercommittee utterly failed and the sequestration *was* implemented—and was indeed as harmful as everyone predicted, cutting funds for everything from cancer research to church-based soup kitchens. So, the President and Congress then had to enact a Plan D for their Plan C for their original Plan B, and struck a deal four years later, in 2015, to repeal both the Supercommittee and the sequestration. And that, ladies and gentleman, is exactly how to negotiate and negotiate—and negotiate—until all sides reach a resounding "no." Feel better?

IT'S THE DUMB-ASS VOTERS, STUPID

When Americans do show up at the polls they are often ignorant—damn ignorant—fools. There, I said it. *The New York Times* reported that some attendees at a Donald Trump rally in Vermont were torn between Trump and Sanders. One said of Mr. Trump, "Bernie is my No. 1 choice, and Trump is No. 2. They're not that different." Another man, a hardwood floor installer who traveled all the way from Ohio for the rally, opined, "I'm a Trump guy, but I do like Bernie. There are a lot of parallels between these two guys. There's a populist appeal that comes with both of them." The article reported, "Voters who were on the fence between the seemingly polar opposite candidates said both communicated well with working-class people and made strong cases for how they would improve the economy."[25]

There's too much childish name-calling in American politics, and responsible citizens should engage in less of it. That being said, I can't help but violate my own admonition by stating that anyone who found it difficult to choose between Trump and Sanders was a friggin' idiot, and that's putting it kindly. The only quality Trump and Sanders shared was the need for better barbers. Equating Sanders with Trump solely because they both draw large crowds is as nonsensical as likening the Pope with Kanye West because they do too. The reality is that Donald Trump is the embodiment of just about everything Bernie Sanders was running *against*. Sure, "they both made strong cases for how they would improve the economy," but, aside from a few small similarities on trade, each of their cases were exactly the opposite—and entirely incompatible—with the other's. It's as if someone wants to believe that putting water into a freezer will both turn it into ice *and* turn it into steam. But as long as so many voters are so willfully ignorant, it's impossible for any president or Congressional leader to effectively govern, don't you think, America?

The kinds of campaign-ending gaffes other pols get caught saying in private on secret tapes or on hot mics are the kinds of things Trump said, repeatedly, in public and proudly. Trump actually boasted that his supporters gave him such unquestioning support that they would back him even if he shot someone in the middle of a crowded street.[26] The Americans who actually voted for him after that proved that they were exactly the kind of gullible morons the Donald claimed they were.*

In general the public has no problem freely calling politicians "idiots," "hypocrites," and much worse, but we flinch from applying those labels to the voters who elect them. I think it's high time we assigned the rightful blame to the voters themselves.

In his book *Democracy without Politics*, Steven Bilakovics demonstrates that, in America and most Western democracies today, the majority of citizens hold both politics and politicians in contempt. But he points out that the least democratic branch of government—the military—is now the most trusted major institution in our country. He addresses different academic theories as to why democracy is now in such disrepute:

> First, in our modern, middle-class, commercial republic, people are otherwise occupied by matters both noble and base and are so "rationally ignorant" of and uninterested in a complex polit-

---

* Dear Donald Trump supporter: If you would like to send me hate mail, please send it to my personal e-mail address: MichaelMoore@MichaelMoore.com.

ical process that daily affects them little; the consumer-citizen chooses to spend finite resources elsewhere ... The ordinary running of government is intentionally ... entrusted to institutional mechanisms, elected representatives and technocratic "experts." Second ... citizens are reduced to spectators of a distant and byzantine political system dominated by organized "special interests" and oligarchic "elites" ... Money is power, and in our pay-to-play political system, the people's putative authority amounts to sound without fury. In the first line of reasoning described here, the reigning popular sovereign happily abdicates direct rule, if not ultimate authority; in the second, a citizenry longing for a more significant political power is institutionally and materially locked out of a political space.[27]

In other words, the first theory posits that citizens give away our political power freely, and the second suggests that our power is taken from us, against our will, by the moneyed elites.

But Bilakovics is not convinced by either explanation and he argues, counterintuitively, that the very idea of democracy itself—"its promise of transcendent freedom and unlimited power"—renders the everyday politics of argument and persuasion absurd by comparison. The very freedom given to us by democracy allows us the free will to neglect it. To fix our democracy, Bilakovics calls on us, the public, to overcome our antipolitical biases and embrace the wonderment that is politics, appreciating that democracy gives average citizens both the right and the obligation to both persuade and be persuaded.

That's pretty highfalutin talk. Let me posit my much simpler theory of why voters don't participate: The citizens who embodied the ideal of ancient Greece have degenerated over centuries into reality show-addicted dumbasses.*

---

*

 +  =

It is certainly true that many voters trust neither their neighbors nor themselves. That explains the popular push for term limits, which are essentially an admission that people think everyone around them, and perhaps themselves too, are too stupid or out-of-touch to know when to reelect or boot incumbents. They want their own choices limited by arbitrary cut-offs, instead of taking responsibility to figure it out for themselves.

Democracies face challenges for the same reasons that restaurants with ultra-long menus do: people can't handle too many choices.

OBAMA'S FATAL OVERCOMPENSATION

People always try overcompensating for the issues that make them most insecure. Show me a man bragging at a bar about his prowess in bed, and I'll show you a man with microscopically small genitals.

Likewise, presidents always overcompensate for their perceived political weaknesses. The media called George Herbert Walker Bush a "wimp," so he invaded Iraq. Bill Clinton was dogged by charges that he avoided military service in Vietnam, so he gave his generals whatever they wanted, including allowing them to continue to prevent LGBTQ people from serving openly in the armed forces. George W. Bush worried that he was overshadowed by his father's legacy, so he decided to not only invade, but also occupy, Iraq. Because Barack Obama is the first African American president, it's likely that he and his political advisors worried that he would be perceived as favoring blacks over whites, and since poverty is incorrectly seen by much of the nation as an issue affecting mostly nonwhites, the Obama team may have thought that, if they were perceived as doing too much to fight poverty, it would also be viewed as favoring people of color over whites.* As a result, particularly in his first term, Obama shied away from discussing race and poverty in public, even though racial issues and poverty were arguably two of the most widespread and serious problems vexing America.

When the President *did* so much as dip his toe into the roiling water

---

* During the Clinton administration, I worked for the first African American secretary of agriculture, Mike Espy, and many white employees assumed, totally incorrectly, that Espy would unfairly favor black employees.

of race—such as when he decried the likely mistreatment of African American Harvard University professor Henry Louis Gates, Jr. by a local law enforcement officer—he was roundly vilified by conservatives, and he quickly pulled his toe back out as though the racial waters burned him. During Obama's reelection campaign, *Politico* noted,

> Obama may have started his political career fighting poverty as a community organizer . . . but he's running for re-election without almost ever even using the word "poor." And when he does, it's not to describe the problem or his administration's efforts to combat it—only an aspirational message of trying to get more impoverished people into the middle class. . . . [W]ith Obama already on defense about the economy—and issues of race and accusations of being a "food stamp president" in the background—he's mostly avoided touching the topic, at least directly. Mitt Romney has not been so reluctant, repeatedly using the poverty statistics in attacking Obama's overall economic record and pointing out Obama's specific failure to improve the numbers. . . . Five years ago, [Obama] railed against poverty under President George W. Bush's watch. . . . When Obama [now] avoids talking about poverty or food stamps, it's in part because "he just doesn't want to draw attention to something that's going to draw the Tea Party claim that you're giving my money to people who didn't earn it," said Gary Burtless, a senior economics fellow at the Brookings Institution.[28]

It is infuriating to me that many supposedly respected analysts and political consultants actually counseled Obama and other Democrats to not "draw attention" to poverty at all. Most Democrats, sadly, followed this ethically challenged and politically naïve advice. In each of the three general election debates of 2012, Mitt Romney attacked Obama on high rates of food stamps (SNAP) participation. Even though Obama was the first president with a close family member (his mother) who received food stamps, he went out of his way to avoid responding to the attacks, instead changing the subject each time.

The conventional wisdom—that if Democrats so much as discuss poverty, it will scare away middle-class voters—is (How shall I put it?) a load of crap. Many middle-class voters have already spent at least a portion of their lives poor, and many more are scared to death of falling into poverty, which will indeed happen to many in our current economy. Moreover, it is a truism of politics that it's a mistake to allow your opponents to define any critical issues on their terms instead of yours. Of course, if the only argument the public hears is the right-wing trope that social programs are all waste-laden, fraud-ridden handouts to work-avoiding nonwhites, they will believe that. The Democrats fail to see that they can't win an argument that they're unwilling to have. And it's not just that they did everything to avoid having a rhetorical debate on these issues—more tragically, they also often shied away from the substantive work necessary to prevent Republicans from slashing anti-poverty programs.

When attacked by Romney, what Obama *should* have said was, "Governor, my mother briefly obtained food stamps when she was putting herself through nursing school and that prevented her from starving. Like most food stamp recipients, she got the help for a short period of time and spent the vast majority of her life giving back to society. I am sick of millionaires, like you, who get all sorts of corporate welfare your whole lives, trying to take food away from our struggling neighbors. We Americans take care of our own. It's the right thing to do morally and the smart thing to do economically."

Had Democrats forcefully explained the reasons why social programs are needed to aid low- and middle-income families alike, they would have both retained many middle-class voters and reduced the massive drop in Democrat turnout in off-year elections, too.

In Obama's last two years in office, with the Senate also in Republican hands, perhaps he felt he had nothing left to lose or had been pushed beyond the limits of his naturally accommodating temperament, and finally began speaking more forcefully about race and poverty. After the 2015 mass shooting at a black church in Charleston, South Carolina, his eulogy for the Rev. Clementa Pinckney delivered what was widely considered his most forceful and direct condemnation of racism and poverty as president. The speech included him spontaneously and emotionally singing "Amazing Grace," and was one of the few times that, as leader of the free world, he directly connected poverty with racism. It was also one of the rare public appearances where it seemed that not only was Barack Obama seeing and feeling economic and racial injustices as a representative of all Americans, but that he was also speaking from the heart as a black man who saw and felt those injustices more keenly:

> He [Rev. Pinckney], embodied the idea that our Christian faith demands deeds and not just words, that the sweet hour of prayer actually lasts the whole week long, that to put our faith in action is more than just individual salvation, it's about our collective salvation, that to feed the hungry, clothe the naked, and house the homeless is not just a call for isolated charity but the imperative of a just society. . . . [Black churches] have been and continue to be community centers, where we organize for jobs and justice, places of scholarship and network, places where children are loved and fed and kept out of harm's way and told that they are beautiful and smart and taught that they matter. . . . That's what the black church means—our beating heart, the place where our dignity as a people is inviolate. . . . For too long, we were blind to the pain that the Confederate Flag stirred into many of our citizens. It's true a flag did not cause these murders. But as people from all walks of life . . . we all have to acknowledge, the flag has always represented more than just ancestral pride. For many, black and white, that flag was a reminder of systemic oppression and racial subjugation. . . . Removing the flag from this state's capital would not be an act of political correctness. It would not be an insult to the valor of Confederate soldiers. It would simply be an acknowledgment that the cause, for which they fought, the cause of slavery, was wrong. The imposition of Jim Crow after the Civil War, the resistance to civil rights for all people, was wrong. It would be one step in an honest accounting of America's history, a modest but meaningful balm for so many unhealed wounds. . . . Perhaps this tragedy causes us to ask some tough questions about how we can permit so many of our children to

languish in poverty or attend dilapidated schools or grow up without prospects for a job or for a career. Perhaps it causes us to examine what we're doing to cause some of our children to hate.[29]

It's unclear whether the President finally found his true voice—or, more likely, felt unencumbered enough to use his real voice—but thank goodness, he did. The truth-telling Obama of his remaining two years was exactly what we were waiting for all along. In his final State of the Union address, he declared, "Food stamps recipients didn't cause the financial crisis; recklessness on Wall Street did." Watching that on TV, I practically leapt through my living room ceiling in excitement.

But what took him so long?

LET THEM EAT SOUNDBITES: OBAMA'S FAILED CHILD HUNGER PLEDGE

Obama, his team, and the public as a whole failed to fully appreciate that all the racism, sexism, classism, and xenophobia—not to mention rampant partisanship and big money control of elections and lobbying—which were key barriers to the nation's progress *before* the election, would continue to be key barriers *after* the election.

Few of his big campaign promises would be implemented easily. A good case study of how the nation's tangled problems hold back progress is Obama's failure to realize his pledge to end domestic child hunger by 2015.

It is very likely that, by the time Obama leaves the presidency, at least one in five American kids will still struggle to get the nutritious food they need. So, while the President reduced the level of child hunger that he inherited, he failed to keep his promise to eliminate it. Why?

The pledge, made in a position paper issued late in the campaign, was pretty shaky from the start. Neither Obama nor Biden actually voiced it themselves. No press release was issued.

Even though the paper was released after the collapse of Lehman Brothers, it's unclear whether the campaign fully understood the enormity of the economic improvements needed, and the cost of the safety net expansions necessary, to entirely eliminate domestic child hunger.

Other than promising a one-time spending boost for SNAP in the economic stimulus plan, the position paper made no dollar commitments. While it mightily praised nutrition aid to pregnant women and infants, school meals, summer meals for kids, and aid to food banks, it offered no new money for any of those efforts. Given that their Republican opponents were slamming Obama and Biden as so-called big spenders, it's no surprise that the campaign refused to put a price tag on the pledge.

By the time Obama was inaugurated, the full extent of the economic collapse was evident. The number of US children in poverty had increased by 2.4 million under George W. Bush. Most mainstream economists agreed that massive new government spending was needed to both boost economic growth and slash poverty. But the campaign hadn't educated voters about the need for such large outlays—and Republican opposition to a proposed recovery package was immediate, fierce, and unified. Not surprisingly, the timid Democrats scaled back their stimulus package and declined to push minimum wage hikes, even though at the time, they controlled the White House and both Houses of Congress. Once the GOP took control of the Congress (or once the Democrats gave it away, depending on your point of view), full austerity became the norm and wage hikes were a nonstarter.

The growth in jobs from 2010 to 2014 was not enough to counteract the devastating impact of low wages, large numbers of workers with only part-time employment, and limits on social service funding. That's why child poverty increased by another 1.5 million between 2009 and 2014, thereby making the child hunger-reduction goal even more difficult to achieve.

The Obama administration did take some steps to carry out the child hunger pledge. The original stimulus act did, as promised, include a significant bump in SNAP spending. Obama's appointees at the US Department of Agriculture courageously and effectively lifted barriers to nutrition program participation.[30] First Lady Michelle Obama fought for—and won—major improvements in the nutrition quality of school meals.

But when future bills to fight hunger were considered, Democrats suffered withering (often racially-freighted) attacks from conservatives for supposedly wanting to turn America into a "food stamp nation." The petrified Democrats never rebutted those charges. Meanwhile, agribusinesses, threatened by potential rationing to their always-open spigot of corporate welfare, for the first time pushed for cuts in hunger programs instead, and since they were big campaign donors, Congress listened.* The President and many Democrats surrendered under pressure (of course . . . see a pattern here?), and agreed to a total of $14 billion in SNAP cuts in both the 2010 Child Nutrition Reauthorization Bill and the 2014 Farm Bill. The Democrats claimed they had no choice, because the Republicans would halt any bill without deep cuts. To respond to that in ultra-technical, highly wonkish terms: that's total ~~bullshit~~ nonsense. The Democrats refused to lead any significant debate over the cuts, even declining to point out that half of SNAP benefits go to children. So, in order to pass bills that supposedly gave more school meals to hungry kids, the Democrats passed bills that took away home-cooked meals from hungry kids.** The President signed the cuts into law (of course). Yes, the Republicans are the bad seeds here, but the Dems seem to be co-dependent enablers.

Media acquiescence also played a role. Political reporters and editors are usually obsessed with polling, insider bickering, big-money fundraising, and personal insults—not substance and certainly not substance relating to poverty. No high-profile media outlet reported on Obama's hunger pledge when he made it, even though, had the promise been kept, it would have transformed American society. Since then, only a few media outlets have reported on the President's progress on the pledge.[31]

A few progressive opinion-makers did speak out. When SNAP cuts in the farm bill were enacted,

---

* Where's Grandpa driving the tractor on the kind of small, idyllic family farm typically aided by farm bills?

** Some brave Democrats, like Senator Kirsten Gillibrand of New York and Rep. Jim McGovern of Massachusetts, did try mightily to defeat the cuts, but they were outnumbered (of course).

Blake Zeff published a piece in *Salon* entitled "DC celebrat‹
letting poor Americans go hungry." Wrote Zeff,

> Based on reports from the Beltway, there's good news out of
> Washington this week. "We are on the verge of achieving major
> reform," touted Sen. Debbie Stabenow, D-Mich. "Things are
> actually starting to work," exclaimed one published analysis.
> "Just the way Congress is supposed to work!" cried another . . .
> Congress, long stymied by dysfunction, was able to pass a farm
> bill . . . In an environment where very little legislation gets
> passed, it's a sign of democratic progress to see an exception to
> the trend. But any celebrating assumes that the only thing that
> matters is *process*. By this way of thinking, if both sides come
> together and pass something (anything), this is intrinsically a
> good thing. In this worldview, all that matters is bipartisanship
> and passing things. But what if *outcomes* matter, too? By that
> standard, the bill's passage looks different . . . 850,000 low-in-
> come households will . . . lose around $90 per month.[32]

Reaching new heights of irony, Obama finally defended the SNAP
program forcefully, but did so at a ceremony in which he signed the
farm bill into law, thereby implementing the very type of cuts he was
decrying. I can't help but wonder if the President considered that he
was slashing the exact type of aid that provided food to his mother.
(I also can't help but wonder if young community organizer Obama
would have picketed middle-aged President Obama.)

In late 2015, Jeb Bush chastised Hillary Clinton for giving Obama
an "A" grade in running the country. Said Jeb, "One in seven people
are living in poverty. That's not an A. One in five children are on food
stamps. That is not an A." Virtually every other Republican candidate
has blamed the President for our high rates of poverty and food stamp
usage. But few in the media questioned those candidates about the role
of longstanding Republican economic and social policies in wrecking
the economy and making it harder for families to climb out of poverty in the first place. In the 2016 presidential primary debates, both
Republican and Democratic, none of the journalists moderating asked

so much as a single direct question about poverty or hunger, although Clinton and Sanders did raise the issues on their own.*

We can't let the American people off the hook either. If the average American can remember the name of the fourth-season winner of *Survivor* or the Cubs's third-string catcher, then they have enough time and mental acuity to take it upon themselves to carefully study the promises of all the candidates, to vote only for those who make realistic pledges, and to hold their elected officials accountable once in office.

THE LIFE OF THE PARTY

Plenty of advice columnists give tips on the proper way to behave at parties. Always flatter your hosts. Don't bring up depressing topics. Be the kind of agreeable guest that is always invited back. The one time I was invited to a White House holiday party by the Obamas, I violated every one of those rules. (And no, I won't do it at your party, America. Wait. Maybe I will. Maybe I already have!)

The invite came in December 2012, coincidentally at the same time that the Farm Bill was being considered by Congress. This was my first—and only—such invitation during the Obama presidency. I had never met Barack Obama, and wasn't sure whether I would get to do so at the party, but just in case, I prepped like a candidate for a big debate. Knowing that, if I was lucky, I'd get five seconds or so with the President, I intended to make good use of that opportunity to lobby him to oppose SNAP cuts. I wrote and rewrote my potential five-second pitch to him. I first considered using a line based on morality by citing how all religions demand that we feed the hungry. Then I tried out an economic argument, that SNAP creates jobs and supports work. Finally, I settled on a more personal approach by making a connection with the First Lady's "Let's Move!" initiative, which encouraged young people to exercise and eat less junk food. I thought it would be best to focus on something that really mattered to him, since "Let's Move!" was his wife's signature project.

---

* Most GOP candidates for president in 2016 did attend a conservative forum on "expanding opportunity" and reducing poverty, but their supposed solutions were—as always—cutting social programs and keeping wages low, so it wasn't a serious poverty forum.

When I got to the White House for the event, no one was handed a ticket for a receiving line as they had at other parties I'd attended under President Bill Clinton, so I figured out that they would not invite each guest to take a picture with him, further proving the accuracy of the media reports that the Obamas dramatically cut down on that practice. I did note early on where the podium was located at the event and I guessed that if I waited right in front of it, without moving for hours until the President spoke, I might just be able to get a few seconds with him as he was "working the rope line," which is political-speak for shaking hands over some sort of barrier (in this case a velvet rope, like in a movie line) between the elected official and the crowd.

Sure enough, after the President and the First Lady each made a few remarks, they started working the rope line. The First Lady got to me first, and I exhaled my well-practiced pitch: "Hi, I'm Joel Berg with the New York City Coalition Against Hunger.* We're honored to support your "Let's Move!" initiative. I hope you understand, Madame First Lady, that you can't achieve your obesity-reduction goals unless the President achieves his hunger-reduction goals. And I hope you understand how important it is for the Senate to pass a farm bill *without* cutting SNAP." The First Lady, the better politician of the couple, listened closely, then warmly agreed and smilingly thanked me for my work. Just inches away, warily watching me out of the corners of his eyes, the President could tell I was pressing his wife a bit, so by the time he got to me, he shook my hand extra-briefly and extra-wearily. That was my interpretation, anyway. I tried to speak as quickly as I could, while avoiding the appearance of being a nutcase on amphetamines (which I get a lot). "Mr. President," I piped up, "I'm Joel Berg with the New York City Coalition Against Hunger. As you may have heard me tell the First Lady, I hope you understand that she can't achieve her obesity-reduction goals unless you achieve your hunger-reduction goals. And I hope you will pledge, Mr. President, to veto any bill that will cut SNAP." The President shrank back, almost imperceptibly, and said, half-jokingly, smiling with his mouth but not with his eyes, "Man, it's Christmas-time. Are you lobbying me at a holiday party?" Just as I started to reply, politely but defi-

---

* The New York City Coalition Against Hunger changed its name to Hunger Free America in 2016.

antly, "Yes I *am*, Mr. President," he moved on to my girlfriend, standing next to me. Perhaps sensing he may have seemed a bit callous, he looked back at me for a second, still holding her hand, and nodded, saying, "but it's for a good cause." I then tried winning his good graces by pointing out that I was one of the few nonprofit leaders who had supported his proposal to decrease tax deductibility for charitable donations, but that was much too wonky to explain in a second and, besides, he was already way past me, and never looked back.

At least I hadn't been kicked out.

While I had a few brief conversations with President Clinton when I worked for his administration, I don't want to pretend that I talk to presidents often or that I am blasé about it. Like a junior high school boy going over and over again a text he got from his crush, I reviewed my exchange with Obama over and over—and over—with my girlfriend, who'd heard the whole exchange, and a few close friends and colleagues. I carefully considered every one of his words (all 17 of them), every bit of his vocal tone, every minute change in his facial expressions, and even the tiny expressions in his body language. What did the President truly mean? What was his real intent? Was he being funny, or was he insensitive? Three theories emerged from discussions with my brain trust, in descending order of whether the theory flattered or denigrated the President.

The first theory was that he was giving me a backhanded compliment. As a tough basketball player who reveled in trash talk, the fact that he was willing to rib me could have meant that he truly respected someone who had the guts to lobby him at a White House holiday party on a vital topic.

The second theory was a more neutral one—which is that he simply might not have wanted to go on the record with me about a position at that time—so he made a joke to avoid giving a real answer.

The third theory was the most negative assessment of him—that he could have actually been annoyed that I was hassling him and his wife at a party at their house. The consensus of my advisers, including my girlfriend who witnessed and photographed the exchange from a few inches away,* concluded that theory three was most likely, that the leader of the free world was ticked off at me. It had been a long journey from the church in Pittsburgh, gospel music swelling, hope rising . . . but, oh well.

In any event, this exchange exemplified why my old boss, Bill Clinton, in his prime was a far better one-on-one politician than Barack Obama. There is no way in the world that if someone ever asked Clinton at a party to save nutrition benefits, that he would brush the person off with a joke—for whatever the reason. Even if, the very next day, Clinton felt he was forced to sign food stamp cuts into law, he still would have assured the partygoer that this was a really, truly, vital issue and that he would do all he could to protect the program. (I can all-but-hear him feeling that person's pain, and know he would continue squeezing their hand tight, and smiling, maybe even pulling them in for a hug before parting.) Finally accepting the theory that Obama was sort of pissed that I bothered him at a party, I then dreamed up three fantasy follow-up responses, which of course, I would never get the opportunity to give:

1) If, Mr. President, you invite me to the Oval Office on Monday to discuss this in detail, I promise not to bellyache to you anymore at your party.

2) It is true that you live here, Mr. President, and that it's your party, but since our tax dollars are paying for both, you owe it to the American people to hear me out.

3) Tens of millions of Americans depend on SNAP to survive, Mr. President. Since none of *them* were invited to your party, it is my obligation to ask you to protect SNAP on their behalf.

At White House parties, like at all parties, you always think of the best quips *after* you leave.

---

* Here's me talking to the First Lady and me near the President, then with eyes smiling, just seconds before he lost the twinkle in his eyes when forced to talk to me.

On my way home from the festivities that day, a panhandler at the Farragut West Metro stop, obviously unaware of the conversation I had just had with the President, yelled out to me, "Tell the President that I need help." I answered, "You won't believe this, but I just did."

2.

Money Can't Buy Happiness
(Just Food, Clothing, Gas, Medicine, and Housing)

F. Scott Fitzgerald: "The rich are different from you and me."
Ernest Hemingway: "Yes, they have more money."

Bobby McFerrin: "Don't Worry—Be Happy"

One popular self-help meme reads, "If you want to feel rich, just count the things you have that money can't buy." Another says, "We tend to forget that happiness doesn't come as a result of getting something we don't have, but rather from recognizing and appreciating what we do have."

That's easy for them to say.

America, I'd bet all the gold in Fort Knox (or my entire collection of mint-condition Robert Reich action figures) that whoever cooked up those quotes never struggled to pay rent or put food on the table.

Of course, having lots of money can't *guarantee* happiness, but a severe lack of money—a problem faced by all low-income and many middle-class Americans—virtually guarantees unhappiness.

So yes, I am going to go out on a limb and say that rich people are, in general, happier than poor people.*

---

* Don't believe me? Then I ask you, which of these people looks happier?

I am certainly not arguing for rampant materialism and over-the-top conspicuous consumption, but when the ultra-wealthy complain that money doesn't bring them joy, they doth protest too much, methinks.

People with mountains of dough have forever lectured people without it that they should at least enjoy their circumstances. Arthur C. Brooks, president of the right-leaning American Enterprise Institute (AEI), has written,

> I learned that rewarding work is unbelievably important, and this is emphatically not about money . . . Economists find that money makes truly poor people happier insofar as it relieves pressure from everyday life—getting enough to eat, having a place to live, taking your kid to the doctor. But scholars like the Nobel Prize winner Daniel Kahneman have found that once people reach a little beyond the average middle-class income level, even big financial gains don't yield much, if any, increases in happiness.[33]

Given that Brooks was paid by AEI more than $1 million in salary in 2014 (more than twice the president of the US), it's a hoot for him to claim that people's jobs are "not about the money." Benjamin Kline, an expert on work and leisure, has pointed out that many jobs are tedious and require very little mental challenge. "Purpose, meaning, identity, fulfillment, creativity, autonomy—all these things that positive psychology has shown us to be necessary for well-being are absent in the average job," he said.[34]

Brooks's characterization of the study he cites—which considers both "life evaluation" and "emotional happiness"—is also extremely misleading. For life evaluation—the most basic question of whether people generally believe their lives are good—satisfaction does rise considerably with rising incomes. For emotional happiness, it is also true that the increases in satisfaction level off at incomes beyond $75,000 annually, but for most Americans, that's a lot of money.[35] Brooks describes that $75,000 level as "little beyond the average middle-class income"; yet in 2009, the year of the study's data, the

American median household income was $49,777. Ask a family earning around 50 grand if they think earning 75K would be just "a little beyond" what they are making now, and they will likely laugh at you. Moreover, 68 percent of American households earned less than $75,000 annually that year.[36]

In other words, the very study that Arthur Brooks claimed proved that money doesn't buy happiness actually proved that people *do* evaluate their lives based on how much money they have, and that the least wealthy two-thirds of the American people are far less happy than the wealthy.

Sure, some ultra-rich individuals might loathe themselves. But to paraphrase my late mother's own paraphrase of an old Yiddish saying, We should *all* be so unhappy.

After all, when was the last time a couple broke up over incessant arguing about having too *much* money?

THE REVERSE ESCALATOR BETWEEN
THE MIDDLE CLASS AND POVERTY

What's the difference between families in the middle class and the poverty class? Not as much as you might think. In fact, many of the individuals and families in both categories frequently swap places more than once over a lifetime.

While many assume (correctly) that low-income people spend virtually every dollar they have, few realize that the same is true for most middle-class families in the US today. American families spent, on average, $53,495 in 2014, but the median family income was only $53,657 that year. Given that so many middle-class households have little or no savings to fall back on, they can slip into poverty after even a relatively minor or temporary economic setback.

While both the right-wing and mainstream media usually portray low-income Americans as some distinct, inferior, small, "other" class of people that is detached from conventional American life, the reality is that poverty is as common as snow in Buffalo and as American as apple pie, jazz, and baseball. Listen up, America: your wealthy elites want the middle class to believe that they have more in common with the rich than the poor. They also want you to buy the myth that, if you are in the middle class, you are likely to be rich someday. It's pitiful, America, that you fall for that shtick as frequently as Charlie Brown falls for Lucy's football trick. The reality, though, is that members of the US middle class have far more in common with the poor than with the wealthy, and that middle-class families are far more likely to sink into poverty than to strike it rich.

Sociologist Mark Rank has discovered that, by the time Americans reach the age of 60, nearly four in five experience "some kind of economic hardship: They've gone through a spell of unemployment, or spent time relying on a government program for the poor like food stamps, or lived at least one year in poverty or very close to it."[37] The chief threats to the middle class—too few jobs and too low wages, combined with soaring costs for housing, healthcare, education, food, and childcare—are the very same factors that are the main contributors to poverty.

Americans are working their tushes off, but the massive increases in US worker productivity have been coupled with a sharp decline in the purchasing power of those same workers' wages.

Countless Americans are solidly middle class one day—but after the car that takes them to work breaks down, their home catches fire, someone in their family gets very sick, their company announces layoffs, or they go through a tough divorce—they are soon impoverished. Tens of millions of families are only one or two setbacks away from financial disaster, especially since the US is the only industrialized Western nation with no paid family or medical leave.

The Financial Times reported, "America's middle class has shrunk to just half the population for the first time in at least four decades as the forces of technological change and globalization drive a wedge between the winners and losers in a splintering US society. The ranks of the middle class are now narrowly outnumbered by those in lower and upper income strata combined for the first time since at least the early 1970s."[38]

The share of working-age households falling into the middle class (with incomes roughly between $30,000 and $90,000) fell from 56.5 percent in 1979 to only 45.1 percent in 2012.[39]

Truly middle-class families are vanishing so quickly that the only reliable way you can see them anymore is on sitcom re-runs on Nick at Nite.*

Too many elites (including Barack Obama and Hillary Clinton) claim that people earning up to $250,000 annually constitute the "middle class." Yet the US median household income in 2014 was $53,657, statistically the same as in 2013, and, adjusted for inflation, 6.5 percent lower than in 2007. Of all US households, nearly half earned $50,000 or below and one in 20 (equaling about seven million households) earned $200,000 or more.[40] Given that nearly half of all Americans have annual incomes below $50,000, it is clear that $250,000 per year is *not* middle class, even in high-cost cities.[41]

Many folks who have been solidly middle class during their working years fall into poverty in retirement, as their savings and pensions are swept away. Nearly one-third of US heads of household ages 55 and older have no pension or retirement savings and a median annual income of about $19,000.[42] Nearly every state has cut back on retirement plans for state workers, many of whom are low-paid.[43] The pension fund of the Teamsters Union, one of the largest labor groups, filed for reorganization under a new federal law and informed its 400,000 members that their benefits had to be cut.[44] Imagine busting your ass for decades driving a dangerous truck or lifting heavy boxes—and a slightly comfortable retirement is one of the few things you can look forward to—only to learn that others have squandered your meager nest egg. Fortunately, Obama's Department of the Treasury rejected the plan.[45]

Millions who are "too poor to retire and too young to die," as the *Los Angeles Times* put it, continue toiling long into their golden years.[46] America, you even treat the elderly—whom many other cultures revere—like crap.

I must again note that it's wrong to assume that most US poverty is passed down between generations of families. Because this point is so central, I must again also cite the fact that, in the 48 months encompassing the years 2009 to 2012, more than a third of all American families experienced poverty in at least two of those months, but less

---

* An endangered species, a middle-class family.

than 3 percent were poor for *every one* of those 48 months.[47] That means that the number of Americans who *sometimes* live in poverty dwarfs the number of those who *always* do.

NUMBER OF MONTHS US HOUSEHOLDS
LIVED BELOW THE POVERTY LINE
2009 – 2012

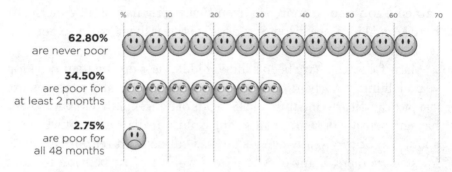

62.80%
are never poor

34.50%
are poor for
at least 2 months

2.75%
are poor for
all 48 months

Again, most families who experience poverty do so sporadically, repeatedly climbing into, and then falling out of, the middle class. Likewise, many middle-class Americans fall into poverty multiple times over a lifetime, often for brief stints. The average length of time most families spend in poverty is now six months—far too long, but hardly a lifetime.

Given the paltry media coverage of poverty, you'd never know that about 100 million Americans (a number greater than the combined populations of California, Texas, Florida, and Illinois) dipped below the poverty line at least once during that four-year period.

Even over one year, 2014, the number of Americans in poverty and near poverty was massive—and incredibly diverse. A third of American households, equaling more than 100 million people, earned below $40,000. In that year, one in seven Americans, or 47.7 million, lived in poverty, a number larger than the populations of California and Virginia combined.* The Census Bureau reported, "For the fourth consecutive year, the number of people in poverty at the national level was not statistically different from the previous year's estimates."[48]

---

* In 2014, a family of three was defined as "poor" if they earned $19,790 or less during the year.

Yet during that same four-year period, the stock market rose by 60 percent. This has been the first time in modern history that massive income growth among top earners and strong overall economic growth did nothing—literally nothing—to reduce poverty, because too many Americans were still either entirely unemployed, had just given up in their job searches, or were working part-time or full-time for lower wages. Fully 9.4 million *more* Americans lived in poverty in 2014 than in 2007, before the recession. Eight percent fewer Americans owned their own homes in 2015 than in 2005, further proof that many never recovered from the 2007–2008 financial collapse. Don't accept this deprivation as the "new normal," America.

From 2010 to 2013, employment in the wealthiest US neighborhoods jumped by more than a fifth, but in the lowest-income neighborhoods, the number of jobs fell sharply and one in 10 businesses shuttered.[49]

In 2014, as has been the case for decades, while people of color were more likely than whites to be poor, the largest number of Americans in poverty was white.[50] The number of poor women exceeded the number of men by five million. While foreign-born Americans had a poverty rate higher than the population as a whole, those who had become naturalized citizens had a lower rate than native-born Americans. The South continued to have the highest poverty rate, 19.5 percent, but even in the region with the relatively lowest level of struggling families, the West, more than one in 10 people lived in poverty. One in 10 suburban dwellers, and one in 16 married couples, suffered from poverty. Even among Americans with college degrees, one in 20 was poor.[51]

And US children continued to be particularly vulnerable, with one in five (more than 15 million) living in poverty. The lazy bums.

Troubled yet? Wait, it gets still worse. "Deep poverty" is generally defined as affecting households that earn less than half the official poverty cut-off; thus in 2014, if you were in a family of three, and you lived in deep poverty, you earned $9,895 or less. In 2014, an appalling 20.8 million Americans (a number larger than the population of Florida) lived in so-called deep poverty.[52]

If you can believe it, it gets worse still.* (I've said it before, but I promise, I really am fun at parties.) Some Americans live in such abject poverty that their Dickensian conditions are similar to those in developing countries. The term "extreme poverty" refers to people who live on $2 or less per *day* in cash, or less than $730 per *year*. We usually imagine that humans suffering from such destitution would live in places like Bangladesh, Haiti, or Mali. Can you imagine living on $2 a day in the United States? I can't. Yet in mid-2011, 2 years *after* the official end of the recession, an estimated 1.65 *million* US households, with 3.55 million children, survived on $2 or less in cash income per person daily.[53] Part of the reason for that is that cash assistance (welfare) is now so limited.

(As I typed the above paragraph, an ad for Emirates Airline appeared on my TV. In it, Jennifer Aniston, in a lush terrycloth robe, is having a nightmare in which the airline she is on—unlike Emirates Airline, apparently—didn't have showers and a bar stocking champagne and fancy liquor. That sure is a nightmare!)

Arguably the most severe symptom of poverty in America is homelessness. An astonishing 2.5 million children—a number greater than the population of Houston and about one in 30 of the nation's children—were homeless in 2013, representing an 8 percent jump in just one year. Nearly half the kids were six or younger.[54] Many of these Americans aren't even included in the Census Bureau counts of poverty.

I am so, so sorry for delivering bummer after bummer, dear reader. You might get the false impression that I am a dreadful, unremitting scold who doesn't want Jennifer Aniston to shower wherever and whenever she pleases, but I want you to know that I am actually a carefree, fun-loving guy.

Here, I'll prove it.

Q: Why did the low-income American cross the road? A: To get to a soup kitchen.

OK, never mind.

"Don't you get tired of being outraged all the time?" my friend once implored me.

"Yes," I said. "So, would you please tell the world to be less outrageous?"

---

* This is so depressing, dear reader, that I think by now you deserve a cute panda picture: Now don't you feel better?

WHAT'S AMERICAN POVERTY *REALLY* LIKE?

In 1651, English philosopher Thomas Hobbes wrote that life is "solitary, poor, nasty, brutish, and short." (And you thought *I* was a curmudgeon.) Hobbes's statement is no longer entirely true for most residents of developed nations anymore because they usually live longer, but most of it is true day-to-day for many Americans in poverty.

For the 1.65 million American households that suffer extreme poverty on $2 a day or less, life is hell. Many are forced to live on the streets, in cars, and/or on a rotating array of couches in the homes of friends or relatives. Many face frequent and acute hunger, and are sometimes forced to rummage through garbage bins for dinner scraps. Some must resort to selling blood, their identity, or sexual favors to survive.[55] The children in these families suffer grave emotional and physical harm. Setbacks pile upon setbacks, and life is all but hopeless.

For the majority of Americans below the poverty line, however, life is marginally less tragic. Many benefit from at least some safety net programs like SNAP, Medicaid, Section 8 subsidized housing, and, if they are working, Earned Income Tax Credits and Child Tax Credits. For millions more, those programs actually lift them above the poverty line.

But just because the living conditions of many low-income Americans are slightly better than those in developing countries, we shouldn't discount the reality that their lives are pretty darn miserable.

Most low-income Americans do work—and in the most tedious, dangerous, and low-paid jobs. For instance, a *New York Times* exposé of nail salon employees found that

> [t]he women begin to arrive just before 8 a.m., every day and without fail, until there are thickets of young Asian and Hispanic women on nearly every street corner along the main roads of Flushing, Queens. . . . They will not return until late at night, after working 10- to 12-hour shifts, hunched over fingers and toes. . . . Jing Ren, a 20-year-old who had recently arrived from China, stood among them for the first time, headed to a job at a salon in a Long Island strip mall. . . . She clutched her lunch and a packet of nail tools that manicurists must

bring from job to job. Tucked in her pocket was $100 in carefully folded bills for another expense: the fee the salon owner charges each new employee for her job. The deal was the same as it is for beginning manicurists in almost any salon in the New York area. She would work for no wages, subsisting on meager tips, until her boss decided she was skillful enough to merit a wage. It would take nearly three months before her boss paid her. Thirty dollars a day. The number of salons in New York City alone has more than tripled over a decade and a half to nearly 2,000 in 2012. But largely overlooked is the rampant exploitation of those who toil in the industry. A vast majority of workers are paid below minimum wage; sometimes they are not even paid. Workers endure all manner of humiliation, including having their tips docked as punishment for minor transgressions, constant video monitoring by owners, even physical abuse. Employers are rarely punished for labor and other violations.[56]

In 2016, when the *Boston Globe* switched paper delivery companies and there were many problems as a result, the newsroom staff pitched in to deliver the Sunday edition once, generating heartwarming media coverage nationwide. But buried in the *Globe*'s own coverage of the story were some disconcerting facts about their long-time workers: "Carriers generally can gross about $1,200 to $1,400 a month for about 25 hours of work each week . . . That indicates an hourly rate of about $12 to $14."[57] Twenty-five hours of work a week is obviously too many for a kid, so their delivery personnel are likely adults, who would be earning between $14,400 to $16,800 yearly, and thus would be living in poverty or forced to take second or third jobs, even though they must wake up obscenely early in the morning and make deliveries in all types of miserable weather, either lugging their kids with them or leaving the kids home alone to get ready for school.

Because low-income folks work so hard—but generally lack the best nutrition and top-notch healthcare—poverty, and the symptoms of it, can literally kill. Leading epidemiologists have found that "approximately 245,000 deaths in the United States in 2000 were attributable to low education, 176,000 to racial segregation, 162,000 to low social support, and 1,119,000 to income inequality."[58] Low-income people are even more likely than others to die in car crashes because they own cars that are older, have lower crash-test ratings, and have fewer safety features such as side airbags, automatic warnings, and rear cameras.[59] Overall, lowest-income Americans die even younger than the lowest-income Costa Ricans, a country with more severe poverty than the US.[60] In the early 1970s, the wealthiest half of American men lived about a year longer than the least wealthy half; by 2013, they lived 14 years longer.[61] As a result, low-income working Americans are subsidizing the old-age Medicare and Social Security payments of higher-income Americans.

Because they have little economic power, and even less political power, low-income people are shafted in every aspect of life—and death.

In a piece in the *New Yorker* entitled "What Poverty Does to the Young Brain," Madeline Ostrander wrote,

> The conditions that attend poverty—what a National Scientific Council report summarized as "overcrowding, noise, substandard housing, separation from parent(s), exposure to violence, family turmoil," and other forms of extreme stress—can be toxic to the developing brain, just like drug or alcohol abuse. These conditions provoke the body to release hormones such as cortisol, which is produced in the adrenal cortex. Brief bursts of cortisol can help a person manage difficult situations, but high stress over the long term can be disastrous. . . . A person whose brain has been undermined in this way can suffer long-term behavioral and cognitive difficulties. . . . [N]euroscientists at four universities scanned the brains of a group of twenty-four-year-olds and found that, in those who had lived in poverty at age nine, the brain's centers of negative emotion were more frequently buzzing with activity, whereas the areas that could rein in such emotions were quieter. Elsewhere, stress in childhood has been shown to make people prone to depression, heart disease, and addiction in adulthood. The story that

science is now telling rearranges the morality of parenting and poverty, making it harder to blame problem children on problem parents.[62]

Recent research proves that when, at the end of each month, low-income people exhaust their government benefits and have diminished food budgets, they suffer from the following:

▸ A drop-off in caloric intake, with estimates of this decline ranging from 10 to 25 percent over the course of the month;

▸ A 27 percent increase in the rate of hospital admissions due to low blood sugar for low-income adults between the first and last week of the month;

▸ An 11 percent increase in the rate of disciplinary actions among school children in SNAP households between the first and last week of the month; and

▸ Diminished student performance on standardized tests, with performance improving only gradually again after the next month's benefits are received.[63]

I once heard a small child in Delaware explain how her mother worked seven days a week but didn't always have enough money to get the food they needed. And US child hunger numbers would be far greater if it weren't for the life-saving impact of federally funded school breakfasts and lunches. Hungry kids actually root *against* snow days.

Forty-seven million Americans, including 12 million children and seven million seniors, were forced to use the nation's food pantries and soup kitchens in 2014.[64] It should break your heart, America, that 70 years after FDR's death, you are again full of breadlines.

All hunger, but particularly child hunger, inflicts great hardship on the most vulnerable of our neighbors. It also makes it nearly impossible for little boys and girls to grow up to achieve the American Dream. The main cause of hunger is poverty. Yet hunger makes it difficult for children to escape poverty, creating a cruel trap. What's more, researchers have produced vast amounts of data in recent decades proving that hunger and food insecurity directly harm children at each stage of their development while also erecting barriers to effective parenting. Hunger impairs physical growth and health, saps energy, and makes it impossible to concentrate, thereby compromising performance at school and at home. It should be no shock that hungry children perform less well on tests. To be schooled, you must be fueled. To be well-read, you must be well-fed.

Even children in families that struggle to put food on the table but manage to avoid extreme hunger still suffer serious physical and emotional damage from the uncertainty, from eating less nutritious but more affordable food, and from the stress. All those factors fuel feelings of despair and inadequacy among children and parents.*

College students also face hunger and homelessness. In a nationwide survey of community college students, one in five said that in the 30 days prior to the survey they had gone hungry because of a lack of money, and a shocking 13 percent had experienced homelessness sometime that year. Far more—just over half—said they were at risk of either hunger or homelessness. Most received financial aid and held down jobs, but it wasn't enough. "Without a home and without meals, I felt like an impostor," one student said. "I was shamefully worrying about food, and shamefully staring at the clock to make it out of class in time to get in line for the local shelter when I should have been giving my undivided attention to the lecturer."[65] It is no wonder why so many students aren't able to stick it out and get degrees.

Ok, I know the facts are unremittingly depressing—yet again. Sigh.**

But even if a family is fortunate enough that their SNAP benefits

---

* Ok, it's time for another cheer-you-up break—now with an adorable baby pig eating an ice cream cone:

** If you still can't get enough of this ultra-fun topic of US hunger, then rush right out and buy my first book: *All You Can Eat: How Hungry is America?*, also published by Seven Stories Press. Not only will you learn more about domestic hunger than you'd ever need to know, you can actually read something nice about Richard Nixon. And by the way, if you want to do something more concrete to fight hunger here at home, go to www.HungerFreeAmerica.org. Do it now.

somehow cover all their food purchases for a month, SNAP can't help them pay for anything else, such as diapers, tampons, or toilet paper.

Meanwhile the cost of everything keeps going up, while wages stagnate. Housing costs are far outstripping wages. The price of healthcare, childcare, and higher education continue to skyrocket.

Even the quintessential public transport system in America—the Metropolitan Transportation Authority in New York City—has gone from being highly affordable to absurdly expensive, due to a combination of factors, including cuts in federal and state subsidies and mismanagement. In 2015, the price of one subway or bus ride increased to $2.75. That was the fourth fare hike in six years, with overall increases doubling the rate of inflation. A one-way bus or subway fare then cost 31 percent of the state's minimum hourly wage, compared to 11 percent in 1970. Meanwhile, key politicians in the state kept bragging that they'd avoided raising any taxes, utterly ignoring the reality that transit hikes *are* tax increases on the working people who can afford it least.

Low-income people often pay *more* for things than the wealthy. They need to rent furniture. They fork over astronomical fees for check-cashing services. They hand over higher security deposits for apartments (which they often never get back). They frequently feel they have no choice but to take out cash advances called "payday loans" (which charge exorbitant, *Sopranos*-level rates of interest) to tide them over until they get their next paychecks. While in El Paso, Texas, I heard a revolting radio ad that claimed a company's payday loans would prevent a family from "choosing between food and rent" and "going hungry." The combination of fear mongering and extortion is appalling. Likewise, Trump University recruiters targeted single parents with hungry kids because they were most desperate to get ahead.[66]

A study by the Progressive Policy Institute found that in 2016 low-income workers paid an average of around $400 each to national tax preparation chains.[67] Damn, poverty is expensive.

Government also gets into the act when it comes to playing on the hopes and fears of low-income families in order to make money. As the *Portland Press Herald* reported,

(Please join me in singing the official campus fight song for Trump U:
"♪♪Go, go, go Trump U / As we seek more desperate students to royally screw / Look
at all the students piled fore and aft / Just some more suckers we can shaft / Our profits
are yuuuge, our accomplishments are small (like Marco Rubio's you know what) /
But you'll forget about the Donald's crookedness if we just build a wall♪♪")

Seidl's tiny roadside convenience store, along a lonely stretch
of Route 1 in an area where unemployment has often been the
highest in the state, sells more lottery tickets per capita than any
other in Maine: $1,313 for every man, woman and child in town . . .
[A]cross the state, lottery ticket sales go up when people lose their
jobs. For every 1 percent increase in joblessness in a given zip
code, sales of scratch and draw tickets jump 10 percent . . . [T]he
lottery is a tax on the poor. Recent research in 39 states has shown
that lottery sales increase with poverty, and economists have long
warned that lotteries prey on societies' most desperate people,
who play disproportionately despite long odds of winning . . .
Residents in Maine's poorest towns spend as much as 200 times
more per person than those in wealthier areas, according to the
data. Disproportionate spending by the poor and unemployed has
helped to boost ticket sales to $230 million annually, more than
what Mainers spend each year on liquor.[68]

After this news broke in Maine, state legislators of both parties (oh, so predictably) sought to restrict the purchasing habits of low-income people, rather than to limit the lottery, or, goodness forbid, enable struggling Mainers to lift their incomes by establishing more jobs or higher wages. As Maine activist Mike Tipping put it, "Most Republicans and far too many Democrats were looking for a chance to spew some bile about Maine's undeserving poor."[69]

Even in natural disasters, the poor suffer more, but at least for a brief moment of time right after each of them, the public seems to notice. Disasters rip the bandages off the festering wounds of poverty, and we all could see that, after Hurricane Katrina, low-income New Orleanians had the least ability to evacuate. Their houses were located in the most at-risk neighborhoods and their dwellings were made with shoddy building materials. Because they also had the least political influence, their neighborhoods were the last to be rescued and the last to be rebuilt—and many homes were not rebuilt at all. After Hurricane Sandy, while some wealthier, white neighborhoods were quickly back in business, I visited Red Hook, Brooklyn, a community of mostly low-income families of color, and much of the neighborhood still had no lights. You need political power to get electric power restored after a natural disaster—now that's a man-made disaster if I've ever heard of one.

So, poverty stinks. I could say, "I don't want to belabor the point," but people who say that, myself included, already have. So let's trudge on anyway, America, because we need to look carefully into the mirror and see what poverty does to our nation's face and why.

SO, WHY *ARE* LOW-INCOME PEOPLE POOR, REALLY?

The facts make it pretty obvious that the main reason low-income people are poor is because they don't have much money. Seriously. It's as simple as that.

Most of us easily accept the reality that the biggest difference between the rich and the nonrich is that rich people have more money, but America's elites trip all over themselves to continually try to imagine complex, unfathomable reasons for poverty.

Much of the endless tut-tutting over the *true* cause of poverty—by academics, policy makers, columnists, and think tank analysts—often comes back to the same conclusion: that poverty is, somehow, mostly caused by poor folks themselves. Conservatives say low-income people are poor because they are lazy, shiftless, drug-addicted, criminal, coddled by government, and promiscuous. But even many well-meaning liberals—particularly if they are white and/or never faced poverty themselves—frequently think that the main cause is inadequate education, job skills, or financial education among poor people. (Granted, those liberals may also think that the substandard education and job training within the ranks of the poor is caused by racism, Republican budget cuts, etc., but in the end, many liberals still believe that the main problem is a knowledge and skills gap, rather than broader societal faults, such as few living-wage jobs in the economy.)

Nobel Prize-winning economics wizard Joseph Stiglitz has written, "Unemployment—the inability of the market to generate jobs for so many citizens—is the worst failure of the market, the greatest source of inefficiency, and a major cause of inequality."[70] In May 2016, the US unemployment rate fell to an eight-year low of 4.7 percent, but that still meant that one in 20 Americans looking for work couldn't get it. The official unemployment rate fails to include people who have stopped looking for work, so a better gauge of unemployment is the labor force participation rate, which was only 62.6 percent that month, which meant more than 77 million Americans over the age of 16 were not officially working outside their homes, although significant numbers of those were raising children full time, attending school full time, working off the books, retired, and/or disabled. Tens of millions of other Americans were working part time, unable to obtain the full-time work they were seeking or needing.

For those who do have jobs, their wages are frequently at levels so low they ensure destitution. In 2013, the median wage of the 55,000 fast-food workers in New York City was $8.90 an hour, equaling about $16,000 for a year. Between 2000 and 2013, the number of fast-food jobs in the city increased by more than 50 percent—10 times as fast as in any other type of private job. Only 13 percent of fast-food workers got health insurance benefits at work. In New York State, three in five have received some form of government assistance over a five-year period.

Meanwhile, fast-food industry executives made out like bandits: executive pay and profits in the industry rose mightily.[71] Are you sitting down? It would take a Chicago McDonald's worker who earns $8.25 an hour more than a *century* on the clock to match the $8.75 million that the company's chief executive made in 2011.[72]

There is the old stereotype that fast-food workers are all teenagers, just earning some extra cash on the side to buy video games. Yet, according to the Center for Economic and Policy Research, "Only about 30 percent of fast-food workers are teenagers. Another 30 percent are between the ages of 20 and 24. The remaining 40 percent are 25 and older. More than one-fourth are raising at least one child. Over 70 percent have at least a high school degree and more than 30 percent have had at least some college education . . . Their wages are very low, even by today's depressed standards. If we look at straight wages—that is, excluding overtime, tips, bonuses, and commissions, all of which are rare in the fast-food industry—about 13 percent make at or below the federal minimum wage . . . [F]ewer than one in twelve make more than $12 per hour."[73]

In 1998, the federal minimum wage was a paltry $5.15 per hour. The 2014 minimum wage level, adjusted for inflation, was equivalent to only $4.99 per hour. As the chart on the next page demonstrates, the low minimum wage was one of the prime reasons that 48 million Americans still couldn't afford enough food in 2014.

But even folks who are making slightly above the minimum wage struggle mightily. Bertrand Olotara, a chef in the cafeteria of the United States Senate, wrote,

> Every day, I serve food to some of the most powerful people on earth, including many of the senators who are running for president: I'm a cook for the federal contractor that runs the US Senate cafeteria. . . . I'm a single father and I only make $12 an hour; I had to take a second job at a grocery store to make ends meet. But even though I work seven days a week—putting in 70 hours between my two jobs—I can't manage to pay the rent, buy school supplies for my kids, or even put food on the table. I hate to admit it, but I have to use food stamps so that my kids don't go

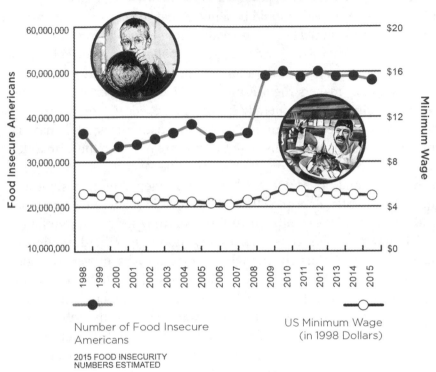

AS PURCHASING POWER OF MINIMUM WAGE SINKS, US HUNGER STAYS SKY HIGH

Number of Food Insecure Americans

US Minimum Wage (in 1998 Dollars)

2015 FOOD INSECURITY NUMBERS ESTIMATED

to bed hungry. I've done everything that politicians say you need to do to get ahead and stay ahead: I work hard and play by the rules; I even graduated from college and worked as a substitute teacher for five years. But I got laid-off and now I'm stuck trying to make ends meet with dead-end service jobs.[74]

Eighty-five percent of US households with children struggling against hunger have one or more adults in the labor force, including almost 70 percent with at least one full-time worker.[75]

"IT'S ALL *YOUR* FAULT" AND OTHER LIES YOUR EX TOLD YOU

If the two greatest causes of poverty and inequality are the lack of money and the lack of hope, it should be a given that the clearest response to those problems should be giving people more earning power and more hope. Yet few of America's existing public policies—and even fewer of today's political leaders—offer tangible means of providing either.

A few policy makers rhetorically recognize the importance of hope, but their solutions are generally in the "just cheer up" or "have more faith" vein, detached from the need to ensure concrete, material improvements in people's lives—or worse, are based on the false (often racially-loaded) assumption that low-income Americans create their own poverty and can escape it if they simply adopt a more positive attitude, work harder, or change their "culture." No matter how much our leaders screw up the country, if you're poor, they say it's all *your* fault.

The downtrodden, conservatives say, don't work hard enough or raise families responsibly enough because they have been corroded by "dependence" on government. Ben Carson, Scott Walker, Rudy Giuliani, Bill O'Reilly, Jeb Bush, Ted Cruz, Rush Limbaugh, Mitt Romney, Marco Rubio, Sean Hannity, Carly Fiorina, and John Kasich (among many others) all make similar claims. The belief of government-induced laziness as the prime source of poverty is such a fixation on the Right that it almost edges out "climate change is a hoax," "guns prevent violence," and "Obama is a Muslim" for the top spots in their greatest hits collection.

Economics writer Neil Irwin, comparing Nordic nations to the US, has thoroughly demolished the myth that robust government safety nets discourage employment: "More people may work when countries offer public services that directly make working easier, such as subsidized care for children and the old; generous sick leave policies; and cheap and accessible transportation."[76]

Yet rather than acting upon concrete evidence of what really works in reducing poverty, most "anti-poverty" proposals from the Right call for cutting the safety net and placing onerous new government controls on the personal lives of low-income Americans. What they call "anti-poverty" plans would be more accurately labeled "punish-poor-people" plans that will increase poverty. Their plans are a political "bait and switch."

Take Speaker of the House Paul Ryan's proposals. Please. First, there is the issue of Ryan's credibility—or lack thereof—on the issue of fighting poverty. Some make fun of Ryan for spending so much time at the gym. We shouldn't. Health is important, and he looks great. The far more important point is that, in the remaining time he is not at the gym, Ryan has spent much of his career trying to take food, housing, and healthcare *away* from poor people. And he's succeeded in helping to cut billions of dollars of aid to the most vulnerable Americans, thereby *increasing* poverty and worsening its impact. Therefore, when he offers what he claims is a comprehensive plan to *reduce* poverty in America, we can be forgiven if we take his proposals with a grain of salt. In fact, we take them with a few Great Salt Lakes' worth of salt.* After all, his anti-poverty ideas to date have been only slightly more helpful than Colonel Sanders's promised "retirement plans" for chickens.

But even as we point out Ryan's flaws as a messenger, it is vital that we seriously examine the substance of his message. He has taken the time to produce a 73-page report on opportunity and poverty, which sets him apart from his compatriots.[77] He's the former vice-presidential nominee of his party and, arguably, the second most powerful elected official in Washington. Any leading political and governmental figure who claims to offer substantive recommendations to address poverty deserves a serious hearing and a serious response. So, let's take a look.

Ryan's plan includes a few positive proposals, such as expanding the federal Earned Income Tax Credit (EITC)—which now gives tax refunds to low-income workers, mostly those with children—to include more childless wage earners. This is a good thing. He has also proposed that workers get their portion of EITC payments spread out over each paycheck, instead of just once a year. Those are not new ideas, but again, they are good ones, and they should receive bipartisan support. But because Ryan and his GOP colleagues refuse to even *consider* requiring wealthy Americans to again pay their fair share of taxes, and because he has pledged that his anti-poverty approach wouldn't add a

---

* The Great Salt Lake contains about 4.5 billion tons of salt.

penny to the federal deficit, he has proposed to pay for the EITC expansion by eliminating some existing low-income programs of proven effectiveness. One of the programs on Ryan's chopping block is the USDA Farmers' Market Nutrition Program, which helps low-income women who are pregnant or who have small children obtain fresh produce at local farmers' markets. Yes, Paul Ryan would rather harm small farmers and literally take fresh, healthy food away from pregnant moms than require billionaires to pay a few more dollars in taxes.

The centerpiece of the Ryan plan, like many conservative proposals of the last few decades, is eliminating the right of individuals to receive SNAP as a guaranteed entitlement if their income is low enough. Instead he would give the money to the states in the form of block grants, allowing them to determine who does, and does not, get nutrition assistance.* Ryan claims that his proposal wouldn't result in benefit cuts, but as the Center on Budget and Policy Priorities has documented, the structure of his plan would virtually guarantee cuts over time, and would provide less help to families in need, because his new system—as is the case with all block grants—would not adequately respond to changing economic conditions or prevent governors from raiding anti-poverty funds for other purposes.[78]

Moreover, the entire Ryan poverty plan, as well as many similar GOP recommendations, is doomed to failure because of reliance on discredited, right-wing beliefs about poverty. It's as if your spouse keeps claiming he's taken out the garbage even though the kitchen trashcan is overflowing, or if he keeps denying he's cheating no matter how many suspicious hotel purchases are on his credit card. But, as in any emotionally abusive relationship, if one side keeps lying often and convincingly enough, both parties start to believe the lies are truth.

To help prevent this from continually happening to you, America, here are some fact-based talking points you can use next time you are arguing with a frothing, prevaricating, right-winger:

Reality #1: While the Right often claims the 1960s War on Poverty was a failure, the Great Society programs actually helped slash poverty in half, greatly reducing the worst symptoms of deprivation, and boosting economic mobility.

---

* Pundits keep calling Ryan's plans "big and bold." So were the plans for the Titanic.

Conservatives say over and over again that the federal "War on Poverty"—the ambitious federal initiative to end impoverishment started by President John F. Kennedy, dramatically expanded by President Lyndon B. Johnson, and largely continued by President Richard M. Nixon—was a failure. But the reality is that, between 1960 and 1973, due to both broad-based economic growth and increased social service spending, the US poverty rate was cut in half and 16 million Americans climbed out of destitution and into the middle class. The truth is that we were winning the war on poverty, until we stopped fighting it by reducing funding for proven poverty-reduction efforts.

Moreover, the main thrust of most federal safety net programs is not, per se, to reduce poverty. Federal nutrition programs are primarily designed to reduce hunger, and they do. Federal housing programs are primarily designed to reduce homelessness, and they do. Medicaid is primarily designed to increase life expectancy, and it does. You will even find, tucked deep in a section of Ryan's report decrying the supposed failure of the War on Poverty, a sheepish admission: "The federal government has helped decrease material deprivation." In other words, even Paul Ryan admits that federal programs help reduce the pain of being poor. That's a pretty startling admission from a powerful man who has made a career of falsely asserting that the safety net never worked, but we shouldn't expect a true apology from him any more than we should expect him (or me, for that matter) to pull his car over to ask for directions when he's lost.

These federal programs *do* reduce hardship overall, indirectly. But right-wingers continue to argue that, because these endeavors haven't wiped out poverty altogether, the programs just don't work. That's absurd. It's like arguing that your marriage is a failure if you and your mate squabble occasionally. It's like arguing that all police forces are failures because crime still exists, or that all military and intelligence efforts are failures because America still has foreign enemies. If government spending significantly reduces the problem it is fighting, then it's obviously working, not failing.

On rare occasions, leading Republicans stray from current orthodoxy and admit the obvious—that, sometimes, government programs are life-savers. US Senator Marco Rubio, when he was near the beginning of his presidential campaign in 2015, rhetorically supported the existence of government social service programs, saying, "I don't take my children to the circus very often, but when I do, I have noticed that acrobats tend to be much more daring when they have a safety net beneath them. [Such support] is essential for the success of the free enterprise system."[79] In fact, the actual policies Rubio proposed, even at the time, would mostly have *cut* the safety net, but his willingness to at least verbally concede the worth of government programs was notable. Unfortunately, as the GOP primaries wore on, and it became obvious that "compassionate conservatism" was being Trumped by a sputtering hatred of all people nonwhite and non-wealthy, Rubio joined former Florida governor (and the brother of you know who*) in blasting Democrats for wanting to supposedly give away "free stuff" to low-income Americans just to get votes.[80] Truth-telling is rewarded in the modern Republican Party about as often as discretion is rewarded on *The Jerry Springer Show.*

Reality #2: While conservatives claim that the only measure of an anti-poverty program's success is whether it reduces the use of those same government benefits, a far more meaningful measure of its effectiveness is whether it reduces poverty and improves the long-term economic and social well-being of communities, families, and individuals.

The Ryan plan states, "Our true measure of success is the number of people who don't need government assistance." Ryan even equates receiving food and healthcare assistance from the government with "servitude."[81]

First, let's tackle the hypocrisy. Speaker Ryan and so many of his cronies decry every government program *except* the many programs from which *they* personally benefit. Ryan himself collected federal social security payments for two years after his father died and he has been on government payrolls, obtaining government healthcare, virtually his entire adult life.

As the *Seattle Times* reported, "The past decade has been very good

---

*

financially for Paul Ryan—the Janesville, Wis., congressman's net worth increased at least 75 percent, and he purchased a historic home once owned by the top executive of the Parker Pen Company. Federal financial disclosure forms show that last year [2011] Ryan, 42, had assets of between $2.1 million and $7.8 million—figures that include a trust valued at between $1 million and $5 million inherited by his wife."[82] Yet Ryan brags that his mom "relies on Medicare."[83] Ayn Rand is rolling in her grave.

Plus, Ryan doesn't consider it a failure if we spend money on the military or a new city transit center in his hometown. What Ryan really means is that government program reductions are a victory only when *low-income people* get less help.

Wisconsin Governor Scott Walker, who, as of 2016, had been on government payrolls for 22 years, often says that success should be measured not by how many people are dependent on government but by "how many people are no longer dependent on government."[84] Yet the same Scott Walker awarded $250 million in taxpayer funds to millionaire basketball team owners, some of whom were his campaign backers, to finance a new sports arena.[85]

Retired neurosurgeon Ben Carson, who once impersonated a presidential candidate, has repeatedly claimed that government programs create dependency and "rob people of incentive." He even had the gall to falsely claim that Dr. Martin Luther King, Jr. opposed such programs, when the truth is that King played a leading role in the fight to expand the anti-poverty safety net.[86] Carson went so far as to accuse Obama of purposely depressing the economy to keep people on welfare.[87] Yet growing up, Carson himself attended public schools, received food stamps, and obtained free eyeglasses from a government program.[88]

I could go on and on. And of course I will. (You knew that was coming, right?)

"Dependence" is in the eye of the beholder. Corporations may not actually be people, as Mitt Romney opined and as the Supreme Court has ruled, but corporate welfare surely goes to people, and very wealthy ones at that.*

---

* Federal government subsidies for nuclear power, for instance, go to oligarch nuclear power plant owners such as C. Montgomery Burns.

Let me tell you about the Republican congressman from Tennessee, Stephen Fincher, who claimed that funding SNAP was the same as "stealing other people's money" and misquoted scriptures to defend cuts to the program. Yet he personally lined his own family's pockets with $3.48 million in federal farm subsidies from 1999 to 2012.[89]

All these self-prophesied religious conservatives seem to have made up the definitive self-serving bible verse: "He who lives in glass houses should throw boulders." If hypocrisy were an Olympic sport, they would be multiple gold medal winners and be on a Wheaties box *and* in a Nike ad by now. Few things break up relationships more quickly than when one party lives by an entirely different set of rules than their partner.

Beyond the double standards, a knee-jerk preference for less government defies logic. Defining the success of a program merely by whether fewer people use it makes as little sense as defining the success of a hospital by how many people leave it—without differentiating between how many people leave it cured, equally ill, or dead. (Hint: It's better when people leave cured.) Likewise, if people are forced off government benefits only to become destitute, hungry, and homeless, then the caseload reduction must be deemed a failure. Yet big government is not always the answer either. For each problem, government should be as small or as big as it needs to be to properly address the challenge. America, let's try common sense for a change.

Besides, recent evidence suggests that safety net programs *do* promote long-term self-sufficiency. In just one example, a Harvard study found that, in families who received federally funded Section 8 housing vouchers to improve their housing and/or increase their housing stability, the long-term earnings of adults in those households increased by 15 percent.[90]

Reality #3: While more money isn't the only solution to poverty, it is clearly the top one.

Poverty is the one and only problem that is defined, first and foremost, by lack of money. Claiming you can solve poverty without money—as conservatives usually do—is like claiming you can solve drought without water or cure baldness without hair.

Conservatives—who seem to be about "money, money, money" when it comes to other issues (especially defense spending, tax cuts for the rich, and Wall Street bailouts)—don't seem to understand that when low-income families earn more money—or get help to pay for food, housing, or healthcare—they live better. When you dramatically increase your income—no matter whether it's because you got a raise as a reward for hard work or because, while "shootin' at some food" on your land, you find "bubblin' crude, black gold, Texas tea"—that extra money is almost certain to increase your standard of living.* While Jed Clampett may have made some bad spending choices after coming into wealth, numerous studies prove that the vast majority of real-life low-income people spend extra income on basics like food, housing, clothing, childcare, and medicine or, as some right-winger might put it, "luxuries."[91]

In the not-too-distant past, conservatives were at least intellectually honest, and admitted they actually thought inequality was a good thing. William F. Buckley once said, "Freedom breeds inequality. Without the freedom to be unequal, there is no freedom."[92] But when Republicans (such as Barry Goldwater) acknowledged that they thought inequality was positive, they got creamed in elections. That's why GOP pollsters then instructed their candidates to make the cockamamie claim that they would reduce poverty and inequality by "liberating" low-income people from dependence on government by cutting the safety net. Trust me, no one has ever been liberated by having their food taken away.

Reality #4: The federal government is often more responsive, quicker, more capable, and less corrupt than state and local governments.

The centerpiece of the Ryan plan is a scheme to scrap all the key federal poverty programs that are currently operated separately at the state level and instead fold them all into one program that would be run by each state but still funded by the federal government.

Conservatives want us to believe that states wear halos but, as corrupt as Washington, DC, is these days, many state capitols are even more crooked. So many state officials have been convicted of

---

* Hey, young 'uns: if you don't get this reference, google the Beverly Hillbillies. You'll be glad you did. You'll quickly learn how much the show has in common with *The Real Housewives of Beverly Hills*.

felonies that prisons could field football teams made up of former public servants: imagine the Attica Assemblymen versus the Joliet Govs.

Plus, there is not one iota of hard evidence that state governments, in aggregate, manage anti-poverty programs—or any other programs—more effectively than the federal government. If you are a low-income Californian living in South Central Los Angeles, a state government bureaucrat in Sacramento (a five-hour drive away) is no more—or less—likely to understand your needs than a federal government worker in Washington, DC (a five-hour flight away).

If the federal government is truly as evil and ineffective as conservatives claim, why do even the most Tea Party-fueled elected officials in the most right-wing states immediately demand that the *federal* government rush in to respond to local disasters such as tornados or chemical plant explosions? When the chips are down, no one argues that state or local governments—or faith-based nonprofit groups—are better suited to respond to tornadoes or floods than FEMA or the National Guard.

Remember when all the right-wing media and Republican pols were yowling that the Ebola virus would decimate the American populace and that it was somehow President Obama's fault? Remember that even the most conservative leaders wanted the federal—*yes, federal*—Centers for Disease Control and Prevention (CDC) to take the lead in solving the problem? Not one of them suggested that an Ebola onslaught could be halted by state or local agencies—or their local churches and synagogues. (Oh, and by the way, the federal CDC *was* remarkably successful, taking just a few weeks to prevent a major outbreak nationwide.) The record is clear that often the federal government is far *more* effective than states.

Moreover, history tells us that the very reason Congress created federal social safety net programs in the first place was precisely because states, on their own, were unable or unwilling to solve large social problems.

It is telling that, even as Ryan and others propose that poverty programs be run by states, they still call for them to be *paid for* by the federal government. Why? The dirty little secret is that many Southern states, which tend to be the most conservative and anti-Washington, are the very states most likely to receive far more federal dollars than their residents pay in federal taxes. For instance, South Carolina residents receive

$7.87 back from Washington for every $1 its citizens pay in federal tax, compared to less than $1 in New York, Ohio, Illinois, and Minnesota.[93] Out of the 20 states with the highest levels of SNAP participation as a percentage of their populations, many are in the South and 16 voted for Mitt Romney for president in 2008.[94] These red states couldn't survive without massive infusions of federal anti-poverty bucks.

Reality #5: Most poverty is short-term and caused by inequality and low wages, not *personal behavior.*

Paul Ryan's plan differentiates between what it calls "situational poverty" and "generational poverty." He implies that situational poverty is due to temporary factors mostly beyond someone's control and that generational poverty is long-term and caused mostly by irresponsible behavior. But the plan includes no serious provisions to create living-wage jobs or even raise wages, so its basic thrust is aimed at generational poverty.

The Ryan proposal claims that people suffering generational poverty lack "parenting skills" and "productive habits," yet it cites no data that low-income people are worse parents or lazier than wealthy Americans. If anyone doubts that wealthy people can also be fundamentally irresponsible, I have six words for you: Lindsay Lohan, Charlie Sheen, and Justin Bieber. (Oh, let me throw in four more words: Robert Durst and Bernie Madoff.)* Ryan also states that individuals in poverty are "at risk of return to substance abuse," as if it is self-evident that all those in long-term poverty previously engaged in substance abuse. (Did I mention Courtney Love?)

When a few states wasted millions of dollars and violated the Bill of Rights (as ruled by courts) in order to drug-test welfare recipients, it turned out that people receiving public assistance actually used drugs at a rate *lower* than the population as a whole.[95] I would be remiss if I didn't point out that Trey Radel, a GOP congressman who previously voted to drug-test SNAP recipients, was forced to resign after he pled guilty to cocaine possession. Yet as money-wasting, civil-liberty-crushing, and hypocritical as such ideas are, the GOP just can't let go of them. In 2016, a more senior Republican member of Congress, Rep. Robert Aderholt of Alabama, pushed to spend billions of dollars to drug-test tens of millions of Americans who rely on SNAP to obtain

---

* For additional examples of very wealthy people behaving very poorly indeed, see TMZ.com.

their food, and yet, as I'll explain later in the book, taxpayers and campaign donors pay for most of Aderholt's meals.[96]

In yet another attempt to correct the supposedly antisocial behavior of low-income Americans, the Ryan scheme allows states to create "opportunity grants" to require low-income families to be held to "a contract outlining specific and measurable benchmarks for success." The contract's benchmarks would include items such as finding a job, enrolling in employment training, participating in financial education and parenting classes, and even meeting "new acquaintances outside the circle of poverty." Sheesh. Anytime a lover tells you that they hate all your friends and family and that you must sever all contact with them, you know that you should have broken up with that jerk long ago.[*]

The Ryan agreement would also provide a "timeline" in which individuals are contractually obligated to meet these goals, allocate bonuses for meeting the requirements early, and impose "sanctions for breaking the terms of the contract." Such punitive mandates amount to massive government intrusion into the personal lives of citizens. This contract is so one-sided and patronizing that it amounts to the worst prenuptial agreement in world history. Just one look at this and this wedding's off, America!

State legislators in Kansas, not to be outdone by the poor-people-bashing in Congress, further injected themselves into the daily activities of impoverished people, as the *Washington Post* reported:

> Not trusting the poor to use their money wisely, [legislators] have voted to limit how much cash that welfare beneficiaries can receive . . . placing a daily cap of $25 on cash withdrawals . . . which will force beneficiaries to make more frequent trips to the ATM . . . Since there's a fee for every withdrawal, the limit means that some families will get substantially less money . . . Since most banking machines are stocked only with $20 bills, the $25 limit is effectively a $20 limit. A family seeking to withdraw even $200 in cash would have to visit an ATM 10 times a

---

[*] Imagine if President Obama had tried to require that defense contractors develop friendships with people who weren't fellow defense contractors. He would have been impeached.

month, a real burden for a parent who might not have a car and might not live in a neighborhood where ATMs are easy to find.[97]

Just to shame people in poverty, Kansas proposed spending tax dollars on bank fees that would otherwise have been used by families to pay for food and rent. Thankfully, after a public outcry, Kansas backed down, but I have no doubt the state is now scheming to find other ways to shaft the most vulnerable.

Conservatives proclaim that they don't want government on their own backs, or on the backs of giant corporations, but when it comes to people living in poverty, they want government on poor folks' backs, fronts, tops, and bottoms.* It's as if your spouse hid a nanny cam in a stuffed animal in your living room not to monitor your nanny, but to surreptitiously keep minute-by-minute tabs on *you*. Again, the Right is using a double—or triple—standard.

Prior to the mid-1990s, conservatives claimed that most poverty was caused by high rates of cash welfare dependency, crack use, teenage pregnancy, and violent crime. But the 1996 welfare reform law dramatically reduced cash assistance, and now fewer than 10 percent of Americans in poverty receive cash welfare. Nationwide, rates of violent crime, crack use, and teen pregnancy have plummeted since 1996. And while poverty dipped in the late 1990s, it has soared since then as jobs disappeared and wages flatlined. Thus, the preponderance of evidence suggests that economics and inequality of wealth, not personal behavior and dependency, continue to be the main causes of poverty.

In direct contrast to the right-wing caricature that low-income people are perpetually dependent upon government programs, the reality is that struggling families usually obtain means-tested benefits when they are facing their worst economic crises, but rapidly leave benefit programs when their fortunes improve. Also, while conservatives have fixated for decades on the supposed catastrophe of single motherhood,

---

* Sometimes conservatives want the government to control even the bodies of people suffering in an irreversible persistent vegetative state, as was the case when then-Governor Jeb Bush tried to use the power of the entire state government of Florida to keep Terri Schiavo alive against the wishes of her husband and legal guardian. Likewise, countless GOP politicians try to restrict women's access to contraception and abortion services by making it nearly impossible for providers to help the low-income women who can't go to another location or another job or another state for such services.

government data proves that married couples generally obtain higher government benefit amounts than households led by single mothers.[98]

As much as I blame conservatives and Republicans (rightfully so), again let's not let liberals and Democrats off the hook. While they are less likely to support massive cuts in anti-poverty programs and are slightly more willing to support marginal increases in funding, it's not as if liberal and Democratic leaders of the last few decades have made ending hardship a serious national priority. The liberal desire to give down-and-out families a few more crumbs is certainly more laudable than the conservative desire to take away even the tiniest tidbits, but strapped Americans deserve a full loaf.*

While many elites of both parties think low-income families need more financial education to lift them out of poverty, the reality is that while additional financial literacy could be useful to Americans of *all* incomes, if a struggling father pays more in basic living expenses than he earns in wages, no amount of money-managing advice will save him or his children.

And the frequent suggestions from some self-proclaimed progressives that hungry Americans would escape their fate if they took cooking and nutrition classes are out-of-touch, even if well-meaning. Certainly, Americans of all stripes could benefit from learning about food preparation and nutrition. For me, it might be nice if I knew how to make something other than spaghetti out of a jar.

Yet all the culinary classes and food budgeting help in the world won't solve the US hunger epidemic if people don't have the money to buy healthy food, can't find affordable nutritious foods in their neighborhoods, or don't have the time to prepare it if they are able to get it. As I'll explain later in the book, the myopic focus of some public health zealots to deny soda to low-income people distracts from accomplishing more meaningful nutrition goals.

---

* No, not this one

America, face the facts: only more jobs, higher wages, and a more robust governmental safety net can end US hunger once and for all.*

Still, even though the data clearly proves that most poverty is due to circumstances beyond the direct control of the people who suffer from them, and that most wealth is gained by a large measure of luck and proximity, it would be a massive mistake for progressives to entirely discount personal responsibility and individual initiative. Americans who work the hardest, sacrifice the most, and contribute to the common good *should* prosper more than those who don't. But we need concrete economic improvements (which I'll propose later in this book), not empty rhetoric, to ensure such earned prosperity. And all people—even those who screw up occasionally, whether rich or poor—should have a right to food, shelter, and healthcare.

Conservatives have raised poor-people-bashing to an art form. Low-income families don't need more scolding, restrictions on their behavior, or exhortations to "cheer up." They need more income. Don't lecture your overweight spouse to unilaterally eat less and exercise more; instead, buy healthier food and offer to go to the gym together.

Can't you see how absurd it is to keep blaming the victims of poverty for their own destitution? It's like when your ex cheated on you with your best friend, then, when caught, yelled at you that it was *your* fault because you introduced them in the first place. That's why that person is now an *ex*. We can deal with your "best friend" later, but for now, isn't it time we broke up with the conservatives?

---

* If you want details about the proven, common-sense ways to end domestic hunger, I urge you to run out—right now—to your favorite independent bookstore to buy that Seven Stories classic, *All You Can Eat: How Hungry is America?* by Joel Berg, a heartbreaking work of staggering genius. Or you can get a "used—very good" copy through Amazon for about eight cents. For $2.23, you can get a signed copy, which the online sellers of the book brag, has "never been read, never been opened." Yes, I know this is the second plug for my own book in a single chapter, and a pathetic one at that, but, you know, a guy's gotta make a living.

3.

Eat, Pray, Love ...
and Then Get Fired for Spending
So Much Time Away from Work

What would *you* do if you were an American woman who had just gone through a bitter divorce?

Would you take a year-long, round-the-world therapy tour, spending four months in Italy, eating and searching for pleasure, three months in India searching for spirituality, and five more months in Bali to find balance and the love of your life (a Brazilian businessman)—and then hope that you'd be played in the movie version of your life by Julia Roberts?*

Or would you get the hell right back to work and perhaps seek a second or third job to pay the bills and support your kids, if you had them—and dream about the day you'd be played in a sitcom by Bonnie Franklin?**

Before you answer that quiz, consider these facts: in 2014, women earned 82 cents for every dollar earned by men; women's median weekly earnings for full-time work were $719 (equaling $37,388 for a year) compared with $871 (equaling $45,392 for the year) for men.[99] Women tend to lose income, while men tend to gain it, after a divorce. In 2014, the 31 percent poverty rate for families headed by single moms was nearly triple the overall rate.

---

* We know Julia Roberts is acquiring some ancient wisdom here because she is sitting on a floor, cross-legged.

** Here is Bonnie Franklin (the redhead), playing the divorced mom Ann Romano, in the groundbreaking sitcom *One Day at a Time* from the olden days of yore. In this ultra-realistic depiction of single motherhood, she received superb parenting advice from her building's super, Schneider.

America, you treat women workers particularly badly, but both men and women workers all too often get a raw deal. Consider that about a quarter of all American private sector workers get no paid holidays and a similar number earn no paid vacation time, according to the Economic Policy Institute.[100] Lower-income workers, who are arguably in greater need of time off, get even less: 66 percent get no paid holidays and 61 percent get no paid vacation time. Among the top 10 percent of workers, meanwhile, 93 percent receive both paid holidays and paid vacation time.

So, who can afford to take an entire year off work, and pay for round-the-world plane tickets, as well as food and lodging for that whole time?* Not everyone has a generous publisher (which paid for the trip) as Elizabeth Gilbert apparently did. Most divorced women would feel lucky to have a boss who doesn't harass them or a job that enabled them to pay their bills on time.

Republican Congressional leaders oppose mandating paid sick leave nationally, even though Speaker of the House—and poor people's champion!—Paul Ryan was able to curtail his weekend work to spend more time with his own family, saying, "I cannot and will not give up my family time." Good for him! Massachusetts Senator Elizabeth Warren responded in a tweet directed at the Speaker, "Family time should not be a privilege reserved for the Speaker of the House. You deserve it—and so does everyone else."[101]

Hell, many American workers don't even get *unpaid* sick leave. The federal Family and Medical Leave Act of 1993, pushed by President Bill Clinton and enacted into law by a then-Democratic Congress, requires employers to provide unpaid leave for up to 12 weeks for employees caring for a new child or a seriously ill family member, to recover from one's own serious health condition, or to deal with certain obligations (including childcare and other related activities) arising from a spouse, parent, or child being on, or called to, active military duty. But due to many loopholes in the bill that were lobbied for by the busi-

---

* On the definitive, foolproof source of all knowledge, Yahoo Answers, "Kasey" asked, "How much money would it cost to take the same trip as the woman did in the movie *Eat Pray Love*?" "Nick" responded, "I'd say around 10,000." How can you argue, dear reader, with such thorough research as that? Sounds right to me! It turns out, though, that Elizabeth Gilbert's moneyed publisher was her true faith healer.

ness community and agreed to by Congressional members, more than 40 percent of workers are ineligible for any leave at all. Not only that, many workers who *are* covered by the act cannot afford to take unpaid leave or do not know about their rights under the statute.[102]

TIME IS *NOT* MONEY

The fact that so many of America's workers earn less than a living wage in their jobs is tied inexorably to the reality that many of those laborers also have little family time away from work, and that, while at their places of employment, they can face dangerous work conditions. All of these hardships are borne from a lack of political power, as well as a sharp decline in collective bargaining power, for average American workers.

Employees covered by collective bargaining agreements earn wages that are 13.6 percent higher, and these workers are 18.3 percent more likely to have health insurance and 22.5 percent more likely to have pensions, than comparable workers in non-unionized jobs.[103]

But from 1968 to 2012, union membership nationwide fell from 28.3 percent to 11.3 percent (the lowest level in 75 years). At the same time, the percentage of the nation's income earned by the middle 60 percent of households dropped from 53.2 to 45.7 percent.[104]

In *The Federalist Papers*, James Madison wrote, "If men were angels, no government would be necessary." Well, if all employers were angels, no union would be necessary. And guess what? Not all employers are angels.

About one in four American jobs pay too little to lift a family of four out of poverty.[105] In 2014, fully 16 million working Americans aged 15 to 65 lived in households in which one or more adults were working but still couldn't afford enough food.[106] Roughly 60 percent of all workers in the bottom 10 percent of wage earners (those paid less than $7.42 per hour) received some form of government anti-poverty assistance in 2012–2014, either directly or through a family member. Similarly, over half of workers in the next 10 percent of wage earners (those paid between $7.42 and $9.91 per hour) received public aid.[107] But many struggling workers earn just slightly too much to qualify for key types of government help. For example, I met a taxi driver in Little Rock who told me he worked 12 hours per day, seven days per week, and was informed by his local social services office that he earned one dollar— one dollar!—too much to qualify for SNAP nutrition assistance. It's crazy to contemplate, but it's true.

President Franklin Roosevelt signed the Fair Labor Standards Act into law in 1938. It created a national minimum wage, introduced the 40-hour work week for many, and prohibited most employment of minors in "oppressive child labor," although it continued to allow children to toil in agriculture. Unfortunately, as recently as 2012, as many as half a million US children harvested up to a quarter of our nation's crops.[108] Eat up, America! Tiny hands worked hard for those juicy tomatoes!

The tobacco industry is particularly rife with child labor, as reported by Steven Greenhouse for the *New York Times*:

> PINK HILL, N.C.—On many mornings, as tobacco plants tower around her, Saray Cambray Alvarez pulls a black plastic garbage bag over her 13-year-old body to protect her skin from leaves dripping with nicotine-tinged dew.
>
> When Saray and other workers—including several more teenagers—get to the fields at 6, they punch holes through the bags for their arms. They are trying to avoid what is known as "green tobacco sickness," or nicotine poisoning, which can cause vomiting, dizziness, and irregular heart rates, among other symptoms.
>
> Saray says that she sometimes has trouble breathing in the middle of all the heat, humidity, and leaves, and that she often feels weary during her 12-hour shifts. . . .
>
> "You get very thirsty," said Saray, who sometimes waits an hour in 90-plus heat for a drink until her crew returns to the opposite side of a field, where the water jugs are parked . . .
>
> Hilda Solis, then the labor secretary, proposed declaring work in tobacco fields and with tractors hazardous—making that type of work illegal for those under 16. . . . Brazil, India, and some other tobacco-producing nations already prohibit

anyone under 18 from working on tobacco farms. The Obama administration withdrew Ms. Solis's proposed rule after encountering intense opposition from farm groups and Republican lawmakers.[109]

Saray Cambray Alvarez, 13. (Travis Dove, *The New York Times/Redux*)

Even Graham Boyd, executive vice president for the Tobacco Growers Association of North Carolina, acknowledged the danger of nicotine poisoning and other tough conditions in the fields. "No one is going to say it's a day at the beach," Mr. Boyd said."[110]

Civilized countries don't allow child labor. Period. But, America, you still do.

In a California study, more than 60 percent of female farmworkers interviewed said they had experienced some form of sexual harassment. In another report, by Human Rights Watch, nearly all the female farmworkers interviewed had experienced sexual violence, or knew others who had. One woman told investigators that her workplace was called the "field de calzón," or "field of panties." As an Iowa immigrant farmworker told her lawyer, "We thought it was normal in the United States that in order to keep your job, you had to have sex."[111]

Agriculture isn't even the most dangerous profession in America: 874 construction workers, disproportionately Hispanic men, died on the job in 2014.[112] If you are fortunate enough to have a cushy office job, before you utter the phrase that you are "dying from boredom," please take a second to consider how many people actually die at their jobs when a crane collapses on them.*

As if deadly working conditions weren't bad enough, low-income employees frequently get their wages stolen outright, as *TalkPoverty* has reported:

> Although Javier, who emigrated from Mexico with his family, routinely worked 50 to 60 hour weeks for four years in a Philadelphia restaurant's kitchen, he was never paid properly. When Javier demanded all the unpaid wages and overtime that had accrued, his employer threatened him with immigration consequences and physical violence against him and his family . . . . Fearing that the abusive employer would act on his threats, Javier and his family spent days without leaving their home.
>
> Javier's experience isn't uncommon. Civil legal aid attorneys have also represented a crew of cleaners who were locked in a restaurant overnight while they cleaned (and not paid overtime for the additional hours) and construction workers strung along for years with partial weekly payments, among others. They have even had to sue the same employers multiple times on behalf of different workers. And the practice is widespread. A report from Temple University's Sheller Center found that in any given work week in the Philadelphia area, almost 130,000 workers will be paid less than minimum wage, over 100,000 will experience an overtime violation, and over 80,000 will be forced to work off-the-clock without pay. Although wage theft is illegal under federal law and under statutes in most states,

---

* And with that last admonition, I win a "Lifetime Achievement Award for Self-Righteous Scolding," a brand-new honor bestowed by the Hollywood Foreign Press Association. I dare you to make fun of *that*, Ricky Gervais.

enforcement is underfunded—sometimes nonexistent. This disproportionately impacts low-wage workers, who are more likely to work in low-regulation and non-union jobs where employers cut corners at their expense. But these workers— who need those wages the most—don't know where to turn for help when they do not receive a paycheck, fear losing their job if they complain, or simply cannot afford to miss work for the several days that it takes to file a complaint and attend a court hearing.[113]

Even after courts find employers guilty of stealing wages, they still find ways to avoid paying. Legal service organizations found that 62 percent of federal and state court judgments against employers for wage theft were not paid, denying workers more $25 million owed to them:

> [T]he most evasive employers simply refuse to participate in the legal system, leaving workers who seek to enforce their rights with only a piece of paper declaring how much they are owed. . . . The restaurant and construction industries ranked highest in avoiding the payment of judgments: 26% of the cases (16 cases) were from the restaurant industry and 34% (20 cases) were from the construction industry. But employers' evasion of judgments occurred across all low-wage industries, including domestic work, garment factories, nail salons, and grocery stores.
>
> The problem is not limited to civil litigation. . . . The New York State Department of Labor was not able to collect over $101 million in wages the agency had determined employers owed to workers over a 10-year period.[114]

THE FADING AMERICAN DREAM

Throughout US history, freshly arrived immigrants (including Donald Trump's family), with the hope of achieving the American dream still intact, usually worked their tails off. My grandparents who came from the Ukraine and Latvia certainly did. And so do today's Guatemalan farmworkers, Nigerian taxi drivers, Polish office cleaners, Chinese post office workers, West Indian nurses, and Bengali newsstand operators. Ditto for mechanics of indeterminate national origin.*

In the beginning, they believe that the harder they work, the more money they will save, and the better off their children will be today and in the future. A generation ago, such hard work and optimism were indeed rewarded with slightly improved lives for themselves, and much better lives for their children and grandchildren. It was real. Their hope was fueled by tangible benchmarks of success. For instance, my grandparents believed that, if they saved enough money, those funds could eventually be used to help their grandchildren go to college, and they did. The United States was the beacon of opportunity for the world. America, you certainly earned your victory lap.

But that was then. These days, while a few immigrants still do eventually get ahead and keep their aspirations alive, too many wind up disappointed. Hard-earned wages and earnings get eaten up by soaring rents, high fees and licenses, and taxes that fall disproportionately on working people. They are stuck doubled- and tripled-up in unsafe housing and their kids often go to rotten public schools. Eventually, many immigrants also lose hope in their American expectations of gold-paved streets as they wake every morning, unable to significantly move up the economic ladder. A Kosovar Albanian refugee that I know, trained as an electrical engineer but now working 80-plus hours a week as a building superintendent in Brooklyn, is grateful that the US took in his family as refugees, but insists that his life was materially better when he was growing up in the old Yugoslavia, a communist dictatorship. Immigrants and native-born Americans alike now believe that—for reasons they can neither control nor sometimes even comprehend—they just can't get ahead. It turns out, America, that your victory lap was premature.

Poverty, like depression, is manifested by tangible

---

* Noted hard-working immigrant mechanic Latka Gravas, from the 1980s hit TV show, *Taxi*.

symptoms but also by invisible social forces, which, like gravity, hold people down.

All of us want to be told yes, you *can* do what you want to do or have something you want to have. Adam and Eve wanted the snake to tell them, "Yes, eat that apple." Cleopatra longed for a "yes" from Marc Antony. After 265,000 words of pain, tedium, beauty, humiliation, and suffering in *Ulysses*, James Joyce's epic novel ended with a joyously shouted "yes I said yes I will Yes."

Any relationship revolving around the word "no" will fail. Yet when you are low-income or otherwise marginalized, the country is telling you "no" over and over again. No, you can't be proud of your heritage, family, religion, race, language, ethnicity, gender, sexuality, birthplace, or your neighborhood. No, you can't expect a good public school education for your children, and, even if they get one, no, they can't expect to afford college. That's a broken relationship if I've ever heard of one, and once again, America, that's on *you*.

TIME IS *NOT* ON OUR SIDE

America, you increasingly force your workers to endure long-ass commutes. The average one-way daily commute for US workers is 25.5 minutes, nearly a one hour round-trip, or five hours a week—five hours a week that are unpaid yet necessary to keep the job. Add that to the average workweek of 47 hours and we're looking at 53 hours per week getting to—and being at—work. Many Americans must commute far longer than that, with 8 percent commuting an hour or longer each way. According to *US News & World Report*, one such mega-commuter is Neil Shapiro, who, to travel each day from his home in New Jersey to his job in Manhattan, has to drive to a commuter train, then ride that train to New York, then take a subway to a location near his employer, then walk even further to his office, taking 1 hour 45 minutes each way, equaling a three-and-a-half-hour commute. And that is dependent on the commuter trains and subways being on time, and they frequently aren't.[115]

Many Americans work more than 47 hours per week. According to Gallup, 11 percent work 41–49 hours, 21 percent work 50–59 hours, and 18 percent work 60 hours or more.[116] It's not surprising that, in 2010, 46 percent of full-time working men and women reported that their job demands interfered with their family lives sometimes or often, up from 41 percent in 2002.[117]

Of course, America, as is the case in every aspect of life, low-income Americans have it the worst. In addition to lacking spare cash, low-income Americans often lack spare free time. Just as many personal relationships collapse when people don't have "quality time" to spend with each other, the time demands of commuting and working wreaks havoc on the efforts of low-income people to participate fully in serious relationships with their families and with their communities, as well as the time they are able to spend on their own health.

Many struggling Americans work two or even three jobs. If they are unemployed, they spend a great deal of time looking for work and proving to a government agency they are looking for work. They often travel by public transportation, laboriously making one, or two, or three connections to shuttle among home, work, social service agencies, houses of worship, and grocery stores. If they work as a nanny caring for someone else's children but can't afford to pay for their own childcare, these hardworking parents must also take the extra time to care for their *own* kids or shuttle them between relatives and friends who act as caretakers. If they work as home health aides to assist someone else's parents but they can't afford home healthcare for family members themselves (which, of course, they cannot), they also must take the time to care for their *own* elders.

While it's true that government safety net programs help tens of millions of Americans avoid starvation, homelessness, and other outcomes even more dreadful than everyday poverty, it is also true that government anti-poverty aid is generally a major hassle to obtain and to keep. Congress, which writes the laws governing the programs, and most states and localities, which implement those laws, purposely make it difficult to advertise these programs and enable families to access them. That's why many low-income people are actually unaware of all the government benefits for which they are eligible, reducing the amount of help going to Americans in need by tens of billions of dollars every year. It's as if your spouse has your money stashed in a secret place and you might not even know you had money at all.*

Even if struggling families *do* know about available aid, the journey to receive it is usually long, onerous, and time-consuming. Put yourself in their places for a moment. You will need to go to one government office to apply for SNAP, a different government office to apply for housing assistance, a separate WIC clinic to obtain WIC benefits,** and a variety of other government offices to apply for other types of help—sometimes traveling long distances by public transportation or on foot to get there—and then once you've walked through the door, you are often forced to wait for hours at each office to be served. Even if you initially apply for benefits online, you often have to make a separate physical trip to one or more government offices to follow up, bring documents, or participate in lengthy interviews. You will need to bring huge piles of paperwork to each office, usually a slightly different combination of records every time. And don't forget, making copies of the paperwork before you arrive also takes time (and money), so plan accordingly. The lines in these offices can seem endless, and sometimes you'll need to wait outside for hours, in the worst kinds of weather. At a social services office in Chicago, the lines start forming long before the 8:30 a.m. opening time; if clients arrive at 8:00 a.m.— merely a half hour *before* the office is scheduled to open—they are told to come back the next day.[118] Imagine that. You'd have to start all over again the next morning, assuming you can get off work at the last minute and keep your job.

Many offices don't have weekend or night hours, so if you work, which you most likely do, you'll likely lose wages by applying for government help, since you'll probably have to take time off work. You could try

---

*

** The federal Special Supplemental Nutrition Program for Women, Infants, and Children, commonly known as WIC, provides extra food of high nutritional content to pregnant women and children, ages 5 or younger.

calling on the phone, but it's rare for a human to answer, and the case-worker voice mailboxes are often full, so you couldn't leave a message anyway.

And when a bureaucrat finally sees you at their office, they will usually ask you many of the same intrusive, detailed, lengthy questions about your finances and your intimate, personal situations as similar government workers did at the last three offices. It's as if you have to explain to 12 different cousins at six different family get-togethers why your marriage fell apart and why you need to sleep on each of their couches for a night—while also having to hand over to each of them your complete tax records to prove why you are too broke to pay rent to them for that night of couch-surfing. In most places, if you have children, you must fill out additional forms, which your kids must bring to school, to qualify for free or reduced-price school meals.

To be sure, these government benefits provide a critical lifeline—and they often are the difference between a family eating and not eating, and between having a home or being homeless. But just because these programs are vital doesn't mean they are perfect. Besides, the wealthy aren't forced to jump through nearly as many hoops when they obtain far more expensive government aid, like farm subsidies or tax deductions for their vacation homes.

To obtain some form of help, regardless of your work or family situation, you may also be required to attend job readiness classes. Often these seminars are worthless time sucks for you and are more about giving large payouts to politically connected contractors that are more interested in punishing you for your poverty than they are with placing you in a real living-wage job. If you quit the classes in disgust, you'll likely lose benefits for yourself and for your children.

More and more Republican-run states are forcing struggling workers to jump through additional hoops to prove they are "worthy" of getting federally-funded SNAP nutrition assistance. As the *Huffington Post* reported,

> Becky Murphy of Summit Lake, Wisconsin, doesn't want to be one of the estimated 1 million Americans kicked off food stamps this year, so she's doing her homework.

"Every week I have to meet with a caseworker, which requires driving about 18 miles to the nearest town, and I have to show him my activity report form" . . .

The form she fills out every week asks her things like whether she applied for a job, what kind of job it was, how far she drove, and whether she sent an email following up on her application. The time Murphy spends on these activities can be added to the 20 hours per week she has to spend either working for pay or doing an approved work-like activity.[119]

Even though Obamacare significantly decreased the number of Americans without health insurance, if you get aid through it, you will also probably need to spend as many hours figuring out which absurdly complicated healthcare options are affordable and workable. And after you do, the options often change, which means even more time spent reviewing more complicated options. *The New York Times* has reported that "insurers in many counties are offering such a dizzying array of health insurance plans with so many subtle differences that consumers have struggled to determine which plan is best for them."[120] Such confusion is cited as being one of the reasons that significant numbers of Americans drop healthcare coverage after receiving it: "Some who signed up for coverage this year lost it within months because they did not understand what information they had to supply or even that they were required to make monthly payments."[121] And Republicans inexplicably want to take even that meager help away.

Are you fed up yet? Are you tired? Well, if you live in poverty, your day has only begun.

Given that the US has literally hundreds of thousands of nonprofit groups providing social services, it is nearly impossible for you, as a struggling American, to determine which of those organizations provides services you need, whether the organization is conveniently located, and for which services you are eligible. If you do figure out that a nonprofit (or multiple nonprofits) could help, you will need to take the time to visit each one, again paying or arranging for transportation to a location where sometimes lines around the block ensure yet another seemingly endless wait, only to fill out even more paperwork, and go through yet more interviews, where you might be asked even more personal questions.*

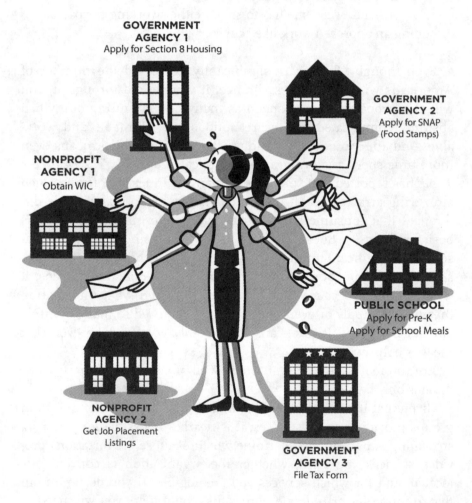

THE GOVERNMENT/NONPROFIT SOCIAL SERVICES STATUS QUO

GOVERNMENT AGENCY 1
Apply for Section 8 Housing

GOVERNMENT AGENCY 2
Apply for SNAP (Food Stamps)

NONPROFIT AGENCY 1
Obtain WIC

PUBLIC SCHOOL
Apply for Pre-K
Apply for School Meals

NONPROFIT AGENCY 2
Get Job Placement Listings

GOVERNMENT AGENCY 3
File Tax Form

---

* At one of the largest and most effective feeding programs and social service agencies I know, the New York Common Pantry in East Harlem, the doors for breakfast open at 8:00 a.m., but the lines can start forming as early as 3:00 a.m. the night before.

And since many government and nonprofit programs require frequent re-applications and re-certifications, you will often be required to jump through all these hoops every few months. Being poor can be a full-time job in and of itself.

Plus, it's rare for the multiple government and nonprofit programs aimed at low-income people to work together in a coherent fashion to bolster families' long-term self-sufficiency. Too often, these programs work at cross-purposes, so that obtaining one benefit might make you ineligible for another. (The reverse is sometimes true, where getting one benefit makes a recipient automatically eligible for other benefits, but conservatives are trying to make that more infrequent.)

Sometimes you can't win for losing, such as when you finally get a raise and then lose your benefits because of it, and the amount of the raise is less than the value of benefits lost. (Other times, getting a job can make you eligible for Earned Income Tax Credit [EITC] payments, the value of which may exceed the amount of benefits lost, but that often depends upon household composition and a variety of other factors, so that, too, is a crapshoot.) It's like having an endless number of squabbling, divorced parents, with one mandating that you save your allowance and the other prompting you to spend it. In the words of anti-poverty activist Sarah Palmer, "It's supposed to be a social safety net, not a ropes course."

And that's not all.

If you don't have a checking account or credit cards (and many low-income people don't), you can't pay bills by mail or online, so you pay for everything in cash, spending money on extremely high fees at check-cashing facilities that prey on people like you who live in poor neighborhoods. Even then you aren't done, because paying bills in cash often requires a personal visit to the phone company, the electric company, the landlord, and the gas company, where more long lines await those who must pay their bills in person, after paying for more transportation and taking more time off work.

There's no rest for the poor and weary.

Yes, you're poor, but like all of us, you also have to file tax returns with the IRS, sometimes paying a tax preparer handsomely to do so, even if the government owes you an EITC refund payment. You might even pay an unscrupulous tax preparer more than your refund is worth.

They might offer to loan you the refund amount in advance and will charge you insanely high interest.

All citizens are asked to serve on jury duty, but because you are struggling, you have fewer ways of getting out of it than wealthy businessmen.* When low-income and/or people of color like you go to vote, your wait times will usually be far longer than those for wealthy white people and you are more likely to find trouble at your polling places, like broken machines.**

If you live in poverty, you are less likely to have a washing machine in your home or apartment building, so you must use laundromats, also requiring time, money, and transportation. There are neither doormen at your buildings nor secured delivery spaces, so if you ever get a package or an important letter, you'll have to make yet another trip to the post office to pick it up—where you will inevitably find even more lines.

If you are poor in a rural area, lost time accessing basic services can take even longer, and cost even more money. For instance, in the small town of Panola, Alabama, the closest place to get a driver's license is an hour-and-ten-minute drive away. Even if you don't own a car, you will often need a driver's license or a non-driver ID from the Department of Motor Vehicles to show when you apply for benefits or conduct business in modern life, so you might need to pay a neighbor $50 to drive you to the license office.[122] You pay it forward, backward, sideways, just about every direction except into your savings account, if you even have one.

Economists often apply the term "opportunity costs" to wealthy people, indicating that if the wealthy are spending time on one task, then they are not performing other tasks that could aid the economy; therefore the time spent on the original task represents value lost to the economy as a whole.*** But the nation's elites rarely apply that term to low-income workers, acting as if poor people's time is essentially

---

* *Business Insider* published a piece in 2009 entitled "9 Ways to Get Out of Jury Duty."
** Long lines at polling locations make it more likely for people to leave before voting and/or be less likely to vote the next time, which is precisely the intent of the Republicans who do everything they can to ensure that the lines are as long as possible and that voting is as complicated as possible too.
*** Look at all the opportunity costs that are lost to our society when this wealthy person is sunbathing on a tropical island rather than generating new income. Even on a deserted island, he makes the laborer, Gilligan, do all the hard work.

worthless. Sort of like the spouse who doesn't count your food shopping, cooking, cleaning, child-rearing, accounting for family finances, shuttling family members to appointments, taking care of your sick parents, etc., etc., as *work*.

For all Americans, including wealthy ones, modern life is complex. There are always a zillion family, work, personal, community, religious, and civic obligations. With ever-shifting and complex options, it's a challenge to effectively juggle them all, and it can feel impossible to plan for the future. But wealthy Americans are able to get professional help in sorting through their options and obligations, utilizing the best personal assistants, financial advisors, and modern technology that their money can buy.

Meanwhile, change is the norm. Government anti-poverty programs (even ones that work spectacularly well) are too frequently cut back or eliminated, always subject to the political whims of whoever is in power. On rare occasions, the safety net is expanded, but sometimes even those enlarged programs are cut back later.* Offices close or move. Income guidelines and responsibilities for benefit recipients change. The only constant is disruption. Good luck planning for the future.

Relationships in which one side has no money, no time, and no ability to plan for the future have about as much chance of lasting as a Kardashian marriage. No wonder low-income Americans are pissed. But what about you, America? Are you pissed yet? Or just worn out from your short walk in a struggling neighbor's shoes? To read the next paragraph please have a seat and wait for about four hours before turning to page 422 in this book and filling out forms 17A and 147F, and please remember to attach the paperwork you filled out in Chapter 1. Get the idea?

That's why we need to enable low-income families to have a coherent *plan* to ensure that all the programs they use work together, in a mutually supportive way, to promote the long-term upward mobility all families crave and work so hard to achieve. That's why we need a whole new way to help struggling Americans clarify their options and sim-

---

* Congress has slashed funding for Section 8 housing vouchers. Congress entirely eliminated funding for the USDA Hunger Free Communities grant program, even though it effectively aided grassroots public/private partnerships to feed the most vulnerable Americans. While Congress significantly increased SNAP funding in 2009, it cut SNAP funding by more than $14 billion a few years later.

plify their lives. Hang tight—I'll explain how we can do all that later in the book.

Then everyone can have extra time to do what all of us want to have the freedom to do: to eat, pray, and love.*

---

* Or at least eat. Atheists likely won't pray. And truly loveless people won't get to love, although I think there's still hope for Louis C.K.

4.

Chicken Soup for the Soul Brothers and Soul Sisters
Why Kind, Personal Gestures Aren't Enough to Overcome Structural Racism

Can—or should—a white guy write about race?

Let's discuss, America.

Yes, as you might imagine from my author photo, I am white.[*] Very white. Both my parents, and all my grandparents, were white. Very white. I was raised in a mostly white neighborhood in a suburb of New York City, went to mostly white public schools, and grew up attending an all-white synagogue, which was, not shockingly, also all-Jewish. I went to Columbia University, an expensive private college, which, by the time I graduated in 1986, had an overwhelmingly white (but increasingly Asian-American) undergraduate population, but very few African Americans.[**]

Many of the workplaces in my career have been mostly white, particularly at senior levels. In the positions in which I've had the power to hire staff, I've tried to build workforces that are diverse at every level, but haven't always been as successful as I'd like. Although I spend significant time visiting and working in communities of color as an anti-poverty organizer, my nonprofit's headquarters is in the Wall Street neighborhood of Manhattan, a few doors down from the New York Stock Exchange, a neighborhood whiter than Norway (except for

---

[*] In the course of this chapter and book, I use the terms black and African American interchangeably. White, however, is just plain old vanilla.

[**] Even by 2014, Columbia's undergraduate population was only 7 percent black. Ironically, while a student there, I took a course taught by the late Amiri Baraka, a famed, fiery Black Nationalist and Marxist poet and playwright, who must have made his own peace with the contradiction that he was working for such a white establishment institution.

the limo drivers, cleaning staffs, and security personnel who commute to work there for the mostly white executives).

I chose to live in Brooklyn, an extraordinarily diverse borough of New York City, which is 57 percent nonwhite, but the neighborhood in which I live, Park Slope, has gentrified dramatically since I moved there, and now it's mostly white.

(America, admit it: most of your white people live similarly white lives.)

And while I have a black Jamaican sister-in-law, am a serious student of black music, culture, literature, and history—and have dedicated my life to fighting for racial and economic justice—I'd be deluded if I thought any of those things made me any sort of expert on what it's like to be black.

Like every white person on the planet (and as I'll argue later in this chapter, like every nonwhite person on the planet too), I occasionally have conscious thoughts (and likely unconscious feelings) based on negative racial stereotypes. Although I believe in racial equality with every fiber of my being, I also know that I can never fully escape the racist brainwashing upon which our society and world are built. I also understand that I benefit, every day, from white privilege. I never worry about being shot by a cop or being followed around by a store security guard. Although, I suppose, there have been times in my career that I may have been marginally harmed by anti-Jewish bias, modern US anti-Semitism—even in an era when Donald Trump's presidential candidacy was widely embraced by white supremacists and neo-Nazis —has only a fraction of the negative impact of contemporary US racism; many African Americans are refused job interviews because the names on their resumes "sound black"—I'm pretty sure there was never a job for which I didn't get an interview because my name "sounded Jewish."*

At the same time, I don't have an iota of white guilt. Guilt is mostly a useless emotion and holds us back when we are trying to solve problems. So, while I acknowledge my white privilege, and surely benefit

---

* Fellow Jews sometime say that our people made it without any governmental help, despite discrimination against us, so other minorities should be able to make it on their own, too. That perspective ignores how much government assistance (such as excellent public schools) "our people" utilized. It also ignores the historical reality that white immigrants (Jews included), fresh off the boat, were automatically endowed with more rights and often faced less discrimination than nonwhite people who had already been in the US for centuries.

from it, I don't beat myself up over it. I merely want to work toward eliminating such privilege, and more importantly, eliminating any of racial privilege's insidious flipside, discrimination.

But make no mistake about it, I am damn white and live a damn white life. And I know it.

So, can I—and should I—write about race?

I think so. Here's why:

Racial issues undergird every molecule of America's past and present. Since this book is seeking to deal with the largest problems facing contemporary America, given that so many of our most pressing national dilemmas are intertwined with racial issues, if this book didn't touch on race, it would be as useless as a book on the Vatican that didn't mention the Catholic Church.

But can a white guy have valid opinions about racial issues?

I think so. Here's why:

All humans should be free to express informed, sensitive views about all other humans. Impoverished people should be able to have opinions about rich people, just as the wealthy should be able to express thoughts on people who live in poverty. People of all sexes should be able to talk about gender and sexism. People all along the gender spectrum ought to be able to discuss sexual orientation, gender identity, and homophobia. It stands to reason, then, that nonwhite people and white people alike should be able to explore issues on how to understand and help each other.

And no, pointing out hard facts about structural racism doesn't make you a divider or a "race-baiter" (as Rupert Murdoch's *New York Post* once called me when I did so). Blaming racism on those who uncover it is like blaming a hurricane on a weatherman who reports it. Conversely, falsely claiming that your community or country are united and that everyone has equal power and rights simply doesn't make it so either.

Can—or should—a white person make jokes about race? Generally not, I think, and I won't.*

---

* While other chapters in this book are chock-full of footnotes with (hopefully) amusing images, this one isn't. Including humorous pictures regarding the sensitive issue of race would be like traveling on my own volition to a minefield just to see if I could walk across it without blowing up.

Now that we've gotten the ground rules down, let's talk about race.

White America, I know you'd rather talk about anything but race. You'd probably prefer to do your taxes or get a root canal before discussing it. But we can't get serious about facing the nation's most profound issues unless we deal with race.

A HOUSE DIVIDED AGAINST ITSELF

For millennia, humans have been divided by tribe, ethnicity, nationality, and religion. But our current concept of race is, at its core, a fake social construct dreamed up by white Europeans—and elaborated upon by their white American progeny—in order to justify chattel slavery and the genocide of American Indians. As Ta-Nehisi Coates has explained, "Americans believe in the reality of 'race' as a defined, indubitable feature of the natural world. Racism—the need to ascribe bone-deep features to people and then humiliate, reduce, and destroy them—inevitably follows from this inalterable condition. In this way, racism is rendered as the innocent daughter of Mother Nature, and one is left to deplore the Middle Passage or the Trail of Tears the way one deplores an earthquake, a tornado, or any other phenomenon that can be cast as beyond the handiwork of men."[123]

Yet much of white America, but particularly conservatives, can't seem to agree on whether US racism: a) doesn't exist much anymore; b) never existed; or c) does exist in large doses, but only because non-white people, they say, are inferior.

The first claim—that America has mostly overcome its racist past due to the success of the Civil Rights movement and the election of a black president—now seems to be the default position for most mainstream conservatives. In the majority opinion for a case overturning a key provision of the federal Voting Rights Act, which thereby made it easier for states to enact laws to restrict the ability of nonwhite people to vote, Chief Justice John Roberts allowed that systematic Southern racial discrimination was in place as recently as the 1960s, but "nearly 50 years later, things have changed dramatically" and voting discrimination has been reduced so much that the "extraordinary" protections of the law are no longer needed.[124]

Aside from ignoring the reality that most of the building blocks of the modern conservative movement (the 1964 Barry Goldwater for President campaign, the *National Review*, etc.) were dead-set against the Civil Rights movement,* the right-wing claims of nearly perfect contemporary racial harmony ignore most known facts on race in America today. In 2014, more than one-quarter of all African Americans (26.2 percent) lived in poverty, a rate two and a half times higher than the rate for non-Hispanic whites. The poverty rate for Hispanics of any race was only slightly lower, at 23.6 percent. Median household income was $35,398 for blacks and $42,491 for Hispanics of any race; both numbers were considerably lower than the $61,317 median income for non-Hispanic whites.[125]

The gaps in assets—what people own—were far vaster. According to Demos, a public policy organization,

> [T]he typical black household now possesses just 6 percent of the wealth owned by the typical white household and the typical Latino household owns only 8 percent of the wealth held by the typical white household. . . . In 2011 the median white household had $111,146 in wealth holdings, compared to just $7,113 for the median Black household and $8,348 for the median Latino household. . . . The US racial wealth gap is substantial and is driven by public policy decisions . . . From the continuing impact of redlining on American homeownership to the retreat from desegregation in public education, public policy has shaped these disparities, leaving them impossible to overcome without racially-aware policy change. . . .
>
> While 73 percent of white households owned their own homes in 2011, only 47 percent of Latinos and 45 percent of Blacks were homeowners. In addition, Black and Latino homeowners saw less return in wealth on their investment in

---

* In a 1957 editorial entitled "Why the South Must Prevail," *National Review* founder William F. Buckley called white people "the advanced race." Senator Barry Goldwater fervently opposed the 1964 Civil Rights Act, ostensibly to defend "states' rights." Dr. Martin Luther King, Jr. wrote, "While not himself a racist, Mr. Goldwater articulated a philosophy which gave aid and comfort to the racist." In the US Capitol building, a sculpture of Barry Goldwater now stands just a few feet away from one of Rosa Parks.

homeownership: for every $1 in wealth that accrues to median
Black households as a result of homeownership, median white
households accrue $1.34; meanwhile for every $1 in wealth that
accrues to median Latino households as a result of homeownership, median white households accrue $1.54.[126]

And the gap is widening. The wealth of white households was 13
times the median wealth of black households in 2013, compared with
eight times the wealth in 2010, according to the Pew Research Center.
Likewise, the wealth of white households was more than 10 times the
wealth of Hispanic households in 2013, compared with nine times the
wealth in 2010.[127]

None of this is accidental. In the post-World War II housing boom,
when federal agencies systematically blocked loans to black people,
they were purposely locked out of the greatest wealth accumulation in
US history.[128]

By 2015, the richest 100 US households, none of which were headed
by African Americans, owned about as much wealth as the nation's
entire African American population of 39 million people. Among the
Forbes 400 that year, just two individuals on the list were African
American—Oprah Winfrey and tech investor Robert Smith, numbers
211 and 266, respectively.[129]

America's public schools are now more racially and socioeconomically segregated than they have been for decades. In 2014, in the
Northeast, 51 percent of black students attended schools where 90 to
100 percent of their classmates were nonwhite, up from 43 percent in
1968. In the country's 100 largest school districts, economic segregation rose roughly 30 percent from 1991 to 2010.[130]

In 2008, white Americans with 16 years or more of education had
life expectancies far greater than black Americans with fewer than
12 years of education—14.2 years more for white men than black men,
and 10.3 years more for white women than black women.[131] Racial, economic, health, and educational divides all reinforce each other.

Black people are far more likely to get their electricity cut off, be sued
over a debt, and/or land in jail because of a mere parking ticket.[132]

Racism, classism, and political powerlessness combine in a toxic brew—over and over again—and nonwhite and nonrich people always get the short end of the stick, if they even get a stick at all. There is just no way that the water-poisoning crisis in Flint would have been allowed to happen in Beverly Hills.

Despite the vast evidence of rampant, structural, nationwide discrimination based on race, many on the Right still imply that white people have better jobs and more money because they simply work harder and are smarter. Yet the National Bureau of Economic Research—a mainstream economics think tank that's not exactly an Afro-centric outfit—found that job hunters with traditionally white-sounding names on their resumes got called in for interviews 50 percent more frequently than those with traditionally African American–sounding names.[133] *The New York Times* found that in 2016, out of the most powerful 503 people in American culture, government, education, and businesses, just 43 were nonwhite.[134]

The myth of a colorblind America is far easier to disprove than the existence of Bigfoot, but many whites still cling to it.

Some white conservatives claim that the problem is black folks' bad behavior. On Fox News, Brit Hume, masterfully combining a racist generalization with a backhanded compliment of President Obama, told Bill O'Reilly that it's a big problem that African American parents don't raise their kids as well as Obama raised his own kids, to which O'Reilly responded that Obama only talked about racial discrimination to appeal to "his crew."[135] White people on Fox understand racial issues less well than my late mother understood the Internet—and she thought e-mail came to our US mail box.

Yet disturbing racial perceptions go way beyond the Far Right. A study found that Americans are far more likely to appreciate a politician's lecture on the need for personal responsibility when the audience for the lecture is black than when it is white. The author of the study, Phia Salter of Texas A&M University, said her research indicated that Americans falsely think black Americans have a tendency to "blame the system too much." First, she pointed out that, "[b]y minimizing or ignoring the ways in which structural inequality persists, we are unlikely to search for, endorse, or enact solutions that might address these forms of societal problems." Second, she said, targeting black

Americans with the idea that they caused their own circumstances by not working hard enough "reinforces the idea that Blacks are ultimately responsible for their own disadvantage, even when structural inequalities persist."[136] Some African American critics have even slammed President Obama for discussing personal responsibility in front of black audiences. "Obama is forced to exaggerate black responsibility," wrote Michael Eric Dyson, "because he must always underplay white responsibility."[137]

While it's true that people of color disproportionately live in single-parent homes—and are disproportionally both the perpetrators and victims of crime—and while the Right blames such problems not only on irresponsible mothers but also on unengaged, deadbeat fathers, the facts suggest otherwise. "Defying enduring stereotypes about black fatherhood, a federal survey of American parents shows that by most measures, black fathers who live with their children are just as involved as other dads who live with their kids—or more so," reported the *Los Angeles Times*. "Among fathers who lived with young children, 70% of black dads said they bathed, diapered, or dressed those kids every day, compared with 60% of white fathers and 45% of Latino fathers . . . Nearly 35% of black fathers who lived with their young children said they read to them daily, compared with 30% of white dads and 22% of Latino dads."[138]

News and social media continue to perpetuate the falsehood that black people are uniquely criminal or distinctly irresponsible. Activist Van Jones pointed out that, after Hurricane Katrina, the Yahoo news website "featured a photo of two white residents, wading through the water with food. The caption read: 'Two residents wade through chest-deep water after finding bread and soda from a local grocery store' . . . Then there is a photo of a Black youth, wading through water with food. The caption read: 'A young man walks through chest-deep flood water after looting a grocery store.'"[139] Civil unrest by black people after a police shooting is usually portrayed by the media as a riot, but protestors in Tiananmen and Tahrir Squares were characterized as heroes. Meanwhile, American whites who riot after sporting events like hockey are usually portrayed as merely rambunctious. Fox pundit Deneen Borelli said heavily-armed Oregon militia who took over a federal building in 2016 were not "thugs," like black protesters; the militia were justified because they fought a "government gone wild."[140]

THE JUICE PUTS TALK OF RACE ON THE LOOSE

On October 3, 1995, Americans gathered around their TV sets to watch the verdict delivered in the O.J. Simpson criminal trial. Most watched either at their homes, schools, or workplaces, locations that were (and still are) highly separated by race.

In Washington, DC, at the mostly white American University, students viewed the not guilty announcement with stunned, mostly disappointed, silence. But, across town, on the campus of historically black Howard University, cheers erupted.

That day I was about two miles away from Howard's campus, working as a presidential appointee in the administration of Bill Clinton at the headquarters of the US Department of Agriculture, one of the most racially divided federal agencies in the country's history, labeled by many African Americans as the "last plantation." The department had, since its creation by President Abraham Lincoln, systematically ripped off nonwhite farmers and rural homeowners, and it generally treated its own (limited number of) nonwhite employees horribly. It was widely felt that the Department's gleaming white marble headquarters building on the National Mall* had been, before the Bill Clinton administration, essentially off-limits to any nonwhites other than cleaning crews. In a rare act of truth-in-advertising, Congress named the building after Mississippian Jamie Whitten, an ardent segregationist member of Congress, who as late as the 1990s addressed a fellow congressman from his state, African American Mike Espy, as "boy." Espy later was appointed by President Clinton to become the nation's first black secretary of agriculture, presiding over the department from the building named after Whitten. While the department's leadership under Espy, and later, under Clinton's second appointee, the first Jewish secretary of agriculture, Dan Glickman, was fiercely committed to stopping new USDA discrimination and compensating

---

* The street on which the building was located was named "Jefferson Drive." When people say to me that Jefferson was a farmer, I correct them and reply, "Actually, Jefferson *owned* farmers."

victims for past bias, resistance from the department's vast bureaucracy, as well as from Congress, ensured that the improvements could
be implemented only at a glacial pace—and that was before "glacial
pace" meant fast.

I watched the O.J. Simpson verdict on a TV, alone in my office.
Then a chorus of cheers emanated from a room down the hall, where
I learned later a number of African American employees had gathered
to watch. Shortly thereafter, a black female colleague, with whom I'd
always had cordial relations, passed me in the hallway and said, "I
guess our side won this one."

Wow.

I responded with silence, rare for me.

I didn't know which bothered me more: that a criminal justice
trial determining whether one human being killed two other human
beings would be primarily boiled down to a referendum on race, or the
assumption that I was on the "side" of white people.*

Countless Americans—of both races—had similar wake-up calls
that day. At the time of the verdict, while about 80 percent of white
Americans thought Simpson was guilty of murder, only about 20 percent of black Americans did.[141]

Despite the massive racial progress that the nation had achieved in
the last few decades, we were reminded that people of different races
still tended to see reality very differently, even tending to enjoy very
different types of entertainment.** Don't believe me? Ask 100 random
black people to name their favorite episode of *Seinfeld* or 100 random
white people to name their favorite moments from the *BET Awards*.***

---

* In college, I was an anti-apartheid activist. When I ran for New York State Senate, at age 22, I
was a rare white candidate who campaigned door-to-door in heavily black, low-income neighborhoods, and even though I lost virtually every majority-white precinct, I won every majority black
district. I cry every time I watch MLK's "I Have a Dream" speech. Yet, as I noted above, I am
only too aware that I benefit daily from white privilege. So while intellectually I fully understand
why a black person would assume I would be on the "side" of white people, emotionally such an
assumption is troubling to me. (Note to self: "Get over it. The systematic oppression of tens of
millions of Americans isn't about *you*.")
** According to Nielsen ratings, the TV broadcasts most likely to be widely viewed by white and
black Americans alike are NFL football games, but such games garner low ratings for Hispanic
Americans. In 2013, out of the top ten non-sports shows watched by black and white Americans,
only *American Idol* was on the top ten list of both groups.
*** Cheat sheet: *Seinfeld*—"The Contest." "Yadda, yadda, yadda." *BET Awards*—"It's All About the
Benjamins." "Nicki Minaj Gives DeJ Loaf a Big Co-sign."

One hundred days after President Obama's inauguration in 2009, a poll found 59 percent of African Americans and 65 percent of white Americans rated race relations in the United States as generally good. Yet a 2016 poll found that 61 percent of blacks and 45 percent of whites said race relations were generally bad.[142] In 2015, when Gallup asked Americans how satisfied they were with how black people were treated by US society, 18 percent of whites and 45 percent of blacks said "very dissatisfied." When asked if racial relations in the US "would always be a problem or would eventually be worked out," 59 percent of whites and only 42 percent of blacks thought that they would ever be "worked out." The more the questions morph from the vague and national to the specific and local, the greater the racial gap in perception becomes. When asked if "blacks in your community stood as good as chance as whites to get any job for which they are qualified," 72 percent of whites said yes, but only 36 percent of blacks did. Only 34 percent of whites thought blacks were treated less fairly by the police, compared to 73 percent of blacks. When Hispanics were asked the same set of questions, their responses were usually about halfway between the views of whites and blacks.

Fascinatingly, though, an equal number of whites and blacks, 32 percent, thought "racism against whites was widespread in America."[143] Also, according to a 2016 Pew poll, 55 percent of whites and 57 percent of blacks thought "family instability is a major reason why black people in our country may have a harder time getting ahead than whites."[144] While white ideologues of both the Left and the Right tend to blame troubles in the African American community entirely on either white racism or black personal behavior, African Americans themselves tend to be aware of the complex intersection of the myriad of economic, political, social, and cultural forces harming their community.

In contrast, white denial can be staggering. In a 2015 Louisiana poll, almost four in five white residents (78 percent) said that Louisiana had "mostly recovered" from Katrina, while nearly three in five African American residents (59 percent) felt it had "mostly not recovered."[145] A 2013 statewide poll in Louisiana found that many whites blamed the dreadful Hurricane Katrina response on Obama, not George W. Bush, even though the storm hit three and a half years *before* Obama became president.[146]

As deep as the splits are today, they are far less severe than decades ago. In 1958, 94 percent of whites and 33 percent of blacks said they opposed intermarriage.* By 2013, only 13 percent of whites and 3 percent of blacks admitted to pollsters they were against racially-mixed marriages. That's some progress, but I certainly understand why Chris Rock isn't impressed:

> When we talk about race relations in America or racial progress, it's all nonsense. There are no race relations. White people were crazy. Now they're not as crazy. To say that black people have made progress would be to say they deserve what happened to them before. . . . The advantage that my children have is that my children are encountering the nicest white people that America has ever produced. Let's hope America keeps producing nicer white people.[147]

Plus, even though some white people are marginally "nicer" now, they sure do say some stupid crap. Beyond the virulently racist rants of professed white supremacists and certain GOP presidential candidates, random people—who have obviously experienced neither slavery nor overt discrimination themselves—cluelessly throw around jokes about their own supposed oppression. On TripAdvisor.com, "Philip G," of Louisville, Kentucky, claimed that, because a pizza restaurant in Marseille, France gave him a tourist table far away from tables where local residents were seated, that action made him experience "segregation . . . like Rosa Parks." Yeah, I'm sure Rosa would have been equally outraged when she was brought a pepperoni instead of a sausage pie.

Tiger Woods's former caddie Steve Williams, a white man who earned an estimated $9 million working for Woods over a span of 12 years, complained, after being fired by the golfer, that the 14-time major champion treated him like a "slave" because Woods forced him to occasionally bend down to pick up discarded clubs.[148]

---

* Intermarriage was illegal, at various times, in 42 different states. The US Supreme Court didn't strike down state bans on interracial marriage until 1967, three years after I was born, in the case of *Loving v. Virginia*, the most aptly titled court case in history.

DON'T KNOW NOTHING 'BOUT HISTORY

Some (i.e., many white people) would like us to believe that slavery and racism were merely incidental sidebars in American history. Yeah, right.

Slavery existed legally in the United States for 337 years, from 1528 until 1865, when it was finally outlawed by the Thirteenth Amendment to the Constitution.* As I write this in 2016, American slavery has been outlawed for merely 151 years. In other words, our country was a slave nation more than twice as long as it's been a non-slave nation.

America, you continually want to obscure the harshest realities of your past. Even liberals today sometimes want to disguise the true cause of slavery. While in 2015, the *New York Times* editorial board indignantly (and appropriately) decried the transatlantic slave trade for sending "12.5 million human beings in chains from Africa to the Americas—killing about two million along the way," the editorial maintained that the trade was "driven not by hatred, but by greed."[149] Not quite. The greed was enabled by hatred. There's a reason that the slave-traders captured Africans, not Europeans.

For many centuries, whites have defined nonwhites as subhuman. Even today, natural history and anthropology museums in both Europe and America showcase nonwhite peoples in display cases similar to those for animals, but rarely do so for white people.

While Northerners may want to easily dismiss slavery as a Southern institution, all 13 of the original US colonies, in both the North and the South, legally allowed slavery at some point in time. According to economist Thomas Piketty, "The total market value of slaves represented nearly a year and a half of the US national income in the late eighteenth century and the first half of the nineteenth century."[150]

Not only were the US Capitol building and the White House built, at least partially, by enslaved African Americans, so was the Colonial-era

---

* The first slaves in what were to become the United States were brought to Spanish-run Florida in 1528. Given the Anglophile nature of most US history books, commonly-taught American history usually begins with the English settlement of Jamestown, which imported its first slaves in 1619. Thus, while many claim that US slavery lasted "only" 246 years, the 337-year calculation is clearly more accurate.

wall after which New York City's Wall Street was named.* Even in
Concord, Massachusetts, the birthplace of the Revolutionary War for
"freedom," half of the elected officials were, at one time, slave owners.[151]

Of course, legalized slavery lasted far longer in the South, and was
more deeply entrenched in the economic and social fabric of that
region. That's exactly why traitorous, Southern terrorists—i.e., Confed-
erates—took up arms to defeat the democratically elected government
of the United States. While revisionists since then have cooked up all
sorts of fake causes for secession, the Confederate leaders themselves
were crystal clear that they were fighting primarily so they could keep
forcing human beings to work against their will, for no pay, and in
sub-animal conditions, solely due to their skin color. South Carolina's
secession declaration, for instance, noted "an increasing hostility on
the part of the non-slaveholding States to the institution of slavery,"
and protested that Northern states had failed to "fulfill their constitutional obligations" by interfering with the return of fugitive slaves to
bondage.[152] The cause for which they fought, under the Confederate
battle flag, was *never* noble.

The retroactive claim that the Confederate rebellion was all about
that age-old amorphous notion of "states' rights" is hogwash. The only
"right" that Confederate leaders truly cared about was their so-called
right to deny millions of African Americans their freedom and make
money off their misery. Case in point: the pre-Civil War federal Fugitive Slave Law, pushed by Southern states, trampled on the sovereignty
of free states by preventing them from allowing escaped slaves to live
in freedom in their states. Thus, the South was *against* states' rights for
Northern states.

The vast majority of those who fought for the Confederacy—
including poor, non-slave-owning whites—fervently supported slavery
and white supremacy. As scholar James W. Loewen has written, many
low-income whites hoped to strike it rich someday so they, too, could
own slaves: "Poor white Southerners supported slavery then, just as
many low-income people support the extension of . . . tax cuts for the
wealthy now."[153]

---

* The wall was built to keep out Native Americans. Trump would have loved it, despite its lack
of fake gold and the absence of his name in "yuuuuge" letters, placed in a prominent location.

The argument that Confederate soldiers were just fighting to "preserve their way of life" (what "way of life"? Slavery, of course!) or were merely following orders rings as hollow as the argument that Nazi soldiers fought and committed atrocities for the same reasons. No modern-day mainstream German politician now defends the Nazi flag as a legitimate expression of their nation's heritage.

In 2015, a century and a half after the end of the Civil War, after a white supremacist killed nine people at the historic Emanuel African Methodist Episcopal Church in Charleston, South Carolina, the Confederate battle flag was finally taken down from its place over the capitol building in Columbia. You'd think that should have been the end of the debate. But as the *New York Times* reported, regarding a nationwide poll,

> About four in 10 whites, and one in 10 blacks, said they disapproved of the decision to lower the flag in Columbia, while 52 percent of whites and 81 percent of blacks favored it. Nearly half of white Southerners disagreed with the decision. . . . When asked how they regarded the battle flag, 57 percent of whites said they considered it mostly an emblem of Southern pride, while 68 percent of blacks said they saw it more as a symbol of racism. The view that the flag represents heritage more than bigotry was shared by 65 percent of white Southerners, including three-fourths of white Southern men. . . . "The Confederate flag is a part of history that should not just be thrown out the door," said Mary Nordtome, 66, a white retired rancher from Fort Sumner, N.M., in a follow-up interview. "It really hurts me that we have to be so politically correct in everything."[154]

Likewise, Jeb Bush, who, the pundits kept telling us, was supposedly the most intelligent "policy wonk" in the 2016 Republican presidential primary field, said, "The problem with the Confederate flag isn't the Confederacy, the problem with the Confederate flag is what it began to represent later. And that's what we have to avoid to heal those wounds."[155] Huh? It is true that the Confederate battle flag was taken

up in the 20th century by the Ku Klux Klan and other white supremacists in their defense of segregation, and that was indeed heinous.
But Bush's implication was that, when the flag merely represented a
defense of slavery, then it was just fine and dandy. If the real-world
consequences of such idiocy weren't so harmful, the claim that the Confederate flag used to represent a good thing, before it was co-opted by
hate mongers, would be merely laughable. Not to be outdone by Jeb!,*
a Ted Cruz super PAC ran a radio ad and sent robocalls that blasted
Donald Trump, who had mildly criticized the Confederate flag once,
saying, "Trump talks about our flag like it's a social disease." Notice the
word "our." When you out-racist Donald Trump, that's quite an accomplishment, especially when you are half-Cuban and born in Canada.

It shouldn't be surprising that the "Don't Tread on Me" flag, which
was a favorite icon of the Klan, also became a preferred symbol of the
Tea Party.**

It takes a certain kind of person to be nostalgic for the 19th century:
"Only straight, white men would like a time machine to travel back
in time," said writer Saeed Jones.[156] I certainly would not relish going
back in history; not only would I detest living in a time when so many
people lacked even minimal rights, I'm pretty sure I'd miss indoor toi-
lets, recorded music, and novocaine.

The greatest irony is that many Southerners who consider themselves white, including many who are openly hostile to blacks, are likely
to have at least some African DNA as a result of the rampant rapes of
female slaves.[157]

The real problem with the systematic denial of history is that it leads
to a systematic denial of structural racism today. Until the South—and
indeed, until the whole country—fully reckons with our 337 years of

---

* After Jeb spent $130 million on his losing presidential candidacy (which made it through only
three states), his campaign was forced to auction off its exclamation point on eBay for 23 cents.
** J.B. Stoner, American segregationist convicted for bombing a black church, with "Don't Tread
on Me" banner in 1964. US Senator Ted Cruz in front of the same symbol in 2013.

chattel slavery and our 100 years of legal segregation and discrimination that followed that, we will never fully accept the reality that racism and discrimination are still deeply woven into every strand of the nation's civic cloth.

In order to understand the present, we must acknowledge the past. In the 1968 general election, segregationist Alabama governor George Wallace, running as an Independent, received 13 percent of the popular vote and won five states. In 1972, running for the Democratic nomination, when many Southern Democrats were still overtly racist, Wallace not only won every county in Florida's Democratic primary, but won the primaries in Maryland and Michigan, before a nearly successful assassination attempt ended his campaign. If more Americans remembered—or even knew—all that, then maybe they'd be less surprised by the success of Donald Trump and realize that his candidacy was just the cherry on top of the hot hate sundae that the Right has been consuming for decades.

BACKLASH BLUES

According to the Southern Poverty Law Center:

> The number of extremist groups operating in the United States grew in 2015—a year awash in deadly extremist violence and hateful rhetoric from mainstream political figures. The number of groups increased from 784 to 892—a 14 percent jump—in just one year. 'While the number of extremist groups grew in 2015 after several years of declines, the real story was the deadly violence committed by extremists in city after city,' said Mark Potok, senior fellow at the center. 'Whether it was Charleston, San Bernardino, or Colorado Springs, 2015 was clearly a year of deadly action for extremists.'[158]

Often perceived by the rest of the country as liberal, New York State had the third-highest number of hate groups.*

---

* Oy, New York. To paraphrase a song, "If you can hate here, you can hate anywhere." That doesn't exactly make a great new advertising jingle for the state.

In 2014, Rep. Steve Scalise (R-LA), then the US House Majority Whip, acknowledged that he spoke to a white supremacist gathering while serving as a state representative in 2002. Not only did this revelation fail to cost him his seat in the House, it didn't even dislodge him from the Whip post, the third-highest leadership position in the chamber.[159]

Did the election of the nation's first nonwhite president actually *increase* racism in America? That's unclear, but it certainly did make unapologetic racists more vocal and more panicked.* Obama's reelection particularly drove them to hysteria—causing a massive spike in guns and ammo purchases—because they could no longer write off his original election as a fluke. They finally understood (either consciously or not) that the days in which white men could unilaterally control every aspect of our nation's government and society were over.

America has a long history of short periods of racial progress immediately followed by retrenchments. After the racial empowerment of Southern Reconstruction after the Civil War, the KKK and other Southern white supremacy groups violently reclaimed political power in what some called "the Redemption." After the successes of the Civil Rights movement of the 1950s and 1960s, race-baiters like Wallace, Richard Nixon, and Ronald Reagan rode to power on a white backlash. Historian Eric Foner fears that, in the age of Obama, we are experiencing "a similar kind of retreat . . . The attack on voting rights, incarceration, obviously, but even more intellectually and culturally, a sort of exhaustion with black protest, an attitude of 'What are these people really complaining about? Look at what we've done for you.'"[160] It is no wonder that a Pew poll in 2016 found that, while 41 percent of blacks expressed "strong support" for the Black Lives Matter movement, only 14 percent of whites did.[161]

There's also the possibility that a fair number of white Americans wanted to believe that merely electing an African American president would shut the door on the nation's troubled racial past, absolving the country from its past sins and abdicating any responsibility to discuss,

---

* The widespread use of the Internet—and the ability to spew hatred anonymously—has also contributed to the ubiquitousness of hate in our society. Now any racist yokel with a computer in his basement can be famous for two seconds by posting a meme even more racist than a meme posted by another racist yokel.

no less redress, centuries worth of systematic oppression, thinking, "We gave the brass ring to a black guy. Done. We're off the hook. America's officially forgiven."

Social psychologists use the term "self-licensing" to describe a phenomenon in which, after people perform an act they think commendable, they feel more justified to do something rotten. Did the act of electing a black president, that one good deed, give some Americans the self-license to more openly express racist thoughts? Researchers at Stanford University believe it did. In a study, they found that people who had an opportunity to publicly proclaim their support for Obama were more likely to think that white people were better qualified for a certain job in law enforcement; people who voiced vocal support for white presidential candidate John Kerry were less likely to express such racially-biased views.[162]

Perhaps this is the same reason that Republican-base voters claimed, in polls taken early in the two most recent presidential election cycles, to support Herman Cain for president in 2012 and Dr. Ben Carson in 2016, even though Cain and Carson were even less qualified then the rest of the mostly unqualified conservatives. Even far-right pundit Jonah Goldberg admitted that Republicans embraced Carson, in part, to shield themselves from charges of racism:

> One could argue that [Carson] is even more authentically African American than Barack Obama, given that Obama's mother was white and he was raised in part by his white grandparents . . . Carson's popularity isn't solely derived from his race, but it is a factor. The vast majority of conservatives resent the fact that Democrats glibly and shamelessly accuse Republicans of bigotry.[163] *

WHO IS RACIST?

Whites who claim that dark-skinned people are intrinsically inferior because of their skin color are obviously racist. But how about everyone

---

* Note to Republicans: If you don't want to glibly and shamelessly be called a racist, don't *be* a racist.

else? In an opinion piece titled "Dear White America," scholar George Yancy wrote,

> I'm asking for you to tarry, to linger, with the ways in which you perpetuate a racist society, the ways in which you are racist . . . As you reap comfort from being white, we suffer for being black and people of color. But your comfort is linked to our pain and suffering. Just as my comfort in being male is linked to the suffering of women, which makes me sexist, so, too, you are racist. That is the gift that I want you to accept, to embrace. It is a form of knowledge that is taboo. Imagine the impact that the acceptance of this gift might have on you and the world.[164]

I don't agree that benefiting, even involuntarily, from racism or sexism automatically makes someone racist or sexist, but I do think that racially-biased thoughts do, at least occasionally, pop into the heads of even the most progressive whites (myself included) and that insensitive thoughts about women do, at least occasionally, pop into the heads of the most feminist men (myself included). It's impossible to live in a society and a world that is as racist and as sexist (and many other "ists") as ours without having just a bit of that rub off on you.

There is no question that white privilege is real, pervasive, and extremely harmful to nonwhites. But there's also an unhelpful tendency for some people to see each and every problem facing Americans *only* through the lens of race. (Just as it's problematic for some on the Left like Bernie Sanders to view every issue almost exclusively through the lens of class.)

Peggy McIntosh, a women's studies scholar at Wellesley, penned one of the most famous essays on privilege, "White Privilege: Unpacking the Invisible Knapsack." While her writing correctly acknowledges that white people generally benefit from more abundant professional opportunities and a society that meets many of their needs and whims, she goes a bit too far, claiming that, as a white person, "I can be pretty sure that my neighbors . . . will be neutral or pleasant to me . . . I can arrange to protect my children most of the time from people who might not like them . . . I can be pretty sure that my children's teachers and employers will tolerate them if they fit school and workplace norms . . .

I can criticize our government and talk about how much I fear its policies and behavior without being seen as a cultural outsider."[165] I am not sure what magical bubble she's living in, but in every society on the planet, all human beings, including white ones, sometimes face unpleasant neighbors, have children that are despised by some people, face great intolerance if they violate work and school norms, and suffer from tremendous ostracization if they publicly oppose popular positions. In addition, not every nonwhite who faces any of those uncomfortable situations faces them solely because of their race. Just as it's absurd to claim that no problem is ever caused by racism, it's equally absurd to argue that every problem is.

Some even argue that every white person in America is intrinsically better off than every nonwhite person. Hardly. Yes, even Oprah can have someone following her in a store once in a while, but there's no question that her life is better than that of a white coal miner in West Virginia who will live his entire existence impoverished and probably will die an early, painful death from black lung disease.

Can black people be racist, or, as it is sometimes called, "reverse racist"? Yes, I think they can—and are—but, before I explain why, let's hear from some of those who claim that's impossible. In the movie *Dear White People*, one of the characters sums up the case: "Black people can't be racist. Prejudiced, yes, but not racist. Racism describes a system of disadvantage based on race. Black people can't be racist since we don't stand to benefit from such a system." Writer Zeba Blay puts it this way in the *Huffington Post*:

> Reverse racism isn't real. No, really. The "reverse racism" card is often pulled by white people when people of color call out racism and discrimination . . . The impulse behind the reverse racism argument seems to be a desire to prove that people of color don't have it that bad, they're not the only ones that are put at a disadvantage or targeted because of their race . . . White people can experience prejudice from black people and other nonwhites. Black people can have ignorant, backwards ideas about white people, as well as other nonwhite races. No one is trying to deny that. But racism is far more complex . . .

At its core, racism is a system in which a dominant race benefits off the oppression of others—whether they want to or not. We
don't live in a society where every racial group has equal power,
status, and opportunity. White people have never been enslaved,
colonized, or forced to segregate. They do not face housing or job
discrimination, police brutality, poverty, or incarceration at the
level that black people do. This is not to say that they do not experience some of these things (like poverty and police brutality) at
all. But again, not on the same scale—not even close.[166]

I don't buy that argument. Claiming that people can be "discriminatory" but not "racist" is self-denial in the extreme. Even in a world
where white people are, in aggregate, more powerful than people of
color, it's simply not the case that whites are more powerful in each
and every interaction. If you claim that blacks can never—ever—have
personal power in a white society, isn't that denying African American
individuals basic human agency?

While, in the course of US history, there has been far more white-
on-black violence than the reverse, when, during the 1992 Los Angeles
riots, a group of African American assailants beat a white truck driver,
Reginald Denny, nearly to his death, the black people in that instance
had more power than the white victim.

It's also outdated to view race as black or white. The US is now full of
multitudinous skin colors and ethnicities, along an endless spectrum of
possibilities. More Americans now identify as Hispanic than black, and
more than ever now identify themselves as being two or more races.[167]

In 2010, 17 million Americans—one in 20—were of Asian descent.
You'd never know that Asian Americans have historically been treated
as subhuman from today's media coverage and cultural expectations—
which give the false impression that Asian Americans are some sort of
super-minority who can do no wrong. In 1871, in one of the worst mass
lynchings in US history,[168] an angry mob of over 500 white Los Angeles
men attacked, robbed, and murdered Chinese residents, with 14 Chinese victims killed.* The very first federal control over immigration to the

---

* Ironically (or not), the street where the massacre took place was named "Calles des Negros,"
otherwise known as "Nigger's Alley."

US, the 1882 Chinese Exclusion Act, barred all immigrants from China. More than 100,000 Japanese Americans were thrown into internment camps during World War II. As late as the 1990s, a number of African Americans in various cities firebombed stores owned by Korean Americans, specifically because they were owned by people of Asian descent; you can call that whatever you like—I call it racist.

Worldwide, there are endless categories of people in endless combinations of religions, races, tribes, and cultures, which also result in endless opportunities for hate, misunderstanding, and resentment. Too often, darker- and lighter-skinned people of color hate each other. There's long been bad blood between Japanese and Korean people, Hatfields and McCoys, secular and ultra-Orthodox Jews, Crips and Bloods, Sunni and Shiite Muslims, Hutus and Tutsis, etc. This list could be longer than my entire book and still wouldn't include every possibility for intolerance.

How much of that is racism versus some other form of hatred? Who knows? But who cares?

This is essentially a pointless debate. What real-world difference does it make how a certain type of hatred is categorized or what it is called? Getting bogged down in purely identity politics—competing over whose group is more oppressed—is the surest way to guarantee that all groups will continue to be oppressed.

Actual human beings often defy expectations. I once met an African American taxi driver in Washington, DC, who described himself as a "Black Power activist." But, he confided to me, he usually did not pick up black people hailing his cab because he worried that they would either attack him or fail to pay the fare.

Yes, groups of people, systems, and structures are complicated, but individual human beings are twice as complex, and bewilderingly inconsistent.

HELLHOUND ON THE TRAIL: THE SORDID INTERSECTION OF POLICING AND RACE

The criminal justice system in America has always been about many things, but, first and foremost, it's been about race, about keeping nonwhite people "in their place." While Thomas Jefferson and James

Madison are now famous for supposedly wanting only limited government, they both supported the creation of a strong government police state to enforce slavery, using law enforcement authorities and courts to prevent—as well as to capture and punish—runaways. In the 19th century, white abolitionist William Lloyd Garrison said, "Hardly any doors but to those of our state prisons were open to our colored brethren."[169]

Throughout US history, African Americans and other people of color have been victims of police brutality, ghastly work camps and inhumane prisons, selective enforcement, vigilante justice, trumped up charges, and false, forced confessions. "If one is carried back and forth from the precinct to the hospital long enough, one is likely to confess to anything," wrote James Baldwin in 1966.[170]

Especially since the riots of the 1960s, urban police departments have been turned into militarized armies of occupation. Here's a 1967 photo from Newark, New Jersey:

(Don Hogan Charles, *The New York Times*/Redux)

One of my very first memories as a child was driving through that city in a car with my parents in 1969, and seeing an armored police vehicle that looked like a tank.

Massive state violence against people of color is nothing new; what's new is the common availability of video cameras and smartphones to document it, and for social media and 24-hour cable news to ensure that such images are seen by millions of people, over and over again—if they choose to cover it.

Given that most American police forces are now more racially diverse than at any time in US history, we have to grapple with the hard reality that some of the police officers who commit brutality against people of color are themselves people of color. For instance, one of the supervising officers at the scene when New York City cops choked Eric Garner to death was Sergeant Kizzy Adonis, a black woman.[171] One of the officers charged in the death of Baltimore's Freddie Gray, a black man killed while in police custody, was Officer William Porter, also black.[172]

I would like to stipulate that I believe that most police officers are brave, selfless, underpaid public servants who perform dangerous, challenging—and usually thankless—work protecting the public. They mostly get media attention only when something goes wrong. Any violence against them, including the mass murder of officers in Dallas, is both morally repugnant and politically backwards.

But we must also acknowledge that too many police have not yet shed their biased, trigger-happy past. According to *USA Today*, "Nearly two times a week in the United States, a white police officer killed a black person during a seven-year period ending in 2012 . . . On average, there were 96 such incidents among at least 400 police killings each year that were reported to the FBI by local police. They show that the shooting of a black teenager in Ferguson, Mo. [Michael Brown] was not an isolated event in American policing. The reports show that 18 percent of the blacks killed during those seven years were under age 21, compared to 9 percent of the whites."[173]

The Guardian compiled a more comprehensive database of police shootings in the US, and found that 1,134 Americans died at the hands of law enforcement officers in 2015, and that black men were nine times more likely than other Americans to be killed by police officers.[174] We don't know how many of those killings were in response to true threats to police officers or community members.

"More than 50 police officers involved in fatal shootings [in 2015] had previously fired their guns in deadly on-duty shootings," according to the *Washington Post*. "For a handful of officers, it was their third fatal shooting. For one officer, it was his fourth. The findings concerned many law enforcement experts, who said that most officers never fire their weapons on the job."[175]

As someone who is pro-union to my bones, it pains me to say that police unions have often not only refused to help weed out their own "bad apples," but they have even engaged in systematized campaigns to blame the victims and tar elected officials who so much as mildly attempt to hold their police forces accountable.

Some police unions and their enablers in the right-wing media are stuck in full denial mode. They don't seem to understand that a public that fears its police, or a police that fears its public, is a threat to democracy. They often imply that people of color who commit crimes somehow represent their entire races, but when nonwhite people are innocent victims of brutality, then race is totally irrelevant. In a *New York Post* piece entitled "The Myth of the Killer-Cop 'Epidemic,'" Michael Walsh wrote about the rash of police killings of unarmed African Americans:

> Each incident is breathlessly reported by a media determined to show that America remains deeply, irredeemably racist. Problem is, it's simply not true. White cops shooting unarmed black men accounted for less than four percent of fatal police shootings. Since the population of the US is about 318 million people, a thousand deaths at the hands of police works out to 1 in 318,000. You have a better chance of being killed in a violent storm (1 in 68,000) or slipping in the tub (1 in 11,500) than being shot by a cop, no matter what color you are.[176]

Calculating one person's personal risk of being shot by cops sure is a twisted way to discount the murders of unarmed Americans. Using this same methodology, you could conclude that, even though 14 innocent people were killed in the San Bernardino mass shooting, an individual would have only a one in 23 *million* chance of being killed that day in a domestic terrorist attack.* Of course, every unnecessary death is tragic.

New York City provides one example of the polarized, racially-charged politics of policing. Thirty-eight percent of the entire city's more than 34,000 police officers—and an astounding 55 percent of the city's white police officers—live outside the city, further increasing the divide between officers and the communities they serve.[177] Nationwide, many urban cops are white, and live in mostly-white suburbs outside the heavily nonwhite cities in which they serve.

Between 2002 and 2015, according to the New York Civil Liberties Union, "innocent New Yorkers have been subjected to police stops and street interrogations more than five million times . . . and the black and Latino communities continue to be the overwhelming target of these tactics. Nearly 9 out of 10 stopped-and-frisked New Yorkers have been completely innocent, according to the NYPD's own reports."[178] In 2013, a federal court judge found these practices unconstitutional.

In 2011 alone, New Yorkers were stopped by the police 685,724 times. New York City Mayor Bill de Blasio, a progressive Democrat who was catapulted into office in 2013 largely on his pledge to stop arbitrary stop and frisks, brought that number down to 45,787 in 2014 and 22,939 in 2015, a whopping 97 percent fewer stop and frisks than in 2001, under then-Mayor Rudy Giuliani.

The city's police unions bitterly fought the reductions in illegal stops, engaging in all sorts of fear-mongering. I am sick of law enforcement officials whining that they can't do their jobs without routinely violating the Bill of Rights. Protecting the Constitution isn't a diversion from law enforcement, it *is* law enforcement. Stopping crimes without violating rights is as central to law enforcement as scoring goals without using hands is in soccer.**

---

* I also note that, in 2015, there were roughly 3.3 million American Muslims. The two attackers in San Bernardino were the only shooters of the Muslim faith to engage in a domestic terror attack in 2015, which means that, if you were a US Muslim in 2015, you had only a one in 1.6 million chance of *conducting* a terrorist attack.

** Perhaps the most repugnant—and gratuitous—act of a New York City police union was when the Sergeants Benevolent Association asked its members and supporters to post pictures of homeless people in humiliating situations to a website it created. Their twisted thinking was that this was some sort of way of harming the progressive mayor with whom they were feuding. So much for "protect and serve."

The scare tactics of the police unions and the city's newspaper tabloids aside, in 2015, New York City was as safe as it had been at any point in modern times, continuing to be the lowest-crime big city in the nation. Overall crime decreased by 2 percent that year, and there were 536 fewer murders than five years earlier.[179]

Still, after two police officers were tragically assassinated on the job, the police unions implicitly blamed de Blasio.* Egged on by their unions, significant numbers of officers did the unthinkable—they physically turned their backs on their mayor (their democratically-elected boss)— at the funeral of one of the fallen officers. Shortly thereafter, the *New York Times* editorial board opined,

> With these acts of passive-aggressive contempt and self-pity, many New York police officers, led by their union, are squandering the department's credibility, defacing its reputation, shredding its hard-earned respect. They have taken the most grave and solemn of civic moments—a funeral of a fallen colleague—and hijacked it for their own petty look-at-us gesture.
>
> None of [their] grievances can justify the snarling sense of victimhood that seems to be motivating the anti-de Blasio campaign—the belief that the department is never wrong, that it never needs redirection or reform, only reverence. This is the view peddled by union officials . . . that cops are an ethically impeccable force with their own priorities and codes of behavior, accountable only to themselves, and whose reflexive defiance in the face of valid criticism is somehow normal.
>
> It's not normal. Not for a professional class of highly trained civil servants, which New York's Finest profess to be. The police can rightly expect, even insist upon, the respect of the public. But respect is a finite resource. It cannot be wasted. Sometimes it has to be renewed.[180]

When government is given the power to use force, accountability

---

* It shouldn't need to be said, but for the record, I must say it again: Violence against law enforcement officers is just plain wrong. In 2015, according to the National Law Enforcement Officers Memorial Fund, 94 officers died on duty in 2015, with 52 dying in traffic-related events and 42 dying from gunfire.

has to be clear, strong, and unwavering. Given that the US military has always reported to civilian elected officials, it's ridiculous that some police seem scornful that they are also required to report to civilians. The police deserve real respect, sincere thanks, as much safety as possible, and good wages and benefits, but not automatic immunity for murder or unconstitutional practices.

Americans of all backgrounds have always offered broad public support for tough, effective law enforcement. But African Americans have long been in a bind, since they have been disproportionately victims of both police misconduct and crime. Starting in the 1960s, key African American leaders—seeing their communities awash in blood and heroin needles—started calling for stricter crime crackdowns. As crime scholar Michael Javen Fortner noted, "Harlem business leaders supported stricter law enforcement and harsher punishments for criminals. In 1973, nearly three-quarters of blacks and Puerto Ricans favored life sentences for drug pushers, and the Rev. Oberia Dempsey, a Harlem pastor, said: 'Take the junkies off the streets and put 'em in camps,' and added, 'we've got to end this terror and restore New York to decent people. Instead of fighting all the time for civil rights we should be fighting civil wrongs.'"[181]

By the early 1990s, a generation of Americans had witnessed ever-increasing crime levels. In 1994, according to the FBI, there were 1.8 million violent crimes reported in America, including 23,000 murders, 102,000 rapes, 618,000 robberies, and 1.1 million aggravated assaults.[182] Low-income communities of color were particularly ravaged. Although, in reality, yearly increases in crime had started to flatten out by 1994, the fear of crime was still being inflamed by the rise in saturation-level crime coverage on ratings-hungry cable TV networks and the advent of shows like *America's Most Wanted*. Bolstered by George Herbert Walker Bush's victorious presidential campaign, which used race-baiting imagery to paint his opponent, Massachusetts Governor Michael Dukakis, as "soft on crime," the Republicans intensified their use of crime as a wedge issue.

Bill Clinton's 1992 presidential campaign sought to neutralize the issue by acknowledging people's real concerns over crime and by embracing a broad package of government anti-crime proposals. In the wake of that campaign, the 1994 federal crime bill, championed by President Clinton, was the largest proposed crime legislation in US history and was an ideological mixed bag. It funded 100,000 new police officers, provided $9.7 billion in funding for prisons, expanded the federal death penalty, required states to create sex offender registries, and eliminated educational aid to inmates—all traditional conservative priorities. That extra money for prisons gave states a serious incentive to increase incarceration. But contemporary Black Lives Matter protestors and other progressives often forget that this same bill—which they retroactively despise—also advanced longtime liberal priorities: providing $6.1 billion in funding for crime-prevention programs (including youth programs, such as "midnight basketball," decried by the Right), banning assault weapons, and allocating $1.6 billion to help prevent and investigate violence against women. Additionally, the extra cops on the street were targeted to community policing activities that engaged neighborhood residents as partners in the anti-crime fight, long a progressive priority. Both because of the progressive provisions of the bill and because low-income communities of color were the ones most devastated by crime, most progressive members of Congress, including then House Member Bernie Sanders, as well as 24 members of the Congressional Black Caucus, voted for the bill.[183] As Fortner explained,

> Black folks have agency. Their voices had a huge impact in changing the narrative around urban crime and drug addiction and pushing it in a way that validated very punitive crime policies . . . You get the sense [from certain black critics of the Clinton crime bill] that crime policy was not developed to solve any problem, that these laws were created just to put away black folks . . . I thought the dominant scholars were completely ignoring the effects of crime on people's lives. I grew up in Brownsville [a high-crime neighborhood in Brooklyn], and I remember what crime felt like. And these academic discussions, these ideological discussions about crime, completely ignore the terror in the streets. They completely ignore how crime shaped whether you went to church at night or how you felt coming home from work. Once you add that to the picture,

I think crime policy becomes less suspicious. That doesn't mean it becomes less problematic. These were dumb policies. But they begin to have a logic that is not strictly tied to racial or economic imperatives. It begins to have a logic that's tied to people wanting to live normal, safe lives in urban communities, and politicians who responded to those pleas.[184]

Beyond the crime bill, the nation even extended its tough-on-crime mode to schools, and did so in a racially discriminatory manner (of course). Once left to parents, teachers, and principals, school discipline was increasingly handled by law enforcement agencies, and increasingly resulted in sending kids to prison.

Seventeen thousand sworn police officers were posted in US schools in 2009, and, in 2014, more than three in four high schools, and the vast majority of large schools, had armed security staff. Schools where at least half of the children were nonwhite, as well as high-poverty schools, were most likely to have in-house police.[185] In the past, when old-fashioned hall monitors found kids misbehaving, the children were likely to be sent back to their classrooms, or, at worst, were sent to the principal's office and got their parents called. Today, when confronted by armed police in schools, they are likely to be referred to the criminal justice system. A water balloon fight in North Carolina, initiated as a senior-day prank, led to eight teens being arrested. A rowdy four-year-old, in pre-kindergarten class in West Virginia, was taken out of her class by police, in handcuffs.[186]

It is true that too many students bring lethal weapons to school, and that a dangerous school punishes the innocent children who most want to learn, but too many of our institutions of learning have lost the balance between student safety and student dignity.

Nationally, in just the 2011–2012 school year, 1.2 million black students were suspended from public school, from kindergarten through high school. Fifty-five percent of those suspensions occurred in 13 southern states and often for relatively minor, nonviolent infractions.[187]

"I came to see the streets and the schools as arms of the same beast," wrote Ta-Nehisi Coates. "One enjoyed the official power of the state while the other enjoyed its implicit sanction. But fear and violence were the

An officer and a narcotics-detecting dog in an Indianapolis public school
(AP Photo/Michael Conroy)

weaponry of both. Fail in the streets and the crews would catch you slipping and take your body. Fail in the schools and you would be suspended and sent back to those same streets, where they would take your body. And I began to see these two arms in relation—those who failed in the schools justified their destruction in the streets. The society could say, 'He should have stayed in school,' and then wash its hands of him."[188]

As the nation cowered in their fear of serious crime, and children were afraid of being assaulted at school, most Americans were all too willing to give great, unfettered powers and huge sums of money to law enforcement and corrections officials, sending them away with the tacit instructions, "Do whatever you need to do to protect us, and we'll avert our eyes from any unpleasant tactics." America, you had the same attitude about our military and intelligence agencies after 9/11. Most Americans willingly outsourced our dirty work. Waterboarding? Fine.* Stopping and frisking millions of innocent people of color? No problem. Unfair targeting of Muslim Americans? You bet. Giving teenagers a criminal record for a water balloon fight? No problem. Just spare us the details, and don't make us look at any pictures or videos of any of that unpleasantness. Only after crime decreased, and after the

---

* Few seriously questioned why the United States was using the very same form of torture, waterboarding, for which the country had previously prosecuted Japanese enemies for war crimes.

country moved further away in time from 9/11, was the public willing to start asking hard questions about the liberty-crushing brutality conducted on its behalf. The public *should* ask tough questions, but those who previously condoned those hard-line tactics should be a little less self-righteous and a little more self-reflective. Let's hold the media and police accountable, sure, but let's also hold *ourselves* accountable. Like most societies, America, you respond badly to fear. But I'll keep pushing you to be *better* than most societies.

WHO IS DOING THE KILLING? WHO IS GETTING KILLED?

Law enforcement sometimes overreacts to perceived threats, but we have to acknowledge that in most cases, they are indeed reacting to actual danger. We need a national conversation on how weapons and violence on all sides merely fuels more of each, and how race, gender, and class intersect regarding this problem.

Barely two months into 2016, Chicago had already logged more than 365 shootings—including at least 70 that resulted in fatalities. During Memorial Day weekend of 2015 alone, Baltimore saw 26 injured and nine killed in shootings. In both cities, the shooters and victims were mostly young black men. Meanwhile, nationwide, African American men suffered from astronomically high levels of unemployment.[*]

The good news, America—rarely reported in a media ecosystem driven by sensationalism and clickbait—is that, between 1995 and 2014, US violent crime dropped by 47 percent and murders dropped 34 percent, partially due to the policing and incarceration trends that had so many troubling side effects. Still, there were 14,249 murders and non-negligent homicides in 2014, a staggering number, more than three times the total number of US troops killed in Iraq over the 11-year period of 2003–2014.

---

[*] In January 2016, the official unemployment rate for African American men, 8.4 percent, was nearly double that of the population as a whole. As bad as that is, the official unemployment rate dramatically underestimates the lack of opportunities for young, black, inner city men. A report from the Great Cities Institute at the University of Illinois at Chicago found that in that city, nearly half of black men aged 20 to 24 were neither working nor in school; the rate was 20 percent for Hispanic men and 10 percent for white men. The report found that in Los Angeles and New York City, about 30 percent of 20- to 24-year-old black men were out of work and school in 2014.

We are accustomed to reviewing crime through the lens of race, but rarely do we do so through the viewpoint of gender (except when it comes to rape). Yet according to the FBI, of the 5,703 crimes classified as homicides in 2014, 90 percent of the murderers, and 70 percent of the victims, were male. Thus, while the nation is convulsed in a debate over the racial aspects of criminology, the greatest correlation to violent crime, by far, is gender. I suppose that's how it's been in every society at every point in history, and that violence has always been closely tied to masculinity. But there is no doubt that the country is truly in the grips of a decades-long "male-on-male" crime wave. But I don't see anyone calling for stopping and frisking *all* men.

Most murderers kill people of their own race. Eighty-two percent of the people killed by white people are white and 90 percent of the people killed by black people are black. Yet, while it is true that the largest *number* of murderers and murder victims are white, the *percentage* of black murderers and murder victims is more than three times that of the proportion of African Americans to the population as a whole.

HOMICIDE OFFENDERS AND VICTIMS VERSUS THE US POPULATION 2014

	% of Homicide Offenders	% of Homicide Victims	% of US Population
Whites, both genders	48%	53%	77%
Blacks, both genders	47%	43%	13%
Men, all races	90%	70%	49%
Women, all races	10%	30%	51%

(Note that in this chart, "whites" includes Hispanics who consider themselves white—
Sources FBI and US Census Bureau)

In 2014, white Americans killed 2,488 white people and 187 black people, while black Americans killed 2,205 black people and 440 white people. In contrast, by one estimate, over the years 2009 to 2014, an estimated 76 unarmed men and women were killed while in some form of police custody, equaling about 15 per year.[189] I'm in no way trying to minimize the senseless tragedy of unwarranted police-committed killings, but I must point out that, in sheer numbers, those deaths are simply dwarfed by the number of civilians murdering each other.

Some African American and progressive activists insist that "black-on-black" crime is a myth, and that the only reason anyone so much as brings up the topic is due to their racism.

In a piece in *The Root* entitled "Don't White People Kill Each Other, Too?," Edward Wyckoff Williams wrote,

> When it comes to America's racial past and present, lies and snake oil are sold in many colors. In the wake of the Trayvon Martin tragedy, conservatives in media have sought to deflect from the racism and racial profiling that precipitated his untimely death by referencing the broader social malaise of supposed "black-on-black violence." What [white critics] failed to mention is the exacting truth that white Americans are just as likely to be killed by other whites. According to Justice Department statistics, 84 percent of white people killed every year are killed by other whites. The term "black on black" crime is a destructive, racialized colloquialism that perpetuates an idea that blacks are somehow more prone to violence. This is untrue and fully verifiable by FBI, DOJ, and census data. Yet the fallacy is so fixed that even African Americans have come to believe it. In fact, all races share similar ratios. Yet there's no outrage or racialized debate about "white on white" violence. Instead, the myth and associated fear of "black on black" crime is sold as a legitimate, mainstream descriptive and becomes [the] American status quo.[190]

That convoluted reasoning is just as wrong-headed, and just as counterproductive, as the right-wing claims that white-on-black police violence isn't a serious problem either. Of course, white people, who are 77 percent of the country's population, commit most of the nation's crimes and are the majority of crime victims. It is also true that when upper class people and/or whites are the victims of violence it receives much more media coverage.

But the double standards shouldn't obscure the heartbreaking reality that, for young black men, murder is the top cause of death. (Murder is not even close to the top cause of death for young white men.) In males 15–24, homicide is the leading cause of death for nearly half of blacks but for less than 10 percent of whites.

HOMICIDE AS CAUSE OF DEATH IN WHITE MEN
VERSUS BLACK MEN, 2013[191]

Age Group	Black Men	White Men
Ages 10–14	2nd highest cause of death 10% of deaths	5th highest cause of death 5% of deaths
Ages 15–19	Top cause of death 48% of deaths	3rd highest cause of death 9% of deaths
Ages 20–24	Top cause of death 50% of deaths	3rd highest cause of death 8% of deaths
Ages 25–34	Top cause of death 34% of deaths	5th highest cause of death 5% of deaths
Ages 35–44	3rd highest cause of death 13% of deaths	6th highest cause of death 3% of deaths

Source: Centers for Disease Control

The numbers speak for themselves. Yes, murder is horrible when white people kill white people (which they do at alarming rates), but the cold fact remains that black people in the US kill other black people at even more alarming rates.

We should certainly have a robust debate over *why* black-on-black murder rate percentages are so high. How much of it is caused by the pain of living in a racist society? How much is prompted by the de-industrialization of large cities and the sky-high unemployment rates for black men? How much of it is fostered by desperate poverty? How much is due to the nation's entrenched housing segregation, which means that blacks mostly live near other blacks exclusively?

How much of it is due to American culture or mass media?* If I even attempted to answer those questions, it would take another five books, so I won't try to do so here. But I will insist that we have to admit that *both* police violence and black-on-black violence are critical problems that urgently need to be addressed. While I am obviously fully aware that some African Americans (and non–African Americans) feel the phrase "black-on-black violence" is misleading, and that it particularly shouldn't be uttered by whites such as myself (or that some other, less direct, words should be used to describe the problem), given the real-life tragic consequences of this problem, I believe it does the victims of such violence and their families a disservice for anyone—of any race—to shy away from accurately describing the full nature of the problem and have an endless debate over word choice.

Spike Lee, whose brilliant and underrated film *Chi-Raq* takes this denial head-on, stated in an interview, "It wasn't a cop that killed and that executed Tyshawn Lee, the nine-year-old boy who was lured into an alleyway in Chicago's Southside . . . To me, I don't care about the complexion or the color of the trigger finger. It does not matter to me. If you kill somebody, you kill somebody. It doesn't matter who you are." Lee also told CNN that black people "can't ignore that we are killing ourselves, too." He condemned the shooting of unarmed black people by police, saying, "those were wrong." But he added, "We cannot be out there [protesting police violence] and then when it comes to young brothers killing themselves, then mum's the word. No one's saying nothing? It's got to be both ends."[192]

I doubt that Lee agrees much with conservative African American pundit Jason Riley, but they seem to find common ground on this issue. Riley has said, "Let's not pretend our morgues and cemeteries are full of young black men because cops are shooting them. The reality is that it's because other black people are shooting them."[193]

---

* Some people assume that the violence and drug use often associated with hip-hop culture is unique to contemporary African American culture. Not true. Historically, there have been other examples of dispossessed classes of outsiders fostering cultures that combined music, illegal vices, and rampant violence. One example is Rembetika, an underground Greek folk music, which originated in the violence-ridden hashish dens of Athens around the turn of the 20th century, as a result of the forced immigration of two million Greek refugees from Asia Minor. Another example, Argentinian tango, originated in the slums of Buenos Aires, and was often associated with prostitution and violence. There are countless other historical examples.

But denial is still pervasive: In a widely-shared blog post, Black Lives Matter activist Shaun King went even further:

> Don't you ever say "Black on Black Crime" again.
> Ever.
> Don't say it.
> Don't think it.
> Don't write it.
> Don't spell it on Scrabble.
> Don't even see what other words you can make with the letters that form *black on black crime.*
> It is the dumbest, most ridiculously racist phrase used to describe crime in the world right now.
> . . . The only reason the phrase black on black crime even exists is in some racist attempt to make it [seem] like black folk have some unique problem with committing crimes against each other that other folk don't have.[194]

The rest of the piece goes on to repeat the same diversionary points almost word-for-word, as other, similar pieces—that most crimes are committed by whites and no one is discussing "white-on-white crime." When a Facebook friend of mine re-posted King's essay approvingly, it generated a lively debate, including this amazing response from a woman named Jean:

> I don't believe it is important how it is referred; the reality is that senseless killings happen far too often in our community. Try & convince a father or mother that it should be referred as something else when their 11 year old African American child was gunned down by 5 African Americans. It would be more advantageous for you young men & women who responded to organize some type of group to focus on changing the mindset of our youth & young adults to manage their anger/rage in a more responsible manner, than kill, kill, kill. Each of you has the potential of becoming another Dr. Martin Luther King, Jr. and leading this community out of bondage.

There's really nothing to add to that.

WITH LIBERTY AND JUSTICE FOR ALL
(WELL, ACTUALLY, MOSTLY FOR RICH WHITE FOLKS)

In the 1963 Supreme Court case of *Gideon v. Wainwright*, the US Supreme Court ruled unanimously that states were required to provide legal counsel to criminal defendants who could not afford them.* While that decision has never been overturned, an increasing number of low-income Americans, particularly nonwhite ones, are routinely denied adequate counsel.

For instance, in early 2016, the New Orleans Public Defenders Office, which mostly defends African Americans, announced that, because it was so underfunded by the government, it could no longer afford to take on new cases. Chief District Defender for Orleans Parish, Derwyn Bunton, wrote,

> It is not an exaggeration to say that fines from traffic offenses, which, in Louisiana, can result in jail time, play a big part in determining whether one of those men in the orange jumpsuits receives an adequate defense required by the Sixth Amendment to the Constitution. . . . Louisiana spends nearly $3.5 billion a year to investigate, arrest, prosecute, adjudicate, and incarcerate its citizens. Less than two percent of that is spent on legal representation for the poor. Public defenders are struggling across the country. A 2013 study in Missouri provided a snapshot of the problem. For serious felonies, defenders spent an average of only nine hours preparing their cases; 47 hours were needed. For misdemeanors, they spent two hours when 12 hours were necessary.[195]

To make matters even worse in New Orleans, a class-action lawsuit

---

* The decision did not apply to civil cases, i.e., personal lawsuits, housing court proceedings, etc.—where low-income, lower-class defendants often get shafted. Neither does the right to counsel apply to nonresident immigrants, who often face deportation proceedings with no legal assistance, even when the outcome could split them apart from family members who are legal residents of the country.

alleged that judges and court officials have been running an "illegal scheme" in which low-income residents are indefinitely jailed if they fall behind on payments of court fines, fees, and assessments. The suit describes how fees are imposed with no hearing on a resident's ability to pay, and how nearly all components of the local criminal justice system—the judges, the prosecutors, the public defenders—benefit financially to some degree. "The extent to which every actor in the local New Orleans legal system depends on this money for their own survival is shocking," said Alec Karakatsanis, one of the lawyers who filed the suit.[196]

Perhaps even more galling is the fact that similar, only slightly less corrupt, practices are actually *legal*—and common—throughout the country, through so-called "legal financial obligations" (LFOs) collected by states and localities. A report from the New York Law School found that

> [s]anctions may include fees, fines, restitution orders, and other legal obligations imposed by the courts and other criminal justice agencies. Other penalties may include fees for supervision, program participation, electronic monitoring services, jail/ prison costs, and health care, and other fees levied in addition to any civil penalties and child support obligations. . . . The aggregate effect is a class of citizen that is . . . financial slave in a system where it is virtually impossible to "pay" one's debt to society. . . . Such penalties keep a lock on individuals long after they leave prison. It is a schema that serves little social or penal purpose. . . . In Washington State, for example, sentencing courts may impose many LFOs without determining whether offenders are able to pay. . . . Most offenders owe around $7,234. At that level, and with the accumulation of interest, offenders who pay fifty dollars per month will still have debt in thirty years. Some are imprisoned for failing to re-pay.[197]

Given how many low-income people lack adequate legal representation, even in serious criminal trials, it should be no surprise that a record 149 people in the United States were found in 2015 to have been falsely convicted of a serious crime, and of those, nearly four in 10 were exonerated of murder. The review by the National Registry of Exonerations found that the inmates spent more than 14 years behind bars on average, with some serving more than three decades. More than two-thirds of those exonerated in 2015 were minorities, and half were African American. Five exonerated defendants had death sentences.[198]

Lack of representation is even more widespread in civil cases. In 2009, more than 2.3 million New York State residents were ensnared in the state's complex civil justice system without a lawyer. According to a state judicial task force, "In the wake of the Great Recession, the numbers were shocking: more than 98 percent of tenants were unrepresented in eviction cases; 99 percent of borrowers were unrepresented in consumer credit cases; and more than 95 percent of parents were unrepresented in child support matters."[199]

AMERICA'S JAIL FAIL

I was at an event once where the chair of the Delaware Republican Party opined that many Americans are in prison because they were previously hungry. That's true. Hungry children are more likely to drop out of school and see no option but a life of crime. More than 60 percent of all prison inmates are functionally illiterate.[200] Hungry adults may purposely commit, and then get arrested for, petty crimes, specifically so they get a roof over their heads and three square meals a day. Prisoners are the only Americans guaranteed a right to food under our Constitution, because courts have ruled that not feeding prisoners would embody unconstitutional "cruel and unusual punishment."

It's becoming increasingly obvious that our nation's sky-high incarceration rate is directly linked to our sky-high poverty rate. Hillary Clinton, having previously been criticized by some activists for the results of her husband's crime bill, said in 2015: "We can't separate the unrest we see on our streets from the cycle of poverty and despair that hollow out those neighborhoods."[201]

The criminal justice system costs taxpayers $260 billion a year and is responsible for about 20 percent of the poverty in America, according to the Brennan Center for Justice.[202] That $260 billion spent on the system annually equals about two and a half times the amount the federal government spends each year feeding low-income Americans through the SNAP, WIC, and school meals programs combined. Meanwhile, millions of law-abiding citizens who work full time at minimum wage jobs struggle against hunger. Talk about perverse incentives.

The US prison and jail population in 2016 was 2.2 million. If that population constituted a city, it would the fourth-largest in America, about the size of Houston and bigger than Philadelphia. One in 28 American children—equaling 2.7 million kids—have one or more parents behind bars.

According to the NAACP, from 1980 to 2008, the number of people incarcerated in our country quadrupled from roughly 500,000 to 2.3 million people. We have 5 percent of the world's population but 25 percent of its prisoners. Combining the number of people in prison and jail with those under parole or probation supervision, one in every 31 adults, or 3.2 percent of the population, is under some form of correctional control. African Americans are incarcerated at nearly six times the rate of whites, and constitute nearly one million of the total 2.3 million people incarcerated.[203] That's why legal scholar Michelle Alexander has written that "mass incarceration is, metaphorically, the New Jim Crow."[204]

If current trends continue, up to one in three black males could go to prison in their lifetimes, compared with one in every six Latino males, and one in every 17 white males.[205] While the oft-cited statistic—that more black men are in prison than college—isn't actually true, the numbers are still uncomfortably close: in 2013, 1.4 million black men were in college and 745,000 were behind bars.[206]

The NAACP has explained that disparities in drug sentencing are a key cause of the high black incarceration rates. About 14 million whites and 2.6 million African Americans report using an illicit drug. Five times as many whites are using drugs as African Americans, yet African Americans are sent to prison for drug offenses at 10 times the rate of whites. Blacks represent 12 percent of the total population of drug users, but 38 percent of those arrested for drug offenses, and 59 percent of those in state prisons for a drug offense. African Americans serve virtually as much time in prison for drug offenses (59 months) as whites do for violent offenses (62 months).[207]

In Vermont, only 1.2 percent of the state's population is black, yet 11 percent of Vermont's inmates are African American. The state's black prison population rose by 252 percent from 1992 to 2014, while the white prison population went up 112 percent. It cost $59,643 to house each Vermont prisoner in 2014.[208] All this occurred in a state in which Obama won landslide victories in the 2008 Democratic primary and the 2008 and 2012 general elections.* This just proves that our justice system and incarceration problems go way beyond the good or bad will of individuals—they are baked into our entire nation and culture.

As you can see from the cost of housing prisoners in a state as small as Vermont, we've made the prison industrial complex damn profitable. Today, for-profit companies oversee about 6 percent of state prisoners, 16 percent of federal prisoners, and inmates in many local jails. While promoted as a way to save tax dollars, private prisons sometimes cost more to run than government ones. These private prisons have also been linked to numerous cases of violence, abuse, and atrocious conditions.[209]

Most perversely, 65 percent of private prison contracts included occupancy guarantees in the form of quotas or required payments for empty prison cells. In other words, taxpayers are forced to pay private companies to ensure that their prisons have large numbers of inmates. Occupancy guarantee clauses in private prison contracts range between 80 and 100 percent, with 90 percent as the most frequent occupancy guarantee requirement.[210] I wish this was an *Onion* story, but it's not. Fortunately, in August 2016, the Obama administration announced that the US government would no longer use private incarceration facilities, but the feds have no authority to shut down state and local private prisons.

A total of 4,446 inmates died in state prisons and local jails—both public and private—in 2013, with more than one-third of the deaths due to suicide.[211]

Those who do make it out of prison alive are often unable to find any employment at all once they get out, but if they do, it is almost

---

* Barack Obama beat Hillary Clinton in the 2008 presidential primary in Vermont by 20 points. He beat McCain by 37 points in the 2008 general election—the second-highest state margin, after Hawaii, where Obama grew up. He beat Romney in the 2012 general election by 36 points there, even though Romney was governor of neighboring Massachusetts.

always low-wage, low-skilled work characterized by low mobility and high turnover. Prisoners are also locked out of democracy: the US is one of the world's strictest nations when it comes to denying the right to vote to citizens convicted of crimes. The Sentencing Project reported that 5.85 million Americans are forbidden to vote because of "felony disenfranchisement," or laws restricting voting rights for those convicted of felony-level crimes. Approximately 2.5 percent of the total US voting-age population—one of every 40 adults—is disenfranchised due to a current or previous felony conviction, a huge jump over the last few decades. One of every 13 African Americans of voting age is disenfranchised, a rate more than four times greater than non-African Americans.[212]

By 2016, it was clearer than ever that America's drug use epidemic had grown far beyond inner cities populated by people of color. In ultra-white New Hampshire, there were more than 400 drug overdose deaths across the state in 2015, double the level in 2013. The number of near-death overdoses was in the thousands.[213] White rural areas across the nation reported similar problems, and more whites, including middle-class and upper-income individuals, were going to prison for drug-related offenses.

There has been some good work performed over the last decade or so on criminal justice reform by both the Left and the Right, but lo and behold, it wasn't until the white people with money started going to prison in higher numbers that the nation started seriously considering whether it had an over-incarceration problem. Jeb Bush, not one for big emotions, opened up about his daughter's drug problems. Chris Christie emoted up a storm about a friend brought down by drugs. Both Bush and Christie suggested that, perhaps, treating drug addicts might be a better approach than imprisoning them. Even the arch-conservative Koch brothers started funding prison reform work.

In an op-ed entitled "When Addiction Has a White Face," Ekow N. Yankah wrote, "It is hard to describe the bittersweet sting that many African Americans feel witnessing this national embrace of addicts. It is heartening to see the eclipse of the generations-long failed war on drugs. But black Americans are also knowingly weary and embittered by the absence of such enlightened thinking when those in our own families were similarly wounded. When the face of addiction had dark skin, this nation's police did not see sons and daughters, sisters and brothers. They saw 'brothas,' young thugs to be locked up, rather than 'people with a purpose in life.'"[214]

FERGUSON

The small city of Ferguson, Missouri—made infamous by the brutal 2014 killing of unarmed black teenager Michael Brown by a white police officer—perfectly illustrates how political inequality results in inequality in the criminal justice system. When it comes to dysfunction, Ferguson has it all: racially-biased, trigger-happy police; a white minority shutting a black majority out of political power; and a massive use of racially discriminatory fines to fund the city.

In 2015, though whites made up just 29 percent of the city's residents, five of Ferguson's six city council members were white, as was the mayor. Six of the local school board's seven members were white.

Many nearby towns, as well as inner-ring suburbs nationally, are similar to Ferguson in this regard. Longtime white residents found ways to consolidate power, continuing to dominate local government despite the massive demographic changes. They kept control of patronage jobs and government contracts awarded to allies.[215] The policy group Demos reported,

> A recent study found that while people of color make up 37 percent of the US population, they account for only 10 percent of elected officials at the federal, state, and county levels. By contrast, white men, who make up 31 percent of the population, account for 65 percent of representatives. . . . One such city [with great underrepresentation of black elected officials], with a population that is 63 percent black but a council with only one black member, is Ferguson. . . . In political science, descriptive representation refers to legislators' having things in common with the groups they represent. It has been linked to confidence in government, positive legislative outcomes, and engagement with the political process. . . . Black legislators

lead to more congressional attention and money for black constituents. Benefits such as these could have stopped the crisis in Ferguson. A black city council may have raised the alarm about police treatment in a city where blacks make up 93 percent of arrests, 91 percent of searches, and 86 percent of stops by the Ferguson police.[216]

Following the Michael Brown shooting, the US Department of Justice investigated Ferguson, found systematic criminal justice abuses, and issued a scathing report. They found that the city "exhorts police and court staff to deliver revenue increases" through fines, and that the "city's emphasis on revenue generation has a profound effect on [the police department's] approach to law enforcement . . . [M]any officers appear to see some residents, especially those who live in Ferguson's predominantly African American neighborhoods, less as constituents to be protected than as potential offenders and sources of revenue." They also found "a pattern of stops without reasonable suspicion and arrests without probable cause in violation of the Fourth Amendment; infringement on free expression, as well as retaliation for protected expression, in violation of the First Amendment; and excessive force in violation of the Fourth Amendment."

They further stated that "[n]early 90% of documented force used by FPD officers was used against African Americans. In every canine bite incident for which racial information is available, the person bitten was African American." As one example, the report found that a 32-year-old African American man, sitting in his car, cooling off after playing basketball in a public park, was, without cause, accused by a cop of being a pedophile, ordered out of his car for a pat-down, and had his car searched. When the civilian cited his constitutional rights, he was arrested at gunpoint and charged with eight violations of Ferguson's municipal code. One charge, "Making a False Declaration," was for initially providing the short form of his first name (e.g., "Mike" instead of "Michael"). The report found that the local courts also caused "disproportionate harm to African Americans." African Americans were 68 percent less likely than others to have their cases dismissed by the court, and were more likely to have had their cases last longer and result in more required court appearances. African Americans were at least 50 percent more likely to have their cases lead to an arrest warrant, and accounted for 92 percent of cases in which an arrest warrant was issued by the Ferguson Municipal Court.[217]

IT TAKES A VILLAGE—AND A PROGRESSIVE FEDERAL GOVERNMENT— TO REDUCE AMERICA'S STRUCTURAL RACISM

Sure, Dr. Martin Luther King, Jr. wanted to change the hearts of bigots in order to convince them to be less prejudiced, but he made it clear—over and over again—that what he *really* wanted to change were government policies, federal legislation, and entrenched, society-wide economic and social structures.

In his landmark "Letter from Birmingham Jail," King wrote, "We have not made a single gain in civil rights without determined legal and nonviolent pressure. Lamentably, it is an historical fact that privileged groups seldom give up their privileges voluntarily. Individuals may see the moral light and voluntarily give up their unjust posture; but . . . groups tend to be more immoral than individuals."[218]

King tackled this topic even more directly in a 1963 speech at Western Michigan University:

> A myth that gets around is the idea that legislation cannot really solve the problem and that it has no great role to play in this period of social change because you've got to change the heart and you can't change the heart through legislation. You can't legislate morals. The job must be done through education and religion. Well, there's half-truth involved here. Certainly, if the problem is to be solved then in the final sense, hearts must be changed. Religion and education must play a great role in changing the heart. But we must go on to say that while it may be true that morality cannot be legislated, behavior can be regulated. It may be true that the law cannot change the heart but it can restrain the heartless. It may be true that the law cannot make a man love me but it can keep him from lynching me and I think that is pretty important, also. So there is a need for

executive orders. There is a need for judicial decrees. There is
a need for civil rights legislation on the local scale within states
and on the national scale from the federal government.[219]

King was adamant that kind personal gestures, and simply trying to
find common ground with people of different backgrounds, weren't
enough to overcome Americans' vast institutional racism. Yet many still
argue, against the historical record, that simple strategies such as "cross-
group friendships" can truly reduce systematic discrimination.[220]

Rodolfo Mendoza-Denton, an associate professor of psychology at
the University of California, Berkeley, has listed his "Top 10 Strategies
for Reducing Prejudice." These strategies include "Travel (somewhere
that challenges your worldview)"; "Take a course on prejudice"; "Laugh
a little"; "Find some mean zombies";* "Soup or salad? Salad, by a long
shot"; and "Make a cross-race friend."[221] Nice suggestions—especially
the one about eating salad to end racism!—but I prefer strong anti-discrimination laws.

To achieve full equality, America, never forget Dr. King's message
that civil rights must go hand-in-hand with economic rights. Recent
research has indicated that, while physical segregation by race is still
deep and pervasive in the US, although marginally less so than decades
ago, economic segregation by class is deepening.[222]

We must remember that the official name of the 1963 March on
Washington was the "March for Jobs and Freedom." Half the agenda
was—and still should be—about economic justice. Shortly before his
death, Dr. King said, "What does it profit a man to be able to eat at an
integrated lunch counter if he doesn't have enough money to buy a
hamburger?"

---

* He writes: "My wife and son are hooked—nay, positively addicted—to the video game *Plants vs.
Zombies*. My heart melts when they play together: The way she scaffolds the game for him, helps
him with strategy, and speaks to him like an equal mind and partner in the game is beautiful to
watch. The upshot here? The way you categorize others ('us' vs. 'them') is more malleable than we
imagine, and really highlights one way in which race, religion, gender, sexuality, disability, or ethnicity are social constructions. Fortunately, you don't need extraterrestrials or zombies to achieve a
common ingroup identity. All you need is a little compassion and flexibility of thought." Perhaps
someday, bigotry can be eroded with something as facile as playing a zombie video game that will
teach us to break down the divide between "us" and "them," but until that glorious day arrives, we
should keep fighting for stronger governmental civil rights laws, an utterly transformed criminal
justice system, and stronger government safety nets for those most oppressed.

BETWEEN THE WORLD, ME, AND TA-NEHISI COATES'S SON

Ta-Nehisi Coates's 2015 book, *Between the World and Me*, was rightly hailed for both its transcendent writing and its unsparing take on modern American racial issues. Couched as a letter to his adolescent son, Coates hones in on the expendability of black bodies in today's America:

> You know now, if you did not before, that the police depart-
> ments of your country have been endowed with the authority
> to destroy your body. It does not matter if the destruction is
> the result of an unfortunate overreaction. It does not matter if
> it originates in a misunderstanding. It does not matter if the
> destruction springs from a foolish policy. Sell cigarettes without
> the proper authority and your body can be destroyed. Resent
> the people trying to entrap your body and it can be destroyed.
> Turn into a dark stairwell and your body can be destroyed.
> The destroyers will rarely be held accountable. Mostly they
> will receive pensions. And destruction is merely the superla-
> tive form of a dominion whose prerogatives include friskings,
> detainings, beatings, and humiliations. All of this is common
> to black people. And all of this is old for black people. No one is
> held responsible.[223]
>
> To be black in the Baltimore of my youth was to be naked
> before the elements of the world, before all the guns, fists,
> knives, crack, rape, and disease. The nakedness is not an error,
> nor pathology. The nakedness is the correct and intended
> result of policy, the predictable upshot of people forced for cen-
> turies to live under fear. The law did not protect us. . . . The law
> has become an excuse for stopping and frisking you, which is
> to say, furthering the assault on your body. But a society that
> protects some people through a safety net of schools, govern-
> ment-backed home loans, and ancestral wealth but can only
> protect you with the club of criminal justice has either failed
> at enforcing its good intentions or has succeeded at something
> much darker. However you call it, the result was our infirmity

before the criminal forces of the world. It does not matter if the agent of those forces is white or black—what matters is our condition, what matters is the system that makes your body breakable.[224]

In response to the book, columnist David Brooks wrote a piece headlined "Listening to Ta-Nehisi Coates While White," in which he praised the book as something every American should read, and then, of course, criticizes it:

> The disturbing challenge of your book is your rejection of the American dream. My ancestors chose to come here. For them, America was the antidote to the crushing restrictiveness of European life, to the pogroms. For them, the American dream was an uplifting spiritual creed that offered dignity, the chance to rise.
>
> Your ancestors came in chains. In your book the dream of the comfortable suburban life is a "fairy tale." For you, slavery is the original American sin, from which there is no redemption. America is Egypt without the possibility of the Exodus. African American men are caught in a crushing logic, determined by the past, from which there is no escape . . .
>
> I read this all like a slap and a revelation. . . . I find the causation between the legacy of lynching and some guy's decision to commit a crime inadequate to the complexity of most individual choices.
>
> I think you distort American history. This country, like each person in it, is a mixture of glory and shame. There's a Lincoln for every Jefferson Davis and a Harlem Children's Zone for every K.K.K.—and usually vastly more than one.
>
> In your anger at the tone of innocence some people adopt to describe the American dream, you reject the dream itself as flimflam. But a dream sullied is not a lie. The American dream of equal opportunity, social mobility, and ever more perfect democracy cherishes the future more than the past.[225]

Brooks thinks of himself as someone who aims for moderation, but, in cases such as this, he just doesn't get it. Brooks claims that the terrible legacy of Jefferson Davis was balanced by the hopeful legacy of Lincoln, and that the shameful record of the KKK was partially compensated for by the existence of a mid-size nonprofit group—the Harlem Children's Zone.

Where do I even start? Let's begin with Brooks's Lincoln versus Davis bit.

Brooks appears to minimize the long-term impact of the reality that millions of humans were brutally enslaved here for 337 years.

Then he wants you, America, to gloss over the next 100 years of Jim Crow, slavery-like sharecropping, and mass lynchings, and instead be contented that an African American man can start a nonprofit education group that helps a few thousand kids in one neighborhood of one city.

But as wrong as Brooks is about the past, he's even more off-base about the present. His implication that the American dream is alive and well today—for every American of every skin color and background—is seriously detached from reality.

But permit me, ever so gently, to differ with Coates too. Others have chided him for being a bit too pessimistic on racial matters, and I agree. He's an even bigger downer than *me*. We all should be able to take at least some comfort in the fact that most of the truly reprehensible things that white people have done to black people over the years are at least now illegal in the USA. While electing an African American president certainly didn't end all our strife (and may have even increased racial hostility in the short term) it set a marker for future progress. An African American man broke the ultimate American barrier, grabbing the highest rung on the ladder, a breakthrough that was previously unimaginable.

Yet, black president or no black president—and no matter how much money and fame Coates earned for his family—it is likely that his son, too, will suffer for his blackness at some point. A store patron may falsely assume he is a store clerk rather than a fellow shopper. A racially-addled taxi driver (including perhaps, a black one) may refuse to pick him up when he needs a ride. And terrifyingly, some dime-store cop, frothing at the sight of a young man with a different skin color, could still shoot him in the back as if he were wild game. Every one of those possibilities is a shameful reality for an African American in our country today. After all, even a world-famous scholar like Henry Louis Gates, Jr. or top White House aides can suffer from racially biased policing.

But almost every one of those shameful outcomes is less likely to happen to Coates's son because his family now has money. Not to mention that his chances of being raped are miniscule because he is male.

So that's what Coates's book seems to miss: that class and gender can have as much impact as race—that both privilege and oppression are allocated based on many criteria—not just skin color.

Yeah, I know, it's damn easy for me, a white guy, to say that race isn't the only decisive factor in America. Sure, I can spew facts on class, gender, and sexual orientation, but to many people living in black and brown skin, that's beside the point.

Still, even if Coates's pessimism *could* be true, I just can't abide it. And neither should you, America.

I don't think the country should give up hope that we will see racial progress. The nation is destined to change, most likely for the better, if for no other reason than simple demographics. The country is becoming more nonwhite by the year; with numbers come the possibility of power, and with power eventually comes better treatment and more safety.

But I don't want to wait that long, and neither should you, America. Every son and every daughter deserve a more just world and nation on his or her first day of life. If, 100 years from now, our country is still so screwed up that a black author stills feel the need to write an open letter to his son about how America *still* ravages black bodies, that should break all our hearts.

No kid should let anyone, not even his or her own father, convince them that nothing can improve, and that they can never change the world.

Change won't happen unless we also attack poverty and sexism. And even then, it won't ever be a perfect fairy tale because humans are not perfect.

While social movements are more energizing (and sometimes fun) when they are engaging in collective action in the streets (in the full glare of TV floodlights), they are often far more effective when they are performing behind-the-scenes drudge work to improve the laws, programs, and policies necessary to make racial (and other) progress a reality. And yes, America, part of *your* job is to get that concrete progress accomplished.

So America, imagine that you are Coates's son and then successfully work to reduce racism. What son wouldn't love proving his dad wrong?

Or build a more racially just nation for yourself—do it for even the slight possibility that we can create an America in which everyone feels safe—perfectly safe—in every corner of the country.

But even if you don't do it for your dad or for yourself, at least do it for your future black sons. That's the best way to ensure that black lives matter.

5.

They're Just Not That Into You
Why Working-Class Whites Are
Rejecting Democrats

Democrats keep sitting by their rotary dial princess phones, pining for the call that just won't come.* They keep waiting—and waiting—for it to ring. They're expecting to hear from White Working Folks (whom I will refer to from now on as "WWF"**), and they have convinced themselves that when the phone finally rings, the WWF will offer them a sobbing, full-throated apology for having left the bed of the Dems for the seductive embrace of the GOP. America, you and I know the Dems are fools for lost love, but they won't accept it.

After all, the WWF were so deeply, loyally in love with the Democrats during the New Deal and the decades that followed, that the Dems convinced themselves that the recent WWF crush on the Republicans was merely a temporary, hormone-addled dalliance.

But the call hasn't come and the WWF keeps voting—big-time—for the GOP.

The Democrats keep waiting . . . for another two years, then another four, then another two, then another four. And still nothing. At this

---

* While the Obama campaign pioneered the mass use of campaign text messaging, many local Democratic Party organizations are pretty behind the times, tech-wise. They are apparently unaware that no one talks on the telephone anymore, not even cell phones. Don't even try to explain Snapchat to them.
** Any similarity between the initials WWF and the World Wrestling Federation is purely coincidental.

point, the Democrats would settle for a drunken booty call. Or even an accidental pocket dial.

The Democrats try not to show their pain. As Greg Behrendt, author of *He's Just Not That Into You: The No-Excuses Truth to Understanding Guys*, and Amiira Ruotola-Behrendt, put it, "Being brokenhearted is like having broken ribs. On the outside it looks like nothing's wrong."[226] All the Democrats get is dead silence. No call. No text. No knock. Ok, "screw 'em," they finally say to themselves. We don't *need* them. We can win *without* them. The country is increasingly nonwhite, so if we just keep bringing more nonwhite voters to the polls, we'll be just fine. After all, we're good enough, we're smart enough, and doggone it, nonwhite people really like us.

Big wins in recent presidential elections gave Democrats the false hope that they'd finally cracked the electoral code. But the nearer the Dems get to the destination of a true electoral majority in all elections, the more the WWF keeps slip-sliding away, finding 50 ways to leave their former Democratic lovers.*

In off-year elections—such as 1994, 2010, and 2014—because overall Democratic turnout, especially among people of color, was so low, the party got totally creamed. In 2014—when Congress, and many governorships and state legislatures, were at stake—only 36 percent of the US voting-age population bothered to vote, the lowest turnout since 1944, 70 years earlier, during the height of World War II.[227] Those in the WWF who did show up at the polls in 2014 voted overwhelmingly Republican, giving GOP candidates nine more Senate seats and control of the chamber with a 54 to 46 majority. Republicans also consolidated their grasp of the House of Representatives, with a 246 to 188 majority.

The Democratic losses at the state level were even worse, placing 70 percent of state legislatures, more than 60 percent of governorships, and 55 percent of attorney generals' offices and secretaries of state, in GOP hands.[228]

Not only did GOP control of states mean they would implement conservative, highly damaging policies, but it also meant that they would

---

* Other Paul Simon songs that contain lessons for the Democrats: "The Bridge to Nowhere over Troubled Water," "The Political Party in a Bubble," and "Me and Julio Deported from the Schoolyard by Obama."

get to determine Congressional district boundaries, and could change them to be so skewed in their favor that it would make it even more difficult for the Democrats to regain the House in the future. The GOP takeover at the state and local levels increased the challenge for Dems to build a "farm team"—i.e., leaders who could advance up the ladder over time—thereby making the long-term rebuilding of the party that much more daunting.

Even in presidential elections, in order to overcome huge losses in WWF areas, Democrats need to have historic levels of nonwhite turn out; Obama was able to generate enough enthusiasm in nonwhite communities to do so, but other Democratic presidential candidates may not. Plus, here's a scary thought: some nonwhite Americans, particularly Latinos and Asians, could eventually start voting more like the WWF, especially if their needs continue to be unmet by the Democratic Party and if the GOP becomes even marginally less racist. It is dangerous for the Dems to base their entire future on the hope that more people will be born someday and will eventually vote for them.

Debating whether Democrats or Republicans have a structural advantage in presidential contests is silly; the side with the most compelling message always wins. Besides, even if a larger Democratic base could ensure continued presidential election wins, that wouldn't be enough to take back the House. Bottom line: if the Democrats offer nothing more than the same muddled message and limited policies to the WWF, they will continue to lose their vote and thus continue to fail to truly be able to govern the whole country.

UNDERSTANDING WHITE WORKING CLASS MEN

Here are a few other pearls of wisdom from *He's Just Not That Into You*—and my explanation of how they apply to the Democrats.

"When it comes to men, deal with them as they are, not how you'd like them to be."

When the Democrats visualize the WWF, they imagine Dan Connor from *Roseanne*, but should really be thinking about Angela from *The*

Office (the American version).* They imagine Dan—and his interest in minimum wage hikes, healthcare coverage, and drywall—but refuse to allow themselves to see Angela—who cares deeply about abortion, religion, guns, and Schrute Farms beets. After elections that Democrats lose, much of the post-balloting handwringing from the Left assumes that red state Americans are too dumb or too bigoted to understand what's in their own self-interest. It is patronizing attitudes such as these that consign progressives to continued failure.

"We're taught that in life, we should try to look on the bright side. Not in this case. In this case, assume rejection first. Assume you're the rule, not the exception."
The Democrats keep inanely assuming that the WWF should instinctively side with them, and that their recent rejection is just a temporary aberration. The party still hasn't fully accepted how even white union members are voting against them.[229] Only after Democrats truly acknowledge, as a fact of life, the enormity of the breakup can they take the concrete steps necessary to win back the WWF.

"Don't be with someone who doesn't do what they say they're going to do."
The Dems keep promising to significantly raise the standard of living for the WWF, but that hasn't really happened since Bill Clinton was president. While things would have been far worse had Romney become president instead of Obama, the fact remains that, as I noted before, the US median household income in 2014, adjusted for inflation, was 6.5 percent lower than in 2007. And no, Democrats won't win points with the WWF by simply blaming the GOP.

"The only way you can find out that there's something better out there is to first believe there's something better out there."

A typical evangelical swing voter, who happens to be married to a closeted gay state senator. *That could never happen!*

Democrats whittled down Obamacare, jettisoning a public option, then ran the hell away from what they did pass.* If Democratic politicians don't act like they believe that they are giving a better future to the country, why should the voters? While much of the white working class *does* realize that the Republicans lie to them, cheat them, and keep breaking their promises, until the Dems can provide proof they will do better, they will lose the WWF. As Leo Martin, a 62-year-old machinist from New Hampshire, said while attending a Trump rally, "The Republican Party has never done anything for the working man like me, even though we've voted Republican for years."[230] If he's sticking with the Republicans no matter how much they've shafted him, we can only image how little he thinks that the Democratic Party offers.

"Big plans require big action . . . A man who wants to make a relationship work will move mountains."

As you have witnessed, America, the Dems have tried all sorts of superficial (and downright embarrassing) ways to win back the WWF. They've dressed up in camouflage clothing to go duck hunting (Kerry), appeared on *SportsCenter* (Obama), and faked a southern drawl (Gore). Now some leading Democrats are trying to prove their "real people" cred by engaging in planned spontaneity, but that works as poorly in a campaign as it does in a bedroom. Given such shallow entreaties, it's no wonder that the Dems still haven't won back the WWF. Every single time I see a new Woody Allen movie, I foolishly hope that it will be as good as his old masterpieces. I keep hoping for another *Annie Hall*, but get *To Rome with Love*. The WWF must feel the same way about Democrats. They keep hoping for another FDR or Truman but all they get are Democrats riding in tanks or shooting birds. Perhaps Democrats should try something novel: giving the WWF large-scale, concrete improvements in their lives. The Democrats should go big, or go home.

---

* All four Senate Democrats who voted against the public option in healthcare—Joe Lieberman, Ben Nelson, Mary Landrieu, and Blanche Lincoln—were all forced out of office within four years of doing so.

WHERE HAVE ALL THE WHITE VOTERS GONE?
LONG TIME, PASSING.

The last Democratic candidate for president to actually win the majority of the white vote was LBJ in 1964. Check out these presidential election stats:

Year	Margin of Loss of White Vote of Democratic Presidential Nominee	Percentage of Total Voters Who Were White
1976	Carter—4	89%
1980	Carter—20	88%
1984	Mondale—32	86%
1988	Dukakis—20	85%
1992	Clinton—2	87%
1996	Clinton—2	83%
2000	Gore—13	81%
2004	Kerry—17	77%
2008	Obama—12	74%
2012	Obama—20	72%

Source: NBC News, *First Read*[231]

As the chart makes clear, given that whites are an ever-decreasing share of voters overall, it is possible for Democrats to win the presidency while still getting clobbered in the white vote, but they need a massive turnout of nonwhite voters to do so. Also, any Democrat who wins the White House while losing the white vote overwhelmingly will be far less likely to gain a Democratic House or earn any sort of broad mandate for governing.

While Democrats have actually been doing relatively well in recent decades among suburban, upper-middle-class whites (especially unmarried women), they have suffered a total collapse in support among low-income ex-urban and rural white voters (especially married women and men).

To drill down deeper into this phenomenon, I analyzed presidential voting patterns for 1992–2012 in a total of 69 rural counties in the swing states of Florida, Missouri, North Carolina, Ohio, and Virginia, selecting counties that were more than 80 percent white and had poverty rates above 20 percent.* The chart below demonstrates the massive Democratic losses in those rural swing state counties since 1992.

POINT MARGIN OF DEMOCRATIC WIN OR LOSS OF WHITE VOTE IN 69 RURAL WHITE, SWING STATE COUNTIES

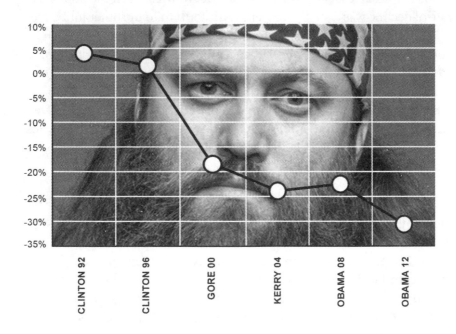

It's been well-documented that these counties have been trending Republican for a while, but even I was shocked by the magnitude of the Democratic decline. Bill Clinton in 1992 won in these counties by

---

* These 69 counties were on average 93.3 percent white, with median family incomes of $35,230 and poverty rates of 21.9 percent.

an average of 4 percentage points, but Obama lost them in 2012 by an average of 30.6 points.

I had always assumed that the steepest part of this decline coincided with Obama's campaigns, and that the drop was tied mostly to his race. But my analysis proved that the rural white vote drop is a multi-decade-long trend. Kerry in 2004 (who was obviously white, very white) did even worse in these counties than Obama did in 2008. Furthermore, two of the Virginia counties that Obama lost by massive margins in 2012 (Buchanan and Wise) were actually won handily by African American gubernatorial candidate Douglas Wilder in 1989. So, while race was clearly a huge factor in these counties, it wasn't the *only* factor. The problem was at least as pronounced in the Midwest as in the South. The rate of decline was actually steeper in Missouri than the other four states.

Although each of these counties has relatively small populations and vote totals, because the Democratic losses in them had become so lopsided, they were decisive in the statewide vote outcomes. These rural losses clearly deprived both Gore and Kerry of wins in Ohio and Florida,* and thus cost them both the presidency. The miniscule Dem support in these counties was the main reason that Obama barely lost Missouri in 2008, and the top explanation for why, in 2012, Obama lost North Carolina and wasn't even competitive in Missouri.

No single issue or factor is the cause of the Democratic decline. If it wasn't just race, you may assume that it was all about guns. But President Bill Clinton pushed through an assault weapons ban in 1994, and while that clearly contributed to the GOP takeover of the House in 1994, Clinton himself performed only 2.5 percentage points worse in these counties in 1996 than in 1992. In 2000, Gore, who did not push for gun control, performed a whopping 17 percentage points worse in these counties than Clinton did in 1996. Some pundits in 2004 attributed the losses to marriage equality ballot propositions, but the Dems did as poorly in states without them. Some blamed the losses on environmental regulations, but most of these counties are outside coal or timber country.

---

* Had all the votes in Florida been counted in 2000, Gore would have actually won the state, but if he had won more WWF there, then the state vote totals would have never been close enough for the election to have been stolen from him.

I know an elderly white woman who has lived in farm country in rural North Central Pennsylvania, in near-poverty conditions, for her entire life. In 2008, she was a passionate Hillary supporter, but when I emailed her in late 2015 to ask if she still was, she responded,

> I am no longer an ardent supporter of anyone at all. Over the last eight years, I have totally lost any faith or confidence in our government, or our system of voting. Only the very wealthy manage to get in, and only the very wealthy control almost every aspect of our lives, and it is always going to be that way. I won't even waste my time voting any longer, I'm just that dissatisfied and discouraged. I'm just thankful I'm not too far from the grave, so I won't have to put up with any of them that much longer. I wouldn't trust one single person that is running for anything at all, for even a moment. They do nothing but lie from day one, so I will have nothing to do with them. So sorry, I'm out.

Her despondent attitude is certainly common. Political writer Alec MacGillis has argued that Dems lose not because rural, poor white people switched sides, but because they stopped voting entirely:

> In eastern Kentucky and other former Democratic bastions that have swung Republican in the past several decades, the people who most rely on the safety-net programs secured by Democrats are, by and large, not voting against their own interests by electing Republicans. Rather, they are not voting, period. . . .
>
> The people in these communities who are voting Republican in larger proportions are those who are a notch or two up the economic ladder—the sheriff's deputy, the teacher, the highway worker, the motel clerk, the gas station owner, and the coal miner. And their growing allegiance to the Republicans is, in part, a reaction against what they perceive, among those below them on the economic ladder, as a growing dependency on the safety net.[232]

MacGillis's explanation is likely correct for off-year elections, including the Kentucky 2015 governor's race, but less correct for presidential years, when overall turnout in these counties is much higher.

In rural white counties, many people are jobless and many others work but earn slightly above the minimum wage and are still struggling economically. While minimum wage hikes might help some in these counties, and they certainly should be implemented, Democrats need to better grasp that raising the minimum wage or blasting Wall Street and trade agreements is not the answer to all of the WWF's economic problems. Rural white areas need far more robust initiatives to create living-wage jobs, bolster education, provide broadband Internet service, and guarantee retirement security. Any of those things would be damn more impressive than a duck-hunting trip.

THE BIG SORT AND THE GROWTH OF PARTISANSHIP

America, in some respects, you're not as divided between red states and blue states as you might think. The winner-take-all nature of the Electoral College exaggerates the differences between the parties because presidential candidates won't spend time and resources in states they know they can't win. Had Mitt Romney seriously contested New York in 2012, he still would have failed to carry the state, but he wouldn't have lost by anything close to his 27-point margin; likewise, had Obama competed seriously in Idaho, he could have lost by far less than his 32-point defeat. I know from my travels that Alabama liberals are just as progressive as liberals in New York, and that conservatives in New York are just as conservative as Alabama right-wingers—there just happen to be more liberals in New York and more conservatives in Alabama.

One of the reasons the country seems so divided is that people of all races are increasingly voting like their neighbors. It's unclear whether people are purposely moving to places specifically to be in a locale in which people agree with them politically—or are moving to places specifically for certain types of coffee shops, churches, jobs, recreational activities, and bookstores, which just *happen to be* in neighborhoods of likeminded politics. I suspect it's both. Bill Bishop, in his groundbreaking book, *The Big Sort*, proved this point:

Communities are not close to being [in a state of] equipoise, even within solidly blue or red states. They are, most of them, becoming even more Democratic or Republican. As Americans have moved over the past three decades, they have clustered in communities of sameness, among people with similar ways of life, beliefs, and, in the end, politics. Little, if any, of this political migration was by design, a conscious effort by people to live among like-voting neighbors . . .

Americans were forming tribes, not only in their neighborhoods but also in churches and volunteer groups. . . . [I]n every corner of society, people were creating new, more homogeneous relations. Churches were filled with people who looked alike and, more important, thought alike. So were clubs, civic organizations, and volunteer groups. . . . [A]s people heard their beliefs reflected and amplified, they would become more extreme in their thinking. What had happened over three decades wasn't a simple increase in political partisanship, but a more fundamental kind of self-perpetuating, self-reinforcing social division. The like-minded neighborhood supported the like-minded church, and both confirmed the image and beliefs of the tribe that lived and worshiped there. Americans were busy creating social resonators, and the hum that filled the air was the reverberated and amplified sound of their own voices and beliefs.[233]

This physical division is mirrored in social media's electronic divisions, where people tend to cluster among those with similar tastes and political beliefs and "de-friend" those who don't.

The number of "swing states" that are true general election battlegrounds is also shrinking. In the 2012 general election, the presidential candidates held public campaign events in only 12 states.[234] That means that citizens in 38 states—including enormous ones like California, Texas, New York, Illinois, and Georgia—never got to meet the candidates, except if they were rich enough to attend private fundraisers. Most of the nation was little more than a passive spectator of a far-off campaign played out in TV-land.

HOW THE GOP RACE CARD TRUMPS EVERYTHING ELSE

The single greatest determining variable in how a person or neighbor-hood will vote in contemporary America is race, and both parties know it. Race is a far more important factor in voting patterns today than income, geography, or gender.* How the modern parties respond to race, however, differs vastly.

It is not commonly known outside the small circle of professional Democratic political campaign operatives, but I know (from having been such an operative) that many Democratic campaigns for top offices waste time, money, and emotional energy by running two separate, but often overlapping, operations—one for white voters in white neighborhoods and an entirely different one for black voters in black neighborhoods. Large campaigns have Hispanic, Asian, and other outreach divisions as well.

Perhaps I've made that sound more insidious than it is, America. A key component of your political system—from the very begin-ning—has been to enable people with varied interests, concerns, and backgrounds to back candidates who best meet their specific needs. That's why most campaigns—Republican and Democratic alike—have separate staffs to reach out to all sorts of constituencies: teachers, women, gun owners, veterans, people with disabilities, LGBTQ com-munities, religious leaders, unions, etc. That's how democracy is *supposed* to work.

So what's so wrong with Democrats running parallel campaigns in different communities? Nothing really, except that, as a practical matter, it diverts the Democrats from their single most necessary task: crafting and delivering messages and policies that will aid, and thus resonate, with *all* races. Unsuccessful campaigns spend a lot of time worrying about whether they should "turn out their base" *or* con-vince swing voters. Successful campaigns do both at once.

---

* When the GOP still had a moderate wing, and most Southern Democrats were segregationist, the black vote was far more mixed. Dwight D. Eisenhower won 39 percent of the African Ameri-can vote in 1956, and Richard Nixon in 1960 (then a public moderate on racial issues) received 32 percent of the black vote against JFK. George W. Bush won 11 percent of the black vote against Ker-ry. McCain won 4 percent and Romney won 6 percent of the black vote. June 2016 polls showed Trump getting zero—yes, zero—percent of the black vote in Ohio and Pennsylvania.

Of course, my small qualms about how Democrats tackle these issues pales compared to my five-alarm fire—combined with a tsunami warning—battle cry over how the GOP exploits race. There's no question that conservatives use every trick in the book—and then write a few more books of tricks—to stoke up racial resentments for their own electoral benefit.

In 1968, eschewing the racial moderation he professed earlier in his career, Richard Nixon launched a "Southern strategy" to appeal to racial animus to win southern states, or at least deny them to the Democrats. In 1980, Ronald Reagan delivered a high-profile campaign speech in Mississippi near a town associated with the murders of civil rights workers, to highlight the need to defend "states' rights," the old Confederate/segregationist rallying cry. Reagan also decried "young bucks" buying T-bone steaks with food stamps. George Herbert Walker Bush used vile racial stereotypes featuring convicted murderer Willie Horton to defeat Michael Dukakis. In the Obama era, GOP leaders Newt Gingrich and Rick Santorum both publicly complained about too many African Americans getting food stamps (SNAP)—claiming that it was all Obama's fault—when the largest number of recipients were (and are) white and when the high overall rates of program participation were due to the Bush recession.

Of course, Donald Trump turned modern race-baiting into an art form, starting with his long crusade to fabricate doubts about President Obama's birthplace, not to mention questioning the intelligence of the President, who earned two Ivy League degrees.

And what, over many years, did the GOP elder statesmen and the big dollar donors—some of whom, presumably, weren't overtly racist themselves—do about this perversion of the party of Lincoln? Nothing. Absolutely nothing, other than grin as the votes rolled in and whine to the media that it was unfair to call their party racist.

The 2016 election further upped the ante on race-baiting. When Wisconsin governor and Republican presidential candidate Scott Walker was asked if President Obama was a Christian, he answered, "I don't know," teasing his audience with the suggestion that he might agree with the false reports that Obama was a Muslim, and by doing so, affirming the common GOP belief that being Muslim was a bad thing.

Senator Ted Cruz said, "I oppose the legalization [of immigrants] . . . today, tomorrow, forever," a formulation obviously similar to Alabama Governor George Wallace's 1963 statement of defiance, "Segregation now, segregation tomorrow, segregation forever."[235]

The GOP is often accused of using racist "dog whistles," but by 2016 they had moved up to wolf-pack air raid sirens of overt racism.* Not to be outdone by the others in 2016, Trump took his racism amplifier "up to 11." He didn't toss racially-loaded grenades only at the President; he also denigrated people with disabilities, Jews, Latinos, women, Muslims, gold star mothers, fire marshals, Mexicans, the Pope, prisoners of war, and [Dear reader: please use this space the fill in the other categories of people Trump vilified after this book went to press: _____ _____.]

Trump's prolific insults became so infamous they even spawned an app called the "Trump Generator," where you can enter a name and "have Donald Trump insult your friends!" In fact, a quick Google search of the words "Trump insult" generates nearly 3.5 million hits (yes, this is the kind of nonsense I seek late at night when I can't sleep—it doesn't help).

By February 2016, more than 60 percent of the tweets that Trump re-tweeted came from the Twitter accounts of avowed white suprem-acists. It is no wonder that, in South Carolina, 70 percent of Trump supporters disagreed with the decision to remove the Confederate battle flag from the state capitol building, 38 percent said they "wish the South had won the Civil War," and one in five admitted to believing that "whites are a superior race." Nationally, nearly 20 percent of Trump's voters disagreed with the freeing of slaves in southern states after the Civil War.[236] (Goodness knows how many additional Trump supporters believed these things but wouldn't admit them to pollsters.)

Does Donald Trump actually mean any of this? It's anyone's guess.

---

*

But for many gullible Americans, his highly dangerous shtick seems to have worked. The difference between P.T. Barnum and Donald Trump is that Trump isn't patient enough to wait a full minute before each new sucker is born. He is a serial, maniacal fabricator, but his fans love him precisely because they say he is a bold truth-teller.* Let's never forget that many of history's most murderous dictators were first considered blustery, semi-entertaining buffoons. People like Trump want the WWF to fear Muslims and Mexicans instead of fearing that people like him will take away their homes and pensions.

Later in the campaign, the GOP establishment tried to distance themselves from the most egregious of Trump's racist comments but still mostly stood by his side in support. Speaker Ryan called one of Trump's rants against an American judge of Mexican heritage "textbook racist," but, as late as October 2016, still refused to pull his endorsement of Trump.[237]

Some pundits and Republican leaders twisted themselves into pretzels to explain the Trump surge as somehow occurring *despite* his racism, when it was obviously occurring *because* of his racism. Hamilton College professor Philip Klinkner found that the single greatest variable in determining whether a voter would support Trump is the degree of racial animus they expressed. Klinkner wrote, "Trump's appeal has little to do with economics. To paraphrase what Marco Rubio once famously said (over and over and over), 'let's dispel with this fiction' that Donald Trump is appealing to the economic anxieties of Americans. Instead, attitudes about race, religion, and immigration trump (pun intended) economics."[238] Similarly, the *Washington Post* found that the greatest correlate to Trump support was racial resentment.[239]

Oh no, some say, there were plenty of other, entirely legitimate reasons why conservative voters supported Trump. Really? Let's see about that.

Opposition to government-run healthcare? Trump has supported massive government involvement in healthcare, and even said about the personal insurance mandate—the most controversial part of Obamacare—"I like the mandate."

---

* Note to Trump fans: Self-proclaimed truth-tellers who loudly, convincingly, and repeatedly lie in order to dehumanize the weak are actually not truth-tellers. In fact they are liars, or, alternatively, fascists:

Family values? Trump, like the previous winner of the South Carolina Republican primary, Newt Gingrich, has been married three times and has been a proud adulterer.*

The sanctity of life? Trump once called himself "very pro-choice."** Shutting down Planned Parenthood? Trump said, "They do some very good work."[240]

Fervent belief that President George W. Bush kept us safe? "The World Trade Center came down during the reign of George Bush . . . [W]e weren't safe," offered Trump.

Dead-set against raising taxes on the wealthy by even a penny? Trump bragged he would take on "the hedge fund guys" and eliminate their tax breaks. He said it was "outrageous" how little tax some multimillionaires paid.

Total opposition to any form of gun control? Trump supported the Bill Clinton assault weapons ban. Unwavering fealty to the National Rifle Association (NRA)? Trump blasted Republicans who "walk the NRA line."[241]

In fact, on just about every issue that supposedly matters most to conservatives in modern times, Trump has held the *opposite* position.

So on what issues *does* Trump agree with the Republican base that supported him?

One thing and one thing only: Hating nonwhite and non-Christian people.

You have a better explanation, America?

(*Long pause.*)

Nah, I didn't think so.

But Republican Party leaders and conservative pundits, who benefited mightily for so many years from their side's slightly veiled racism, are now aghast at their compatriot's overt, in-your-face racism. They happily lured the racist genie out of the bottle, which was just fine

---

* Exodus 20:14 says, "You shall not commit adultery." Deuteronomy 22:22 states, "If a man is found sleeping with another man's wife, both the man who slept with her and the woman must die." Leviticus 20:10 exhorts, "If a man commits adultery with another man's wife—with the wife of his neighbor—both the adulterer and the adulteress must be put to death." I don't agree with those sentiments, but I thought I'd point them out since Trump told Christian Right audiences that he was a big reader of, and believer in, the Bible.

** Though, like the vast majority of those in the GOP who call themselves "pro-life," Trump also supports the death penalty, unfettered weapon ownership, and new wars.

when said genie was bestowing them with all sorts of electoral gifts, but when the genie became more forthright in its racism, and it threatened to destroy the entire Republican Party, they claimed to be appalled by Trump's crude ethnic attacks (but would support his candidacy when push came to shove anyway).

The GOP is like the wife of a crystal meth manufacturer or mobster who loves all the money her husband is bringing in, until there is some chance that he might get caught, and all of a sudden she gets indignant.*

The real trouble that Trump brought to the GOP is that his popularity exposed as a myth the notion that their most loyal voters were all tied together by opposition to big government or abortion, when the thing that most united them was bigotry.

So, given that the modern GOP dives to the lowest possible level to win, should the Democrats play that game too? Not on your life.

First, it's immoral. To paraphrase Michelle Obama, when they go low, we should go high. Second, in the long run, the more diverse America becomes, the more that campaigning on the country's divisions will fail.

Rather, the Democrats need to develop progressive, common-sense policies and messages that will take away the fuel that powers racism: broken dreams. Sure, even if the Democrats offered a more persuasive economic vision (as I'll propose later in this book), some hardcore racists would still vote against them—and that would be just fine—but the racist vote will dwindle over time as many of the most die-hard racists will, in fact, eventually die.

HOW GOP RACE-BAITING WORKS

Historically, GOP race-baiting focused on claims that the Democrats were "weak on crime" and opposed to "states' rights"—but the states' rights issue faded away somewhat as the South was eventually

---

*

forced to accept the basic provisions of federal civil rights laws, and the crime-based attacks subsided after President Bill Clinton pushed through a tough-as-nails crime bill and violence plummeted in most parts of the nation.

The GOP routinely demonized "welfare"—commonly defined as cash assistance to low-income families. But Bill Clinton de-fanged this issue too when he made good on his promise to "end welfare as we know it." As of 2015, less than 1 percent of Americans overall, and only 6 percent of Americans living in poverty, received cash welfare.[242] Substantively, both the crime and the welfare bills resulted in decidedly mixed outcomes for America, but they did dilute some key Republican lines of attack.

So what did the Republicans and conservatives do when they didn't have cash assistance welfare to kick around anymore? They falsely started characterizing other government programs such as SNAP and Medicaid as "welfare," and fabricated claims that such programs increased dependency and sapped able-bodied adults (Reagan's "young bucks") of a willingness to work. They then sneakily implied that most of the people getting help were nonwhite (which, of course, is also false). Hell, a few Republicans even claimed that school lunches and summer meals for kids were some sort of welfare, and called for children to work in exchange for eating at school.

Jeb Bush, the supposedly "moderate," "sensible" GOP candidate in 2016 (according to pundits), implied that Democrats lure black voters with welfare programs: "Our message is one of hope and aspiration. It isn't one of division and 'Get in line and we'll take care of you with free stuff,'" Bush said. And he lost the racist vote anyway.[243]

For Republicans, other than the politically inept Jeb!, such attacks have been reliable vote-getters. It is amazing how many white people—and particularly low-income whites—have been conned into thinking their problems are caused by low-income nonwhites. For an odd reason I can never understand, people waiting in a very long line seem less agitated if they know there are other people even *further* back in the line than they are.

In a piece that posed the question, "Why do working-class Americans vote as they do?" columnist Eduardo Porter concluded,

Perhaps even more than economic status, racial, ethnic, and cultural identity is becoming a main driver of political choice. It suggests that the battle over the purpose and configuration of the American government—what it's for, who it serves—may become more openly about "us" versus "them," along ethnic lines. . . . The reaction of whites who are struggling economically raises the specter of an outright political war along racial and ethnic lines over the distribution of resources and opportunities. Racial animosity has long helped foster a unique mistrust of government among white Americans. Nonwhite voters mostly like what the government does. But many white Americans, researchers have found, would rather not have a robust government if it largely seems to serve people who do not look like them.[244]

As scholars Alberto Alesina, Edward Glaeser, and Bruce Sacerdote have explained, Americans have a much smaller safety net relative to Europe, mainly because of American racial heterogeneity: "Racial animosity in the US makes redistribution to the poor, who are disproportionately black, unappealing to many voters."[245]

Even in a state like Kentucky, which is 88 percent white, and in which the vast majority of social service program beneficiaries are white, similar forces are at play. After Obamacare became law, then-Kentucky Governor, Democrat Steve Beshear, courageously expanded Medicaid and created an online exchange, Kynect, which healthcare experts called one of the best in the country. In 2015, with Beshear soon to leave office due to term limits, the gubernatorial election in Kentucky revolved around whether those new healthcare programs would continue. After the Dems lost the election, "Carolyn Bouchard, a diabetic with a slowly healing shoulder fracture, hurried to see her doctor after Matt Bevin was elected governor here this month," reported the *New York Times*. "Ms. Bouchard, 60, said she was sick of politics and had not bothered voting. But she knew enough about Mr. Bevin, a conservative Republican who rails against the Affordable Care Act, to be nervous about the Medicaid coverage she gained under the law last year. 'I thought, before my insurance changes, I'd better go in,' she said as she waited at Family Health Centers, a community clinic here."[246]

At least some people who desperately needed healthcare knew fully well that conservatives would try to take it away. Ms. Bouchard knew that so well that she rushed to get treatment before they did it. This story clearly reinforces my contention that dumb-ass voters (and, indeed, nonvoters) need to be held accountable for their dumb-assness.

But this is also a case of political malpractice on the part of other Kentucky Democrats. The 2014 Democratic candidate for US Senate against Majority Leader Mitch McConnell failed to forcefully defend the healthcare changes, and she refused to even say whether she voted for Obama. She lost in a landslide. The 2015 Democratic nominee for Kentucky's governor, Attorney General Jack Conway, did a bit more to try to defend Beshear's healthcare advances, but he never effectively refuted the main GOP charge—that Obamacare was essentially an "alien" imposition of a DC power play on the good people of Kentucky.

In any other country in the world, a candidate's chances of being elected or reelected would be destroyed if it turned out that the candidate had opposed healthcare. Only in America do candidates *brag* they denied healthcare to the public, and then actually win because of that.

WHAT'S THE MATTER WITH THE WWF?

Kansas native Thomas Frank, in his best-selling book *What's the Matter with Kansas?*, makes the argument that Republicans moved Kansas from a progressive state to a far-right-wing one over the last few decades by duping voters into caring only about meaningless social issues instead of their own economic self-interest. While Frank makes some vital points, I think he misses the mark in a number of ways.

First, while it is true that Kansas previously had many progressive strains and even a significant number of Democratic elected officials in some parts of the state before the 1990s, it's not as if the overall state has actually been liberal at any time in the last 100 years or so. In the 24 presidential elections between 1920 and 2014, Democrats won merely three times—in 1932, 1936, and 1964, when FDR and LBJ won national blowouts. The last time a Democrat won a US Senate seat in the state was 1936. So any implication that Kansas was a leftie hotbed until the religious Right hijacked the state in the 1990s just isn't accurate.

Second, Frank downplays the role of race in the GOP takeover of the state. But Kansas was segregated back in the day (remember *Brown v. Board of Education of Topeka?*) and in Kansas, as elsewhere, the racial composition in any electoral division is the top determinant of how it will vote.* But let's examine the heart of Frank's message:

> People getting their fundamental interests wrong is what American political life is all about. This species of derangement is the bedrock of our civic order; it is the foundation on which all else rests.
>
> If you earn over $300,000 a year, you owe a great deal to this derangement. Raise a glass sometime to those indigent High Plains Republicans as you contemplate your good fortune: It is thanks to their self-denying votes that you are no longer burdened by the estate tax, or troublesome labor unions, or meddling banking regulators. Thanks to the allegiance of these sons and daughters of toil, you have escaped what your affluent forebears used to call "confiscatory" income tax levels. It is thanks to them that you were able to buy two Rolexes this year instead of one and get that Segway with the special gold trim. . . .
>
> While earlier forms of conservatism emphasized fiscal sobriety, the backlash mobilizes voters with explosive social issues—summoning public outrage over everything from busing to un-Christian art—which it then marries to pro-business economic policies. Cultural anger is marshaled to achieve economic ends. And it is these economic achievements—not the forgettable skirmishes of the never-ending culture wars—that are the movement's greatest monuments . . . In fact, backlash leaders systematically downplay the politics of economics.[247]

He is correct that the main Republican/conservative discourse in Kansas (where I served as the Clinton/Gore press secretary in the 1992 campaign) over the last few decades has been about abortion, gay

---

* In 2012, Obama won only two counties out of 105 in the state: Obama won 60 percent of the vote in Douglas County, home to the liberal college town of Lawrence, and 67 percent of the vote in Wyandotte County, home of the Kansas side of Kansas City, which is 58 percent nonwhite and is the only majority nonwhite county in the state.

rights, prayer in school, and other issues vital to the religious right. But the Republicans definitely delivered clear messages about economics too—with a consistent low taxes/small government theme—which, they told voters, would aid *all* of them through economic growth.* The economic and social themes were often intertwined, with some religious leaders telling voters that Jesus opposed tax hikes on the wealthy almost as strongly as abortion. The WWF were particularly receptive to this argument. "Socialism never took root in America because the poor see themselves not as an exploited proletariat but as temporarily embarrassed millionaires," John Steinbeck may (or may not) have said.[248]

Yet, as we've seen in the case of Gingrich and Trump, Kansas Tea Partiers retained support from the religious Right, and key blocks of evangelicals happily supported candidates that personally flouted family values, as long as those candidates also flagellated nonwhite people. Sure, religious and moral issues were rolled out to distract and rile up the WWF. But the historical record seems to indicate that it's impossible to separate those from the racial and economic issues. The Kansas GOP's welfare-bashing was thinly veiled race-baiting, and even much of the anti-abortion crusading was combined with anti-black imagery and rhetoric.

That being said, it is a bit presumptuous to call people "deranged," as Frank does, for either having a different definition of self-interest than he, or perhaps placing a higher value on the well-being of society than the material benefits for your own family.

If you believe your family is in danger—including spiritual danger—from what you consider rampant social ills all around you—unfettered sexual deviancy, soaring rates of "baby murder," and the removal of God from your kids' schools—then you *are* voting in your self-interest if you are supporting candidates who pledge to protect your family from those things you find so threatening.**

But let's say, for the sake of argument, that you don't think your

---

* The Kansas GOP slashed funding for public schools, and even threatened to de-fund courts that opposed them. Their low-tax crusade finally imploded when far-right Governor Sam Brownback just couldn't make his budget numbers add up, and even key Republicans in the legislature rebelled.

** I personally don't think those issues are a threat to anyone's family, but I am trying to understand the beliefs of people who do.

family is *personally* threatened by any of those issues, and that your only worry is that those values are destroying the broader society and the nation over time. In that case, if you vote for people who agree with you, wouldn't that actually be idealistic?

If you believe that Democrats might get you a wage hike but the Republicans will save the entire country's soul, wouldn't it be noble, in a sense, for you to vote against your self-interest?

In truth, though, very few people would actually vote for broad moral uplift instead of an increase in their incomes if they were given a clear choice between the two. The reason so many people are voting based on morals is that they don't believe the Democrats will actually get them a raise (and mostly they're correct), so they settle for the side that agrees with them morally.

Unfortunately, there is some truth to the conservative claim that coastal liberal elites look down at the rest of the nation. As just one tiny example, near where I live, a trendy Brooklyn bar holds a regular "White Trash Bingo" night. As Atlanta-based writer James Swift has noted, "When examining the universally despised hipster subculture, the one aspect of it no one ever seems to decry is its unabashed promotion of classism. The entire hipster aesthetic these days is an insincere mocking of white poverty—really no different than staging a white-faced minstrel show."[249] It's hard to imagine that openly mocking people doesn't get them on your side.

As J.D. Vance, author of *Hillbilly Elegy: A Memoir of a Family and a Culture in Crisis,* put it in an interview, "If you're an elite white professional, working class whites are an easy target: you don't have to feel guilty for being a racist or a xenophobe. By looking down on the hillbilly, you can get that high of self-righteousness and superiority without violating any of the moral norms of your own tribe. So your own prejudice is never revealed for what it is."[250]

But the main reason that the moral Right's issues have resonated so well and so consistently over the past 25 years is that they are filling a *vacuum* in the national political debate that has been created by the *absence* of a true, solutions-oriented debate on economic justice. When will the Democrats learn that a simplistic, fact-adverse message from the other side beats no message from their side every single time?

ECONOMIC HAPPY TALK AND THE POLITICS OF DENIAL

In the late Obama era, Democrats couldn't seem to get their message straight about the economy. Was it soaring because of the visionary leadership of President Obama or failing because of the intransigence of Congressional Republicans? Their answer depended on the day.

In 2014, Obama stated, "Since I have come into office, there's almost no economic metric by which you couldn't say that the US economy is better . . . None." But the previous year, Obama delivered a very different message:

> Starting in the late '70s, [the nation's] social compact began to unravel. . . . As good manufacturing jobs automated or headed offshore, workers lost their leverage, jobs paid less and offered fewer benefits. . . . [B]usinesses lobbied Washington to weaken unions and the value of the minimum wage. . . . [M]illions of families were stripped of whatever cushion they had left . . . The combined trends of increased inequality and decreasing mobility pose a fundamental threat to the American Dream, our way of life. . . . [P]eople's frustrations run deeper than these most recent political battles. Their frustration is rooted in their own daily battles—to make ends meet, to pay for college, buy a home, save for retirement. It's rooted in the nagging sense that no matter how hard they work, the deck is stacked against them. And it's rooted in the fear that their kids won't be better off than they were.

You'd never know he was talking about the same country, being led by the same president. Other Democratic leaders exhibited similar confusion. One week they praised job growth and GNP expansion under Obama; the next they decried low wages and high inequality.

With such mixed messages, it's no wonder the Democrats lost the Senate in 2014, and made no inroads in the House. On a political level, contradictory messages ensure defeat. On a substantive level, claims of a flourishing economy ring hollow to many Americans because poverty is soaring and the middle class is treading water.

What can we do about it?

First, all progressive leaders should thoroughly and consistently own up to America's dire economic state, making it clear they understand the people's pain. Next, they should communicate that these problems are mostly the fault of conservative policies that crush unions, prevent minimum wage hikes, outsource jobs, and slash spending for vulnerable families. And finally, they should propose concrete plans to reverse those policies. Explaining how you will improve people's lives is always a better strategy than trying to convince suffering families that they never had it so good.

WINNING BACK THE WWF WILL TAKE MORE
THAN FLOWERS AND CANDY

The trend of the WWF fleeing the Democratic Party won't reverse itself. The laws of physics apply to politics as much as they do to nature. Objects at rest (such as the Democratic Party resting on its decades-old demographic laurels) tend to stay at rest unless acted upon by an outside force (changing their damn message and fighting harder for serious policy change). Objects in motion (such as the Republican Party gobbling up more white voters) tend to stay in motion unless acted upon by an outside force (like Democrats with smarts and guts). In the post-mortems following all losing campaigns, the left and the centrist sides of the Democratic Party continue to skew data to support their own preconceived notions that their candidate would have won if only he or she had steered either more to the left or more to the center/right. But both claims are simplistic and wrong.

America, your average voters hold complex—and often contradictory and muddled—ideologies. Look at the fact-averse voters who claimed in 2016 they couldn't decide between Donald Trump and Bernie Sanders. Democratic candidates usually don't lose because their positions aren't liberal or conservative enough—they lose because their positions aren't credible enough. Real people generally don't think the Democrats have real solutions to their real problems, partially because they don't think Democrats share their values, so they won't even consider their policy ideas. As Bill Clinton proved in his campaigns, before you can even have a prayer of connecting with the WWF, you need to prove to them that you champion, or at least understand, their values. Does that mean that the Democrats should sell their souls, shoving nonwhite voters or LGBTQ people off cliffs? No way.

Rather, progressives need to do better connecting their values with mainstream values. We need to explain that we are pro-immigrant because our society is stronger and richer thanks to a robust, diverse population of energetic newcomers, and because every major religious figure in history—including Christ—commanded their flock to welcome strangers. We are against mass deportations because we don't want to break apart families.

We support marriage equality because we want everyone to have the right to a loving, stable, life-long relationship.

We're pro-life because we want to make it harder for toddlers to kill themselves* with guns lying around the house and because we want pregnant women to have good nutrition.

We're pro-minimum-wage hikes because we want work to pay more than welfare.

We're pro-choice because we want every baby to be well cared for and loved, and we are pro-contraception because we think fewer women should have no choice but to get abortions.

We're against hunger and poverty because the Old Testament, the New Testament, and the Quran all tell us we ought to be, and because if we let our neighbor's house burn, the whole block will soon go up in flames.

Once we've connected on values, progressives need to prove to the WWF that we have real-life achievable plans to fix their real-life problems. Stay tuned for that in the last part of this book.

In the meantime, you can at least *start* by sending WWF flowers.**

---

* In 2015, according to the *Washington Post*, at least 13 toddlers accidentally killed themselves, and two killed others, with guns.
**

6.

Your Best Life Is Actually Someone Else's
The Politics of Resentment

"Hurting people often hurt other people as a result of their own pain. If somebody is rude and inconsiderate, you can almost be certain that they have some unresolved issues inside. They have some major problems, anger, resentment, or some heartache they are trying to cope with or overcome. The last thing they need is for you to make matters worse by responding angrily."
—Joel Osteen, *Your Best Life Now: 7 Steps to Living at Your Full Potential*, 2004[251]

"It's human; we all put self-interest first."
—Euripides, *Medea*, 431 BCE

Pretend you are Plato,* the ancient Greek philosopher, and you are lounging in an ornate marble bathhouse, being fanned and brought wine by one of your numerous slaves.** Like many "great thinkers" that came after you (see *Jefferson, Thomas*), you have plenty of time to think greatly and philosophize up a storm because your enslaved laborers are doing all your work.

But wait, you overhear one of the slaves tell another that they're thinking about rebelling. Gee, if they did, that would sure put a cramp

---

* This . . .   not that.

** The average ancient Athenian "citizen" household owned three or four slaves. So much for being the "cradle of democracy." Plato himself reportedly owned at least five at the time of his death.

in your lifestyle. You might even be forced to stomp your own grapes or carry your own quills and parchment. Oh, the calamity. So what do you do?

You bolt up, ask your slaves to towel you off, and then run home in your slave-made sandals, where you ask your slaves to bring you papyrus and immediately start writing the *Republic*, in which you provide a philosophical and ideological justification for slavery. You come up with this great scheme: let's tell everyone that we need to create an ideal state, and that, to do so, there must be lots and lots of slaves to get the work done, with "citizens" overseeing the slaves, then elite citizens, called "guardians," presiding over the rest of the citizens, and then there really must be one great "philosopher king" (clear your throat, look at your sandals, then shuffle your feet a bit, until they point to you as the natural choice, but of course!) to rule over the elites and everyone else, including the slaves. Then you come up with the idea—get this—that the slaves will actually *benefit* from the system because of the super-wise decisions that you will make as part of your philosopher-kingship. And if any of the slaves don't buy that, just slaughter them. Even if you have to kill a few slaves now and then, you can do so with no recriminations (no less guilt) because you've convinced yourself and the elites serving under you that such an action would be somehow *good* for the slaves.

Fast-forward a millennium or so, and imagine that you're a king in medieval Europe. Back in the beginning of the age of royalty, some kings were selected in elections, of sorts, by fellow nobles. Eventually you grow tired of begging for support from those prissy-pants fops, which is humiliating for a monarch of your exalted stature. Not only that, you worry that someone else will convince the nobles to vote for them instead of for you, and then you'd be shipped to a dreary, second- or third-rate, backwater little island to preside over herds of swine.* So, what do you do?

You hold a big-ass coronation, and pay off (or threaten) a bishop so that he announces at said coronation that God *picked* you—yes, you—

---

* I'm not talking about England, so don't get so defensive, British readers. I meant another dreary isle. And please don't whine about what a great empire you once were—at least you still have Gibraltar (that's some big rock). And we all still love the Beatles and scones, though it was idiotic of you to vote to leave the EU.

to be sovereign. No, it wasn't a vote of vassals that made you Top Dog, and no, it wasn't just the dumb luck of your birth into a family horribly deformed by inbreeding. It was *Divine Intervention*. Yeah, that's the ticket. You have a "divine right" to be the ruler. Hey, the church and the Lord say so, and *ipso facto*, it's gotta be true. If anyone questions your celestial selection, you quickly behead the nonbeliever and then announce that the beheading, too, was God's will. It's really quite elegant in its simplicity.

Now imagine that you are in late-19th-century Gilded Age America and that you are mega-ultra-obscenely rich—wealthier than anyone's dreams (income tax didn't exist back then). You got that way by luckily finding a gold deposit or by using your family's money to start a railroad and then you built a monopoly and crushed all competition. Soon, some of your workers complain that they aren't paid enough to feed their families and are forced to work insane hours, six days a week, while you don't seem to do much actual work yourself, and your vacation home in Newport is larger than the entire housing compound for your workers. These ingrate workers are even starting to use an ugly, scary word: "union." Egad! What do you do?

You hire some toady* to come up with the idea of "Social Darwinism," which proclaimed that you did so well because you were "naturally fitter" and more virtuous than your workers. If any of the workers don't buy that, you direct your henchman to hire private security forces that kill or beat the crap out of the union organizers. Simple.

Lastly, think of yourself as a modern-day Silicon Valley tech zillionaire. A social outcast, you dropped out of college, then came up with one idea**—which was funded with seed money from your parents—and since other Silicon Valley dropouts also thought it was a cool idea, even though your company has never earned any profit, venture capi-

---

* Either of these make fine "number twos" who specialize in "the dirty work."

** Perhaps you founded the tech startup—"Wow-ME!" which automatically projects selfies on every surface you pass and adds self-confidence-building subliminal messages to your iPhone music playlist.

talists gave you scads of money, which made your personal net worth larger than the combined GNP of all sub-Saharan African nations combined. But the people who blow leaves off the lawns at your eight luxury homes are living out of their cars, and there was a nasty story about that on *BuzzFeed* that embarrassed you just as your private jet was about to land at Davos. So, what do you do?

You and your pals declare that America is a "meritocracy"—and that only the smartest, hardest-working, most creative, innovative people get ahead—and you darn well deserve every penny you earn and every bit of power you exert. Then you fund a sycophant 20-something "journalist" to tag along with you, in ultra-luxury, to all the "ideas conferences" that you attend and all the ribbon-cutting ceremonies for all the charter schools you fund, until the journalist writes a fawning magazine profile about how your life is the epitome of "meritocracy," how we are all lucky that you donate in such an effective, metrics-based manner to charities, and oh, by the way, how those poor slobs who mow your lawns just don't merit higher pay in "the free market" because they don't have more advanced education levels and probably like working outside anyway. When your lawn crews join the Fight for $15 movement to seek a $15 minimum wage, you fund a libertarian think tank to publish a detailed policy paper (full of impressive-sounding, but untrue, charts and graphs) that says that the real problem with minimum wage increases is that they would really hurt the workers themselves. If your workers don't buy your claim that your biggest interest is *their* well-being, then call your buddy, the local mayor (a liberal, of course, to whose campaign treasure chest you donated big bucks), to get your workers arrested for violating the municipal ordinance that bans people from sleeping in their cars, then replace the workers with undocumented immigrants who will be less likely to complain and who will be "grateful" to blow leaves off your lawns for sub-minimum wage.

All these historical imaginings of various lives as rulers illustrate that, throughout history, people first seize money and power, and then, utilizing that power and money, they fabricate ideologies defending their ruling status and lucre not only as entirely natural and just, but also as a very good thing for the people *without* money and power. Then they use that money and power to brutally tamp down any opposition. It is a truism that power corrupts, and that absolute power corrupts absolutely, so the elites always act in their *own* self-interest. But like the cheating spouse who claims that he is doing *you* a favor by letting you off the hook from having sex with him frequently, the self-serving elites always tell you they are doing it for *you*.

Make no mistake about it, America, the idea that the contemporary US is a true meritocracy—that people are rewarded only for talent and hard work—is as much of a myth as the idea that the Lord personally picked Prince Charles to be a ruler.*

Ironically, when British left-winger Michael Young first coined the term "meritocracy" in 1958, he meant is as satire, as a warning that moneyed, educated elites would consolidate power, wealth, and standing, but then claim that they earned their success through hard work and smarts. Young later wrote, "It is good sense to appoint individual people to jobs on their merit. It is the opposite when those who are judged to have merit of a particular kind harden into a new social class without room in it for others."[252]

The US has the best meritocracy money can buy. The combined net worth of the Forbes 400 in 2015 was a staggering $2.29 trillion, up $270 billion from the previous year.** The average worth of each person on the list was $5.7 billion. If each one of the 400 multi-billionaires gave away all their money in excess of a billion dollars, and resigned themselves to being mere billionaires, that mountain of remaining money would equal $1.8 trillion, which is four times the entire US federal budget deficit.

Those 400 people—who were just one part of the top one-tenth of 1 percent of the wealthiest Americans—comprised 16,000 families

---

*

** In 2015, you needed to have at least $1.55 billion to make the Forbes 400. Imagine having only $1.54 billion on hand, thus failing to make the list, then kicking yourself the whole year because you lost a million dollars investing in the movie *Waterworld*.

with combined assets of $6 trillion in 2012, more than 12 times the US budget deficit. That top one-tenth of 1 percent owned a greater share of the nation's wealth than during any time in the last hundred years. And the wealthiest 10 percent of Americans had, in 2012, more money than the bottom 90 percent of all Americans combined.[253] America has been very, very good to its rich.

Now that I've thoroughly depressed you, let me pile on. The Institute for Policy Studies has found that America's 20 wealthiest people—a group that could fit comfortably in one single Gulfstream G650 luxury jet—now own more wealth than the bottom half of the American population combined, a total of 152 million people in 57 million households. They also found that the Forbes 400 own more wealth than the bottom 61 percent of the country combined, which is comprised of a staggering 194 million people.[254]

As Robert Reich has pointed out, "We're on the cusp of the largest inter-generational wealth transfer in history. The wealth is coming from those who over the last three decades earned huge amounts on Wall Street, in corporate boardrooms, or as high-tech entrepreneurs. It's going to their children, who did nothing except be born into the right family. The 'self-made' man or woman, the symbol of American meritocracy, is disappearing. Six of today's ten wealthiest Americans are heirs to prominent fortunes. Just six Walmart heirs have more wealth than the bottom 42 percent of Americans combined (up from 30 percent in 2007)."[255]

Poor kids who do everything right don't do better than rich kids who do everything wrong, explained Matt O'Brien in the *Washington Post*:

> Inequality starts in the crib. Rich parents can afford to spend more time and money on their kids, and that gap has only grown the past few decades . . . Between 1972 and 2006, high-income parents increased their spending on "enrichment activities" for their children by 151 percent in inflation-adjusted terms, compared to 57 percent for low-income parents. It's an educational arms race that's leaving many kids far, far behind . . .
>
> Rich high school dropouts remain in the top [income bracket] about as much as poor college grads stay stuck in the

bottom. . . . These low-income strivers are just as likely to end up in the bottom as these wealthy ne'er-do-wells. Some meritocracy . . .

Rich kids who can go work for the family business, or inherit the family estate, don't need a high school diploma to get ahead. It's an extreme example of what economists call "opportunity hoarding." That includes everything from legacy college admissions to unpaid internships that let affluent parents rig the game a little more in their children's favor. But even if they didn't, low-income kids would still have a hard time getting ahead. That's, in part, because they're targets for diploma mills that load them up with debt, but not a lot of prospects.[256]

Our elite universities are privilege mills. Sixty-eight members of the Columbia College class of 2018, my alma mater, were sons and daughters of Columbia alums. More than two-thirds of those went to private secondary schools.[257] Talk about affirmative action for kids who don't need it.

Much of America's wealth is inherited, but the media still salivates over so-called "self-made" men. Aside from that notion being darn insulting to the parents of those men, it's often untrue even financially. *The New York Times* described one billionaire as "self-made" even though he started his investment businesses during his sophomore year in college with "$265,000 from family and friends."[258] The vast majority of Americans don't have family and friends who can give them $265,000 ever, no less in their second year of college.

In the most comprehensive takedown of modern meritocracy, the book *Twilight of the Elites*, journalist Chris Hayes writes,

The meritocracy [. . . creates] a new hierarchy based on the notion that people are deeply unequal in ability and drive. It offers a model of society that confers vastly unequal compensation and resources on the bright and the slow, the industrious and the slothful. At its most extreme, this ethos celebrates an "aristocracy of talent," a vision of who should rule that is in deep tension with our democratic commitments. . . . [T]his parody of democracy has facilitated accelerating and extreme economic inequality of a scope and scale unseen since the last Gilded Age.... It is precisely our collective embrace of inequality that has produced a cohort of socially distant, blinkered, and self-dealing elites.[259]

Economic research has repeatedly debunked the notion that what's good for the elites is good for the rest of us. "One should be wary ... of conventional wisdom that modern economic growth is a marvelous instrument for revealing individual talents and aptitudes," wrote Thomas Piketty, in *Capital in the Twenty-First Century*. "There is some truth to that, but since the early nineteenth century it has been used all too often to justify inequalities of all sorts, no matter how great their magnitude and no matter what their real causes may be, while at the same time gracing the winners in the new industrial economy with every imaginable virtue."[260]

For any readers who still believe that the rich are rich because they are smarter, harder working, or more virtuous than the rest of us, I have a final two-word rebuttal: Donald Trump—a man who inherited a boatload of money, dodged the draft, committed serial adultery, and drove multiple businesses to bankruptcy.

Because the meritocracy delusion helps people with power and money maintain both—as well as their self-esteem—the hoi polloi do everything possible to foster it. As a result of the persistent mythmaking by media owned and run by elites, most Americans still believe that there is far more upward mobility in America today than there actually is.

When the elites fail to persuade, violence is always an option. As John Steinbeck wrote in 1936 about farm workers forming unions, "Attempts to organize have been met with a savagery from the large growers beyond anything yet attempted. The usual repressive measures have been used against these migrants: shooting by deputy sheriffs in 'self-defense,' jailing without charge, refusal of trial by jury, torture and beating by night riders."[261]

THOU *SHALT* COVET

The "other Joel,"* as I like to think of the mega-church pastor, Joel Osteen, teaches us that resentment hurts not only yourself, but also others. That's surely true, but resentment and spite are two of the top defining features of American politics today. The middle class resent the rich, the merely rich resent the richer, and everyone—including poor folks—resent the poor.

The twin engines of resentment are envy and disgust. America, you damn well want things that others have, but are indignant that they have them whether or not we have them too. In 2013, a person needed $7.9 million to be in the wealthiest 1 percent of Americans but needed $1.3 billion—165 times that—to get on the Forbes 400 list.[262] No wonder millionaires are envious of billionaires. Columnist Ginia Bellafante lampooned the "rise in tension between the very affluent and the exceptionally rich" in the Hamptons over the noise from helicopter landings: "It is easy, of course, to mock the grievances of those driving their $40,000 Volvos to $1 million summer houses against those spending thousands on helicopter rides to their $10 million houses as distinctions without a difference. Every fall, this dynamic of envy-repulsion finds renewed context in the private-school world of the city's most exclusive neighborhoods, where parents who trudge to school with their children on foot find themselves exorcised by those who drop them off in Town Cars; and parents who spend $2,000 a year on SAT tutors mine their outrage over those who are able to afford 10 times that or more."[263]

A blogger that covers the travails of Manhattan's Upper East Side elites quoted a multi-millionaire as complaining, "Just when you think you've made it with your Mack-daddy $10 million apartment, your wife comes home and says, 'So and so just bought a $35 million apartment,' and you feel like a loser."[264]

---

* People who confuse this Joel for me: absolutely no one, ever.

It's fun watching the super-rich fight the super-duper-rich. In Los Angeles, when Fred Rosen, who built Ticketmaster into a multi-billion-dollar household name and who was spending an estimated $150 million to build a mega-mansion of 90,000 square feet—with five swimming pools*—his rich neighbors fought a down and dirty battle to prevent the construction.[265]

Perhaps because they are spending so much time in their uber-mansions, glass-walled corner offices, and private jets, the wealthy don't socialize as much as low-income Americans, spending, on average, 6.4 fewer evenings per year in social situations and spending an estimated 10 minutes more time alone in a day, as well as 26 fewer minutes per day (158 hours per year) with family.[266] Perhaps that's one key reason why, as scholars have proven, lower-income people demonstrate more "dispositional compassion" than the wealthy.[267]

What's even more amazing than the wealthy envying the even wealthier is when either cohort takes time out of their very busy days going to spas or running the world to claim they envy the poor. In 2012, then-New York City Mayor Michael Bloomberg (who was worth $27 billion at the time, even though he accepted only one dollar a year as compensation for working as mayor of the largest city in the US) said that the reason the number of homeless people in city shelters jumped by 18 percent in just that year was that "[w]e have made our shelter system so much better that, unfortunately, when people are in it—or fortunately, depending on what your objective is—it is a much more pleasurable experience than they ever had before."[268] Pleasurable? The luxurious nature of homeless shelters, complete with rampant vermin and overcrowding, is exactly why Bloomberg offered to switch places with a homeless family that year so he could live in a shelter and they could move into one of his 14 homes around the world—not. He wouldn't even live in Gracie Mansion, the historic official home for New York City mayors, so maybe he is just against government-owned housing altogether.[269]

Starbucks CEO Howard Schultz, who, in 2013, took home $20 million—equaling the yearly salary of 1,250 of his typical baristas—

---

* For the record, I could probably muddle through with only four swimming pools at my mansion.

bemoaned the nation's "food stamps dependency,"* even though many of his workers were paid so little they were eligible for such benefits.[270] In 2015, when asked about the improving economy, US Senate Majority Leader Mitch McConnell scoffed, saying business leaders tell him they have "a hard time finding people to do the work because they're doing too good with food stamps, Social Security, and all the rest."[271] *Too good?* At the time, SNAP (food stamp) payments equaled about $1.40 per meal, far too meager to live on, especially since recipients could not use them to pay for rent, clothing, transportation, childcare, diapers, or medicine. Yet right wingers keep promulgating the myth that SNAP recipients seem to always be just ahead of them in the grocery checkout line buying steaks and lobsters that their own families couldn't possibly afford. They inevitably add their false claims that those lucky duckies on food assistance also wear absurdly expensive shoes, use high-priced iPhones, and drive luxury cars.**

In a national poll in 2015, more than three-quarters of self-described conservatives and more than half of respondents who described themselves as "financially secure" believed "poor people have it easy because they can get government benefits without doing anything."[272] Yes, poor folks sure are lucky bastards.

When a number of high-profile conservative corporate, business, and government leaders discovered that close family members were gay, their views flip-flopped and they came out in favor of gay rights. If only they ever would have a low-income relative (which they rarely would), perhaps they could develop some empathy for families that struggle against poverty, too.

The poorest Americans overwhelmingly want stable, full-time work. As Kathryn J. Edin and H. Luke Shaefer wrote in their book, *$2.00 a*

---

* One definition of the Yiddish word "chutzpah" is when a person kills both his parents then pleads for mercy in court because he is an orphan. Another definition is a CEO who pays his workers so little they need food stamps and then complains that so many Americans need food stamps.

** The right also implies that SNAP recipients don't want to work. Yet according to the Center on Budget and Policy Priorities, "The overwhelming majority of SNAP recipients who can work do so. Among SNAP households with at least one working-age, non-disabled adult, more than half work while receiving SNAP—and more than 80 percent work in the year prior to or the year after receiving SNAP. The rates are even higher for families with children—more than 60 percent work while receiving SNAP and almost 90 percent work in the prior or subsequent year."

Day: Living on Almost Nothing in America, about a destitute woman in Chicago, "Jennifer rejects the idea of taking 'handouts' even now in her third spell of two dollar per day poverty in as many years, and so she won't even apply for welfare. Her vision of a good life is astonishingly humble: she dreams of a full-time job paying $13 an hour, a set schedule, and decent working conditions."[273]

Even self-styled progressives resent and fear their low-income neighbors and people of color. As 1960s radical songwriter Phil Ochs sang in the song "Love Me, I'm a Liberal," "I love Puerto Ricans and Negroes, as long as they don't move next door."

People who are homeless elicit particular fear and loathing, even among those who proclaim themselves to be on the Left. I recall a time in 2002, when St. Joseph's, a Catholic cathedral in Prospect Heights, Brooklyn, near my home, was full of angry neighbors. A significant portion of the neighborhood was still quasi-industrial, including empty lots filled with barrels of chemical waste. But the outraged crowd of mostly yuppies was there to protest what they perceived to be a much greater risk than toxic poisoning: a proposed small transitional shelter for homeless women and children. The signs advertising the meeting included a map with concentric circles drawn around the proposed shelter, showing the distance each block would be from it, as if charting fallout from a nuclear blast.

Liberal bumper stickers adorned many of the neighborhood cars at the time—"Visualize World Peace," "No Farms, No Food" were some favorites—but only three of the hundred or so people there (two friends and myself) supported the shelter. Some attendees, who lived in the neighborhood for merely moments—and were obviously unaware that many of the shelter residents were lifelong Brooklynites—loudly decried the "invasion" of "their neighborhood."

Some forecast that property values would plummet. The church's priest warned of a massive wave of rape. When I pointed to the church's crucifix, reminded the crowd that Christ was once homeless, and challenged them on whether they would let *him* live in the neighborhood, I was shouted down with clenched fists. No kidding.

The tabloids further whipped up the fear and ignorance. Writing in the *New York Post,* Robert George opined that the homeless families were the ones with true power, since they have "plenty of politically connected activists and sympathetic judges in their corner," but that the real "victims" were the local homeowners.[274]

Despite the fear mongering, Mayor Michael Bloomberg's administration did go ahead and place that small shelter on that site. Subsequently in Prospect Heights, crime continued to plummet and property values skyrocketed as the neighborhood gentrified. An artisanal mayonnaise store opened (and has since moved to a larger space elsewhere), though I never saw a customer in there.* In 2010, the shelter was torn down to make way for a parking lot for the new Barclays Center arena, which frequently sells tickets to events for hundreds and thousands of dollars.**

Most people who are homeless simply don't earn enough to afford rent, especially in 21st-century New York City. Yet the elites assume that all homeless people are mentally ill and/or substance abusers and the major problem is that they annoy upstanding citizens. Demagogues blow dog whistles with those stereotypes, and use them to prey on, dehumanize, and threaten our most vulnerable neighbors. Ever-compassionate former Mayor Rudy Giuliani offered this advice on the homeless issue: "You chase 'em and you chase 'em and you chase 'em and you chase 'em, and they either get the treatment that they need or you chase 'em out of the city."[275] But even the supposedly liberal media often makes homeless people sound intrinsically dangerous, often equating homeless people with crime, dirtiness, and disorder. The vast majority of crimes are committed by people who have homes. Yet in the relatively rare instances when homeless people do commit serious infractions, the perpetrators are almost always described in mainstream media accounts as homeless, where the reverse is rarely the case. And even worse, the media rarely report on the too-frequent crimes *against* homeless victims.

In supposedly ultra-progressive Port-

---

* No, I did not make up the artisanal mayonnaise store. While there wasn't much visible foot traffic there, apparently they sell their wares to the likes of Whole Foods and Fancy Expensive Groceries You Can't Afford.
** Home of the Brooklyn Nets, which at one time was partially owned by Jay Z.

land, Oregon, a homeless woman was charged with third-degree theft when she plugged her cellphone charger into an outlet on a public sidewalk planter box. As *Street Roots News* reported, "According to the Electrical Research Institute, it costs about 25 cents a year to charge the average mobile phone. If the phone in this scenario had gone from zero charge to full charge, the cost would have amounted to mere fractions of a penny."[276] Yet Portland spent a minimum of thousands of dollars to get two police officers to issue the summons, prosecutors to bring the case to court, and for a court to consider the case.

America, you should be ashamed of how you often treat low-income people as subhuman. The dehumanization of the poor is as old as human civilization. It is referenced (and condemned) in the Bible. In 1700s New York, low-income residents who received public aid were required to visibly wear a badge of blue or red cloth. Some of the first people the Nazis imprisoned in concentration camps were homeless people. After a homeless person was arrested for trespassing in Sarasota County, Florida, a police officer tossed peanuts into the man's mouth, as if feeding an animal at the zoo, and then he gave the homeless man "dog commands."[277]

The heartbreaking reality is that the lives of wealthy elites are always treated as more valuable than those on the bottom economic rungs.*

A NATION OF ANTI-IMMIGRANT IMMIGRANTS

"The Donald" sure does have a short memory. Friedrich Drumpf, Donald's grandad, immigrated to the US in 1885, decades before the federal government formally regulated most immigration. In "No, Your Ancestors Didn't Come Here Legally," blogger Ben Railton wrote,

> It's almost impossible to find any conversation about immigration—between elected officials, pundits, online commenters— in which at least one participant doesn't use the phrase ["My ancestors came here legally"]. It's an understandable position,

---

* When the Titanic sank in 1912, 39.5 percent of first class passengers died, but 75.5 percent of third-class passengers and 76.2 percent of crew members perished. Even when portrayed by Leonardo DiCaprio, the lowest income passengers *still* died.

through which the speaker can both defend his or her family history and critique current illegal immigrants who choose to do things differently. It helps deflect charges of hypocrisy (since most Americans are descended from immigrants). It's hard to argue with. And it's also, in nearly every case, entirely inaccurate.

If your ancestors came before the 1920s and weren't prostitutes, criminals, or from one of those Asian nations, they remained unaffected by any laws, and so were still neither legal nor illegal. This might seem like a semantic distinction, but it's much more; the phrase "My ancestors came here legally" implies that they "chose to follow the law," yet none of these unaffected immigrants had to make any such choice, nor had any laws to follow.[278]

People who push their way onto a crowded subway train at one stop tend to be the people angriest when someone else does it at the next stop. America, you are the same way when it comes to immigrants. We think that the last legitimate immigrants were *our* people.* Many Americans have awfully short memories. Cuban-American senator and presidential wannabe Marco Rubio proposed stricter immigration screenings, which, had they previously been in place, would likely have resulted in the deportation of his own grandfather, the man Rubio has called his "mentor and closest boyhood friend."[279]

Personally, I have a long memory. On February 25, 1923, my mother (then called Bejla), two months old, arrived at Ellis Island on the *S.S. Minnekahda*, along with her two parents, Etel and Levi.**

---

* Considering that European colonists barged into the country without permission from Native Americans, you'd think we'd be a little more hesitant to bolt the door behind us when new refugees seek to land on our shores.

** This is the ship on which my mother and her parents arrived. Their "ethnicity" was listed as "Hebrew" and their hometown was listed as Czortków, Russia (which, in 2016, was in the Ukraine and had previously been part of Poland, the Ottoman Empire, and the Austro-Hungarian Empire). *The New York Times* reported that the city had been so cold that the harbor was "ice-clogged" that day and that coal deliveries across the Hudson were made "under great difficulty." The city was also in the throes of a deadly influenza epidemic.

My father's two parents were also immigrants from Eastern Europe. While none of them were legally classified as refugees, they were clearly fleeing the anti-Semitic violence and destitution so common in their homelands. Odds are, had they not escaped, they would have been killed during the Holocaust or in a pogrom, as were many other members of my family who stayed. Thus I, and tens of millions of fellow descendants of immigrants, literally owe our lives to welcoming US immigration policies when our families arrived. If you are a child, grandchild, or great grandchild of immigrants (as most of us are), and yet you now oppose innocent refugees entering our nation, ~~screw you~~ I urge you to reflectively contemplate whether you may be hypocritical.

America, your anti-immigrant fervor is sickening. The 19th-century political party that opposed immigration was called the "Know-Nothing Party"—and today's anti-immigrant Americans wallow in similar ignorance. The only emotion that leads humans to do dumber things than greed and lust is fear, and the anti-immigrant crowd specializes in fear. One such demagogue, Congressman Steve King (R-IA), has compared Mexican newcomers to cockroaches and dogs, likened illegal immigration to terrorism and the Holocaust, and has joked about deporting liberals.[280] I am surprised King hasn't called for the humanitarian group Doctors Without Borders to institute borders. Apparently lacking any sense of irony, King originally endorsed Canadian-born Ted Cruz for president.

Most of the contemporary fears of immigrants are based on utter nonsense. I have never understood how opponents simultaneously claim that migrants are lazy, welfare-dependent, slacker criminals while somehow also stealing all our jobs. A landmark report by the National Academies of Sciences, Engineering, and Medicine found

> [i]ncreased prevalence of immigrants is associated with lower crime rates—the opposite of what many Americans fear. Among men ages 18–39, the foreign-born are incarcerated at a rate that is one-fourth the rate for the native-born. Cities and neighborhoods with greater concentrations of immigrants have much lower rates of crime and violence than comparable nonimmigrant neighborhoods.[281]

Hey, Trump, King, and Palin! Did you hear that? Immigration *decreases* crime? The report also noted,

> Concern about immigration is also fueled by misconceptions about immigrants and the process of integration. Americans have been found to overestimate the size of the nonwhite population, to erroneously believe that immigrants commit more crime than natives, and to worry that immigrants and their children are not learning English. A sense of cultural threat to national identity and culture, rooted in a worry about integration, therefore seems to [underlie] many Americans' worries about immigration. . . .
>
> Policies designed to block the integration of undocumented immigrants or individuals with a temporary status can have the unintended effect of halting or hindering the integration of US citizens and [lawful permanent residents] in mixed-status families.[282]

In other words, the very thing that anti-immigration leaders complain about most—foreigners supposedly not fitting into our society—is made worse by the very policies pushed by those very same leaders to make newcomers' lives more difficult.

Out of all the bogus right-wing attacks against Obama, few are more absurd than the charge that he broke US laws to allow in multitudes of new undocumented migrants. In fact, the reverse is true, and, as the chart on the next page proves, Obama became the "deporter in chief." Obama reportedly believed that deporting many immigrants would enable him to build GOP support for comprehensive immigration reform, which it obviously did not.

One of my most frequent fantasies is for every immigration opponent in America to be injected with truth serum so they would honestly admit how much their own lives are aided, each and every day, by those they proclaim to hate. I'd love to hear Congressman Steve King say, "The people who pick, cook, and serve our food deserve to live in the US without fear and should earn a living wage, because without them, I'd starve."

When it is to their financial advantage, business leaders—even Donald Trump—happily use immigrant labor, and big time. For example, Disney laid off 250 employees in 2015, replaced them with

DEPORTATIONS FROM THE US
1892 - 2013

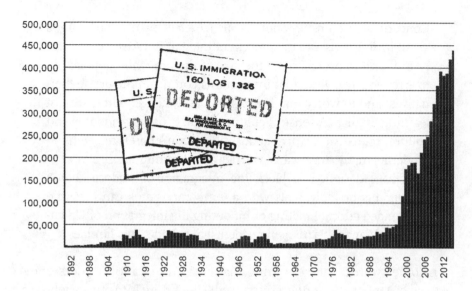

Number of immigrants removed or returned

SOURCE: THE NATIONAL ACADEMIES OF SCIENCE

immigrants on temporary visas for "highly skilled technical workers," and then expected some of the soon-to-be-unemployed Disney employees to train their immigrant successors. Technology giants like Microsoft, Facebook, and Google repeatedly press the government to allow more foreign workers under the same visa program.[283]

Pope Francis has said, "Migrants and refugees are not pawns on the chessboard of humanity. They are children, women, and men." Vital point. But in 1947, French philosopher Jean-Paul Sartre identified the United States's hypocritical identity crisis even better. "An American said to me: 'The trouble is that we are all eaten by the fear of being less American than our neighbor.' I accept this explanation: it shows that Americanism is not merely a myth that clever propaganda stuffs into people's head but something every American continually reinvents in his gropings."[284]

TEA PARTIES ARE ALL THE RAGE—AND ALL RAGE

The Tea Party movement was a combination of true grassroots, anti-Obama, and anti-government anger and outrage manufactured by health insurance companies and members of the Republican ruling class from the safety of their country club verandas.

The movement vaulted into the public consciousness in the summer of 2009 by sending angry groups to Congressional town hall meetings about healthcare reform, stoking their fears with outrageously false claims by Sarah Palin and others that President Obama's proposal included "death panels."

At a forum held by Rep. John Dingell, a longtime Democratic congressman from Michigan who supported Obamacare, a man pushed the wheelchair of his son, an adult man with a disability, to the front of the room and said to Dingell, who, at the time, used crutches himself, "Why do you want to kill my son?" An uninsured woman, Marcia Boehm, who attended the meeting to support health reform and who happens to be a short person with a disability and uses crutches, was booed, heckled, and physically intimidated. A very large man got down on his knees so he could be face-to face with her and said, "They are using you. You're stupid. They're going to euthanize you."[285]

Valerie Przywara, another pro-Obamacare organizer in attendance, described the scene at the meeting: "I've seen a lot—but last night was like nothing I've experienced. . . . There was a huge picture of President Obama, distorted, to look like Hitler. . . . [There was] shouting, vulgar language and physical intimidation. . . . Perhaps the saddest thing I saw was a father and his six-or-seven-year-old son—the father was trying to provoke a fight with reform supporters by calling them 'stupid fuckers' and poking his finger in people's chests, all while his son stood by with his fingers in his ears to shut out as much as he could of the aggressive shouting."[286]

As historian Rick Perlstein chronicled in his essay, "In America, Crazy Is a Pre-existing Condition," other extreme scenes played out nationwide:

> In Pennsylvania . . . a citizen, burly, crew-cut, and trembling with rage, went nose to nose with his baffled senator: "One day

God's going to stand before you, and he's going to judge you
and the rest of your damned cronies up on the Hill. And then
you will get your just deserts" . . .

In New Hampshire, outside a building where President
Obama spoke, cameras trained on the pistol strapped to the leg
of libertarian William Kostric. He then explained on CNN why
the "tree of liberty must be refreshed from time to time by the
blood of tyrants and patriots."[287]

Liberal Illinois Sen. Dick Durbin explained these tactics: "They want
to get a little clip on YouTube of an effort to disrupt a town meeting
and to send the congressman running for his car. This is an organized
effort. . . . [Y]ou can trace it back to the health insurance industry."[288]

The Tea Party protestors were hopping mad, not only because of their
belief that Obamacare was a massive increase in federal involvement in
healthcare (although, in reality, at the time the bill was being considered,
the federal government already provided healthcare to nearly a third of
Americans and Obamacare would only marginally increase that), but
also at the very idea that government could be useful or could perform
any function other than repressing the country's taxpayers. They seemed
to willfully ignore the reality that in a democracy like the United States
(notwithstanding the 2000 presidential election theft), government isn't
some alien force antithetical to the beliefs of the American people, but is
actually the embodiment of the voters' will, for good or bad.

What truly distinguished this new brand of extremists is that, unlike
previous fringe groups that were mostly kept outside of mainstream
political parties, the nuttiest elements of the Tea Party were warmly
embraced by the GOP. Key figures with official positions in the Republican Party would routinely say things so outrageous that they would
out-Tea Party the Tea Party. At a "How to Take Back America" conference, Rep. Trent Franks of Arizona called President Obama "an enemy
of humanity."[289] Jack Kingston of Georgia, then a high-ranking Republican congressman, proposed that low-income children be forced to
sweep floors in their schools in exchange for free lunches. Glen Urqu-
hart, Republican Party nominee for the US House in Delaware, said
the phrase "'separation of Church and State' came out of Adolf Hit-

ler's mouth,* that's where it comes from. Next time your liberal friends talk about the separation of Church and State ask them why they're Nazis."[290] (And the GOP had the chutzpah to hand-wring in 2016 about how Donald Trump brought uninformed anger into their party?)

In a 2016 forum on "opportunity," Republican House Speaker Paul Ryan said that he never sees himself as part of government and that he still thinks of himself as fighting against government—a stunning level of disingenuousness from a man who heads a house of the Congress in which he has served since 1999. If the man who is arguably the second most powerful person in the US government claims he has no stake in that government, it's no wonder that rank-and-file conservatives feel they don't either.

Rallying against government, just for its own sake, is pure nihilism. It's like painting all your bedroom walls pitch black even if you don't like the color. As the writer and TV producer David Simon aptly said, "Sneering at government and walking away is like having an argument with a 14-year-old."[291]

Some pronouncements made by high-ranking Republicans are worse than jaw-dropping—they're practically jaw-obliterating. Republican Senator Thom Tillis from North Carolina actually suggested that restaurant employees should be allowed to "opt out" of mandatory hand washing.[292] *US News & World Report* is primarily centrist, and most of their online polls skew to the conservative side, but when the publication quizzed readers on the senator's suggestion online, a whopping 93 percent disagreed with it.**

Another usual sign of our times is how many Americans claim to hate all government programs while personally receiving substantial amounts of government aid. For instance, most members of Congress who angrily decry socialist, evil, government-run healthcare for the masses happily take it for themselves, utilizing one of the most generous health insurance programs in the country offered to them at low or no cost.

America, I can't remind you enough times that the most right wing states with the heaviest Tea Party presence, particularly those in the South, benefit most from federal government largesse, taking in far more in federal spending than they pay in taxes. In Mississippi, for instance, state residents receive $2.43 from the feds for every dollar they pay in federal taxes. In 2015, out of the 15 states most dependent on

---

* Actually Thomas Jefferson coined the phrase, but close.
** Please remind me never to eat dinner at Senator Thom Tillis's house.

the federal government financially, 13 voted for Romney over Obama in the 2012 election.[293] Not coincidentally, these tended to be the states with the highest levels of poverty and the lowest average incomes.

The GOP persistently refuses to define tax cuts as spending, or to even so much as admit that tax cuts take revenue *away* from the budget. Yet these same Republicans often say that we should treat government budgets like family budgets. But in family budgets, if you have a choice between cutting vital expenditures you need to live (like food, housing, and healthcare), or bringing more income into your home through a raise, of course you'd bring more income into your home. Well, tax hikes on the rich bring more income into the government, just as surely as tax cuts for the wealthy take away income from all of us who live here.

In his book *Welfare for the Wealthy*, Christopher G. Faricy states, "Tax breaks are just government spending by another name and a major component of the American social welfare state . . . [A] tax expenditure program is a type of off-budget spending executed through the tax code, and therefore allows policy makers to increase social spending without being accused of explicitly expanding the size of government."[294]

Faricy contrasts the negative public view of the welfare queen with the positive public view of "the private social system" (i.e., benefits funded by tax breaks) which accrue substantial benefits to wealthy, white professionals in corporations. Although these privileged groups receive substantial federal social benefits and services, they are rarely called "welfare recipients." As the chart below (adapted from his book) demonstrates, in 2013, tax breaks, which disproportionately went to the wealthy, cost the US government $1.145 trillion, which equals 14 times the amount of money that the government spent on SNAP nutrition assistance that year.

Right-wingers often equate freedom with less government, but the freedom to starve is no freedom, especially to anyone actually at the risk of it. Besides, when the chips are down, the Right often jumps to expand big government when it suits their interests. In 2013, Republicans in control of the House were unable to pass a stand-alone Farm Bill, supposedly because many of their members could not stomach the SNAP funding that has historically been in the bill. So, for the first time since 1973, the House took SNAP out of the Farm Bill and tried to pass a separate bill only with farming and other solely rural programs in it. They pretended to eliminate

FEDERAL SPENDING, IN BILLIONS OF US DOLLARS

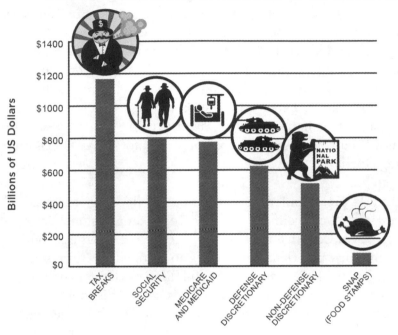

the most unpopular types of corporate welfare farm subsidies, but mostly they renamed and repackaged them by spending $9 billion more on a crop insurance program. The bill also created new subsidies for peanut, cotton, and rice farmers, gave new money to fruit and vegetable growers, and restored insurance programs for livestock producers. It also made changes to, but largely left intact, a dairy program that sets limits on the amount of milk produced and sold in the United States—a socialist provision if there ever was one.[295] All in all, the revised bill, *sans* SNAP, was an orgy of corporate welfare and big government, precisely the kind of thing that Tea Party Congressional members claimed they were elected to *stop*. So, how did they vote? Every Democrat in the House voted against the bill but it passed with 216 GOP ayes and only 12 GOP nays.[296] Most members of the far-right House Freedom Caucus and of the Tea Party Caucus voted *for* it. When push came to shove, this vociferously anti-government crowd voted for an immense expansion of big, socialist government because it a) aided many of their districts and b) aided many of their campaign donors. Yes, the Tea Party is a fraud.

Sometimes, progressives gave Tea Party types this backhanded compliment: "They may be nuts, but at least they are standing up for true, consistent beliefs in smaller government." But that's not even true. The stand-alone Farm Bill vote proved that the GOP isn't really against big government—it's against big government only for low-income people and the non-rich.

Plus, it turns out that ultra-conservatives temporarily become more liberal than Ted Kennedy when a tornado, drought, or hurricane impacts their home state. As *Politicus USA* reported in a piece headlined "Ted Cruz Demands Federal Money for Texas Floods after Blocking Hurricane Sandy Relief,"

> During a press conference on the deadly flooding in Texas, Cruz said, "I am confident that the Texas congressional delegation, Sen. Cornyn and I, and the members of Congress both Republicans and Democrats will stand united as Texans in support of the federal government fulfilling its statutory obligations, and stepping in to respond to this natural disaster."
>
> Sen. Cruz sang a completely different tune in 2013 when he called federal aid for the victims of Hurricane Sandy (which hit the Eastern US) "wasteful . . . The United States Senate should not be in the business of exploiting victims of natural disasters to fund pork projects that further expand our debt." Cruz's claim that the Sandy relief bill was wasteful was debunked by PolitiFact.[297]

Shock of all shocks: right-wing Republicans will quietly embrace even the hated Obamacare when it helps their states—and their reelection hopes. John Thune of South Dakota, the third-ranking Republican in the US Senate, voted to repeal Obamacare and ravaged it in remarks on the Senate floor. A week later, his state's Republican governor, Dennis Daugaard, announced that he would use his executive authority to make 55,000 additional South Dakota residents eligible for Medicaid under the law. A far-right Republican governor of Arizona, Jan Brewer, also expanded Medicaid, adding 78,000 state residents to the federal healthcare rolls in the state. "I am very reluctant to take positions that counter the decisions made by the governor," said senior US Senator John McCain, Republican from Arizona, also a virulent opponent of Obamacare. Why

did some in the GOP find shifty ways to expand Obamacare while trying
to claim they want to repeal it? Because it's simply better to offer healthcare to voters and to take federal money to pay for it than not. Duh.[298]

Even the most famous critics of big government, Tea Party darlings the
Koch brothers, somehow have found a way to benefit mightily from it. An
Arkansas steel mill, in which they are the largest investors, was funded
by $125 million in state bond issues, as well as over $200 million in tax
credits for buying and installing recycling equipment. In response to
a media inquiry about this, a Koch spokesman said in an e-mail, "Koch
Industries has consistently opposed and actively lobbied against all forms
of corporate welfare, including those we currently benefit from. With that
said, we will not put ourselves and our employees at a competitive disadvantage in the current marketplace." Translation: they have no problem
at all lining their own pockets with the very dirty, immoral, un-American,
corporate welfare they claim to have opposed their whole lives.[299]

The Tea Party fancies itself as full of no-compromise purists, often
bandying about the historic "Don't Tread on Me" flag with that danger-
ous-looking snake. But their real motto is, "Tread on me all you want,
as long as you pay me off. As for the tea, not so much so—I'd gladly
take coffee instead, if the price is right."

THE COLLAPSE

It's a misnomer to say that our American economic system is entirely a
"free market" one. As Robert Reich explains,

> Markets depend for their very existence on rules governing
> property (what can be owned), monopoly (what degree of
> market power is permissible), contracts (what can be exchanged
> and under what terms), bankruptcy (what happens when pur-
> chasers can't pay up), and how all of this is enforced. Such
> rules do not exist in nature. They must be decided upon, one
> way or another, by human beings. The rules have been altered
> over the past few decades as large corporations, Wall Street,
> and wealthy individuals gained increasing influence over the
> political institutions responsible for them.[300]

Nobel Prize-winning economist Joseph E. Stiglitz also wrote that

> [p]rogressive tax and expenditure policies (which tax the rich
> more than the poor and provide systems of good social protec-
> tion) can limit the extent of inequality. By contrast, programs that
> give away a country's resources to the rich and well connected
> can increase inequality. . . . [These are many of the ways] by
> which our current political process helps the rich at the expense
> of the rest of us. . . . [This] takes many forms: hidden and open
> transfers and subsidies from the government, laws that make
> the marketplace less competitive, lax enforcement of existing
> competition laws, and statutes that allow corporations to take
> advantage of others or to pass costs on to the rest of society.[301]

I won't detail the economic and political causes of the 2008 Wall
Street collapse, because so many books and movies have already done
so in mind-numbing detail.* All I'll say about it is this: the collapse
shouldn't have been the least bit surprising. Of *course*, the wealthiest
rigged the system on their own behalf. Why? Because they *could*.

As always, the elites find a way to win whether they are betting for
or against the economy. America, you seem surprised that very few of
the perpetrators of the Wall Street debacle were prosecuted. That's why
you need to understand that the crimes of the plutocrats—which would
have certainly violated the law in most other developed countries—
were, and still are, mostly *legal* in the United States. That's right. The
cliché that "he who has the gold makes the rules" is truer than ever.

International financial consultant Sam Wilkin, in his book, *Wealth
Secrets of the One Percent*, argues that many of the world's wealthiest
people created their fortunes by changing the rules in their own favor;
others did it by entering fields or doing business in countries with little
or no regulation; and most created monopolies for themselves, by ruth-
lessly eliminating competition.

Wilkin counsels businesspeople to "spin laws into gold" by getting

---

* In the movie *The Big Short*, actress Margot Robbie provided an excellent explanation of CDOs
(collateralized debt obligations) while taking a bubble bath. In the movie version of my book,
John Goodman will explain the most technical argument I make while showering.

governments to create legislation and regulations that both help them and are too complex for the general public to understand:

> In a well-functioning market economy, one should not be able to make hundreds of millions of dollars year after year after year (which is what is usually required to earn billions of dollars in a single lifetime). . . . Indeed, economic theory implies that in a healthy, perfectly competitive market economy, business profits should be fairly close to zero. The stupendous fortunes of the world's billionaires, therefore, imply the existence not simply of a few market imperfections but of giant, gaping holes in economic reality—holes into which you can plunge your hand and extract a billion dollars.[302]

The combination of greed and power should not be unexpected. What is stunning is that, once we found out that we were all colossally defrauded, the political movement that had the greatest concrete impact that emerged from the collapse—the Tea Party*—took up pitchforks to go after the *victims* of the crisis, instead of the wrongdoers. Right-wing leaders made this case by convincing middle-class families that America's real enemy is "the poor" instead of the wealthy elites that got us into this mess. As I explained in a previous chapter, much of that was due to racism, but there was also more going on.

Conservatives contradictorily claimed to advocate for smaller government, but spent billions to pay federal employees who were *not* working when they shut the government down with their budgetary bullying. At least when Wile E. Coyote sawed himself off a cliff, he didn't take the whole country with him.**

When any of us so much as dared to raise the Tea Party's inconsis-

---

* As I explain later in the book, while the Occupy movement and the Sanders for President campaign were certainly responses to the Wall Street collapse, they did not significantly remake American politics.
**

tencies, much of the media, often now controlled by giant corporations, parroted the lines that we were "socialists" engaging in "class warfare." Yet the elites have been waging—and winning—that battle since time eternal. Their real worry isn't class warfare: it's that the other side will fight back.

Oh, and by the way, pointing out verified facts about class divisions isn't warfare—it's democracy, dummy.

This story is far from new. In an 1873 editorial called "The Growth of Corporate and Decline of Governmental Power," the *Nation* stated,

> Such sayings as "The world is governed too much," "The less government you have, the better," "Individual enterprise will accomplish everything, if you only give it the chance" were adopted as incontrovertible maxims, and society set itself to giving individual enterprise all the chance it asked. At the same time, the science of government, which had received so much attention from our earliest statesmen, was allowed to die out in this country. . . . [T]he immense power of great and concentrated wealth which is actively employed [by the growth of corporations] made itself immediately felt.[303]

WHEN SOMEONE HAS BEEN GIVEN MUCH, MUCH WILL BE REQUIRED IN RETURN

Since the elites benefit more from society than others, they have more freedom to act altruistically, right? Not so much. Actually, the wealthy are more likely to lie and cheat, as one study found:

> Are society's most noble actors found within society's nobility? That question spurred [researcher] Paul Piff . . . to explore whether higher social class is linked to higher ideals, he said in a telephone interview. The answer Piff found after conducting seven different experiments is: no. The pursuit of self-interest is a "fundamental motive among society's elite, and the increased want associated with greater wealth and status can promote wrongdoing" . . . The

"upper class," as defined by the study, were more likely to break the law while driving, take candy from children, lie in negotiation, cheat to raise their odds of winning a prize, and endorse unethical behavior at work, the research found.[304]

Yes, you read that right: they are more willing to take candy away from children. "Smithers, take away that little girl's Hershey Bar immediately!"

The 2015 poster child for behaving badly was Martin Shkreli, a former hedge fund manager who was founder and chief executive for Turing Pharmaceuticals, which acquired the life-saving drug Daraprim and then raised its price overnight from $13.50 a dose to $750.[305] The very same Martin Shkreli threw down $2 million to own the one and only copy of Wu-Tang Clan's hip-hop album *Once Upon a Time in Shaolin.* To no one's chagrin—perhaps not even his mother's—Shkreli was later arrested on securities fraud charges.

If people knew that they would never get caught for smashing a rock into a jewelry store and stealing diamonds, burglaries would flourish. Likewise, when corporations know that, if they put the health and safety of the public or their workers at risk that they will rarely get caught or punished, they will do it. Left to their own devices, people and corporations with unregulated power and money often do truly awful things.

For years, the DuPont Company hid the dangers of an obscure chemical pollutant, perfluorooctanoic acid (PFOA), and bamboozled regulators into allowing their toxic contamination to continue long after the perils were known to the company.[306] Fiat Chrysler Automobiles significantly underreported to regulators the number of death and injury claims linked to possible defects in its cars that resulted in at least 124 deaths.[307] Fifteen people died and more than 260 others were injured when a chemical plant in the town of West, Texas, exploded. Nearly 20 fertilizer plants in Texas alone, and others nationwide, have the same dangerous proximity to schools, parks, nursing homes, and housing as the one in West, according to federal officials. A lack of regulations has put other communities at risk.[308] Due to budget restrictions, the main federal agency that protects worker safety, the Occupational Safety and Health Administration (OSHA), as well as its state partners, have a total of only 1,840 workplace safety inspectors to protect 130 million workers in more than eight million workplaces across the country. This means there are enough inspectors for federal OSHA to inspect workplaces only once every 145 years, on average, and for state OSHA agencies to inspect workplaces once every 97 years.[309]

The activities—good and ill—of all the world's elites are now linked together in a global economy. According to *Forbes*, the number of billionaires worldwide increased from 146 in 1987 to 1,826 in 2015.

New York Magazine declared that "the New York real estate market is now the premier destination for wealthy foreigners with rubles, yuan, and dollars to hide."[310] A *New York Times* exposé found that one $15.65 million condo purchase was financed, at least in part, by profits made off of Angola's long civil wars. Here are some other examples in the *Times* article:

> On the 74th floor of the Time Warner Center, Condominium 74B was purchased in 2010 for $15.65 million by a secretive entity called 25CC ST74B L.L.C. It traces to the family of Vitaly Malkin, a former Russian senator and banker who was barred from entering Canada because of suspected connections to organized crime.
>
> Another shell company bought a condo down the hall for $21.4 million from a Greek businessman named Dimitrios Contominas, who was arrested a year ago as part of a corruption sweep in Greece.
>
> A few floors down are three condos owned by another shell company, Columbus Skyline L.L.C., which belongs to the family of a Chinese businessman and contractor named Wang Wenliang. His construction company was found housing workers in New Jersey in hazardous, unsanitary conditions.[311]

Showing how the media can be schizophrenic, the same *New York Times*, in its obsequious "Wealth" section, explained in glowing terms why buying a $100 million condo can be a great investment, even if you keep it empty and never use it.[312] In 2014, when 54,000 people were sleeping in New York City's homeless shelters, nearly a third of all apartments in the quadrant from 49th to 70th Streets between Fifth and Park Avenues were vacant.[313]

The *Times* even planned an "International Luxury Conference" in

France—at Versailles, where else?—as they explained in their promotional materials:

> Hosted and moderated by *New York Times* fashion director, Vanessa Friedman, and award-winning *New York Times* journalists, the International Luxury Conference addresses the most critical challenges—and unexpected opportunities—in today's luxury battlefield.
>
> Rigorous analysis and lively cross-border debate among top C.E.O.s, prestigious economists, technology mavericks, entertainment and sports icons, and artists will provide crucial insights, fresh ideas, and new strategies for winning the hearts and minds of luxury consumers.
>
> To participate in this unprecedented event—where you will join interactive sessions led by global experts, dine in the spectacular Chateau de Versailles, and connect with luxury influencers from around the world—please request an invitation today.
>
> Participation at the *New York Times* International Luxury Conference is by invitation only . . . Please note there is a fee of €3,495 payable to attend this conference.
>
> *The Times* works meticulously with sponsors to integrate them into the conference . . . *The Times* can deliver on a wide variety of goals—thought leadership, V.I.P. client treatment, generating media interest (via print, online, social), introductions to individual delegates, showcasing products and designs, branding, use of conference content or content generation, media relations, or other objectives.[314]

When it comes to their interactions with global plutocrats, the *Times*, like many other media outlets, whipsaws from exposing and chastising them to toadying up to and profiting from them.

For America's masters of the universe, what they eat is as over-the-top as their housing. In 2012, attendees at the Golden Globes[*] awards ate desserts covered with edible gold flakes,

---

[*] Ricky Gervais at the Golden Globe Awards. He was paid—and fed—very well to pretend to bite the golden hand that feeds him.

which retailed at $135 a gram. "There is gold dust on there for the Golden Globes," pastry chef Thomas Henzi explained, adding that the dessert would pair ideally with the Moët & Chandon Grand Vintage 2002 magnums of champagne created for the special night.[315]

For a 2014 Thanksgiving dinner, which cost $35,000 for each group of four guests, the Old Homestead Steakhouse in the Meatpacking District of Manhattan served farm-raised organic turkey stuffed with seven pounds of ground Japanese Wagyu filet mignon. The meal included the "finest wines in the world," and the dessert featured "chocolate dipped in gold." Each foursome was also provided its own private butler.[316] Giving thanks indeed.

It seems like those who need it least get the most in handouts. 2016 Oscar presenters and prominent nominees (including Leonardo DiCaprio, who earned $29 million that year), were given a free swag bag worth $230,000, including a round of laser skin tightening treatments valued at $5,500, a $45,000 junket to Japan, and a $275 roll of Swiss toilet paper.[317] (For the record, I never pay more than $250 per roll for *my* toilet paper.)

In today's America, such conspicuous consumption occurs just across town from searing poverty. The Oscars, with their self-congratulatory toilet paper for their expensive, surgically-lifted buttocks, are celebrated a mere 16 minutes (without traffic) from the infamous Skid Row, where Angelinos who cannot afford rent come to find shelter—or to sleep on the streets.

Mind-boggling inequality of wealth and the resulting vast social divisions are the chief defining features of our time. The nation's big metropolitan areas are increasingly divided into two kinds of neighborhoods: those that hire nannies and those that supply them. Every time I watch *It's a Wonderful Life* I get despondent as I must acknowledge that the Mr. Potters are now firmly in charge of the land.

THE WORLD'S WORST WHITE WHINES

Considering that rich white men pretty much get to run the country and the world, it's amazing how much they whine.

Pundit Fareed Zakaria once asked Jamie Dimon, chief executive of JPMorgan Chase, why banks didn't increase their lending significantly post-crisis: "What do you say to the average American taxpayer who says, 'Guys, we bailed you out, now do something in return?'" In response, Dimon whimpered, "There's good and there's bad . . . Well, not all bankers are the same. And I just think this constant refrain 'bankers, bankers, bankers,'—it's just a really unproductive and unfair way of treating people. And I just think people should just stop doing that."[318]

By 2012, the elites were so out of touch that even famed far-right scholar Charles Murray was scolding them: "As the new upper class increasingly consists of people who were born into upper-middle-class families and who have never lived outside the upper-middle-class bubble, the danger increases that the people who have so much influence on the course of the nation have little direct experience with the lives of ordinary Americans, and make their own judgments about what's good for other people based on their own highly atypical lives."[319]

THE WORTH OF WORK

Under the myth of meritocracy, worker wages are supposedly determined by unseen free market forces worldwide, beyond any human's control, based on immutable laws of supply and demand. Balderdash. If that were the case, jobs that fewer people want to perform—like picking vegetables or cleaning bathrooms—would pay more than jobs that everyone would love, like rock star or restaurant critic. In truth, both wages and prices are arbitrary, set by people in power, usually for their own benefit. A New York street food pretzel can be two dollars on one corner and four dollars a few blocks away, just as the same handbag can differ in price by tens of thousands of dollars depending on which designer label is slapped on it. Wages are similarly set in a nonsensical manner.

In her column "Do we value low-skilled work?," waitress/writer Brittany Bronson explained,

We're raised, in the culture of American capitalism, to believe . . . that the value of work is defined by the complexity of the task and not the execution of it, that certain types of work are not worthy of devoting a lifetime to.

The terms "unskilled" and "low-skilled labor" contradict the care and precision with which my co-workers, who have a variety of educational backgrounds and language fluencies, execute their tasks. . . . A skilled server assistant can clear a table in one trip versus two, simply with more careful placement of dishes along his forearm or between his knuckles . . .

The labels "low-skilled" or "unskilled" workers—the largest demographic being adult women and minorities—often inaccurately describe an individual's abilities, but play a powerful role in determining their opportunity. The consequences are not only severe, but incredibly disempowering: poverty-level wages, erratic schedules, the absence of retirement planning, health benefits, paid sick or family leave, and the constant threat of being replaced.[320]

Companies will go to extraordinary lengths to avoid paying a living wage to their workers. Over the last 20 years every major US airline has been through bankruptcy once or more, mostly to avoid paying out on labor contracts to which they previously agreed. Under federal bankruptcy laws (largely written by credit card companies and bankers), workers who are owed money often rank at the lowest priority for being repaid.[321]

Ignoring that they use government bankruptcy laws to shield themselves, wealthy businesses then turn around and try to make the claim that government setting wage floors is an un-American, almost-communist, intrusion into the free market. When the New York City Council tried to set living-wage standards for a development project that received hefty government subsidies, then-Mayor Michael Bloomberg compared that effort to Soviet-style communism, even though this same mayor wanted to micromanage the portion size of sodas sold by even the smallest businesses. When such philosophical arguments against wage hikes fail, opponents cherry-pick data to misleadingly claim that wage hikes significantly reduce employment and raise prices.

Just as the Right absurdly claims that safety net programs harm the people who participate in them, they stick to the time-worn and thoroughly discredited claims that they oppose minimum wage hikes because they harm the workers who receive them. Business groups and their cronies continue to make the claim—with straight faces— that workers are just too unsophisticated to know wage hikes will hurt them. Oh please. A billboard paid for by the fast food industry in Times Square actually stated that fast food employees would work less hard if they were paid higher wages. Give me a break. Billionaire tech investor Nick Hanauer, who supports wage hikes, has helpfully explained that many of his fellow mega-wealthy business owners fabricate reasons for their opposition to minimum wage hikes to cover up their prime motivation: greed. Here's a thought: What if poor people claimed the main reason they opposed more tax cuts for the rich is because the extra money would somehow oppress the rich?

The claim that the free market will fix everything is one of the oldest chestnuts of the business community. In 1939, FDR offered a biting retort: "If millions of citizens starve, it is no answer to the starving to say that in the sweet by-and-by, business, left to itself, will give them a job. But if we do not allow a democratic Government to do the things which need to be done, and if we hand down to our children a deteriorated nation, their legacy will be not a legacy of abundance or even a legacy of poverty amidst plenty, but a legacy of poverty amidst poverty."[322]

Minimum wages are generally poverty wages. Forty-three states allow even lower wages for tipped workers—whether a waiter will be able to feed his or her family that week will depend upon a wild game of Russian roulette revolving around whether their customers were in a good mood or were feeling generous or if there were even customers in the restaurant that week.

Don't believe the hogwash that the US economy just can't afford to pay higher wages. Wall Street bonuses in 2014 —$28.5 billion—were double the combined annual pay for all 1.007 million US full-time minimum wage workers.* The Wall Street bonus pool alone was so

---

* These $28.5 billion in bonuses were an additional reward *on top of* base salaries in the securities industry, which averaged $190,970 in 2013.

large it would be far more than enough to lift the wages of all 2.9 million restaurant servers and bartenders, all 1.5 million home health and personal care aides, or all 2.2 million fast food preparation and serving workers up to $15 per hour.[323]

The CEO of McDonald's, who made nearly $14 million in 2013, can surely ensure his workers earn enough to eat. If McDonald's still claims it can't afford to pay its workers a living wage, perhaps they should trade in their golden arches for bronze ones. In 2013, fast food CEOs made 1,000 times the wages of their workers—the highest pay disparity of any industry. And then they spent millions of dollars on lobbying and media campaigns to oppose wage hikes.*

It's not just industries that are typically associated with low wages—like fast food and agriculture—that pay poverty salaries. Nearly four in 10 New York City bank tellers and their family members earn so little that they are enrolled in some form of public assistance program.[324]

Nick Hanauer has argued persuasively that those corporate leaders who oppose wage hikes are unknowingly the ones harming their own self-interests: "The fundamental law of capitalism is that when workers have more money, businesses have more customers and need more workers . . . The more money workers have to spend, the more incentive there is for entrepreneurs and investors to create new products and services that can increase our standard of living."[325]

Still, since human beings are so messy and demanding, more and more companies are replacing a multitude of jobs—from supermarket checkers to auto workers—with robots.**

Meanwhile, corporate executives never seem to make their own jobs superfluous, and they stack their executive compensation committees with people sure to give them towering raises whether they succeed or fail.

"In 1965, CEOs of America's largest corporations were paid, on average, 20 times the pay of average workers," according to Robert

---

* A few progressive leaders in the fast food industry, such as Danny Meyer, who founded the Shake Shack chain, do pay well above minimum wage because they know it's both good business to retain workers and it's the right thing to do. At the fancier restaurants he also owns, Meyer has eliminated tipping and significantly raised salaries, so that his employees are no longer subject to the daily whims of customers to pay their bills.
** Perhaps, once workforces are entirely automated, the robots will rise up and form unions. Meet new union shop steward Rosie:

Reich. Now, the ratio is over 300 to one. Companies with the highest-paid CEOs returned about 10 percent less to their shareholders than their industry peers. Larry Ellison, the CEO of Oracle, received a pay package in 2013 valued at $78.4 million, a sum so stunning that Oracle shareholders rejected it. That made no difference because Ellison controlled the board.[326]

In 2012, average compensation for a board member of an S&P 500 company was $251,000, for three to four meetings per year. CEOs help select their board members, and vice versa, so it's a pretty nifty system for everyone involved.

In 1999, Carly Fiorina was tapped to lead Hewlett-Packard, a company with $40 billion in revenue. She set her sights on becoming the biggest computer maker in the world. The board gave her a $3 million signing bonus and stock worth $65 million, and agreed to pay to ship her 52-foot yacht from the East Coast to the waters near San Francisco Bay. Under her leadership, the company shed half its market value and slashed more than 30,000 jobs amidst what rivals called "the dumbest deal of the decade." *The Washington Post* reported,

> As [the company's] fortunes sank, Fiorina's take-home pay soared. She averaged $3 million in salary and bonuses every year, not counting her tens of millions of dollars in stock options . . . HP replaced two aging planes with Gulfstream IV jets and leased a fifth plane—particularly beneficial for Fiorina, whose contract allowed her personal use of the company's air fleet. . . . [After she was fired] she drifted to earth with a golden parachute, pocketing a cash severance of $21 million plus stock and pension benefits worth about $20 million. . . . On the day of her firing, its stock surged upward 7 percent.[327]

This experience, Fiorina's one and only stint as a company CEO, led her to conclude that she has exactly what it takes to run for US Senate. After losing her Senate race by a million votes, she ran a losing campaign for president of the United States. I guess her motto—as well as Trump's—is, "If at once you don't succeed at all, try, try, and try again for jobs for which you are spectacularly unqualified."

Can someone please explain to me how some people make massive amounts of money running businesses that consistently lose money? Oh, you can't? I thought so.

One key reason for soaring CEO compensation is that our tax policies encourage it. But another reason is that the values of our corporate leaders have changed. Robert Reich explained,

> A half-century ago, CEOs typically managed companies for the benefit of all their stakeholders—not just shareholders, but also their employees, communities, and the nation as a whole. . . . For thirty years after World War II, as American corporations prospered, so did the American middle class. Wages rose and benefits increased. American companies and American citizens achieved a virtuous cycle of higher profits accompanied by more and better jobs.
>
> But starting in the late 1970s, a new vision of the corporation and the role of CEOs emerged—prodded by corporate "raiders," hostile takeovers, junk bonds, and leveraged buyouts. . . . CEOs began to view their primary role as driving up share prices. To do this, they had to cut costs—especially payrolls.
>
> Corporate statesmen were replaced by something more like corporate butchers, with their nearly exclusive focus being to "cut out the fat" and "cut to the bone." Ordinary workers lost jobs and wages, and many communities were abandoned. Almost all the gains from growth went to the top.[328]

Our national values are so distorted that when Dan Price, the CEO of the Seattle credit card processing firm, Gravity Payments, announced that he would pay all his employees (including the support staff) a new minimum annual salary of $70,000, a few customers, dismayed by what they viewed as a political statement, withdrew their business. Others, anticipating a fee increase—despite repeated assurances to the contrary—also left. Two of the company's most trusted employees quit, in part because they thought it was unfair to double the pay of some new hires while the longest-serving staff members got small or no raises. Other corporate leaders in Seattle were also upset that the company's action made them look stingy in front of their own employees.[329] Our national values are upside down.

AH, THE JOYS OF INEQUALITY

There's now a cottage industry in academia defending inequality, at least some forms of it, as a net good. Economist Tyler Cowen has written,

> Income inequality and economic immobility are often lumped together, but they shouldn't be. Consider the two concepts positively: Income equality is about bridging the gap between the rich and the poor, while economic mobility is about elevating the poor as rapidly as possible. Finding ways to increase economic mobility should be our greater concern. . . . Still, we should be cautious in using "inequality" as an automatically negative term. A lot of inequality is natural and indeed desirable, because individuals have different talents and tastes and opportunities can never be fully equalized.[330]

Ah, glorious inequality! Similarly, Nobel Prize-winning economist Angus Deaton has noted that

> [t]he tale of progress is also the tale of inequality . . . Living standards are vastly higher today than a century ago, and many people escape death in childhood and live long enough to experience prosperity. . . . [I]nequality can sometimes be helpful—showing others the way, or providing incentives for catching up—and sometimes unhelpful—when those who have escaped protect their positions by destroying the escape routes behind them. Inequality is often a *consequence* of progress. Not everybody gets rich at the same time, and not everyone gets immediate access to the latest life-saving measures, whether access to clean water, to vaccines, or to new drugs preventing heart disease. Inequalities in turn affect progress. This can be good; Indian children see what education can do and go to school too.

It can be bad if the winners try to stop others from following them, pulling up the ladders behind them.[331]

That's easy for him to say, considering that he and his family are surely those that benefit first from each new wave of health advances, though he does acknowledge the downside of inequality: "If those who get rich get favorable political treatment, or undermine the public health or public education systems, so those who do less well lose out in politics, health, or education, then those who do less well may have gained money but they are *not* better off. One cannot assess society, or justice, using living standards alone."[332] But his use of the word "if" to begin that sentence demonstrates that he doesn't seem to fully accept that the systems are rigged by the elites just about every time.

Yet another academic economist, the Canadian William Watson, doesn't worry too much about inequality:

> This preoccupation with inequality is an error and a trap. It is an error because inequality, unlike poverty, is not the problem it is so widely presumed to be. Inequality can be good, it can be bad, and it can be neither good nor bad but benign.... Evaluating the different types of inequality requires moral judgments that it would be wrong to try to finesse ...
>
> Inequality is also a trap ... because concern with it leads us to focus on the top end of the income distribution when our preoccupation should instead be the bottom, where the bulk of human misery almost certainly resides. Not everyone miserable is poor and not everyone poor is miserable. Some currently poor people are med students, law clerks, and other varieties of the future rich working through their apprenticeship. But other poor people are stuck in poverty for the duration— for their duration, which may be shorter as a result of their poverty—and miss out on many advantages the rest of us take for granted. Their relative or even absolute deprivation may not prevent them from leading good lives, nor even the good life that has preoccupied philosophers since philosophy began. But it drastically limits their opportunities and in particular their

chance to enjoy the fascinating and alluring gadgets, entertainments, and experiences, notably travel, that define modern
affluence.[333]

His quaint notion—that low-income people miss out on "fascinating
and alluring gadgets, entertainments, and experiences, notably travel,
that define modern affluence"—showcases almost laughable class
bias. Sure, low-income people miss out on some cool gadgets and fun
travel, but he seems to leave out the little tiny part about them missing
out on food, shelter, and healthcare. I do agree generally with Cowen,
Deaton, and Watson that we should be far more concerned with people
not having enough money than with people having too much, but they
significantly underestimate how inequality fuels poverty through distorted wage and tax structures mandated by the whims of the wealthy.

HEADS, IF YOU'RE WEALTHY YOU WIN—TAILS, IF YOU'RE NOT WEALTHY, YOU LOSE

Do the world's elites secretly gather in one place to precisely plan how
they will purposely screw everyone else? I don't think they do. But, as
they globetrot, they do spend most of their time with people in similar
bubbles of mega-privilege, and they share a groupthink that reinforces
their previous beliefs that they are deserving and anyone else is undeserving.

Not only do they decide what to pay themselves and their workers,
they often decide what they will pay—or, more frequently, not pay—in
taxes and other revenues that governments need to survive and thrive.
The net effect—enabling the wealthiest to essentially write our tax
codes—is the equivalent to having arsonists write our fire codes.

The tilt of the tax system away from the wealthy to the shoulders of
the middle class has been decades in the making. Family trusts that
provide tax relief used to be limited to about 90 years, but changes
implemented under President Reagan extended them in perpetuity,
and "dynasty trusts" now allow super-rich families to pass on to their
heirs money and property, mostly tax-free, for generations. President
George W. Bush's biggest tax breaks helped high-income workers

but gave even more money to people living off accumulated wealth. While the top tax rate on income from work dropped from 40 percent to 35 percent, the top rate on dividends went from 40 percent (taxed as ordinary income) to 15 percent, and the estate tax was completely eliminated. (After polling on this issue, conservatives labeled the estate tax the "death tax," which sounds far more ominous.) President Obama and Democrats in Congress have since marginally rolled back some of these cuts, but many still remain.[334]

Substantial tax cuts for the rich are sold to working-class Americans by telling them that the enormous riches bestowed on the pluto-crats will eventually "trickle down" to them. That's never been close to true, but the myth persists. Responding to statistics that proved the Big Apple in 2013 was the poverty capital of America—and had greater wealth disparities than even Mexico or Sri Lanka—then-Mayor Bloomberg opined, "If we could get every billionaire around the world to move here, it would be a godsend . . . They are the ones that pay a lot of the taxes, and we take the tax revenues from those people to help people throughout the entire rest of the spectrum."[335] But, when the total tax burdens are considered, the wealthiest New Yorkers pay proportionately less into the system than everyone else. Besides, New York's levels of both poverty and inequality dwarf the levels in other world cities such as Paris, Tokyo, London, and Berlin. Also, cities with the most poverty—Mumbai, Cairo, Mexico City—also have the most inequality of wealth; thus the claim that having a lot of wealth sloshing around reduces poverty is bunk. Plus, at the time, New York already had 53 billionaires and no, they had not magically saved New York.

As Nobel Prize-winning economist Paul Krugman wrote,

> You might think that there was a defensible economic case for the obsession with cutting taxes on the rich. That is, you might think that if you'd spent the past 20 years in a cave (or a conservative think tank). Otherwise, you'd be aware that tax-cut enthusiasts have a remarkable track record: They've been wrong about everything, year after year.
>
> Some readers may remember the forecasts of economic doom back in 1993, when Bill Clinton raised the top tax rate.

What happened instead was a sustained boom, surpassing the Reagan years by every measure.

Undaunted, the same people predicted great things as a result of George W. Bush's tax cuts. What happened instead was a sluggish recovery followed by a catastrophic economic crash.[336]

Even Ronald Reagan's archconservative budget director, David Stockman, became convinced by 2014 that the national GOP tax and spending priorities were little more than an irresponsible sop to the rich: "The Ryan Plan boils down to a fetish for cutting the top marginal income-tax rate for 'job creators'—i.e., the supser wealthy—to 25 percent and paying for it with an as-yet-undisclosed plan to broaden the tax base."[337]

In 2015, at a time when the State of New York claimed that it didn't have enough money to comply with a court decision mandating that the state fund education more equitably, the Democratic governor, the Democratic State Assembly, and the Republican State Senate all agreed to a provision in a secret budget deal that exempted very expensive boats from sales taxes.* "The so-called 'yacht credit' has not been part of the budget discussion this year, but it appeared quietly over the weekend in a revenue bill and would exempt any portion of the purchase of a boat above $230,000 from sales tax," reported *Politico New York*.[338]

In supreme actions of anti-patriotism, many US companies are now using so-called "inversions" to avoid paying even minimal US taxes. Johnson Controls, an auto parts company that had its ass saved by the federal auto industry bailout, and which has received hundreds of millions of dollars' worth of tax breaks from states like Michigan and Wisconsin, renounced its United States corporate citizenship by selling itself to Tyco International, based in Ireland, a deal that reduced its US tax bill by $150 million annually. Other major companies—including pharmaceutical giant Pfizer, the medical device maker Medtronic, and Coca-Cola's largest bottling company—have tried to head overseas, at least on paper, to avoid paying US taxes.[339] All that is despite the fact

---

* Since that time, the heads of both the Assembly and Senate were arrested and convicted on corruption charges.

that, for each dollar America's fifty biggest companies paid in federal taxes between 2008 and 2014, they received $27 back in federal loans, loan guarantees, and bailouts.[340]

Every year ultra-wealthy families find more ways to avoid paying taxes. Hedge fund magnates Daniel Loeb, Louis Bacon, and Steven Cohen have billionaire investors. Each has exploited an obscure tax loophole that saved them millions in taxes by routing money to Bermuda and back. They and others utilize a battalion of expensive lawyers, estate planners, lobbyists, and anti-tax activists who exploit and maintain the loopholes. It won't shock you to know that they also donate heavily to political campaigns.[341]

Despite all this, even people who are generally liberal, if they are in the highest classes, often oppose taking dramatic action to reduce wealth accumulation at the top. Daron Acemoglu, an economist at MIT who supports more public investment in education, infrastructure, and social services, wrote that a wealth tax—which could pay for those things—could prove "very distortionary and naturally discouraging of saving, not a good thing in the current US context."[342]

Billionaires even gain special tax breaks—supposedly designed to boost affordable housing for low-income people—for absurdly expensive luxury dwellings, as *NBC News* has reported:

> The billionaires paying more than $90 million for top apartments at the new One57 tower in New York have some very special amenities. They get more than 10,000 square feet, 75 floors above Manhattan. They get VIP concierge and doorman services, along with some of the best views in the city.
>
> But they may also get a less publicized benefit: tax breaks of more than $150,000 a year from a program aimed at low-income housing. . . .
>
> One57 may receive tax abatement under a long-existing city program designed to provide more low-income housing. . . .
>
> Take the "penthouse" on the 75th and 76th floor. The apartment, at 13,554 square feet, reportedly sold for more than $90 million to an unknown billionaire. Normally, the annual real-estate taxes on the apartment would be around $230,000

a year. With the special abatements, however, the taxes are projected to be only $20,000 a year—saving the owner $210,000
a year in real-estate taxes.[343]

America, your greatest crimes still are legal, including condoning
these practices. I've simply run out of synonyms for "appalling."

Why do we collectively let this happen as a society? Because those of
us who are not among the elites are too pissed off at each other to go
after the real villains.

The price of resentment is much too high—both for ourselves and
for the nation—but, as I explain later in the book, there are concrete,
realistic ways to reduce both resentment and inequality. In the meantime, don't take advice on either governing or toga design from Plato.

7.

The Rules
Time-Tested Secrets for
Capturing Mr. Right Wing

Play hard to get. Make them approach you. Don't put out until you get a ring. Be clear that you will only accept a relationship on *your* terms.

Those are the central premises of the 1990s blockbuster, *The Rules: Time-Tested Secrets for Capturing the Heart of Mr. Right*, by Ellen Fein and Sherrie Schneider.[344]

And that's essentially how, over decades, the mainstream Republican Party won over the American far-right wing and, until very recently, kept it in its corner. The Grand Old Party made it clear to ultra-conservatives that they would be damn lucky to be allowed into the party and would need to come to the GOP, not the other way around. The GOP would keep promising home runs but wouldn't even allow them to get to second base on the third date—or even the 300th—even if the Right kept buying really expensive dinners. In fact, the party would only accommodate ultra-conservatives when they helped the GOP win; when the Right became a liability, the party would try to hide these embarrassing extremists under a fake cloak of "compassion."

The feelings between the Republican Party and its ultra-right wing were never quite reciprocated, as E.J. Dionne, Jr. explained in *Why the Right Went Wrong*:

> Conservatives have won many of the elections since their movement began to take control of the Republican Party more than half a century ago. But these victories produced neither the lasting electoral realignment that conservative prophets kept predicting nor the broad policy changes the faithful hoped

for. For the rank-and-file right, the sense that their leaders had deceived them and that the political system had shortchanged them created a cycle of radicalization. . . . We are living with its fruits today.[345]

But other than a brief dalliance with George Wallace's Independent 1968 bid for president, in which the perceived "outsider" Wallace carried five southern states in the general election with primarily right-wing votes, uber-conservatives have remained stubbornly loyal to the GOP. Even when hardcore conservative hero Pat Buchanan ran as an Independent candidate for president in 2000, he won less than one-half of 1 percent of the popular vote (about one-sixth of the votes that left-wing Independent candidate Ralph Nader received).

The rise of the Tea Party stretched those bonds to a near-breaking point, and the attention-seeking bottomless-pit-of-a-reality-star Donald Trump and the election of 2016 may have finally shattered them, but up until those junctures, the GOP kept the Right enthralled and in line for decades. How did they do it?

WE HAVE NOTHING TO FEAR BUT EVERYTHING

Historian Richard Hofstadter, in his classic 1965 book, *The Paranoid Style in American Politics*, chronicled how hundreds of years' worth of America's hate mongering and conspiracy theories spurred reactionary forces.[346]

In colonial times, Hofstadter explained, some Americans were terrified by what they thought was a grave threat to their land by an international conspiracy led by what they called the "Bavarian Illuminati." (Don't ask.)[*]

Then, in the 19th century, many Americans were freaked out by the influx of Catholics into the country. A Protestant militant wrote, "Jesuits are prowling about all parts of the United States in every possible disguise, expressly to ascertain advantageous

---

[*] This is the symbol of the Bavarian Illuminati, an Enlightenment-era secret society founded in Europe that was opposed to "obscurantism." (See, I told you not to ask.)

situations to disseminate Popery . . . The western country swarms with them under the names of puppet show men, dancing masters, music teachers, peddlers of images and ornaments, barrel organ players, and similar practitioners."[347] I get the hatred of puppets, but not Catholics.

In the 1930s, moneyed interests opposing the New Deal learned to tap into the deep well of the nation's paranoia, and that's when, I'd argue, the seeds of the modern conservative movement were planted. The plutocrats hated FDR so much they wouldn't even allow themselves to speak his actual name, instead sputtering the phrase "that man in White House." They claimed he was a secret Jew (yes, they meant that as an insult, just as secret Muslim is meant as an insult today), and they labeled his much-despised wife Eleanor a "nigger lover."* They spread rumors that his disability was caused by syphilis, not polio.

What angered the Right most was that Roosevelt greatly expanded the role of the federal government in aiding working people and the unemployed. The minimum wage and mandated overtime pay were steps "in the direction of Communism, Bolshevism, fascism and Nazism," the National Association of Manufacturers fulminated in 1938.[348] A leader of the American Liberty League, founded by business leaders to oppose the New Deal, said, "You can't recover prosperity by seizing the accumulation of the thrifty and distributing it to the thriftless and unlucky."[349] That's eerily similar to Mitt Romney's remarks about the 47 percent.

While FDR's enormous support from the general public empowered him to push through much of his agenda, key parts of it were still blocked by the interlocking forces of a reactionary Supreme Court, big business interests, and southern segregationists. The Right mostly lost, but they developed a taste for blood.

Historian Rick Perlstein makes a persuasive case that ultra-conservatives have been both angry—and nuts—for decades:

In the early 1950s, Republicans referred to the presidencies of

---

* I debated myself over whether to include the actual word "nigger" in my book, but I decided to do so because it's important to make the historical record clear that the vilest forms of racism have long powered the American Right.

Franklin Roosevelt and Harry Truman as "20 years of treason" and accused the men who led the fight against fascism of deliberately surrendering the free world to communism. . . . Vice President Richard Nixon claimed [the Democrats had] a blueprint for "socializing America."

Thousands of delegates from 90 cities packed a National Indignation Convention in Dallas, a 1961 version of today's tea parties; a keynote said he was for "hanging" [Supreme Court Chief Justice Earl] Warren.

There were right-wingers claiming access to secret documents from the 1920s proving that the entire concept of a "civil rights movement" had been hatched in the Soviet Union.

So, crazier then, or crazier now? Actually, the similarities across decades are uncanny. When Adlai Stevenson spoke at a 1963 United Nations Day observance in Dallas, the Indignation forces thronged the hall, sweating and furious, shrieking down the speaker for the television cameras. Then, when Stevenson was walked to his limousine, a grimacing and wild-eyed lady thwacked him with a picket sign. Stevenson was baffled. "What's the matter, madam?" he asked. "What can I do for you?" The woman responded with self-righteous fury, "Well, if you don't know I can't help you."[350]

After Dwight Eisenhower left office, the Right felt unleashed, as historian Sean Wilentz has noted:

Rejecting reasoned compromise as perfidious, [the Far Right] would settle only for total victory over the foe, whose ranks ranged from bedraggled postwar communist and socialist left to the supposedly traitorous Eisenhower administration. No class or economic interpretation could explain the new Right's frenzied attacks on the Supreme Court and the United Nations, as well as the income tax and social welfare legislation. Nor could economic self-interest explain why pseudo-conservative fervor had gripped so many Americans in lower-middle-income households—voters whose material lives would not be improved, and in some respects would suffer, if right-wing extremists prevailed.[351]

In the 1963 book, *The Radical Right*, Daniel Bell warned,

> The ideology of the right wing in America threatens the politics of American civility. The radical right is only a small minority, but . . . social groups that are dispossessed invariably seek targets on whom they can vent their resentments, targets whose power can serve to explain their dispossession . . . [A] significant number of corporations have been contributing financially to the seminars of the radical-right evangelists. What is uniquely disturbing about the emergence of the radical right of the 1960s is the support it has been able to find among traditional community leaders."[352]

In 1965, Richard Hofstadter wrote that uber-conservatives felt that:

> The Goldwater movement [has shown] how much political leverage can be gotten out of the animosities and passions of a small minority . . .
>
> I call it the paranoid style simply because no other word adequately evokes the qualities of heated exaggeration, suspiciousness, and conspiratorial fantasy that I have in mind. [They are] pseudo conservatives. Although they believe themselves to be conservatives and usually employ the rhetoric of conservatism, [they] show signs of a serious and restless dissatisfaction with American life, traditions, and institutions. They have little in common with the temperate and compromising spirit of true conservatism in the classical sense of the word . . .
>
> Their political reactions express a profound if largely unconscious hatred of our society and its ways. It is the tendency of status politics to be expressed more in vindictiveness, in sour memories, in search of scapegoats, than in realistic proposals for positive action.[353]

Hofstadter also noted that ethnic and racial animosities prevented the working classes from uniting. Sound familiar? Yet this was written in 1965, not 2016.

For decades after that, the far Right continued to be hate-filled and violent. The Ku Klux Klan and neo-Nazi groups flourished. In 1994, popular right-wing radio host and convicted Watergate felon G. Gordon Liddy hosted fellow law-breaker and US Senate candidate Oliver North on his show; shortly thereafter on the same program, Liddy urged his listeners to shoot federal law enforcement agents between their eyes so they wouldn't be protected by flak jackets. Right-wingers had so demonized government that they started detesting even the types of law enforcement officers they previously lionized.[354] Through all this, conservative extremists generally voted Republican, primarily because they hated, just despised, the Democrats. Traditional Republicans continued to find it easier to foment opposition to the dreaded "other" than to conceptualize and implement a coherent governing philosophy of their own.

In the Obama era, people tended to forget just how much the GOP abhorred, loathed, hated, reviled, and detested Bill Clinton. The Right had almost as many words to describe their dislike of Bill Clinton as Inuit (Eskimos) have for snow.* It was during the Clinton years that the new Right, fueled by talk radio, extremely conservative websites, and 24-hour Fox News, started infiltrating all aspects of American pop culture. From 1995 to 2015, the proportion of Republicans who called themselves "very conservative" increased by 74 percent.[355]

The Tea Party and the Trump campaign were hardly brand-new movements, but rather the culmination of decades' worth of conservative organizing and messaging, fueled by racism, sexism, xenophobia, homophobia, and fear of modernity, with a dollop of faux anti-big business populism thrown in.**

Yes, everything old is new again. Thus, I have one bit of good news (if you can call it that) for you, America: our nutty contemporary times may not actually be any nuttier than previous nutty times. Every relationship has its ups and downs. Especially downs.

---

* Inuit have 50 words for snow, including "aqilokoq" for "softly falling snow" and "piegnartoq" for "the snow that is good for driving sled," according to the *Washington Post*.

** Sometimes business interests would even fund fake grassroots groups that would use rhetoric slamming both big business and big government, so they would seem more credible to the public, but the actual policies they pushed would always quietly advance the businesses interests that funded them. This is the ultimate political bait-and-switch.

WAS REAGAN A LIBERAL?

Ronald Reagan, journalist Jacob Weisberg wrote, "supported the biggest amnesty bill in history for illegal immigrants, advocated gun control, used Keynesian stimulus to jump-start the economy, favored personal diplomacy even with the country's sworn enemies, and instituted tax increases in six of the eight years of his presidency. The core beliefs that got Reagan elected and reelected were conservative: lower taxes, smaller government, and a stronger, more assertive military. But Reagan was also a pragmatist, willing to compromise, able to improvise in pursuit of his goals and, most of all, eager to expand his party's appeal."[356]

In a 1980 debate between presidential candidates Ronald Reagan and George Herbert Walker Bush (for you young'uns, that's W's dad), a young audience member asked, "Do you think the children of illegal aliens should be allowed to attend Texas public schools free?" Bush responded,

> I'd like to see something done about the illegal alien problem that would be so sensitive and so understanding about labor needs and human needs that that problem wouldn't come up. But today if those people are here, I would reluctantly say, I think they would get whatever it is that the society is giving to their neighbors. But the problem has to be solved. . . . Because as we have kind of made illegal some kinds of labor that I'd like to see legal, we're doing two things: we're creating a whole society of really honorable, decent, family loving people that are in violation of the law and secondly, we're exacerbating relations with Mexico. . . . If they're living here, I don't wanna see a whole thing of six- and eight-year-old kids, being made totally uneducated and made to feel they're living outside the law. . . . These are good people, strong people, part of my family is a Mexican.

And this is how "ultra-right-winger" Reagan responded:

The time has come that the United States and our neighbors, particularly our neighbor to the south, should have a better understanding and a better relationship than we've ever had. And I think that we haven't been sensitive enough to our size and our power. They have a problem of 40 to 50 percent unemployment. . . . Rather than . . . talking about putting up a fence, why don't we work out some recognition of our mutual problems, and make it possible for them to come here legally with a work permit and then while they're working and earning here, they pay taxes here and when they want to go back, they can go back, and they can cross, and open the border both ways by understanding their problems.[357]

Leading Republicans, including the sainted Ronald Reagan, were indeed far more moderate on immigration than they are today, but notice that both Bush and Reagan focused on the need for Mexican "workers." Then, as now, one of the greatest tensions in the GOP is that large corporations, including agribusinesses, which fund the party desperately want more immigrants in the US (who generally work for low wages), even as the Republican voter base mostly despises immigrants.

Still, Reagan was no liberal. When Medicare was first considered, he warned it would lead to the "destruction of freedom." Sean Wilentz has noted, "Reagan was also a denizen of the pseudo-conservative intellectual underground and advanced its hatred of the federal government as a collectivist monster. . . . Reagan built a new coalition of right-wing Protestant segregationists, urban Catholics, former southern segregationists, and Sunbelt Republican entrepreneurs who appeared to specialize in the politics of paranoia."[358]

As president, Reagan said that all peace protestors were essentially KGB dupes, crushed the air traffic controllers' union, invaded Grenada mostly for show, and presided over the start of America's deindustrialization and outsourcing of jobs. He ridiculed those who supported abortion or opposed prayer in school. Reagan's press secretary literally laughed at the growing AIDS crisis (and much of the White House press corps laughed along).[359] In order to pay for the largest peacetime military build-up in history and massive tax cuts for the mega-rich, Reagan slashed funding for vital social services, creating our modern hunger and homelessness crises from which America has yet to recover.

While Reagan occasionally moved marginally, and temporarily, toward the center when it was in his strategic interest to do so, the larger truth is that he, more than any other figure in history, gave respectability to the far-right demons still haunting America.

Sure, there was a time when conservative Republicans such as Senators Howard Baker of Tennessee and Bob Dole of Kansas were willing to come together and at least cut deals with Democrats, but those days are long gone. Now, when Republicans want to give the impression that they're "moderate" and "compassionate," they're usually faking it, mostly to win votes from more moderate suburban middle-class voters. (Yet even faking moderation, as Chris Christie tried, can mean political death within the GOP).

As then-President Bill Clinton said in 1999 about then-presidential candidate George W. Bush, days after W. chided the GOP party for some harmful budget cuts, "One reason Bush is doing so well is because he criticized one thing on the right . . . But it's a fraud because he is really for them on everything else."[360]

During the 2012 presidential election, GOP vice-presidential candidate Paul Ryan, who, consistently supported anti-hunger funding cuts, tried to showcase his compassion by stopping by a soup kitchen in Youngstown, Ohio for 15 minutes. *The Washington Post* reported, "The head of a northeast Ohio charity says that the Romney campaign last week 'ramrodded' their way into the group's Youngstown soup kitchen so that GOP vice presidential candidate Paul Ryan could get his picture taken washing dishes in the dining hall. Brian J. Antal, president of the Mahoning County St. Vincent De Paul Society, said that he was not contacted by the Romney campaign ahead of the Saturday morning visit by Ryan . . . 'We are apolitical . . .' Antal said. 'It's strictly in our bylaws not to do it. They showed up there and they did not have permission. They got one of the volunteers to open up the doors.' By the time he arrived, the food had already been served, the patrons had left, and the hall had been cleaned. I certainly wouldn't have let him wash clean pans, and then take a picture,' Antal said."[361] I wonder if

Paul Ryan goes to his mother's house to re-wash her clean laundry? Probably not, since there aren't any news cameras there.

THE DUMBING DOWN OF US POLITICS

Some blame Donald Trump for the dumbing down of modern US politics, and others trace it back to Sarah Palin, but it truly dates back to Ronald Reagan. As conservative as Herbert Hoover and Barry Goldwater were—and as criminal and dangerous as Richard Nixon was—they were at least intelligent and hard-working.

Reagan, a B-movie actor by trade, shattered the previous expectation that US presidents would be among the "best and brightest" and most industrious. He claimed, for instance, that 80 percent of pollution was caused by trees. When asked by a reporter what kind of governor he'd be, he said, "I don't know. I've never played a governor." He also famously said, "It's true hard work never killed anybody, but I figure, why take the chance?" As president, he once confused the only African American in his cabinet—Housing and Urban Development Secretary Samuel Pierce—with a mayor. Believing that his gut instincts were more important than facts—an early practitioner of what Stephen Colbert would later call "truthiness"—Reagan said, "If you're explaining, you're losing."

Way before he had Alzheimer's disease, Reagan often confused fact and fiction. He once urged British Prime Minister Margaret Thatcher to read a Tom Clancy novel, *Red Storm Rising*, to better understand the "Soviet Union's intentions and strategy."[362]

George W. Bush further lowered the bar on presidential rationality and intellect, as Paul Krugman recounted:

> When Mr. Gore tried to talk about policy differences, Mr. Bush responded not on the substance but by mocking his opponent's "fuzzy math"—a phrase gleefully picked up by his supporters. The press corps played right along with this deliberate dumbing-down: Mr. Gore was deemed to have lost debates, not because he was wrong, but because he was, reporters declared, snooty and superior, unlike the affably dishonest W. . . . Then

came 9/11, and the affable guy was repackaged as a war leader. But the repackaging was never framed in terms of substantive arguments over foreign policy. Instead, Mr. Bush and his handlers sold swagger. He was the man you could trust to keep us safe because he talked tough and dressed up as a fighter pilot. He proudly declared that he was the "decider"—and that he made his decisions based on his "gut."[363]

At the time that President George W. Bush decided to invade Iraq, he was reportedly unaware that there were two distinct primary sects of Islam—Sunni and Shia—even though the rift between the two had violently divided the region for nearly 1,400 years. After advisers spent considerable time explaining to W. that there were two different sects in Islam, Bush responded, "I thought the Iraqis were Muslims!"[364]

While the bar was already low enough for a very challenging game of limbo, John McCain lowered it further by picking Sarah Palin as his vice presidential nominee. Perhaps he did so to make Dan Quayle look good.

It was a bit rich when the GOP elites faulted Trump for not being in command of policy details. Peter Wehner, who worked in the Reagan and George H.W. Bush administrations, as well as in the White House for George W. Bush as a speechwriter, lamented that "during the course of this campaign [Trump] has repeatedly revealed his ignorance on basic matters of national interest."[365] Those Trump gaps in knowledge certainly should be shocking disqualifiers for higher public office, but a Reagan and W. aide complaining about ignorance in another leader is like a Kardashian complaining about the narcissism of Kylie Jenner.

Describing the mainstream GOP reaction to crazy statements by Trump, Senator Ted Cruz, Dr. Ben Carson, etc., Paul Krugman wrote,

How can this be happening? After all, the antiestablishment candidates now dominating the field, aside from being deeply ignorant about policy, have a habit of making false claims, then refusing to acknowledge error. Why don't Republican voters seem to care? Well, part of the answer has to be that the party taught them not to care. Bluster and belligerence as substitutes for analysis, disdain for any kind of measured response, dismissal of inconvenient facts reported by the "liberal media" didn't suddenly arrive on the Republican scene . . . On the contrary, they have long been key elements of the party brand. So how are voters supposed to know where to draw the line? . . . [George W. Bush's] subtext was that real leaders don't waste time on hard thinking, that listening to experts is a sign of weakness, that attitude is all you need. And while Mr. Bush's debacles in Iraq and New Orleans eventually ended America's faith in his personal gut, the elevation of attitude over analysis only tightened its grip on his party . . .[366]

DIRTY TRICKSTERS

Dirty tricks have been a staple of US politics since John Adams's acolytes called Vice President Jefferson "a mean-spirited, low-livered fellow, the son of a half-breed Indian squaw, sired by a Virginia mulatto father," and Jefferson's camp said Adams had a "hideous hermaphroditical character, which has neither the force and firmness of a man, nor the gentleness and sensibility of a woman."[367]

The use of the mass media for attack politics was pioneered by Republican operatives—backed by big money, including that of the Hollywood studios—in the 1934 campaign to defeat left-wing Democrat Upton Sinclair in the race for California governor. Sinclair ran a mostly positive campaign focused on the need to reduce poverty, but the opposition swamped him with negative (often misleading or downright false) radio ads, direct mailings, and flyers. The studios even produced newsreels—which were then projected in movie theaters statewide as if they were actual news—featuring actors hired to pretend to be hordes of hobos supposedly crossing to California in advance of the massive new welfare opportunities that Sinclair would provide.[368]

Nixon's political operatives faked letters from political opponents with damaging language, and then leaked them to a gullible media. In the 1988 campaign for president, George H.W. Bush's political henchman Lee Atwater not only masterminded the race-based use of the Willie Horton issue, but he also fabricated, out of whole cloth, a rumor that Governor Michael Dukakis's wife, Kitty, had once burned a flag.[369]

Sometimes, Republicans turn on each other in the vilest ways: before the 2000 South Carolina primary, George W. Bush's accomplices spread false claims that John McCain was mentally ill, the father of a nonwhite child, and a traitor to his country.[370] The Democrats haven't always been altar boys, but when it comes to sleaze, they are still Little Leaguers compared to the GOP Yankees.

Another way the Republicans (legally) cheat is when Republican-controlled state legislatures rewrite Congressional district lines in ways that lump all the Democratic voters into just a few districts, also called gerrymandering, thereby minimizing the Congressional seats they win. In 2012, Obama won five million more popular votes than Romney, but, because the Congressional district lines were so skewed, it was the first time since 1960 that the winner of the election did not win the popular vote in a majority of Congressional districts.[371] Even though Democratic House candidates won about 1.4 million more votes overall than Republican candidates, gerrymandered lines ensured that Republicans won 31 more seats than the Democrats.[372] Sure, when the Democrats are in charge, they also write slanted district lines, but modern Republicans have taken this, like much else, to new extremes.

WINNING ISN'T EVERYTHING—IT'S THE ONLY THING

The Right has placed a far higher priority on gaining power than in helping to effectively govern the nation. That may sound harsh and partisan, but it's demonstrably true. By the time of the Gingrich revolution in the mid-1990s, when the GOP decided it was far better to scorch the Earth than live on it with Democrats, even former dealmakers such as Senator Bob Dole turned into ardent obstructionists. Dole had previously cosponsored a bill to create a program of civilian national service, but when President Clinton proposed a similar bill (which created the AmeriCorps national service program), Dole, hungry for the presidency, filibustered against it. Sort of like your boyfriend/girlfriend, in a fight, blasting you for doing something that they themselves did yesterday.

In 1983, Bill Kristol, a top conservative strategist, wrote a lengthy memo to GOP leaders urging the defeat of President Bill Clinton's proposed healthcare plan because—get this—if it became law, it would actually *work* and help people, and as a result people would vote for Democrats in the future:

> Health care will prove to be an enormously healthy project for Clinton. . . . It will relegitimize middle-class dependence for "security" on government spending and regulation. It will revive the reputation of the party that spends and regulates, the Democrats, as the generous protector of middle-class interests. And it will at the same time strike a punishing blow against Republican claims to defend the middle class by restraining government.[373]

Gee, it would be horrible if people benefited from a government program, then thought more highly of the government because of that. It would be positively awful for the nation.

Still don't believe me that the modern Republican Party puts its own power first? In 2010, then-Senate Minority Leader Mitch McConnell (R-KY) said, "The single most important thing we want to achieve is for President Obama to be a one-term president." Couldn't he have least pretended the single top thing he want to do was eliminate the deficit or defeat ISIS—and that burying Obama politically would be, let's say, priority two or three?

They will twist any issue and distort any reality to win. Sometimes they contort their ideology to win, but other times, they convince themselves that contradictory ideals are absolutely consistent. Sometimes they even believe this stuff.

CONSTITUTIONALLY INCAPABLE OF CORRECTLY READING THE CONSTITUTION

Conservatives read the Constitution as selectively as they read the Bible, ignoring the parts of each that contradict their preconceived notions. You'd never know from them that the Constitution doesn't mention filibusters, for instance. When it was convenient, they ignored the clause that said the president "shall" nominate a Supreme Court justice (and there is no exception for election years). They read half, and only half, of the Second Amendment—the part about the right to bear arms—but completely ignore the first part of that sentence about how arms are needed for a "well-regulated militia" (i.e., government troops).

I once met with a top aide to then-House Majority Leader Eric Cantor who ostentatiously carried a pamphlet-sized copy of the Constitution with her. Twice in the meeting she implied that the existence of federal nutrition assistance programs, which have been in existence, in some form, since the 1930s, violated the US Constitution. After the second time, I asked her directly if she thought those programs were unconstitutional. She responded by saying that the Republican leadership only wanted to specifically support programs "authorized by the Constitution." I then responded, "Well, the Constitution doesn't specifically authorize the Air Force. Do you think the Air Force is constitutional?" Soon after, Cantor lost to someone even further to the right (gasp at the thought).

Not only does the Constitution fail to include the word "God" so much as once, it explicitly prohibits the creation of an official state religion and specifically bans any religious tests for office. The text is crystal clear that no one religion or no one set of religious beliefs should ever rule the nation. Case closed, right? Hardly. In 2012, then-House Majority Whip Tom DeLay (R-TX) told evangelical Christians that he pursued Bill Clinton's impeachment in part because Clinton violated the Bible by holding "the wrong worldview."[374] Top GOP leaders keep claiming the US is a "Christian nation," but, on occasion, they throw a sop to us Jews by lamely calling it a "Judeo-Christian nation." Screw the Muslims, Hindus, etc., and doubly screw the atheists!*

---

* The stigma against atheism in American politics is still so great that even an official of the Democratic National Committee suggested that it could harm Bernie Sanders's campaign if Sanders was tagged (falsely) as an atheist.

THREE OTHER TIME-HONORED CONSERVATIVE BAITS

Beyond race-baiting and Bible-thumping, the top three GOP storylines that keep their base excited are a) only they can keep the nation safe; b) tax cuts for the wealthy aid the middle class; and c) the Dems want to take away your guns.

Let's start with the safety bit. Did George W. Bush purposely cause— or fake—the terrorist attacks on 9/11? No, he did not. Not only are there countless witnesses and massive video and forensic evidence proving otherwise, I saw the Twin Towers burn and then fall with my own eyes, out of my bedroom window in Brooklyn. Anyone on the Left who believes that W. planned or fabricated 9/11 is a nut. Crazy. Loco. Wackadoodle.

But 9/11 *did* happen when George W. Bush was president, and there is plenty of hard evidence he and his national security team negligently overlooked multiple warnings (such as subtle little signs like a memo with the title "Bin Laden Determined to Strike in US" . . . Oh, *that* memo). It's now obvious that the invasion of Iraq made America and the world *less* safe. But rather than run away from this ineptitude, the Republicans consistently found ways to *own* the security issue, even having campaign surrogates of draft-dodger George W. Bush attacking war hero Kerry for *his* battle record.

There are only two consistent strands in all Republican defense and war policies: a) pretend to be stronger than the other side to win votes and b) shower defense contractors (who just happen to be huge donors) with ever more riches, whether their defense systems are needed or not.

In 2014, former Vice President Dick Cheney* said in a speech that the most important spending priority should be the military, "not food stamps, not highways or anything else."[375] Uh huh. You'd think from his statement that the Pentagon was starved for cash and the SNAP and highway maintenance programs were just rolling in dough. The chart below shows how much money each of the three actually got.

I bet you are not shocked that Cheney's implication was untruthful. The GOP has adopted the basic concept of the Big Lie, by which they attempt to turn an untruth into a truth by saying it loudly, frequently, and adamantly.

---

* Cheney's weapon of choice: Death Star.

Speaking of untruths, let's examine their repeated claims that tax cuts for the richest Americans reduce the deficit and aid the middle class. They don't. Next.

How about the promise by key GOP leaders that we can get a better country by eliminating the IRS? That's like promising you can lose weight by getting rid of your scale. Next.

Now let's talk about guns. Please don't shoot me for doing so. Pro-gun mania has gripped the nation for decades. After JFK was assassinated, a bill to tighten the sale of firearms through the mail was considered but opposition from gun owners was fierce. Three men drove 2,500 miles from Arizona to the nation's capital to whip up a fervor against it, saying that any curtailment of gun sales constituted

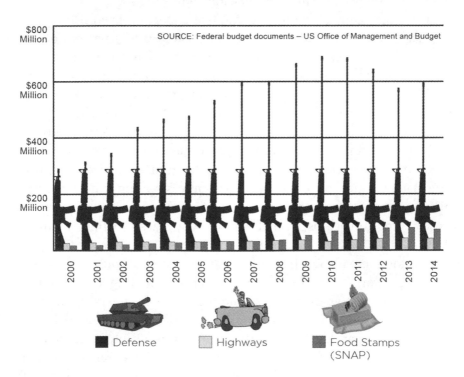

**GUNS vs. HIGHWAYS vs. BUTTER:
FEDERAL SPENDING ON DEFENSE, HIGHWAYS, AND SNAP**

SOURCE: Federal budget documents – US Office of Management and Budget

(Source: Federal budget documents, U.S. Office of Management and Budget)

"further attempts by a subversive power to make us part of one world socialist government."[376]

Between 2001 and 2013, guns killed more Americans in 12 years than AIDS, war, and illegal drug overdoses combined. By the fall of 2015, as the *Washington Post* reported, 13 babies had accidentally killed themselves that year with guns. "Roughly once a week this year, on average, a small child has found a gun, pointed it at himself or someone else, and pulled the trigger. In thirteen of the forty-three total incidents, a child's self-inflicted injuries were fatal. In two other cases, another person died after being shot by a toddler: a father in Alabama, and a one-year-old in Ohio. In one instance, a three-year-old managed to wound both of his parents with a single gunshot at an Albuquerque motel."[377] And yet, states only *loosened* rules on gun ownership. How scared are elected officials of the NRA? Very scared. More scared than they are of diaper-wearing shooters, apparently.

The NRA claimed five million members in 2015. Even if that were an exaggeration, it would still equal only about 6 to 7 percent of gun owners in America, and less than 2 percent of the population as a whole. Polls consistently show that most gun owners are far more supportive of common-sense gun safety standards and crime prevention measures than is the NRA. Even a third of NRA members support banning assault-style weapons (like those used in the San Bernardino and Orlando shootings) and high-capacity ammunition magazines.[378]

So, how is it that the NRA has exerted almost total control over the national gun policy agenda, not only stopping any legislation they oppose, but even preventing the government from so much as researching gun deaths, no matter how many mass shootings victimize the country? How do they keep the majority of members of Congress (including some liberals from rural states, such as Bernie Sanders) and state legislators under their mesmerizing spell, getting leaders to veto even the mildest attempt to regulate the use and ownership of guns, which have killed more than 400,000 Americans since 2001? Part of the reason is that the NRA and their supporters simply intimidate the nation: they often give the impression that, if the federal government passes even marginal restrictions on guns, they would literally start a civil war. Trump echoed that threat, implying that his gun-toting supporters should assassinate Hillary Clinton. After the *New York Times* front page editorial calling for sensible gun safety measures, the far right website *RedState* posted a photo of that editorial with seven bullet holes in it, a none-too-subtle message.[379]

Another reason for the NRA's success is that there is a small kernel of truth to the NRA argument that guns are not the sole reason for violence in America; many Canadians, for instance, do own guns and they *don't* all kill each other.* It is true that the NRA spends lots of money on lobbying and campaigns, but so does the other side. In 2015, the NRA spent $32.5 million, but Americans for Gun Safety, backed by billionaire Michael Bloomberg, spent $36 million. The biggest reason they wield such power is that NRA members vote—boy, *do* they. They vote in every single election and make the gun issue the top issue on which they vote. They also are more likely to contact their elected officials than are the public as a whole.[380] As much as the Left doesn't want to admit it, the success of the NRA is actually an example of representative democracy as it was designed to work. If you agree with me that some common-sense gun protections are in order—even if they save only a handful of lives—then I hope you will accept the reality that the only way to make that happen is to convince average American voters who agree with us to actually base their votes on that issue.

THE CRACK-UP

There's always been good money to be made by whipping up the far Right into a foaming, angry, frenzied mob.

Richard Hofstadter noted as early as 1965 that "[w]ealthy reactionaries try to use pseudo-conservative organizers, spokesmen, and groups to promulgate notions of public policy, and that some organizers of pseudo-conservative and 'patriotic' groups often find this work a means of making a living—thus turning a tendency toward paranoia into a vocation asset, probably one of the most perverse forms of occupational therapy known to man."[381]

---

* I said "small kernel" of truth, and I meant a pretty small one. Canada aside, countries with more guns generally have more guns deaths and countries with fewer guns generally have fewer gun deaths.

More recently, the presidential campaigns of Michele Bachmann and Dr. Ben Carson were at least as much fundraising machines as they were serious quests for the presidency. Some on the Right have started to catch on to these scams, which may be another reason they have grown tired of the Republican Party.

The failure of the Right to actually deliver on most of their promises (other than to protect guns, which they have done spectacularly) has caught up with them, as noted by E.J. Dionne, Jr.:

> The history of contemporary American conservatism is a story of disappointment and betrayal. For half a century, conservative politicians have made promises to their supporters that they could not keep. They offered stirring oratory that was not commensurate to what was possible. They described a small government utopia that was impractical and politically unsustainable because it required wrenching changes to the government that most American didn't want. They denounced decades of change, pledging what amounted to a return of the government and the economy of the 1890s, the cultural norms of the 1950s, and, in more recent times, the ethnic makeup of the country in the 1940s. This proved far beyond the capacity of politics. Most Americans—including a great many who were neither very liberal nor radical, and especially the young—did not want to go back.[382]

Perhaps that's why, through their support of Trump and Cruz in 2016, conservatives were finally telling the establishment GOP to take a hike. Large numbers of conservatives and Tea Party activists told pollsters they felt "betrayed" by the party.

One piece of advice from *The Rules* is "Don't Meet Him Halfway or Go Dutch on a Date." In other words, the other side is supposed to pay for everything but you are *still* not supposed to put out. The GOP has followed this advice for decades, and now their extremist right wing has a severe case of blue balls.

8.

Friends *Without* Benefits
or Why Buy the Voter When You Can Get the Milk for Free?

Is the entire American political system, awash in mountains of campaign cash, now for sale to the highest bidder?

Yes.

Ok, now that we've gotten that settled, on to the next chapter, America.

But wait. It's actually just a bit more complicated that. Sometimes the candidates with the most money lose, including Jeb Bush, who, in his 2016 race for the presidency, raised and spent more than $140 million (including $84 million on positive ads about himself, $15,800 for parking, and $4,837 for pizza),[383] spending about $1,376 per vote.* In 2012, the super PAC run by Republican strategist Karl Rove,** American Crossroads, spent $104 million, but failed to elect any of the candidates it supported and helped defeat only two of the candidates it opposed, achieving its desired result only 1.29 percent of the time.[384]

In 2010, Republican Meg Whitman, the former CEO of eBay, spent $175 million of her own money on a losing race for California governor, and Linda McMahon, a former executive at World Wrestling Entertainment, spent $49 million of her own money on a failed campaign for US Senate in Connecticut. Self-funded candidates mostly lose: in 2012, 11 out of 12 such candidates for US Senate lost and, over the previous decade, only 14.5 percent of self-funded Congressional candidates won.[385] Fortunately, America, sometimes you are a little bit discerning with your love.

---

* In contrast, when I ran—and lost—a race for New York State Senate when I was 22, I spent 24 cents per vote, and drove around the block a lot so I got all my parking for free.

** The only mystery greater than why so many French people think Jerry Lewis is a genius is why so many political journalists and insiders think Karl Rove is.

Despite that, the candidates with the most overall money usually still win. Why the paradox? Because, when candidates raise lots of campaign cash (from people and entities *other* than themselves), that is usually a sign of—as much as it is a cause of—broader political strength.

America, even though you claim to hate Congress as a whole, 95 percent of the members of the House won reelection in 2014, about in line with historic trends. Yes, most of the incumbents have massive piles of campaign dough, but most of them would likely get handily reelected without it, so people donate to them to curry favor more than they do to influence the outcome of elections.

In many state legislatures, the elected officials have such high reelection rates that they are more likely to be removed in handcuffs or a coffin than through competitive elections.* A third of state legislative candidates face no campaign opponents at all.[386]

If having the most money doesn't always obtain or preserve political power, then why is our political system so controlled by it?

Why do so many politicians claim to be the friends of their voters, but time and time again shower the *real* benefits of their power on the moneyed elites instead of their rank-and-file constituents?

Why do leaders who could win elections without lots of money spend goldmines worth of it on campaigns anyway? Why *do* they buy the voter when they can get the milk for free?

STARTING ON THIRD BASE

Congress is full of very wealthy people, who almost always get far richer while in office. In 2015, half of those entering Congress for the first time were millionaires upon arrival. According to the Center for Responsive Politics, the median net worth of a member of Congress was $1.029 million in 2013, and 271 of the 533 members were millionaires. The average lawmaker has as much money as 18 average US households.[387] The prosperity is bipartisan: six of the 10 richest members of Congress are Democrats.[388]

---

* In New York State, between 1999 and 2010, 96 percent of the legislators were reelected. The top leaders of each of the two houses of the legislature were convicted for felonies, as well as many rank-and-file members.

In 2016, while the base Congressional salary, $174,000, was more than triple the median US family income, that equaled only 2 percent of the salary of CEOs at the nation's 500 largest corporations.[389]

Members of Congress get to keep their outside investments while they serve, and oh, do they have investments! For instance in 2014, 66 members of Congress (26 Dems and 39 Republicans) owned stock in General Electric, which is both a large defense contractor and a builder of nuclear power plants; 47 (14 Ds and 33 Rs) owned stock in Chevron,* the energy giant.[390] And—you guessed it—there is no rule that requires them to recuse themselves from voting on bills that could directly impact the value of their investments.**

Wait, it gets better. Many members of Congress use their vast campaign accounts to essentially subsidize lavish lifestyles. The House Ethics Committee (a phrase that is funny in and of itself) explains,

> While House rules provide that campaign funds may be used for "bona fide campaign or political purposes" only, the rules do not include a definition of that term. The Ethics Committee has long advised that each Member has wide discretion to determine whether any particular expenditure would serve such purposes, provided that the Member does not convert campaign funds to personal or official uses. Put another way, the rule is not interpreted "to limit the use of campaign funds strictly to a Member's reelection campaign," but instead is interpreted "broadly to encompass the traditional politically related activities of Members of Congress."[391]

Here's my English language translation for that: House mem-

---

* A Congressional investment at work.

** The House Ethics Committee advises, "Since legislation considered by Congress affects such a broad spectrum of business and economic endeavors, a Member of the House may be confronted with the possibility of voting on legislation that would have an impact upon a personal economic interest. This may arise, for example, where a bill authorizes appropriations for a project for which the contractor is a corporation in which the Member is a shareholder, or where a Member holds a kind of municipal security for which a bill would provide federal guarantees. Longstanding House precedents have not found such interests to warrant abstention." *Translation: "Ethics. We don't need no stinkin' ethics."*

bers can use campaign funds to pay for lavish meals and drinks, first-class plane travel, luxury hotels, gifts, etc., just as long as they claim (and few ever check on such claims) that the spending is necessary for either their campaign or to support their official duties. The Federal Election Commission (comprised of both Democrats and Republicans) makes it clear that campaign funds can even pay for congresspeople to take spouses and children along on travel, as long as they can make some vague claim that the travel is related to official or political duties.[392] Sweet deal. Many state and local elected officials are similarly allowed to use their campaign accounts to subsidize luxurious lifestyles.

It's no wonder that so many elected officials spend so much of their time raising money—night and day, week after week, year after year—even if they never face any serious competition for their jobs.

There are other reasons that elected officials in non-competitive seats keep raising gobs of cash. They want to use the funds to scare off potential opponents, springboard themselves to higher office, or prepare for the possibility that their district lines might be changed (remember gerrymandering from the last chapter?) in case they someday *might* face a tough challenge. Some use the money to make donations to local charities, whose officials often then turn around and donate to their campaigns. Others give money to general campaign committees or other candidates in their party, thereby increasing their leadership roles and the chits owed them. Others use the funds to keep family, friends, and/or campaign workers on their payroll year-round, whether they are needed or not, just to keep them loyal.* Members of Congress often raise money for themselves at events from coast to coast, usually in treasured hot spots like New York, California, Florida, and Texas. That's why the greatest expenses are often for the money search itself, paying for the salaries and commissions of professional fundraisers, and for venues and food for events nationwide. Yes, they raise tons of money to pay for raising more tons of money.

---

* Fun fact: Members of Congress can't use campaign funds to mail holiday cards to family and friends unless these family and friends donate to, or volunteer for, their campaigns. Can you imagine getting that Christmas card: "Dear Dad: Merry, jolly Christmas! Please don't forget to send me that campaign donation.—Your loving son, Congressman Bob Spends-His-Holidays-Alone-A-Lot."

In 2014, there were 31 members of Congress (16 Ds and 15 Rs) who ran unopposed in the general election. One of those was Rep. Ted Deutch (a liberal Democrat from Florida) who only faced a token primary challenger that year, winning 92 percent of the vote in the primary. Robert Aderholt (a conservative Republican from Alabama) was entirely unopposed in both the primary and the general election. Yet in the two-year period leading up to the 2014 election, Deutch raised $1.05 million and spent $1.01 million, and had $530,000 left over by the time of election (because virtually all members of Congress have significant cash in their campaign accounts even after election years). Aderholt raised $1.175 million, spent $910,000, and had $419,000 left over at the end of the cycle.[393]

Deutch's money came largely from a mix of business interests, labor unions, employees of the Disney Company, and supporters of Israel; Aderholt raised much of his money from agricultural interests, lawyers, and employees of the Boeing Company.[394]

And how did these unopposed candidates manage, over two years, to spend nearly two million dollars between them? The Deutch campaign committee gave over $300,000 to the Democratic Congressional Campaign Committee (which funds Democratic candidates for the House) and directly to other Democratic candidates. His campaign paid $225,000 to the Katz Watson Group for "fundraising consulting services," spent $975 for florists, and spent thousands for lodging in DC, Dallas, Beverly Hills, and New York. The Aderholt campaign account gave over $300,000 in "dues" to the Republican Congressional Campaign Committee (which funds GOP candidates for Congress), paid $60 grand to Hooks Solutions for "fundraising consulting fees," reimbursed his wife for more than a thousand dollars of travel expenses, and spent $258 at a gift shop in Vail, Colorado. In addition to 51 individual payments for "event food," the Aderholt account also paid for "food" or "food and beverages" an additional 141 times, meaning that the congressman used his campaign account to purchase 192 meals during one two-year period.*

---

* In just those two years, he used his campaign account for 27 meals at Bullfeathers, a delightful Washington, DC, eating and drinking establishment on Capitol Hill.

That doesn't even include when lobbyists or event hosts paid for his meals directly. Thus, it is likely that Congressman Aderholt rarely pays for his own food. Yet Congressman Aderholt voted to cut $40 billion from SNAP nutrition assistance for low-income Americans. As you may recall from earlier in this book (there *will* be a quiz), the very same Congressman Aderholt also introduced a bill to require the drug testing of SNAP recipients, saying, "This bill provides states with the ability to identify those who are gaming the system . . . The goal is not only to break welfare recipients' dependence on government programs but also on their addiction to drugs."[395]

Of course, large sums of money are indeed spent on actual campaigning. When the politicians *do* have contested races, they deem massive campaign spending to be even more vital. In 2008, in 93 percent of House of Representatives races and 94 percent of Senate races, the candidate who spent the most money ended up winning.[396] Those statistics are slightly deceptive since many of those races weren't really competitive, in part because the candidate with the most money often scares away a strong challenger.

Part of the reason campaign spending is so out of hand is what I call the "campaign-consultant-media-industrial-complex." Journalist Jacob Weisberg explained, "The presidential campaign of 2016 will most likely cost upward of $5 billion, more than 10 times the one that elected Reagan in 1980. A lot of people get rich in a $5 billion industry, and some are politicians."[397] Well-funded campaigns hire full-time campaign staff, as well as media consultants to create TV and radio ads, media buying consultants to place the ads, direct mail persuasion consultants to send direct mail intended to win votes, direct mail fundraising consultants to send a different kind of direct mail intended to raise money, individual donor consultants, Spanish-language outreach consultants, political action committee fundraising consultants, pollsters, voter targeting consultants, and turnout consultants. They often also hire "general consultants," whose job it is to coordinate all the other consultants. Many of the people in these roles are friends, former colleagues, lovers, ex-lovers, frat-mates, etc., and they often recommend each other for high-paying gigs on campaigns, in party campaign committees, in consulting firms, and (when their candidates win) in government. Many of these consultants and aides are also drinking buddies of—and/or insider sources for—the political media, who breathlessly report that campaigns will only be taken seriously if their friends, the "star" consultants or aides, are hired and if the campaigns raise boatloads of money to pay for their services and broadcast their ads. This incestuous circle goes beyond back scratching—it is back _____. (Fill in the blank with your gutter gerund of choice).

As the *Washington Post* reported about Charlie Dent, an unopposed Republican from Pennsylvania with a huge campaign war chest, "Without being able to see the specifics, David Wasserman, who handicaps House races for the Cook Political Report, said the generous support for Dent is more symbolic because he is representative of interests that reach far beyond his district. 'He doesn't need help (winning reelection), but what he needs help at is building influence as the de facto leader of the Main Street mind-set,' Wasserman said."[398] How's that for twisted Beltway logic? A congressman needs to raise lots of money from Beltway special interests—money which he doesn't even need to get reelected—just to be credible with "Main Street." That's tortured thinking, a specialty of the DC elite.

Perhaps the most insidious contribution to soaring campaign spending is the fact that most media consultants are actually paid on commission, as a percentage of all the TV and radio ads bought. In a hotly contested House race, media consultants can earn 10 to 15 percent of all ads purchased; in presidential races the commission can be as high as 6 percent of all ad spending.[399] That means that in a House race, media consultants can make hundreds of thousands of dollars; in expensive governor, US Senate, or presidential races, they can personally take in millions. They have a built-in incentive to advise the candidates not to worry about paying people to go door-to-door, or even worse (to the consultants), recruiting lots of volunteers, because either cuts down on the need for ads and thus the commissions they will pocket. Even though door-to-door operations can be more effective than blanket advertising blitzes, which often become overkill, few top-rank media consultants would ever admit that because it won't fill their pockets. They also have a built-in incentive to convince losing presidential primary candidates to stay in the contest—raising more money to buy more ads—far after the rest of the world understood they had no chance of winning.

In the middle of the 2012 campaign cycle, the *Huffington Post* calculated that the top 150 campaign consulting companies—media, fundraising, digital/social, direct mail, and others—had grossed $465.76 million, out of a total of $1.24 billion spent on campaigns. They estimated that, by the end of that campaign year, they could rake in three billion dollars.[400] Media consultants—many of whom are, first and foremost, wily and adroit salespeople for themselves—play on the insecurities of politicians by telling them that their careers will be dead—simply dead—if they don't spend all their time raising money to provide the astronomical sums of cash they need. Because politicians spend their whole lives seeking public approval—for a living!—most are insecure at heart, and when the consultants say "jump," the politicians ask "how high?" and "should I bring my trampoline?"

CALL ROOMS AND OTHER INDIGNITIES

It's illegal to make fundraising calls from federal offices, and most state and local government facilities as well, so even incumbent elected officials, including very high-ranking ones, must often leave their government offices to travel to "call rooms" to spend hours and hours of "call time" begging and cajoling donors for support. Actually, many of these rooms are little more than Dilbert-like cubicles. Here's how returning Congressman Steve Israel described the demeaning process in an illuminating and brutally honest op-ed:

> I'll be leaving Congress at the end of this term—sentimental about many things, but liberated from a fund-raising regime that's never been more dangerous to our democracy. . . . There were hours of "call time"—huddled in a cubicle, dialing donors. Sometimes double dialing and triple dialing. Whispering sweet nothings and other small talk into the phone in hopes of receiving large somethings. I'd sit next to an assistant who col-

lated "call sheets" with donor's names, contribution histories and other useful information. ("How's Sheila? Your wife. Oh, Shelly? Sorry.") . . . Since then, I've spent roughly 4,200 hours in call time, attended more than 1,600 fund-raisers just for my own campaign, and raised nearly $20 million in increments of $1,000, $2,500, and $5,000 per election cycle. And things have only become worse in the five years since the Supreme Court's Citizens United decision, which ignited an explosion of money in politics by ruling that the government may not ban political spending by corporations in elections.[401]

As blogger Georgia Logothetis reported, "Senator Al Franken explained that a candidate's time isn't spent 'kissing babies or shaking hands or having serious policy debates. It's spent on the phone, raising money.'"[402] She continued, "A consultant (who desired to remain anonymous) disclosed the maxim of modern campaigns: 'I stress they can never do enough call time. Dialing for money is going to be 80 percent of their role as a candidate.' Indeed, on many days and in the hardest fought races, 100% of a candidate's time can be devoted to call time."[403] *The Huffington Post* broke this depressing development in 2013:

A PowerPoint presentation to incoming freshmen by the Democratic Congressional Campaign Committee . . . lays out the dreary existence awaiting these new back-benchers. The daily schedule prescribed by the Democratic leadership contemplates a nine or 10-hour day while in Washington. Of that, four hours are to be spent in "call time" and another hour is blocked off for "strategic outreach," which includes fundraisers and press work. An hour is walled off to "recharge," and three to four hours are designated for the actual work of being a member of Congress—hearings, votes, and meetings with constituents. If the constituents are donors, all the better. The presentation assured members that their fundraising would be closely monitored.[404]

It's fairly amazing that a major political party would be so seemingly unembarrassed by this and so matter-of-fact that they would actually put it in writing.

Fundraising requirements turn all politicians, no matter how esteemed their offices, into pathetic supplicants. In 2014, I received a fundraising e-mail from then-US Senator Kay Hagan with the subject line, "Joel, I'm begging."

All campaigning and governing is now indistinguishable from fundraising. The vast majority of e-mails and letters that I now receive from elected officials are either thinly veiled fundraising pitches or overt ones.

For all the media handwringing over campaigns promoting fluff instead of substance, the media spends far more time reporting on how much money candidates do or do not raise than they do on their records or their policy positions. It's like having a lover who is indignant that you support ending government funding for PBS, but all they want to actually watch is celebrity cooking shows.

YOU GET WHAT YOU PAY FOR

America, if you were ever able to put Washington on trial for the crime of placing the interest of donors above that of the people, then federal agriculture subsidies, which mostly go to huge agribusinesses and are widely reviled, would be "Exhibit A." The right-wing Heritage Foundation has slammed them as "corporate welfare" and the Libertarian Cato Institute wrote that "farm subsidies make no sense."[405] In general, I agree with them, making this just about the only issue on which I and other progressives agree with the far right.*

Six liberal-to-conservative Washington think tanks that prepared major deficit-reduction plans with grants from the Peter G. Peterson Foundation, the organization founded by a centrist budget hawk, all proposed abolishing or greatly reducing these payments.[406]

The agricultural subsidies status quo is opposed by the Left, the

---

* I do support some aid to small farmers to promote conservation practices and growing fruits and vegetables. What I oppose is the status quo of massive amounts of taxpayer dollars going to gigantic agricultural concerns to support growing grains, cotton, and sugar-producing plants— or to wealthy landowners who've never even visited their properties.

Right, and the Center—a truly rare point of ideological agreement—but the last time Congress considered a Farm Bill, in 2013, it made only cosmetic changes in the subsidies. *USA Today* editorialized, "The House bill retains lavish subsidies for an agriculture sector that is doing much better than many other parts of the economy—so lavish that they make a mockery of House Republicans' attempts at cost cutting. The measure would cost roughly $200 billion over the next decade. That's nearly 10 times the much-maligned bank bailout, which is now expected to cost $21 billion."[407] The vast majority of newspaper editorial boards nationwide—across the ideological spectrum—also condemned continued corporate agriculture subsidies, pointing out that they both help explode the deficit and promote obesity by making sugar cheaper than produce.

"It's hard to understand how anyone in the House who calls himself a conservative could support this, but many did," said Chris Chocola, president of archconservative Club for Growth, which opposed the bill and lobbied against it. "With the federal debt and deficit we have, to be subsidizing millionaire farmers makes absolutely no sense," he said.[408] Again, I shockingly agree with the Far Right on this issue.

So how is it that a corporate welfare regime condemned by the Left, the Right, and the Center—and the vast majority of newspapers nationwide—continues on, year after year, virtually unscathed?*

If you guessed the answer was lobbying—and the accompanying giant piles or cash and favors—you'd be a winner.**

Agribusinesses donated a total of $505 million ($169 million to Democrats and $333 million to Republicans) to federal campaigns from 1990 to 2016, according to the Center for Responsive Politics, while, in 2015 alone, 1,033 lobbyists spent $131 million lobbying Congress on behalf of 435 agribusiness clients. In contrast, anti-hunger advocates spent a pittance on campaign donations

---

* Rep. Paul Ryan—then Budget Committee Chair—voted for the bill, under pressure from then-Speaker John Boehner, even though Ryan said he opposed it. Wha?

** You can pick as your prize (from left to right) either a very angry horse, a penguin in a Rastafarian hat, or a befuddled stuffed dog.

and lobbying to oppose the accompanying Farm Bill SNAP cuts. So if you are surprised that the Farm Bill which eventually passed favored corporate agribusinesses over hungry Americans, I have a bridge to sell you or at least a bridge on which Chris Christie can block traffic so you can take the day off.

Senator Kirsten Gillibrand (D-NY) proposed an amendment to the Farm Bill that would have avoided the SNAP cuts by instead cutting corporate welfare to crop insurance companies, a number of which are foreign-owned. Under normal circumstances, a vote to fund food for hungry Americans—instead of corporate welfare for foreign companies—should have passed the Senate easily. Yet this common sense amendment was defeated by a vote of 70 to 26. Not a single Republican voted "yes," and half of Senate Democrats, including liberal stalwarts such as Tom Harkin, Barbara Mikulski, and Al Franken, voted "no." The dominance of big money in politics and the undue deference to Tea Party demands doomed the amendment.

But even the minor cuts in farm subsidies were too much for some. US Senator Steve Daines (R-MT), who has received over half a million dollars in campaign donations from agribusiness, delivered a speech on the Senate floor in which he indicated that, after a lengthy business career, he was elected to the Senate to "get Washington, DC's reckless spending and record debt under control," and that the first bill he introduced was to mandate a balanced budget. Then he segued to complain about cuts in agribusiness funding: "The crop insurance program was gutted as a way to make this deal work. Where was the voice of Montana? Where was the voice of rural America as this backroom deal was cut?"[409] Oh gag.

Agribusiness donations and lobbying spending is only the tip of the iceberg. In 2015, Congressional lobbyists spent $525 million on behalf of miscellaneous business interests, $509 million lobbying for the healthcare industry, $487 million representing finance, insurance, and real estate interests, $382 million on behalf of the communication and electronics industries, and $325 million for energy and natural resources companies.[410]

As for campaign contributions, between 1990 and 2016, donations to federal campaigns were gobsmackingly enormous: $2.3 billion

($1.278 billion to Republicans, $970 million to Democrats) from the finance and real estate sectors, $607 million ($319 million to Rs, $283 million to Ds) from the securities and investment industry, and $350 million ($213 million to Rs, $133 million to Ds) from insurance interests.[411] Are you seeing any patterns yet? This vast spending was surely an investment for these industries, which received far more back in tax breaks and corporate welfare than they ever spent on donations and lobbying. Politics, like any relationship, is really all about give and take—but what the donors give is dwarfed by what they take.

In a tweet, I once accidentally spelled "U$ Capitol" with a dollar sign, and then realized that it was totally appropriate, even if subconscious.

Remember that old Saturday morning cartoon about how a bill becomes a law ("I'm just a bill, here on Capitol Hill . . .")? As my two charts on the following pages prove, that civics book version of good government is sadly outdated.

In state legislatures, city councils, and county legislatures across the country, big money also sloshes around indiscriminately and bills become laws in similar, undemocratic ways.

At every level, power and money seem interchangeable. When two campaigns spent massive amounts of cash to flood my mailbox to win a State Assembly seat that officially paid $79,500 per year, the cynic/realist in me thought, "Hmmm."

GOVERNMENTS FOR RENT

While a top reason wealthy voters support campaigns is to obtain policy outcomes that benefit them, sometimes the top motivation for big donors is to simply flatter themselves with the notion that they are truly Big Shots. How else can you explain how two gay businessman, who were high-profile supporters of marriage equality and owned a hotel that catered mostly to the gay community, hosted an event at their home for virulently anti-gay presidential candidate Ted Cruz?[412] People will do anything to feel like they are movers and shakers—and to be perceived as such.

But most give the big bucks because they want a tangible payback. Former Louisiana senator John Breaux once said, "My vote can't be

HOW A BILL IS <u>SUPPOSED</u> TO BECOME A LAW

A bill is introduced in either Chamber of Congress
(House of Representatives or Senate)

Committee
★ Debate
  • Amend
★ Vote
  • Table
  • Defeat
  • Pass

Floor Action by Chamber
★ Most bills require a simple majority vote

The bill moves to the other chamber

Committee
★ Debate
  • Amend
★ Vote
  • Table
  • Defeat
  • Pass

Floor Action by Chamber

Pass WITH amendment

Pass WITHOUT amendment

Conference Committee
★ Members of the House and Senate work out differences between versions

President

Bill fails to become law
★ When the president vetoes it and Congress does not override the veto
★ When left unsigned for 10 days and Congress is adjourned (pocket veto)

Bill becomes law
★ When the President signs it
★ When left unsigned for 10 days while Congress is in session

HOW A BILL **REALLY** BECOMES A LAW

Special interest lobbyist drafts text of a bill, delivers it to a friendly Member of Congress to whom he donates, who then introduces the bill, word-for-word

A special interest lobbyist takes the friendly committee members on a duck-hunting trip and tries not to shoot one of them by accident (see Cheney, Dick)

Before the committee votes on the bill, lobbyists make especially large campaign donations to each of the committee members

A special interest lobbyist writes floor speeches for the members to whom they've made more big donations, and the members read those speeches, word-for-word, on the floor of the chamber

The extra-powerful Congressional conference committee members can be especially helpful, so lobbyists hire their spouses or offer high-paying summer jobs to their kids

Special interest lobbyists spend millions of dollars to produce fake grassroots support – so-called "astroturf" – generating fake letters and calls of support to Congress before the floor vote

A special interest lobbyist makes such a massive donation to the President's re-election committee that he gets invited to sleep in the Lincoln Bedroom at the White House. Of course, the lobbyist never speaks to the President about business while there (wink, wink)

President

Bill fails to become law

A special interest lobbyist who fails to push a bill into law convinces the special interests paying him exorbitant sums to raise his salary even more, so he will have even more clout the next time

Bill becomes law

At the signing ceremony, the President and Members of Congress speechify about how the passage of the bill is a triumph of democracy, embodying the "People's Will" bought, but it can be rented." Lots of his colleagues in politics continue to make boatloads of money off such rent payments, and, the vast majority of times, it results in policies that favor the wealthy at the expense of everyone else, even if it requires lawmakers to do backflips to reverse their previous stances. America, your so-called friends are giving you *no* benefits.

Right-wing legislators claim over and over again that the more local—and closer to the people—that government is, the better. But Republicans in state legislatures entirely ignore such federalism when localities pass laws banning fracking or raising the local minimum wage, and then moneyed interests who would be harmed by such moves get the state legislatures to overturn the will of the localities.

State lawmakers in Alabama, Idaho, Illinois, Minnesota, Montana, Pennsylvania, and Washington introduced legislation in 2016 to curb or outlaw local minimum wage increases. In Indiana, Kansas, and New Mexico, state legislators tried overruling local fair-scheduling laws, which require employers to give reasonable notice of workers' hours.[413] In Alabama, the governor signed a bill to nullify the Birmingham City Council's vote for a citywide minimum wage of $10.10 an hour. Birmingham City Council President Johnathan Austin responded, "The very people who have refused to expand Medicaid in the state to help the most vulnerable amongst us receive critical medical care are once again keeping their boots on the necks of people in desperate need of financial relief. People cannot pull themselves up by their bootstraps if they can't afford to buy boots."[414]

The cable TV industry relies heavily on government-approved monopolies, so it spends an especially large amount of money and effort on influencing government, as Robert Reich explained:

> Comcast ranked thirteenth of all corporations and organiza-
> tions reporting lobbying expenditures and 28th in campaign
> donations, and also made Michael Powell (former Chair of the
> Federal Communications Commission) head of the industry's
> lobbying group. The National Cable and Telecommunications
> Association ranked twelfth in lobbyist spending in 2014. Com-
> cast is also one of Washington's biggest revolving doors. Of its
> 126 lobbyists in 2014, 104 had worked in government before

joining Comcast. Former FCC member Meredith Attwell Baker, for example, went to work for Comcast four months after voting to approve Comcast's bid for NBCUniversal in 2014.[415]

It's key to again note, America, that such corruption is legal. That's because the people who engage in such practices pay the politicians to pass laws to ensure that they *stay* legal.

There are now so many revolving doors in DC that the average power brokers spin their heads more than that demon-plagued kid in *The Exorcist*.

One time I was on an Amtrak train leaving Washington, DC, and some loudmouth near me, obviously a lobbyist, bragged that the only people who stay working for government instead of going into lobbying are those that are too lazy to find lobbying clients. He repeatedly dropped the name of a senator he used to work for, but the idea that someone would voluntarily and/or altruistically devote their life to public service was a truly foreign concept to him. Unfortunately, that mindset is all-too-typical in modern politics, yet that wasn't always the case, as lobbying was essentially illegal in much of the country for much of our history. In some states, such as Georgia, lobbying was a crime. And even where lobbying was not outlawed, courts often refused to enforce contracts for lobbying on the ground that such conduct was contrary to public interest.[416]

The notion that we should disallow any practice that places a private good over a public good seems almost quaint today. One politician I worked for asked for my advice on how he should vote on a bill that pitted one group of campaign donors against another group of campaign donors. When I responded, "Do what you think is best for the American people," he just laughed.

In 2015, in what the *Miami Herald* called a rare show of unity, all but one of the US House members from Florida (Republicans and Democrats alike), including then-Democratic National Committee Chair Debbie Wasserman Schultz, fought federal regulations on the nefarious payday loan industry. It's probably only a coincidence that they received significant funding from that industry, including $31,250 received by Wasserman Schultz over the previous two years.[417]

A favorite goal of business interests is to get Congress to shield them from any legal liability, no matter how much they screw up. Vaccine manufacturers paid Congress to protect them from being sued, even if their vaccines make people sick.[418] Nuclear power plant builders also convinced Congress to give them total immunity, even if one of their plants melts down and wipes an entire city off the map.

The pharmaceutical industry used its lobbying might—spending $272,000 in campaign donations per member of Congress in 2014, paying for more lobbyists than there were Congressional members—to prevent the government from bargaining for drug prices in Medicare. That result equals a $50 billion annual gift to drug companies.[419]

It is no shock that the top goal of ultra-wealthy campaign donors is to pay less in taxes. "There's this notion that the wealthy use their money to buy politicians; more accurately, it's that they can buy policy, and specifically, tax policy," said Jared Bernstein, who served as chief economic adviser to Vice President Joe Biden. "That's why these egregious loopholes exist, and why it's so hard to close them."[420]

EVERYTHING GETS WORSE WITH KOCH

In the 2016 campaign, just 158 families, along with companies they own or control, contributed $176 million in the first phase of the campaign, about half of all early campaign spending combined.[421]

At the top of this heap is the Koch family. Family patriarch Fred C. Koch, the father of billionaires Charles G. and David H. Koch, helped construct a major oil refinery in Nazi Germany that was personally approved by Adolf Hitler. Fred also financed the extreme right-wing John Birch Society, even though the founder of the society called President Eisenhower a "communist" and the group was deemed too wacky-out-of-his-mind-conservative by even William F. Buckley.[422] The sons, who built on daddy's wealth to earn their billions, didn't fall far from the ultra-right-leaning tree. With campaign spending unencumbered after the Supreme Court's "Citizens United" ruling, the Koch brothers planned to personally spend and raise about $900 million in 2016 alone to impact the campaigns; in comparison, in the previous presidential election, the Republican National Committee and the party's two Congressional campaign committees spent a total of $657 million.[423]

The Kochs are so influential among conservative lawmakers that in 2011, then-House Speaker John Boehner visited David Koch to ask for his help in resolving a debt ceiling stalemate.[424] But now the Kochs want to tackle poverty, so they say, as *Politico* reported,

> Charles and David Koch [are] quietly investing millions of dollars in programs to win over an unlikely demographic target for their brand of small-government conservatism—poor people.
>
> The outreach includes everything from turkey giveaways, GED training, and English-language instruction for Hispanic immigrants to community holiday meals and healthy living classes for predominantly African American groups, to vocational training and couponing classes for the under-employed.
>
> The efforts include a healthy dose of proselytizing about free enterprise and how it can do more than government to lift people out of poverty.
>
> "We want people to know that they can earn their own success. They don't need the government to give it to them," [said] Koch network official Jennifer Stefano . . .
>
> "Sometimes, we have not been as good at explaining the virtues of economic freedom and individual liberty to people who are struggling," said Americans for Prosperity's president Tim Phillips. . . .
>
> In post-election strategy sessions, Charles Koch and his inner circle fixated on an exit poll finding that highlighted a so-called "empathy gap" that plagued GOP presidential nominee Mitt Romney. . . . [Koch] concluded that winning over empathy-seeking voters could help them tilt the electoral map in their favor.[425]

What is a proper reaction to the idea of bribing hungry people with turkeys to get them to vote against their own interests? "Splendid, simply splendid, Smithers."*

As is often the case, the *Onion* nailed it best: "Koch Brothers Get

---

* I actually wrote a respectful e-mail to the Koch "anti-poverty" initiative asking whether we could talk over the phone or meet in person to discuss areas of potential agreement. They never responded.

Each Other Same Election for Christmas . . .. 'After he got me Wisconsin's right-to-work bill last year, I knew I had to get him something really good this Christmas,' David added. . . . According to reports, the brothers agreed they would avoid making the same mistake next Christmas by simply giving each other a $25 million gift card that could be spent at any lobbying firm in the United States."[426]

THE POWER OF THE PURSE

The central role of money in politics is so overwhelming that it trumps the will of the people. In 2015, nearly six in 10 Americans said government should do more to reduce the gap between the rich and the poor.[427] The public clearly wants policies to reverse inequality, but the donor class wants the opposite. We know who wins. That's why at no time in modern history has our public policy-making been more detached from the public will than today. America, you know you've been sold out.

When the stakes are low, public opinion matters a bit. But when the stakes are high regarding money, the wealthy almost always win, shafting everyone else. Martin Gilens of Princeton and Benjamin I. Page of Northwestern found that, in policy-making, views of ordinary citizens mostly don't matter. They examined 1,779 policy issues and found that attitudes of the rich and of business organizations significantly impacted the final outcome—but that preferences of average citizens were almost irrelevant. "The majority does not rule. Majorities . . . actually have little influence over the policies our government adopts."[428]

NO MONEY, NO HONEY (NO BREAD, NO MEAT, NO NOTHING)

Because our entire political system is so oriented towards the money—and thus the needs and concerns—of the wealthy and the upper middle class, even liberals generally rarely think about poverty issues anymore. Journalist Thomas Edsall pointed out,

> Democrats now depend as much on affluent voters as on low-income voters, Democrats represent a majority of the

richest congressional districts, and the party's elected officials are more responsive to the policy agenda of the well-to-do than to average voters. The party and its candidates have come to rely on the elite 0.01 percent of the voting age population for a quarter of their financial backing and on large donors for another quarter. . . . The gulf between the two parties on socially fraught issues like abortion, immigration, same-sex marriage, and voting rights remains vast. On economic issues, however, the Democratic Party has inched closer to the policy positions of conservatives, stepping back from championing the needs of working men and women, of the unemployed, and of the so-called underclass.[429]

In 2016, I received a mailed questionnaire—i.e., fundraising ploy—from the national Democratic Party signed by Nancy Pelosi. Not one of the 19 issues queries on the questionnaire was about poverty, wages, hunger, or homelessness. Of course, we can totally forget about the Republicans raising these issues in any serious way.* When these concerns are literally out of mind and sight of both parties, it's easy for both to agree on cuts to housing and food for struggling families.

America, you should be far more upset that the top activity and top priority of your elected officials is raising money. Priority number two isn't even close. It is the corrosive role of money that has caused one side of our political system to be evil while the other side is soulless.

That's what happens when average voters give away our love (and votes) to our leaders, but demand little in return. We're not even getting the milk anymore. Later in the book, I'll propose a specific Constitutional Amendment to fix all this.

But, in the meantime, damn it, America, let's at least demand that our friends give us the benefits they promised in the late-night, drunken text!

---

* Bernie Sanders did talk about poverty a fair amount in his campaign, but other than calling for minimum wage hikes and new government jobs programs, he offered few specific anti-poverty proposals. While Hillary Clinton did, in the primaries, propose a fairly significant anti-poverty agenda under the rubric "Breaking Every Barrier," her campaign did little to promote that.

9.

How to Lose Friends and De-Influence People
How the Left Turns Off the Public and Turns On Itself

Did the Occupy Wall Street movement and the Bernie Sanders campaign change everything, as some progressives claim?

Did they take any power or money away from Wall Street or the 1 percent? No, they did not. The plutocrats only got richer and more powerful.*

Did they force regulatory improvements or taxes on large corporations? No, Congress and many state legislatures only accelerated their tax-cutting and regulation-nullifying zealotry.

Did they elect candidates that have stood up for the 99 percent or, alternatively, boot out of office anyone that coddled the plutocrats? Not really.**

Did they unite people of all races, truly bring together the working class and students, empower the masses, and build long-lasting organizational structures that could effectively take on the status quo? Hardly.

Did they at least leave a handful of autonomous communities, taking care of their own needs, without help from the corporate power structure? No, they didn't even do that.

---

* The Sanders campaign did force some progressive improvements in the Democratic Party platform, but in modern times, such party platforms are all-but-meaningless, having little significant impact on actual policy-making.

** While some Sanders supporters still may think he actually won the 2016 Democratic nomination (just as a few ancient Japanese soldiers on some deserted islands may still think Japan won World War II)—or that the nomination was somehow "stolen" from him, the reality is that Sanders actually received 3.7 million *fewer* popular votes than Hillary Clinton in the primaries and caucuses. (See: http://www.realclearpolitics.com/epolls/2016/president/democratic_vote_count. html) And no, minor tinkering by some DNC staffers against Sanders did not significantly impact that vote total. In 2013, socialist Kshama Sawant, affiliated with the Occupy movement, did win a seat on the Seattle City Council; yet this one City Council victory was dwarfed by massive Tea Party electoral victories at the federal, state, and local levels.

Don't get me wrong—I'm thrilled that activists in the Occupy and Sanders movements rose up to fight against inequality, but if we ever want to achieve their goals, then we simply must unflinchingly examine why they mostly failed.

In contrast, the Tea Party movement radically influenced federal and state policies (almost always for the worse) and elected significant numbers of supporters at all levels of government, while defeating key opponents (including right-wingers who weren't quite far-right enough), forcing mainstream Republicans to bend to their will, and fundamentally remaking US politics from coast-to-coast. The Tea Party overhauled America, but the Occupy movement and the Sanders campaign were barely blips.

Having spent many pages excoriating the extreme conservative Republicans and spineless Democrats, this chapter, dear reader, is the one in which I piss off some of the only people remaining: the hard Left. Well, at least my cat still loves me . . . I think.

UNCIVIL DISOBEDIENCE

Many wishful-thinking liberals noted Occupy's success in raising the profile of the issue of inequality. Robert Borosage, president of the Campaign for America's Future, a leading progressive advocacy organization, wrote,

> Occupy was scorned for not having a platform; its organizers were dismissed as idealistic anarchists; and its time in the sun was brief. But its message—"We are the 99 percent"—and its indictment of Wall Street and the greed of the 1 percent were electric. Occupy transformed the national debate and gave Americans a new way of looking at things . . . The limits of the old debate were shattered.[430]

While many progressives were writing about—and organizing around—the issue of inequality for decades before protesters camped out in Zuccotti Park, it was certainly helpful that the Occupy movement briefly generated intense, worldwide media coverage. Problematically, though, the media and public debate soon devolved into a distracting side issue: whether protesters in New York and elsewhere had a right to indefinitely stay in public spaces, which, by their own admission, was breaking the law in order to "occupy."

Many of the Occupy protesters and others on the Left, who still practice what they call "civil disobedience," misunderstand the history and true meaning of the term. In 1846, Henry David Thoreau was jailed after he refused to pay his poll tax, which he argued supported slavery and the Mexican-American War, both of which he opposed. He later penned the essay, "Civil Disobedience," in which he called on citizens to violate "unjust laws." In the century or so that followed, civil disobedience almost always involved breaking specific laws that were, in the eyes of the protesters, inherently immoral. It was illegal for women to vote, so suffragettes illegally voted. It was illegal for Indians living under British rule to make their own salt, so Gandhi led his followers to break the law by making salt. It was illegal for black people in the South to sit at integrated lunch counters, so they sat at lunch counters in order to integrate them. Vietnam War protesters blocked military recruiting stations to try to stop people from enlisting. In these examples, the entities and people being challenged by the protests were institutions and officials directly responsible for enforcing specific laws resulting in oppression or injustice.

But in recent times, protesters have sought to violate a law (usually a trespassing law)—no matter how unrelated to the cause at hand—simply to register their objection to a broader societal or worldwide ill. Such unfocused actions dilute the moral and practical impact of civil disobedience.

Today's diffuse left-wing demonstrations rarely effectively target the power structure; instead they mostly piss off working people who should be allies. Sometimes marchers block public streets or bridges, choking traffic, chanting, "Whose streets? Our streets!" The taxi and truck drivers who use those streets to earn their livings and pay for those streets with their taxes "own" the streets just as much as the protesters do.*

A central tenet of true civil disobedience

---

* Here's another example of someone who needlessly blocked traffic to make a political point.

is that those doing it take responsibility for breaking a law, albeit an unjust law, and are willing to suffer the consequences for doing so. Gandhi and King actually *chose* jail over capitulation to reinforce their resistance to unjust systems. (Thus it was silly when some Occupy protesters actually *complained* that they were arrested for breaking the law.*) Getting arrested for trespassing, just to advance a broader cause, provides the demonstrators with a feeling of cheap virtue, and the false sense of thinking they are doing something radical and powerful.

When I was in college at Columbia University in the 1980s, I joined a blockade of a key academic building to protest university investments in the apartheid government of South Africa.** I'm still proud I did that. But when fellow protesters and I weren't arrested, we upped the ante by sitting in the lobby of the Park Avenue building that housed the executive offices of Rolls-Royce, which provided equipment to South Africa's military and whose CEO, Samuel L. Higginbottom, was also the chairman of Columbia's board of trustees, which had refused to divest the parts of the university's $864 million endowment that were propping up apartheid. In a piece of theater that the activists pre-arranged with the police, we were arrested without violence, detained at a police station for an hour or so, and then sent on our way. A bunch of us then went to V&T Pizzeria, a Columbia hangout, to celebrate our own courage and radicalness. A few months later, those of us who were arrested—all of whom were students at an elite university, and most of whom were white and from upper-middle-class or wealthy families—participated in a court hearing which lasted about 15 seconds, at which the judge dismissed our arrests on First Amendment grounds. Walking out of the courtroom, I was pretty proud of my courage and radicalism, until I noticed benches full of young African American men literally in chains, guarded by

---

* I should be clear that the police were often in the wrong for using violence against Occupy activists, destroying their lawful property, and arresting people who were merely innocent bystanders. But the police who nonviolently arrested those who were actually breaking the law were mostly working-class folks just doing their jobs.

** At the time, US conservatives, including the Reagan administration, implied that Nelson Mandela was a dangerous communist and that black South Africans could never be trusted to govern their own nation. We claimed that Mandela was a man of peace and that blacks were perfectly capable of governing their own affairs. They alleged that any change in the South African government would result in massive bloodshed. We insisted that change could happen peacefully. We were right. They were wrong.

heavily armed police, waiting for their hearings—the "real" criminal justice system.

Certainly there are times when the offense you are protesting is so grievous, or the system you are trying to change is so undemocratic, civil disobedience is still in order. But in most situations in America today, so-called civil disobedience is usually a self-indulgent distraction from the much harder, long-term work of trying to effectively convince the population to take your side on an issue. Sometimes, it's a tacit admission that you are on the losing end of a public argument. Moreover, while many people mistakenly believe "any media attention is good media attention," that's just not true—media coverage that reinforces negative perceptions about your cause is counterproductive. If you lead people to think you care more about shutting down a bridge than the broader issue you are trying to advance, you lose.

The day Occupy became more about holding onto patches of ground—and about whether those sites were sanitary or safe—rather than about inequality, was the day that Occupy lost the hearts and minds of the American people and the movement's ability to enact meaningful change. While many of the protestors felt that holding onto communal space was somehow critical to the movement, the broad public never shared that belief.

IT TAKES A VILLAGE—AND A COHERENT MESSAGE— TO BUILD A MOVEMENT

Zuccotti Park, a one-block-long concrete plaza that was home to Occupy Wall Street's main New York City encampment, was just a few blocks away from my anti-hunger advocacy organization's office, so I visited a few times over the weeks that the protesters were there. They were mostly white, even though New York is more than half nonwhite. Judging from the high-priced Apple products many employed to condemn world capitalism, I'd say many of them were from upper-middle-class or upper-class backgrounds. Rarely were there more than a few hundred campers at a time. It was impossible to find anyone who would claim to be a leader—since the working ideology of the movement was that it was "leaderless." Many of the demonstrators claimed to be anarchists. The open general assemblies—at which consensus on key issues was theoretically intended to be reached—were chaotic. The system they came up with to ensure that the crowd could hear the speaker-participants (who didn't have microphones)—where successive rows of protesters repeated what the person in front of them said, like a grade school game of "Telephone"—made more noise than sense, and became just a silly affectation. Millionaire celebrities, including Kanye West and Alec Baldwin, dropped by to express their solidarity. When actual homeless people started hanging around, looking for food, and camping out in the park too, at least some activists seemed threatened.

The Occupiers in New York and elsewhere seemed to spend an inordinate amount of time discussing the process for governing the encampment (such as whether using hand signs were a less repressive way of expressing an opinion than clapping) but spent far less energy considering concrete strategies for reducing world inequality. In the assemblies I listened to, there was little discussion on the most harmful impacts of inequality: poverty, hunger, and homelessness; rather, their complaints were more generic, focusing on how everyone, except the 1 percent, was screwed out of power and money by those elite few at the top. A mix of idealism, resentment, and Starbucks fueled the crowd.

All too often, members of the movement were tone deaf to the existence of their own class and racial privileges. Progressive writer Kenyon Farrow commented, "One of the first photos I saw from the Occupy Wall Street protests was of a white person carrying a flag that read 'Debt = Slavery.' White progressive media venues often compare corporate greed or exploitation to some form of modern-day slavery . . . Arguing that white working- and middle-class people are slaves to debt or corporations undermines not only the centrality of the African slave trade to the birth of the modern corporation but the distinct ways in which debt prevents many blacks from achieving middle-class status."[431] Incredibly, at an Occupy rally in Atlanta, after a 10-minute debate on the matter, the crowd voted *against* having civil rights icon and congressman John Lewis (who was beaten almost to death at Selma) speak to the gathering.[432]

Given that fighting inequality has been a central component of my work for a few decades, I was initially happy that so many people had taken up the cause with altruism and passion. But when I went to Zuc-cotti Park to try to recruit protesters to go knock on doors with me in low-income neighborhoods to organize the people most affected by inequality, none offered to join me. Annoyed by agitators' lack of both organization and focus, I concluded, sadly, that too many of the Occu-piers were posers.*

There were no public bathrooms in or near the park; many of the protesters relied on local private businesses for their bathrooms. All the food was brought to the site, either by the campers themselves or by outside supporters. Once the protest received global attention, some faraway supporters bought the dissenters pizza remotely via Internet or by phone, and then the pizza was delivered to the park. (Ironically, many were likely purchased with credit cards from big banks, and the pizzas were probably made and delivered by low-wage, possibly undocumented immigrants, demonstrating how even the protestors benefitted from privilege.) An Occupy supporter called me to find out if our organization could help provide extra meals to the demonstrators; I politely explained that since half the soup kitchens and emergency food pantries in New York City at that time lacked sufficient supplies to meet the needs of truly hungry New Yorkers, we could not use our meager resources to help feed mostly non-poor people who had chosen to camp out, no matter their cause. In the smallest—and perhaps most self-serving—gesture I could muster, I did donate my first book (on US hunger) to the Zuccotti Park Occupy library.**

Sure, the mainstream media mischaracterized the movement, but it was easy to do so because Occupy did not fully define itself. One Occupy website (there were a number of them, but none dared to call themselves the "official" website) included this self-description: "Occupy Wall Street is a leaderless resistance movement with people of

---

* This photograph shows some of the drummers who were ubiquitous at Zuccotti Park. As *Gawker* reported, Occupy activists spent weeks in fruitless mediation with the drummers at Zuccotti Park to try to limit their hours of drumming, which also greatly agitated those who lived and worked in the neigh-borhood. Again, when you are arguing about drumming, not inequality, you are losing.

** In a legal settlement, the City of New York agreed to pay Occupy Wall Street protesters and lawyers over $230,000 for the destruction of books during a police raid.

many colors, genders, and political persuasions. The one thing we all have in common is that We Are The 99% that will no longer tolerate the greed and corruption of the 1%. We are using the revolutionary Arab Spring tactic to achieve our ends and encourage the use of nonviolence to maximize the safety of all participants."[433]

Even after the New York City General Assembly of Occupy agreed, by consensus, to a very vague "State of Solidarity," the statement still included this disclaimer: "This is an official document crafted by the Working Group on Principles of Consolidation. The New York City General Assembly came to consensus on September 23rd to accept this working draft and post it online for public consumption. The Working Group on Principles of Consolidation continues to work through the other proposed principles to be incorporated as soon as possible into this living document."[434] In other words, they hadn't truly "decided" anything, and their hemming and hawing with buzzwords was so lame that the disclaimer could have been issued by the very type of corporate lawyers they derided.

"The Declaration of the Occupation of New York City," also "accepted by the NYC General Assembly," did not propose a plan for reducing inequality, and instead issued a detailed list of 23 grievances, including

▶ They have taken our houses through an illegal foreclosure process.
▶ They have taken bailouts from taxpayers with impunity, and continue to give executives exorbitant bonuses.
▶ They have poisoned the food supply through negligence, and undermined the farming system through monopolization.
▶ They have profited off of the torture, confinement, and cruel treatment of countless animals, and actively hide these practices.
▶ They have continuously sought to strip employees of the right to negotiate for better pay and safer working conditions.
▶ They have held students hostage with tens of thousands of dollars of debt on education, which is itself a human right.
▶ They have used the military and police force to prevent freedom of the press.
▶ They have donated large sums of money to politicians, who are responsible for regulating them.

▶ They have purposely covered up oil spills, accidents, faulty bookkeeping, and inactive ingredients in pursuit of profit.
▶ They have perpetuated colonialism at home and abroad.
▶ They continue to create weapons of mass destruction in order to receive government contracts.[435]

Their claim that freedom of the press has been destroyed was disproven by the fact that they could print and distribute these very grievances freely. I'd also quibble with their assumption that all corporations—no matter their size and their mission—are equally, intrinsically evil; I don't agree that the original Ben & Jerry's is exactly the same as DuPont.* Plus some of their language—such as claiming that students are "held hostage" by student debt—was a bit self-serving and over-the-top. But other than that, their list was so broad and vague that most progressives, including me, could readily agree with them on most of the points. At the end of their laundry list of grievances, they included an asterisk leading to a footnote that read, "These grievances are not all-inclusive." They surely weren't.**

Plain vanilla liberals and progressives heatedly denied that Occupy Wall Street was an anarchist movement, and asserted that any such suggestion was merely an invention of the right-wing media. Yet many of the demonstrators themselves happily admitted to being anarchists. The liberal establishment desperately wanted the protests to be considered mainstream by the public, but they weren't; much of Occupy's rhetoric was about replacing, not improving, capitalism. The movement called itself "revolutionary"—a phrase sure to turn off most

---

* Good corporation: Evil corporation:

** Some other potential grievances they could have added: "They forced us to recognize 'humpday' on Wednesdays, when it should be on Mondays." "They convinced Caitlyn Jenner to be a Republican." "They conned the populace into frequently using the phrase 'It's all good' when it's never all good."

mainstream Americans*—although, in practice, the "revolution" for some of the Occupiers equated to doing little more than hanging out in that park indefinitely. When one Occupy activist, interviewed on live TV,[436] was asked what promise the country could make to get them to agree to leave the park, the protester essentially said that they didn't want any promises and they didn't want to ever leave the park because living collectively in a public space was their idea of a perfect society.**

Some more thoughtful progressives, including Occupy cheerleaders such as Robert Borosage, did acknowledge deep problems within the movement:

> Occupy's tactical means—asserting a grassroots control of public space—spread like wildfire across the country, but it couldn't be sustained. For a short time, Occupy did galvanize attention—and inspired millions. But the central challenge of a movement—an independent institution that can attract large numbers of people and broadly educate them—remains unfulfilled. . . . Movements must do more than merely shatter the cultural acceptance of a particular injustice as "normal" or "natural"; they must also propose bold alternatives that offer a way out. And they must engage their activists and the broader public in a battle of ideas with the defenders of the status quo. . . . As awareness grows, movements must offer a real hope that things can change. . . . Movements must offer more than solidarity; they must offer the hope that the time for change has come. . . . This requires a vehicle, an organizational form that sustains change.[437]

Given that many of the Occupiers were upper-middle-class whites,[438] detached from the people they claimed to represent, and unwilling to propose specific solutions, it's no wonder that their actions did not lead

---

* Bernie Sanders and his supporters keep using the word "revolution" as well. While that pumped up his crowds, his use of the term also turned off most swing voters.

** Protesters, who slept in tents made and distributed by giant corporations, used computers and smartphones made and distributed by giant corporations, used bathrooms in local small businesses, and then ate food that someone else grew, cooked, and delivered to them (and even sometimes purchased for them), and then patted themselves on the backs for being a self-sufficient, autonomous, anarchist community, were pretty self-deluded.

to a long-term movement that could achieve concrete victories. (The same was true of the Sanders presidential campaign.)

Every effective movement needs to include all segments of the village—or the city, state, or country. Every effective movement needs a coherent message that not only explains what's wrong, but exactly how those things can be fixed. And every effective movement needs a long-term plan and a structure to carry it out. Occupy had none of those things.

What troubled me most about the Occupy movement is how many of the protesters refused to accept the possibility of any serious role for government—either the US government or international governments—in redressing inequality. Many identified with anarchism and had a knee-jerk anti-establishment stance, but that placed them—unintentionally, no doubt—close to the Tea Party in terms of anti-government fervor.

Contrast this to 40 years prior, when most progressive demonstrators made it their top priority to push the federal government to do more to reduce racial discrimination and fight poverty. Those protesters helped force the government to enact anti-discrimination and anti-poverty laws, which did succeed spectacularly in ending legalized segregation and were highly effective in slashing poverty. For much of the 20th century, from the Progressive Era through the '70s, government power was seen as a critical tool to solve major problems. But then conservatives who didn't believe in government took it over, ran it horribly (see Katrina, Iraq, corporate deregulation, etc.), and then said, "See, we told you so—government is crap."

It's not shocking to me that the Right did that—it's shocking to me that they suckered the Left into believing it. To me, conservatives' single greatest success has been to convince the country—including self-proclaimed progressives—that government is *not* a big part of the answer. Many Occupy activists seemed blind to the reality that government was the only entity with enough power to check the vast powers of corporations they so despised.

True, government can be repressive, ineffective, and murderous, so it's never the *only* answer. But throughout the centuries, in instances when starvation, warfare, and poverty were reduced, government was usually the driving force (although, I acknowledge, government was also usually a driving force when such problems were worsened.) I challenge self-described anarchists (or libertarians, for that matter) to provide a specific example in all of human history when people have voluntarily, on their own, with no help from government, solved a major societal problem. It's never happened. Government is an inconsistent and flawed partner for progressive change, but only governments have the size, scope—and yes, legitimacy, at least in democracies—to solve big problems. As Chris Hayes has written, "When people come to view all authority as fraudulent, good governance becomes impossible, and a vicious cycle of official misconduct and low expectations kick in."[439]

After Superstorm Sandy hit New York, and some government and private relief efforts moved too slowly (including established charities like the Red Cross), some Occupy Wall Street veterans founded Occupy Sandy, which they defined as "a grassroots disaster relief network that emerged to provide mutual aid to communities affected by Superstorm Sandy." This effort focused mostly on volunteer-driven direct community service to redress the results of the storm, not on the political advocacy necessary to reduce poverty and stop climate change, which together caused the storm and ensured low-income neighborhoods in New York (and, previously, New Orleans) would suffer most from it. The original Occupy Sandy volunteer events were fairly effective, but they—again unintentionally, I'm sure—communicated to the rest of the public the Reaganesque message that volunteer work within the community, not big government action, was a better solution to community problems.

But Occupy Sandy eventually faded away, and its volunteers moved on to other causes and projects. As of June 2016, the most recent posting on the website was from October 2014.[440] Meanwhile, key New York neighborhoods had still not fully recovered from Sandy, and it was city, state, and federal agencies and programs that were still working on long-term rehabilitation.

WE ARE THE 20 PERCENT

Occupy Wall Street, the Bernie Sanders for President campaign, and many progressive writers and activists have said over and over that the 1 percent is fleecing America for their own benefit, while everyone in the remaining 99 percent are being duped and screwed. Really? The entirety of the 99 percent is a blameless, suffering victim?

I certainly get why it's vital to point out the myriad problems caused by such staggering wealth at the very top. In fact, in my first book (written way back in the pre-Occupy Stone Age of 2008), I wrote, "While all of the merely rich and very rich certainly did far better than the poor, the near-poor, and the lower middle class, even the merely rich and the very rich were all left in the dust by the ultra-rich." I had a field day excoriating the wealth of the Forbes 400 and detailing just how obscenely ultra-rich the obscenely ultra-rich were. Of course since then, they've only become more obscenely ultra-rich.*

Many of us tended to equate the top 1 percent with all things bad about our plutocracy. Chris Hayes wrote, "The one percent and the nation's governing class are more or less one and the same. If you are a member of the governing elite and aren't a millionaire, you're doing something wrong. And if the divide between the one percent and the 99 percent really is a defining feature of our politics, how can the 99 percent trust that some wealthy, governing elite will zealously pursue its interests?"[441]

But in retrospect, all this focus, including my own (*mea culpa!*), on just the very, very top of the moneyed elites likely had the unintended negative impact of oversimplifying the problem and letting many residing in the top 20 percent, including the families of some of the Occupy protesters, off the hook for their own complicity in our rotten system.**

---

* Here's how the obscenely super-rich watch football games.

** Full disclosure: my 2016 income placed me in the top 20 percent of wage earners, although near the bottom of that group. Now, if you buy 10 million copies of this book in bulk to distribute to all your friends, you can get me closer to the top 1 percent, at which time I will take back all the mean things I have said about them.

America had 536 billionaires in 2015, which was just a small subset of the 16,000 families that comprised the top 1 percent. Moreover, the US had more than 10 million millionaires in 2014.[442] Yes, you read that right, more than *10 million* households (about 12 percent of all US households)—owned more than one million dollars or more in investable assets, a 500,000-person jump over the previous year. That means not just the top 1 percent, but actually the entire top 12 percent of Americans lived in millionaire households (while 15 percent were poor). That is why, in suburbs or ex-urbs outside virtually any big or medium city in America, there are large developments of McMansions.

Economist Joseph Stiglitz, who played a key role in popularizing the progressive focus on the top 1 percent, has explained how some of the money distinctions between elites and non-elites can be a bit elastic: "I often use the term 'the one percent' loosely, to refer to the economic and political power of those at the top. In some cases, what I really have in mind is a much smaller group—the top one-tenth of one percent; in other cases, in discussing access to elite education, for instance, there is a somewhat larger group, perhaps the top five percent or 10 percent."[443]

As for earnings (as opposed to assets) in 2014, 5.5 percent of US households, one in 20, earned over $200,000, and another 5 percent earned between $150,000 and $199,000. An additional 13.54 percent earned between $100,000 and $149,000. All told, a nearly a quarter of American households earned more than $100,000 a year, about the same percentage as those who earned below $25,000 per year.[444] While plenty of families earning that hundred grand might complain they're not wealthy, given that they earn nearly double what the median household earns, they should think twice before complaining, even if they live in areas with high costs of living and have to work hard to save for their kids' college tuition. While the top 1 percent (of course) has vast wealth, even after paying taxes, the next 19 percent still had almost as much money as the middle 60 percent and the bottom 20 percent *combined.*

Why are these numbers important? Because they help us understand the reality that the entire top 20 percent of Americans—tens of millions of families—have done very well indeed over the last decade. And it's the top 20 percent that often support the policies that keep the 1 percent so flush, hoping that they too will become millionaires or billionaires.

The focus on just the top 1 percent also allows the 20 percent to deny their role in all that's wrong with the country, smugly blaming those that are even richer for all of society's ills. That's why you could see multimillion-dollar brownstones or luxury cars in well-to-do Park Slope, Brooklyn with a sign saying, "We are the 99%" in their windows. That slogan makes them feel virtuous and whitewashes away whatever role they—or their family—may have played in increasing inequality in America. When the sub-billionaire wealthy publicly place themselves in the lower 99 percent, it allows them, in their own minds at least, to be in the same boat as their plumbers and the lady behind the counter at the DMV, and they are better able to convince themselves they are one of the "good guys" (whoever they are) and that they play a very different role in society than they actually do. Even the upper middle class are doing far, far better than the poor, given that the middle 60 percent of income earners take home 45 percent of the nation's income—while the bottom 20 percent of workers only see 3 percent of the nation's total income. *Three percent.* The upper middle class is often just as clueless about true poverty as are the rich. They don't want to admit it, but they, too, are America's elite.

UPPER-MIDDLE-CLASS SOCIALISM

The Bernie Sanders presidential campaign suffered a bit from another kind of elitism, which most of its supporters wouldn't acknowledge, or even understand. The campaign and its boosters often bragged that, unlike Hillary Clinton's "dirty Wall Street" money, the Sanders operation was a massive group of working-class revolutionaries, funded almost exclusively by millions of average Americans, as if his donors were all just run-of-the mill, middle-class working stiffs.

According to the Center for Responsive Politics, as of April 30, 2016, the Sanders campaign had raised $207 million, and spent $203 million.[445] Even including political action committees (PACs) that aided either Clinton or Sanders, Bernie ended up spending just about as much as Hillary during the primary season. The money the Sanders campaign spent, most of which went to TV and radio stations owned by massive multinational corporations (with millions going to a few top campaign consultants),[446] equaled federal spending for 35,000 Pell Grants. By spending far more money on media advertising than grassroots organizing, Sanders further limited the ability of his campaign to build a true long-term progressive movement; after the campaign, even some of his former campaign staffers complained about that point.

Yes, most of Sanders's huge treasure chest came from relatively small contributions, but a whopping $80 million came in donations of $200 or more. While few of his donors were likely hedge fund managers, few were paupers either. Out of the top 10 employers of Bernie donors, seven are the very kind of huge corporation Sanders routinely blasts: Alphabet Inc. (the parent company of Google), Microsoft, Apple, Amazon.com, Kaiser Permanente, Boeing, and AT&T.[447]

The Sanders campaign, like Obama strategists in 2008, sold the media on the narrative that the campaign was far less dependent on donations from the wealthy than it really was.

Of the top seven zip codes from which Sanders received donations, all were wealthy areas in San Francisco, New York, and Seattle, plus Burlington, Vermont in Sanders's home state. Excluding Burlington, the average income in these zip codes was $91,160, a full 70 percent higher than the median US family income. While most of Sanders's donors weren't likely in the top 1 percent, it is clear they were primarily in the top 25 percent. They may not have been "limousine liberals," but they were often Prius faux-socialists. The vast majority of the Sanders campaign donations were made online, requiring credit cards,* but about a third of Americans, mostly low-income ones, don't have credit cards.[448] Bottom line: it is likely that very few of his contributions came from the true working class, and even fewer came from low-income voters.

---

* The "socialist" Sanders campaign kept bragging about its fundraising prowess. Online donors to the Sanders campaign needed either a credit card or PayPal. Even if a small percent of that went to credit card processing fees, that means that the bank and credit card company-hating Bern-ers gave millions of dollars to those dreaded entities.

Like Springsteen fans, Sanders fans like to think of themselves as average, working-class Joes, when very few of them actually are.*

The Sanders campaign and most of its supporters were never able to grapple with the reality that they couldn't come close to winning the majority of nonwhite voters, or the majority of very poor voters.[449] Many Sanders champions were in denial of this reality since many people they personally knew that were either low-income or of color were Sanders supporters, just as liberal supporters of Walter Mondale in 1984 couldn't believe that he lost to Reagan in 49 states, because everyone they personally knew was for Mondale. (Likewise, some Hillary supporters were loath to admit—and concede the importance of—the reality that she was getting creamed among younger voters, including younger women.)

Why did the Occupy and Sanders movements mostly fail to catch fire with low-income voters and people of color? The main reason, I think, is that Americans who are especially oppressed on a daily basis have very little patience for pie-in-the-sky, theoretical notions of "revolutions" that fail to realistically explain how their living conditions will be concretely improved. They've seen lofty promises come and go over generations and are far more interested in tangible, real-world results. Yet neither Occupy nor the Sanders campaign were able to convince these voters that they could deliver on their high-minded goals.

Even worse, when it became clear that low-income voters and people of color favored Hillary, some Bernie lovers patronizingly blasted those populations for being too dumb or too easily duped to understand what was in their own self-interest. Yeah, low-income Americans, and people of color do really love it when upper-middle-class white people claim to know their interests better than they do. Despite having marched for civil rights decades earlier, Sanders himself continued to be a bit tone deaf on some racial issues, even once implying that all black people lived in poor ghettos—a "racial land mine," to quote Kirsten West Savali, writing for *The Root*,[450] a gaff which haunted Sanders's cam-

---

* For the record, I have many friends (at least until they read this chapter) who were fervent Bernie supporters. I am not criticizing them as people—I greatly respect that most of them are dedicated progressives—but I am challenging Sanders-ism as a movement to acknowledge what it truly was and wasn't—and what needs to be done better in the future to achieve the "revolution" they seek.

paign. These disconnects exhibited by both Sanders and the Occupy movement are emblematic of the serious class and racial divides, even among progressives. Upper-middle-class white progressives need to engage in deep soul searching—and ever deeper listening—to learn from low-income families and people of color as to why the sides are so far apart. And older progressives need to engage in similar soul searching and listening to learn why younger voters are so disconnected from the current political system.

CIRCULAR FIRING SQUADS

The Left has a long history of spending more time and energy eating its own than defeating the Right. On many of the issues that mattered most, Hillary Clinton and Bernie Sanders held positions and records that were similar.* In any case, the differences between Bernie and Hillary were absolutely dwarfed by their shared divergence with the ultra-nutty GOP contenders in 2016. But that didn't prevent Clinton and Sanders and their supporters from ripping each other apart, sometimes viciously, and often unfairly.

Michael Moore implied that the demise of the Michigan auto industry was because of the NAFTA trade agreement (and thus the Clintons), but his movie, *Roger and Me*, which detailed how General Motors screwed his Michigan hometown of Flint, came out years before Bill Clinton was elected president. And according to the Bureau of Labor Statistics, there were more auto manufacturing jobs in Michigan at the end of Bill Clinton's administration than there were at the beginning.[451]

Too many Sanders online supporters—so-called "Bernie bros"—made vile, widely misogynistic attacks on Clinton. I saw one claim that a reason to vote against Hillary Clinton was the death of Vince Foster, echoing the extremist, fringe-right rumor that Clinton had one of her best friends killed. Despicable. When the self-professed Left gloms onto fanatic conservative talking points, you know they are themselves unhinged.

Hillary Clinton's campaign and supporters were hardly blameless.

---

* The two biggest substantive differences were that Hillary voted to authorize the Iraq War but Sanders voted against it, and also that Hillary was generally far more supportive of gun control than was Sanders.

If Sanders so much as hiccupped near her, he was falsely blamed for being sexist. There is no doubt that misogyny in our country is still prevalent—and that she was the frequent victim of large and small slights due to her gender—but not every criticism of Clinton's record should have been attributed to out-of-control sexism by Sanders supporters, as some of her defenders charged.

The Sanders versus Clinton fight pitted wives against husbands and friends against friends—when the party should have been particularly united in gearing up against the outcome of the Republican primary contest, full of the least-qualified and downright craziest challengers in the history of American presidential elections.

Progressives can't always seem to tell the difference between their committed enemies and their true friends. In the mid-1990s, when Al Gore was vice president, the Clinton administration advanced the vast majority of the environmental movement's agenda. In contrast, the Congressional Republicans, led by Newt Gingrich, came out against every environmental priority. Yet, at the time, I received a fundraising call at home from Greenpeace, which slammed the Clinton administration on their management of national forests, conveniently omitting from their script that the objectionable forest policies were mostly forced on the US Forest Service by Congressional Republicans. That's so typical of the Left, going after their friends for disagreeing on a few small things, rather than battling the other side for opposing them on everything.*

Just as many conservatives heap especially heavy scorn on those Republicans not far-right-wing enough—calling them RINOS (Republicans in Name Only)—many on the Left are obsessed with crusading against center/left-leaning members of their party who have called themselves "New Democrats." Liberals claim that New Democrats sold out progressive causes when Bill Clinton was president. They heap extra-special distaste on the now-defunct centrist Democratic Leadership Council (DLC) and its affiliated think tank, the Progressive Policy Institute (PPI), the organizations which pioneered many of the New

---

* Now, I am fully aware that some might laugh at me—of all people—complaining that others are too verbally combative. But I'd like to think that my verbal jousting is focused on big picture issues of life and death, not petty squabbles. But I guess that's what petty, combative people always think.

Democrat ideas, and for which I worked from 1989 through 1991.* In 2016, New Democrat-bashing became particularly fashionable as a way for the Left to slam Hillary's campaign. In *Salon*, writer Walker Bragman wrote,

> In the '90s the Democrats figured out the prevailing narrative and adapted. Ultimately, they accepted the GOP rhetoric and economic platform—that's what the New Democrats were; Reagan Democrats. While this move got Bill Clinton elected president (along with the fact that George H.W. Bush couldn't fix the Reagan economy), since then, we have had a hard time recovering. Getting anything passed has not been easy since we willingly tied our legs together. . . . But now we face a different situation than we have in 50 years. The country is moving left out of desperation for change after years of Republican dominance. The GOP is unable to tap into this shift, like the Democrats of yesterday. Now, we must show courage and not settle for anything less than a New Deal-style overhaul.[452]

In *What's the Matter with Kansas?*, Thomas Frank blamed the demise of Democratic Party fortunes among the white working class on the DLC, which he claimed "was pushing the party to forget blue-collar voters and concentrate instead on recruiting affluent, white-collar professionals" and "to make endless concessions on economic issues, NAFTA, Social Security, labor law, privatization, and the rest of it."[453]

Most of these characterizations of the New Democrat movement were off the mark. While the DLC, PPI, and their acolytes were far from perfect,** their main goal was to win *back* working-class votes, and, with Bill Clinton's leadership, they mostly succeeded. Far from harming the party at the ballot box, the party's mainstream orientation enabled the Clinton/Gore ticket to nearly win even Kansas in 1992,

---

* The Progressive Policy Institute is still going strong and I still do write some policy papers for them.
** The organization's staffs weren't as diverse as they should have been and were a bit too aligned with big corporate interests for my taste (although I happily accepted my salary despite who paid for it), and sometimes they chose confrontation over cooperation with other Democrats who could have been allies, but they were still far more progressive than critics on the Left have charged.

the closest showing by a Democrat in that state since 1964.* Clinton won two landslide national elections.** If you claim that the country would have been just the same had George Herbert Walker Bush won a second term in 1992, or had Bob Dole won the presidency in 1996, I say you are off your rocker.

Perhaps the greatest failure of the New Democrat movement and Bill Clinton's affiliation with it were that they gave the country the false impression that they embraced Center/Left ideas for the mercenary reason that they wanted to gain power or reward donors, when they also did so because they believed these types of policies were the best for the country. While I'll be the first to admit that welfare reform certainly had significant flaws (especially in the form pushed through by the Gingrich Republicans and that was eventually signed into law), the bottom line was that focusing on work as the centerpiece of social policy was a continuation—not a deviation—from the legacy of FDR, who made work a focal point of all his relief efforts, such as the Civilian Conservation Corps and the Works Progress Administration. The New Democrats proposed many policies that were truly progressive, including Individual Development Accounts to help low-income families save money, higher taxes on the rich, expanded tax credits for the working poor, a plan to enable all Americans to pay for college through civilian national service (which became AmeriCorps), and empowerment zones and enterprise communities to target increased aid to some of the nation's lowest-income rural communities and urban neighborhoods.

Far from the caricature that they were merely trying to turn the Democratic Party to the Right, they were trying to modernize it, thereby—in their minds—saving it and its core progressive values. The proof was in the pudding: under President Bill Clinton, 2.8 million people who'd been previously unemployed entered the labor force, median worker wages rose, and poverty dropped, with black and Hispanic poverty

---

* In 1992, I was the Clinton/Gore statewide campaign press secretary in Kansas. We lost the state by only 4 percentage points that year, compared to losing neighboring Nebraska by 11 and Oklahoma by 17. Whatever was—and is—the matter with Kansas, I still feel love for its BBQ and its people. Well, many of them.
** I am no doubt biased because I worked for Bill Clinton and the New Democrat movement, but the facts are the facts.

sinking to historic lows. Yet some on the Left now, incomprehensibly, seem to team up with the Right in their claims that the 1990s were a nightmare for America. Thomas Frank even called the Bill Clinton presidency "odious."

In 2014 Bill Curry, former White House advisor to President Bill Clinton and two-time losing candidate for governor of Connecticut, urged progressives to abandon the Democratic Party in order to fix it:

> Some say the Democratic Party is beyond saving. Others say it's our last hope. I see progressives taking leave of Democrats not as abandonment but more like tough love. In the end it may be the only thing that can save Democrats or for that matter progressives, whose reputation has been tarnished by the party that betrayed them.[454]

Throughout this book, I have excoriated Democrats for their spinelessness. But any implication that what the party really needs is a yet another spell of Republican-run governance is lunacy.

But whether the attacks against the New Democrats are deserved, or whether my defense of the movement (admittedly defensive and personal) is warranted, I think the bigger point is that progressives need to move beyond endlessly fighting past battles and holding ideological witch trials.

In 1934, (true) anarchist Emma Goldman noted how the Soviet Union's quest for ideological purity crushed progressive causes:

> All political movements are at each other's throats—more bitter, vindictive, and downright savage against each other than they are against their common enemies. The most unpardonable offender in this respect is the so-called Union of Socialist Soviet Republics. Not only is it keeping up a process of extermination of all political opponents in and outside its territory, but it is also engaged in wholesale character assassination. Men and women with a heroic record of revolutionary activity, persons who have consecrated themselves to their ideals, who went through untold sufferings under the Romanovs,

are maligned, misrepresented, dubbed with vile names, and hounded without mercy.[455]

Any political movement that seeks 100 percent purity will, in the long run, lose or collapse. Human beings aren't 100 percent pure or even 99. That's why my top ideology is effectiveness. Getting stuff done that actually helps people is always preferable to being so hamstrung by ideological purity that you lose every fight.[*] I once got a fortune cookie that said, "Thought that leads to no action is not thought—it is dreaming." Exactly.

FRIENDSHIP-WINNING IN THE 21ST CENTURY

While most American liberals are not nearly as elitist as conservatives make them out to be, many of them, especially the more privileged white ones, are uncomfortably out of touch with the needs of their working-class and racially-diverse neighbors.

How to Win Friends and Influence People, written by Dale Carnegie in 1936, was one of America's earliest popular self-help books, selling 16 million copies worldwide by 2016, marginally more than *All You Can Eat: How Hungry is America?* or; *Soul on White Rice: The Rachel Dolezal Story*.[**] There are some rules in the Carnegie book that the Left should consider following:

Become genuinely interested in other people. Be a good listener. Encourage others to talk about themselves.

Progressives really need to get out more, spend quality time in low-income and diverse neighborhoods, and learn from the people who actually live in those communities what they truly need and want.

Smile.

Too many of my fellow Lefties are humorless scolds. (As opposed to

---

[*] The only thing that drives me more nuts than purists who are upset when they lose fights, are purists who believe their losses further prove the righteousness of their ideological purity, a stance that is incredibly self-indulgent.

[**] *All You Can Eat: How Hungry is America?* is a cult masterpiece (or maybe just required reading in compounds led by cult leaders). *Soul on White Rice: the Rachel Dolezal Story* doesn't exist.

me, a *humorous* scold.) Liberals seem to constantly barrage the social media world and elsewhere with images of people angrily marching with clenched fists. Progressive activists need to look less angry, and *be* less angry, myself included.*

Talk in terms of the other person's interest.

You may want to talk about some amorphous attack by the 1 percent, but if the people you're trying to convince really want to hear how they'll get jobs or raises, then you'd really better talk about *that*.

If you're wrong, admit it quickly and emphatically.

Lately, liberals have been adopting conservatives' bad habit of believing wacky conspiracy theories that just aren't true. You lefties shouldn't do that: stop it. Stop it now. If facts prove your preconceived notions wrong, just admit that. It will get you votes, I promise.

Appeal to the nobler motives.

Movements, and especially progressive ones, need to provide more than just an opportunity for like-minded people to vent about what pisses them off. By that count, both Occupiers and Bernie-istas have not yet succeeded. If we want to not only maintain the moral high ground, but also actually win policy fights and govern the nation, progressives need to transcend the politics of resentment.

We must persuade based on voters' self-interest, explaining how we will improve their daily living conditions. In addition, we should appeal to the nation's fundamental altruism, explaining how all of us will benefit from a more inclusive America. Simply scapegoating the 1 percent just won't cut it.

If we truly want to win over the country, we need an inclusive message that says: "We are the 100 percent."

---

* Okay, so maybe I need to learn how to smile, too. And, yes, I realize this whole book is a giant angry scolding bullhorn of clenched fist-typing.

10.

Republicans Are from Mars, Democrats Are from Venus

"You can always tell when a man is well-informed. His views are pretty much like yours."
—Bob Hope

"It's a darn sight easier to slip on bullshit than it is to slip on gravel."
—Lyndon Baines Johnson

America, the supporters of your two political parties don't just live on separate planets—they live in separate universes. They have less chance of meeting and interacting as equals than do Superman and Spider-Man.*

But if you don't think we've always been very seriously divided by ideology and region, please google a little thing called the "US Civil War."

Even when we weren't shooting at each other over cotton fields, we were yelling at each other across village greens and screaming at each other through hyper-partisan newspapers and broadsheets. Throughout US history, not only have opposition forces been truly nasty to one another, they have usually ignored evidence that contradicted their preconceived worldviews.

Tribalism, and the biases that come with it, are baked into human nature. An academic study that compared the views of Palestinians versus those of Israelis, as well as those of Republicans versus Dem-

---

* Note to any readers who are *not* comic book fans: The Superman character is owned by DC Comics, while Spider-Man is owned by Marvel Comics. In comic book parlance, the characters live in two separate universes. Note to any readers who *are* comic books fans: Superman and Spider-Man are *not* actually real people. Get a life. By the way, I do realize that sometimes Republicans and Democrats are actually married to each other, but that doesn't mean they are on the same planet with each other, politically-speaking.

ocrats, discovered "motive attribution asymmetry," meaning each side attributed virtuous motives to their own side but nefarious ones to the other.[456] It is sobering to consider that the political divides in the US may now be almost as entrenched as those in the Middle East.

When an evangelical Christian kills people, Christian conservatives shrug their shoulders and say he's just a lone, crazed madman, nothing like them. But when a fanatical Muslim kills people, those same right-wingers angrily claim he represents all the earth's 1.6 billion Muslims. Likewise, when a deranged right-winger goes on a shooting rampage, some liberals might label all conservatives as a murder-loving fringe.

We see in issues, and in people, what we *want* to see. In an experiment, six different professional Australian photographers were each asked to take photos of the same man, but each of them was told different backstories about the man, who was actually an actor. They were told he was a millionaire, an ex-convict, a psychic, an alcoholic, a life-saver, and a fisherman. Despite photographing the same man in the same studio with the same props, the results were radically different, proving that preconceptions dramatically alter how we see each other.[457]

Each of us sees the world through our own lenses, but personal bias now often blends with greater ideological bias. Too many conservatives wear special virtual non-reality glasses that prevent them from ever seeing the Mexican gardener mowing their lawn as a hard-working family man, and too many progressives wear rose-colored glasses through which they visualize Bernie Sanders being sworn in as president of the United States.

What's different about us today is that all the long-standing differences are shoved in our collective faces—24/7—through cable TV and social media. These differences incubate and fester until they emerge as a full-blown infection of hate, further corroding our national discourse and fueling our political dysfunction.

A TALE OF TWO SETS OF CHARTS

Things are so bad these days, America, that even when both sides agree on basic statistics, they form entirely different conclusions as to what the numbers really mean.

For instance, according to USDA caseload statistics, SNAP (food stamps) participation rose by 171 percent from 2001 to 2012 (a 27.4 million-person jump). First, examine this chart from the liberal-leaning Center on Budget and Policy Priorities (CBPP):

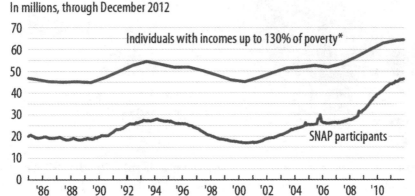

SNAP Caseloads Closely Track Changes in Number of Poor and Near-Poor
In millions, through December 2012

*Poverty numbers are annual estimates. Spikes in SNAP participants are from disaster benefits (i.e., after hurricanes).

Sources: Department of Agriculture (SNAP program participants); Census Bureau (annual estimates of individuals below 130% of poverty).

Center on Budget and Policy Priorities | cbpp.org

Notice that the CBPP's chart clearly demonstrates that a) the SNAP rolls went up when the number of people living in or near poverty increased, in both George W. Bush's and Barack Obama's presidencies, and b) the SNAP rolls declined during the strong economy of the Bill Clinton presidency. It clearly indicates that economics, not laziness, is the greatest variable determining levels of SNAP participation.

Now check out the very same numbers, displayed in two charts from the right-wing Heritage Foundation's publication, "The 2013 Index of Dependence on Government."

The first difference you'll notice is that the CBPP chart contains a smaller scale for the "year" access, making for a more horizontal chart and making the SNAP rise look modest, while the Heritage charts span

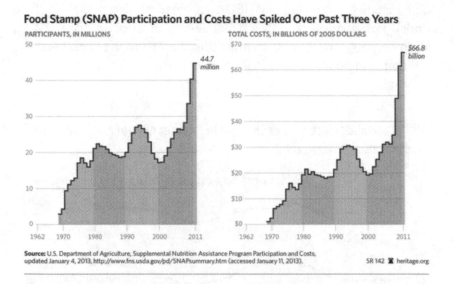

Food Stamp (SNAP) Participation and Costs Have Spiked Over Past Three Years

Source: U.S. Department of Agriculture, Supplemental Nutrition Assistance Program Participation and Costs, updated January 4, 2013, http://www.fns.usda.gov/pd/SNAPsummary.htm (accessed January 11, 2013).   SR 142 ⬛ heritage.org

more years and are more vertically oriented, making the SNAP rise look scarily severe. The second difference is that the Heritage charts omit any reference to poverty, while highlighting SNAP's increasing costs. (It won't shock you to know that their "dependency" report doesn't include stats on skyrocketing payments to defense contractors). Third, the Heritage chart's headline reports a spike "over the past three years," thereby implicitly blaming Obama, while the numbers make it clear that the spike started under Bush. (Between 2013, when the Heritage report came out, and January 2016, SNAP participation actually *declined* by 2.5 million people, mostly due to the improving economy under Obama, but subsequent Heritage reports never highlighted the decline.) Based on the exact same set of numbers, the liberal chart reinforces the progressive belief that government should help people who, through no fault of their own, need assistance to avoid starvation, while the conservative charts reinforce the conservative trope that government aid busts the budget and reinforces dependency.

As Chris Hayes wrote, "Choose nearly any important public issue—the long-term solvency of Social Security, the effect of taxes on growth, the importance to student performance of merit pay for teachers—and you will find smart, well-credentialed, and energetic advocates arguing for mutually exclusive positions. In this way, the voter is asked to referee a series of contests for which he or she has absolutely no independent expertise."[458]

Beyond the tendency to cherry-pick data, many "experts" at think tanks, especially those on the Far Right, have no idea what they are talking about and are often laughably out of touch with facts on the ground that relate to the topic on which they are opining. One time, while debating a so-called "food stamps expert" from a conservative think tank on a live radio show, I asked her, "When was the last time you actually met a family receiving food stamps?" There was dead silence. I then answered my own question, "I thought so."

ALL THE NEWS THAT'S FIT TO STINK

While some newspapers have always been highly partisan, there was a time not so long ago when much of the news media at least pretended to play the role of an impartial referee. No more. Even the media that isn't far to the right generally refuses to plainly separate the truth from widely believed lies and delusions.

If, let's say, a progressive has a press conference on a Wednesday, and announces, "Today is Wednesday," but then a conservative think tank holds a press conference on the same day and announces, "Today is Thursday," the media will generally dutifully report both sides, and then ask their audiences, "Which side is correct?" You can expect one of two clichés for their suggested answer: "You decide, dear reader," or "Only time will tell." What they should do instead is state unequivocally, "We checked the calendar and the progressive was telling the truth and the conservative was lying." Ah, I can dream. Some media do now have "fact-check" features, but those are still too few and far between.

Because all humans lie at least sometimes, and because all politicians are human (at least until the robots take over),* all politicians lie at least sometimes. But some people tell small white lies, and do so infrequently, while others tell Everest-size lies, repeatedly and seri-

---

* By 2037, this robot army will run Congress. They will never—
ever—shut down the government to make a political point; they
will only shut themselves down for a hard reboot, when necessary.

ally. Just as it would be absurd to say that, since no human beings are 100 percent truthful, therefore all human beings are 100 percent deceitful, it's absurd to make that same formulation about politicians. But that's how the public—and the media—treat them. We are told that mild fallibility and pure evil are one and the same. Yet the facts prove that some politicians lie more frequently and far more dangerously than others.

Angie Drobnic Holan, editor of PolitiFact, a nonpartisan, political fact-checking website, wrote in December 2015, "Donald J. Trump's record on truth and accuracy is astonishingly poor. So far, we've fact-checked more than 70 Trump statements and rated fully three-quarters of them as Mostly False, False or 'Pants on Fire' (we reserve this last designation for a claim that is not only inaccurate but also ridiculous)." PolitiFact determined that all the other serious Republican presidential candidates lied somewhat less frequently than Trump but far more frequently than Bernie Sanders or Hillary Clinton. The two most truthful politicians that they rated were Barack Obama and Bill Clinton, both of whom the opposition routinely accuses of being serial liars.[459]

Yet even Holan's column, which made it clear that the parties differed significantly in their honesty, hedged a bit with its Melba toast headline, "All Politicians Lie. Some Lie More Than Others." A far more accurate headline should have been, "Leading Republicans Lie Far More Than Do Leading Democrats."

Mainstream media outlets now regularly report the most senseless rumors fabricated by conservatives as if they were facts, but explain themselves by claiming they are merely "reporting on the controversy." As historian Sean Wilentz has written, "It was bad enough that once-respected outlets became flagship 'talk radio' stations; even worse, the *New York Times*, *Washington Post*, and other leading newspapers, under the label of investigative reporting, allowed their news columns to become soapboxes for right-wing cranks and political moderators, thereby giving the cranks credibility."[460] The best example is the mainstream media reporting on the preposterous—and demonstrably false—charge that President Obama was born in Kenya. It wasn't always this way, as Rick Perlstein points out:

It used to be different. You never heard the late Walter Cronkite taking time on the evening news to "debunk" claims that a proposed mental health clinic in Alaska is actually a dumping ground for right-wing critics of the president's program, or giving the people who made those claims time to explain themselves on the air. The media didn't adjudicate the ever-present underbrush of American paranoia as a set of "conservative claims" to weigh, horse-race-style, against liberal claims. Back then, a more confident media unequivocally labeled the civic outrage represented by such discourse as "extremist"— out of bounds. . . . Conservatives have become adept at playing the media for suckers, getting inside the heads of editors and reporters, haunting them with the thought that maybe they are out-of-touch cosmopolitans and that their duty as tribunes of the people's voices means they should treat Obama's creation of "death panels" as just another justifiable political claim.[461]

Fox News has taken the outright lies and fantastical delusions industry to a stratospheric level. It doesn't just occasionally give airtime to fact-averse cranks: its entire business model is fact-averse crankery (plus rampant sexual harassment). The nonpartisan blog *PunditFact* checked a wide array of claims by Fox News pundits, columnists, bloggers, political analysts, hosts, and guests, and found that 10 percent were true, 12 percent were mostly true, 19 percent were half true, 29 percent were false, and 9 percent were characterized at "pants on fire" lies.[462] That means that nine out of 10 Fox items checked weren't entirely true. If you gave a tic-tac-toe–playing chicken* a multiple-choice test on current events, the chicken (or mere random chance) would have a far higher accuracy rate than Fox. I think the only job in America more rare today than a telegraph operator is a Fox News fact-checker.

Defending Fox against *PunditFact*'s findings, the archconservative *National Review* published a piece, "How Stupid Happens."[463] They meant that *PunditFact* was stupid for uncovering the lies, not that Fox was stupid for promulgating them.

---

* In a gaming parlor in New York City's Chinatown in lower Manhattan, there really was a chicken that played tic-tac-toe.

Fox host Chris Wallace once questioned Illinois Democratic Senator Dick Durbin about the budget, but then asked him to not get "too deep in the weeds" on budget issues. Translation: "Don't confuse viewers with actual facts."

Because Fox is *expected* to get it wrong, they are held to even lower standards than the rest of the media. Bill O'Reilly claimed he was in a "war zone" to cover the Falklands War, but he never got closer than 1,100 miles away. In contrast, Brian Williams was indeed in a war zone, but he exaggerated how much danger he was in. Williams was fired from his anchor post and managing editor job at *NBC Nightly News*, but O'Reilly kept his job (though a few months later, NBC brought Williams back on the air on their cable channel, MSNBC).

Fox has made a specialty out of demonizing people who live in poverty, as President Obama pointed out:

> Over the last 40 years, sadly, I think there's been an effort to either make folks mad at folks at the top, or to be mad at folks at the bottom. And I think the effort to suggest that the poor are sponges, leeches, don't want to work, are lazy, are undeserving, got traction, [and] it's still being propagated. If you watch Fox News on a regular basis, it is a constant menu. They will find folks who make *me* mad. I don't know where they find them. They're like, I don't want to work, I just want a free Obama phone—or whatever. And that becomes an entire narrative—right?—that gets worked up. And very rarely do you hear an interview of a waitress—which is much more typical—who's raising a couple of kids and is doing everything right but still can't pay the bills.[464]

Joe Scarborough, who, by early 2016, was the only token conservative with his own show on MSNBC, blew a gasket in response to Obama's comments. After saying that "the arrogance of it all is staggering," and that he was "a little embarrassed" for the President, Scarborough implied that no Fox clip existed that characterized poor people so negatively. Really? In 2004, Bill O'Reilly said on Fox, "You gotta look people in the eye and tell 'em they're irresponsible and lazy. And who's gonna wanna do that? Because that's what poverty is, ladies and gentlemen. In this country, you can succeed if you get educated and work hard. Period. Period." In 2012, O'Reilly said the "true causes of poverty" included "poor education, addiction, irresponsible behavior, and laziness."[465]

In 2013, I had my own run-in with Fox News. They contacted me to see if I would agree to a series of taped interviews for a special they were producing on the SNAP program, which they still referred to as food stamps. I knew they were going to do a hatchet job, but I think it's vital for progressives to at least try to offer their voice of truth in response to every right-wing attack, so I agreed to do it. They ended up taping three different interviews with me, collectively talking to me, on camera, for a number of hours.

My final interview was with Bret Baier, one of the most popular Fox personalities. I came prepared. Check out this exchange:

Baier: "Joel, don't you think the higher levels of food stamps dependency sap the American spirit of independence which made America great?"

Me: "Bret, you graduated from DePauw University, didn't you?"

Baier: "Yeah, why?"

Me: "Well, Bret, about 55 percent of DePauw students receive student aid. And your boss, Roger Ailes, the CEO of Fox News, attended Ohio University, a state school, arguably a socialist institution, which receives massive government funding. I don't think the fact that my tax dollars helped your classmates and your boss go to college weakened the spirit of independence that made America great. I think my country became stronger when my tax dollars helped your classmates and your boss go to college, just as I think my country is stronger when my tax dollars go to SNAP benefits that help prevent my neighbors from starving."

Guess what? They didn't use any of that exchange.

At one point, Bret asked me about whether their example of one person engaged in possible SNAP fraud made me less supportive of the SNAP program. My response: "The fraud rate in SNAP is only about 1 percent. It's wrong to imply that tens of millions of law-abiding people who get help from a program are criminal for the misdeeds of one person, just as it would be wrong to assume that all Fox News employees are criminal just because a few top executives of News Corp, your parent company, have been arrested for felonies." They didn't use that either.

Over and over, Baier kept trying to bait me to say that I thought more food stamps were the top solution to hunger, and over and over again I answered that the top solution to the hunger problem was more living-wage jobs, and that if the GOP was serious about either slashing food stamps use or reducing domestic hunger, they'd drop their opposition to minimum wage hikes. Wanna guess if they ran that response either?

Although I had given them hours of interviews, they only used a few seconds in the final broadcast. In one of the interviews that nearly made the cut I said, "The top answer is living-wage jobs, but when those aren't enough, everyone who needs it should be able to get SNAP benefits." Of course, Fox edited out the first half of my sentence about jobs, so that my quote gave the impression that I thought everyone should simply get government aid. The report did label me "One of America's most energetic proponents of food stamps." I'll take that as a compliment, but they pointedly left out my equally passionate advocacy for more jobs and higher wages.

The final Fox report, which ran nearly an hour in prime time, was a master class in distortions, half-truths, and outright lies. If it weren't for the report's half-truths, it would have had no truths at all. Focused on just a handful of Americans they claimed were frequently or inappropriately using SNAP (including an unemployed rock musician/surfer named Jason who said he'd rather surf and eat SNAP-funded sushi and lobster than work—where did they find that guy?), the show quoted a conservative pundit as saying, "Jason has cousins in every town in America." That spurious guilt-by-association is the worst sort of anti-poor-folks McCarthyism. This show was about as fair as a North Korean propaganda film and about as balanced as a fight between a sumo wrestler and a baby. It should have won a Pulitzer Prize—but for fiction.

Demonstrating exactly how the Fox echo chamber works, O'Reilly, on his own show, responded to the Fox SNAP report by saying that Obama "encourages parasites to come out and take as much as they can with no remorse."[466]

Yet another Fox show had a segment commenting on the SNAP special. Peter Boyer, a Fox News editor-at-large, lamented, "Three billion dollars a year we spend just in administering the Food Stamp Program. Three billion for the bureaucrats to shovel the dough out the door." The anchor on that broadcast, Lauren Green, then relayed her own family's story, almost as an aside, at the end of the segment: "You know, when my mother was little, they were on welfare and it was the most embarrassing thing for her ever. And they didn't want to be on welfare, and not only that, they didn't hand out checks, they handed out goods, which was a different kind of concept."[467] Like many conservatives who grew up receiving government help, Green seems to have no problem participating in the shaming of others who need help.

The only thing worse than O'Reilly's claim that hungry Americans are "parasites" is when he claims that they don't exist at all. In 2015 on his show, O'Reilly said, "If you look at the studies of poverty, most poor people in this country have computers, have big screen TVs, have cars, and have air conditioning. This myth that there are kids who don't have anything to eat is a total lie." His guest, Democrat Kirsten Powers, responded, "There actually are students in New York City, there are kids in New York City who go all weekend without anything to eat except when they eat in the schools. That is absolutely a fact." O'Reilly then bombasted,* "Oh, that is such the biggest baloney. You produce one. You produce one. You can't."[468]

After O'Reilly threw down the challenge for anyone to produce proof of a hungry child, the nonprofit anti-hunger advocacy organiza-

---

* Yes, I am using "bombast" as a verb because it uniquely applies to anything that Bill O'Reilly says.

tion I run immediately contacted his show to relay that we had found a mother who had agreed to appear with O'Reilly and explain how she couldn't always afford enough food for her child. An O'Reilly producer kept promising us they would have the mother on the show, but kept postponing the segment with excuse after excuse. We repeatedly followed-up for months, but they never kept O'Reilly's promise. Nor did they accept my challenge to have me on the show to debate O'Reilly. Not only is O'Reilly a liar, he's a phony and a coward.

Out of all the truly awful things Fox News did, among the most abominable is when they routinely questioned Obama's legitimacy as president, or even as a human being. When Obama cried while recounting gun deaths of children in Chicago, Fox actually disputed whether the tears were authentic; host Andrea Tantaros suggested Obama had used a "raw onion" to produce fake tears. Oh, yes she did. What a lovely human being.*

As truly nasty as Fox News is, right-wing talk radio, which I force myself to listen to when I travel nationwide, is often even worse. Fox at least feels the need to veil its racism and sexism in code words, but talk radio hosts feel no such compunction. Compared to talk radio, Fox is practically PBS. I remember when Paul Ryan was being considered for Speaker of the House, I heard both Rush Limbaugh and Sean Hannity on the radio complaining about how Ryan was too *liberal*. (Can you hear me choking—even now—from here at my desk in New York?)

Blogs can be equally awful, with the crazy, shrill, liberal ones sometimes sinking almost as low as the ones on the Far Right. The left-leaning *Daily Kos* ran a headline, "Paul Ryan ready to take being a partisan prick to a new level over immigration." In response to Hillary Clinton's proposal to send education experts to low-performing public schools, the conservative *National Review*'s website proclaimed in a headline, "Hillary's Federal Education Jackboot Squad."

---

* Screenshot of Tantaros showing how Obama faked his tears. Now that it turns out she was one of the many victims of Fox chief Roger Ailes serial sexual harassment, I actually do feel sympathy for her, but I wish she shared such basic human empathy for those who disagree with her on politics.

DENIAL AIN'T JUST A RIVER IN EGYPT

Perhaps the only thing more troubling than the nastiness of our current media and online culture is the frequency with which it denies clear scientific facts. Some of the denial is bipartisan, such as the dingbat belief that vaccines cause autism. Some of it is spouted by liberals, like the exaggerated fears that Genetically Modified Organisms (GMOs) in food cause cancer. But most of the denial comes from conservatives on topics ranging from evolution to global warming.

I had to laugh at this *New York Times* headline: "Measles Outbreak Proves Delicate Issue to G.O.P. Field." If you are pro-measles, then you've reached Taliban-levels of anti-science.

As for climate change, not only do scientists carefully measure global warming and sea changes, year after year, but also we can see the changes with our own eyes. In Glacier National Park a century ago, there were 150 ice sheets. By 2014 only about 14 survived, and by 2044, there may be none.[469] At some point, the park will need to change its name to the "Park Full of Tropical Beaches That Were Formerly Glaciers."*

Not only does the Right deny the basic science behind climate change, they claim that anyone who does accept the science is a mortal enemy of free enterprise. Influential conservative radio host and *RedState* website founder and editor Erick Erickson wrote,[470]

> Many environmentalists are watermelons. Green on the outside, inside they are as red as any communist ever was. It is not a coincidence that the environmental movement picked up strength after the Soviet Union collapsed. The propagandists for communism against capitalism had to go somewhere. They went to the environmental movement. With demands for state subsidy, an agenda hostile to western powers, and a deep antipathy toward free markets and capitalism, the two groups

---

* This will soon be . . .   this.

merged. Like Stalinists before them, environmental elite wish to purge society of capitalists, anyone who challenges them, and free market ideas. Like communists before them, they wrap themselves in a moral banner for war—against rising sea levels, against drought, against all sorts of things no right thinking person could be against.[471]

Not content to call environmentalists mere communists, he compares them to Stalin, who killed millions of innocent people.

When a NASA scientist and astronaut, Piers Sellers, discovered he had stage four pancreatic cancer and would soon die, he announced that he wouldn't retire, but would rather use his remaining days to do everything he could to study and slow climate change. Writing about it, Sellers posed this question: "Was continuing to think about climate change worth the bother?" James Delingpole, for the right-wing website *Breitbart News Network*, ridiculed that, saying, "At the risk of being ungracious to the terminally ill, the correct answer to that question on any number of levels is 'No.' . . . Sorry, but no. Sellers's cancer says no more about the validity of global warming theory than Einstein's having shagged Marilyn Monroe says about the validity of his theory of relativity. . . . Interesting biographical details and personal tragedy have nothing to do with the scientific method. . . . I'm genuinely surprised that NASA thought it was at all a good idea to publish this emotive piece."[472] I try to have a bit more empathy than this writer—or many conservatives—but I must admit, if this guy Delingpole owns a beach house, and, someday it is submerged under 50 feet of sea water, I likely won't grieve.

TURN THE OTHER CHEEK—BUT ONLY WHEN MOONING THE SIDE THAT'S CONSPIRING AGAINST YOU

The nastiness and know-nothingness of much of the media reinforces the nastiness and know-nothingness of too many of our political leaders, especially on the GOP side. Before President Obama's 2016 State of the Union address, when Speaker Paul Ryan was asked what he would suggest that Obama say, the speaker essentially urged the President to repudiate his own presidency by saying, "I take it all back."[473]

And it's not just the President they hate. Congressman Trey Gowdy called Minority Leader Nancy Pelosi "mind numbingly stupid." Senator Ted Cruz labeled his own party's Senate Majority Leader, Mitch McConnell "a liar." Rep. Alan Grayson (D-FL) said, "blood drips from Dick Cheney's teeth when he talks."* A study found that members of Congress spend more than a *quarter* of their time just taunting each other.[474] **

One of the worst tendencies of some in politics is slamming your opponents for doing the exact same thing you did five minutes before. For instance, whether one party claims that the executive or legislative branches are given more power under the Constitution is entirely a function of whether that party happens to control either branch at the time. Dick Cheney thought the president should have virtually unlimited power when he was ~~president~~ vice president, but later he claimed Obama was overstepping his powers. Conversely, when W. was president, Democrats Harry Reid and Nancy Pelosi claimed that the president had limited executive authority, but they expressed far more expansive views about presidential power when Obama was president. Republicans who howled when Democrats voted down GOP judicial nominees whom the Democrats claimed were extreme, are the same Republicans who have bawled that it would be oh so wrong for them to even meet, no less have a hearing or a vote on, a moderate Obama Supreme Court nominee. The greater the hypocrisy becomes, the greater the vitriol.

Many elected officials seem to be in denial about the destructive impact of their own hate-filled rhetoric on our national politics and on how the world sees us. Near the end of his 2016 presidential race, Marco Rubio expressed his concern that Trump was leading the country to "chaos" and "anarchy." Rubio worried, "You wonder if we're headed in a different direction today where we're no longer capable of having differences of opinion but in fact now protests become a license

---

* I do realize that I previously compared Cheney to Darth Vader, but when I did so, I did it lovingly. And I'm not an elected official. No "Honorable" in front of my name.
** Congressional floor debates can be amusing—in a sort of post-modern, meta-ironic way: a speaker will call their nemesis "my good friend" or "the distinguished gentleman" just before accusing their good friend of having anal sex with an underage hedgehog, while being married to a baboon.

to take up violence and take on your opponents physically. This is what happens when a leading presidential candidate goes around feeding into a narrative of bitterness and anger and frustration." Yes, this is the same Rubio that accused Obama of purposely "undermining this country" and that "all this damage that he's done to America is deliberate"—essentially alleging treason by Obama, an offense punishable by death.[475]

SOCIAL MEDIA IS NEITHER SOCIAL, NOR MEDIA

Given that members of Congress—who are supposed to abide by rules enforcing decorum (thus, "my friend" the ~~necrophiliac rodent~~ good senator from wherever)—are so uncivil, it is no surprise the Wild West world of social media, where anonymity gives cover to vicious bigotry and hatred, is even worse.

Social media is one step further below the old media on the information food chain, and it's a veritable factory of untruths. Right-wing myths about Obama abounded: born in Kenya, taking away your guns and bibles, secret Muslim, gay, and a Communist, as well as the Anti-Christ, just to name a few. But progressive aversion to facts is also all-too-common. After Bernie Sanders lost five key states (three of which were lost by landslides) to Hillary Clinton on March 15, 2016, any plausible analysis of the results proved that Sanders got creamed and that he had virtually no chance, by simple math, of being the Democratic nominee—with or without the controversial superdelegates. But a blog post entitled "Bernie Sanders Had a Phenomenal Night — Here's Why" was all the rage on progressive social media. Even after Bernie lost California, New Jersey, and New Mexico in landslides in one night, many of his supporters still convinced themselves he was somehow winning. Bernie boosters were in as much denial as the spokesperson for Saddam Hussein who kept insisting Iraq was winning the war against the US. Some Bernie followers even posted pictures of massive crowds, which were supposed to be rallies for Bernie in the US, but were obviously taken from a mass gathering in Paris.* Zealots of any stripe see what they want to see. As David Auerbach wrote in a piece for *Slate* called "The Bernie Bubble,"

> There is also a structural social issue that has enabled Sanders's rise: the ability of the Internet in general and social networks in particular, to cloister off and amplify political ideologies on the left and right alike. . . . Just as Fox News and talk radio carved off a group on the right that brooked our current era of no compromise, the architecture of how we consume and share information online has begun to do the same to a very different class of left-wing voters. . . . This generation has partially replaced traditional mainstream establishment narratives with localized media bubbles. This effect is sometimes called a filter bubble. . . . In 2016, leftist politics—and leftist media— feels larger and more austere and purist . . . the more time you're spending with people who think just like you do. . . . Little wonder, then, that the fights over the Democratic primary on my Facebook wall feel so much nastier than the ones that took place in 2008: Everybody seems to have forgotten how to interact politely with others with whom they disagree.[476]

The left-wing extremists on social media take quotes from Republicans and even Hillary Clinton supporters out of context, and then magnify them with scary headlines; conservatives do the reverse even more frequently, and then repeat. And repeat. And repeat.

---

*

This above image, which Bernie supporters claimed was of his April 2016 rally in New York City, was really taken in Paris, France in January 2015, following the Charlie Hebdo terrorist attacks.

I have no doubt that a fair number of people who are reading this book were Sanders acolytes, and may be pretty pissed at me by now for continually picking on Bernie and his boosters. The reason I am doing so is that I fear terribly that, if the Left becomes almost as fact-averse as the Right, the progressive movement, such as it is, will entirely sink for good.

That being said, keep in mind that the conservative extremists are still far worse. Psychologist Bradley M. Okdie found that right-wingers are more likely to share a given piece of content than progressives are, especially if it provokes a negative emotion. "Conservatives tend to be a lot more reactive to negative information, and they also tend to be a lot more insular in nature, and they also tend to have less tolerance for ambiguity," Professor Okdie said. "Conservatives would prefer a negative concrete statement to a slightly positive, uncertain statement."[477]

Unfortunately, a lack of even basic human empathy in social media is now bipartisan. Just minutes after Supreme Court Justice Antonin Scalia died, progressives were savaging him on Twitter and Facebook. Even though I thought that Scalia spent his whole career putting a fake intellectual sheen on dangerous bigotry, I was still taken aback by the ferocity of attacks—and outright glee in his death—against someone whose body had not yet cooled. When I pleaded online for liberals to wait just a few days before attacking Scalia's memory, out of respect, I was castigated by some people for making even that small statement of compassion for his family. Likewise, conservatives have cheered when liberals have faced tragedy.

When Hillary Clinton gave George W. Bush a brief hug at Nancy Reagan's funeral—a small human gesture—Bernie Sanders supporters took that image viral and treated it as some sort of betrayal of Democratic values, similar to the way that Chris Christie's half-embrace of President Obama after Hurricane Sandy was treated as a betrayal of Republican values. When we don't even allow our leaders to so much as treat other leaders as fellow human beings, we are all in trouble.

It is both amusing and distressing that the more you respond on social media with facts, the more opponents get personal and nasty. One respondent, a stranger to me, sent me 60 different tweets in an argument *she* started, but when I responded with facts, and requested a "reasoned public discourse," she tweeted, in capital letters no less, "STOP TWEETING AT ME . . . I never wanted or asked for your 'reasoned public discourse'. STOP tweeting at me you virtue signaling loser." Alrighty then. So sorry for signaling virtue.

Some twisted folks seem to take it as some sort of virtuous act to proudly proclaim their bigotry. It's easy to shout your racism while sitting in your underwear in front of the TV alone while eating nachos and tweeting from the relative anonymity of the web and using only your first name or a nickname. A man calling himself "Brannon" tweeted, "The future of the west depends on those brave enough to be called racist, bigot, sexist, homophobe, xenophobic and not flinch or back down." In another tweet, he added, "I became tired of being called a racist bigot so I just stopped caring and actually became a racist bigot." Oh, that explains it.* When people claim they aren't racist or misogynist—just funny—they are usually wrong on all counts. LOL.

A Facebook friend of mine, who I didn't know well, posted an anti-Obama screed and a friend of his then posted a reply with the suggestion that Obama meet the same fate as Mussolini, who was assassinated. This same Facebook friend of mine later posted a graphic—including a lascivious image of a woman about to be sexually assaulted by a man—that implied that liberals were pro-rape. I do try to keep friends with opposing views, but I did finally unfriend him, for my own sanity, if for nothing else.

THE PC WARS

While I've made it clear that merely spouting the phrase "I'm not PC" shouldn't be a "get out of racism or sexism free card" for anyone who wants to spew something racist or sexist or any of the other -ists, it is true that too many progressives, including some on college campuses, are now too intolerant of and overly sensitive to basic free speech. Some examples:

▶   Students at Yale were livid that some in the university admin-
     istration defended the right of other students to wear cultur-

---

* Here's another gem from "Brannon": "#FeminismIsCancer because feminists are a malignant growth that feeds on a healthy host society." Of course, this genius is a Donald Trump supporter, who later tweeted, "Media has turned @realdonaldtrump, who is a powerful, victorious, politically astute billionaire, into a sympathetic underdog. LOL." And later: "Obama is Trump's final level bad guy. In Trump style, he won't only roll back his policies but expose Obama for the faggot man-child he is."

ally insensitive Halloween costumes. A handful of students angry about that surrounded one faculty member that they felt was particularly insensitive, as one of them screamed at the professor, "Be quiet . . . It is your job to create a place of comfort and home for the students . . . [Y]ou should step down! Why the fuck did you accept the position? Who the fuck hired you? It is not about creating an intellectual space! It is not! Do you understand that? It is about creating a home here! You are not doing that. You're going against that."[478]

▶ Fordham University prohibited its students and faculty from using their computer systems to "post or transmit any information, data, text, file, link, software, chat, communication or other content (hereinafter, collectively, 'Content') that is harmful, abusive, discriminatory, hostile, combative, threatening, insulting, embarrassing, harassing, intimidating, defamatory, pornographic, obscene, or which negatively affects the University, another User, or any third party."[479]

▶ Smith College activists blocked media from a student sit-in unless reporters agreed to explicitly state support for their movement in the coverage of the event, and the Smith administration backed that position.[480]

▶ The University of California distributed a piece of training literature to some of its administrators (which since has been taken down from the university's website) which suggested that it might be a problematic "micro-aggression" to state any of the following things on campus: "I believe the most qualified person should get the job," "America is the land of opportunity," or "Everyone can succeed in this society, if they work hard enough."

Before I mock these examples mercilessly, let me note why a more nuanced approach is in order.* Suzanne Nossel, the executive director of PEN American Center, a membership association of prominent

---

* On Twitter once, I praised the Melissa Harris-Perry Show (since taken off the air by MSNBC), for "nuance." A right-winger responded, "'Nuance.' The favorite word of a liberal. It's so flexible." I responded, "'Nuance' means life is complex, without pat, easy answers for everything. Exactly opposite of your point."

literary writers and editors with the mission of "defending free expression," argued, smartly,

> Some student rights advocates seem convinced that their needs and safety can be assured only by restricting speech. They demand "trigger warnings" on syllabuses, safe spaces on campus where unwelcome views are excluded, and de facto prohibitions on potentially offensive forms of expression—including poor-taste Halloween costumes.
>
> On the flip side, among defenders of free speech, conservative and liberal alike, the students' outbursts are met with dumbfounded incomprehension, laced with ridicule. Students are brushed off as a misguided generation of hothouse flowers. Their fears for their own physical and emotional "safety" are dismissed as Salem-style hysteria.
>
> Both sides are wrong. The dispute is too often framed as a binary match between an emphasis on individual rights—to speech, opinions, and Halloween costumes—and the communitarian drive to create campuses bound by shared values and girded against outside intrusion. But these are hardly mutually exclusive. . . .
>
> Student protesters needn't give up their drive to nurture and protect diverse communities in order to accommodate free speech. In fact, free speech is an essential dimension of vibrant campus communities. . . . Free speech has long been a potent weapon for disenfranchised groups, used to expose repression and prevent the powerful from silencing dissent.[481]

I agree with every word of that, but I still must offer some mockery. The Yale student's idea—that "safe" spaces and "intellectual" spaces are somehow contradictory—is flat-out totalitarian. If "combative" language were against the rules everywhere, as per the Fordham policy, I'd be serving consecutive life sentences in a maximum-security penitentiary for a decades'-long crime spree of verbal combativeness. I also don't fully agree with the statement "America is the land of opportunity," but there are thousands of fact-based methods to legitimately defend that statement without saying anything that is even remotely racist. Reporters should never—ever—be required to agree in advance on how they will report a particular story.

At Amherst College (where starting tuition, room, board, and fees exceeded $70,000 in 2016), protesting students, calling themselves "Amherst Rising," issued a list of demands for the college administration, including

▸ President Martin must issue a statement of apology to students, alumni and former students, faculty, administration, and staff who have been victims of several injustices including but not limited to our institutional legacy of white supremacy, colonialism, anti-black racism, anti-Latin racism, anti-Native American racism, anti-Native/indigenous racism, anti-Asian racism, anti-Middle Eastern racism, heterosexism, cis-sexism, xenophobia, anti-Semitism, ableism, mental health stigma, and classism.

▸ President Martin must issue a statement to the Amherst College community at large that states we do not tolerate the actions of student(s) who posted the "All Lives Matter" posters, and the "Free Speech" posters that stated that "in memoriam of the true victim of the Missouri Protests: Free Speech." Also let the student body know that it was racially insensitive to the students of color on our college campus and beyond who are victim to racial harassment and death threats; alert them that Student Affairs may require them to go through the Disciplinary Process if a formal complaint is filed, and that they will be required to attend extensive training for racial and cultural competency.

▸ Dean Epstein must ask faculty to excuse all students from all 5 College classes, work shifts, and assignments from November 12th, 2015 to November 13th, 2015 given their organization of and attendance at the Sit-In.[482]

Ah, where to begin my mocking? It's absurd to demand that a private college president personally apologize for every injustice committed in the United States over hundreds of years. Why not also ask him to apologize for the Franco-Prussian War of 1870? It's downright scary that students would want other students punished for complaining that free speech was in danger. (Have those students had any sense of irony surgically removed from them?) Some seem to think that, if anyone ever disagrees with them on anything, that automatically constitutes hate speech. Lastly, the request that the college provide time off from classes or work for civil disobedience proves that these self-professed radicals are mostly privilege-clinging, overgrown babies.

All that being said, at no college in the country, as far as I'm aware, was someone fired or disciplined for expressing their free speech rights on campuses, so the conservative claim that there is no freedom of expression at colleges today is bunk. Newt Gingrich tweeted in 2016 that the "[f]ascism in modern America is on the left—on college campuses, in left wing groups." Oh please. In each of the cases the Right cites, they were fully able to make their opposing views known. If they feel too intimidated to do so, it's only because they also are cowardly. Both sides are now competing in the victimization Olympics.

HEARING EACH OTHER AND SEEING EACH OTHER

In the book, *Men Are from Mars, Women Are from Venus: The Classic Guide to Understanding the Opposite Sex*, counselor John Gray wrote, "Men mistakenly expect women to think, communicate, and react the way men do; women mistakenly expect men to feel, communicate, and respond the way women do. We have forgotten that men and women are supposed to be different."[483]

The same can be said about Democrats and Republicans. We want them—and expect them—to think and act as we do. Gray also wrote, "When men and women are able to respect and accept their differences then love has a chance to blossom." Perhaps that's a lesson for politics as well. We don't have to agree with each other, but we at least can start by accepting the basic humanity of even our opponents. We also must keep open minds. Reading and hearing from people with whom we fervently disagree is both infuriating and absolutely vital. Here's a crazy idea: if the facts prove a preconceived notion you have is wrong, why not change it? I know, that seems rich, coming from me, but I do change my opinions when facts change—I swear.

After the 2000 election, I was absolutely convinced that George W. Bush stole it in a bloodless coup. So, a few days before my Clinton-appointed job at the USDA ended, just prior to a Bush appointee getting my office, I took a bunch of post-it pads, wrote on every one of them, "Your boss stole the election," and I placed them in every desk and cabinet drawer in my office. But on my last day, I changed my mind. I took all the notes out and ripped them up. For the good of the country, I decided that, no matter how they got there, the people who served the public after me deserved a fresh start.

Continuing a presidential tradition started by Ronald Reagan, President George H.W. Bush left a note in the Oval Office desk for his successor, Bill Clinton, revealing that Bush also believed in a clean slate for each new leader:

January 20, 1993

Dear Bill,

When I walked into this office just now I felt the same sense of wonder and respect that I felt four years ago. I know you will feel that too. I wish you great happiness here. I never felt the loneliness some Presidents have described. There will be very tough times, made even more difficult by criticism you may not think is fair. I'm not a very good one to give advice; but just don't let the critics discourage you or push you off course. You will be our President when you read this note. I wish you well. I wish your family well. Your success now is our country's success. I am rooting hard for you.

Good luck –

George[484]

Every few years, our politics need a fresh start and we at least must try to have a civil conversation—earth-to-earth, human-to-human, eye-to-eye—with the other side. It's easy to forget, in the heat of battle that is our day-to-day society, we are really on the same team—or should be.

IT'S ALL GIVE AND TAKE: THE MYTH OF THE MUSHY MIDDLE

Given that too many people want to pull our relationship with the nation to the extreme right and some want to yank it to the extreme left, surely there's a middle course—the slightly warm porridge—that's exactly what our relationship (and Goldilocks) needs?

Not so fast.

Compromise smack dab in the middle of two extremes only makes sense if there is an objective, reasonable reality in that course and if everybody stands to benefit from taking it. On relatively small matters, and if a decision is a based on a judgment call that can reasonably vary based on subjective values or tastes, a compromise in the middle makes all the sense in the world.

But if you were suffering from brain cancer, and all your city's most qualified doctors agreed (based on a series of scientific medical tests) that you needed brain surgery, yet there was some quack psychic down the street who thought (based on a Ouija board) that your real problem was a blister on your big toe, it would make no sense to "compromise" between those two positions by agreeing to open-heart surgery. If you took that advice, not only would you fail to build common ground between the experts and the quack, you'd soon be dead. That's the problem with many of the political compromises pushed by elites today—they often seek compromise for compromise's sake, regardless of whether the agreement would heal or kill the body politic.

A true compromise isn't combining objectively dumb ideas in a package with objectively smart ideas—a true compromise is finding common ground on ideas of proven merit which aid everyone.

FALSE MODERATES AND ENDANGERED PORPOISES

A huge part of the problem is that the elites and the public as a whole love to traffic in false equivalency—because neither is perfect, it must mean that both sides are equally dreadful. Nonsense!

A good example of this false equivalency would be claims that Texas Senator Ted Cruz is the mirror image of Massachusetts Senator Elizabeth Warren since both are outsiders and close to the ideological edges of their respective parties. Balderdash! Warren is generally even-keeled temperamentally and data-driven; while Cruz is almost always in amped-up attack mode and even his fellow Republicans say he often fabricates things.*

The media and other arbiters of conventional wisdom try to anoint hardline conservatives, such as John McCain and John Kasich, as moderates—usually based on some singular, isolated act, such as McCain opposing torture or Kasich expanding government healthcare coverage in Ohio.

Yet McCain has supported a foreign policy more hawkish than that of George W. Bush, opposed federal minimum wage hikes, opposed gun safety legislation, opposed federal equal pay protections, and opposed reproductive choice. He even voted against a bill that would have banned employment discrimination against gay workers.

Kasich was House Budget Committee chairman when Newt Gingrich was Speaker and was a key leader of the effort to enact the far-right "Contract with America." As Governor of Ohio he tried (unsuccessfully) to crush public employee unions and pushed (successfully) to make it easier for people to carry concealed weapons. He is anti-choice, against federal action on climate change, and opposed to federal minimum wage hikes.

If McCain and Kasich are moderates, Kanye West is quiet, modest, and unassuming. In reality, true Republican moderates are now more of an endangered species than the Yangtze finless porpoise.**

Thomas E. Mann is a senior fellow at the Brookings Institution and Norman J. Ornstein is a resident scholar at the American Enterprise Institute. They are both longstanding, mainstream, moderate observers of Washington, and fixtures of the DC establishment. For decades, they have always been the epitome of "on the one hand x, while on the other hand y" reasonableness. So, it was particularly striking that, in 2012, they teamed up to write an op-ed for the *Wash-*

---

* Maybe there should be an app just to help politicians keep their lies straight too.

** This is a Yangtze finless porpoise. According to the World Wildlife Fund, there are only 1,800 of these cute little guys left, which means there are 1,800 more of these smiling creatures in the world than there are moderate Republicans. Or smiling Republicans, for that matter.

ington Post titled "Let's Just Say It: The Republicans are the Problem," which concluded,

> We have been studying Washington politics and Congress for more than 40 years, and never have we seen them this dysfunctional. In our past writings, we have criticized both parties when we believed it was warranted. Today, however, we have no choice but to acknowledge that the core of the problem lies with the Republican Party.
>
> The GOP has become an insurgent outlier in American politics. It is ideologically extreme; scornful of compromise; unmoved by conventional understanding of facts, evidence and science; and dismissive of the legitimacy of its political opposition.
>
> When one party moves this far from the mainstream, it makes it nearly impossible for the political system to deal constructively with the country's challenges.
>
> "Both sides do it" or "There is plenty of blame to go around" are the traditional refuges for an American news media intent on proving its lack of bias, while political scientists prefer generality and neutrality when discussing partisan polarization. Many self-styled bipartisan groups, in their search for common ground, propose solutions that move both sides to the center, a strategy that is simply untenable when one side is so far out of reach.[485]

When discussing important issues, Americans often say they "don't want to make it political." Actually, that's the most political statement of all, and it really means, "Don't take a position with which I disagree." Most things in life that really matter are controlled, to some degree or another, by government actions (or non-actions), including the quality of our water, air, schools, parks, roads, jobs, and housing. The reason we have so much hunger in this country is due almost entirely to politics—and especially the domination of our national discourse by the Right. Even matters perceived by the public to be mostly beyond the scope of "politics"—love and death—are intensely political. Government has decided which of its citizens who are in love get to be married and government has decided whether people who aren't rich can receive lifesaving healthcare or earn enough money to afford a decent burial. Claiming to be non-political doesn't make you "above it all" or inoculate you from life's problems any more than an ostrich sticking its head in the sand saves it from predators such as spotted hyenas.*

TRUTH IN LABELING

Basing your civic views and decisions on ideology alone can be problematic. Strict adherence to dogma is a crutch for the intellectually lazy. On the other hand, claiming you have no principles at all is usually a dodge. Most of us do have firm positions on issues, although those positions often contradict each other, as in the case of people who want cleaner drinking water but less regulation on businesses that pollute, or they want to see fewer homeless people in their neighborhoods but less government spending on housing and jobs.

Having a coherent worldview, and accurately understanding which political party or candidate more closely bolsters your viewpoint, is a critical component of being an informed and responsible citizen in a democracy.

That's why the "No Labels" movement—funded by some big-money types such as Michael Bloomberg—is bound to fail. Their motto is "Stop Fighting. Start Fixing," as if the problem is merely petty squabbling for which each side is equally at fault. As I think I've persuasively proved, the charge of equivalency between the parties is a load of a crock of a wagon of horse manure. It is also problematic to posit the idea that labels are intrinsically bad. Labels are actually pretty helpful—they can help consumers know if a bottle—or a political party—contains poison

---

* Well, there you go.

or vital nutrients. The reality that today's political parties are ideologically diverse is both good and bad. It's harmful when it prevents the parties from working together for the common good. But it can be good for voters in that they now have a much better idea of what they are getting when they vote for a particular party.

Some from the left, like blogger Mark Sumner, have argued that the No Labels movement is merely a front for right-wing business interests:

> The whole point of the No Labels organization, from its Washington lobbyist creators to the moneymen hiding in the shadows, is to take far-right positions and give them a (thin) wash of mainstream patina. The organization exists to present ideas that are as out there as anything in the tea party, while giving a good tut-tut over how we just can't get those lefties to sign onto our *entirely mainstream ideas*. . . .[486]

I am slightly less cynical about the motivations of No Labels, since some good people of varying political backgrounds are involved in it and few of their positions are truly "far-right." Still, their self-professed goals are startlingly naïve:

> We need solutions to our most pressing problems now, and we need buy-in from both Democrats and Republicans to find them.
>
> For No Labels, the prevailing hurdle preventing our nation's progress isn't disagreement over particular policies. It's an attitude—specifically, the hyper-partisan viewpoint that leads far too many of our leaders (and citizens) to completely dismiss, ignore, or question the motives of people from the other party.
>
> We don't operate like that. Any member of Congress—conservative, liberal, or in between—can win our approval, so long as she or he is willing to work with any other member to find solutions.
>
> The primary goal of No Labels is to start a national movement that will culminate in a Federal government that sees the presidential administration and both houses of Congress

working together to achieve mutually agreed-upon goals that will solve the nation's problems.[487]

No, decades' worth of big-money influence—coupled with deeply-entrenched ideological, racial, and regional differences—won't magically evaporate if elected officials merely show more goodwill.

In a similar, pie-in-the-sky vein, No Labels has adopted four big, broad policy goals:

1. Create twenty-five million new jobs over the next 10 years
2. Secure Social Security & Medicare for another 75 years
3. Balance the federal budget by 2030, and
4. Make America energy-secure by 2024.

Those goals are so vague and popular that Hillary Clinton, Ted Cruz, John Kasich, Marco Rubio, Bernie Sanders, and Donald Trump all endorsed them, rendering them meaningless. I'm surprised they didn't ask the candidates to sign on in favor of puppies.* If the No Labels crew is unwilling to offer specifics on how they would achieve any of these big goals, they are the opposite of the brave problem-solvers they purport to be.

But when you drill down to some of the few specifics on minor items the No Labels group actually wants the federal government to implement, much of it is even more shallow and superficial than the traditional policies of the two parties that they are trying to bring together. One of their top 10 asks is for federal agencies to cut 50 percent of their travel and replace it with video conferencing. I'm not sure that's a good idea, because in my time in the federal government, I found it critical to get out of my DC office and personally visit program sites nationwide to see on-the-ground activities with my own eyes and hear from local residents

---

* Are *you* in favor of cute little wiggling puppies, or are you an anti-American supporter of ISIS? We demand to know your answer to this terribly difficult question.

directly about what is and isn't working. But even if the government could operate just as well using video conferences instead of face-to-face meetings, that would save a mere pittance in tax dollars. A suggestion like that is symbolic, meant only for show, exactly the kind of false political gesture that No Labels was, in theory, founded to move beyond.

Other self-professed anti-ideological centrist reformers have a tendency to, when they are proposing big changes in society, almost always focus on placing more burdens and sacrifices on low-income and working people. The Holy Grails of these reforms—Social Security and Medicare "fixes"—almost always include proposals to cut long-term benefits and/or raise retirement ages. (It's easy for someone who writes memos all day in an air-conditioned office to say that workers can retire a few years later—tell that to someone who performs back-breaking construction work for a living.)

RADICAL CENTRISM

By now, America, you may be damn confused about my point. I've criticized the Far Right, the Far Left, *and* the Mushy Middle. So, who could I support? What point of view could I get behind?

I'm for more fighting over true principles, and less fighting over knee-jerk contrarianism. I'm for less fighting over power, party, and pettiness. As writer George Packer put it, "Ideology knows the answer before the question has been asked. Principles are something different: a set of values that have to be adapted to circumstances but not compromised away."

I'm for more compromises in which the deals truly help the country as a whole. For instance—and I know even this is a long shot—perhaps more conservatives could be persuaded to support comprehensive, free birth control as a way to decrease the need for abortions in America. Wouldn't that be a win-win, America?

Mostly, though, I am for what I call "radical centrism"—a new wave of large-scale, society-changing, progressive advances which aid both the middle-class and low-income Americans, but do so based on smart, realistic reforms anchored in mainstream values. The last part of this book will propose such reforms.

Arthur C. Brooks, president of the right-leaning American Enterprise Institute, has written,

> Pessimists see people as liabilities to manage, as burdens or threats that we must minimize. This manifests itself on the political left when we construct welfare programs that fail to boost unemployed Americans back into the work force. On the right, it shows up in strains of anti-immigrant sentiment or throw-away-the-key criminal sentencing . . . Maximum progress would come not from convergence on an unsatisfying centrism, but from a true competition of optimistic visions for a better future. What happens if one side unilaterally breaks out of the current negative equilibrium? I predict it will see victory—especially if the other side doubles down on pessimism and division.[488]

I rarely agree with Arthur Brooks, but he's spot-on here. A true competition of realistic, practical ideas will be far more helpful to the nation than throwing up our hands, giving in to the notion that the best we can hope for is some microscopic, meaningless, counterproductive give-and-take just to say we tried.

Compromise *is* what binds relationships together, but it must work for *both sides*. Merely accommodating one side and only reaching agreement on ways for the relationship not to suck so much won't save it and make it stronger. Papering over your differences, and kicking the can down the road on major problems, just draws out the time before the inevitable divorce, making a final break-up even messier and costlier.

Benjamin Franklin once said, "Never confuse motion with action." Meaningless compromises provide motion, but not action to move our country forward.

Relationship bliss may require giving up something, but it is also predicated on getting something meaningful back, not just a vague promise of warm porridge. It means not just settling for motion, but holding out for true action. Even if you must meet in the middle, you have to be able to go forward, together.

11.

Three Cups of Crime Spree
Why the Nonprofit Sector Is Too Crooked, Self-Aggrandizing, and Ineffective to Save America

We all love feel-good stories.* We all rejoice when everything works out well in the end, without too much muss or fuss.

That's why the public is so drawn to tales of magical successes from nonprofit groups, who claim to bring endless happiness and unimaginable progress to the most downtrodden people—all for just pennies in donations for each person helped. The charities broadcast smiling, ever-so-grateful aid recipients and brag that they accomplished all this magnificence without a cent of government funding—which, by their implication, is somehow tainted. Such stories are even better if the founder of the organization undergoes some harrowing tale and then experiences a startling personal transformation in her or his outlook on life that leads her or him to change professions to start that nonprofit group.**

We *want* to believe all this.

That's why we wanted to believe that Greg Mortenson, author of the inspirational 2007 book, *Three Cups of Tea: One Man's Mission to Promote Peace*, really did build 140 schools, mostly for girls, in remote parts

---

* When I write, "We all love feel-good stories," the "we" doesn't include me, and the "all" doesn't include any reader who has made it this far in my "feel-bad" book.

** Nonprofit fundraising experts all agree that it's vital for nonprofit CEOs to have a "relationship" (albeit not a physical one) with top donors so the donors really feel they know the leaders as people, thereby making it more likely for them to give generously. When I meet with potential donors for my nonprofit group, they all want to know not only what kind of work my organization does, but *why* I am motivated to do such work. I generally answer that I obtained my commitment to social justice from my grandparents and parents, but I do wish I had a better story, such as: I was stranded on a life raft for seven months, battling for my life each day, having to capture all my own fish and seagulls just to survive, which made me more appreciative than ever of everyone's need for food. Come to think of it, the truth—my inspiring immigrant foremothers and forefathers—is even better.

of Afghanistan and Pakistan. He has recounted incredibly riveting tales of how he got lost trying to climb K2, the second-highest mountain in the world, was saved by Pakistani villagers, vowed to return there to build a school for girls, then later, was captured by the Taliban during his quest to end extremism by building even more schools for girls across the culturally misogynist, war-torn region.

Virtually everyone believed him. The book sold four million copies and became required reading for US troops sent to Afghanistan. President Obama donated $100,000 of his Nobel Prize money to Mortenson's nonprofit group, the Central Asia Institute, which raised millions of dollars, ostensibly for school-building. America, you were shocked when *60 Minutes* exposed many of his stories to be fabrications, including his claims about the number of schools he built. The report even cast doubt on whether or not he had indeed been kidnapped by the Taliban.[489]

Where did the money *really* go? An investigation by the Montana Attorney General's Office found that the charity allocated $4.9 million for advertising Mortenson's two books, spent another $4 million buying copies of the books to give away to schools and libraries, paid inappropriately high speaking fees to Mortenson, and footed the bill for the founder's charter flights for family vacations, clothing, and Internet downloads.[490]

Like all hustles, which require the grifter to obtain the confidence of the mark, "nonprofit" con jobs rely upon the goodwill that the charitable sector has earned from the public. Few bothered to ask many questions about Mortenson's stories or his charity because they desperately *wanted* it all to be true. Similarly, few people ask questions about the effectiveness and honesty of the nonprofit sector in general, because we *want* to believe charities can painlessly solve the world's problems and thus relieve that guilt we feel for prospering while much of the earth suffers. Donating to charities makes us feel even better than reading a self-help book.

CRIME AND (LITTLE) PUNISHMENT

Is the Mortenson story a rare aberration in the otherwise pristine world of perfectly managed, entirely honest charities? Hardly. It's only the tip of the iceberg of nonprofit crookedness and mismanagement. Let's talk about some other recent inductees into the "Charity Hall of Shame."

The Federation Employment and Guidance Service, widely known as "FEGS," was a massive social service organization in New York City, with a budget of $200 million, which claimed to help 12,000 low-income people, with and without disabilities, per day with job placement services. Its CEO earned $638,880 in total compensation in 2012, more than two and a half times the official salary of the city's mayor. In October 2014, the organization awarded its executive vice-president a bonus of $92,000, on top of his salary of $343,000. Just a month later, the organization announced that it had somehow lost $19.4 million, and just a few weeks after that, the group filed for bankruptcy and shuttered its doors, terminating all its services. Now, get this—just a few months later, at a time when many of its thousands of former employees were still without jobs, the former CEO—yes, the one who earned $638K in one year—sued the bankrupt agency for $1.2 million in deferred compensation.[491] That's like a car bomber suing her victims to get repaid for the car. As of September 2016, no one had been charged with a crime for any malfeasance.

An exposé in the *New York Times* blew the lid off highly questionable spending practices at one of the country's highest-profile veteran's charities, the Wounded Warrior Project, which recently had doubled its staff and raised its highest annual budget to $225 million. The organization spent millions on "travel, dinners, hotels, and conferences that often seemed more lavish than appropriate. The organization has also spent hundreds of thousands of dollars in recent years on public relations and lobbying campaigns to deflect criticism of its spending and to fight legislative efforts to restrict how much nonprofits spend on overhead . . . About 40 percent of the organization's donations in 2014 were spent on its overhead." The article also charged that the group—known for its constant barrage of emotional television ads featuring veterans who have lost limbs wearing prosthetic devices and talking about how much they've been helped by the charity—fudged its records to imply that it helped more veterans, and was generally far more effective in providing services, that it really was.[492] Shortly after the exposé ran, the group's board of directors fired the nonprofit's two top executives.

Feed the Children, one of the country's largest domestic and international anti-hunger charities, became famous through the ubiquitous TV ads of its charismatic founder, the Reverend Larry Jones, who intoned, "For only $8 a month, you can help feed a child. Would you go to your phone?" Jones was eventually forced out after being accused of taking bribes, giving large amounts of the charity's money to family members, secretly wiretapping employees, and collecting incest-related porn in his office.[493] The organization gave him an $800,000 payout when he was fired.[494] Again, as of March 2016, he was never prosecuted for a crime.

AARP, the powerful and respected national charity that effectively advocates for older Americans and provides them supplemental health insurance, lost more than $230,000 to embezzlement and billing irregularities in 2001. No one has been charged in those incidents either.[495]

My alma mater, Columbia University, disclosed in 2011 that it had been defrauded of $5.2 million in "electronic payments." In a rare instance of accountability, an accounting clerk and three associates were later convicted of stealing what turned out to be $5.7 million.[496] Maybe the difference is that it is more acceptable to prosecute low-level employees, rather than the powerful and often highly-paid CEOs.

The American Legacy Foundation, based just a few blocks from the White House in Washington, manages hundreds of millions of dollars drawn from a government settlement with big tobacco companies, and uses those funds to support health research and inform the public of the dangers of tobacco. It reported to the IRS that it had lost more than $250,000 due to a "diversion" of funds. Yet a *Washington Post* investigation found an estimated $3.4 million in theft, linked to purchases from a business described sometimes as a computer supply firm and at other times as a barbershop, and to an assistant vice president who now runs a video game emporium in Nigeria.[497]

I could go on—and on—with tales of charitable misdeeds. The nation is in the throes of a charitable crime spree, making a mockery of the word "non" before the word "profit." Very few perpetrators face serious criminal penalties, indicating that, for too many, charity crime *does* pay. *The Washington Post* found that, in federal tax filings from 2008 to 2012, there were more than 1,000 organizations that reported they had discovered a "significant diversion of assets, disclosing losses

attributed to theft, investment fraud, embezzlement, and other unau-
thorized uses of funds."[498] Keep in mind that those are just the ones
who discovered—and publicly reported—such theft.* No one knows
how much stealing there is that we don't even know about.

One in three Americans had lost faith in charities in 2015, according
to a national poll. And 41 percent thought nonprofit leaders were paid too
much. But, because nonprofit groups still, for the most part, wore haloes in
the public's perception, more than 80 percent of respondents in that poll
said charities do a "very good" or "somewhat good" job helping people."[499]

Because we still assume that most charities are intrinsically virtuous, the nation's nonprofit sector is massive—and growing. The
Urban Institute estimated that, in 2010, 2.3 million nonprofit organizations operated within the United States, and approximately 1.6
million nonprofits were registered with the IRS in 2010, an increase of
24 percent from 2000. The nonprofit sector contributed $804.8 billion
to the US economy in 2010, making up 5.5 percent of the country's
gross domestic product (GDP). Public charities, the largest component
of the nonprofit sector, reported $1.51 trillion in revenue, $1.45 trillion
in expenses, and $2.71 trillion in assets (yes, all three numbers are "tril-
lion" with a "t").[500] If those numbers seem too large to be believed, keep
in mind that most colleges and universities and many of the nation's
largest hospitals are classified as nonprofit organizations. Harvard
University's endowment alone was $36 billion in 2014.**

2.3 *million* charities in America. Think about that. That equals about
one charity for every 133 Americans.

So many organizations get away with fraud and mismanagement

---

* Perhaps these guys could also run nonprofit groups:

** Harvard's endowment equals the combined GNPs of the 29 countries on the planet with the
smallest GNPs: Guyana, Maldives, Lesotho, Liberia, Bhutan, Cape Verde, San Marino, Central
African Republic, Belize, Djibouti, Seychelles, St. Lucia, Antigua and Barbuda, Solomon Islands,
Guinea-Bissau, Grenada, St. Kitts and Nevis, Samoa, The Gambia, Vanuatu, St. Vincent and the
Grenadines, Comoros, Dominica, Tonga, São Tomé and Príncipe, Micronesia, Palau, Marshall
Islands, Kiribati, and Tuvalu. But I'm totally sure Harvard needs the money more than all those
countries do.

because the nonprofit sector—although gargantuan—is actually the least regulated major sector of US society, under far less oversight than either the public or private sectors. While there are more than 1.6 million tax-exempt groups in the US, the IRS only has about a hundred employees to determine whether new organizations should obtain such a designation, and there is virtually no federal oversight after they do. State and local monitoring of nonprofit groups is also scant.

It's as if there is a separate country within the borders of the United States, comprised of self-professed do-gooders and operating with trillions of dollars relatively independently, and with almost no accountability. The founder and editor of *Inside Philanthropy*, David Callahan, has written,

> [Philanthropy] is a world with too much secrecy and too little oversight. Despite its increasing role in American society, from education to the arts to the media, perhaps no sector is less accountable to outsiders . . . The charitable sector is a bit like the Wild West—by design. Foundations have long been granted expansive freedom, on the view that the diversity of America's civil society is one of the country's signature strengths, as Alexis de Tocqueville famously said, and that government shouldn't mess with this magic. Both political parties have been content to impose a minimum of rules on philanthropy . . .
>
> Foundations don't have to prove that they're making good use of billions of dollars of tax-subsidized funds . . . The law even permits donors to get an immediate tax break for charitable gifts that may sit in investment accounts for decades, never helping anyone. . . . It also makes it hard to answer the simplest questions about charitable giving, such as what society is getting for the $40 billion in tax breaks that donors receive annually.[501]

I should note that most people who work for nonprofit groups—including many of my closest friends—are honest, effective, underpaid, and hard-working, but when the sector overall has so little oversight, problems are bound to occur.

STRIKING IT RICH

Some of the shameless nonprofit executives who turned out to be the most crooked or incompetent were those who previously argued the loudest that charitable leaders should be paid very high salaries in order to compete with the private sector for the best leadership.

Too many nonprofit leaders earn more than the president of the United States ($400,000 per year in 2016), and they never have to decide whether to send troops into battle or whether to pardon someone on death row. University presidents, museum directors, and hospital heads often make millions of dollars per year. The president of Columbia University earned $4.6 million annually in 2013, more than 10 times the US president, while incoming undergraduate students paid $69,000 in tuition and fees for one year ($16,000 more than US median family income)—and graduate students paid even more. Meanwhile, some of the university's low-level employees were so poorly paid that they needed to use neighborhood food pantries.

In 2014, WNET, the nonprofit PBS affiliate station in New York City, earned $144 million in revenue, of which at least $23 million came from government. Their president earned more than half a million dollars, two other executives earned more than $300,000, and eleven employees took in more than $200,000 apiece.[502] Yet while the station has sponsored some important programming on poverty, it also repeatedly broadcasts insipid reunions of 1960s pop stars to bolster the station's seemingly nonstop pledge drives, which give viewers the false impression that the station will close up shop if each of them does not personally donate.*

America, you falsely think nonprofit leaders are saints but government officials are sinners; therefore, we overpay many nonprofit leaders, but underpay those in some higher-level government jobs.

---

* Cutting edge pledge-drive favorites are

"Motown 25," "Doo Wop's Best on PBS," and "Peter, Paul & Mary: 25th Anniversary Concert."

The head of the Central Park Conservancy earned \$656,735 in 2014 for his charity, which raises private money to aid Central Park in Manhattan (which comprises 843 acres of land, much of which borders extraordinarily wealthy neighborhoods). Yet New York City's parks commissioner, who manages 29,000 acres of land at 1,700 parks, playgrounds, and recreation facilities citywide—including Central Park—earned \$205,180 that same year.

Often nonprofit leaders compare their salaries to those of executives in the corporate sector or to those of their well-heeled friends in their social sets. But charities are *not* supposed to be the same as for-profit companies, which is exactly why such organizations are exempt from paying taxes.

I do think it is reasonable for nonprofit leaders to compare their salaries to those of the leaders of comparable nonprofit entities, but here's a shocking suggestion: they should also compare their salaries to those of their own lowest-paid employees. Some charity leaders receive compensation packages that are hundreds of times greater than those of their most poorly paid employees, ratios similar to those at some of the largest, greediest corporations.*

Here's an even more radical suggestion for my fellow nonprofit leaders: also compare your salary to those people you represent or serve. If you run a museum, you should contrast your salary to the incomes of the average families that fork over entrance fees to that institution. If you run an anti-poverty organization, you should compare your salary to that of people who live in poverty; I am *not* suggesting that nonprofit group leaders, me included, should get paid poverty wages, but simply that we at least think about the discrepancy between us and the people we aid when we (and our boards, which are legally responsible for setting our salaries) consider the pay levels for us and our executive staffs.

Goodness knows, it's hard for most nonprofit organizations to raise money for anything, and it's especially difficult to raise money for staff salary increases because many funders don't want their money going to what they consider "overhead." But I still think the entire nonprofit

---

* In 2016, I earned about three and a half times my organization's lowest-paid full-time employees and about seven times the salary of a family living in poverty. I consider myself damn fortunate, and I'm working hard to raise more money to pay our lowest-paid staff even more.

sector, as a whole, should do more to ensure that our own employees can earn solidly middle-class salaries and benefits. CEOs like me should prevent our employees from going hungry before we convince our boards to give us stratospheric levels of executive pay.

Not only do some highly compensated nonprofit leaders pay their frontline workers garbage, some of them—amazingly—even oppose minimum wage increases, claiming that their groups, and the rest of the nonprofit sector, can't "afford" to keep up. For example, in 2015, an organization called Quality Services for the Autism Community testified at a New York State Wage Board hearing to oppose a proposal to raise the minimum wage to $15 per hour for only fast food workers. The organization claimed that, even though their own workers would not be directly covered by this wage hike, it would be far harder for them to recruit and retain their employees if they had to compete against a $15 wage at fast food establishments. Yet in 2013, that organization took in $48 million in revenues, provided its CEO with $433,898 in total compensation, and paid three other executives more than $200K each.[503] I don't know how poorly entry-level workers there are paid, but if the group is worried about losing their work force if the local Wendy's was forced to pay their workers $15 per hour (which equals only about $31,000 per year, hardly a living wage), their workers must be very poorly paid indeed. If, let's say, their lowest-paid employees earned $12 per hour, the CEO could drop his salary from $433,000 to merely $200,000 and the savings from doing so could enable 46 of his lowest-paid employees to get raises to $15 per hour. It's all about priorities.

PINK RIBBONS, FOOD DRIVES, AND CHARITY FEEL-GOODISM

Many Americans believe that we can end US hunger one person at a time, one donated can of food at a time. They also believe they can cure breast cancer one pink ribbon at a time. The people who believe those things are well-meaning. But they are wrong.

US history proves that major societal problems can only be solved by massive, coordinated, society-wide action, led by the only entity capable of organizing such action: the government.

Yes, the *government*. I'm perfectly aware that, in today's political climate, it's downright shocking to claim that government must take the leading role in solving major social problems, such as domestic hunger or breast cancer, but history proves that my claim is demonstrably true.

America's dominant political narrative now tells us that our own government is somehow an evil, alien, occupying force that does nothing except violate the Constitution and steal our money. We're told that government is the antithesis of community. And we're told that government programs rarely, if ever, work.

That narrative is problematic for many reasons, not the least of which is that it's utterly untrue.

While the Tea Party movement seeks to claim that centralized government programs are a violation of the US Constitution, the truth is that the original Constitution was created to replace the weak Articles of Confederation precisely so that the federal government would have *more power* to engage in coordinated action on behalf of the states and the people.

In a democracy such as the United States, government is the most legitimate embodiment of community. Of course, all the components of civil society—including businesses, nonprofit groups, civic and religious organizations, families, and individuals—have important roles to play in addressing social problems. Yet leaders of nonprofit organizations aren't elected by the public. Neither are business leaders. (Small, self-selected boards of directors generally pick both.) In contrast, the reason we call elected officials by that name is that they were elected by a majority of voters. Whether you like them or not, the fact remains that elected officials are the only leaders empowered by the community to act on behalf of the interests of the entire society. And they are the only ones we can replace if we don't like the job they are doing.

Moreover, the knee-jerk hatred of all things governmental ignores the historical reality that government efforts have often been extraordinarily successful at accomplishing their goals. When I worked for the US Department of Agriculture for eight years and insisted to others that agency programs like those I helped run were vital in tackling major social problems, I would often hear that I was biased and that if I ever got a "real job" outside of government I'd understand. The reverse happened. As of 2016, I had spent 15 years in the nonprofit sector, and I believed even more strongly than ever in the role of the government versus that of the charitable sector. I had seen firsthand that all the things people say they hate about government—waste, inefficiency, turf battles, self-serving vanity, and outright corruption—were actually far more prevalent in the nonprofit sector than in government. Government programs generally have far more transparency and accountability than do nonprofit programs.

But because Americans these days often hate government and anything labeled "political," our media and culture continue to champion one-on-one do-gooding instead of efforts that fight for systemic policy improvements. For a number of years, CNN has awarded "hero" status to nonprofit groups, proclaiming that CNN Heroes showcase "10 organizations started by everyday people who ended up doing some pretty extraordinary things." All the honored institutions focused on direct service rather than policy advocacy, even though advocacy efforts have been proven to have a much higher bang for the buck in tackling social problems. For instance, CNN honored a group that provides services to teen moms (certainly a noble goal), but I doubt it would ever honor an organization fighting to ensure that government provides free birth control to anyone who needs it, which could dramatically reduce the number of single mothers needing help.

The news media, as well as your average Joes on social media, generally prefer to exalt one-off, one-on-one charitable gestures—like the man who took his own shirt off to give to a homeless person on the subway—than broader efforts that focus on structural changes. Another one-time incident—in which a police officer, called in to monitor a domestic dispute, bought a family dinner after he discovered they were fighting over not having enough to eat—spread like wildfire through numerous social media posts. I am glad the officer was kind-hearted enough to do what he did, but the resulting publicity made it seem like his gesture was a serious response to the nation's hunger epidemic—or even a solution to that one family's hunger problem. Asked about that by the media, I gave one of my trademark, scolding responses: "Having one police officer charged with defeating hunger makes as much sense as one social worker charged with defeating ISIS."[504]

Americans typically want their charitable giving and volunteer work to be fun, and preferably to involve celebrities in some way. That's why the ice-bucket challenge was far more popular than substantive discussions of how to cure the disease ALS.

Imported from the UK to the US, Red Nose Day describes itself as a "campaign dedicated to raising money by simply having fun and making people laugh. Money raised is spent to help lift children and young people out of poverty in the US and some of the poorest communities in the world." Their motto is "Have fun. Raise money. Change lives." The campaign asks people to purchase a red nose—the type that clowns wear—at Walgreens and Duane Reade pharmacies nationwide for one dollar. A Walgreens press release quoted a customer as saying, "Giving $1 is easy enough to make a big impact. It feels so good to give back to charity." Red Nose Day also sponsored a star-studded telethon complete with pop stars, comedy, and maudlin videos of celebrities comforting the dangerously impoverished. The telethon featured pictures of emaciated African kids sleeping on mats. Jack Black asked a small African child, "What about your mother and father, where do they live?" The child responded, "My mummy's dead."* Gag.

Red Nose Day claimed to have raised $23 million in 2015. That's great. The money seems to have gone to some excellent groups such as Oxfam, the National Council of La Raza, and the Boys & Girls Clubs of America. I'd be thrilled if, in the future, the advocacy organization I head, Hunger Free America, received donations through this or similar efforts.

Still, celebrity events such as this, which convince consumers that they

---

*

In a piece for CNN, Nathalie Dortonne wrote, "Social media is inundated with posts about the importance of being thankful for family, friends, and well-being because there are starving children in Africa who wish they had a quarter of your good fortune. Cue the images of an emaciated child with flies buzzing around his face, protruding rib cage, runny nose, and extended hands toward the camera—also known as poverty porn. Poverty porn is a tactic used by non-profits and charity organizations to gain empathy and contributions from donors by showing exploitative imagery of people living in destitute conditions. It leaves many of us feeling uncomfortable, disconnected, and guilty." Nathalie Dortonne, "The dangers of poverty porn," CNN.com, December 24, 2015, http://www.cnn.com/2015/12/24/living/poverty-porn-danger-feat/

can "make a big impact" for one dollar, are troubling. Celebrities in the telethon spouted such maxims as "Imagine a world with no poverty"—as if $23 million spread out over 12 different organizations worldwide could cure poverty for the 2.1 billion people who suffer from it. ($23 million equals about *one penny* for every poor person on the globe.) Even more troubling, none of the Red Nose Day activities so much as mentioned that the public could fight for changes in the underlying economic and political conditions that cause poverty. No one mentioned that if, for instance, a mass people's movement forced every nation on the globe to raise their national minimum wages by just one dollar per hour, it would absolutely dwarf the anti-poverty impact of the $23 million raised. (I doubt, though, that Walgreens, their sponsor, would be too keen on sponsoring an event to push for wage hikes.)*

That's my basic problem with pink ribbons to raise awareness of breast cancer, food drives, Facebook "likes for charities," and yellow ribbons to support the troops. They provide a mirage of easy virtue while letting the public off the hook from asking—and acting upon—the more fundamental questions.

For example, it's nice that the Denver International Airport collects "loose change" to help homeless people, but how much nicer would it be if Denver residents supported government policies that ensured that everyone there had a home of their own? Likewise, it's commendable when people donate their old winter coats to homeless people (as long as the coats are not too ratty, which the donations sometimes are), but few stop to consider that the beneficiaries of their largess wouldn't need so many heavy coats if they lived indoors.

Most returning troops likely appreciate seeing yellow ribbons of support, but I'll bet they'd be far more grateful to have adequate healthcare and living-wage jobs upon their return—and many probably would have also preferred not to have their legs blown off because their nation's leaders (most of whom have never fought in a war, nor have sons or daughters who will ever fight) send them off to pointless battles based on fabricated intelligence, with unquestioning support from the ribbon-sporting populace. Boy, howdy.

---

* In 2015, Walgreens was forced to settle a suit from workers alleging that they were given meaningless "promotions" in order to make them ineligible for overtime.

In my first book, the best-selling, award-winning (ok, barely-read and occasionally on sale now for less than a dollar—but with my signature!) treatise on US hunger (*All You Can Eat: How Hungry is America?*)—I extensively demolish the myth that private charities can end US hunger. I won't rehash all those arguments here, but I will point out that the most popular type of anti-hunger effort—the food drive—is an awful, truly awful, way to fight hunger.

In a piece for *Slate* entitled "Can the Cans: Why Food Drives are a Terrible Idea," Matthew Yglesias explained how economically inefficient they are:

> Having 100 different people go out and pay retail prices for a few cans of green beans is extraordinarily inefficient relative to pooling those funds to buy the beans in bulk (what food banks usually do) . . .
>
> But it's even worse than that. All across America, charitable organizations and the food industry have set up mechanisms through which emergency food providers can get their hands on surplus food for a nominal handling charge. [Charity expert] Katherina Rosqueta . . . explains that food providers can get what they need for "pennies on the dollar." She estimates that they pay about 10 cents a pound for food that would cost you $2 per pound retail. You'd be doing dramatically more good, in basic dollars and cents terms, by eating that tuna yourself and forking over a check for half the price of a single can of Chicken of the Sea. . . .
>
> Charities are naturally reluctant to turn down donations for fear of alienating supporters or demoralizing well-wishers, but the reality is that dealing with sporadic surges of cans is a logistical headache. A nationwide network of food banks called Feeding America gingerly notes on its website that "a hastily organized local food drive can actually put more strain on your local food bank than you imagine."[505]

Besides, if your own grandmother couldn't afford prescription medicine, you'd never ask your neighbors to hold a prescription drug drive, and go into their medicine cabinets to donate old drugs they think your grandmother might need. Of course not. Well, food drives are essentially the same thing, people donating food they often don't want any more to total strangers, having no clue as to the medical, nutritional, or cultural needs of the family getting help.

Volunteering at food pantries and soup kitchens just on Thanksgiving and Christmas is equally counterproductive. I've been forced to become quite the public Grinch on this topic. As *CNBC* reported:

> Some seemingly obvious moves to create charitable children have surprisingly little effect. And some can actually backfire, according to Joel Berg. . . . Take soup kitchens. A family outing to serve meals to your needy neighbors, especially around a holiday like Thanksgiving when many people are planning elaborate meals, seems like it ought to go a long way toward teaching charity. . . . Guess again, Berg says. . . . "The 7-year-old is making more work for the agencies, they're too young to move stuff around, and they can't really be around anything hot, or knives. The time it would take to instruct them is more than it would take for an adult." That's not the only problem. "Even very young kids have a built in b.s. detector," Berg said. "If you send them to a food pantry or kitchen on Thanksgiving that normally has 10 people volunteering, and there are 55 people there, they're going to see in a heartbeat that there are people standing around and doing nothing, and they'll get cynical."[506]

On a killjoy roll, I wasn't done. *The New York Times* wrote, "What is the sound of one eye rolling? Call Joel Berg and tell him you want to engage in that wonderful holiday tradition of volunteering on a soup line in the third week of November. 'Thanksgiving is to hunger groups what Halloween is to a costume company,' he said. 'Sometimes people actually get mad at us when they call a day or two before Thanksgiving or a day or two before Christmas and want to volunteer, when in fact many of these agencies have waiting lists months in advance.'"[507]

The very holiday volunteer activities that are supposed to reinforce our idealism have now morphed, for some, into the supreme form of

American narcissism by placing a volunteering family's own needs to "feel good" or "learn a lesson" above the concrete needs of the charities supposedly being helped.*

But my real problem with food drives and holiday volunteerism is that they distract from us understanding—and more importantly, acting upon—the fact that the true causes of hunger are low wages and massive holes in our social safety net.

That's also what's wrong with the organizations that give the false impression that pink ribbons, "increased awareness," and private research alone are all that's needed to tackle breast cancer, when there is plenty of evidence that unhealthy foods and environmental hazards greatly exacerbate the problem. Anti-cancer crusades that don't tackle environmental causes are as ineffective as anti-hunger campaigns that fail to tackle economic causes.

It's not just a theoretical concern that donations and volunteerism undermine the push for broader social change; there's science behind that worry. Studies have found that performing good deeds can liberate individuals to engage in behaviors that are immoral, unethical, or otherwise problematic, behaviors that they would otherwise avoid for fear of feeling or appearing immoral.[508] That goes for societies as well as individuals. Thus, donating or volunteering can make people feel better about supporting public policies—such as huge tax cuts for themselves or decreasing regulations of chemical plants—that may end up increasing hunger or cancer or other societal ills.

WHO DONATES TO CHARITY AND WHY?

One of the top justifications the Right often gives for passing huge tax cuts for the rich is that the wealthy are then more likely to turn around and give more money to charities. That sounds great, but the myth of "trickle down" charitable giving isn't true. According to the *Chronicle of Philanthropy*,

---

* Fortunately, there *is* a better way. Go to www.hungervolunteer.org, a state-of-the-art web portal launched by Hunger Free America, to find out how, year round, you can engage in skills-based and/or high impact anti-hunger volunteer work that truly makes a difference by helping people access government nutrition assistance, by fighting for public policy improvements, and by offering your professional skills to emergency feeding agencies.

As the recession lifted, poor and middle class Americans dug deeper into their wallets to give to charity, even though they were earning less. At the same time, wealthy Americans earned more, but the portion of the income they gave to charity declined. . . . The wealthiest Americans—those who earned $200,000 or more—reduced the share of income they gave to charity by 4.6 percent from 2006 to 2012. Meanwhile, Americans who earned less than $100,000 chipped in 4.5 percent more of their income during the same time period.[509]

The amount of money that the wealthy donate to charities is dwarfed by the amount of money that they no longer pay in taxes due to decades' worth of tax cuts. Not only that, when the wealthy *do* give to charities, they are most likely to donate to hospitals, universities, and cultural institutions that provide services to *their* families.

Many disturbing variables also impact how generously—or not-so-generously—donors will act. For example, one study found that all-white religious congregations became less charitable as the share of black residents in their communities rose.[510]

Buildings on college campuses used to be named after national heroes, famous scholars, or particularly accomplished deans or university presidents, but now they are almost all named for big donors. Livingston Hall at Columbia University used to be named after a Columbia grad, Robert Livingston, one of the key founding fathers who helped draft the Declaration of Independence; but, when Columbia renovated the building in the 1980s, it changed the building's name to that of a donor, Ira D. Wallach, CEO of Central National-Gottesman, the largest privately-held marketer of paper and pulp products.[*]

Sanford I. Weill, a Wall Street billionaire, and his wife, Joan, decided not to donate $20 million to a struggling northern New York college after a judge ruled that it could not be renamed for Mrs. Weill (though they did get their names plastered on New York City's New York-Presbyterian Hospital/Weill Cornell Medical Center and the Joan and

---

[*] Central National-Gottesman's motto is "It's Not Just Paper." Their largest competitor is Dunder Mifflin, which, after a disastrous foray into the laser printer business, retreated to its core paper business, and adopted the motto "It's *Only* Just Paper."

Sanford I. Weill Department of Medicine at the Weill Cornell Medical College,[511] and the Weill Cornell Graduate School of Medical Sciences, and the Weill Institute for Neurosciences at the University of California at San Francisco,[512] and . . .).[513]

Music mogul David Geffen donated $100 million to renovate Avery Fisher Hall, home of the New York Philharmonic at Lincoln Center, but on the condition that $15 million of that amount would be used to buy off the Fisher family so that the hall could be renamed after Geffen. Lincoln Center also had to pay workers to change 61 different signs from Avery Fisher Hall to David Geffen Hall.[*]

Major donations often have as much to do with flattering the ego and advancing the uninformed biases of the donors, as they do to concretely aid the cause at hand—what philanthropist Peter Buffett has described as "Philanthropic Colonialism":

> People (including me) who had very little knowledge of a particular place would think that they could solve a local problem. Whether it involved farming methods, education practices, job training, or business development, over and over I would hear people discuss transplanting what worked in one setting directly into another with little regard for culture, geography, or societal norms . . .
>
> As more lives and communities are destroyed by the system that creates vast amounts of wealth for the few, the more heroic it sounds to "give back." It's what I would call "conscience laundering"—feeling better about accumulating more than any one person could possibly need to live on by sprinkling a little around as an act of charity . . .
>
> But this just keeps the existing structure of inequality in place. The rich sleep better at night, while others get just enough to keep the pot from boiling over. But as long as most folks are patting themselves on the back for charitable acts, we've got a perpetual poverty machine.[514]

---

[*] The $15 million that Geffen paid the Fisher family to substitute his name on that building instead of theirs could have paid for 9.1 million school breakfasts—but who's counting?

DON'T BELIEVE THE HYPE: BRING BUSINESS SENSE
TO CHARITY WORK

Americans love "social marketing," through which they can aid charities when they buy products. Subaru once heavily advertised, "If you
purchased or leased a new Subaru between November 19 and January
2, we'll donate $250 to a choice of charities that benefit your commu-
nity. By the end of this, our eighth year, Subaru and its participating
retailers will have donated over $65 million to charity." That sounds
great, but the public had no way of knowing whether Subaru jacked
up the price of each car by $250 to pay for this promotion. In any case,
a $250 donation equals only about 1 percent of the sales price of their
average car. But again, if Subaru wants to donate money from each car
to Hunger Free America, then they would be the greatest auto company on the planet!

Today's entrepreneurs use the word "disruptive" in practically every
sentence. They proclaim to be so proud to overturn the status quo in
everything they do. How ironic, then, that their charitable endeavors
tend to be wedded to a broken status quo, the tech equivalent of type-
writers or slates, giving to the "same ol', same ol'" organizations. Sure,
they may require the charities they fund to report detailed "metrics" or
use snazzy new apps, but, in the end, their favorite charities usually
perpetuate the failing establishment.

Sometimes, the entrepreneurs do think a little bigger, but then they
make the mistake of wanting to start their very *own* nonprofit, as Mark
Rosenman pointed out in the *Chronicle of Philanthropy*:

> Many people probably rejoiced when they heard about a
> study . . . showing that 12 million baby boomers want to start
> their own nonprofit or socially oriented business over the next
> decade . . .
>
> Adding millions more of such entities is not good for this
> nation. . . . While existing organizations need to provide
> expanded services and economic opportunities, they have
> the capability to care for people in need, if given adequate
> money and creative support. . . . At a time when nonprofit

organizations are being pushed to greater program efficien-
cies, mergers, and other administrative economies, why do
boomer entrepreneurs seem to think that starting millions of
brand-new entities is the most effective way to make a societal
contribution? Why can't they work through existing organizations to start their creative new programs, improve existing
ones, or concentrate resources instead of multiplying administrative and overhead costs?

When businesspeople want to aid the public good, but don't want
to be bogged down by niceties such as the laws that govern nonprofit
groups, they have increasingly started "social enterprises," which
are for-profit businesses that earn money while supposedly serving
a greater public purpose. One famous model is TOMS, which calls
itself a "one-for-one company," because it gives away one pair of shoes
(to people "in need") for every pair it sells. Kentaro Toyama, in his
must-read book, *Geek Heresy: Rescuing Social Change from the Cult of
Technology*, takes apart the TOMS business model:

> Since its founding in 2006, it has handed out over 10 mil-
> lion shoes, which implies cumulative revenues of about half
> a billion dollars. . . . Despite its performance, TOMS has come
> under some scathing criticism. Some say giving away shoes
> to poor communities stunts local economies and perpetuates
> a culture of dependence. Others note that TOMS could direct
> its spending to something more lasting than straw-and-canvas
> shoes. . . . Still others find TOMS to be little more than a sweat-
> shop, exploiting cheap Chinese labor and photos of children
> for hefty profits. . . . But the real problem is deeper still. . . .
> Though TOMS trumpets its commitment to addressing "hard-
> ships faced by children growing up without shoes," it's not very
> open about what its customers are actually paying for. TOMS
> doesn't disclose its financial statement. What we do know
> is this: thanks to a recent agreement with Bain Capital, [the
> TOMS CEO] stands to gain as much as $300 million on top of
> whatever he's paid himself so far as sole owner and CEO. . . .

Imagine if you made a $50 donation to a nonprofit, and out of that, say, $10 went to the cause, while $10 came back to you as a thank-you gift, and $30 facilitated the executive director's multimillion-dollar bonus. You wouldn't stand for it, yet this is effectively the TOMS "business model." And from it, the founder not only richly profits from it but then is widely hailed as a social activists' hero. . . .

By misleadingly presenting itself as primarily interested in charity, the company diverts the goodwill of people who might otherwise engage more deeply in the cause. . . . There's a good chance that TOMS customers skimp on more worthwhile efforts, something they probably wouldn't do if they bought their shoes from Nike. . . . The greater jeopardy, though, is that . . . by playing up efforts like TOMS, we as a society fool ourselves into believing that the world's problems can be solved by enlightened consumerism.

That's the problem with social-enterprise hyperbole in general. Its noisy buzz draws attention away from effective government and nonprofit approaches to social causes.[515]

People who want to start social enterprises (often based on what they believe are new technologies) to fight hunger often coming knocking on my door, but their ideas are usually impractical. I hate to break their earnest hearts, but I must frequently inform them that, not only is their idea not new, but something nearly identical to what they are proposing was tried before and didn't work. Then I tell them what *does* work in fighting hunger—building an economy with living-wage jobs for all and ensuring that everyone who needs it can get SNAP. I close by suggesting that it would be far better for them to use their prodigious talents and inspiring idealism to aid an effective anti-hunger organization that already exists (*hint, hint*). Some of the advice-seekers realize that it makes sense to work with an existing organization, but too many still decide to go off on their own, and they usually fail. As Kentaro Toyama put it,

Many [technology utopians] believe that *every* kind of problem can be solved by some invention, often one that is right around the corner. Whether the issue is poverty, bad governance, or climate change, they say things like "There is no limit to human ingenuity," and "When seen through the lens of technology, few resources are truly scarce." Besotted with gadgets, technological utopians scoff at social institutions like governments, civil society, and traditional firms, which they pit as slow, costly, behind the times, or all of the above.[516]

WHAT *SHOULD* THE ROLE OF NONPROFITS BE?

In 2012, after his lies and financial shenanigans were exposed, a settlement with the Montana Attorney General's Office forced Greg Mortenson to return over $1 million to the Central Asia Institute and prohibited him from having any future financial oversight role in the organization. But in 2014, Mortenson was still the group's highest-paid employee, earning $169,330, and the charity continued to use the fabricated accounts from his book for their marketing.[517] Yet regulators and the media mostly moved on. As far as I can tell, Obama never got his $100,000 back.

Despite all the scandals and despite our increased cynicism about charities, the nation continues to give the nonprofit sector a pass on any serious, systematic scrutiny.

But even if all US nonprofits were well-regulated, well-run, scrupulously honest, and incredibly effective, should they continue to take over functions, particularly social service work, previously performed by government? No, they should not.

Many of these groups do provide vital services and perform good work. But while they may pioneer some best practices or help a few thousand people at a time, they rarely are able to fundamentally solve major societal problems on their own.

What wealthy elites choose to fund is highly subjective, and biased towards their class beliefs and goals. As David Callahan put it, "Donors to nonprofit groups can get the same tax break for bankrolling a libertarian push to abolish food stamps as they do for giving to a food pantry . . . Philanthropy still does enormous good, perhaps now more than ever. But it's alarming how in an era of high inequality, private funders have a growing say over central areas of civic life like education and public parks, and how this influence is often wielded against a backdrop of secrecy."[518]

As Joanne Barkan, a critic of big philanthropy, wrote, "The mega rich increasingly use their foundations and their celebrity as philanthropists to mold public policy to an extent not possible for other citizens."[519]

Too often, nonprofit leaders give the impression that the only concrete action that corporations and wealthy Americans need to take to be socially responsible is donating to their nonprofit organizations. It's great when folks donate, and we certainly appreciate it (go to https://www.hungervolunteer.org/donate now!). But we all need to be clear that it's even more important for Americans to hold corporations accountable for generating living-wage jobs, ensuring safe conditions for workers, limiting negative impacts upon the environment, and ending support of trade associations that lobby against all those things. The very best way for wealthy individuals to be generous is to pay their fair share of taxes that will support an adequate governmental safety net for everyone in our national community.

I am *not* saying that all nonprofit groups should go out of business. I am saying that, at a minimum, the entire nonprofit sector needs more constructive oversight from government, the media, and an informed public. More broadly, we need to restore a greater balance between what the government and nonprofits should be doing and what we expect from both sectors.

The government should be working with the business sector to ensure a robust economy full of living-wage jobs. For those who still can't find work, are unable to work (including children and people with severe disabilities), are retired, or for whom available jobs pay too little, government should provide an adequate safety net, ensuring high-quality education, childcare, food, housing, and healthcare, either for free or at affordable rates. But when government fails to adequately perform one or more of those functions—which it has frequently done over the last few decades—too many nonprofits are forced to provide regularly recurring services that should really be provided by government, such as basic food and housing for the masses. So long as charities are laden with the colossal burden of making up for all of government and society's deficiencies, they will never be able to succeed. As President Obama has said, "Feed the hungry, clothe the naked, and house the homeless is not just a call for isolated charity but the imperative of a just society."

If government went back to doing what it should be doing—ensuring basic survival of the populace—then nonprofits would be far more successful in doing what they do best—filling in the gaps in government services, testing out innovative new approaches that could later be adopted by government, and providing personal and spiritual guidance to people at times of crisis. Most importantly, nonprofits could do more to fulfill their most vital role in civil society: prodding every institution in our country, including government, to do a better job in meeting the nation's most pressing needs. More nonprofit groups should be prophetic voices of justice, but it's hard for them to do so if they are busy treading water—or worse, sinking—just trying to meet the basic human needs of millions of struggling families.

HOW TO PROVIDE A ZILLION CUPS OF TEA

America, please move beyond your eternal quest to support nonprofits because the founder has some incredible personal story (which may be untrue anyway). Please transcend the belief that magical nonprofits can effortlessly solve huge problems on their own. Please allow yourself to realize that, if the main reason you donate or volunteer is to "feel good about yourself," that's yet another form of counterproductive narcissism.

One person, or even one nonprofit group—no matter how honest and effective—can only provide so much tea. To have a truly meaningful impact on the large scale necessary to make significant progress, we need the public, business, and nonprofit sectors to mutually reinforce each other's strengths, and serve as a check on each other's weaknesses. Only when each sector does what it does best can we can ensure that everyone gets as many cups of tea as they need.

12.

The Seven Habits of a
Highly Unsuccessful Nation
Why the US Is Lagging

Have you ever crossed the US/Canadian border by car, perhaps to visit Niagara Falls or Montréal, or by taking a scenic train between Seattle and Vancouver? If so, did you see hoards of bedraggled, desperate, Canadian-born refugees teeming at the border, willing to risk their lives on a harrowing journey to illegally cross to the US—just so they could avoid the totalitarian oppression they suffer because their government guarantees healthcare and delicious maple syrup?

Or did you see happy—gosh darn happy—Canadians everywhere, quite content to stay in their country, not having to worry about whether they would ever be denied life-saving medical treatment, eh?* I thought so. You betcha. It's not just your imagination: 92 percent of Canadians consider themselves satisfied or very satisfied with their lives. In contrast, only one in three US residents say they are happy, according to a 2015 Gallup survey.[520]

So why are Americans less happy than Canadians, and less happy than many people in many other industrialized western nations? Perhaps it's because, on most significant measures of well-being, the US trails them.

The Stanford Center on Poverty and Inequality analyzed data on poverty, employment, income and wealth inequality, economic mobility, educational outcomes, health inequities, and residential segregation

---

* Look how gosh darn happy people are to be Canadian.

and found that, among 10 developed Western countries, the US ranked worst overall.

When the Center compared the US with 21 countries, including less developed European nations, in four areas (employment, social safety net, inequality, poverty), the US ranked 18th overall, with only Spain, Estonia, and Greece ranking lower. The report also found that in some US states, including Alabama and Kentucky, levels of average health and health inequality are comparable to those in post-Soviet-bloc countries such as Bulgaria, Estonia, and Latvia.[521]

Rankings for 21 Countries:

Country	Labor Markets (Unemployment Rates)	Poverty	Safety Net	Income Inequality	Overall
Australia	10	6	18	11	13
Canada	6	8	15	9	9 (tie)
Czech Republic	7	11	16	6	11
Denmark	13	5	4	5	4
Estonia	16	20	21	15	20
Finland	15	7	6	8	8
France	5	12	2	14	7
Germany	1	15	3	12	6
Greece	20	18	14	21	21
Iceland	3	1	19	1	2 (tie)
Ireland	21	16	1	19	15 (tie)
Italy	18	17	9	16	17
Luxembourg	4	2	11	13	5
Netherlands	2	3	5	4	1
Norway	9	4	8	3	2 (tie)
Poland	14	21	12	10	15 (tie)
Slovak Republic	8	14	17	2	12
Slovenia	11	13	7	7	9 (tie)
Spain	19	19	13	17	19
United Kingdom	12	10	10	18	14
United States	17	9	20	20	18

Note: From "Pathways, The Poverty and Inequality Report 2016," Stanford Center on Poverty and Inequality, page 7. The ranks presented here were secured by (a) converting the scores on the indicators in Table 3 to country rankings, (b) averaging across the rankings comprising each domain and converting these averages to domain-specific rankings, and (c) averaging across these domain-specific rankings to produce an overall country ranking.

America, over the last few, flailing decades, your operating philosophy seems to have been to see what works well in the rest of the world,
and then do the *opposite*. It's crazy that we continue to refuse to learn
from either our mistakes or other nation's successes.

In his groundbreaking business advice book, *The 7 Habits of Highly
Effective People*, Stephen Covey comprehensively studied how successful people operated. He then gave his readers concrete tips for
emulating the methods that lead to accomplishment, often suggesting
that readers needed to make wholesale changes in how they operate
in order to achieve their goals. Covey wrote, "We see the world, not as
it is, but as we are—or, as we are conditioned to see it . . . If you want
small changes in your life, work on your attitude. But if you want big
and primary changes, work on your paradigm."[522] Similarly, America,
if you want to improve your dismal rankings on many key international
indicators, you'll need to do many things entirely differently. Covey's
seven habits are: be proactive; begin with the end in mind; put first
things first; think win-win; seek first to understand, then to be understood; synergize; and sharpen the saw. Let's examine how the US is
falling behind many of our international peers precisely because our
habits are the *opposite* of those winning ones.

Habit 1: Be Proactive

America, you are reactive, not proactive, on so many fronts. We
spend tons of money on the back-end to deal with problems that could
have been largely prevented if we spent more on the front-end. For
instance, 11 states spend more on prisons and jails than on their public
colleges. State budgets for public universities have been cut about 20
percent since 2008, but, since 1986, funding for prisons has spiked 141
percent.[523] If we spent more on making public education—starting for
toddlers and continuing through college—more effective and affordable, we'd have far less need to spend on criminal detention.

US hunger and food insecurity cost the American economy an estimated $167.5 billion annually.[524] And by 2018, obesity is expected to
account for 21 percent of healthcare spending, equaling $334 billion
per year.[525] Yet, America, you could end hunger entirely and dramatically reduce obesity for a small fraction of that simply by ensuring

that all Americans can afford nutritious foods and obtain them in their neighborhoods.

Another thing that our international competitors do far better than we do is invest in infrastructure. Public transportation schedules in Germany, Japan, and Scandinavia, for instance, are so reliable that I'd literally be willing to bet my life on them.*

The US used to invest heavily in effective infrastructure, but now—not so much. Our nation's train system is a joke, often characterized by slow and outdated trains, slow and outdated tracks, and slow and outdated signals. *The New York Times* reported,

> New Jersey Transit [train] riders had a truly torturous experience. There were major delays on four days because of problems with overhead electrical wires and a power substation, leaving thousands of commuters stalled for hours. One frustrated rider, responding to yet another New Jersey Transit Twitter post announcing a problem, replied, "Just easier to alert us when there aren't delays."
>
> These troubles have become all too common on the Northeast Corridor, the nation's busiest rail sector, which stretches from Washington to Boston and carries about 750,000 riders each day on Amtrak and several commuter rail lines. The corridor's ridership has doubled in the last 30 years even as its old and overloaded infrastructure of tracks, power lines, bridges, and tunnels has begun to wear out. And with Amtrak and local transit agencies struggling for funding, many fear the disruptions will continue to worsen in the years ahead . . .
>
> [The delays] have a ripple effect, sending more traffic onto roads and wasting hours for commuters who could be working. The shutdown of the corridor for one day could cost the country $100 million in added congestion, productivity losses, and other effects.
>
> While President Obama called for $2.45 billion for Amtrak—about $1 billion more than the previous subsidy—

---

* If I ever need a respirator which requires that its doses of oxygen be calibrated to exact time intervals, I'd be delighted if they were based on the schedule of the Helsinki tram system, which is lovely and efficient, no matter the weather.

Republicans in the House passed a bill to reduce spending on Amtrak by about $250 million.[526]

Our reactivity also fosters even bigger problems, such as violence in our country and hemisphere. We ignore festering problems in our own inner cities and rotting rural areas—as well as impoverished nearby powder kegs like Mexico and Honduras—and then we wonder why violence envelops our nation and region. Smart spending that reduces poverty and bolsters a social safety net here and abroad could prevent so many more security issues down the road.

America, you simply can't imagine how many headaches you'd forestall if you'd become proactive.

Habit 2: Begin with the End in Mind

If we seek to intervene in another nation's problems, we had better first look five—or ten—steps ahead to consider every conceivable outcome down the road.

One of the top reasons the US is falling behind much of the developed world is that we simply refuse to learn the lesson that wasting money on endless, pointless wars—and propping up murderous, freedom-crushing regimes—only makes us weaker and poorer in the long-run.

In 1898, after the Spanish-American War, reformer Carl Schurz wrote, "The indiscriminate screaming of the eagle could really gratify the American people only in their boyish days. We have got beyond that now. What the people want is a just, sober, sensible, and dignified foreign policy."[527] Ah, how wrong he was. Even a "mature" nation remained addicted to that bird's screaming and hollering.

After every counterproductive US military adventure abroad turns sour, those who pushed for them in the first place inevitably try imposing amnesia on the populace by claiming that no one ever could have predicted that things would go awry. That's rarely true. In 1954, a decade before the Gulf of Tonkin Resolution pushed America into full-scale war in Vietnam, journalists Bernard Fall and Frances FitzGerald warned,

Politically, the situation looks even more hopeless for the West. France has not succeeded in convincing the Vietnamese that it will make good its promises of full independence. . . . Now, however, the French are obviously eager to stop the fighting in any way possible [as they face] hopeless stalemate in the jungle swamps. We need have no illusions about Ho's regime. It is of course Communist-dominated. . . . A farsighted policy based on well-administered aid might do more to stem the Communist tide in Southeast Asia than sending a few technicians or a few additional plane-loads of napalm.[528]

In 1968, following the heavy US bombing of the Viet Cong–held city of Bến Tre, an anonymous US major was quoted as saying, "It became necessary to destroy the town to save it." Though some have disputed the veracity of the quote, it became one of the iconic utterances of the Vietnam War, symbolizing the US military's indifference to civilian casualties. As Joshua Keating wrote in *Slate*, "That line comes to mind after reading [about] Ramadi, which was mostly retaken by US-backed Iraqi forces . . . but now features a panorama of wreckage so vast that it was unclear where the original buildings had stood."[529]

Throughout history, humans have always used their most sophisticated technologies to kill each other, proving that intelligence is not the same as wisdom. We seem to never accept the senselessness of warfare. Given that humans don't live in caves too often anymore (even Osama bin Laden didn't, it turns out), why do we still so frequently resort to violence? Why are we only half-evolved? A drone strike actually isn't that different, in its end result, than bashing a bunch of people in the head with a rock or pushing them in front of a stampeding mastodon.

We also never seem to understand that, when the US intervenes violently overseas, we almost always suffer from unintended results. The Old Testament traces how generations of Middle Eastern residents "begat" each other and goes on for some time in this vein. Let me update these Middle Eastern genealogies to explain how US interventions begat unintended negative results.

THE GENEALOGY OF US-CREATED TRAGEDY IN THE MIDDLE EAST

MOHAMMAD MOSSADEGH WAS A DEMOCRATICALLY ELECTED PRIME MINISTER OF IRAN.

HE TOOK THE NATION'S OIL INDUSTRY AWAY FROM THE BRITISH, SO THE BRITISH AND US INTELLIGENCE AGENCIES REMOVED HIM WITH A COUP.

THAT COUP BEGAT THE MURDEROUS, US-BACKED REGIME OF DESPOTIC SHAH OF IRAN, MOHAMMAD REZA PAHLAVI.

THE REPRESSIVE REGIME OF THE SHAH BEGAT THE IRANIAN REVOLUTION OF 1979, WHICH BEGAT THE RULE OF THE GRAND AYATOLLAH SAYYID RUHOLLAH MŪSAVI KHOMEINI, WHO REALLY, REALLY, REALLY DIDN'T LIKE THE US, PRIMARILY BECAUSE WE BACKED THE SHAH FOR SO LONG.

THE US CIA TRAINED FUNDAMENTALIST MUSLIMS, INCLUDING PERHAPS OSAMA BIN LADEN, TO FIGHT AGAINST THE SOVIET UNION IN AFGHANISTAN, WHICH BEGAT SOME OF THE MOST VIOLENT MUSLIM FUNDAMENTALIST OPPOSITION TO OUTSIDERS IN THE REGION.

THE US THEN BASED TROOPS IN SAUDI ARABIA TO FIGHT SADDAM HUSSEIN, WHICH BEGAT YET ANOTHER WAR IN IRAQ 10 YEARS LATER.

OPPOSITION TO US TROOPS IN THE HOLY LAND OF SAUDI ARABIA BEGAT AL QAEDA.

THE US BACKED SADDAM HUSSEIN IN THE IRAN/IRAQ WAR.

SADDAM THEN UNLEASHED POISONOUS GAS ON IRAQI KURDS,
AS AMERICAN OFFICIALS LOOKED THE OTHER WAY.

BUT THEN SADDAM THREATENED THE PERSIAN GULF OIL SUPPLY, SO THE US
GOT RID OF HIM, LEAVING A MAJOR POWER VACUUM IN IRAQ THAT BEGAT ISIS.

For 100-plus years, the US has sent military aid to military dictatorships, claiming they supported vaguely defined US interests, sometimes economic, sometimes security-related, and usually both. Time after time, the strategy of "an enemy of my enemy is a friend" backfired on us, but we continue to use it to side with the most odious regimes.

For the life of me, I can't understand why we still defend Saudi Arabia, for example. Fifteen of the 17 hijackers on 9/11 were Saudi.

While there is no evidence that the Saudi government was directly behind the 9/11 plot, the Saudi regime did actively promote and fund some of the most extreme forms of Islam. The Saudi Kingdom is a religious dictatorship which, according to Human Rights Watch, in 2014:

▶ Convicted and imprisoned political dissidents and human rights activists solely on account of their peaceful activities.

▶ Sentenced prominent Eastern Province activist Fadhil al-Manasif to 15 years in prison, a 15-year ban on travel abroad, and a large fine after it convicted him on charges that included "breaking allegiance with the ruler," "contact with foreign news organizations to exaggerate the news," and "circulating his phone number to news agencies."

▶ Prohibited public worship by adherents of religions other than Islam and systematically discriminated against those who practiced forms of Islam different than Saudi Arabia's official form of it.

▶ Convicted activist Raif Badawi and sentenced him to 10 years in prison and 1,000 lashes for "insulting Islam" by establishing a liberal website critical of the government.

▶ Detained political opponents, including children, who commonly faced systematic violations of due process and fair trial rights, including arbitrary arrest and torture, as well as ill treatment in detention.

▶ Filed 191 cases of alleged sorcery—a crime punishable by death—including some against foreign domestic workers. Executed at least 68 persons, mostly for murder, drug offenses, and armed robbery. Thirty-one of those executed were convicted for non-violent crimes, including one man sentenced for "sorcery."

▶ Sentenced prominent Shia cleric Nimr al-Nimr to death on a host of vague charges, based largely on his peaceful criticism of Saudi officials.

▶ Forbade women from driving, obtaining a passport, marrying, traveling, or accessing higher education without the approval of a male guardian, usually a husband.[530]

Ladies and gentlemen, I present you the Kingdom of Saudi Arabia—our close friend and ally! When ISIS beheads people for heresy, it's correctly considered barbaric. When our "ally" Saudi Arabia does it, we consider that just an internal matter.

The US gave Saudi Arabia a green light for its counterproductive war in Yemen, which was conducted with complete disregard for indiscriminate mass civilian casualties. Obama grumbled about this conduct in Yemen a bit in an interview, but we mostly stuck with them. If this was only about oil, I'd understand it (although still find it appalling), but given the major increase in US oil production and conservation, Saudi oil is no longer critical to our economy. According to the US Department of Energy, in 2014, "Net imports accounted for 27 percent of the petroleum consumed in the United States, the lowest annual average since 1985." Only 13 percent came from Saudi Arabia, slightly more than what came from Mexico or Venezuela.[531] Why our government still considers them an ally is a mystery to me.

We still support *many* dictators who claim to be our friends. In 2015, we gave $1.3 billion in military aid to Egypt's brutal dictatorship; that funding could have instead paid for an additional billion meals for low-income Americans in the SNAP program or contributed mightily to aiding refugees fleeing Syria. (Note to the Left: neither does it makes sense to support brutal dictatorships in places like Cuba and Venezuela just because the US government is at odds with them.)

Will we never learn from history that dictators can never be true allies of democracies? Not only is supporting repression always immoral, but from a pure *realpolitik* point of view, doing so will most always come back and bite us on the ass. America, we wouldn't have these problems if we began with the end in mind.

Habit 3: Put First Things First

America, you have your priorities ass backwards. One of the traditional bedrocks of conservatism is supposedly fiscal moderation, but the neo-cons have thrown that out the window to feed their bloodlust for war. As of Fiscal Year 2013, the US had spent $1.7 trillion (equaling $5,000 per second) on the Iraq War alone. Since the war was paid for with borrowed money (because the Right refused to follow the long

US tradition of raising taxes on the wealthy to pay for our fighting), it cost the country a projected $7 trillion more in interest payments on the national debt. Of the money spent, $20 billion went to KBR, a contractor responsible for equipment and services. (Pentagon auditors found $3 billion of these payments "questionable.") The military lost $546 million in spare parts alone. American subcontracting companies really cleaned up as they received $75 billion, with the largest payments going to Halliburton, where Dick Cheney was formerly CEO.[532] I'm not a conspiracy theorist by nature, but when a vice president leads us into a war based on false pretenses, and his former employer makes billions of dollars off that decision, a long "hmm" is certainly in order.

Elites around the globe make tons of money off combat and armaments. The US may be trailing the developed world in healthcare and education, but it's oh so comforting that we're still leading it in foreign arms sales. On Christmas Day 2015, it was reported that foreign arms sales by the United States jumped by almost $10 billion in the previous year to $36 billion, a 35 percent jump over the year before that. Some of our biggest customers included Qatar, Saudi Arabia (oh, so *that's* why we still side with Saudi Arabia!), and South Korea. The US remained the single largest provider of arms around the world, controlling just over 50 percent of the market. The next highest-grossing arms suppliers, in ranking order, were Russia, Sweden, France, and China.[533]

Part of the reason that elites—who never seem to fight in wars themselves or encourage their children to do so—love ever-more wars is the bundle of money to be made, but part of it is also that (perhaps *because* of the money to be made) they've conned themselves—and much of the world—into believing their rhetoric that bloodshed advances freedom and security. But the neo-cons' permanent war economy—combined with their brilliant strategy of tax cuts for the rich—is bankrupting you, America.

We can only be as strong abroad as we are at home, and given that, as of 2014, we had 48 million residents who couldn't afford enough food, the US is pretty weak at home. No superpower in the history of the world has remained a superpower if it failed to feed its own people. Let's get our own house in order before we presume to tell the world what to do.

In contrast, other countries that spend less on armaments spend far more directly aiding their residents. I have a friend who lives in Paris and received 800 Euros in 2015 just for having a baby.* Parents there also receive €400 per child for school supplies, up to €1,200 for three kids. No, she doesn't have to show the government receipts for the items she bought for her child—the government there trusts her and other mothers (gasp) to use the money wisely. She pays only €145 per month for high-quality childcare for her infant, and that is heavily subsidized; in New York, a parent would need to pay, on average, six times that, at least, for the care for an baby under one year old. Of course, she and her family receive excellent free healthcare also.

Part of the difference between the US and France is how we *think* of ourselves. The French strive to achieve their national motto, "liberté, égalité, and fraternité" (liberty, equality, and fraternity). They consider economic equality vital. In contrast, America rarely considers any sort of food, housing, or money support to be a right. The US Declaration of Independence merely seems to suggest the *"pursuit* of happiness." Our country's message, since the nation's inception, has basically been, "If you can't achieve happiness yourself, well, then, you're on your own, buddy."

How does France afford to pay for their expansive safety net? It's pretty simple: they require their wealthiest citizens to pay their fair of taxes (what the US used to do, but hasn't in decades). That's why, while the share of the national income earned by the top 1 percent has soared in the US, it has remained relatively modest in France.

Countries with far larger safety nets than the US generally do not define poor people's programs as distinct from everyone else's programs. They define government benefits, by and large, as stuff everyone in society gets. Everyone is eligible for healthcare (most of which is free), and heavily subsidized public transportation, childcare, higher education, unemployment benefits, maternity leave, etc. They view these as benefits to the society as a whole, and everyone, especially the wealthiest, chip in adequate taxes dollars, to support these activities in the name of the mutual good.

You might expect that the countries that have the most generous gov-

---

* At the time I wrote this, the value of the Euro was very close to that of a US dollar.

ernment benefits and the broadest safety nets would have the highest
levels of official corruption, but the reverse is true. Countries with the
most robust social services—such as Denmark, Finland, Sweden, and
Norway—have some of the world's lowest levels of pilfering from government programs (according to Transparency International, which
tracks international levels of public corruption); nations with virtually invisible safety nets—such as Haiti, India, and the Congo—have
rampant corruption. Why? I think the reason is that, in countries with
more robust government services, residents tend to feel that "they are
all in this together," and thus social norms make it both less likely for
someone to commit fraud and more likely for someone to turn them
in. Conversely, in societies that provide less government support, more
people have the attitude that "it's every man for himself"—and thus,
they have fewer misgivings about stealing (they likely don't see it as
plundering it from themselves, because they don't reap the rewards of
a strong government anyway) and more of their peers have the incentive to be collaborators, not whistleblowers.

Most other developed countries also have wages far higher than
ours, even for jobs typically characterized as "low skilled." In Denmark,
the base wage for fast food workers was the equivalent of twenty US
dollars in 2014. Danish Burger King worker Hampus Elofsson said,
"You can make a decent living here working in fast food. You don't
have to struggle to get by." John Schmitt, an economist at the Center
for Economic and Policy Research, a US think tank, agreed: "We see
from Denmark that it's possible to run a profitable fast-food business
while paying workers these kinds of wages."[534] Of course, right-wing
US business interests claim that Denmark is too small and homogenous to be a fair comparison to America.[535] Conservatives who claim
to worship the universal laws of economics trip all over themselves to
justify why those rules somehow don't apply to high-wage countries.

Sweden recently moved to a six-hour working day in a bid to increase
productivity and make people happier. *The Independent* reported,
"Toyota centers in Gothenburg, Sweden's second largest city, made the
switch 13 years ago, with the company reporting happier staff, a lower
turnover rate, and an increase in profits in that time. Filimundus, an
app developer based in the capital Stockholm, introduced the six-hour

day last year. 'The eight-hour work day is not as effective as one would think,' Linus Feldt, the company's CEO told Fast Company. 'To stay focused on a specific work task for eight hours is a huge challenge. In order to cope, we mix in things and pauses to make the work day more endurable. At the same time, we are [finding] it hard to manage our private life outside of work.'"[536]

Higher pay than the US for *less* work than the US? That must really suck, at least according to US conservatives. Right-wing scholar Charles Murray has written that he "feels sorry" for the Europeans for preferring time off to work. Murray bemoans the "restrictions" that the European model imposes on the economic behavior of both employers and employees. (He considers high wages and short workweeks to be "restrictions.") While he admits that "the citizens of Europe have (so far) gotten economic security," he concludes that this is a "bad trade. . . . When the government intervenes to help, whether in the European welfare state or in America's more diluted version, it only diminishes our responsibility for the desired outcome."[537] I'm still flabbergasted that anyone takes such arguments seriously.

These countries have indeed put first things first and have their priorities in order. Disturbingly, though, there is now a pattern throughout some of the developed world in which, in the name of some theoretical "austerity," neoliberal* policies are eliminating jobs, depressing wages, increasing workweeks, and slashing social safety nets. In many places, it seems, the lowest-income populations make the easiest punching bags for politicians, enabling the wealthiest to make out like bandits. In 2015, the top 1 percent of the world's richest people had accumulated more wealth than the rest of the world put together, and the richest 62 citizens had the same wealth as the bottom half of humanity, which consists of 3.6 billion people.[538]

It's not just capitalism that's the problem. China, which still pretends to be a communist country, gained *242 new billionaires* in 2015, giving the country 596 billionaires, exceeding the US in this mind-boggling statistic for the first time.[539] China now has the inequality of

---

* "Neoliberal" usually means the belief in laissez-faire, supposed "free market capitalism," and is a conservative philosophy, not to be confused with the way "liberal" usually means "progressive" in US politics.

wealth found in capitalism, but still has the totalitarian repression of communism.*

Globally, elites are teaming up to shaft workers. Joel Rogers explained in the *Nation*, "This new world has disrupted labor movements across the globe and eliminated any trace of the home-country loyalty previously displayed by big business. But its greatest casualty has been public confidence in liberal democracy itself. At no time in the past century has that been lower than today. You can't blame the public for this. Politics has truly failed them."[540] Actually, as this whole book argues, we *can*—and *should*—blame the public (at least in democracies) for letting this happen, but he's certainly right about the twisted values of the world's elites. The Brexit vote surely is another example of a public taking out their anger in asinine, counterproductive, ways.

The new pressures on workers can be intense. In Hambach, France, the managers at Smart cars, owned by the German auto giant Daimler, asked the plant's 800 workers to take a pay cut and temporarily abandon the cherished 35-hour workweek, implying the plant would shutter altogether if they didn't. Workers worried that the company's call to "lift competitiveness" was little more than a charade to sucker-punch workers to increase profits. "What they're asking is for people to work more and earn less," said Didier Getrey, a local labor leader, who led the opposition to the deal. "We cannot live in a world where we're always scraping savings off the backs of the little guy to enrich the one percent. Those are Chinese labor standards. We are not going let it happen in France."[541]

The 2008 world economic collapse further increased strains on the safety nets of many nations. Conservatives and neoliberals used the crisis to advance their long-held view that the welfare states were harming their nations. *The New York Times* reported on this phenomenon in Greece:

> In a society that has lived off the generosity of the government for decades, the cash crisis has already had a shattering

---

* At least China still has many wonderful people and some world-class food, but as writer Jennifer 8. Lee has proven, while there was indeed a General Tso, he had nothing at all to with the Chinese-American fried chicken dish later named after him (yum!), which, by the way, is still a favorite food for Jews to eat on Christmas.

impact . . . For a generation of Greek politicians who saw government spending (and borrowing) as a national birthright, the
idea of deploying only the money at hand has been jarring. But
for other Greeks who are eager to break from the country's tradition of dispensing political favors to the well-connected, these
years of imposed restraint have also provided a valuable lesson.
"There are no free rides in this country anymore," said Kostas
Bakoyannis, 37, the governor of the Central Greece administrative region. "Now we have to live on what we can make and
produce."[542]

Perhaps it's true that the Greeks' level of government and bureaucracy was just too big to be sustainable. When I visited Athens in 2015,
I was struck that municipal garbage pickups occurred seven days a
week in the nice Athenian suburb where I stayed; in contrast, the garbage was picked up only twice per week in the middle class New York
City suburb where I grew up. Yet it was clear that some Greek elites
and other European countries were pushing Greece for cutbacks that
would harm struggling residents the most.

There is plenty of evidence that developed countries, such as those
in Scandinavia, which started off with hefty safety nets before the fiscal
crisis—and maintained or expanded them during and after it—not only
avoided significant deprivation for their most vulnerable residents, but
also boosted their overall economies.

Angel Gurría, secretary-general of the Organisation for Economic
Co-operation and Development (OECD), wrote, "Survey research in a
number of OECD countries suggest strong support for maintaining
social spending in key areas. That will not always be easy, but where
cuts are needed they must be done in ways that do not undermine the
prospects of the most vulnerable or compromise the long-term well-
being of children and young people. That means, in the words of a
popular mantra in policy circles, 'doing more with less.' But it also
means that resources for crucial areas of support, such as social safety
nets for the poorest, may need to be increased."[543]

In a report, the OECD found that "[m]aintaining and strengthening
support for the most vulnerable groups must remain a crucial part

of any strategy for an economic and social recovery." The report also concluded that, like in the US, the recession hit hardest the long-term dispossessed in all developed countries: "Growing numbers of people without recent work experience, depreciating skills, and employers' reluctance to hire them, swell the ranks of discouraged job seekers, i.e., those who want to work but no longer actively look for a job. Lengthening jobless spells make turning a hesitant recovery into a job-rich economic upswing much more difficult, and can lead to rising structural unemployment."[544]

A United Nations report on the impact of the recession in developed countries found that children suffered most from the recession, but that countries who spent the most on safety nets did the best job of reducing the harm on children. It noted, that "with the persistence of the recession, however, national revenues fell and deficits increased significantly in many countries. Increasing pressure from financial markets forced many governments to make budget cuts. The Eurozone's U-turn was particularly abrupt."[545]

If one of the key reasons that much of Europe originally developed a more robust safety net than the US was that their populations were more homogenous than that of America, it is clear that one of the reasons that they have starting cut back those safety nets is the influx of immigrants, and that their communities are less likely to support programs for people with different nationalities, races, religions, and languages. This effect will only increase with the unprecedented numbers of escaping refugees moving across the countries of Europe from desperately hungry war-torn regions like Syria, Iraq, and northern Africa.

While much of the continent has reacted nastily to the recent, mostly Muslim, refugees and other immigrants, parts of Central and Eastern Europe have been the harshest. Hungary hastily built a 100-mile chain-link and razor wire fence along its eastern border, and guarded it heavily with police officers and soldiers. Laszlo Toroczkai—the 37-year-old mayor of Asotthalom, a rural Hungarian town near the Serbian border, used the refugee crisis to bolster his status as an ultranationalist star of far-right European politics. After the fence was built, he posted his version of a "Dirty Harry" video on YouTube, which included images of stern Hungarian border guards on motorcycles and horseback. Stone-faced and wearing a black jacket, Toroczkai warns illegal immigrants that "Hungary is a bad choice." He stared straight into the camera. "Asotthalom is the worst."[546] The nations that participated in the Holocaust by aiding the Nazis (yes, I am talking to *you*, Hungary, not to mention Austria, Poland, Russia, etc.) haven't shed their historic hatreds in the few decades since.

Some countries are pushing back against the right-wing tide, though. In 2015, Swedes voted to reduce recent tax cuts for the wealthy to spend more on social welfare and education programs. Despite success of the previous moderate ruling party in steering the country to a rapid and sustained recovery after the global economic collapse, many Swedes were very concerned that the government was easing away from their cherished welfare state, and rebelled against that by electing a left-wing party that pledged to bolster it.[547] (It is important to keep in mind that, even when Center/Right parties in northern and western Europe marginally restricted their welfare states, still those governments' benefits dwarfed those of the US in both scope and spending per capita.) In 2015, Canadians also elected a more progressive government dedicated to undoing some of the nation's austerity. In response, former US Treasury Secretary Larry Summers, often thought of as a moderate on fiscal issues, tweeted, "Around the world, austerity is a political & policy loser for progressive parties. Infrastructure is a winner."

Sweden and Canada are putting first things first. America, isn't it about time you did so too?

Habit 4: Think Win-Win

America, you continue to pursue lose-lose policies. By failing to seriously address global warming, for instance, you not only threaten the long-term survivability of the human race, you cost the US countless jobs that could be created by developing and utilizing new technologies to reduce carbon emissions. We should pivot to win-win scenarios that protect the planet for our grandchildren while boosting the economy.

Rather than continuing other lose-lose endeavors, such as destroying other countries in skirmishes that kill thousands of Americans and drain our treasury, why don't we dramatically expand the Peace Corps, and ensure that any American who serves for two years gets to go to college for free? That would aid the world far more than our drones, and would build our economy too with a more educated and productive workforce. That's another a win-win!

The ultimate lose-lose for any nation is to allow its own people to go hungry, which not only destroys the moral fabric of a nation but also hampers economic growth.

This isn't about food production, it's about political power. Some of the world's most agriculturally abundant nations are also the hungriest. For instance, in 2014, India exported 30 million metric tons of food, worth twenty-three billion US dollars.[548]

Meanwhile, India's food-insecure population is 255 million people, constituting about 36 percent of the people who are hungry *on the planet*.[549] That means that India exports about 270 pounds of food per year for every hungry Indian.

Why is this allowed? The main reason is that successive Indian governments have placed a higher priority on earning large sums of money for agribusinesses and exporters than on feeding the nation's own hungry populace.

According to *Forbes*, in 2015 there were more than 100 billionaires in India, with a combined wealth of USD $346 billion, up more than a third from $259 billion in 2013.[550] Mass numbers of Indians literally starve in the streets just feet from gleaming luxury skyscrapers. In Delhi alone, about 3,000 people die homeless on its streets every year, and a "sleep mafia" even charges homeless people for the right to be able to sleep on the sidewalks on small bits of cloth.[551] As hardened as I am by visiting impoverished neighborhoods in the US and abroad, the wretchedness that I saw in some parts of Delhi took my breath away. Of course, it's the skyscraper owners who have the political power to decide how food stocks are utilized.

In the US, our leaders also generally prioritize wealth creation for the richest over feeding Americans. While the severity of the hunger in our country is generally far less than in India, US hunger is far worse than in any other Western industrialized country. Yet in 2013, the US exported $144 billion worth of food, equaling $2,938 worth of food for every American struggling against hunger.[552]

It's obviously the case that if nations have enough food to export vast amounts of it, they have enough food to feed their own people. The main cause of food deprivation in both countries is the inability of mass numbers of people to either grow their own food or be able to afford to buy enough food, which in turn is caused by mind-boggling inequality of wealth. While defenders of inequality trip all over themselves to manufacture supposedly unalterable economic or cultural reasons for inequality of wealth, its main cause is inequality of political power.

In fact, in every nation on earth that has significant hunger, poverty, and economic inequality, there is significant political inequality. The converse is also true: The countries that do the best job of meeting the basic living needs of their residents also have political systems in which most citizens have an active and effective stake in their governments. In the last few years, I have visited India, Singapore, Australia, Mexico, France, Germany, Russia, Colombia, and all the Scandinavian countries, and this correlation was crystal clear everywhere.

Political power results in public policies favorable to those who hold that power, and public policies *do* matter, in nation after nation.

Because of the broader social safety net in Europe, the poverty rate across Europe (even including its poorest nations) in 2014 was 9 percent, compared to 15 percent in the US.

Scandinavia is doing even better than Europe as a whole, and the poverty rate in Sweden is only 1 percent. Scandinavia used to be very poor. That's the main reason why, between 1820 and 1940, 19,592 people from Finland, 335,025 people from Denmark, 697,095 people from Norway, and 1,325,208 people from Sweden immigrated to the United States. Scandinavian art and literature from the 19th century is replete with references to mass hunger and other serious forms of deprivation.

Today, these same Scandinavian countries have virtually no hunger and food insecurity, and minimal poverty. It's not that their basic cultures changed. It's not that they developed new natural resources that brought in wealth (with the exception of Norway's major increases in oil production). It's that their public policies changed. These nations eliminated hunger and virtually eliminated poverty because they made conscious societal decisions to transform their economic and social policies.

America, when I suggest to you that the US should model its programs and policies on Scandinavia, you respond that those countries are just too small and just too homogenous to be appropriately compared to the US with its 320 million people and diversity.

So let's compare the US to France, a large, diverse country that has recently attracted many immigrants, including very low-income ones. Yet France also has much less poverty and hunger than the United States, even per capita.

In 2013, 6 percent of the population of France (or 3.7 million people) lived below their poverty line, giving them a poverty rate[*] far less than half that of the US.[553]

Happy now, America?

About 6 percent of Paris residents lived in households suffering from food insecurity or hunger in 2010. In the lowest-income Paris neighborhoods, the rate was 14 percent. In contrast, 17 percent of all New York City residents, and 29 percent of the residents of the Bronx (the lowest-income borough of New York City) lived in food-insecure households in 2013, according to federal data calculated by Hunger Free America. The Bronx had more than twice as much food insecurity as the lowest-income areas in Paris.

The difference between the US and France is that France has higher wages and a more robust social safety net. Outbursts of violence, racism, xenophobia, and anti-Semitism in France have demonstrated that their society is far from perfect, but compared to the US they still have far less violence, poverty, hunger, and food-related disease.

The US isn't just lagging behind countries with big safety nets and significant wealth such as Sweden and France. Check out the chart below which demonstrates that, out of the 34 members of the OECD, the US had the sixth-highest rate of residents saying they cannot afford

---

[*] France measures poverty differently than the US. If they used the same criteria as the US, their poverty rate would actually be only about a third of that in the US.

enough food, with a food deprivation rate higher than struggling countries like Greece, Poland, the Slovak Republic, Spain, and Italy. America, if you'd be humiliated at the Olympics to lose to the Italy in synchronized swimming or to Spain in team handball, shouldn't you be about a zillion times more embarrassed that we lose to them in feeding our own people?

PERCENTAGE OF RESIDENTS WHO CAN'T AFFORD ENOUGH FOOD: US DOES WORSE THAN GREECE AND SLOVAK REPUBLIC

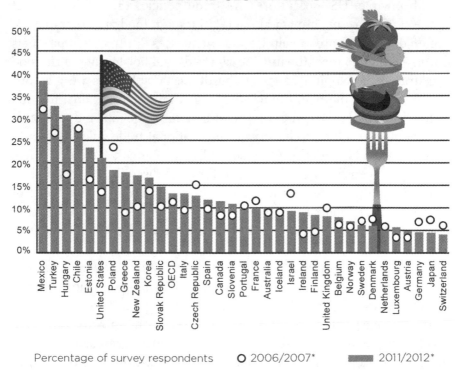

Percentage of survey respondents   O 2006/2007*   ▬ 2011/2012*

Share of "yes" responses to the question "Have there been times in the past 12 months when you did not have enough money to buy food that you or your family needed?"

*2008 data for Iceland; 2007 data for Luxembourg; 2009 data for Switzerland (instead of 2011/12)

SOURCE: OECD SECRETARIAT CALCULATIONS BASED FROM GALLUP WORLD POLL

Yet the US Right isn't particularly worried. Representative Darrell Issa (R-CA), the richest man in Congress (worth $448.4 million in

2014), said, "If you go to India or you go to any number of other Third World countries, you have two problems: You have greater inequality of income and wealth. You also have less opportunity for people to rise from the have nots to the haves." The United States, he claimed, has made "our poor somewhat the envy of the world."[554]

It's true that poor and food-insecure people in the US have slightly less horrendous lives than those in developing countries. But America, should you really be proud that you're not quite that awful? I think not.

Meanwhile, US agriculture and trade policies often have the net impact of *increasing* hunger abroad. US foreign food aid programs are often designed more to help US agribusinesses dump excess products overseas than to meet the nutritional needs and bolster long-term food security of developing nations. The domestic subsidies we give our producers give them an unfair advantage in the international market. Then the US has the gall to complain that domestic food aid programs in countries such as India violate international trade rules. As world hunger experts Timothy A. Wise and Biraj Patnaik have explained, "It was hypocrisy [for the US] to call for close disciplines on payments to some of the poorest farmers in the world in order to feed some of the hungriest people in the world when US farmers are far better off and recipients of US government food assistance get four times the amount of food."[555]

Despite the harmful policies of the US and other developed nations, hunger and poverty have actually been decreasing worldwide over the last few decades. (Don't be shocked, dear reader, that I have *good* news for a change.) Due to a combination of economic growth, improved technology, and some effective international aid programs, the number of hungry people across the globe dropped by 216 million from 1990 to 2014, declining from 23 percent to 13 percent of the world's population.[556] Severe poverty and infant mortality are also decreasing, while educational attainment is improving.[557] (Yay!!!)*

This progress is encouraging, but we still have our work cut out for

---

* I do believe that is the first time in this book, so far, that I've use an exclamation point in a non-ironic manner. It may also be the first cheerful news I've been able to impart, other than reporting on the happiness of our friends, the Canadians.

us. In 2015, 800 million people suffered from chronic undernour-
ishment worldwide. That not only directly causes mass suffering and
death, but is also a major factor in the spread of disease, war, and
terrorism. United Nations Food and Agriculture Organization Direc-
tor-General José Graziano da Silva estimated that, over the following
15 years, an additional investment of $160 per year per person living in
extreme poverty would be needed to end hunger once and for all. "This
represents less than half a percent of global income in 2014. And it is
only a small fraction of the cost that hunger and malnutrition impose
on economies, societies, and people," he said.[558]

Still, just as it's troubling that many developed countries are following America's lead by reducing safety nets, it's equally concerning
that they are also taking a dangerous page from the US playbook by
replacing their safety nets with inadequate charitable aid.

Corporate food businesses across the globe are supporting the creation and growth of food banks, modeled on American emergency food
warehouses, to distribute excess food products to low-income people.
According to the Global FoodBanking Network, there are now food
banks in more than 30 countries. Having visited a few in Australia,
I can attest that they are nearly identical to the industry-backed food
banks in the US.*

As in the US, international food banks do—and should—help
dispose of excess food in an environmentally friendly way and fill in
some holes in government safety nets. But in no city or country in the
world are charitable food banks coming even close to fully filling in all
those gaps. In most, if not all, of the nations in which food banking
is growing, hunger and food insecurity are growing far faster than is
charitable food distribution.

Making matters even worse, just like in the US, governments
sometimes use the existence of food banks to give the public the
false impression that these charities are solving the problem, thereby
diverting attention away from failing public policies.

As Nelson Mandela once said, "Like slavery and apartheid, poverty
is not natural. It is man-made and it can be overcome and eradicated

---

* Some food banks worldwide even use the architectural blueprints of US food banks to build
their warehouses of charitable food distribution.

by the actions of human beings. Overcoming poverty is not a task of charity, it is an act of justice."[559]

Let's end US and world hunger, which would both save the world's soul and reduce wars and conflicts. Nothing would be "win-winnier" than that.

Habit 5: Seek First to Understand, Then to be Understood

America, you dictate to the world, and almost never listen to what they want. You're a nation-state narcissist extraordinaire. Those on the Right that brag they don't even own—or want—a passport are the worst.

But if American conservatives spent more time reading, and less time condemning or burning, the Koran, we'd all be a lot safer. No one has to agree with the tenets in it—or the Old Testament or New Testament or any religious sacred text for that matter—but we all need to understand these texts and their traditions more before we go to war over them.

One of the other bedrocks of traditional conservatism—dating back to Edmund Burke—is a belief that government only has a limited ability to remake basic human nature. That's why it's so odd that modern-day neo-conservatives think we have the power to stop violence in Syria, but not in Orlando or Charleston.

Few American policy makers understood—or even tried to understand—the history and culture of Iraq or Afghanistan. So how is the Republican record on either freedom or security, especially given that they refuse to even try to understand places we invade? Well, the Iraq War resulted in 89,000 direct war deaths, which doesn't include the hundreds of thousands more that died due to war-related hardships; 4,488 US service personnel killed directly; 32,223 troops injured (not including post-traumatic stress disorders); 134,000 civilians killed directly; and 655,000 persons who have died in Iraq since the invasion who would not have died if the war had never occurred. There have been 150 journalists killed. And 2.8 million people were either internally displaced or forced to flee the country. The country is neither secure, nor free.[560]

Of course, Iraq was a big mess, but how about Afghanistan, where we fought the "just, smart" war? As of 2016, not only was that country still in bloody chaos, and not only were most women still severely oppressed, but the country continued to be one of the world's largest opium suppliers. From 2002 to 2015, the United States spent more than $7 billion to fight Afghanistan's runaway poppy production. Tens of billions of US funds were spent on governance programs to stem corruption and train a credible police force. Yet, in districts such as Garmsir, poppy cultivation not only is allowed, but is one of the main sources of funding for the local government. Revenue is kicked up the chain, and opium money remains a significant source of funding for the national government in Kabul as well.[561]

It's not just progressive peaceniks who declare the wars in Iraq and Afghanistan as failures. Many of the more self-reflective military leaders and fighters have spoken out, as retired Lieutenant General Daniel P. Bolger did:

> As a senior commander in Iraq and Afghanistan, I lost 80 soldiers. Despite their sacrifices, and those of thousands more, all we have to show for it are two failed wars. This fact eats at me every day . . .
>
> In 2003, the United States invaded Iraq and toppled a dictator. We botched the follow-through, and a vicious insurgency erupted. Four years later, we surged in fresh troops, adopted improved counterinsurgency tactics, and won the war. And then dithering American politicians squandered the gains. It's a compelling story. But it's just that—a story . . .
>
> The surge in Iraq did not "win" anything. It bought time. It allowed us to kill some more bad guys and feel better about ourselves. But in the end, shackled to a corrupt, sectarian government in Baghdad and hobbled by our fellow Americans' unwillingness to commit to a fight lasting decades, the surge just forestalled today's stalemate . . . The remnants of Al Qaeda in Iraq and the Sunni insurgents we battled for more than eight years simply re-emerged this year as the Islamic State, also known as ISIS . . .
>
> We did not understand the enemy, a guerrilla network embedded in a quarrelsome, suspicious civilian population.[562]

Even today, none of our national leaders can be fully honest about what we are still doing in the region. President Obama kept sending more troops back to Iraq and Afghanistan, but insisted he was not placing more "boots on the ground." Unless new US troops there were wearing sandals, or magically levitating, Obama wasn't telling the truth either.

At a time when 18,000 foreign troops, including 10,600 Americans, were stationed in Afghanistan—and not for sightseeing trips or rug-weaving classes—the US government claimed the war was over, an obvious sham claim. Modern wars are sort of like a roach motel—once you're in, you can't get out.

Yet instead of learning anything at all from these bitterest of bitter lessons, neo-cons, most of whom are chicken hawks who found extraordinarily creative ways to keep themselves out of harm's way, continue to call for more—ever more—attacks and interventions in even more places we don't understand. When you hear warmongers call for "boots on the ground," you know that neither their feet, nor their children's feet, will be filling those boots. The stridency of the neo-con pro-war rhetoric seems directly proportional to how often they are demonstrably wrong.

The top priority of the neo-cons was once getting rid of President Bashar al-Assad in Syria, but then they switched the goal without ever admitting it—to a different purpose: getting rid of Assad's top enemy, ISIS. Had we armed the anti-Assad rebels as conservatives originally sought to do, much of those arms would likely already be in the hands of ISIS.

Despite having little natural ice, the Middle East has more slippery slopes than any region. Yet we never seem to comprehend that history teaches us that military interventions almost always result in unexpected, negative results.

Why is the only national debate over *how* to go to war against ISIS and never over *whether* yet another battle would be counterproductive and ultimately unwinnable? How did we get to the point where the US starts new wars by default?

Why does the failure of air wars always seem to justify the need for ground wars, rather than prove the fruitlessness of war in general?

While ISIS is obviously a ghastly presence on the world scene, we ignore the fact that their US-backed opponents aren't exactly freedom- and diversity-loving pluralists. *USA Today* once ran a headline, "Iraq looks to retake Anbar from extremists."[563] But the paper glossed over the fact that the troops doing the "taking back" should also be characterized—by any reasonable definition—as extremists themselves. Our allies in that fight were recruited by Iraq's top Shiite cleric, Grand Ayatollah Ali al-Sistani, who issued what is known as the "righteous jihad fatwa," encouraging Iraqis to take up arms to defend "their country and their people and their holy places," as well as join the security forces.[564] I fail to see how the US government backing one band of extremists to exterminate another group of extremists makes the world either safer or freer.

We must ask: how much of the "global war on terror" is actually responding to existing threats versus inciting new ones? What makes anyone think that bombing more tent camps—yet again—will protect us from terrorism? Indiscriminate violence and destruction against the families and communities of terrorists usually breeds more terrorists and does not "wipe out the enemy." Our biggest mistake in the war on terror is the false belief that there are a set number of terrorists who can be killed or captured, ignoring how many new ones our actions create.

The rise of ISIS was fueled by decades and decades of US foreign policy mistakes, so, of course, it's all Barack Obama's fault. Pundits have faulted Obama for refusing to give a pat, false solution to global violence, which has been around since caveman times. None of them seem to even consider for a second that the problem is too much war and too much killing, not too little of it.

When Obama sought to advance peace through a nuclear pact with Iran, Congress demanded to be allowed to vote down the peace deal, but then it totally shirked its Constitutional responsibility to actually authorize the new war we were already fighting against ISIS. Yes, their motto was "Vote Against Peace, Not War." (Thank goodness Tolstoy didn't go with *that* name.)

The only constant is that the neo-cons will always seek to impose our national will rather than seek to truly understand what other nations want. (If I thought Dick Cheney would read it, I'd send him Covey's book).

Habit 6: Synergize

Covey says, "To put it simply, synergy means 'two heads are better than one.'" Rather than the US thinking we know everything—on our own—perhaps we should seriously consult a bit more with the world on what works and what doesn't. Here's one hint that the rest of the developed world could share with the US: higher wages and larger social safety nets work and make nations more peaceful and prosperous. Here's a second hint they could give us: if you don't kill as many people or spend as much money in endless wars based on self-delusional lies, your country will be much safer and happier in the long run. Third hint: multinational coalitions are far more effective than go-it-alone US cowboy missions. Damn it, America . . . synergize.

Habit 7: Sharpen the Saw

Covey says that "Sharpen the Saw" means preserving and enhancing the greatest asset you have—you. It means having a balanced program for self-renewal in the four areas of your life: physical, social/emotional, mental, and spiritual. He's so right—that's why I am going to stop writing this chapter right now and go for a jog . . .

. . . Ok, I'm back. Now that I've cleared my head and sharpened my saw, I'm ready to get back to scolding you, America, on how to follow the good habits of the rest of the world.

13.

The Granivore's Dilemma
Can the Foodies Survive on
Foraged Seeds Alone?

"Eight dollars for a dozen eggs sounds outrageous, but when you think
that you can make a delicious meal from two eggs, that's $1.50. It's really
not that much when we think of how we waste money in our lives."
—Michael Pollan, food writer[565]

America, now I'm going to tell you how you can live a healthier, happier life through eating better, using one life—mine!—as the catch-all example of the food experiences of all 323 million people in the US. Not really, but read on anyway.

One morning, I craved waffles but I thought we had no maple syrup in the cupboard. So I went to Key Food, a medium-size food market across the street from my home, which offered 17 varieties of syrups, which are about 16 or 17 more choices than I would find in most grocery stores in most other countries. Examining the choices for 12-ounce bottles, I found that the least expensive option, only $2.19, was "Key Food Quality Syrup Original," which contained the following ingredients: Corn Syrup, High Fructose Corn Syrup, Water, Cellulose Gum, Caramel Color, Salt, Sodium Benzoate and Sorbic Acid (Preservatives), Artificial and Natural Flavors, and Sodium Hexametaphosphate. Mmm. Delicious.

I then checked out a better-known brand, the unhappily named "Aunt Jemima Original Syrup," which sold for $3.69, and contained nearly identical ingredients as the Key Food brand.*

---

* A few years ago, the company made the label slightly less racist, transitioning from the label on the left to the one on the right, but the name itself, Aunt Jemima, is still more than a little problematic.

I decided that I wanted actual maple syrup tapped from actual maple trees—and I also wanted to earn a bit of extra virtue by purchasing a product certified "organic" by the USDA—so, because I could afford to do so, I was just about ready to plunk down $13.49 for a 16-ounce bottle of organic real maple syrup from Coombs Family Farms, based in Brattleboro, Vermont. But then a worry popped into my head: shouldn't I be buying local? I checked my smartphone on the spot and learned that Brattleboro was a 201-mile drive from where I live in Brooklyn, so I figured that any benefit to buying organic was eviscerated by buying something that used so much fossil fuel to reach my neighborhood store. Très uncool. If anyone saw me buying non-local, I could be drummed out of Brooklyn by a ferocious gang of handlebar mustache-sporting, fixed-gear bike-driving foodie hipsters (who would, of course, adamantly deny being hipsters, as they indignantly sipped on their Pabst Blue Ribbon beer, even though they no longer wear fedoras or man-buns because those are *so* 2015).

Inspired to do the "right thing," I trudged 1.1 miles from the Key Food to the Gowanus Souvenir Shop (nestled on the banks of the pastoral Gowanus Canal—nicknamed "Perfume Creek"—an EPA superfund site containing PCBs, coal tar wastes, and heavy metals—and where baby whales go to die), where I could spend $16 for 12 ounces of what they labeled "Gowanus Slurp Maple Syrup—Good for You, Really."* Ah, *local* at last! I could finally be admitted to foodie heaven. But wait: the fine print on the label says: "*Vermont Maple Syrup, New Day Farm™." I looked up the farm (again, thanks to the Android in my pocket), and it was based in Ira, Vermont (I guess if Vermont can have a Bernie, it can also have an Ira)—and was further away from my apartment than Brattleboro. Busted! Oh the horrors! Oh the calamity! This is the worst Brooklyn food scandal since a famed artisanal brick oven

*

pizza restaurant pawned off Quattro Formaggi pizza that turned out to have only three cheeses. What to do? What to do? How could I buy real maple syrup for my Eggo and still save my soul? Would I have to go to Prospect Park and tap a maple tree myself? Does Prospect Park even have maple trees? And would they be organic? Then I remembered: there was still a bit of genuine New Hampshire local (to New Hampshire at least) maple syrup left in the refrigerator. I had purchased the small plastic jug for $6.99 at a touristy general store on a recent trip to New London, New Hampshire.

Whew. Crisis averted, for now.

This story encapsulates what is both wondrous and abhorrent about today's foodies and the foodie lifestyle, both of which have saved and ruined how you eat, America. On one hand, all the attention to local, organic, fresh, and nutritious foods has dramatically improved the taste—and enormously expanded the variety—of foods available to Americans who can afford to buy them, while aiding the environment and boosting small- and medium-sized businesses. You can even now buy organic milk and eggs in small, poor towns like Clarksdale, Mississippi. Farmers markets are popping up all over the country. Big kudos, foodies! On the other hand, too much of this privileged movement merely exacerbated the vast racial and class divides over food access that had always existed in this country. Shame on you, foodies!*

Even as foodies have helpfully raised public consciousness on nutrition and sustainability issues, too many have been far too sanctimonious, patronizing, and elitist, preventing them from building a truly broad-based, effective national food movement.

Foodies unintentionally made artisanal food the latest status symbol of privilege and a way to display false virtuousness. Not only that, many of them have proven to be first-class suckers—paying boatloads of money for products that are supposed to be local but are anything but, like Brooklyn-labeled maple syrup that is really made in Vermont.

---

* I am well aware that not everyone who considers him or herself a "foodie" is involved in the movement to make the US food system more sustainable, and not everyone who is involved in the sustainability movement considers themselves as a "foodie"—and that in fact, some food activists hate the term "foodies." But, for the sake of simplicity, I am using the term "foodie" in the broadest possible manner. So, shoot me—preferably with a cookie-making gun. (OK, I know it is formally called a "cookie press," but give me a break, will ya?)

THE SEARCH FOR FOOD PURITY

Some of what we see in the current "food movement," such as it is, is a natural—and welcome—outgrowth of the environmental and consumer crusades, but some of it is little more than a silly revolt against the inevitable onslaught of modernity.

America, of course we should try to empower shoppers to make informed decisions about the personal and societal impacts of their food purchasing choices. Of course we should try to create a food system that does as little damage to the environment, and commits as little cruelty against animals, as possible. To the extent any food movement advances those goals, that's splendid.

But the myth that hoards of people in modern American society can become self-sufficient in their food production and consumption is laughable. Few of us would claim that we should sew, weave, or knit all our own clothing anymore—and virtually none of us would argue that we should all manufacture our own autos, computers, or smartphones—but some urban and suburban residents cling to the absurdity that they and some of their more "socially responsible" buddies can somehow be food self-sufficient by aiding a community garden, shopping at a farmers market, or belonging to a Community Supported Agriculture (CSA) project. Most of these efforts—while laudable—are seasonal, because in most areas, growing and harvest seasons usually last only a few months. Personally, I enjoy eating 52 weeks out of the year, not just during the few that truly "local" produce happens to be in season in my part of the world. (Admit it, you do too, America.) Even if people happen to live in patches of the southernmost US or in regions of California with year-round growing seasons, the vast majority still buy much of their food (such as grains and spices and oils and other pantry staples, as well as fruits and vegetables) from markets that have themselves purchased products that have been transported long distances, through a vast, international corporate food system. But many foodies don't want to acknowledge that to their peers—or even themselves.

Why does the foodie culture cling so persistently to the illusion that they are in control of their own food? I postulate that such thinking is a last-gasp attempt to mentally hold off the tides of modernity. They are troubled—rightfully so—that our contemporary corporate world is exerting more control over how and when they work, how and where they live, what they buy and where they can buy it, and what food is grown and how it is produced. It seems to me that some foodies want to believe that the last bastion of individuality and control is their own bodies, so by striving to control what goes in them, they regain a sense of empowerment and independence and feel they are, at the same time, sending a message to corporate America. But the reality is they can't even truly control everything that enters their bodies, not unless they want to starve. At some point, the vast majority of locavores, even those who live on rural farms, must consume some food products that other people, usually working for big corporations and usually in faraway places, have created for them to eat. I'm not saying that's a good thing—I'm just saying it's reality.

I want to be clear that I am not knocking folks who try very hard to ensure that their eating represents their personal values and health preferences—far from it. Locavores, vegetarians, and vegans: congrats on your commitment! I am certainly open to your reasoned argument for why everyone should adopt your eating rules. (Given that I specialize in telling other people what to do—and indeed, telling the whole country and world what to do—I'd be a hypocrite if I didn't at least *pretend* to hear your explanation for why it's bad for me and for the world to put cow's milk, even if it's organic, on my "natural" Kashi cereal, which, by the way, is also produced by a huge multinational corporation, Kellogg's, so *mea culpa* yet again). But please don't lecture me that your particular lifestyle choice is the *only* moral, healthy way to live.

If you really want to play the "my food morality is better than your food morality" game, someone can always top you. A vegan can always look down on a mere vegetarian. A fruitarian (who eats only fruits, nuts, and seeds) can be appalled that vegans have the gall to eat processed grains or the occasional Boca Burger made out of soy. Lastly, dear food purist, if you really want to take me to the mat, I challenge you—yes, *you*—to live your life as a granivore who survives only on seeds from existing plants.* And you couldn't just eat artisanal seeds; you'd be so famished all the time that you'd be forced to eat any ol' seed that you were

---

* This photo is of a strawberry damaged by a granivore mouse that ate just the seeds. If you, too, were a granivore, you couldn't even eat the rest of the strawberry.

lucky enough find on any random piece of dropped fruit. That big, juicy steak is looking pretty good now, isn't it?

The following sounds like parody but I swear it's true: the *New York Times* published an illustrated guide by Philip B. Stark, a professor at the University of California, Berkeley, on what kinds of public weeds are edible, which included this caveat: "This guide is not intended to teach you how to identify whether a plant is edible. Rather, it's a sketch of the flavor of some edible plants, and how you might use those plants in your cooking. If you want to learn how to identify edible plants, please consult authoritative field guides and get instruction from an expert forager or botanist."[566] In a related op-ed, *Times* food writer Mark Bittman ticks off the advantages of eating weeds: "They're organic. (They may be soiled by whatever happens on the street, but they're not intentionally doused with chemicals.) They require no cultivation, no care, and they're drought- (and for that matter flood-) tolerant, or you wouldn't find them. And many of them are nutritionally superior to their tamed counterparts . . . They're also free for the intrepid forager." In a related video, Bittman suggested that weeds are especially good food for people living in "underserved urban neighborhoods."* And the Berkeley professor shrugged off this possible concern for the apprehensive beginning forager: "A dog might may have peed (on a weed) but I can wash that off." Uh, okay, you first, professor.

THE LOCAL AND SEASONAL MYTH

How do we define "local?" The definition is in the eye of the beholder— or the profit maker. Here's how Whole Foods squirms out of providing a real definition of the term: "How do we define local? Well, mostly we like to leave it up to our stores. Generally though, we try to use state lines. But, when a state is enormous (like California, for example) we might get a bit more specific about it and divide the state into growing areas like 'The Bay Area' or 'Central California Coast.' Ask your local Whole Foods Market how to find products from your area!"[567] In practice, at least in Whole Foods stores in New York City (which, in 2015, agreed to pay half a million dollars in fines for mislabeling products

---

* Bon appétit, underserved urban people!

and overcharging), much of the produce marketed as local comes from more than a hundred miles away. Ditto for a sizeable amount of the food sold at farmers markets in New York City, which often originates hundreds of miles away in upstate New York, southern New Jersey, or Pennsylvania—and sometimes even Vermont; to my mind, such food should be more accurately called "regional" rather than "local."

Baldor Specialty Foods distributes produce to restaurants, hotels, and other facilities in the New York area.[568] They produced a 75-page glossy color catalogue headlined "Baldor Local," showcasing their "local farms," including spots in Maine, New Hampshire, North Carolina, South Carolina, Massachusetts, Georgia, and even Florida, which is at least 916 miles (a 13-hour drive) from New York City. That stretches the definition of "regional," no less "local." But Baldor openly lists the areas in their catalogue, which means their customers obviously don't think too hard about their own definition of "local." "Seasonal" is also a slippery term, as chef Amanda Cohen explained:

> There are two words that make me die inside: seasonal and local . . . They're well-intentioned but have come to represent eating vegetables as a lifestyle statement rather than something you do because they're delicious. These two words slam the door on people who don't have access to local produce or who want to enjoy a lime in their gin and tonic in February . . .
>
> For the most part, your local grocery is not selling local produce. Don't panic. Eating local is great, and it's wonderful to support your local farmers, but I think you do that by creating demand for vegetables rather than by location-shaming shoppers . . .
>
> Worried about how your groceries affect your carbon footprint? Me too, but I don't have the money to move. No matter what time of year it is, if you live outside of Florida or Southern California, every single lemon, orange, or nectarine you've ever eaten in your entire life has probably taken an airplane trip to your mouth. Want a local lime? Move to Mexico. Do you like olive oil? That's mostly coming from Spain (via Italy) on ships . . . The fact is, we live in a post-seasonal world. The vast

majority of our fruits and vegetables comes to us on trucks and planes from faraway farms, and everything is always in season somewhere. Make your peace with it.[569]

Amen, sister. Alongside "local" and "seasonal," other phrases that are too frequently meaningless are "farmers market" or "farm fresh." At the Charlotte, North Carolina airport, there is a kiosk labeled "Farmers Market," which mostly sells a large array of sugary beverages (what farmer is growing my Coke?). At Houston's George Bush Intercontinental Airport, there's a stall labeled "Farm Fresh Belgian Beer Café," which sells mostly potato chips, packaged cookies, beer, soda, and a few apples wrapped in cellophane. Sure, those examples are particularly ridiculous, but the bottom line is there is no official national definition for those terms.

THE PRICE ISN'T RIGHT

Because healthier food is more expensive and harder to find in low-income neighborhoods, and often takes more time to prepare (and low-income people are extra-strapped for time), hungrier and poorer Americans are more likely to become obese than higher-income Americans. Hunger and obesity are truly flipsides of the same malnutrition coin.

A study by the Harvard School of Public Health found that, between 1999 and 2011, the gap widened between the high nutritional quality of what wealthy people ate and the low nutritional quality of what low-income people ate.[570] Frank Hu, one of the study's authors, called the growing gap between the rich and poor "disturbing," saying America's overall nutritional intake couldn't improve significantly as long as low-income families had no choice but to eat such unhealthy diets.[571]

Famed organic farmer and food philosopher Joel Salatin charged $14.83 in 2015 for one pound of his skinless chicken breasts, raised on his Virginia farm, about eight times the cost of regular, factory-farmed chicken breasts in my Brooklyn neighborhood. This is how he defends the astronomical prices of his and other organic farm products:

Plenty of money already exists in our economic system to pay for good food. Can you think of anything people buy that they don't need? Tobacco products, $100 designer jeans with holes already in the knees, KFC, soft drinks made with high fructose corn syrup, Disney vacations, large-screen TVs, jarred baby food? America spends more on veterinary care for pets than the entire continent of Africa spends on medical care for humans . . . If you took all the money people spend on unnecessary baubles and junk food, it would be enough for everyone to eat like kings. We could all be elitists.[572]

That's pretty tone deaf to people living in poverty. One pound of his chicken costs two hours of earnings at the national minimum wage. Millions of low-income working Americans aren't going on vacations to Disney—they are barely making enough money to pay for rent and utilities, let alone food.

It is true that you can "make delicious meals from two eggs," as Michael Pollan said, but the vast majority of human beings would require a heck of a lot more than that to have a full meal and a satisfied belly. (Toast? Butter? Potatoes? Tortillas? A vegetable?) $1.50 for two eggs may not sound like much money to some, but the average SNAP allotment in 2016 was only $1.40 *per meal*. Foodies need to realize that we live in a country where tens of millions of Americans would have to beg for an extra dime to be able to afford even that last morsel of the second egg.

But there are key figures in the food world, such as chef Tom Colicchio and TV personality Rachael Ray, who are pushing back, consistently pointing out that we must make food both affordable and sustainable, and they agree that too much of the food movement glosses over affordability.*

---

* Both Colicchio and Ray have been key allies in the anti-hunger and nutrition fights, and have taken some heat for their views, but they have not backed down. They know that if you can't stand the heat (from both ovens and TV lights, as well as politics), then you shouldn't be in the kitchen.

INVISIBLE FOOD WORKERS

The average shopper at a farmers market or a Whole Foods learns more about whether their produce was planted in chemical-free soil and whether their chickens roamed free than whether the humans who produced and picked the food were paid fairly and given safe working conditions. This is starting to change (for products mostly from outside the US, like coffee, chocolate, and bananas, where the "free trade" label can sometimes be found on a product), but not by much. Consumers often falsely assume that "organic" or "local" are stand-ins for all things politically correct (if they consider it at all); they assume that organic and local food is both worker- and environmentally-friendly. Hardly. If you think about it for a second, you'd realize that even the worst, mega-polluting, animal-oppressing, corporate-owned agribusinesses are "local" *somewhere*. Plus, much of the organics industry is now controlled by large corporations, not small family farmers. For example, even if your chickens are labeled organic, what does the farmer do with the waste? There are all kinds of pollution, not only chemical. Are the chickens ever seeing the light of day? Cage-free doesn't mean that the egg-laying chickens walk around a barnyard, eating insects all day. Often that label merely means that the poultry is stuck in a warehouse with thousands of other chickens, with little room to move, even though they are not in a "cage."

But at least our own small farmers we chat with at our local farmers markets are all good guys, right? It's not that simple. Consumers tend to think that "Farmer Joe" and "Farmer Ann," the friendly (sometimes) faces at the markets, are the only ones doing all the real farm labor, perhaps along with some cheery-faced family members. That's rarely the case. Most major farmers market vendors employ teams of migrant farm laborers (often undocumented workers, though many are brought in legally under a federal program for seasonal employment) who do much of the farm tasks. And workers on organic farms are often treated as poorly as their conventional counterparts, as *Grist* reported:

> When Elena Ortiz [not her real name] found a job on an organic raspberry farm after working for nine years in conventionally

farmed fields, she was glad for the change. The best part about her new job was that she no longer had to work just feet away from tractors spraying chemical herbicides and pesticides. An added bonus was the fruit itself — "prettier," she said, and firmer, which made it easier to pick . . .

But when it came to how Ortiz was treated by her employers, little was different. Her pay remained meager: $500 a week at peak berry-picking season, but as little as $200 a week during much of the year, leaving her and her farmworker husband with little money to buy fruits and vegetables for their five children. The supervisors at her farm, Reiter Berry, were often "aggressive" and capricious. . . .

When organizers from the United Farm Workers (UFW) encouraged the Reiter employees to form a union, the company allegedly responded with intimidation and harassment. "There was an atmosphere of fear. People were afraid they would be laid off," Ortiz said in a recent interview.

A majority of 188 California organic farms surveyed do not pay a living wage or provide medical or retirement plans. In fact, most organic workers earn the same as those in conventional fields—less (adjusted for inflation) than they were making in the 1970s, when the famous UFW boycotts occurred. . . .

And while organic's profitability would suggest that there is plenty of money to pay workers better—for those so inclined— much of the profits go to retailers and wholesalers higher up the food chain. . . .

Another obstacle toward improving conditions is that, simply put, the treatment of farm laborers doesn't rate high on most people's list of concerns. [A survey of consumers] found that workers' rights ranked fifth on a list of food-related issues that interested respondents—right behind the treatment of animals. . . . Farmer Jim Cochran put it bluntly: "Everybody cares about how the bugs are treated, but nobody cares about how the workers are treated."[573]

When a bill was considered in the New York State Legislature to better protect farm workers, many sustainable agriculture activists and small farmers quietly opposed it because they claimed it would increase their operating costs. I bet their consumers would be shocked to know that.

TELLING LOW-INCOME PEOPLE HOW TO LIVE AND WHAT TO EAT

Over the last 20 years, I have delivered hundreds of speeches on US hunger in dozens of states from coast-to-coast, after which I usually take questions. One of the more frequent questions I get is some variant of this one, typically asked by an upper-middle-class white person: "If low-income people just grew their own food in gardens, and learned to shop better and cook more beans in a crockpot, couldn't we end hunger?" Reading between the lines, the inquiry indicates that the questioner mistakenly believes that hunger is mostly hungry people's fault, because struggling Americans allegedly lack the do-it-yourself initiative, the drive for self-care, and the common sense life skills that the rest of us (the "deserving" folk) obviously have in spades. Every time I get a question like this, I have to work hard not to entirely blow a gasket, though if you look closely, you can probably see my left eye twitching.

Let's dispense with the gardening claim first. Even during the harvest seasons, backyard and community gardens can produce only a small fraction of the food people need to survive and thrive. Most Americans in poverty don't own their own land, and few have access to community gardens. Not only that, gardens are incredibly time-intensive, and since most low-income people are working one, two, or three jobs, they have little time left over to produce their own food. Then there are droughts, freezes, and damage from insects and animals and the cost of seeds, fertilizer, and even water. So no, low-income people *can't* always grow their own food any more than you can build your own electric dishwasher.

It's a false stereotype that low-income people primarily eat at fast food restaurants. Given that SNAP benefits can't generally be used for prepared foods, it's not surprising for studies to show that middle-class people eat at fast food establishments more frequently than do poor people. Nearly 80 percent of low-income families eat at home five or more days a week.[574]

Preparing meals is always tough, but it's especially challenging for families strapped for time and money. Sociologist Sarah Bowen found that preparing a family dinner could be an onerous and unpleasant task for moms overall, but that those in lower socioeconomic brackets faced a particularly hard time getting fresh produce because of its cost and because of the difficulty of getting transportation to a store.[575]

In a piece entitled "I Get Food Stamps, and I'm Not Ashamed—I'm Angry," Christine Gilbert detailed her challenges in preparing meals for her family:

> My larder relies on a few staples: canned beans and tomatoes, potatoes and onions, canned tuna, bouillon cubes. Rice and noodles. A few canned or frozen veggies. Dried beans and lentils for days I have time to cook them properly. . . .
>
> Fresh veggies are pretty much limited to carrots, celery, and the occasional head of cabbage or broccoli. They keep a lot longer than other veggies, and the kids will eat them raw for snacks. Protein is usually chicken—I can get a 10-pound bag of leg quarters for $7.99, split them into smaller bags, and freeze them separately. Occasionally when I find sausage on sale, I'll buy several packages and freeze that too. Hamburger is cheaper than steak but not as cheap as chicken, and sometimes pork steaks are cheaper than beef of any kind, so I guess it's a good thing we don't have any religious restrictions on our diets. . . .
>
> Fruit? Bananas, or sometimes apples or oranges when they're in season and therefore on sale. Maybe a melon in the summer when they're dirt cheap. . . .
>
> Organic? Nope. Precut? Double nope. Worried about chemicals leaking into canned food? I'm a lot more worried about getting enough calories to keep going. . . .[576]

Yet many elites still feel no compunction about lecturing low-income families on what they should or should not eat, even if those prescriptions are entirely different from what they themselves consume. Foodies who have no qualms about gobbling down artisanal pork belly sandwiches on thick slices of freshly-baked sourdough bread are among the first to hector poor people for buying cheap bags of potato chips, even though the snacks are likely to have less fat and fewer calories overall than a giant sandwich of pig fat and refined carbohydrates.

Note that the food police never call for outright bans on food they deem to be unhealthy—since bans would theoretically also apply to themselves. They only cry out for taxing such foods or barring them from programs that only aid people in poverty.

Mark Bittman called for taxing what he described as "bad" foods, "things like soda, French fries, doughnuts, and hyper processed snacks."[577] Yet Bittman subsequently published detailed instructions in the *New York Times* for how anyone could make their own homemade donuts, including jelly, glazing, and extra sugar.* He wrote,

> Places that serve fried food—French fries, fried chicken, tempura, you name it—either serve it straight from the fryer, at its peak, or they find some way, often a heat lamp, to keep it as crisp as possible. So why don't doughnuts get the same love? Most are so far removed from that bubbling bath of oil by the time you eat them that they've almost entirely lost their fresh-fried luster. That's why, I'm sorry to say, if you want a truly great, hot, crisp doughnut, chances are you're going to have to make it yourself.[578]

Some of the calls to restrict what food low-income people can eat are class-biased, racially-loaded, and based on the false belief that low-income people are purposely making irresponsible choices. *Washington Post* food writer Tamar Haspel opined,

---

* This is the photo the *New York Times* ran to accompany Bittman's donut recipes. The photographer was Sam Kaplan. The food stylist was Claudia Ficca. They do look delicious. And in fairness, Bittman had a turnaround a few years ago, after suffering health problems, and now advocates a more middle-of-the-road approach: eating a healthy vegan diet before 6 p.m. and whatever you want for your supper, having less healthy foods occasionally as treats. Not only that, he's begun to frequently speak out in favor of higher wages for food workers.

Scrap the Supplemental Nutrition Assistance Program (a.k.a. food stamps), which is a cash subsidy for buying foods—almost any foods, even unhealthful ones—and reinvent it as a program that ensures Americans have access to healthful foods in their time of need . . . And, along with it, perhaps recruit some food people—lots of us either write about or cook food for a living—to volunteer to teach classes. Let government food assistance be a ticket not just to the healthful foods we all should be eating more of but also to help with figuring out what to do with them. That would also create demand in some "food deserts," where wholesome foods are less available—an important step in righting that imbalance.[579]

How phenomenally patronizing. She seems to have no recognition that low-income people often can't afford healthier food, and assumes that the only reason that food deserts exist is that low-income people haven't created a "demand" for it. The topper—that she and her social set should descend into the 'hood to teach those ignoramuses how to properly eat and cook—is enough to make you want to chug some Pepto-Bismol (the organic version, of course).

Time after time, many elites have a different set of rules for themselves than for everyone else. I once spoke at an anti-obesity conference in Australia at which speaker after speaker blasted the food industry and chastised the masses for eating junk food. They then held a banquet for conference participants where they served copious amounts of wine (about 150 calories per glass, though being Australia, one expects large amounts of alcohol at every function). When attendees were offered a choice of pastries or fresh fruit for dessert the vast majority chose pastry. The anti-obesity conference organizers then gave me, as a gift for speaking, a large box of fancy chocolates so beautiful they could be considered art. I may have gained three pounds at that anti-obesity conference, but who's counting?

THE SODA WARS

Above all, the food police really hate—just hate—sugary soda (that's "pop" to you foreigners in the Midwest or western New York). Boy, they really despise it and frequently compare it to cigarettes and heroin. They want it taxed. They wanted it barred from programs that supplement food for low-income families. Some foodies have even told me that they want it banned entirely because soda "is not food" and it can serve "no good purpose." Can you imagine all the foods—ahem, I meant "nonfoods"—that would fit into this category?

And how about the fact that drinking soda can provide a human with—gasp—*pleasure?* Sodas and other sugary drinks often taste pretty good. There, I said it. Have me drawn and quartered now. I don't drink much soda myself, but absolutely no beverage—not even tea—goes better with Chinese dim sum than a classic Coca-Cola. (Don't ask me why, but try it yourself and you will see I'm right.) Improved public health certainly should be a top personal priority that needs to be balanced with the rights of individuals to get pleasure out of their food and drinks. But I would argue that low-income people, who can't afford many of the other types of satisfactions that the rest of us typically enjoy—like going to an occasional movie, taking a walk in a safe, local park, or vacationing at Disney World—especially deserve the right to relish their food and beverages.

While the food police are sanctimonious on many fronts, when it comes to soda, they go into their full Torquemada mode.* Now, if you really press them (and I *do* press them), the vast majority of people who say that soda should be taxed or barred in food programs will sheepishly admit that they do, occasionally, drink sodas—but that they are "responsible enough" to drink it in limited quantities.

Dr. Marion Nestle is perhaps the best-known critic of US food businesses, but her language is more moderate and her reasoning more nuanced and better researched than many of her peers who oppose "Big Food." In her book, *Soda Politics: Taking on Big Soda (And Winning)*, she concedes, "An occasional sugary drink is hardly a health concern." But, she wrote, "many Americans—especially those who are young, members of minority groups, and

---

* Tomás de Torquemada (1420–1498) was the Spanish Inquisition's chief enforcer. Had soda been around then, he very well could have tortured people who admitted to enjoying it.

poor—habitually drink large volumes of soda on a daily basis at great harm to their health."[580] Notice that she lumps nonwhite people and low-income people into the same group as children, implying (perhaps unintentionally) that each of those groups have to be protected from deciding, on their own, how much soda to drink or not to drink.

The desire to micromanage the lives of poor people is ancient. In Medieval Europe, "sumptuary laws" were passed to prevent non-royalty from wearing fancy clothing or eating gourmet food that was determined to be "above their station."

Throughout US history, one of the few things that wealthy conservatives and upper-middle-class liberals always seemed to unite upon was proclaiming that poor people should behave more virtuously than they themselves do. In the early 20th century, some of the most ardent proponents of alcohol's prohibition were progressive women's rights advocates (who wanted to reduce domestic violence) and reactionary KKK supporters (who wanted to keep booze away from Catholics and blacks).

In 2010, New York City Mayor Michael Bloomberg, having failed in his attempt to get the state legislature to tax soda, wrote to the USDA asking them to prevent SNAP recipients from using their benefits to obtain soda or other types of sugary beverages. I led the opposition to that proposal. A battle royal ensured. Everyone assumed that the powerful multibillionaire mayor would automatically get his way, but I knew we had both the law and the facts on our side. It wasn't quite David versus Goliath. More like Lisa Simpson versus Mr. Burns, except in this case, many of my usual liberal allies (usually upper-middle-class white ones) were also siding with Mr. Burns.

Mt first argument was that, whether the USDA thought the proposal was good or bad public policy, the Department was forced to reject it (as it had rejected similar requests in the past), because the USDA simply had no legal authority to unilaterally ban foods, including soda, that are currently allowed in SNAP under federal law. If opponents of the program wanted to ban soda or any other product in SNAP, then only the president and Congress could jointly do so by changing the law. The USDA ultimately agreed with this argument and rejected Bloomberg's request.

But I also knew that, while the legalistic approach would likely win in this one instance, since prominent leaders would keep pushing to ban either soda or all junk foods in SNAP, we would need to explain our broader argument that such bans would be both unworkable and counterproductive.

For the record, let me first state that I believe Americans of all economic levels should drink fewer sodas and eat less junk food, and that I think the food industry should be ashamed of itself for marketing to children and opposing clearer nutritional labeling.* I have long supported banning sodas and junk foods in public schools, which the President and Congress eventually did.**

That being said, limiting the consumer choice of adults in SNAP is a horrible idea. With billions of dollars at stake, the battle to define what "junk" food is would be epic, with nutrition experts pitted against food-industry lobbyists and even activists like myself, slugging it out one food item at a time. Should chocolate milk be banned? How about caramel apples, ketchup, or Fig Newtons? There would be protracted battles every year as new products are introduced and as the ingredients of existing products changed, requiring a massive government bureaucracy to continuously make such determinations.

America, there is also the issue that such a ban would send the appalling message to low-income Americans that they are uniquely unsuited to make decisions about what is best for their own bodies, essentially for their own lives. In "Why Do Americans Feel Entitled to Tell Poor People What to Eat?" writer Bryce Covert weighed in:

> Why do people think they're entitled to decide how food stamps, in particular, are used? Not all government benefits elicit such feelings. When we give people assistance through the home-mortgage interest deduction, we don't feel entitled

---

* No one—ever—needs a soda this big.

** Some people don't understand why I support banning junk food in schools but not banning junk food for adults in SNAP. They miss the obvious point that society shouldn't be treating adults as children.

to tell them what house to buy or what neighborhood to live in; when we subsidize a college education through student loans, we don't tell students what school to go to or what to major in. When we tax capital gains income at a lower rate than income made from labor, we certainly don't tell those stock pickers what to do with the extra cash. . . .

The reason people in line at a grocery store get to feel morally superior to someone on food stamps is because she has to whip out a card that tells the world that she gets assistance buying food. No such card exists when applying for a mortgage or getting a federally subsidized student loan. The other difference, of course, is that food stamps help the poor.[581]

When I asked self-righteous SNAP soda ban supporters why it was ok for them personally to drink soda but not low-income beneficiaries of the program, they would piously respond that they are "not using public money to do so." Nonsense. Taxpayers subsidize virtually every soda consumed in America, even those purchased with "private" dollars. The beverages contain government-subsidized corn syrup and sugar, and are delivered over government roads and through government ports. Virtually every American who lives to 65 will get Medicare, so if people become less healthy as seniors because they drank too much soda, our tax dollars eventually pay for their medical treatment, whether they received SNAP or not. And most low-income workers move in and out of poverty. When they make higher wages, their increased tax dollars also contribute to the very program that helps them when times are tough.

At the time Bloomberg proposed banning soda in the SNAP program, those same beverages were being given out at City Hall, where he worked, and at events held at Gracie Mansion (where he did not live but where he officially entertained). The employees at Bloomberg L.P., the company he founded and ran, were entitled to unlimited free sodas at work.

At the time, I had a radio debate with the New York State commissioner of health, who was supporting the SNAP ban. I asked him if he would ban soda machines in the office buildings in which his employees worked. He replied, "No, that's different." Sure, it's different—the people who worked for him generally weren't low-income.

But even if you don't buy my philosophical objections to treating poor people differently than everyone else, you should understand that banning certain foods in the SNAP program would almost certainly *not* advance the anti-obesity objectives of proponents. A study by the USDA Economic Research Service found that banning soda in SNAP would *not* likely lead to reduced obesity.[582] It is probable that people would still use some of their limited non-SNAP dollars to buy soda and/or people with a sweet tooth would buy other products with sugar to compensate for their loss of the sweetened beverage.

There is no evidence that low-income people who receive SNAP benefits shop any less nutritiously than others with similar low incomes. The problem isn't that they make poor choices—the problem is that they can't afford to make better choices.

As I detailed in my first book (yes, *another* plug), when I lived for a week on the allotment of food I could purchase under the SNAP budget, I was unable to afford a single beverage, other than tap water. I wanted to eat whole-wheat pasta, but even on sale, at $1.50 a box, it was just too expensive, and I could only afford plain old white pasta at 59 cents a box.

Proponents of SNAP bans assume that if we just eliminate a few "bad foods" from our diets, we will all be healthier. That's bunk. Good nutrition and reaching and maintaining a healthy weight are all about balance and adopting improved eating and exercise habits for a lifetime.

Decades ago, many weight loss programs banned specific foods and gave participants strict guidelines for eating certain "healthier" (and often less tasty) foods. (Remember the weekly calves' liver requirement in 1970s Weight Watchers? No one thinks liver is a health food nowadays.) Dieters would often lose weight rapidly, but then gain it all back just as quickly. In contrast, the most effective weight control programs today emphasize controlling portion sizes, and bar few or no foods, but emphasize healthful balance and moderation: if participants consume a higher-calorie, less-nutritious food at one meal, they simply make up for it by eating lower-calorie, more nourishing foods at other meals. The most effective and popular weight-loss plans also place a priority on encouraging consistent activity throughout the day and also deliberate exercise, such as walking. This approach acknowledges human nature and thus allows participants to gradually change their habits, leading eventually to a healthy lifestyle where they primarily eat nutritious foods and exercise, while still enjoying occasional guilty pleasures.

It's all about balance. The claim by some that soda is just as bad as tobacco or heroin is simply medically false. Just one cigarette raises your blood pressure and one hit of heroin can kill you, but one can of soda, as part of an otherwise healthy diet, will not harm you at all. I am *not* saying that everyone should drink tankers full of soda, but a standard 12-ounce can of Coke contains 140 calories, about equal to a handful of walnuts, only 10 calories more than a small bag of nutritionally empty but hipster-friendly Pirate's Booty, and one-sixth the 830 calories of a (delicious) organic Caramelized Peach Shake at a Shake Shack. Of course, if you eat unlimited amounts of any of those things you will blow up bigger than a dirigible, but that's why our key message needs to be *moderation*. We need everyone in every income bracket to be able to better balance "sometimes treats" with everyday sustenance.

A much better approach than taxing or banning so-called "bad" foods is doing far more to make healthier food affordable and physically available for struggling families. As I'll explain more later, government should do much more to encourage farmers markets, affordable community-supported agriculture projects, produce stands, and full-service supermarkets to establish in low-income neighborhoods and ensure that they accept SNAP benefits. Congress and the president should also increase the purchasing power of SNAP, thereby giving low-income families what we all want: the ability to make their own smart choices and to improve their own lives.

Foodies need to work to ensure that *all* Americans have physical and economic access to the most delicious and nutritious foods, which should be sustainably grown and harvested by well-paid workers in safe conditions. Let's work toward a future where all Americans enjoy both pleasure *and* health when they eat, so that none of us are forced to spend our lives crawling on the ground looking for edible seeds or weeds.

14.

America's
Virgin/Whore Complex
Our Obsession with
Sex and Shaming

When a 35-year-old virgin who just wanted to "get the monkey off his back" wrote to a *Chicago Sun-Times* columnist, Cheryl Lavin, for her advice on how to lose his virginity, she offered this surprising response: "I have a feeling your unhappiness over your virginity is inhibiting you with women. What if you went at it the other way? What if you lost your virginity first, then tried to have a connection with a woman? Your whole personality on a date might blossom. Prostitution is legal in some counties in Nevada. And even where it's illegal, it's widespread."[583]

America, that's your virgin-whore complex—quite literally—in a nutshell. Even a female writer suggested that there are two kinds of women: those who you screw just to screw them and those with whom you let your "personality blossom."

In 1925 Sigmund Freud first identified this phenomenon, which he called "psychic impotence," (which others have called the "Madonna[*]/ whore complex"), writing, "Where such men love they have no desire and where they desire they cannot love."

The duel obsession with both sex and female purity is as old

---

 * This one . . .   not this one.

as humans. Ancient human civilizations seemed freaked out that women had supposedly unleashed evil upon the world, and the evil discussed is *always* a metaphor for female sexuality, which apparently scared the hell out of men from the get-go, likely because they had little control over it. The story of Adam and Eve is allegedly about illicitly enjoying the fruits of knowledge through the bite of the apple, but to my mind, the subtext is clearly about improperly enjoying sex.* The ancient Greek myth of Pandora's box is surely about women unleashing their sexuality—also defined as evil—upon the world. The ultimate presentation of this conflict is the story of Christ's birth to a virgin mother. The reproductive act is sanctified, but the dirty sex act that usually accompanies reproduction never happened.** And let's never forget that any debate over sex is ultimately a debate over power and women's broader place in society.

In today's America, the pure-as-driven-snow Madonna versus the evil-but-alluring slut is the dichotomy splashed over each and every surface of our society. On the one hand, it seems as though our American culture is saturated with hyper-sexualized images and sounds everywhere—music, sports, TV, politics, the Internet, product ads, and even religion—you name it. I suppose you'd expect that the delivery mechanisms that are a perfect fit for porn—such as the Internet and pay-per-view TV—would have lots of sexual content, but what's more surprising is that everything else—no matter how nonsexual at inception—is now more about the sex than about everything else. Sport broadcasts leer over the cheerleaders with more intensity than they replay touchdowns. Entertainment awards shows—and the endless news coverage and social media frenzy that surround them—are more about the female celebrities' cleavages, side-boobs, and shapely posteriors on the red carpet than they are about whatever art form was supposedly being celebrated. Even politics—which used to be considered a semi-sacred civic religion upon which the fate of the nation and world hangs—is now indistinguishable from a night of drunken hookups on *Jersey Shore*. One leading presidential candidate (yes,

---

* Or maybe it's just about an apple. Sure, and a cigar is just a cigar.
** Avoiding controversy—for perhaps the first time in my life—I will not weigh in on whether I believe Mary had a son without having sexual intercourse with a human.

Donald Trump again . . . sigh) even bragged in a national debate about the size of his penis, argued on social media and to journalists and supporters that his wife was "hotter" than opponent Ted Cruz's wife, bragged about sexual assault, and said that his daughter is so attractive that, if she hadn't been his daughter, he'd date her. (Ultra-yuck.) And his supporters—including self-professed Christian conservatives—cheered him on.

Yet we also hate all this sex stuff, or so we say. If we are all about sex, and, at the same time we despise sex and consider it shameful, maybe it's ourselves that we really hate.

Perhaps this dichotomy is why our nation is becoming more sexually squeamish—at least towards women. Conservative federal lawmakers were trying to crucify Planned Parenthood, on the pretext that the health organization "killed babies," but really it was because the group helped women have sex. The Supreme Court was sharply divided over whether it was an imposition on an employer's religious liberty to be forced to provide employees with contraception, but the court never seemed to consider whether, for the employees who practice religions in which contraception is not prohibited, having birth control denied to them could be an imposition on their religious liberty. Again, it's really about keeping women in their *place.*

And, America, your prevalent views on rape still imply that act is about sex—or what clothing the victim was wearing or whether she was drinking—when it's all really about violence and power in our culture that gives lip-service to sexual equality only so long as it benefits men.

Meanwhile, in state after state, right-wing legislators are racing with a fury to prevent transgender citizens from ever—ever—using what conservatives considered to be the "wrong" bathroom, as if transgender individuals are sexual predators or their sexual identity is contagious. In Kansas, the government wanted to pay students a $2,500 bounty to turn in transgender students who use the "wrong" bathroom.[584] Too often in this country, taking one step forward prompts 15 steps in the opposite direction.

In the same way that we often joke about death to avoid truly dealing with it, our society turns human sexuality into comedy—or absurd melodrama—because we can't deal with sexuality in any sort of matter-of-fact way. While so-called reality TV, as well as scripted dramas and comedies, are filled to the brim (and beyond) with references to previously taboo topics such as masturbation, anal sex, adultery, polygamy, threesomes, sex toys, etc.—they infrequently include honest, realistic depictions of sexual relationships. Sex on TV or in movies often results in comedy, humiliation, or regret, and when it is none of those three, sex leads the partners to unfettered, head-over-heels love and frequently, marriage (after which, the sex supposedly ends). Our society still rebels against unpunished pleasure. Describing the sad state of sex education in America, Peggy Orenstein noted,

> Even the most comprehensive classes generally stick with a woman's internal parts: uteruses, fallopian tubes, ovaries. Those classic diagrams of a woman's reproductive system, the ones shaped like the head of a steer, blur into a gray Y between the legs, as if the vulva and the labia, let alone the clitoris, don't exist. And whereas males' puberty is often characterized in terms of erections, ejaculation, and the emergence of a near-unstoppable sex drive, females' is defined by periods. And the possibility of unwanted pregnancy. When do we explain the miraculous nuances of their anatomy? When do we address exploration, self-knowledge?[585]

ABORTION RESTRICTIONS

Men overall, but conservative men in particular, seem absolutely flummoxed by female body parts, which must be why they idiotically say such things as "Rape can't lead to pregnancy." Amazingly, in 2014 (not 1814), conservative pundit Rich Lowry claimed that "forced kissing" isn't sexual assault.[586] For many on the Right, pregnancy is all about the evil act of enjoying sex—unless you're married, when the sex act becomes perfectly acceptable, sort of. As much as some conservatives claim that their anti-abortion crusade is about being "pro-life," given that many of them are also in favor of the death penalty, war, and cuts in child nutrition programs that prevent infant mortality,* it's more than fair to conclude that their real opposition is to sex (at least for women).

In 2016 a House Republican committee, over loud objections from Democrats, unilaterally issued subpoenas to a company that supplies biological specimens for research, a university conducting medical research using fetal tissue, and an abortion clinic in Albuquerque. In addition to requiring these groups to produce exhaustive documentation about how exactly they procure and handle fetal tissue, the subpoenas demanded that the organizations identify personnel, including medical students, who were in proximity to abortions and their aftermath.** Given that anti-choice domestic terrorists have previously used such information to assassinate doctors who perform abortions, this was a dangerous game indeed.[587]

Across the nation, states run by Republicans—particularly those in the South and the Midwest—have been passing harsh restrictions on reproductive choice. Supreme Court Justice Elena Kagan noted that she was struck by the clear relationship between abortion restrictions in Texas and the closing of abortion clinics there. "It's almost like the perfect controlled experiment as to the effect of the law, isn't it?" she said. "It's like you put the law into effect, 12 clinics closed. You take the law out of effect, they reopen."[588] Women in those states with enough money and time will travel to other states to get abortions; other women without means are forced to take more ghastly measures. There is now evidence that because of such restrictions, women are

---

* The US has an infant mortality rate worse than 57 countries, according to the CIA's *World Factbook*. This is likely because of our high rates of poverty and inadequate nutrition for pregnant mothers.

** These are the incredibly diverse House GOP committee chairs, circa 2012, who helped decide legislation regarding women's reproductive issues and other vital matters to women (and men, for that matter).

attempting extraordinarily dangerous self-induced non-medical abortions. In 2015, there were about 700,000 Google searches in the US looking into self-induced abortions. The state with the highest rate of these searches was Mississippi, where all but one abortion clinic in the state had been closed.[589]

The reality that those most likely to be harmed are low-income women and women of color—because they have less power—is one of the main reasons that there has not been more widespread political pushback against these restrictions on reproductive choice.

Some of the women who have benefited most from feminism—those who make a lot of money in their careers—are now some of the same women who reject even the label "feminist," and will do little to help other women, especially those who are poor and voiceless, and who are under the boot of misogynist oppression.

While the US Supreme Court eventually struck down Texas's absurdly restrictive abortion laws, the state-by-state battles to restrict reproductive choices continues.

Just as wealthy business leaders make the absurd claims that they are protecting workers by opposing minimum wage hikes, male lawmakers insist they are protecting women from needing to choose what to do with their own bodies. The anti-abortion group Americans United for Life proposed state legislation with names such as the "Women's Health Protection Act" and the "Women's Health Defense Act." As Emily Bazelon wrote,

> Abortion opponents have started arguing that for the sake of women seeking abortions—to protect their health and safety— the state must impose strict new regulations on clinics. . . . The language of fear has been even plainer in the recent push by conservative Republicans to deny Planned Parenthood government funding. "Planned Parenthood is not a safe place for vulnerable women," the president of the conservative group Concerned Women for America said . . . claiming that the group "coerces women into abortion" and "sells their baby parts." . . .
>
> These claims are not backed by evidence. But still the alarms ring, playing into our usual assumptions that the impulse to

protect is benevolent and, perhaps, that women are especially deserving of solicitude. The association between "protection" and women is deeply embedded in culture.[590]

Again, the real push is to deny women their agency and to impose on them instead the will of conservative men. But the good news is that House Republicans also voted to cut federal funding for Viagra. (Just kidding! I wrote that line for my group's annual April Fools' Day press release. In reality, 92 percent of House Republicans are men—they would *never* take Viagra out of federally-funded health plans.)

MADAM ~~WHORE BITCH CUNT~~ SECRETARY, POSSIBLE PRESIDENT

Early in the 2008 primary season, I was one of the few people I knew who predicted that Barack Obama would best Hillary Clinton. I knew her vote for the Iraq War would hurt her with Democratic primary and caucus voters, and that Obama's freshness and dynamism would be compelling. But I made one other prediction, which also turned out to be completely true: African Americans would feel more comfortable voting for a fellow African American than women would for a fellow woman. In the decisive South Carolina Democratic primary in 2008, Obama beat Clinton by 59 points among black voters, but also beat her by 24 points among women, partially because black women over-whelmingly favored Obama. In the 2016 New Hampshire primary, Secretary Clinton lost the women's vote to Bernie Sanders by 11 points. A large part of both of these losses were due to weaknesses in Clin-ton's campaign message, and to the unique strengths of Obama and Sanders, but part of it was undeniably her gender. The hard truth is that many women still didn't trust other women in positions of authority.

The torrent of misogyny unleashed against Hillary Clinton in the 2016 campaign from the far Right, as well as the self-proclaimed Left, was astounding and nonstop. As Tracy Clark-Flory and Leigh Cuen documented on *Vocativ*,

It only took one post from Hillary Clinton's official Instagram account for the sexist comments to roll in. She was called a "bitch" on her very first post, which featured an image of her predictably red-white-and-blue clothing rack. "If this bitch can't decide what to wear how will she decide what to do for her country, and shit like this is why we shouldn't have a female president," wrote a commenter . . .

A Vocativ analysis reveals that the most common sexist insult directed at Clinton on Twitter is the word "bitch." In a survey of more than 25,650 tweets aimed at her, there were over 1,980 uses of the term. It was hands-down the most popular gendered insult leveled at Clinton. The runners up: "Cunt," with 370 mentions, and "slut" with 114 instances. . . .

On Instagram, predictable insults like "slut," "bitch," "shrew," and "witch" were thrown around, while some users got a bit more creatively horrible. Some actually spelled out their sexist beliefs: "As far as I'm concerned women don't have the same rights as men for a reason. It should stay that way." . . .

It's a mindset that casts the role of a female president as wife to the entire nation. Within that mentality, Clinton is shirking her responsibilities not just to her husband, but also to all men. It calls to mind how during her first presidential campaign she was heckled by guys ordering her to "Iron my shirts!" and antagonized by the Facebook group "Hillary Clinton: Stop Running for President and Make Me a Sandwich." That's how little the sexist rhetoric around Clinton has changed in the past seven years: at its core, it's still about her not knowing her place.[591]

Clinton has been criticized for yelling, but also for talking too softly.* She is slammed for smiling and vilified for being too serious. As Sady Doyle put it in *Slate*, Hillary Clinton could do no right:

---

* Here are pictures of just some of the emotions for which Hillary Clinton is hated:

Hillary Clinton absolutely cannot express negative emotion in public. If she speaks loudly or gets angry or cries, she risks being seen as bitchy, crazy, and dangerous. (When she raised her voice during the 2013 Benghazi Senate committee hearings, the cover of the New York Post blared, "NO WONDER BILL'S AFRAID.") But if Hillary avoids emotions—if she speaks strictly in calm, logical, detached terms—then she is cold, robotic, calculating . . .

It turns out that people hate it when Hillary Clinton smiles or laughs in public. Hillary Clinton's laugh gets played in attack ads; it has routinely been called "a cackle" (like a witch, right? Because she's old, and female, like a witch) . . .

She can't be sad or angry, she can't be happy or amused, and she can't refrain from expressing any of those emotions. There is no way out of this one. There is no right way for her to act . . . How long would you make it, if people treated you the way you treat Hillary Clinton? . . . Bizarre, then, that Hillary Clinton has developed a reputation in the press for seeming distant—even secretive or paranoid! It's almost as if, after a quarter-century of being attacked for her appearance, personality, and every waking move, breath, and word, Hillary Clinton is highly conscious of how she is perceived and portrayed, and is trying really hard to monitor her own behavior and behave in ways people will accept.[592]

Sanders supporters chanted, and posted on social media, the phrase "Bern the witch." At nearly all Trump rallies, vendors sold a tee shirt that said "Trump that bitch" on one side, with photos of Hillary and Monica Lewinsky on the other side, along with the words, "Hillary sucks, but not like Monica."[593] Charming.

Beyond Hillary Clinton, rampant sexism continues to swamp all levels of US politics. A male state senator in South Carolina told a fellow female senator in public that women are inferior because they are a "lesser cut of meat," referring to the passage in the Bible saying God made Eve from Adam's rib.[594] That occurred in 2015, not 1815. I've seen my own US senator, Kirsten Gillibrand, repeatedly referred to as a "bitch" and a "cunt" online. Congressman Blaine Luetkemeyer (R-MO) commented that people need to "find a way to neuter" Massachusetts Senator Elizabeth Warren. In response to a right-wing blog post questioning whether Nancy Pelosi was suffering from severe mental illness, these little nuggets of delightfulness were posted online by various people: "I very much wish you'd not mentioned Pelosi and naked in the same sentence because that's an image I dearly wish I could have avoided"; "Nancy Pelosi is a monkey"; and "This bitch."

Conservative women have sometimes faced the same invective. After Fox News host Megyn Kelly sharply questioned Donald Trump in a debate, Kelly's name and the word "cunt," "whore," "bitch," or "slut" exploded on social media. And Trump only fanned the flames.

America, your hatred of powerful women, even fictional ones, is vast and visceral. The actress Anna Gunn wrote about the misogyny she faced when playing the powerful character Skyler White on the popular TV show, *Breaking Bad*:

> My character . . . has become a flash point for many people's feelings about strong, nonsubmissive, ill-treated women. . . .
>
> I was unprepared for the vitriolic response she inspired. Thousands of people have "liked" the Facebook page "I Hate Skyler White." Tens of thousands have "liked" a similar Facebook page with a name that cannot be printed here. . . .
>
> A typical online post complained that Skyler was a "shrieking, hypocritical harpy" and didn't "deserve the great life she has." . . . The consensus among the haters was clear: Skyler was a ball-and-chain, a drag, a shrew, an "annoying bitch wife" . . .
>
> Vince Gilligan, the creator of "Breaking Bad," wanted Skyler to be a woman with a backbone of steel who would stand up to whatever came her way, who wouldn't just collapse in the corner or wring her hands in despair. He and the show's writers made Skyler multilayered and, in her own way, morally compromised. But at the end of the day, she hasn't been judged by the same set of standards as Walter.* . . .

---

* Walter repeatedly killed people and made and distributed the purest crystal meth, leading users to addiction, poverty, and death—but *she* was the only one everyone hated?

It's notable that viewers have expressed similar feelings about other complex TV wives—Carmela Soprano of "The Sopranos," Betty Draper of "Mad Men." Male characters don't seem to inspire this kind of public venting and vitriol . . .

Already harsh online comments became outright personal attacks. One such post read: "Could somebody tell me where I can find Anna Gunn so I can kill her?" Besides being frightened (and taking steps to ensure my safety), I was also astonished: how had disliking a character spiraled into homicidal rage at the actress playing her? . . .

But I finally realized that most people's hatred of Skyler had little to do with me and a lot to do with their own perception of women and wives. Because Skyler didn't conform to a comfortable ideal of the archetypical female, she had become a kind of Rorschach test for society, a measure of our attitudes toward gender.[595]

Such dehumanizing language and thoughts about woman surely foster rape and other forms of violence against women, devastating consequences for both the women involved and the world as a whole. When Everytown for Gun Safety, a gun control group, analyzed FBI data on mass shootings from 2009 to 2015, it found that 57 percent of the cases included a spouse, former spouse, or other family member among the victims—and that 16 percent of the attackers had previously been charged with domestic violence.[596] I'm sure that last figure would be higher if male batterers were more frequently reported and charged with that crime. Marital rape only became officially illegal in all 50 states as late as 1993, when North Carolina was the final state to criminalize it, and even today, in several states, marital rape is treated differently than rape that happens outside of marriage.[597]

THE ECONOMIC BACK OF THE BUS

The cultural, sexual, physical, and legal repression of women goes hand-in-hand with the economic oppression of women.

Between 1948 and 2013, there was a massive increase in mid-

dle-income American women working outside the home. I stress
"middle-income women" because there is this myth that virtually no
women worked outside the home before the modern feminist movement, but the truth is that low-income American women have *always*
needed to work to survive.* (Meanwhile, women in high-income households, especially on any number of reality shows with the word "real
housewives" in the titles, seem to have little work to perform, either
inside or outside of their multiple homes.**) In 1948, 35 percent of
women worked outside the home in the United States; that figure rose
to 74 percent by 2013. There is no doubt that one significant cause of
that increase was many women's desire to gain personal fulfillment
through their own careers, independent of their spouses; but there
is also no question that many women were forced into the workforce
because their spouse's income alone could no longer pay the bills. In
2013, employed married women's earnings comprised 44 percent of
their family's total income, up from 37 percent in 1970.

As of 2016, American females still earned less than 80 cents for
every dollar men made. A study found that when women enter fields in
greater numbers, pay for those jobs declines—for the very same work
that more men were doing before. The earnings of information technology managers (who are mostly men) were 27 percent higher than
human resources managers (who were mostly women). Janitors (who
are often men) earned 22 percent more than maids and housecleaners

---

* Here are some low-income women, working hard outside the home, way before Betty Friedan
was born.

** Believe it or not, this show occurred long *after* the feminist revolution:

(who are often women).[598] Even female medical doctors earn about $20,000 per year less than their male counterparts.[599]

Despite all the work they now perform outside the household, women still do most of the work caring for children, cleaning the home, and preparing meals. Even when families are impoverished, and men are more likely to be unemployed then women, the females still must produce the food; in 2015, women comprised more than 80 percent of the total number of people that called the USDA National Hunger Hotline to find where they could get free food.*

Because many men still have relatively few responsibilities for raising children, male political leaders still don't understand why paid family and medical leave is particularly important to women. In explaining why he opposed such a measure, Ohio governor and losing Republican presidential candidate John Kasich, said, "The one thing we need to do for working women is to give them the flexibility to be able to work at home online. The reason why that's important is, when women take maternity leave or time to be with the children, then what happens is they fall behind on the experience level, which means that the pay becomes a differential."[600] Kasich was clueless that many jobs that working-class women hold—such as taking care of elderly patients, providing day care, or working cash registers—can't be done from home online.

Throughout the entire world, women are paid less than men, even for identical work. In 2014, according to the World Economic Forum, US women earned only 66 percent of a man's salary, but that was far better than the rates of 48 percent in Italy and 47 percent in Israel. The only country where women earn more than men is Denmark (ah, those great Danes!).[601]

GIVE ME THAT OLD-TIME RELIGION

There is a strong case to be made that, even though Europe is far more secular than a hundred years ago, much of the rest of the world is far more fundamentalist. I think that, in aggregate, practicing Muslims,

---

* The National Hunger Hotline, run by Hunger Free America on behalf of the USDA as of 2016, can be reached at 1-866-3-HUNGRY (1-866-348-6479).

Christians, Jews, and Hindus have become more religiously conservative; and those believers who became more liberal tended to become less
religious overall. I'd argue that there is only one thing that truly unites
the most reactionary strands of all these religions: the oppression of
women. The head of the UN Women agency, Phumzile Mlambo-Ng-
cuka, said that one of the new dangers facing women throughout the
world is a "growing and extremist resistance" to equality between the
sexes. And a major report for the Commission on the Status of Women
found that "[e]xtremism and conservatism are on the rise, manifested in
diverse forms across different contexts," adding that examples include
"tolerating or even promoting violence against women and limiting
women's and girls' autonomy and engagement in the public sphere."⁶⁰²

BACKLASH: WOMEN'S RIGHTS ARE HUMAN RIGHTS

As many societies started to move beyond the bedrock belief that the
only roles for women were to raise children, work inside the home,
have sex whenever the husband wants, and speak and think exactly as
the men demand, a fierce backlash was provoked, since the changing
role of women was the greatest direct threat to men unilaterally ruling
the world, or at least their own households. In pre-feminist times, a
man may have been dirt poor, at the lowest rung of society, with no
political or economic power, and having virtually no voice or standing
within the culture as a whole, but, in his own home, he was an all-powerful dictator, able to exercise power on matters major to petty, all while
commanding respect, obedience, and (in his mind) love, even if those
things were forcefully extracted. Not only were men threatened by
losing their power, many women were too afraid, beaten down, and
ashamed to fully embrace their new influence and the vast array of
potential new life choices, so it was natural that many men (and far too
many women) gravitated to extreme religions that promised to restore
the previous, male-dominated status quo. People were willing to accept
rigidity, so long as it produced certainty.

The unequal role of women today exacerbates virtually every major
problem on the planet, from poverty to war to disease. In India, women
are more likely to be undernourished than men because they feed

themselves last. "These mothers are the last persons in their families to have food," said Dr. Shella Duggal, who works in a mobile clinic aiding the destitute in Delhi's slums. "First, she feeds the husband and then the kids, and only then will she eat the leftovers."[603]

In Saudi Arabia, women who are merely discovered walking in public with men who are not their relatives can be lashed. A woman who was violently gang-raped in Saudi Arabia was sentenced to 200 lashes and six months in jail after being found guilty of indecency and talking to the media.[604] Yes, you read that right, they wanted to punish a woman for the crime of being a *victim* of gang-rape, although the late King Abdullah—ever so magnanimously—pardoned her.

In China, government restrictions on the number of children a family is allowed to have encouraged infanticide, but there and throughout the world, baby girls are far more likely to be killed than baby boys.

In 1903, W.E.B. Du Bois wrote that "the problem of the Twentieth Century is the problem of the color-line." In 2016, it seems clear that an equally big problem of the 21st century is the gender line. If we want to fix the world, we must ensure that all women have an equal stake and an equal say.

To end poverty and hunger, women must be empowered.

To reduce war and terrorism, women must be empowered.

To raise world education levels, women must be empowered.

You get the point.

Of course, the empowerment of women goes way beyond issues of sex, and full equality for women must be viewed independently from issues of sexuality. Highly sexual and asexual women alike—and every woman and human being in between those opposite ends of the scale—must have equal rights and equal standing.

But we can't ignore the centrality of sex to many aspects of discrimination. Women will never have equality unless both men and women accept the basic reality that, to both make babies and feel physical pleasure, both men and women, equally, must be able have sex without shame.

But, America, you still warn women not to dress too prudishly or too suggestively. You still punish women for being weak and for being strong. You still objectify women and put them on pedestals. You do all this, America, when to have a healthy relationship with your citizens, what you should really be working toward is enabling women to experience the miracle of not being seen as either virgin *or* whore, but simply, as fellow humans with all the complexities and passions and responsibilities that implies.

Suck on that, Sigmund!

15.

A Non–Purpose Driven Life
How Our Reality TV Culture Is Stripping America of Soul, Sense, and Meaning

"Humility is not thinking less of yourself; it is thinking of yourself less.
Humility is thinking more of others."
—Pastor Rick Warren[605]

America, both the religious right and secular humanists agree on something big—very big—and they don't even know it. Both agree that each and every human life has a higher purpose that serves a greater good. Both agree living well should encompass more than just personal pleasure and achievement.

Most people in the religious right not only believe in prayer and spiritual devotion, they also believe in performing good works in the here and now—as do most people on the religious left. That's why so many soup kitchens and emergency food pantries in America are run by people of faith, and are frequently housed in churches, synagogues, and mosques.

Secular humanists, by definition, believe it is the duty of each individual to help humanity as a whole.

Thus many on both the Left and Right concur on the central definition of what it takes to be a "good" human being. In essence, they agree that each life has a larger meaning within the world—perhaps the single most important value on which to find common ground.

They also have a common enemy—and they don't know that either. Their common enemy is America's vapid, narcissistic, self-serving, pleasure-at-all-costs culture*—in which the top goal is to be famous for

---

* For the record, I am not against personal pleasure, *per se*. In fact, I am a big fan of pleasure. I just think it needs to be balanced with other values that serve the entirety of the human community.

five minutes. (We can't afford to spare even 15 minutes to focus on our individual fame these days.)

Overall, religious conservatives want our culture to obsess less with sex and to stop glorifying irresponsibility, and liberals want our culture to obsess less with violence and to stop glorifying moneymaking. In the end, both sides' major objection is the same: our media and our society should stop proclaiming that the only thing that matters is personal gratification.

AMERICA'S NARCISSISM EPIDEMIC

"Selfies" may be relatively a new invention—and the ultimate sign of our times—but, America, you've always been more obsessed with your own navel, suntan, speed boat, trophy spouse, powdered wig, fishing hut, jazz records, and sparkling new Model T Fords than with the common good.

However, the most recent foray into a public celebration of all things selfish really took off in the 1970s. According to Steve Salerno, the author of *Sham: How the Self-Help Movement Made America Helpless*, Werner Erhard, founder of the New Age self-help course "est," "made palatable the notion that the end justifies the means . . . Which is partly responsible for the climate of what I call happyism. If your happiness is all that matters, anybody who stands in the way becomes detritus in the ruthless pursuit of individual perfection."[606]

It's no coincidence that the quintessential symbol of American happiness—the cloying yellow smiley face—was so popular in the 1970s.*

The "Me Generation" took over. Self-help books exploded, social action became passé, and mega-churches that placed self-fulfillment ahead of piety sprouted up. Personal happiness was everything to you, America. According to Ronald W. Dworkin, "By 1972, an estimated 13 percent of men and 29 percent of women were using some kind of prescription psychotherapeutic drug. One of the decisive factors underlying this aggressive prescription behavior was a rather revolutionary new belief: even without definitive proof, primary-care doctors

---

* The warm, inviting, (vaguely cult-like) smiley face of the bell-bottoms age 😊 was replaced by the cold, robotic emoji of the skinny jeans digital age ☺. Now, everyone's favorite is this: 💩

and the public alike had decided that unhappiness, even in some cases everyday unhappiness, was the result of a chemical imbalance in the brain—which drugs could fix."[607]

By 2014, our society was so self-centered that even *Scientific American* noted that Americans were more concerned with "personal happiness" (defined as "experiencing pleasure, positive emotion, or success") than people in other cultures.[608]

A 2009 national poll of college students found that 57 percent of them believed that their generation used social networking sites for self-promotion, narcissism, and attention-seeking, while almost 40 percent agreed with the statement that "being self-promoting, narcissistic, overconfident, and attention-seeking is helpful for succeeding in a competitive world."[609] Filed under "hilarious but sadly true": researchers from Australia's University of Queensland found that "[b]oth passive and shunned users [of social media] experienced feelings of exclusion and felt 'invisible' and less important as individuals. Shunned users also experienced lower self-esteem and control."[610]

As if having a zillion selfies posted around the Internet—in every conceivable social media location—was not enough for Kim Kardashian, she actually published a book of selfies (yes, an old-fashioned book with paper, binding, and everything), but at least (with a bit of truth in advertising) she called it *Selfish*.

THE GREAT DUMBING DOWN

And if it isn't bad enough that our culture is obsessed with individualism—in fact, *defined* by it—it's even more focused on making everything simple, one-dimensional, and yes, dumb. Everything that used to be detailed, nuanced, or complex now must be boiled down to just one headline or 140-character tweet—which explains why so many online headlines claim that one, just one! "perfect" tweet or statement can sum up "everything." Some examples of real-life online article headlines from "news" websites:

> "The Star Wars actress puts her critics in their place with one delightfully vulgar tweet"

"The One Perfect Tweet Which Put Megyn Kelly's Duggar Daughter Interview in Context"

"Adele's Comment about Her Son's Sexuality Is Absolutely Perfect"

"Brilliant: @BetteMidler takes down Steve Harvey, Miss Universe & George W. Bush in one perfect tweet"

"In One Quote, Viola Davis Nails The Academy Awards' Diversity Issue"

"America's Top Union Leader Just Destroyed Scott Walker in Six Words from Rolling Stone"

"One Perfect Tweet Demonstrates How Utterly Ridiculous the World Is"

Apparently, it's always got to be "one" tweet saying it all, because it would simply be too taxing for us if we had to read two whole tweets.*

But on a very rare occasion, when even the media acknowledges that an issue is so complex that one mere tweet might not be enough—such discussions as the difficult tradeoffs between the need to protect privacy versus the need to combat terrorism, for example—sometimes something marginally more substantive, like one cartoon, is required to explain it: "The Essence of Apple's Standoff With the FBI, in One Comic." Or "White Privilege: Explained in One Simple Comic." Sometimes an absurdly complicated issue can be explained in one chart, as in, "Here Is the Stunning Utter Failure of the Republican-Led Congress in One Chart," or "Voter Anger Explained—in One Chart," or "How Hijackings Have Changed Over the Years—in One Chart." How about this: "How to Fix All of America's Problems—in One Self-Help Book for the Nation." I like that last one.

Sure, there is just too much information out there, and it *can* be overwhelming, so we all appreciate when the media uses charts, cartoons, or even pithy one-liners to give us the most salient points. If nothing else, this

---

* When I googled "one perfect tweet," I came up with 5,840,000 results in 0.46 seconds. The previous sentence, by the way, at 82 characters, is One Perfect Tweet.

book, too, is an attempt to break down major problems into their simplest terms. That being said, if we are giving the public brief, cursory information, we should not try to claim we are explaining "everything" in one line.

Sometimes the clickbait headlines assume we all agree that a topic which, in previous times, might have been extraordinarily trivial, is now of grand, earth-shattering significance to the entire planet, as in the headline, "The world was not ready for the gown she wore." The "world," huh? Yeah, I'm sure villagers in Burkina Faso were waiting on the edge of their stools to see that dress, and, when they did, they were all knocked into a stupor.

This may be the most epoch-altering headline of all time: "The 20 Totally Rare Times We Saw Taylor Swift in Jeans." But I'll just shake that off because haters are just gonna hate, hate, hate.*

Since your current working assumption, America, is that everything that mattered in the past—or will be important in the future—can appropriately be reduced to its essence in 140 characters or less, I analyzed Richard Lattimore's classic 1951 translation of the ancient Greek epic poem, *The Iliad*, by Homer—which is 727 pages long, each riveting page full of powerful imagery, cruel warfare, essential history, indelible characters, and timeless moral quandaries. I believe I "perfectly" summed it up in "one" tweet of 140 characters: "Wine-dark sea, multitudes die because swift-footed Achilles is prideful jerk with one weak spot in heel. Mourn, oh, mourn."

It's not just pop culture and the media that's been dumbed-down. All key American institutions are now oversimplifying in our age of quick bites (and bytes) of information. Business leaders and nonprofit leaders are encouraged to abbreviate complex restructuring and strategic plans into concise PowerPoint presentations, sometimes as short as one page. According to Helen Thomas, President George W. Bush preferred policy memos extraordinarily condensed and simplified, no matter how complex or urgent the issue.** She wrote, "In White House

---

* For those of you who don't get that reference, ask your kids—or more likely, your grandkids.
** President Bill Clinton would read long memos and respond to them by hand. A man of large literary appetites, Bill Clinton reportedly devoured up to 300 books per year, and he and Hillary owned a book collection of about 4,500 volumes by the time they moved into the White House, requiring additional bookshelves in their private quarters because there weren't enough. Barack Obama famously writes terrific books. So, not all our modern presidents are book-avoiding dumbasses.

meetings his anti-intellectual bent sometimes took the form of kidding experts for being nerds or geeks if their presentations became too complicated."[611] The daily intelligence briefing memo given to President Bush on August 6, 2001, entitled "Bin Laden Determined to Strike the US," was only 486 words long. (It is likely that even such piddling memos would still be too long for Donald Trump's concentration.)

Americans don't always understand the price we pay for our current culture's idolatry of ignorance, short attention spans, and superficiality—and the even bigger price we pay by electing to national office the "regular guy you could sit and share a beer with at the local bar."

OUR SHALLOW POLITICAL AND MEDIA CULTURE

Does our media create, or merely reinforce, our contemporary shallow American culture? Both.

The Lincoln Memorial reflecting pool in Washington, DC is only 18 inches deep, but that's about 18 inches deeper than our current media, entertainment, and political cultures, which are now virtually indistinguishable from each other. Washington is now a lot like Hollywood—but without Hollywood's sincerity and diversity.

Long before Trump ran for president, our media treated politics as one long reality show. Who was winning or losing—who was mad at or infatuated with who—all became the daily—hourly, really—tropes of recent news coverage of governance and politics.

Much, though not all, television news coverage has devolved into short appearances by politicians and "political analysts," with pundits snappily quizzing each other over "who won the week?" or worse, "who won the day?"* Readers are asked to vote online or via text message about the most recent political "winners" and "losers." Everything—and I mean everything—is now seen primarily through the lens of whether it makes the politicians temporarily look better or worse. A major deal to prevent Iran from getting nuclear weapons? The media focused on whether it was a "win or loss" for Obama. Even wars are now given the same

---

* Often the people on cable TV billed as "political strategists" have little, or no, professional experience providing anyone or any campaign with actual political strategy. They either just look good or give good sound bites—preferably both.

thumbs-up or -down treatment. (Too few bother to ask the families of the soldiers or civilians killed, or the residents of cities or towns decimated, if they think the war is a "win" or a "loss"—or if journalists do ask, editors and producers nix it for time or space considerations.)

An insider political publication in New York even pondered whether the way New York Governor Andrew Cuomo reacted to his partner's breast cancer treatment was a political "win" or a "loss." CNN ran a graphic that described domestic bombings as "wins" for Trump. Reprehensible.

Coverage of political campaigns is now so horse-race focused I think the media should just skip the pretense of hiring political analysts and simply replace them all with sports reporters, who are some of the best literary writers in the business anyway.

When assessing the qualifications of presidential candidates, it is generally far easier to objectively examine the records of governors than it is to judge those of senators or businesspeople, because it is easier to see governors' tangible results and/or the consequences of specific actions they took. Did unemployment, poverty, or wages rise or sink in their state while they were in office? Did the state's budget deficit increase or decrease? There are many clear measures of whether a governor is effective, but in 2016, when seven of the original GOP presidential candidates were current or former governors, there was scant media coverage over whether they were good, mediocre, or bad at their jobs. For instance, in a 7,280-word profile of Chris Christie in the *New York Times Magazine*, exactly 45 words (six-tenths of 1 percent) were on his record as governor. (By the way, Christie destroyed his state's finances and seriously harmed its economy.)

Instead, the press was focused on made-for-tabloid insult exchanges between the Republican rivals and endless polls—most unprofessionally conducted and far too early in the process to have any meaning—as to which candidate was up or down by a point or two in Iowa or New Hampshire.* They never bother to tell their readers, listeners, or viewers

---

* The most respected political polls usually have a margin of error of between 3 to 5 points. If a poll has a margin of error of 5 points, that means that, if the poll finds a candidate is getting, let's say, 45 percent of the vote, that really means they could be getting as little as 40 percent or as much as 50 percent of the vote. Thus, when the media blares headlines that a candidate is surging because they had a 1 or 2 point increase, or plummeting because they had a 1 or 2 point drop, that's a load of BS. Since the news media spend a small fortune on polls, they will always make it seem like there are newsworthy changes, even if there aren't.

that, despite the months and months of buildup, the Iowa caucus and the New Hampshire primary are poor indicators of who will get each party's nomination.*

The already pithy average TV sound bite in presidential campaign coverage dropped dramatically in length, from 43 seconds in 1968 to a mere nine seconds in 1988.[612] It's likely even shorter now. By next campaign season, the candidates will just wave and not speak at all (too bad this development didn't arrive in time for Donald Trump's campaign). The media rarely covers actual substance, but they often poll the public on issues, and then feign shock at how little the public knows about those issues. It is not entirely surprising (but is highly demoralizing) that 15 percent of Americans could correctly identify Supreme Court Chief Justice John Roberts, while 27 percent knew Randy Jackson was a judge on *American Idol*.

In the rare instance that cable TV news interrupts mindless, endless speculation about who is ahead in the presidential race, it is only to engage in mindless, endless speculation about whether a knife found in Los Angeles County years ago belonged to O.J. Simpson or whether a missing plane is still missing.

Often the media blame consumers for their senseless coverage, claiming they're only giving the public what they want. Fair point. Even the supposedly sophisticated readers of the *New York Times* usually choose horse-race stories over substance; in one two-week period in the winter of 2016, five of 10 of the *Times's* "most popular" articles in each week were about who was up or down in the presidential race, and not a single issues-related article made either week's list.[613] Still, that's a lousy excuse. If none of their readers were particularly interested in reading or watching stories about the collapse of the Soviet Union, the AIDS epidemic, or the 9/11 attacks when those stories were most fresh, would—or should—the media have failed to cover them? Of course not. News is supposed to be an objective judgment of what's most important—not a popularity contest.

---

* Out of the last seven seriously contested Iowa GOP caucuses, only two of the winners became the nominee. Out of the last eight seriously contested New Hampshire Democratic primaries, only four of the winners became the Democratic nominee. In 2008, seven times the number of Democrats voted in the New York primary as in the New Hampshire primary, but the New York primary received only a tiny fraction of New Hampshire's media attention.

The media have even dumbed-down presidential debates, which were originally supposed to be the ultimate forum to discuss issues. In the 1960 John F. Kennedy/Richard Nixon debates, the moderator questions focused on weighty issues facing the nation and the world. By the 2016 primary debates, the questions leaned heavily on polls, attacks, counterattacks, and juvenile name-calling. Thank goodness neither Lincoln nor Douglas had to suffer through such inane faux questions from TV stars masquerading as journalists.

News commentators just can't get enough of using boxing clichés to describe the debates—"knockdown," "take a punch," and "come out swinging" are favorites. Pundits now almost always rate the debates as "performances," which makes as little sense as rating operas as public policy seminars. In a supposedly straight news story on a debate, the New York Times reported, "[Sanders] smiled a few times, but it felt awkward. Mrs. Clinton laughed a few times, but it felt forced."[614] Any time a reporter is using a passive construction, such as "it felt," that's their underhanded way of giving their personal opinion. In any case, how could the journalist, who is supposed to be focused on facts, have read the minds of Sanders and Clinton to know if the smiles or laughs were genuine?

One day in 2016, the "story of the day" in much of the political media was criticism of presidential candidate and senator Marco Rubio's boots, and the New York Times devoted 769 words to the subject, an obsession Rubio called "craziness." "So let me get this right," Rubio said, "ISIS is cutting people's heads off, setting people on fire in cages. Saudi Arabia and Iran are on the verge of a war," but the media was asking him about his footwear choice instead of what he would do, if elected president, in response to those threats.[615] That was a rare time I agreed with Rubio. The same day, in a different article, the Times wrote that Chris Christie's response to a personal attack gave the governor "a chance to showcase his talents as a political performer." When political reporters are indistinguishable from theater critics, we all are in trouble.

When the candidates were finally asked in debates about serious issues, the questions were usually focused on topics like the deficit or global terrorism, rather than about working-class voter concerns.

In every 2008 and 2012 presidential primary and general election debate—and in all the 2016 presidential primary debates through April 2016—(dozens of debates in all) I don't believe there was a single question on poverty, hunger, or homelessness, even though these problems have a devastating, direct impact on tens of millions of Americans.

Beyond campaign season reporting, mainstream media coverage is often preposterously class-biased. In a *Wall Street Journal* video titled "Do You Make $400,000 a Year but Still Feel Broke" (yes, that is a real video), a reporter ticked off all the absolute necessities for families (including $30,000 per year on food eaten at home—three times what the average family spends—and $25,000 per year on vacations) and concluded that a family earning $400K annually could feel truly down and out.[616]

On the MSNBC show *Morning Joe*, popular among political insiders, journalist John Heilemann said that people making over $200,000 a year "aren't rich," even though that amount is about four times what the average family earns and is in the top 5 percent of the nation's incomes.* All too often the media assumes the entire country earns as much and enjoys the same pampered living conditions as their well-heeled friends and neighbors. A story in the *New York Times* seriously considered whether a private jet ride from New York to Los Angeles, costing $3,600, plus a $2,500 membership fee for the privilege of renting the plane, was affordable.[617] *The Times* also ran a story implying that lots of people customarily get Fridays off from work in the summer (and get paid for that), when such a perk is almost always limited to privileged white-collar job holders.**

One day an ad for a $10,300 Louis Vuitton watch (the cost of which equaled 1,420 hours of minimum-wage work) appeared on the front page of the *Times* right next to a story on the record number of US residents living in poverty. Hey, at least they were covering poverty.

In 2012, Wisconsin's Republican US Senate candidate (who lost, thank goodness) said he was sick and tired of reading sad stories about

---

* Many leading elected officials, including Barack Obama and Hillary Clinton, have proposed tax plans based on the assumption that $200,000 a year earnings aren't considered "wealthy," demonstrating how the media elites reinforce the class bias of the political elites and vice versa.
** Nurses, cops, construction workers, cashiers, etc. do *not* get paid to take Fridays off in the summer. They are lucky if they get Saturdays or Sunday off—unpaid, of course.

people struggling in the recession, saying, "I see a reporter here . . . Stop always writing about, 'Oh, the person couldn't get, you know, their food stamps or this or that.' You know, I saw something the other day—it's like, another sob story, and I'm like, 'But what about what's happening to the country and the country as a whole?'"[618] Yet *National Journal* looked at the nation's five largest newspapers and counted how many times "unemployment" or "deficit" appeared in their headlines or first sentences. The analysis found that unemployment was covered significantly less than the deficit. "Mentions of unemployment have been dwindling since they spiked to 154 in the month ending August 15, 2010; over the month ending [May 15, 2011], there were 63."[619]

What news gets covered and what doesn't is strikingly arbitrary. Between 2001 and 2015, an estimated 250,000 people died in warfare in Syria. That is obviously a horrifying number, and it was appropriate for that bloodshed to receive significant coverage. But between 1998 and 2003, an astounding five million people—about 20 times the number who died in Syria—died in the Congo, and that mass slaughter barely dented the media consciousness. The news organizations' pack mentality works both ways—lots of media rush to cover stories that others are covering, but they also rush backwards to ignore stories that others are ignoring. The Pew Research Center's Project for Excellence in Journalism found that, in 52 major mainstream news outlets, the combined coverage of poverty amounted to far less than 1 percent of all front-page articles.[620] In the first quarter of 2016, neither the *CBS Evening News* nor ABC's *World News Tonight* ran a single story on poverty; the *NBC Nightly News* ran only two.[621]

Cable news coverage is astoundingly non-substantive. One winter morning while watching TV at the gym, I learned two startling things: 1) Nancy Grace thinks murder is bad and 2) massive blizzards are cold and make it hard to drive. A few months later, also at the gym (where my only TV viewing choices are bad and worse—chosen for me by sullen muscular 20-somethings who are looking at their iPhones instead), I watched journalists make another probing and insightful discovery: hurricanes are windy and wet. Morning show folks seem especially adept at jarring, clueless juxtapositions, jumping cheerfully from mass shootings to cooking segments. I once watched a segment on the weekend edition of NBC's *Today* show (at the gym, where else?)

that used a snippet of the song "What's Going On," Marvin Gaye's searing anthem against war and injustice, as a background for a segment on celebrity gossip. A TV news producer once told me that the only way she could guarantee that her bosses would place one of her segments on air was for her to include footage of a panda. I thought she was joking until I experienced it firsthand one snowy weekend as I was bumped off an MSNBC news show where I was scheduled to talk about how snow days deprived hungry kids of school meals. After two hours of waiting in the green room, where I sat looking at what seemed to be the same two half-eaten mini muffins that had been there every time I'd sat in that room for the past three years, I was told that they were sorry but the segment was cancelled "for time." Instead they ran repeated loops of a panda playing in the snow in DC. I kid you not.

Ironically, comedy shows like *The Daily Show* and *The Colbert Report*—and more recently, *The Nightly Show with Larry Wilmore*, *Last Week Tonight with John Oliver*, and *Full Frontal with Samantha Bee*—have provided more in-depth, fact-based coverage than the supposedly serious news channels. The satires were news shows masquerading as entertainment; meanwhile Fox and CNN were mostly comedy networks masquerading as news.

The print media isn't much better these days. Even though there are thousands of reporters based in New York City, only one reporter showed up at a crucial 2014 City Council hearing on hunger and homelessness. The very media that sanctimoniously fulminate when they are excluded from *private* events frequently fail to attend *public* hearings of vital importance.

"Object permanence" is a psychology term that means you know and understand that an object exists after it is no longer right in front of your eyes. Human babies usually develop that knowledge by the eighth month of life. But our modern media, and indeed our entire culture, seem never to have reached the object permanence level of development. We forget any issue once it is no longer discussed, and there's rarely substantive follow-up. It's like our whole country has regressed to an infant state.

Remember the Y2K scare, when we were all warned that the world's computers were going to crash at the start of the year 2000 and bring the modern world, as we knew it, to a screeching halt? Why was there virtually no media coverage after that to explain why the expected calamity never happened?

Remember when the news coverage was all Ebola, all the time? Do you recall that we were told that the disease was supposed to ravage America because our government was ineffective and Obama was incompetent?—or worse, that he purposely wanted to harm America with the disease?* Why was there little to no follow-up coverage in the mainstream media concerning how the government succeeded in stopping Ebola from harming Americans and how Obama was incredibly successful in managing that fight?

Why did media start ignoring Libya virtually days after Muammar Gaddafi was toppled?

A culture and a people unwilling to examine what actually occurred, in even the very recent past, are highly unlikely to effectively tackle the future.

NO, TECHNOLOGY WON'T SAVE US

The Net Delusion: The Dark Side of Internet Freedom is a lengthy, fact-filled polemic (obviously my favorite kind) by Evgeny Morozov, pushing back against the net utopianism that trumpets technology as the panacea for all our problems. For example, Morozov eviscerates Gordon Brown, then-prime minister of the United Kingdom, for this quote, which claimed that the Internet would prevent future genocides: "You cannot have Rwanda again because information would come out far more quickly about what is actually going on and the public opinion would grow to the point where action would need to be taken."[622] Obviously, since then, the existence of the Internet did little to stop mass slaughters in Syria, Rwanda's neighbor the Congo, Sudan, and elsewhere. Morozov also explains why we are fooling ourselves if we think that "slacktivism" (online activism)—as well as online charitable donations—will replace the need for on-the-ground organizing and programming:

---

* As Nicholas Kristof reported in the *New York Times*, Dr. Keith Ablow, a Fox News contributor, suggested that Obama perhaps wanted America to suffer because his "affiliations" are with Africa and not America. Trump even called on Obama to resign because of his supposed mismanagement of Ebola.

While Facebook-based mobilization will occasionally lead to genuine social and political change, this is mostly accidental, a statistical certainty rather than a genuine achievement. With millions of groups, at least one or two of them are poised to take off. But since it's impossible to predict which causes will work and which ones won't, Western policymakers and donors who seek to support or even prioritize Facebook-based activism are placing a wild bet. . . .

Digital activism provides too many easy ways out. Lots of people are rooting for the least painful sacrifice, deciding to donate a penny where they may otherwise donate a dollar. While the social science jury is still out on how exactly online campaigning may cannibalize its offline brethren, it seems reasonable to assume that the effects are not always positive. Furthermore, if psychologists are right and most people support political causes simply because it makes them feel happier, then it's quite unfortunate that joining Facebook groups makes them as happy as writing letters to their elected representatives or organizing rallies without triggering any of the effects that might benefit society at large.[623]

FAKING IT RATHER THAN MAKING IT

Technology not only allows us to fake our activism, it now enables us to fake virtually everything—an app allows students to con their parents and tell them they are studying when they are really on a date or sleeping over in a lover's dorm room.* There are myriad ways to electronically fake reality, as *Computerworld* explains:

How much does it cost to fake popularity? On the cheap side, you can buy 1,000 Twitter followers for $14 on a site called Inter-Twitter; 5,000 followers cost $43; 100,000 cost $487 . . . Higher-end sites like Buy Active Fans promise not just followers, but

---

* I preferred the old system: "Of course, Mrs. Schwartz, Ethan's at the library at 7:00 a.m. on a Sunday. When he gets back from the library, I'll be sure to tell him you called."

engaged followers—and even American ones. But those higher quality followers will cost you: 1,000 global followers cost $10, but 1,000 Americans will set you back $50. A global 100,000 runs $460, but the same number of Yanks costs $4,650. . . .

For $5, you can even have a fake girlfriend on Facebook. A site called GirlfriendHire lets you browse and pick a phony companion—and that person will actually provide the service of posting on your wall, etc., so your family and friends think you really are dating someone. . . .

An iOS app called Fake a Fish lets you take one of your actual photos and add an image of a big fish, so it looks like you caught it.[624]

Well, at least lying about the length of your fish remains constant, or so I'm told.

THE END OF CIVILIZATION

Once, while at the gym (where else?), I had no choice but to watch the show *Next*, an MTV reality series that ran from 2005 until 2008. The show's premise—a sort of TV forerunner to Tinder—was that one man would make an instant judgment on the beauty of five women, or one woman would instantly rate the hotness of five men, before picking one of them for a date.* The man or woman doing the judging would quickly look up and down at the bodies in front of them and then say "next" if they wouldn't want to date them. The day I watched (I was forced!), a young woman rejected a guy because she said the bulge in his pants looked too small and a young man eliminated a female hopeful because he said her chest looked like "mosquito bites." Other contestants were waiting in a bus,

---

* These were some of the classier people featured in the show. Raj, pictured below, called himself the "sultan of sweat" and proudly said that he "hates the sound of old men coughing." How adorable. I wonder where he is now.

and watched the women and men being rejected live, on closed circuit TV, and then promptly made disparaging comments about the rejected contestants in real time, while also supposedly spontaneously commenting on their own chances. The following exchange occurred between several young female contestants in the back of that bus:

> Contestant one: "Would you ever have sex with a homeless man?"
> Contestant two: "Well, some are pretty hot. They are all very tan."
> Contestant three: "You mean like sex under an underpass?"
> Contestant one: "Yes, like sex under an underpass."
> Contestant three: "Well yes, yes, I would. I'd have hot homeless sex."
> Contestant one: "Yeah, that could be pretty hot."*

This show may have been—or should have been—a warning sign of the End Times. In any case, these young competitors—as well as the TV producers who put them up to participating in this swill—obviously see *no* meaningful purpose in their lives. Religious conservatives, secular liberals—and everyone in between—should agree that they, and every member of our reality television society, would be far better off if we all understood that every life actually *does* have a purpose and it is bigger than any one small sound bite.

---

* I tried blocking all this from my memory, so I may have gotten a few of these words slightly wrong, but I swear this was the gist of their exchange.

16.

Deal Breakers
When to Work on a National Relationship
and When to Walk Away

"If he doesn't want to change now, he never will. And if he is capable of changing, waiting for tomorrow robs you of your dreams for today."
—Dr. Bethany Marshall, *Deal Breakers: When to Work on a Relationship and When to Walk Away*

"Let's Stay Together"
—Al Green

Is the relationship that we Americans have with our country and society *worth* saving? Of course. Does the country *want* to change? I think so. But, like Dr. Marshall said, we shouldn't give up our dreams by waiting for tomorrow. We need to fight for progress *now*. We must work to save our relationship with the country *immediately*.

To explain why all those things are true, to try to convince America to stay together with its government, I've written a love poem to America. It's imploring, but hopefully not *too needy*. America, you must, simply must say that you are committed to saving this relationship. But in case you are still wavering, imagine that this poem is being performed for you in song, in a super sexy voice, by the good Reverend Al Green himself. How can anyone say no to Al Green?

Love Poem for America

(apologies to Walt, Gwendolyn, Allen, Adrienne, Langston,
LeRoi/Amiri, and William Carlos)

I.

Your gumbo, America, is African. Is French. Is Caribbean.
Is a cry out from the dank hulls of slave ships and a shout out to
flowered Paris bistros.
Is kicked out of Canada. Is stolen from Nigeria.
Is roux, is soul, is spicy sausages, is juju, is Mississippi mud
water.
Is, you, America.
Your jazz, America, is Italian arias. Is howl of the whip's lash.
Is Ghanaian funeral dancing and drumming. Is whorehouses.
Is the envy of the world, copied everywhere. Is living memory
and forgetting all history. Is, you, America.

II.

so much depends
upon
a working citizenry
glazed with clear
water (from anywhere but Flint)
beside the nonwhite (but also white allies)
free-range chickens

III.

Why stay together?
Because I won't be hauled off to prison for this book.
Because of the twin poles of "Red's"—"Red's Eats," a lobster
shack in Wiscasset, Maine, and "Red's" juke joint, in Clarksdale, Mississippi, one of the last places on earth to hear Delta
blues performed live by impossibly old men.

Because this country took in my mother.

Because this country took in my mother's mother, and my mother's father, and my father's mother, and my father's father.

Because many of us would give our lives before we'd let that motherfucker Donald Trump keep out the next generations of refugees.

Because five minutes of the Grand Canyon is worth five years on the Seine.

Because we let Hemingway be such an asshole.

Because we didn't send Ali to prison.

Because even when we don't live up to our ideals and promises, we sometimes remembered we have them and made them, and sometimes tried.

Because we have copyright laws that protect the hard work of photographers, writers, and artists, but also "fair use exceptions" to those copyright laws that also protect parody, which will (hopefully) protect me from being sued for the way I parody copyrighted materials in this book.

Because there's a restaurant in Brighton Beach, Brooklyn, Kashkar Cafe, where Uyghur people, an ethnic minority of Turkic Muslims from the northwest of China (closer to Kabul than Beijing), serving manty dumplings filled with lamb, hand-pulled noodles, kabobs, and gusht non (flatbread with meat and onion baked in a pan), to anyone, of any race or nationality, who has at least $2.50 in his or her pocket to purchase their cheapest dish.

Because at least some Native Americans don't hate me too much for living on their land.

Because Bob Dylan was born a Jew, became a fundamentalist Christian, then a fundamentalist Jew, and then Bob Dylan again.

Because Elizabeth Cady Stanton and Lucretia Mott said "enough."

Because I can travel to the most spectacular places on the globe and still miss home.

Because of the Bronx, because of South Central.

Because Yellowstone is a national park and not a copper mine.
Because our country could produce both Flavor Flav and
Chuck D. and because at least one of the two still makes our
nation proud.
Because Allen Ginsberg lived almost long enough to get
legally married.
Because Jews go out for Chinese food, and at least occasion-
ally (at Katz's Delicatessen on Houston Street in New York)
Chinese people go out for Jewish food.
Because Dred Scott wasn't the last word.

IV.

I am inside a country
that hates itself. I look
out from its eyes. Smell
what fouled tunes come out
from its chemical plants and Republicans.
Both love and hate
wretched and scared women and men.

V.

I want you back, I want you back, I want you back, Michael
Jackson. Lou Reed, I don't care if you would have hated my guts,
but I want you back too. I want back MLK and Emma Goldman
and Crazy Horse but only the Malcolm who had renounced hate.
I want Coltrane blowing and blowing and blowing back at the
Village Vanguard. I want a country, again, that produced art, and
love, and peace, and a middle class.

VI.

We real cool. We
Left school because our financial aid ran out.
Jazz June. Hip Hop rest of the year.

VII.

Yadda, and yadda, said he.
Yadda and yadda, said she.
And soon, there were three.

VII.

First having read the book of national myths,
and aimed the iPhone camera,
and checked the edge of the knife-blade, and semiautomatic
weapons (legal practically
everywhere)
I put on
the body-armor of not looking at the news
the absurd blinders
the grave and awkward mask.

VIII.

America, remember, when post-9/11, you mostly sought under-
standing and justice instead of revenge?
America, remember when you learned from the mistake of
Prohibition?
America, remember when you made it illegal in all 50 states for
a husband to rape a wife?
America, remember when you took in those no one else would?
America, remember when you gave some payments to some
Alaska natives for their land?
America, remember when, after World War II, you bailed out
the very nations that attacked us?
America, remember your soul. Remember your soul.

IX.

I saw the worst minds of my generation destroyed by Trumpness.

America I'm putting my hetero-normative shoulder to the wheel and then discarding that, to fight to make LGBTQ employment discrimination illegal in every state.

I hear America singing, the varied carols I hear, and I hear America wailing, of fear and fear and fear.

And I hear Walt pleading with us to discard the fear, and just see, really see, their faces and bodies.

    X.

I, too, sing America.
I am the lighter brother.
I am ashamed when you are sent to eat in the kitchen, or to not eat at all.
Why won't we see how beautiful you are?
I too, you too, we too, are America.

    XI.

You hurt us more than you can imagine, America.
Don't you *dare* tell us to forget.
The Manzanar internment camp. Selma. Wounded Knee. Stonewall.
No, we *can't* forget.
Tamir Rice.
No, we *won't* forget.
And no, it's not our right, or even in our power, to *forgive*.
(Even reparations couldn't buy that.)

But if you move on and if we move on
Let's at least try
to make this work.

A Twelve-Step Program for Fixing
Our Relationship with America:
Concrete Ways to Find Common Ground
and Take Personal Responsibility to Solve
Our National Problems

Step One:

"Hi, I'm American . . . and I'm an Alcoholic / Spend-aholic / Gun-aholic / War-aholic / Selfie-aholic"

America, much of the traditional Alcoholics Anonymous 12-step program for ending addiction also applies to fixing our nation, but since the steps were originally based on a singular type of Christianity, they must be tweaked a bit to acknowledge that fixing today's national problems requires us to call upon the collective resources of *all* the nation's extraordinarily diverse religious and secular ethical traditions. As I argued earlier in the book, religious and secular Americans have a lot more in common than either side believes. So based on that, here's how we should apply a modified 12-step program to ending America's addictions to counterproductive habits:

1. Admit that—under the current state of our screwed-up politics—we are currently powerless over greed, gun violence, racism, xenophobia, self-interested government spending and campaign financing, sexism, unworkably low taxes for the rich, and rampant cultural narcissism—and admit that our collective lives have become unmanageable as a result and that this powerlessness is killing our national relationship.

2. Come to believe that a power greater than ourselves—collective action, with citizen-empowered government in the lead—should restore us to sanity. Admit it is troubling that many Americans know every *Bachelorette* winner but not the name of their two US senators. We must reject the myth of rugged individualism for the fabrication it is, and instead accept that we all need each other's help sometimes—whether it's in protecting our drinking water or ensuring that our kids go to high-quality schools.

3. Make the decision to turn over at least part of our will and at least part of our lives to the care of each other as we solve problems together as a nation. Since virtually all religious and ethical traditions say that one of the best ways to honor God or our fellow humans is to repair our own society, this act of letting go would require us to move beyond our own personal needs and desires to aid the greater good. (Recycle that selfie stick—now!) Jesus commanded, "Render unto Caesar that which is Caesar's," directing followers to pay any taxes and obey secular authorities that are just. That's pretty good advice for anyone, whether you're Christian or not. Following that dictate could, for instance, require turning over a bit more in tax dollars to ensure that your neighbors can visit a doctor or feed their families.

4. Make a searching and fearless moral inventory of ourselves by systematically cataloguing our national flaws. Check. (In case you missed that, please reread the first few hundred pages of this book.) Look in the mirror, America, and see yourself, warts and all.

5. Admit to God, to ourselves, and/or to all other humans the exact nature of our collective wrongs, using actual facts to access and solve our national problems. If you've paid good money for this book, feel free to take a photo of any of the charts in it with your cell phones (now that they are not being used for selfies) and text them to anyone who is still fact-resistant.

6. Allow ourselves to embrace the collective will of the nation to act upon a spiritual or ethic imperative (or mere self-interest)—to remove all these defects of national character. In other words, let's all get to work.

7. Humbly ask the whole nation to work together to actively repair our shortcomings. Let's push the president and every elected official and business leader to fix this mess.

8. Make a list of all persons and institutions we have harmed, and become willing to make amends to them all and to fight for a society

that welcomes and honors every group we've dishonored. That's a darn long list but we can start with American Indians, move on to African Americans, women, Asian Americans, LGBTQ people, Latinos, Jews, people with disabilities, people falsely convicted of crimes, Donald Trump's wives, and on and on.

9. Make direct amends to such people and institutions wherever possible, except when doing so would injure them or others. Our apologies won't mean squat unless we actually start helping all the people we previously shafted. (See # 8.)

10. Continue to take personal and collective inventory, and when we are wrong, promptly admit it. Admit how each of us screwed up. (Come clean, 2000 Florida Ralph Nader voters!)

11. Seek, through a careful examination of objective facts on the ground, to improve our conscious contact with our society we as understand it, actively seeking knowledge of verifiable earthly reality, in order to have the power to carry out the change we need. That's a lot of mumbo jumbo that I'll sum up this way: we need to build our collective confidence that we *can* fix the nation's biggest, most seemingly intractable problems.

12. Be both ethically and politically awakened as the result of these steps, and try to carry this message to other Americans, and practice these principles in all our affairs.

The rest of this book spells out my own version of a 12-step program for the nation, but to sum it up in one sentence: let's preach collective responsibility for everyone, then let's practice what we preach.

Step Two:

Breaking *Good*
How the Nation Can Create a "Responsibility-for-All" Society

In the TV show *Breaking Bad*, all the main characters lived up fully to the show's title. They were *bad*, very bad. The show's chief protagonist, Walter White, was a high school chemistry teacher turned crystal meth manufacturer and murderer. His wife was an adulterer, tax cheat, and ultimately, an enabler of his drug empire. His partner was a drug addict, petty thief, and, ultimately, a murderer too. Walter's one-time drug lord boss was a mass murderer, hooking multitudes on deadly drugs, wiping out rival gangs, and killing far more people by giving them diabetes and hypertension through his fast-food fried chicken chain, "Los Pollos Hermanos." Perhaps the worst of the bunch was Walter's lawyer, who draped himself in the Constitution (quite literally), while actively abetting deadly mayhem and mass criminality.

As with *The Sopranos* and *The Wire*, what made *Breaking Bad* so compelling was that even the characters who committed the most heinous acts had some relatable human qualities, such as loyalty, bravery, love of family, or a (twisted) code of justice. But I think a central point of all three shows was that each act of misconduct, each moral lapse, fueled a series of subsequent, escalating evils, which ended in tragedy both for the victims and the perpetrators. Walter's actions led to the crippling of his brother-in-law by would-be assassins. Tony Soprano murdered his beloved nephew. *The Wire*'s Avon Barksdale had to take out his partner and best friend. The characters were rotten to the core because the societies they inhabited were, with every cell of their surrounding ecosystems, infused with immorality, causing a downward spiral that dragged down everyone—even previously innocent bystanders—in a long, fiery, painful decent into Hades. Whoa. No wonder those shows were on cable.

While I don't think America is today quite as dystopian as any of those portraits, we're not that far off. Each misdeed in Congress encourages a misdeed on Wall Street, and then another on Main Street. Before you know it, a sports hero says, "Oh what the hell, since everyone is cheating, I'll take banned substances or deflate footballs too." A doctor defrauds an insurance company. A pampered rich kid cheats on an exam. Each lie, each fraud, each deception—and even each act that may be legal but that involves someone putting their own self-interest before everyone else's good—lowers our national bar of acceptable behavior.

Too many of our leaders have corrupted our American politics into a perpetual blame game. Rather than seriously and honestly dealing with the central problems of the nation—a still-lagging economy, an educational system losing out in competition with the world, an increasing national debt, sky-high poverty, crazy numbers of gun deaths, and declining opportunity—they simply seek to win the daily cable TV sound bite wars to gain any millimeter* of temporary partisan advantage. Politicians reverse their positions at the drop of a hat, and then denounce their opponents for holding views they themselves held just seconds before. They spend more time in TV studios than on street corners or factory floors. And they spend the most time of all at fancy fundraisers hobnobbing with the rich, or in cramped cubicles with a phone, cajoling the wealthiest to donate to their ever-bulging campaign war chests. The only job many seriously care about saving seems to be their own. And they then let their corporate buddies flush America's economy down the toilet for their own massive profit.**

It is vital to note that countless Americans already live their lives performing backbreaking work and exhibiting rock-solid personal and civic virtue. The few times I ride the New York City subway at 5:00 a.m., the car is full of people dressed for working-class jobs (many women in nurse and home health attendant uniforms and many men

---

* Dear Americans reading this: that's a reference to a thing called the Metric System. Look it up. Note to people in other countries: never mind—you obviously already know.
** Again, I stress that not all political leaders are equally bad, but the system, as a whole, is horrid.

in construction worker or security guard clothes)—busting their asses to support their families. I have no doubt that, across the US, hundreds of millions of others are making supreme sacrifices daily to be productive Americans and important contributors to our complex society. That's why I am especially outraged that the people at the top so frequently let them down.

This abrogation of duty by our political, business, and cultural leaders creates a nation of "trickle-down irresponsibility." While most parents who are forced to receive temporary public assistance struggle mightily to get back on their feet by finding a good job, too many give up because they believe those at the top aren't playing fair. And they would be right. Angry at the lack of opportunity, young men far too often falsely excuse senseless violence by blaming society's injustices. Other men sometimes also use a similar justification after they've created children but then walk away. Our reality show culture glorifies sex, violence, vanity, and selfishness over hard work, community, service, and responsibility.

Enough.

A BETTER WAY

Let's replace our current "Responsibility-for-*None*" society with a "Responsibility-for-*All*" society. Every American must serve our society and our society must serve every American.

This new commonwealth should be different both in mindset and in practical action than the failing status quo. America, you should usher in a far higher set of ethical standards for everyone, but also craft concrete public policies that move beyond the dysfunctional left/right debate by promoting a new brand of 21st century patriotism in which everyone from corporate executives to welfare recipients works for the greater good of the commonweal. This era should enable progressives to retake values co-opted by the Republicans, including faith, freedom, work, security, ambition, family, and personal responsibility. This is not about retooling campaign rhetoric to include more middle-of-the road language; it is about a fundamentally new way of governing— building on, and significantly improving upon, many efforts begun in the Bill Clinton and Barack Obama eras—in order to harness mainstream values to achieve progressive goals.

Now is the time to build a new generation of greatness, in which *all* of us take personal responsibility for each other for jointly tackling the nation's most pressing challenges.

If you are a parent, it's our society's responsibility to provide your children with the world's best schools, but it is your responsibility to get them to school on time, ensure they do their homework, read with them at home if you are able, and consistently encourage them to make education a priority. If a college-age student is willing to perform a year or two of national service—tutoring in schools, delivering food to shut-in seniors, fighting fires in national parks, or responding to natural disasters—then the federal government should pay the entirety of their post-secondary education.

It's our nation's responsibility to make food more affordable, convenient, and physically available, and to ensure that parks are safe and recreation centers are accessible so all Americans can exercise. But it is parents' responsibility to ensure that their children eat healthier food and spend less time in front of the TV and more time moving their bodies. While it is our government's responsibility to make healthcare a right and a reality for all Americans, it's everyone's responsibility to smoke less, drink in moderation, avoid hard drugs, eat better, and exercise.

In our generation, America must end domestic hunger and homelessness once and for all. The government must ensure a safety net of secure and adequate housing, nutritious food, and work support, and must build an economy with sufficient living-wage jobs. Effective, well-regulated, nonprofit groups should fill in the gaps. But people who can find private sector work should do so, and public service positions should be created for those who can't. We need a modern day Civilian Conservation Corps (CCC) and Works Progress Administration (WPA)—because, since the time of President Franklin Roosevelt, we've known that the best social program is a living-wage job. As FDR said, "Continued dependence upon relief induces a spiritual and moral disintegration fundamentally destructive to the national fiber. To dole out relief in this way is to administer a narcotic, a subtle destroyer of the human spirit. It is inimical to the dictates of sound policy. It is in violation of the traditions of America. Work must be found for able-bodied but destitute workers."[1]

To compete in the 21st-century economy, we must make job and skills training, as well as life-long education, more available and more affordable to more workers. But Americans must take the personal responsibility to gain the skills they need to compete in the global economy.

Getting ahead through honest, hard work isn't easy, but it's necessary.

Men who father children must take responsibility for them. Gang members who deal drugs and kill innocent children in their cross-fire must stop destroying their communities and falling back on the excuse that "the system is stacked against them." As I've documented throughout this book, racism and poverty are pernicious, ingrained, and widespread. Plus the youngest people involved in the drug trade and gang warfare are often not mature enough to completely internalize the full implications of their deeds. All that being said, selling poison to kids and bringing mayhem to your own blocks where you and other families live isn't the answer. Even the most oppressed, downtrodden people must—simply must—take personal responsibility to better, not worsen, the world around them.

Of course, those at the top bear a special responsibility. Since government continues to invest precious resources in the infrastructure that businesses use, and continues to subsidize higher education institutions that prepare workers to thrive in those same businesses, then companies have an even greater responsibility to their workers and to society as a whole. They must do their best to reduce pollution and create safe products. They must support the right of their workers to engage in collective bargaining, and must pay them a living wage and provide good benefits, even if that means offering slightly lower compensation packages to their executives.

At a time of war and global terrorism threats, the wealthy must remember that paying their fair share of taxes is the *least* they can do to meet their patriotic duty. My father taught me that if you fail to pay your taxes, you aren't ripping off some amorphous "government," you are stealing from neighbors. Having offshore accounts or moving your entire company overseas to lower your tax burden—or, as Trump did, bragging that it's "smart" to pay no taxes—may be legal, but that's certainly not patriotic. Forcing working families to bear the entire burden of paying for the military, highways, national parks, drinking water systems, homeland security, etc. (all of which benefit you and your family)—while you get a free ride—is reprehensible.

Wall Street must be free to invest as they see fit and support businesses that innovate, but the investment community must also play by the rules and build wealth and value for the society-at-large, not just for themselves. A rising Dow must be accompanied by increasing jobs and rising wages. Wall Street should be about building up America, not being bailed out by America. I also challenge the wealthy—especially those who are against even meager government assistance to struggling low-income families—to reject any corporate welfare for themselves.

I reserve my greatest personal responsibility challenge for our political leaders. They must again put country ahead of party. They must again tell the public the hard truths, even if they are politically unpopular. They must reduce the role of money in politics. They must engage in more listening and less yelling and name-calling. They must follow the law and try to remember they are role models for the country's citizens and for people around the world. They must again challenge *all* Americans to move beyond their personal comfort to work for the greater good.

"Responsibility-for-All" must also include those with criminal records and ex-offenders, America. The Center for American Progress found that between 70 million and 100 million Americans, or as many as one in three US adults, have some type of criminal record. Many have been convicted of only minor offenses and many only have arrests that never led to a conviction. Between 33 million and 36.5 million children in the United States—nearly half of American children—now have at least one parent with a criminal record. Parental arrest records significantly exacerbate existing challenges within low-income families by limiting their future income, keeping them in debt, making it harder for them to get education and training, and reducing access to affordable housing.[2] The federal government and states should work together to remove these barriers. Even for those who did commit serious crimes, it's unfair and counterproductive for them—and for their innocent family members— to suffer for a lifetime if the ex-felons have paid their full debt to society. More states need to emulate the efforts of Connecticut Governor Dannel Malloy's "Second Chance Society" initiative, which is trying to reduce the number of people going into prison and make it easier for those already behind bars to get out and have a chance at a law-abiding life. His reform plan reclassified simple drug possession from a felony to a misdemeanor, eliminated mandatory minimum sentences for nonviolent drug possession, expedited parole hearings for people convicted of nonviolent crimes, and simplified the pardon process.[3] Many of those with records want to be more responsible by working hard and giving back—our society must let them.

States should also eliminate voting restrictions on former felons. If we want ex-offenders to see their fellow citizens as peers, not future victims, we must treat them as fellow citizens and allow them their full rights as Americans.

OPTIMISTIC, ASPIRATIONAL, "RADICAL CENTRISM"

Republicans from Reagan to George W. Bush have promised "optimism" for the country, but they confused optimism with a willful attempt to ignore the nation's most pressing problems. The aspirations they raised were largely unmet for the majority of Americans.

In contrast, the two most successful Democratic politicians of the last century—FDR and Bill Clinton—practiced the truest form of aspirational politics, by implementing concrete programs and initiatives that significantly improved the daily lives of Americans. In short, they both took on the title of "optimist" the old-fashioned way—they earned it—by giving Americans something meaningful to be optimistic about.

That's why we need a brand new set of aspirational politics, taking as an inspiration the generations of American immigrants who have been willing to make sustained sacrifices to ensure a better life for their children. While politicians of both parties like to pander to the lowest common denominator by offering voters something for nothing (such as tax cuts at the same time as increased spending on favorite programs), the new aspirational politics would call on today's Americans to sacrifice, but only in explicit exchange for future upward mobility for themselves and their families.

When left-wing pundits call on the Democratic Party to be "bold" again, they usually mean that they think the party should be left-wing again. What they forget is that when the party was most bold and most politically successful—under FDR—it wasn't consistently left-wing.* Franklin Roosevelt campaigned for deficit reduction and made work a centerpiece of virtually all his social programs. Bold, progressive actions are far easier to accomplish when they are in tune with the mainstream values of average Americans.

Conversely, when centrist or right-wing pundits call on the Democratic Party to be mainstream again, they usually mean the party should move to the right, and should take only tepid, non-controversial steps towards addressing major social problems. But they overlook the fact that average Americans want big solutions to big problems, even though they usually distrust *big government* solutions to their problems.

Thus, the new Democratic aspirational politics should call for fundamental, massive social progress, but base that progress upon realistic, common-sense, easy-to-explain plans that will resonate with most Americans. It will mean sometimes stealing back themes from Republicans that they previously lifted from Democrats (such as the centrality of work). That's what I mean by "radical centrism"—a politics that promises (and most importantly delivers) massive, transformational reforms to American government and society, but does so in an incremental way, based on mainstream values. Radical centrism is meant not to just pass temporary programs or small pilot projects, but to develop a new governing paradigm for the country with enough long-term support to ensure that progress made is progress maintained.

Radical Centrism should also make use of the most up-to-date technologies. Technology can't bridge every ideological divide, but it can help with some thorny issues like gun violence. For instance, we should be able to develop bipartisan support for efforts to develop

---

* Hard-core American communists and socialists *hated* FDR, because the success of his bourgeois reforms undercut their calls for revolution.

"smart guns" that won't fire unless intentionally fired by their owners. As the *Los Angeles Times* reported,

> Gun-safety technologies like these wouldn't have prevented mass violence such as the Nov. 27 attack on a Planned Parenthood clinic in Colorado Springs or the San Bernardino shooting attack. The goal instead is to reduce firearms injuries caused by unauthorized or unintended users, including suicide victims, especially youths, and children who encounter loaded guns in the home, and criminal suspects who get their hands on officers' weapons. . . .
>
> Of 33,636 deaths from firearms counted by the Centers for Disease Control and Prevention in 2013, some 62%, or 21,175, were suicides, and about 11% of those were of people ages 5 to 24. Accidental shootings accounted for 505 deaths, including 69 victims ranging in age from less than 1 year to 14 years. "If guns were personalized, none of these would happen," says Stephen Teret, a gun-policy expert. Suicides, he observes, tend to be "means-specific"—if a gun isn't at hand, many suicidal youths would abandon the effort. The roughly 200,000 stolen guns reported each year would be rendered effectively worthless if they were "smart" guns.[4]

THE PRICE OF CIVILIZATION

To get America back on track, everyone needs to pitch in with both their sweat and their financial resources. One of the main things that breaks down relationships is squabbles over money; especially when one side believes the other side isn't carrying their equal share of the financial load. That's why, to fix the relationship of Americans with the nation, it is imperative that the wealthy pay their fair share of taxes again. Patriots—and good neighbors—pay their fair share of taxes.

Keep in mind that the wealthiest Americans in the "Greatest Generation," those who reached adulthood during the Depression and World War II, paid far, far more in taxes than the wealthiest Americans do today. When Eisenhower was president in the 1950s, the top marginal federal income tax rate for the wealthiest was 91 percent.* Yes, when a Republican military man was in charge of the nation, the richest Americans were required to give nine out of every 10 dollars they earned to Uncle Sam—and, by and large, they complied as part of their loyal duty to the nation. As of 2015, the wealthiest only paid only about a third of their total income to the US government in all forms of taxes.[5] The low rate of taxation on the top earners is the single greatest reason why both our deficit is so high and our national investments on social programs and infrastructure are so inadequate. In 1927, fabled Supreme Court Justice Oliver Wendell Holmes wrote, "Taxes are what we pay for civilized society." We seem to have forgotten what it's like to be civilized, America.

Even I don't think we should go back to the full 91 percent rate; a level that high could discourage some investment and entrepreneurship. Rather, I suggest that the most prosperous among us be required to pay a meager 45 percent of their incomes in total federal taxes. Yeah, that's the ticket. If we did that, a whopping $276 billion in extra federal revenues would be generated each year. Even taking into consideration state and local taxes, the average household in this group would still take home at least $1 million a year—I think that somehow they'd muddle through.[6]

What would the American people be able to achieve with that extra $276 billion each year?

First, we could end US hunger, entirely eliminating food insecurity for the 48 million Americans who suffered from it in 2014. (You knew that was coming, didn't you?) Because hungry children can't learn, hungry workers can't work, and hungry seniors can't stay independent. Domestic hunger robs our economy of $167.5 billion annually.[7] I have calculated that we could end hunger here by spending an extra $31.3

---

* Our last socialist president.

billion each year to increase the food purchasing power of low-income people through a combination of employment support and extra SNAP (food stamps) benefits.[8] If you subtract that $31.3 billion from the $276 billion in extra taxes we've collected, we'd still have about $245 billion left over, quite a tidy sum. What should we do with the rest?

As I propose a bit later in this chapter, we should create a new "Service Patriots America" plan to engage two million Americans a year in work for their country through military or civilian service, and reward them with significant benefits to boost their upward mobility. This program would cost about an extra $55 billion per year (although, down the road, it would save us far more than we spend).

Even with those two expenditures we'll still have $190 billion left. I'd allocate a third of that to social and education programs to bolster the middle class and boost people in poverty (paying for other proposals in this book), and a third of that on a national infrastructure jobs program—targeted to repairing our existing infrastructure, making the nation more energy independent, and bringing the fastest broadband Internet service to isolated rural towns and urban neighborhoods. I'd put the remaining third—about $63 billion—toward deficit-reduction and paying down the national debt, smart things to do both economically and politically.

As Bill Clinton did, progressives and radical centrists need to take back the concept of fiscal responsibility from the conservatives, who have proven time and time again that they don't really mean it. It's easy for progressives to advocate for cutting wasteful military spending, but we should also be disciplined and brave enough to call for specific cuts in other types of government costs that are less vital. Democrats must make it clear that they are only in favor of efficient government programs that provide crucial services, and they are not statists that support any and all government efforts just for the sake of supporting government. To give just one specific example, now that *Sesame Street* has moved from PBS to HBO,* and the public has so many additional easy-to-access entertainment and educational television options, perhaps progressives should finally agree that the time has come to eliminate most of the $445 million in federal funding for the Corpora-

---

* Now that Big Bird moved to HBO, we should patiently await his cameo on either *Veep* or *Game of Thrones*.

tion for Public Broadcasting (although I'd keep the financing for public radio intact because it is often the only serious news coverage that still in exists in many areas of the country); $445 million is a tiny chunk of the federal budget, so eliminating most of that wouldn't do much to reduce the deficit, but doing so would send an important signal that progressives are willing to make hard choices.

SERVICE PATRIOTS AMERICA

The embodiment of my calls for a "Responsibility-for-All" society and radical centrism is my Service Patriots America plan for the federal government to engage two million Americans per year in work for their country through greatly expanded service opportunities in the military, the Peace Corps, and AmeriCorps (a sort of domestic Peace Corps started by President Bill Clinton, where Americans perform domestic community service and receive a small stipend and educational award in return).* The plan would cost-effectively accomplish concrete tasks vital to the national interest, while rewarding those who successfully serve with upward mobility. The program could help rebuild the great American middle class, as did the original GI Bill.

In 2015, about 180,000 Americans joined active duty military service, 3,400 served in the Peace Corps, and 80,000 enlisted in AmeriCorps, equaling about 263,000 new Americans per year serving their country.** By setting a goal of two million people annually, the Service Patriots America plan would spur an eightfold increase in full-time service.

While other plans to increase service would promote a wide spectrum of diffuse service opportunities (making it harder to explain to the public and even harder to quantify successes), Service Patriots America

---

* I helped the Clinton administration launch the AmeriCorps program in 1993, the proudest accomplishment of my life, other than scoring a 440 out of a possible 450 on a Keansburg, New Jersey Skee-Ball game in 1991.
** These figures are for the first year of service. While about 1.4 million people are in active duty military service, about 180,000 new recruits join each year. While 6,800 people currently serve in the Peace Corps, since the normal term of service in the Peace Corps is a little over two years, about 3,400 people join the Peace Corps each year. While some AmeriCorps members serve for more than one year, the vast majority serves only one year (or less), so, for the sake of simplicity, this book assumes that all 80,000 people in the current AmeriCorps program serve for one year.

would tackle a few pressing national problems and demonstrate significant, cost-effective progress in addressing them.

Service Patriots America would promote a more equitable civic compact in which all successful participants—including those from low- and middle-income backgrounds—significantly boost their own economic well-being by obtaining a tax-free voucher to pay for college, home ownership, or a business startup. In contrast, the current Ameri–Corps post-service educational awards are too small to be meaningful and can usually be used only for education.

Meanwhile, federal, state, and local government budgets—as well as nonprofit organizational budgets nationwide—continue to be starved of revenue and staffing, forcing continuing cutbacks in vital services. At the same time, there are a number of pressing national problems for which Service Patriots America members are ideally suited to fill in the gaps and can come to the rescue.

Roughly four million Americans turn 18 each year; this plan anticipates that around two million would participate for at least a year in Service Patriots America. To achieve that goal, using existing, but expanded, government structures:

▶ 180,000 people per year—the current level—would continue to join active military service.
▶ 30,000 would serve in the Peace Corps, slightly more than four times the current number.
▶ 1.8 million would serve in AmeriCorps, 22 times the current level.

To effectively engage 30,000 Americans in the Peace Corps, the volunteer activities would be more sharply focused on advancing the United Nations Millennium Development Goals, with a special emphasis on advancing seven basic goals:

1) Eradicating extreme hunger and poverty.
2) Achieving universal primary education.
3) Promoting gender equality and empowering women.
4) Reducing child mortality.
5) Improving maternal health.

6) Combating HIV/AIDS, malaria, and other diseases.
7) Ensuring environmental sustainability.

To effectively ramp up AmeriCorps to a 1.8 million-person level, roughly two-thirds of AmeriCorps funds would be allocated to state commissions appointed by governors (as they are today), and the remainder would continue to be allocated directly by the federal government.

All AmeriCorps grants and programs now in effect would also be increased tenfold, bringing the AmeriCorps program as it is currently instituted to about 800,000 members.

The additional one million AmeriCorps/Service Patriots America members would serve in six new corps focusing on big ticket items:

1) Aiding older Americans by delivering food, conducting basic health screenings, and providing company to shut-ins, thereby increasing their independence, and potentially significantly reducing spending on Medicare and Medicaid;
2) Reducing high school drop-out rates by serving as teacher's aides and mentors in high-risk schools;
3) Aiding universal pre-kindergarten classes;
4) Caring for and improving public lands (national, state, and local parks, forests, and wildlife refuges);
5) Bolstering our police forces with an ROTC-like policing program; and
6) Boosting energy conservation by retrofitting buildings.

People who successfully conclude military service would continue to receive current GI Bill benefits, which often exceed $60,000 per year. Both AmeriCorps and Peace Corps graduates would receive a $20,000 post-service award for each year of service, which they could use to pay for college, graduate school, previously-held student loans, job training, a down payment on a first home, or start-up costs for a new business. Post-secondary institutions, federal housing lending agencies, and the Small Business Administration would be asked to provide added assistance to graduates. Post-secondary institutions that accept the post-service awards would be required to agree to cost containment policies (including reigning in the salaries of their top administrators) so they simply don't jack up their tuition because more federal funds are available.

Former military bases and other abandoned government facilities would be used to house AmeriCorps members who serve in programs (such as those on public lands) in which the program participants may need to be housed on site.

To further ease the costs of service for low- and middle-income Americans who relocate to other parts of the country to serve, a special system could be set up to enable Americans to invite participants to stay for free or at greatly reduced cost in empty rooms provided by homeowners or apartment owners in the communities where they serve—an idea already being piloted by Airbnb.*

The federal government would also produce an official transcript for every graduate of Service Patriots America, detailing performance on specific skills and traits sought by future educational institutions and employers—a reference letter of sorts.

All of the above would be measured in three very basic ways: whether any American who wants to serve can do so productively; whether higher education, housing, and businesses are more attainable and affordable for all Americans who are willing to serve; and whether service projects are making a concrete impact in advancing vital goals, such as enabling more seniors to stay independent and reducing high school drop-out rates.

I estimate that the combined costs of the entire proposal would be about \$55 billion annually.[9] That is indeed a sizable amount of money, but it equals only 3 percent of the net worth of the 400 wealthiest Americans (\$2.29 trillion), and, as I explained above, could be easily paid for with just a portion of an absurdly small tax increase on the top 1 percent.

Another point of comparison for the \$55 billion service plan cost is to the federal prescription drug entitlement program, enacted by then-President George W. Bush and Republican Majority Leader Tom DeLay, which costs more than \$50 billion per year, and provides

---

* Given that political campaigns often get wealthy supporters to give campaign workers free places to stay—often for months at a time—this suggestion is not as outlandish as it seems.

a huge boost to pharmaceutical companies, as well as some relief to the seniors who receive lower-cost medications (although the GOP refused to take serious action to reduce the price of pharmaceuticals). It is simply not correct to say that DC is incapable of enacting big new programs anymore; it can do so if there is substantial political will. The Service Patriots America plan, communicated correctly, could be extremely popular.

Following World War II, the nation experienced a tremendous long-term economic boom, which created the most prosperous middle class the world had ever known. Most Americans now assume that such growth was solely a result of the independent productivity of the private sector. But government efforts, most notably the original GI Bill, played a critical role in this growth. The GI Bill enabled returning soldiers to obtain government help to pay for college, enabling millions of Americans, including my father, to become the first in their families to attend college. The cost of the original GI Bill dwarfed the cost of this proposed plan for Service Patriots America, but it paid remarkable dividends to the American people. It's hard to imagine today, but leaders of some of the most elite universities opposed the education provision of the bill, assuming that people who couldn't afford to pay for college probably weren't smart enough to succeed there. Then-president of the University of Chicago, Robert Maynard Hutchins, said of the GI Bill, "Colleges and universities will find themselves converted into hobo jungles," and James B. Conant, then-president of Harvard, found the bill "distressing" because it failed "to distinguish between those who can profit most by advanced education and those who cannot." Many of these same leaders later retracted their criticisms, admitting that the students who attended their institutions with GI Bill benefits were the most serious and hardworking they ever had. In the peak year of 1947, veterans accounted for 49 percent of college admissions. By the time the original GI Bill ended on July 25, 1956, 7.8 million of 16 million World War II veterans—nearly half—had participated in an education or training program paid for by the federal government.

Before the GI Bill, America's universities were exclusionary bastions for the nation's upper-crust elites. After the law, the nation's campuses were opened, at least briefly, to people from diverse economic backgrounds.

The GI Bill also helped returning veterans put a down payment on a first home or start a small business. From 1944 to 1952, the government backed nearly 2.4 million home loans for World War II veterans. Service Patriots America, like the original GI Bill, can also become a serious engine of economic growth and upward mobility for the masses, and, over time, pay forward to our country much more than its costs. While in theory I agree with Senator Bernie Sanders's position that all college should be free, in practice it's unlikely the American people would provide all that money for what many would deride as "free rides." But if we create a system to enable Americans to earn their education costs through service, that plan would be broadly embraced by the American people.

Moreover, expanded national service would bring together diverse Americans to work side by side as equals, with forged bonds of "sweat equity." This could eventually help replace the divisive identity politics that are cleaving our society with a more communitarian harmony.

We must restore the basic American belief that we are all in it together, that we are all pulling our weight, paying our fair share, and putting all our lives on the line for our country.

In this "Responsibility-for-All" society, we all must do better. It is a small price to pay for a better America for ourselves and our children.

Step Three:

We the Voters—How We Can All Own
American Politics Again

Jesse Unruh, a Democratic politician and power broker in California in the 1960s through the 1980s (who went by the nickname "Big Daddy"), famously said, "Money is the mother's milk of politics."* He was right, but since most political leaders now seem to be choking on it, perhaps it is time to cut them off, and instead place them on a restricted diet of infant formula.

In March of 2016, the *Economist* estimated that at least five billion dollars would be spent on the 2016 presidential campaign. (To put that number in perspective, it equals about 1.3 million average Pell Grants that help low-income students pay for college.)[10]

An estimated four billion dollars more would be spent on US Senate and Congressional races in 2016. Billions more are spent each year on campaigns for governor, state legislature, mayor, city council, county executive, county legislature, and town council. Tens of millions of dollars are now even being spent each year on judicial races. In Pennsylvania in 2015, three swing seats on the Pennsylvania Supreme Court were at stake, and six candidates spent a combined $12.2 million, with two independent groups spending an additional $3.5 million on the campaigns.[11]

In addition to all that campaign spending, special interests paid $3.21 billion to 11,504 lobbyists in 2015 to influence Congress and federal

---

* Here is "Big Daddy" at work, with a "very big gavel."

agencies, according to the Center for Responsive Politics.[12] Goodness knows how many billions more are spent to lobby at the state, county, city, and town level.

Jesse Unruh also said, "If you can't eat [lobbyists'] food, drink their booze, screw their women, take their money, and then vote against them, you've got no business being up here." Aside from his misogynist claim that "their women" are just another commodity of bribery offered by lobbyists and campaign donors, it's just absurd to claim that anyone would be fully indebted to special interests and then consistently vote against them.

Given that the political system is buried so deeply in the pockets of the wealthiest, it's no wonder that low-income Americans simply give up on politics. The Pew Research Center found that, in 2014, almost all of the most financially secure (94 percent) said they were registered to vote, while only about half (54 percent) of the least financially secure were registered. Financially insecure Americans were also far less likely than those at the top to be politically engaged in other ways. For example, just 14 percent said they have contacted an elected official in the previous two years; by comparison, 42 percent of the richest had done this. And when it came to overall awareness of the political landscape, about six out of 10 (61 percent) of the most financially secure Americans could correctly identify the parties in control of both the House and Senate, compared with just 26 percent of struggling Americans. But support for Democratic candidates did not correspondingly increase with financial insecurity: 42 percent of the most secure group preferred or leaned to the Democrats, the same as among the least secure group. Instead, at higher levels of financial insecurity, greater percentages indicated that they had no preference or preferred another party. Wealthier people were more likely to vote for Republicans than low-income people; but low-income people didn't necessarily vote Democratic—many just stayed home.[13]

When so many Americans are disengaged, our democracy is fundamentally broken. Even some right-wingers, such as conservative Richard W. Painter, now argue a conservative case for serious campaign finance reform:

All Americans should be alarmed about the effects of money in politics. But it is conservatives who should be leading the fight for campaign-finance reform. . . . Big money in politics encourages big government. . . . Campaign contributions also breed more regulation. . . . Companies in heavily regulated industries such as banking, health care, and energy are among the largest contributors. . . . Politicians sometimes say they want to roll back regulations wholesale, but they rarely follow through because they know that less regulation will remove the incentive for future contributions. . . . Social conservatives and faith-based voters should care about big money in politics because it drowns out their voices on issues from abortion and euthanasia to gambling and pornography. . . . If religious conservatives want to accomplish their goals, they first need to drive the big spenders out of the temples of our democracy.[14]

Any serious effort to place the American government back in the hands of the voters instead of the special interests must start with joint efforts to restrict both campaign money *and* the influence of big-spending lobbyists.

To do so, we'll need to enact a new Constitutional amendment. The Supreme Court and business interests, along with the American Civil Liberties Union,* have concluded that campaign spending is "free speech," a basic civil liberty protected by the First Amendment. That makes no sense to me to me, since by definition, a civil liberty is something that *every* American can benefit from equally, but campaign spending is highly unequal. No matter, though: the Supreme Court has ruled that campaign spending *is* a Constitutional right, so unless the Supreme Court dramatically changes its position on this matter,**

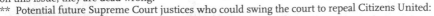

* I strongly support the overall work of the American Civil Liberties Union—I just think that, on this issue, they are dead wrong.
** Potential future Supreme Court justices who could swing the court to repeal Citizens United:

the only way for the American people to significantly restrict campaign donations and spending is to amend the Constitution.

The First Amendment does say, "Congress shall make no law . . . abridging the right of the people . . . to petition the government for a redress of grievances." Lobbying is essentially petitioning the government, so there's a strong case to be made that lobbying is protected by the Constitution too, so we'd need a Constitutional amendment to restrict spending on lobbying as well as spending on campaigns.

It's also insane that some municipalities make it so damn hard for even registered voters to vote. In Maricopa County, Arizona (where Phoenix is located), the number of polling booths was reduced from 200-plus in the 2012 presidential primary to only 60 in the 2016 primary, causing many residents to wait three or more hours just to vote. In general elections, too, voter access, particularly in low-income neighborhoods of color, is colossally screwed up. While apathy and hopelessness are the top causes of nonvoting, ballot access restrictions also contribute to the sad reality that the US is the only Western democracy where less than half of its eligible voters go to the polls, even for elections in which all of the seats in the lower house of the national legislature are in play.[15] America, you fight never-ending wars under the justification that you are saving democracy, but then you hand off that precious democracy on a silver (or a Chinet) platter. That's why the Constitutional amendment I propose would also make voting much easier by allowing everyone to vote by mail or by secured online systems, and require more voting places and shorter lines in communities or neighborhoods where access to voting has been historically difficult. If everyone can pay their taxes online or by mail, they certainly should be able to vote that way.

While we are at it, let's change the US Senate, a fundamentally undemocratic body. It was specifically created by the white, male, landowning (often slave-owning) founding fathers to *limit* the power of individual voters. Why should the 11 million people of Ohio and the 10 million residents of Georgia have exactly the same power in that legislative body as the fewer than one million people each in North Dakota and Delaware? I still think it's a useful check and balance to have two houses of Congress, and for each state to *elect* two US senators, but their votes in the Senate should be counted as proportional to their state's population.

And since the Electoral College is based on inequality within Senate representation, let's replace that archaic institution too and do what every other serious democracy does: give the top job to the person who wins the most popular votes.* The Electoral College is fundamentally undemocratic; people in Wyoming get one electoral vote for every 195,000 people, while voters in California get one for every 711,000 people.** Thus each voter in the least populous states are "worth" two or three times as much as the voters in the most populous states.

As for the presidential nominating system, few people understand this, but it is now set up in such a way that each of the two major political parties, on their own, set the rules for selecting their nominees for president. The system is such a crazy hodgepodge. The Democrats have superdelegates but the Republicans don't. The Republicans have winner-take-all-primaries but the Democrats don't. Whether each party in each state has a primary or a caucus is entirely arbitrary, up to each party in each state, and occasionally a state will have both, with only one actually selecting delegates. Caucuses often require participants to travel significant distances to limited locations, to show up at specific times, to spend hours at the caucus, and then to announce their vote in public, possibly requiring them to even move to a certain corner of the room to express their preference. That's why, compared to primaries in which people go to polling places during the day or night and vote in private like most other elections, caucus turnouts are usually microscopically small, and are frequently limited to a handful of ideologically extreme party activists. Because of the extra time commitment and

---

* Sorry, Al Gore, but my proposed elimination of the Electoral College would *not* be retroactive.

** Wyoming   California

It just makes no sense why voters in tiny states each have more per-person power than voters in huge states.

the fewer locations, caucuses tend to discriminate against low-income people who can't afford paid childcare or who rely on public transportation. Because turnouts in caucuses are generally far smaller than those in primaries, each caucus voter generally has more power than each primary voter. On the Democratic side, caucus states have tended to be much whiter than primary states; so the caucuses tend to violate the "one person one vote rule" by giving more power to white people than to nonwhites. For example, in 2016, 1,202,306 racially diverse people voted in the Ohio Democratic primary won by Hillary Clinton, which allocated 143 pledged delegates. In contrast, 230,000 mostly white people voted in the Washington State Democratic caucuses won by Bernie Sanders, which allocated 101 pledged delegates. Consequently, it took 8,407 votes to allocate each delegate in Ohio, but only 2,227 to do so in Washington; the mostly white voters in Washington had about four times the power as the racially diverse voters in Ohio. It is also absurd that we give the mostly white, rural, non-representative states of Iowa and New Hampshire* so much power every four years, ending the campaigns of much of the presidential field on both sides.

For all these reasons, I suggest eliminating all caucuses and ending the tradition in which Iowa and New Hampshire always go first. Instead I would require each party to select their candidates based on the popular vote, as determined in nine regional presidential primaries (New England, Middle Atlantic, South East, South Central, Great Lakes, Great Plains, Rocky Mountains, South West, and Pacific Coast), with one regional primary every two weeks, their order determined by random selection every four years. Superdelegates not directly elected by voters to represent candidates would be banned.

Constitutional amendments are darn hard to pass—requiring support of two-thirds of both the House of Representatives and the Senate, in addition to the support of three-quarters of state legisla-

---

* Before you get on my case, New Hampshire, let me reiterate that I love—just love—New Hampshire maple syrup and many things about your state. Also, if your main justification to keep the "first in the nation" status of your primary is that you weed out non-serious candidates, or that you refuse to support candidates who are driven mostly by media and are unwilling to spend quality time with rank-and-file voters in "retail politicking," then you lost all credibility on both of those fronts when Trump handily won the New Hampshire Republican primary in 2016.

tures—which is why the Constitution has not been amended since 1992 (in an amendment regulating Congressional salary hikes, which took 202 years, 7 months, and 12 days to pass). That's why, America, we'll need to build the greatest grassroots movement in US history to get it passed.

Let's call it the "We the People—for Real—Amendment" (WTPFRA). I suggest the amendment have the following components:

▶ All primary and general election campaigns for president, US Senate, and US House are paid for entirely by federal tax funds. (Trust me, this would cost the American people far *less* than it costs us to pay for all the pork barrel waste fueled by campaign donations.)

▶ No individual, organization, or business could spend any private funds to influence the general public on how to vote in federal campaigns. (A small exception should be made to enable organizations to spend limited amounts of money to communicate about federal elections with only their own members.)

▶ Prohibit candidates for federal office from using campaign money for meals, lodging, or travel for themselves or their families unless those expenses are explicitly used for specific campaign purposes. Prohibit Senate candidates from spending campaign funds outside their home state, and prohibit House candidates from using campaign dollars outside their home districts.

▶ All federal candidates would be required to participate in at least two public debates before each primary and five public debates before each general election. Stream every debate online.

▶ Replace the Electoral College with the popular vote.

▶ Require the US Senate to count its internal voting proportionately to the population of each senator's home states.

▶ Require states to allow legally eligible citizens to vote in federal elections over at least a week, by mail, or on secured online systems, and require states to allow people to register at the same time they vote.

▶ Require the Democratic and Republican parties to pick their presidential nominees through the popular vote in nine regional primaries.

▶ Limit federal lobbying expenses of individuals, organizations, or businesses to $100,000 annually. (A small exception should be made to enable groups to spend limited amounts of additional money to communicate about pending legislation or agency policies with their *own* members.) The federal government should host an online database that lists all lobbying spending and clients, as well the past employment, board participation, and other key affiliations of clients of each lobbyist.

Prohibit lobbyists, businesses, organizations, or any outside entity from paying for travel, meals, or lodging, or any other expenses or in-kind favors for federal elected or appointed officials.

The amendment should also include language making it crystal clear that it only covers *spending* on campaigning and lobbying. Campaigning and lobbying conducted by Americans entirely as volunteers, either electronically or in person, would still be considered protected free speech, which would be neither limited by anyone nor reported to any government entity. We want all Americans *more*, not less, involved, in fighting for the candidates and causes in which they believe.

I do realize that it would be nearly impossible to get small states to accept the provisions that would limit their clout in the Electoral College or the Senate, so, if we really needed support from such states to pass the amendment, I'd grudgingly agree to drop those two provisions.

This movement to pass such an amendment would take considerable time to educate people, gather steam, and to win votes, so in the meantime there are other things we can do to place government back in the hands of the people.

First of all, candidates themselves should push back forcefully against the 24/7 fundraising that both ruins their lives and is an affront to democracy. They need to stop listening only to their money-grubbing campaign consultants who get a cut of all their TV ad buys—and decide to find grassroots methods to win that don't require them to spend every waking moment in a small cubical calling rich people and begging them for money. Wouldn't you be much happier, dear candidates, if you spent more time meeting actual voters at fun county fairs where you could munch on corndogs without your spouse giving you the evil eye for your bad dietary choices, and less time toadying up to the mega-wealthy in stuffy conference rooms? You know you hate it.

And while you're at it, dear elected officials, please consider other ways to communicate with your supporters other than asking for money. I get countless e-mails from politicians each day—and plenty of phone calls from their staffs—and it seems like, for the vast majority of them, the *only* thing they ask people to do is donate money.

In 2016 I received an e-mail, supposedly from President Obama, with the subject line "Joel I need you to speak up," (He calls me by my first name, which means I'm special, or at least as special as the tens of millions other people who received this computer-generated e-mail). So far so good. The e-mail explained the progressive priorities in his budget proposal, "And I need you to speak up if you share that priority, Joel." Great! But *how* does he want me to prove that I share that priority? By voting for candidates who agree with me? No, he doesn't ask me to do that. By calling members of Congress to ask them to pass his budget priorities? No, he doesn't ask me to do that either. The *only* thing he asks me to do is donate to the Democratic Party. Thus, Obama and every other politician who sends similar e-mails essentially sent the message that, if you don't have money to donate to campaigns, your voice really doesn't matter. So, politicians, please, I beg of you, ask us not only to donate, but to give our voices and our time.

And America, as voters, when you get e-mails and calls asking you for money, push back hard and not only on their records—but also on why they aren't asking you for other types of help, or even better, for why they are not calling or e-mailing to ask your opinion or to figure out some other way to help you. If you were in a relationship where the only thing your partner ever asked you for was money, you'd dump them. I argue that it's time for us to dump the politicians who act that way.* Most importantly, every voter needs to be properly informed

---

* Some campaigns, notably Bernie Sanders's campaign, have been better than others in asking for help other than money. But in general, money is the top thing—and the top 10 things—that campaigns ask for from their supporters.

before they reach the voting booth. Remember that campaign spending doesn't actually *buy* votes, it buys the ability to *influence* votes. If you stay un-influenced by massive campaign spending, you win. As Jeb! Bush's disastrous presidential campaign proved, a candidate can have zillions of dollars but that doesn't guarantee victory.

On Election Day, every American voter (of *every* race, gender, sexual orientation, income level, etc.) has as much power as the president of the United States or a billionaire. That's the one day that the 99 percent actually have more power—99 times the power, in fact—than the 1 percent. But, America, we only have that power if we *use* it.

Mr. Smith, Ms. Sanchez, Miss Patel, Ms. Jones, and Mr. Wang Go to Washington
How All of Us Need to Make Political Activity a Noble Calling Again

"There are people who will say that democracy is neither an intelligent nor fair system, and that those who have the money are the best rulers. But I say, first, that what is meant by the demos, or the people, is the whole State, whereas an oligarchy is only a section of the State; and I say next that, though the rich are the best guardians of money and the best counsellors are the intelligent, it is the many who are the best at listening to different arguments and judging between them. And all alike, whether together or as separate classes, have equal rights in a democracy."
—Athenagoras, as quoted by Thucydides in *The Peloponnesian War*, 4th century, BCE

"I don't want to belong to any club that would accept me as a member."
—Groucho Marx, 20th century, CE

Well, there you have it, America. All of democracy boils down to this one conflict: the belief that all citizens are equally capable of governing versus the belief that we ourselves are unworthy of governing and that therefore any democracy that would allow us to be in charge, is, by definition, unworthy too. In modern America, we've skewed far too much toward the Groucho theory of governance, often incorporating his other dictum, "Whatever it is, I'm against it."

There was a time when Americans were more welcoming of democracy. In 1939, when Frank Capra directed the film *Mr. Smith Goes to*

Washington, politics could still be portrayed as the noblest of callings. Senator Jefferson Smith—portrayed by Jimmy Stewart with all the man/boy charm and gee-whiz idealism he could muster—could still think that serving the American people is, gosh golly, just about the greatest honor anyone could have.* Yeah, he encountered some bad guys in Washington who were perverting the nation's inherent civic virtue, but they are outliers, sure to lose out in the long run against one man, backed by idealistic young people from around the nation, who is determined to do the right thing and make politics work for *everyone*. It wasn't just Washington that was idealized; it was the whole enterprise of politics that was idealized. It was politics, after all, that would get that much-needed boys camp built.

But today, most Americans hate, just hate politics. They'd rather do or say anything than admit to the heinous crime of "being political" or "taking sides" in campaigns. In 2000, at the height of their main-stream popularity, members of the country band the Dixie Chicks told the media, through a spokesperson, that they were too busy touring to have a preference in the race for president between Al Gore and George W. Bush. Thus it was particularly ironic that, three years later, lead singer Natalie Maines sent the band's career into a tailspin by saying in a concert in London, just before the start of the impending US invasion of Iraq, "Just so you know, we're on the good side with y'all. We do not want this war, this violence, and we're ashamed that the president of the United States is from Texas." They didn't know it at the time, but their refusal, and the refusal of many like them (both famous and not)

---

* One of these movies is an entirely accurate portrayal of American democracy.

to "take a side" in 2000, was one of the many factors that allowed Bush to become president and then invade Iraq.*

In 2016, Brandon Stanton, the creator of the popular photo essay blog *Humans of New York*, posted an open letter to Facebook slamming Donald Trump, writing, "I try my hardest not to be political. I've refused to interview several of your fellow candidates. I didn't want to risk any personal goodwill by appearing to take sides in a contentious election. I thought, 'Maybe the timing is not right.' But I realize now that there is no correct time to oppose violence and prejudice. The time is always now. Because along with millions of Americans, I've come to realize that opposing you is no longer a political decision. It is a moral one." Note that, even though he has photographed countless domestic homeless people and international refugees (whose conditions are caused primarily by politics), his note made it seem as if it is somehow dirty to "be political." He then differentiates "political" decisions from "moral" ones when, in fact, all political decisions have moral dimension and most issues of morality have political implications.

People hate the term "political" so much that they even absurdly deny that even actual politics, when they agree with it, is "political." That's like not wanting to admit that fish get wet. Attending a 2015 campaign rally for Bernie Sanders (who, by then, had served for 33 years in political office), supporter Gwen Harvey said, "He is telling the truth, and not giving political speeches."[16] It is both hilarious that she thinks a campaign speech isn't a political speech while also troubling that she equates the word "political" with lying.

Democracy, at its heart, is the practice of politics—people collectively choosing the options that they think are best for the country. Unless we stop being so ridiculously squeamish about politics, we'll never fix our democracy.

Many people who claim that being "nonpolitical" or "above politics" gives them an aura of purity, but to me that's really saying, "I am too

---

* Had Gore won either his home state of Tennessee, which he lost by 80,000 votes out of more than two million cast (and in which Natalie Maines lived at the time); Florida, in which Gore had 573 fewer votes counted than Bush of more than six million votes cast; or Missouri, in which Gore lost by 78,000 votes out of more than two million cast, he would have become president. Given that the vote margins were so tiny, anything, including an endorsement by the Dixie Chicks, hugely popular in those states, could have provided the margin of victory for Gore in one or all of those states.

weak-willed to publicly express the kinds of opinions that all citizens are supposed to have and communicate in a democracy."

Sure, politics can be dirty (but so is farming) and slimy and bloody (but so is open heart surgery), but the practice of politics is absolutely necessary to ensure an effective society. One bit of good news, America, is that you are now more socioeconomically diverse than at any time in our history, so Americans of all backgrounds and ethnicities now have unprecedented opportunities to gain power.

In the old Norman Rockwell conception of America, being a good citizen—showing up to speak at a New England town meeting, for instance—was an essential component of being considered a "good" person in a community. Now, we've entirely wiped out that conception by collectively saying that all people need to do to be "good" is to work hard at their job, raise an upstanding family, and perhaps, occasionally, volunteer in the community to clean up trash in a public park, support a walkathon against lupus, or aid a food pantry—or, even worse, retweet something or "like" a cause on Facebook. Our definition of virtue rarely includes serious civic duty anymore, and that's a problem.

I am not going to personally judge what makes any particular person a good human being or even a good American, but I will strenuously argue that, most broadly, our national definition of being a good American must include being a good citizen.

What does it mean to be a good citizen? At a minimum it means seriously studying candidates and ballot initiatives, and then voting in each and every election. I have shocked some friends and colleagues by noting that my greatest disdain is *not* for far-right conservatives who are active in politics: I hold the greatest scorn for nonvoters. At least right wingers active in politics are acting upon what they think is best for the country; as misguided as I think they are, that's far better than doing nothing. Note to millennials: It's not enough to encourage other people to vote on your Facebook page, you must actually *vote yourself.* (At least five celebrities who appeared in a 2014 Rock the Vote public service announcement—*Girls* creator Lena Dunham, comedian Whoopi Goldberg, *Orange is the New Black* actress Natasha Lyonne, *Rich Kids of Beverly Hills* star E.J. Johnson, and actor Darren Criss from *Glee*—did not vote in the previous midterm election.)[17]

Two, good citizens should show up for jury duty when called, and not pull strings to get out of it.

Three, you should pay your fair share of taxes, especially if you have more money than God.* Yes, I know I've made this point before, but I'll keep making it until my keyboard falls apart, which, at this rate, may happen soon, America.

Fourth, if you really want to win that good citizen merit badge, you should, at least occasionally, attend a town board, city council, or community board meeting—or watch C-Span if you have cable. (Better yet, let's make C-Span like public TV, something that everyone can watch without paying for it.)**

There are a zillion ways to be a good citizen. The researcher Robert D. Putnam, in his renowned book, *Bowling Alone: The Collapse and Revival of American Community*, worried that Americans had been becoming increasingly disconnected from one another and that traditional social structure—such as the PTAs, churches, or political parties—had disintegrated.[18] But in the book *Loose Connections: Joining Together in America's Fragmented Communities*, Robert Wuthnow argues back that Americans are still engaged, just in different ways, such as more likely being involved in special interest groups than in civic organizations. "Although the demise of civil society is a specter that has alarmed many social observers, a close look at civic involvement today reveals that many American still care deeply about their communities and make efforts to connect with other people. But [those efforts] take different forms."[19]

TERM LIMITS AND POLITICAL AMATEURS

The ultimate form of Groucho-like political self-loathing is when voters enact term limits, which in effect say that we simply don't trust ourselves or our neighbors to make the right choices. I grudgingly support term limits for the presidency (because that position, uniquely, has the ability to amass dangerous, secret power), but it makes no sense to have

---

* This guy, for instance, really, really needs to pay his fair share of taxes.

** If you do attend or watch any of those, I'll bring the popcorn.

term limits for other positions. If you were the boss in a workplace, would you indiscriminately fire anyone who has been there 12 years, even if they are superstar workers, or would you wait 12 years to get rid of an employee who sucked? I hope not. Indiscriminately getting rid of both the best and the worst elected officials after a set number of terms is juvenile abrogation of your voting responsibilities, America.

Plus, experience and institutional knowledge matter. If you got on a plane, and the person in the pilot's seat announced that they had neither flown a plane before nor received training on how to do so, you'd get the hell off of that plane immediately. Likewise, you would jump out of your gurney in any operating room if you learned that the person about to cut into you had neither experience nor training as a surgeon.

Then why in the world would you hand over an entire state to a heavyweight wrestler or an actor with no political or government experience? Even worse, why would you even consider handing over the nuclear codes and the presidency to someone with no applicable on-the-ground experience? Insanity. The only Americans more fraudulent than "amateur" politicians are "amateur" porn stars (or so a friend of a friend, who knows a guy, who knows a woman, tells me).

Americans just to love bashing "career politicians." We have this idealized notion of the Jeffersonian-era citizen legislator, who supposedly governs a little before going back to their lives as a simple farmer (or in Jefferson's case, going back to his plantation in which the real work was performed by 170 slaves), but, given how much more complex society is today, we desperately need our leaders to come to understand complex issues, and see patterns over time, and hopefully learn from them. Most people, myself included, are a heck of a lot better in our jobs after we become a little more experienced in them; we should insist that our political leaders have that experience too.

And what's the deal with the fact that we hate it when politicians honestly express ambition? We expect an NBA rookie to say they want to be someday better than Jordan or LeBron, and that they will work hard to become the best there ever was. We expect a recent graduate of business school to openly say they want to someday run the most successful and effective business in the land. But if a city council member dared admit that, someday, they would want to be president of the

United States, they would be a laughing stock. That's gotta change. We should *want* our best and our brightest of all backgrounds to enter politics, and we should encourage them to work so hard and effectively that someday they can rise to the very top and become president.

While some immigrant-haters think diversity is a weakness for the country, I think it's our greatest strength. Ambitious people from around the world who made intense sacrifices to get here, as well as extremely talented native-born Americans, combine to give the United States one of the greatest pools of collective ambition, wisdom, and energy on the planet. Let's use that not only to build the best new ride-sharing and dating apps on the planet, but also to give ourselves the best government on the planet.

We all need to make politics noble again. We need to stop taking the lazy way out by just knee-jerk bashing the "politicians" or the "system". We need to accept the responsibility or the reality that our leaders are only as good—or as awful—as the American people who elected them by voting, or worse, by not voting. We need to appreciate and thank people who are willing to make sacrifices for the common good.

I've surely bashed elected officials—repeatedly—in this book. But I bashed them for their specific bad acts, not for engaging in public service. Most elected officials work very long hours, usually six or seven days a week, and many nights, and they suffer through all sorts of insults and humiliations, whether they deserve it or not. They rarely have true "down time"; even if they are merely shopping at a grocery store for a carton of milk, a constituent can come up to yell at them to fill a pothole.* That's why, wherever I meet with public officials, even ones with whom I disagree, I thank them for their public service. Americans treat them like dirt, indiscriminately.

Just as we need to hold elected officials accountable for doing something with which we disagree, I think we should publicly praise them when they do the right thing. Voters must be far more discriminating between good politicians and bad politicians, and roll out the red carpet for the good ones. We need to make politics honorable again.

---

* Poor Senator Chuck Schumer (who lives in the same neighborhood as I do) had to face me at 7:00 a.m. one morning when he left our local polling place as I was also leaving. I implored him to vote a particular way on a pending hunger bill. Of course, I'd do the same thing again in a heartbeat, but I still felt kinda sorry for the guy.

Besides, politicians are sort of like your children. If you treat them as if you expect them to misbehave, they often will; but if you give them a bit of respect and responsibility, they will often rise to the occasion; we should do the same for our political leaders (but perhaps let them keep their candy *and* their rattle.)

Mr. Smith, Ms. Sanchez, Miss Patel, Ms. Jones, and Mr. Wang should *all* want to go to Washington to make a better America, and we all need to build a political environment to encourage them to do so.

Step Five:

If Corporations Are People, Make Them *Good* People
Holding Businesses Accountable

"Corporations are people, my friend."
—Mitt Romney, 2011

"Soylent Green is People!"
—*Soylent Green* (movie), 1973

In the cult classic *Soylent Green*, a giant corporation runs the Earth and it turns out that the food rations they distribute to everyone are made out of the remains of mass-euthanized humans. I don't think that's what Mitt Romney meant, but who knows?

Now, America, multinational corporations are not the root of *all* evil. After all, I am composing this book on a computer created by a multi-national corporation, and transmitting it to Seven Stories Press through a high-speed Internet connection provided by one of the biggest cable corporations in the country. No matter how much I or Seven Stories do to promote this book to independent bookstores,* the reality is that most copies of this book will be sold online though enormous corporations and many will be read on electronic devices produced by other humongous corporations. Big bank credit cards will be used to purchase this book, and people may drive to see me speak about it in cars made by yet other corporations, using gas produced by yet more corporations.

Most of the food I eat (other than farmers market produce) comes from corporations, and I am pretty fond of eating. Ditto for most of the

---

* Dear reader: please, please, please shop as much as you can at brick and mortar bookstores, especially ones that carry fine Seven Stories Press titles!

clothes I wear. If I need to fly anywhere, I take a plane operated by a big corporation. I brushed my teeth this morning using a toothbrush and toothpaste made by mammoth corporations, too.

Plus, all corporations create jobs (although not as many as they should) and most pay taxes (although not as much as they should).

The fact is that we are all heavily dependent on corporations, usually giant ones. Let's make peace with that basic reality. So, if we have no choice but to live with them, let's make corporations as good (or at least as harmless) as possible.

THE CORPORATE/MEDIA BUBBLE

While I don't agree with Mitt Romney that corporations *are* people, they are certainly run and (mostly) staffed by human beings, so we can first try to appeal to their leaders as people.

The problem is that corporate leaders are mostly isolated from the public at large, plus corporate media and corporate executives are so intertwined socially and economically that they spend much of their time telling each other how wonderful and deserving they are. For instance, *Bloomberg Markets* rated eight CEOs as *"underpaid"* (yes, you read that right) when their salaries ranged from $4 million to $9.3 million per year.[20]* If any of you readers happen to be on the board of a behemoth corporation and you want to "underpay" *me* by that much, please contact me immediately and I'll be on the first plane to your tax-free corporate headquarters in Turks and Caicos.

Given all the media and societal coddling they get, it's no wonder that CEO salaries, often set by themselves in collusion with their hand-

---

* One of those on the "underpaid" CEOs list was William Rogers, who earned $8.5 million in one year to run SunTrust Banks, based in Atlanta, Georgia, where the median family income is $34,770 and starting Atlanta police officers earn $34,726 annually, equaling 1/224th of what Rogers earns. I am pretty sure I have a different definition than *Bloomberg Markets* of the word "underpaid."

picked boards of directors, are so outrageously out of sync with the salaries of their employees.

We should use any means necessary—including letter-writing campaigns, consumer boycotts, shareholder activism, and plain old moral persuasion—to try to get CEOs to lessen the vast and growing divide between themselves and their employees.

NEED A REFEREE?

But let's assume, for a moment, that not every corporate executive decides to increase their workers' salaries just because it's the right thing to do. That's when we need government to step in—and be the referee in this lopsided game—and provide both points and penalties to the corporation's actions to ensure that employees are adequately rewarded for their hard work.

In 2015, a State Senate committee in California passed a bill that would cut the state taxes for companies that can demonstrate lower ratios between their chief executives' pay and the salaries of their median workers. At the same time, the bill would raise taxes on companies with vast gaps between chief executive and median worker pay. As columnist Harold Meyerson explained, "The bill doesn't compel CEOs and their corporate boards to either raise their employees' wages or cut their own. It merely presents them with a choice. Those who overpay themselves and underpay their employees can continue to do so but thereby subject their company to higher taxes. Or they can diminish the discrepancy in compensation and thereby lower their company's taxes. . . . Once you get past the ranks of CEOs themselves, it's hard to find defenders of this pay gap. A [national poll] found that 66 percent of Americans—including even 58 percent of Republicans—thought that CEO pay was too high."[21] Robert Reich handily dispelled objections to the bill:

> What about CEOs gaming the system? Can't they simply elim-inate low-paying jobs by subcontracting them to another com-pany—thereby avoiding large pay disparities while keeping their own compensation in the stratosphere? . . .

No. The proposed law controls for that. Corporations that begin subcontracting more of their low-paying jobs will have to pay a higher tax . . .

For the last thirty years, almost all the incentives operating on companies have been to lower the pay of their workers while increasing the pay of their CEOs and other top executives. It's about time some incentives were applied in the other direction.[22]

Unsurprisingly, after the bill passed out of committee, business interests killed it. But it makes so much sense that such legislation should be fully enacted in California, and in every state nationwide. I'd even argue that federal legislation would make an even bigger impact.

If I had a magic wand, I'd go even further than that: I'd change the tax codes and shareholder governance laws to encourage companies to limit top executive salaries to no more than 100 times the salary of their lowest-paid employee. (For example, if an executive wanted to earn $2 million annually, their lowest-paid workers could earn no less than $20,000 annually.) That's probably politically unattainable at this point, so the least we could do is to provide incentives for change by passing laws such as the one proposed in California.

In addition to the soaring gaps between executives and their employees, another pernicious trend has emerged: that of a US-based multinational corporation merging with a foreign counterpart, with the intent to pay taxes at the other country's lower rate. It's called an inversion, and pharmaceutical giant Pfizer has tried to use this loop-hole to move—at least on paper—to Ireland, to reduce its effective tax rate from 26 percent to 17 percent. Such inversions will deprive the US government of an estimated $33.6 billion over the next decade.[23] The Obama administration took some initial steps to make inversions more difficult, but the next president and Congress will need to team up to change tax laws to prevent them altogether.

Some corporate leaders have even argued that their shareholders could sue them if they ever *did* give a higher priority to paying workers more or protecting the environment than making as big a profit as possible for their shareholders. I think the chances of shareholders filing, no less winning, such lawsuits are extraordinarily slim. But let's remove this excuse altogether by encouraging the federal government and states to change corporate governance laws to clarify that the public interest should take preference over the companies' profit, or at the very least limit lawsuits resulting from actions taken to reduce inequality.

WORKERS OF THE WORLD UNITE: BUY YOUR EMPLOYERS

The best way to increase corporate profits while boosting the greater good is for companies to do more to embrace employee profit-sharing and/or employee ownership.* In the 2016 campaign, Hillary Clinton wisely proposed providing tax credits for companies that adopt profit-sharing for their workers, saying, "Profit-sharing that gives everyone a stake in the company's success can boost productivity and put money directly into employees' pockets." Professors Richard Freeman, Joseph Blasi, and Douglas Kruse of Harvard and Rutgers have found "strong evidence" that profit-sharing has "meaningful impacts on workers' wealth" because "workers with profit-sharing or employee stock ownership are higher paid and have more benefits than other workers."[24]

In April 2016, Chobani (whose "Greek" yogurt is actually Turkish) gave each of its 2,000 employees shares in the company, up to 10 percent of its total value. Beyond that, as *USA Today* reported that

> the two most prominent ways to give workers significant stakes—employee stock ownership plans (ESOPs) and worker cooperatives—go quite a bit further [than what Chobani did], handing as much [as] 100% of a company to its employees. An ESOP, which is far more common, sets up a retirement trust for all full-time employees and contributes shares annually. On average, the trusts are granted 30% to 50% ownership, but four in 10 ESOPs own, or eventually will, 100% of the companies. . . . Although employees must wait until retirement age to draw the

---

* Here are some deliriously happy employees, ecstatic that they are sharing in their company's profits. Actually not—this is just a stock photo of random people—but you get the idea.

funds, ESOPs create far more wealth than 401(k) plans, with participants accumulating about three times the assets of employees in comparable companies. . . .[25]

Employee profit-sharing is exactly the kind of "win-win" Stephen Covey and other business strategy gurus told us to achieve. Turning workers into productive co-owners is a much smarter move for corporations than turning them into liquid food.

Step Six:

We Are the World
Why We Need to Bolster the Planet to Fix America

1985's insipid "We Are the World," written by Michael Jackson and Lionel Richie and sung by a cast of thousands, pleaded with Americans to save the world, and especially those pitiful starving little African kids.* That's the quintessential America attitude—that it's *our* job to unilaterally save everyone else, and to do so through a shallow, easy activity will actually save very few. That's one of the best things—and the worst things—about us as a country.

I'm darn proud, America, that our nation, after seeing suffering and oppression anywhere, has the immediate reaction of wanting to do something about it, even if, as the song says, it's "just you and me."

But I'm also a little embarrassed to be part of a nation that's so arrogant and condescending that we think we can, on our own, "fix" things worldwide, especially since we ignore the major problems in our own country. It's especially embarrassing when many of the issues we are seeking to address overseas are troubles that we created in the first place. It's also problematic that we think we know what's best for other nations far better than the people who live there do, and that we tolerate no opposing views.

While our impulse to help is praiseworthy, our desire to help in our typical "my way or the highway" approach is troublesome and alienating.

Not only do we fail to see how we have frequently screwed up the rest of the world, we don't understand how our

---

* If you want to figure out how to truly save the world, please carefully study self-aggrandizing, one-time celebrity events such as this, then do the complete opposite.

strong-armed interventions worldwide have warped our national character and skewed our own priorities. This is by no means a new insight. In 1967, Dr. Martin Luther King, Jr. explained why the US couldn't end domestic poverty as long as it was engaged in perpetual wars overseas:

> Now what are some of the domestic consequences of the war in Vietnam? It has made the Great Society a myth and replaced it with a troubled and confused society. The war has strengthened domestic reaction. It has given the extreme right, the anti-labor, anti-Negro, and anti-humanistic forces a weapon of spurious patriotism to galvanize its supporters into reaching for power, right up to the White House. It hopes to use national frustration to take control and restore the America of social insecurity and power for the privileged. . . .
>
> The war in Vietnam has produced a shameful order of priorities in which the decay, squalor, and pollution of the cities are neglected. And even though 70% of our population now live in them, the war has smothered, and nearly extinguished, the beginnings of progress toward racial justice. . . .
>
> It is disgraceful that a Congress that can vote upwards of $35 billion a year for a senseless immoral war in Vietnam cannot vote a weak $2 billion to carry on our all too feeble efforts to bind up the wound of our nation's 35 million poor. This is nothing short of a Congress engaging in political guerilla warfare against the defenseless poor of our nation.[26]

We can start by stopping counterproductive, immoral actions overseas, as or President Obama put it, "Don't do stupid shit." We need to go way beyond the absence of a negative. We need to harness the full forces of globalization and world interdependence to enhance, rather than harm, American society.

The world is more entwined than ever, just as each of the states of the United States are. America learned in our Civil War—the hardest of hard ways—how much all our states really needed each other. The North won that war for many reasons. The most obvious was that any system of government that chose to keep the majority of its population in slavery was immoral and destined to fail. The North also had more troops and more ability to manufacture weapons. But I would also argue that the invention of telegraphs, railroads, and steamships bound together all of the American states with the pull of economic self-interest, making obsolete the idea that any individual state could be an independent, self-sufficient economic entity. The simple consequence was that, in the long run, the South would do better connected to the North than separated from it, no matter what it believed at the time. Likewise, I would argue, the invention of jet passenger and cargo planes, the Internet, and satellites have economically bound together nation-states as never before, rendering equally obsolete the idea that countries could be economically self-sufficient. When you add to that reality the fact that air and water pollution know no national borders, and that if country A attacks country B with a nuclear bomb, fallout could land on country C, we must accept that in the 21st century, all nations are in this—the world—together.*

It is true that developing countries will need some extra help—at least in the short-term—from developed countries, including the United States, to reduce their poverty, hunger, and deadly diseases. But it is also true that the United States needs the rest of the world in order to reduce our own poverty, protect our own freedom, rebuild our own middle class, and save our own environment.

GLOBAL PROBLEMS, GLOBAL SOLUTIONS

America's inequality is inexorably tied to the soaring inequality worldwide. That's why I support the call of French economist Thomas Piketty to create a worldwide tax on wealth:

> The ideal policy for avoiding an endless inegalitarian spiral . . . would be a progressive global tax on capital. . . . [Such a tax would also] expose wealth to democratic scrutiny, which is a necessary condition for effective regulation of the banking system and international capital flows. . . . A tax on capital

---

* Yes, the UK voters who supported the Brexit were history-ignoring ignoramuses.

would promote the general interest of private interests while preserving economic openness and forces of competition. . . .

If democracy is to regain control over the globalized financial capitalism of this century, it must also invent new tools, adapted to today's challenges. The ideal tool would be a progressive global tax on capital, coupled with a very high level of international financial transparency.[27]

The time is also ripe for the implementation of an international minimum wage, tied to local economies. Not only would that help workers in countries where the lowest-paid employees live in extreme poverty, but it would also aid the workers in the United States and other industrialized nations by limiting the incentive to drive down domestic wages to compete with the lowest-wage countries. The idea for the global minimum wage has been around for nearly a hundred years, but it's never been enacted due to both the challenging world politics for doing so and the difficulties of agreeing on what that correct wage should be, given that countries vary so dramatically in their wage levels. The hourly minimum wage in 2014, in US dollars, ranged from \$15.58 in Australia to \$7.25 in the US to 20 cents in Guinea-Bissau. The costs of living also vary dramatically in those countries. Rather than have an international minimum wage set at a specific amount that would be the same in each country, I propose that wages be calibrated based on economic conditions in each country, relative to the earnings of both the average and the wealthiest families in each country. Specifically, I propose that each country's minimum wage be set at either 50 percent of the median household income or 14 percent of the income of the top 5 percent of earners in each country, at whichever level is higher.

Here's how that would work, using the United States as an example: In 2014, the US federal minimum wage was \$7.25 per hour; if an employee worked 35 hours per week for 52 weeks, that employee would earn \$13,195 for the year. The median family income was \$51,937; 50 percent of that would equal \$25,968. The income of the top 5 percent was \$206,568; 14 percent of that would equal \$28,918. Under my proposal, the minimum wage would be set at the highest of those two numbers, \$28,918, which just so happens to equal just slightly more than the $15 per hour rate currently being fought for by the US labor movement. Setting rates in this way—using objective, country-specific benchmarks—would make far more sense than the rather arbitrary way in which they are set by governments today. If the wages of average workers and/or the top of the income scale do better over time, minimum wage workers would also automatically earn more. What could be fairer than that?

Some may claim my proposal is socialism. It is not; socialism would pay everyone equally the *same*. I am suggesting that the lowest-paid workers receive, at most, only one-seventh the income of the more highly-paid crowd. The remaining wage differentials would still give both the wealthiest and the working class incentives to innovate and work hard to move up.

As for trade agreements, we need to move beyond either knee-jerk opposition or support for them. All sides need to acknowledge a few basic truths. First, globalism is inevitable—in fact, it's a train that has already left the station and without everyone on it—and can be either helpful or harmful; it can both create and destroy jobs, and share both helpful new technologies and harmful pollutants. Stopping trade agreements won't stop the movement of capital, jobs, and pollution between nations. Many of the manufacturing jobs lost in America would have left the US anyway, even if trade agreements such as NAFTA had never been enacted. Second, real people face real suffering because of economic dislocations due to trade; the idea that increased trade might aid the nation as a whole is cold comfort to those families and communities that have been devastated when a factory closes because those jobs are now overseas.

Future trade negotiations—and US domestic policies in response to them—must focus more on employee income, worker safety, and environmental considerations, as well as real job and income support for the communities harmed. Whether or not we ever adopt an international minimum wage, all future trade negotiations should push to lift wage floors, and focus on increasing income for all the workers involved, but especially women, who usually bear the worst brunt of world poverty.

REPLACING RELENTLESS WARS WITH MUSCULAR PEACE-MAKING

One way the US can improve its relationships with the rest of the world is to stop bombing the hell out of it and to also stop playing footsie with dictatorships. Doing so would make the US safer, wealthier, and more well-respected around the globe.

We must also move beyond our selective freak-outs over isolated acts of terrorism. Terrorists don't win when they kill scores of innocent people; they win when they create fear that leads nations to curtail their own civil liberties or launch counterproductive wars. We must stand up against the absurd premise that ISIS has "won" or that radical Islam is a serious threat to the existence of the US. There are millions of Muslims in our country, so the fact that two in San Bernardino or one in Orlando turned out to be crazy killers shouldn't turn our whole society upside down. Now, before any right-wingers go off on me for saying those things, first I want to be clear that terrorism is never—ever—justified. Resorting to violence usually means that your message is failing to convince the public. I also want to be clear that I think any single death from a terrorist, in the US or anywhere around the globe (whether in France, the Ivory Coast, Pakistan, Israel, Belgium, Nigeria, or any other country) is one too many. That being said, Americans are still far more likely to be shot by a Christian or killed in a drunken driving accident than they are to be killed by Muslims or foreign terrorists. Let's deal with actual reality, America, and ensure that our response to our terrorism worries is fact-based, smart, and proportional.

More warfare and more abrogation of civil liberties should not be our default response.

Our national debate (or lack thereof) on whether to go into battle continues to be warped by the reality that the sacrifices resulting from that choice continue to be borne by a small, mostly non-wealthy sliver of the country who serve in the military—and by the American people who must finance not only the wars themselves, but also the aftermath of them, which includes the rebuilding of—and peacekeeping in—those nations, as well as long-term physical and mental healthcare for veterans.

There are fewer military veterans in Congress now than at any time in modern history. And for those policy makers with children over 18, it's not as if many of them are encouraging their own kids to serve.[*] This, too, is an ancient concern; Athenian leader Pericles noted, in the 5th century BCE, that he thought only leaders who had children in the military should have a say over whether Athens fought a war. If only.

I'd also make this point to my fellow Americans and citizens of other Western nations with a history of colonialism and military aggression: if you don't want so many refugees to keep showing up at your borders, please stop screwing up their homelands.

Beyond the human costs of wars are the vast economic costs. How insane is it that we keep spending vast sums of money to blow places up only to turn around to spend vast sums of money to put them back together again?

We need a sober, data-based national discussion of what will really, truly make us safer, not what will merely make us *feel* safer. To be safer, we need to get more of the world on our side, rooting for us again. Just as domestic policing works best when cops obtain active support and information from the local neighborhood residents where they are patrolling, international terrorism prevention works best when the local populace provides safe havens and actionable intelligence to Americans and our allies. Bombing civilian hospitals is clearly making it less likely, not more, that we will get that necessary support.

Do we really think that our own bomb threats deter terrorists who are planning to blow themselves up, along with innocent bystanders?

We'd have far more friends and fewer enemies if we fed the world instead of armed it. Too often, when we sent military aid, our former allies turned against us, or the weapons fell into enemy hands. Yet food aid has *never* been used against us as a weapon.[**]

---

[*] Many members of Congress, rightfully so, have criticized the US Department of Veterans Affairs (the VA) for poor treatment of wounded veterans. But they also forget that we would have far fewer wounded veterans if we fought fewer unnecessary wars. Congress also glosses over its own role in cutting funding for VA programs. At a bare minimum, we all ought to agree that we must guarantee combat vets a hell of a lot more when they come home than their own sleeping spot on a sidewalk.

[**] Here is a US export that is *never* used against us.

But American international food aid, which for too long was designed mostly to benefit special interests back in the US, should be recalibrated to enable nations to achieve long-term food security and economic prosperity. The Obama administration's State Department deserves great credit for its "Feed the Future" initiative that began to help countries achieve food self-reliance.

At some point, I hope humans advance enough as a species to end wars altogether, finally recognizing that we should be a level or two above most chimpanzees. I hope the US can replace Memorial Day with "Can You Believe That Humans Were Once So Stupid They Went to War Day."

But for now, war and terrorism are deadly realities; so, how should we deal with them? First let's learn from history. We didn't beat the Soviets through direct wars or even proxy wars. We beat them because we proved that our political and economic systems were better and more desirable to many of their citizens. That is still a winning formula to defeat all forms of radicalism and oppression. We need to do that again, through a strategy I call "Muscular Peace Making" in which the US—and our true, democratic, human-rights-abiding allies—stand together to systematically advocate for peace, security, and human rights around the world. Some may falsely believe that a focus on non-violence would be a passive, ineffective response that avoids dealing with serious global problems. Yet while some wrongly dismissed Gandhi and MLK for advocating nonviolence, which some equated with passively accepting mistreatment, both were the antithesis of passivity—constantly agitating, pushing, and challenging. Similarly, muscular peacemaking would constantly agitate, push, and challenge the world to achieve and/or keep the peace, ensure human rights, and reluctantly, but effectively, use multinational force when needed to do so. This strategy would persistently work to undermine the top forces that cause terrorism and war: intolerance, sexism, inequality, racism, poverty, and famine.

That's *not* weak. Building a wall to keep out impoverished Mexicans or scapegoating all innocent Muslims—that's weak. Balancing force with restraint is the essence of strength. Think of the late Muhammad Ali defeating bigger, stronger George Foreman. It's not always the boxer who throws the most punches or swings the hardest who wins—it's the boxer who throws the right punches at the right time.

The neo-cons would say that such a philosophy is naïve and that such good intentions won't play out in the vicious world we live in.

Well, we've tried *their* response—bombing and torturing—and they failed miserably, harming the US and the world on every level.

What if, instead, the world's democracies tried to implement a consistent policy of muscular peacemaking?

First, we would make economic development and poverty reduction our top way of interacting with the developing world, carried out through smart, targeted aid and a dramatically expanded Peace Corps.

Second, we would need to do something big to slow down climate change. Secretary of State John Kerry was absolutely correct when he explained how climate change increased the likelihood of war and terrorism:

> Generals, admirals, three-star, four-star, retired—have all said [climate change] is a major threat multiplier. And there are many different ways in which a security challenge can emerge. You have drought, therefore, perhaps, huge food shortages. Where there is water today, there may not be in the future. That could cause mass migrations. That creates conflict. The water itself—there are wars over water. Already, tribes are fighting in part of the Sahel and other places where water once existed, and now it's dried up. There's a history of conflict where resources are finite or scarce . . .
>
> So if you look around the world, the potential for mass dislocation is rising exponentially right now. We saw massive numbers of people uprooted in Syria and moving into Damascus. The drought in the region did not cause what happened, but it exacerbated what happened. It creates greater instability.[28]

Third, we need to get serious, really serious, about human rights. It won't be good enough anymore for our leaders to make a few soaring speeches on freedom or for our government to write a few well-intentioned reports slapping the hands of "friendly" human rights violators—all the while giving them most-favored-trading status, all the weapons systems they need, tons of military financing, and even carte blanche to torture those people they don't like whom we don't like either. We'd have to move away from the reasoning that "engaging" with dictatorships is the best way to get them to improve. South Africa dropped apartheid, not when the Reagans of the world "engaged" with it, but when the rest of the world fully isolated the country. Granted, it won't change every totalitarian regime, but it will help with most. Conversely, we should do more economically, diplomatically, and, if need be, militarily, to protect fledgling democracies.

Fourth, we should only go to war as a very last resort, and only to fight to worst kinds of human rights oppression, genocides, true humanitarian crises, or to repel military aggression against democracies. (If we fight yet another war that is perceived by the world as bolstering our own self-interest—if we are seen as fighting more for the Halliburtons of the world or for oil rather than for freedom—all is lost.) But if there is absolutely no viable option other than warfare, let's only participate as part of a united coalition of democracies, and make it clear that our collective goal is liberation, not occupation.

America, let's make the United States and other democracies the good guys again. Villagers worldwide will be far happier if we bring them water wells, instead of bomb craters. And, oh yeah, it will also help us solve our own problems.

The whole globe will be happier if we help bring it peace, security, and prosperity—and not just another dumb celebrity sing-along.

Step Seven:

From the Middle Out
Rebuilding the Working Class

"I believe that the way you grow the economy is from the middle out. I believe in fighting for the middle class because if they're prospering, all of us will prosper."
—President Barack Obama, 2012

Every American who works hard and contributes to the nation should get ahead. It's that simple.

The central economic challenge of our time, America, is to create enough sustainable jobs (that won't be eliminated tomorrow because of robots or outsourcing) and to ensure that workers are paid enough to support a thriving middle class. If we did that, it would both bring back the middle class and open doorways of opportunity for tens of millions of those mired in poverty.

Some pundits, such as columnist Josh Barro, claim that there's little the government can do to grow the middle class: "An awkward truth for politicians looking to help the middle class is that there's much less the government can do for them than for the poor. So, the president has picked an opportune time to set his mantra to 'middle-class economics': a time when middle-class economic fortunes are already improving for reasons not much related to policy."[29]

First, the minimal improvements experienced by the middle class in the United States have had a great deal to do with public policies, not the least of which were the government efforts that saved the economy from a full-scale depression in 2009. Second, given that wages are still mostly stagnant, housing is still out of reach, college is still unaffordable, and retirement savings are still in jeopardy for most middle-class

Americans, it's a bit of a stretch to say their "economic fortunes are already improving."

Others, including Nobel Prize–winning economist Joseph Stiglitz, have argued that the decline in the middle class can certainly be stemmed by government actions:

> We can achieve a society more in accord with our fundamental values, with more opportunity, a higher total national income, a stronger democracy, and higher living standards for most individuals. It won't be easy. There are some market forces pulling us the other way. Those market forces are shaped by politics, by the rules and regulations that we as a society adopt, by the way our government financial institutions behave. We have created an economy and a society in which great wealth is amassed through rent-seeking, sometimes through direct transfers from the public to the wealthy, more often through rules that allow the wealthy to collect "rents" from the rest of society through monopoly power and other forms of exploitation . . .
>
> What's been happening in America has also been happening in many countries around the world. But it is not inevitable. It is not the inexorable workings of the market economy. There are societies that have managed things far better, even in a world where market forces and the dominant policy paradigm lead to substantial inequality because of differences in ability, effort, and luck. Those societies produce a standard of living higher than that of the United States.[30]

IT'S THE WAGES, STUPID

A lot of ink has been spilled (and more accurately, a lot of keystrokes have been typed) in discussing varied, complex ways to help more Americans enter—and stay in—the middle class. But let's cut to the chase: the most critical thing we need to do is make work pay more.

The best place to start is immediately raising the federal minimum wage to at least $15 per hour, whether an international minimum wage is enacted or (more realistically) not. Of course, doing so would help people in poverty or at the edge of it. When Arkansas raised its minimum wage by only 25 cents an hour, that enabled some working families to be able to (barely) afford disposable diapers for the first time.[31] Since many salaries that already pay above the minimum wage are set to certain percentages above the minimum wage, when minimum wages go up, salaries tend to increase for lower-middle-class workers too.

David Cooper of *Talk Poverty* estimated in 2015 that raising the federal minimum wage to $12 by 2020 would lift wages for more than 35 million workers nationwide and generate about $17 billion annually in savings to government assistance programs.[32] That would certainly be better than the abysmal federal minimum wage in 2016 of $7.25 an hour, but even $12 an hour would still equal only about $25,000 for a year of full-time work; if a single parent with three kids earned that amount, the family would still be living below the meager federal poverty line and eligible for government food benefits like SNAP. That's why, to truly change lives, we need to raise the national minimum wage to $15 per hour, as California and New York have done, and automatically index future raises to the rate of inflation. Given that nearly two-thirds of minimum wage workers are women, raising the minimum wage would also help narrow the national gender wage gap.[33]

Not only are minimum wage hikes the right thing to do, they are also wildly popular. In 2014, when minimum wage initiatives were on the ballot in four solidly red states (South Dakota, Arkansas, Alaska, and Nebraska), the wage hikes won a whopping 25 percent more of the vote than did the Democratic nominees for US Senate in those states.

As they always do, business interests will make the discredited claim that such wage hikes will reduce jobs. However, FDR explained in a 1939 speech to the National Retail Federation why wage hikes ultimately aid the business community:

> One third of our population . . . is ill-clad and ill-housed and ill-fed. That third—forty million Americans—can buy very little at the stores and, therefore, I do not have to tell you that their local stores can order very little at the factories. Some of

my friends laugh at me when I stress that, laugh at efforts to establish minimum wages and to get more purchasing power for the lowest income groups. But the little and the big store-keepers understand, and know that they will sell more goods if their customers have more money. I want, and I think I have your help, to build up the purchasing power of the average of your customers and mine.[34]

The federal government should also expand the Earned Income Tax Credit (EITC)—which currently provides additional tax refunds for low-income working families with kids—to childless adults. We should also expand the Child Tax Credit to give middle-class families with kids an even bigger boost. We should also provide tax credits to select companies—and particularly small businesses—that pay higher wages, so that there is less incentive for low-wage companies to be, in effect, subsidized by EITC and SNAP payments to their workers.

Comprehensive, humane, fair immigration reform would also lift wages by enabling tens of millions of workers to exit the shadows, making them far harder to exploit with sub-minimum wage pay and life-threatening working conditions. Let's make America even greater by being even *more* welcoming to immigrants.

I also suggest that the next president launch a "Working America" partnership, a public/private initiative somewhat similar to President Bill Clinton's welfare-to-work partnership. The president would convene corporate leaders and other wealthy Americans in order to get them each to pledge to create a set number of jobs here at home, ensure that those jobs pay a living wage, and expand career ladders to help their workers obtain promotions and higher wages in the future.

More broadly, all federal subsidies and tax breaks that go to corporations should be redesigned to focus on creating US jobs and raising US wages. Any subsidy or tax break that does not support one or both of those objectives should be eliminated.

Our leaders also need to do far more to help Americans balance work and family. For starters, Congress and the president should enact the Family and Medical Insurance Leave Act of 2015, sponsored by Senator Kirsten Gillibrand of New York and Representative Rosa DeLauro of Connecticut (Democrats, of course). That bill would provide up to 12 weeks of paid leave to care for a new child or seriously ill family member, and would be funded by joint contributions from workers and employers.[35] America, let's finally enter the rest of the civilized world that makes such leave available. The federal government also needs to significantly increase funding to make high-quality childcare affordable for all parents.

Between 20 to 40 percent of the US population lacks bank accounts and must rely on expensive check-cashing facilities and other rip-off financial services. In response, University of Georgia professor Mehrsa Baradaran has proposed creating a "central bank for the poor," which she describes as a "public version of the Federal Reserve Bank" that would "provide the same short-term credit help to individuals so that they, too, can withstand a personal credit crunch and get back on their feet," with the services delivered at existing US Postal Service offices nationwide.[36] This an excellent idea, just as long as you don't have to wait in line for two hours at the post office behind all those people buying Harry Potter stamps.

TAXES AND DEATH

As Jared Bernstein, the former chief economist for Vice President Joseph Biden, explained, "We have a real problem in regard to federal revenue. Under current law, I simply don't see us collecting what we need to meet the fiscal challenges we face—such as aging baby boomers, crumbling infrastructure, or climate change—that the private sector will not solve for us."[37]

First, let's fully restore—and make permanent—the estate tax, which the Republicans laughably labeled the "death tax." No, it is not taxing death; it is taxing the massive accumulation of wealth (often protected by other tax breaks) that is handed down to extra lucky descendants. For any pampered heirs who whine about this proposal, I'll use a retort that I stole from the Right: "Get a job!"

Second, as Robert Reich has proposed, we need to "eliminate the 'stepped-up-basis on death' rule. This obscure tax provision allows heirs to avoid paying capital gains taxes on the increased value of assets accumulated during the life of the deceased. Such untaxed gains account for more than half of the value of estates worth more than $100 million."[38]

Third, as Reich has also proposed, let's institute a small annual tax on the value of stocks and bonds, the major assets of the wealthy.

RIDING THE WALL STREET BULL

Of course, Wall Street and our entire financial sector need to be effectively regulated again so than a handful of plutocrats don't once more wreck the world economy. Joseph Stiglitz has proposed concrete, meaningful steps to do so:

> Since so much of the increase in inequality is associated with the excesses of the financial sector, it is a natural place to begin a reform program. Dodd-Frank is a start, but only a start. Here are six further reforms that are urgent: (a) Curb excessive risk taking and the too-big-to-fail and too-interconnected-to-fail financial institutions. . . . (b) Make banks more transparent, especially in their treatment of over-the-counter derivatives, which should be much more tightly restricted and should not be underwritten by government-insured financial institutions. . . . (c) Make the banks and credit card companies more competitive and ensure that they *act* competitively. . . . (d) Make it more difficult for banks to engage in predatory lending and abusive credit card practices, including by putting stricter limits on usury (excessively high interest rates). (e) Curb the bonuses that encourage excessive risk taking and shortsighted behavior. (f) Close down the offshore banking centers (and their onshore counterparts) that have been so successful both at circumventing regulations and at promoting tax evasion and avoidance.[39]

What he said.

HOW TO DEAL WITH ROBOTS

On one hand, technological advances can dramatically decrease inequality and drudgery by making so much information free and so many products cheaper, by making many difficult tasks easier, and by freeing up more time for workers. If such improvements are used to reduce the total number of hours people work—but still keep their pay high or increase it, if need be—as has been in the case in some parts of Europe, that's an ideal outcome.

On the other hand, the global elites in control of technology are often much more likely to use the high-tech improvements to slash jobs and lower wages.

Yes, we all really do need to worry about being replaced by robots or other machines.* Many US pharmacies and grocery stores have already installed automatic check-out lines through which customers can scan their purchases themselves and then pay into a machine. In a Paris McDonald's (which I entered only to use a bathroom, I swear) in 2015, there were 10 automated kiosks to take the orders, but only three humans at the counter to hand the food to customers. In manufacturing over the next decade, robots are expected to cut labor costs by 33 percent in South Korea, 25 percent in Japan, 24 percent in Canada, and 22 percent each in the United States and Taiwan.[40] Oxford University researchers forecast in 2013 that machines might be able to perform half of all US jobs within the next two decades.[41] The jobs that will be replaced by automation are mostly low-wage ones, which are usually held by people with lower educational levels.[42]

Derek Thompson, in the *Atlantic*, suggested ways industrialized societies would respond to this decline of tasks that need human workers:

---

* The robots that take away our
jobs will likely look like this. . . .   Not this.

The United States might take a lesson from Germany on job-sharing. The German government gives firms incentives to cut all their workers' hours rather than lay off some of them during hard times. So a company with 50 workers that might otherwise lay off 10 people instead reduces everyone's hours by 20 percent. Such a policy would help workers at established firms keep their attachment to the labor force despite the declining amount of overall labor . . .

The simplest way to help everybody stay busy might be government sponsorship of a national online marketplace of work (or, alternatively, a series of local ones, sponsored by local governments). Individuals could browse for large long-term projects, like cleaning up after a natural disaster, or small short-term ones: an hour of tutoring, an evening of entertainment, and an art commission. The requests could come from local governments or community associations or nonprofit groups; from rich families seeking nannies or tutors; or from other individuals given some number of credits to "spend" on the site each year.[43]

Some have suggested that we merely replace work for many unemployed workers unable to find jobs with a "universal basic income," or UBI. As writer Farhad Manjoo put it, "Rather than a job-killing catastrophe, tech supporters of UBI consider machine intelligence to be something like a natural bounty for society: The country has struck oil, and now it can hand out checks to each of its citizens. These supporters argue machine intelligence will produce so much economic surplus that we could collectively afford to liberate much of humanity from both labor and suffering."[44] But I think that would be a mistake. While I think the Right often idealizes the pleasure that workers get from their labors—especially back-breaking or repetitive labor—I do agree that, in general, humans, like all advanced animals, are happiest when they take some sort of action to support their own survival.

One better way the US government can help workers to adapt to the 21st century job market is to work hand-in-hand with the private sector and community colleges to implement a major apprenticeship system, like that in Germany, to enable those without four-year college degrees to obtain good jobs and move up the career ladder over their lifetimes. As Angela Hanks and Ethan Gurwitz from the Center for American Progress have explained,

> Apprenticeship is a proven worker training strategy that combines on-the-job training with classroom instruction, but is notably underused in the United States. For workers, apprenticeship means a real job that leads to a credential that is valued in the labor market. Apprentices are paid for their time spent on the job, accumulate little to no student debt, and are generally retained once they have successfully completed their programs. Apprenticeship completers also make middle-class wages; according to the US Department of Labor, which administers the Registered Apprenticeship system, the average wage for an individual who has completed an apprenticeship is $50,000. Over a lifetime, this can add up to approximately $300,000 more in wages and benefits compared to their peers.[45]

I would also argue strenuously that even work generally classified as "low skilled" should be paid a living wage. No matter the advances of automation, our society will continue to need such work. So I must always push back against the neoliberal argument that, if we merely made everyone well-educated, poverty would go away. You don't need a bachelor's degree to wash windows or take care of someone's children, but you should still earn enough to feed your family. And how many college-educated workers are in low-skill jobs now because they cannot find higher-paying ones that would better utilize their expensive educations?

But there is also no doubt that many future jobs will need higher levels of education, so, in order to be able to ensure that our middle class thrives in the long run, we also need to make public education in the United States work again—for every child in every neighborhood. America's post–World War II greatness was built on excellent public—not private—schools.

I won't rehash all the debates over charter schools or nonstop testing, but I will say that two of the claims of the so-called "education reform" movement are demonstrably false. Some blame all the problems with education on teachers' unions—but many of the very worst schools are in the parts of the United States (such as the South) where the teachers are least likely to be unionized. Some reformers also like to imply that they can make a school an "island of excellence"—even if every other factor in that school's neighborhood is dysfunctional and even if the local economy, criminal justice system, housing stock, nonprofit sectors, and family units are fundamentally broken. That's not true either. I dare those who make such claims to provide a single example in human history when one key societal institution has thrived while all other institutions around it failed. Fixing public education must go hand-in-hand with fixing all the nation's most pressing problems.

Also, we can't fix public education without ending child hunger (yes hunger, yet *again*!), which in 2014 affected nearly 16 million America children. The good news is that we can easily end domestic child hunger by making free school breakfast available for every student in their first-period classrooms, ensuring universal free summer meals for kids, and increasing the SNAP allotments for all families with children. Well-nourished kids are far more likely to be superstar students, and thus become superstar workers and earners.

Yet again, the evidence proves that the fates of Americans in poverty are inescapably tied to those in the middle class, and vice versa. When we bolster the middle, America, everyone wins.

Step Eight:

How to Overcome Depression with Feathers
Or, A Trope about Hope and How It Will Defeat Poverty

Hope is the thing with feathers—
That perches in the soul—
And sings the tune without the words—
And never stops—at all—
—Emily Dickinson

What happens to a dream deferred?

Does it dry up
Like a raisin in the sun?
Or fester like a sore—
And then run?
Does it stink like rotten meat?
Or crust and sugar over—
Like a syrupy sweet?

Maybe it just sags
Like a heavy load.

Or does it explode?

—Langston Hughes

Report—Poor People Pretty Much Screwed
—The Onion

Are you depressed, America? Seriously depressed? Clinically, perhaps suicidally, depressed?

Can't sleep? Can't focus? Can't work?

Well, just cheer up, will you? Buck up. Smile. Get your shit together. Get back to work.

Focus on the positive! Think of Pharrell Williams. Rainbows. Unicorns. Flowers. Preferably all at the same time.* As well-known sage Dolly Parton once admonished, "Smile! It increases your face value!"**

(Pause.)

Didn't work, huh?

Of course it didn't work. Clinical depression is usually caused by a biochemical imbalance, a deep physiological or psychological trauma, or crushing life circumstances—and often a combination of two or three of those things. True depression can't be overcome merely by thinking positive thoughts or even by reading a zillion self-help books (including this one). Depression can only be ameliorated through carefully targeted medicines, effective psychological therapy, lots of exercise and self-care, or a concrete improvement in life circumstances—and often requires a combination of those solutions.

In fact, the very *worst* advice you can give someone suffering from depression is to "cheer up." Don't believe me? Well, try saying that to a loved one who is depressed and see how that works in your relationship. Go ahead. Do it. I'll wait.

(Pause.)

So, you're sleeping on the couch now, huh? I told you so.

Likewise, the very worst advice our leaders can give you, a depressed nation, is to merely be optimistic and "believe in the American dream."

---

*

** Yes, I've watched *Steel Magnolias*. I didn't like it but couldn't avoid it in my house.

Telling a country that has lost its middle class to cheer up is like telling someone who just lost his or her spouse to hurry up and marry someone else and, for crying out loud, quit moping. That's why Americans are so angry at our leaders that we've essentially told them to sleep on the couch, or even worse, force them to sit in a debate green room with Donald Trump.

While experts believe that personal depression is often caused or exacerbated by physiological chemical imbalances, it is often the case that behavioral factors and life challenges play significant roles. If your husband dies or your company lays you off, you *should* be depressed, at least for a while.

That's why depression is often defined as "learned helplessness," a condition under which people feel that circumstances utterly beyond their control are in charge of their lives.

And when you, America, feel that you are no longer in control of your own destiny and national decline seems inevitable and irreversible, the entire country sinks into a funk. Personal and national depression are, in the end, about a lack of hope.

But this can all be solved with feathers. No. Really.

Now, mind you, feathers can be problematic. They tickle and itch. They make you sneeze. They can smell. After a really hard-fought pillow fight, they are impossible to vacuum.

But anyway, many people, from Emily Dickinson to Liberace, love—really love—feathers.[*]

I get it. Feathers are colorful. They're frivolous. They represent a lightness of spirit and the ability to instantaneously fly—and most of all, they represent the opportunity to get away from it all and leave your dreary circumstances behind.

---

[*] Liberace and Dickinson may also have had something other than feathers in common. She once wrote, "They put me in the Closet—Because they liked me 'still.'"

So yes, while clinically depressed individuals may need pharmaceuticals and professional counseling, above all we need feathers. We need hope.

Hope is the strongest engine of personal and national renewal.

But real hope won't come from holding hands and singing "Kumbaya." Real hope will come when Americans know, truly know, that concrete, tangible improvements in their daily living conditions—and in the futures of their children—are attainable.

We know what happens when people—and particularly those who are oppressed because they are low-income, of color, LGBTQ, or women—are denied hope. As Langston Hughes said, they fester, rot, then explode. They shoot each other in Baltimore. They commit suicide on the Pine Ridge Indian Reservation. They riot in Ferguson. They go on a shooting rampage at a Planned Parenthood clinic in Colorado. They take crystal meth in Appalachia.

Hopeless people either self-destruct, destroy others, or give up entirely.

Since a main cause of depression is helplessness, it should be no shock that low-income Americans—who have the least control over their destinies—have higher rates of depression and other forms of mental illness (often untreated) than wealthier Americans.

The only thing worse about living in poverty than having no money is having no hope.

You have no hope to get a job that will pay for your rent *and* your food. No hope that your heat and hot water will stay on the entire winter. No hope that you will be treated fairly by the criminal justice system. No hope that you'll live as long as the rich people in the fancy part of town. No hope for a promotion or a better neighborhood.

And, worst of all, no hope that your kids will have a better life.

And while plenty of wealthy Americans commit crimes, are violent, lack initiative, and abuse alcohol and drugs—and while most low-income Americans never commit crimes, are peaceful, work hard (at one or more jobs), stay away from drugs, and only moderately use alcohol—the hard truth is that Americans living in poverty are somewhat more likely than the rich to engage in self-destructive behavior. There are many complicated reasons why, including the very-present and ever-harmful impacts of racism, sexism, and classism. But the two central reasons why low-income Americans can be more likely to self-destruct are actually pretty simple: lack of money and lack of hope. Their relationship with you, America, is fundamentally ruptured. And once again, America, it's mostly *your* fault.

CO-DEPENDENCY, FORCED PASSIVITY, AND THE DEATH OF HOPE

America, you force low-income people to bow to the daily whims of a vast web of governmental and nonprofit social service agencies. Although created with mostly good intentions—and staffed largely by idealists who are sincerely trying to help—these massive bureaucracies are often called "command-and-control structures" because their detailed rules and regulations radiate from centralized federal administrative offices to centralized state administrative offices to city or county offices and then to neighborhood offices that actually serve clients. At each stop along the way, the bureaucracies accumulate inertia and further slow their actions. Collectively, these government and nonprofit agencies employ hundreds of thousands of people. They usually utilize antiquated, staff-heavy organizational structures and rarely employ the most modern technologies. While most aspects of modern living have been utterly transformed by technological improvements, visiting a government social service office is often like stepping back in time to 1970.*

Robert L. Woodson, Sr., a black conservative anti-poverty activist, has written, "Since the War on Poverty was launched in the 1960s, a virtual poverty-industrial complex has emerged, staffed by armies of psychologists, social workers, and counselors . . . Priorities have followed from government grant possibilities, which has meant that

---

* I couldn't afford to pay for the rights for a more modern picture, but many social service offices still look like this, I swear.

providers are rewarded not for solving problems but, in effect, for pro-
liferating them: The larger and more diversified the problem set is, the
larger the grants and salaries must be, and the more extensive the staff
to justify it all."[46]

While Woodson wildly exaggerates the percentage of funding that
goes into bureaucratic overhead instead of benefits, and consistently
overlooks the tremendous successes of safety net programs, there's
a kernel of truth to his point. While government program managers
are mostly woefully underpaid, some heads of "nonprofit" social services groups now earn more than the $400,000 annual salary of the
US president. While it is doubtful that many people who work in this
system purposely perpetuate poverty to keep their jobs, the deeply
entrenched nature of the social service status quo makes it far more
difficult for people within it to envision and fight for fundamental over-
hauls of the system.

Meanwhile, America, you consistently provide your most vulnerable residents with sub-par service. If a wealthy dowager or even a
middle-class electrician walks into a department store and applies for
a credit card, he or she can usually be approved for credit on the spot.
Yet, if a hungry person walks into a government social service agency
to apply for SNAP, the state or county can, under federal law, take up
to 30 days to determine whether they are poor enough to get benefits.
That 30-day deadline was created in 1977, before e-mail was available
and when bureaucracies still communicated through tan internal mail
envelopes, which inexplicably had air holes.*

Not only do such old-style systems take precious time away from
struggling families while denying them needed benefits, they cost taxpayers a bundle due to their inefficiency. (Even nonprofit agencies are

---

*

usually funded by government grants and contracts, and are subsidized through funders that receive tax deductions for donating to them, so they also waste taxpayer dollars when they are also behind the times and inefficient.)

Perhaps the most harmful defining feature of the social service status quo is the passivity forced on its recipients. If you live in poverty, you usually must go exactly where others want you to go, do what they want you to do, and do so at the precise time they want you to do it. You must quietly wait in line, rarely being told how long the experience will take, and even more rarely given an appointment so you can come back at a time convenient for you. You must accept whatever paltry amount of food, money, or other assistance is offered, and you must act grateful for that on top of it all.

America, the people who staff your more than 40,000 nonprofit soup kitchens and food pantries nationwide are extraordinarily big-hearted people. Most are unpaid volunteers. Many have been volunteering for decades and often take money out of their own pockets to feed their neighbors, even though they frequently come from modest means themselves. These emergency food programs help, just a bit, to fill in the holes in the government safety net, and the lives of hungry families would be even worse without them. Cherish and honor these selfless servants, America.

But at the same time, we must also consider what life is like on the receiving end for the people obtaining such services. At even the best-run food charities, getting help is usually a demeaning, disempowering experience. Clients are often forced to accept pre-selected food that someone else picked out for them, whether the recipient has a special medically restricted diet, whether they have no cooking facilities, or whether they happen to hate rice and beans. The system turns adults into infants, requiring someone else to feed them. And too few of the programs empower the recipients to help run or staff the programs.

Likewise in government programs, low-income Americans are also usually passive recipients of aid. Some programs incredibly discourage recipients from pursuing higher education. The system tries to create co-dependency of the worst sort, dampening down the natural desire of people to work hard, use their ingenuity, and express their independence. So much for men and women fighting for their own dignity and humanity. The message you send, America, is something very different: Just go away. Just give up. Or remain an infant forever, but one we never have to look at or think about. Despite all these obstacles, many impoverished Americans are so strong and so determined that they are somehow able to maintain their self-respect and continue to fight for their futures despite all attempts to strip them of both, but it's a constant struggle.

Dr. Mariana Chilton is a progressive anti-poverty researcher who created a pioneering program in Philadelphia to empower low-income women to document their own lives in photographs and helped them speak out to the media and to elected officials to call for policy improvements. She has said that she's learned from her work that the "welfare system is a form of slavery." Some on the far Right also use the word "slavery" in relation to the social service safety net.[47] * Unlike conservatives who claim any problems with the safety net are caused by the recipients' laziness and dependency, Chilton argues the root causes of programmatic dysfunction are "racism, discrimination, and misogyny." It is notable, though, that both sides agree that the anti-poverty status quo is fundamentally broken.

Even the most well-intentioned efforts can have unintended negative results. One example is the growing trend for food charities to create "backpack programs" through which low-income children receive school backpacks filled with canned and boxed food to take home to eat over weekends and vacations.** What could possibly be wrong with something so positive? After all, hungry kids are fed. But few of the sponsors of these programs stop to think about the impact upon the

---

* I think it's a bit over-the-top to use a truly radioactive word like "slavery" to address anything other than its specific, historic meaning—people held in chattel servitude due to their skin color—but emotions do run high when people argue these issues and I understand why debaters on both sides feel they need to use words with shock value, although I still don't agree with them doing so.

**

parents. It's one thing for their kids to eat someone else's food when they're away at school or at a summer meals site, but it's another thing entirely for their kids to eat someone else's charity food in their *own* homes. Many parents are surely grateful for this help, but, somewhere in the backs of their minds, they are being forcefully reminded that they are incapable of providing for their own children. Researcher Edward A. Frongillo, Jr. has found that hungry children sometimes falsely tell their parents they are full so their hungry parents will eat the food that is remaining. Imagine the humiliation and pain that a hungry parent must suffer when he or she is forced to choose between: a) sitting by while their children eat but they themselves don't eat, or b) or asking their children to share a little bit of their food with them. Many hungry parents do indeed go without eating themselves to ensure that there is enough food for the children, but backpack programs only exacerbate that horrible parental dilemma. The parent-child relationship is turned upside-down. In addressing one problem (kids without food over a weekend or vacation), such programs sometimes create other, different problems, sapping families of pride and will.

Economic and psychological forces are always intertwined. For economically struggling Americans, the inability to earn enough money to support their families simply crushes hope.

Fortunately, there is a better way.

MOVING FROM OWING TO OWNING

I continue to preach that progressives must propose a fundamentally new way of governing—using mainstream values to achieve progressive goals. Core to such radical centrism is replacing the politics of resentment with what I call "aspirational politics"—which would convince Americans—including middle-class families who worry about falling into poverty, low-income families trying to climb into the middle class, and new immigrants looking to grab a slice of the economic pie—that their hard work will once again (as it did in previous generations) pay off with a chance to fulfill the hopes and dreams to which they aspire.

While the most obvious difference between wealthy and non-wealthy Americans is that the non-rich earn less income, an even far bigger dif-

ference is that the non-wealthy have bigger debt loads, own less, and
have miniscule financial assets. *Half* of all Americans have *zero net
worth*. According to the Pew Research Center, "the gap between America's upper-income and middle-income families has reached its highest
level on record. In 2013, the median wealth of the nation's upper-income families ($639,400) was nearly seven times the median wealth
of middle-income families ($96,500), the widest wealth gap in 30
years since the Federal Reserve began collecting this data. America's
upper-income families have a median net worth that is nearly 70 times
that of the country's lower-income families, also the widest wealth gap
between these families in 30 years."[48] The wealth and home ownership
gaps by race are even vaster. America, your income gap is a deep valley,
but your wealth gap is the Grand Canyon.

When wealthy and upper-middle-class families have assets to fall
back on if they are down on their luck, they can always sell a boat,
cash in an investment, or draw down on a savings account. But when
people with debt instead of assets are down on their luck, they have no
cushion, much less a full sofa of support, to fall back on.

Wealth usually generates more wealth, and poverty usually fosters
more poverty. Of the wealthiest fifth of Americans, 87 percent own
their own homes; of the lowest-income fifth of Americans, only 39 percent do.[49] When you pay down a mortgage for your home, you usually
build up a long-term investment for your own family, but when you
pay rent, all you are doing is increasing the wealth of your landlord's
family.

Due to the magic of compounded interest, people who start with a lot
of money in the bank almost always end up with a lot more money in
the bank. The stock market has always risen over time, and real estate
values almost always increase. In contrast, people in poverty have to
pay extra for basic things, such as check-cashing services, furniture
rentals, and storage facilities.

Public policies only widen this divide. The Corporation for Enterprise Development has found that more than half of the $400
billion provided annually in federal asset-building subsidies—policies
intended to promote homeownership, retirement savings, economic
investment, and access to college—flow to the wealthiest 5 percent of

taxpaying households. Meanwhile, the bottom 60 percent of taxpayers receive only 4 percent of these benefits, and the bottom 20 percent of taxpayers receive almost nothing. Black and Latino households are disproportionately among those receiving little or no benefit. Unless key policies are restructured, the racial wealth gap—and wealth inequality in general—will continue to grow.[50]

For instance, the federal mortgage interest tax deduction cost US taxpayers about $76 billion in 2015. Households with incomes between $40,000 and $75,000 obtained average tax savings of just $523, while households with incomes above $250,000 enjoyed an average write-off of $5,459, or more than 10 times as much.[51] Families who are too poor to own a home get no help at all from this program, yet billionaires can also take deductions for a vacation home in addition to their primary home.

The rich get richer. The broke get broker.

In order to eliminate US poverty once and for all—and build a harmonious, long-term relationship between struggling families and the nation—we need to enable all families to accumulate assets and move from owing to *owning*.

America, you could move beyond your current stalemate in poverty politics by enacting an "Aspiration Empowerment Agenda," which would give all families the opportunity to advance their dreams through learning, earning, and saving their way out of poverty. We must move beyond the conservatives' selective focus on those rare stories of poor people who climb their way out of poverty, supposedly on their own, against all odds, just as we must move beyond the limited liberal focus on those rare people with so many problems they can't possibly move to self-sufficiency no matter how much help they get. We need a clearheaded new approach, based on the reality that the majority of struggling Americans could climb out—and stay out—of poverty, but only with significant help.

The basic idea of empowering low-income people to develop assets has been around for decades and has been advanced by a number of national and grassroots organizations. But we need to go bigger and bolder, fully realizing our "Responsibility-for-All" ideal. A full Aspiration Empowerment Agenda would provide an array of government-funded benefits and work supports at levels higher than what is available today, sufficient to enable low-income families to develop assets and move out of poverty. The agenda would emphasize the importance of personal responsibility for *all* members of society (including the wealthiest), but also design public policies that reward— not punish—low-income people for positive behavior.

All federal and state social programs and tax provisions would need to be reformed to ensure that they aid low- and moderate-income Americans, not just those at the top. As Lauryn Hill put it, "We need to change the focus from the richest to the brokest." We must also make it easier for all families—including those that obtain means-tested benefits—to save their money so they can pay for a down payment on a first home, start a business, pay for higher education for their children, or build a retirement account. We should eliminate provisions in means-tested social programs that automatically kick people off the rolls when they get raises at their jobs, get better jobs, or save money, and replace them with benefits that taper off slowly as people achieve greater economic security.

One example of the assets accumulation concept is the federal Individual Development Account (IDA) program, proposed by Professor Michael Sherraden, popularized by the Progressive Policy Institute (which gave me my first job in DC), and enacted into law in the 1990s by an ideological odd couple: then-President Bill Clinton and then-chair of the House Budget Committee (and later governor of Ohio), archconservative John Kasich. These accounts enable low-income families to match their own savings with funds from government and private sector sources in order to save for job training, home ownership, or business start-ups. Unfortunately, IDAs are still only available in a few dozen small pilot locations, and too few people have been able to utilize the existing IDAs because most people in poverty now lack even minimal disposable incomes to save. Furthermore, even though IDA projects are very labor-intensive to operate, most of the money given to nonprofit groups to run them is set aside for the benefits themselves, with little or no administrative funding going to the organizations. Thus, whether the country continues to use IDAs—or creates another type of savings-matching program—the federal government should make such accounts universally available as a benefit for people in poverty, both increasing the matching funds for families and also providing more realistic funding for administrative support to the entities that operate such efforts.

America, your national leaders should also create a federal "Kids Accounts" program in which every child born in the nation automatically receives a savings account with a small deposit in it. Each child's parents would be provided long-term incentives (with additional rewards for low-income families) to save more for education, job training, home purchases, or retirement. In the United Kingdom, a Labour government created such a program in 2005, but it was scrapped by the Conservatives there in 2011 in order to save money over the short-term, well before the program could prove its long-term advantages. If such a program was created in the US and if it were truly universal, then it could earn broad-based support from the public, as has been the case with other universal programs, such as Social Security.* If you want to prove that you value *all* your children, America, put your money where your mouth is, and enable *all* kids to start their lives with a nest egg.

The assets agenda proposed here would also build upon the good work that some state and local governments and nonprofit groups are already conducting to ensure greater availability of low-cost banking services. We must also crack down on payday loans, high-fee check-cashing facilities, and other financial services that rip off poor folks.

America, you should also dramatically ramp up governmental and private efforts to provide microloans to start very small businesses, so-called "microenterprises." Helping someone open his or her own shoeshine stand or sidewalk food cart or home-based computer repair service could help budding entrepreneurs enter the economic mainstream and perhaps later expand their efforts by hiring employees. What's more American than a Chinese fried dumpling truck, growing into a brick-and-mortar restaurant, and then expanding into a chain of restaurants across a city or even across the entire country, turning an immigrant family with very little means into a financially secure household name?**

I'll even agree with the conservative critique that too many people

---

* In order to offset the fact that some wealthy children would also benefit from this, the US should also restore inheritance taxes for the rich to the much higher rates they were in the past.
** I do look forward to the day when the golden woks of the Zhu Ji dumpling chain replace the golden arches as the nation's top food symbol.

starting out in trades and starting small businesses face too many government licensing requirements and that some regulatory and tax burdens are too heavy. Worker and public safety, wage protection, and environmental regulations should be tougher than ever, but any regulations or fees that are more about earning income for the government and protecting jobs for bureaucrats should be rolled back. (Happy now, Koch brothers?)

If all these steps are taken together, the agenda would be both revolutionary in its ambition and mainstream in its values. The goal is to give all families the tools they need to achieve and maintain at least a middle-class lifestyle—with a good job, a safe place to live, and a hopeful future for their kids and grandkids.

In a "normal" political climate, efforts such as these, which promote both personal responsibility and economic opportunity, would be supported by liberals, conservatives, and moderates alike as bold, common-sense solutions to poverty. But these are not normal political times. Even reasonable, mainstream reforms are now doomed by the nation's political paralysis, which is caused mostly by the intractability and illogic of the Right. That's why, in other chapters, this book argues that it is the job of *every* American to take concrete actions to fix our political system.

Beyond the challenging politics of getting an assets agenda implemented, a major caveat to this type of program is that, even if it is fully enacted, an assets agenda will only work in the context of broader economic and poverty policies that increase what people earn and decrease what they pay for basic necessities. For instance, if a family earns $20,000 per year in salaries but pays $24,000 in rent, then not only won't they be able to develop assets, they will go into debt. Thus, an absolute prerequisite for assets building to succeed is ensuring more jobs, higher wages, and an adequate safety net that helps families afford necessities such as food, housing, childcare, utilities, transportation, healthcare, medicine, and clothing.

PUTTING HOPE INTO THE PALM OF YOUR HAND

America, the time is long overdue for you to replace the failing, antiquated social service landline status quo with an up-to-date smartphone benefits access system. We must use modern technologies and business practices to simplify the lives and boost the long-term self-sufficiency of our most struggling neighbors. One powerful way to do this is for our federal, state, and local governments to create HOPE (Health, Opportunity, and Personal Empowerment) accounts and action plans that I am proposing here. Building upon the Aspiration Empowerment Agenda, a HOPE program can transform national anti-poverty activities by incorporating both a liberal focus on economic mobility and investments in proven safety net programs with a conservative focus on personal responsibility and reduced bureaucracy. Most critically, HOPE would enable the lowest-income families to simultaneously obtain both economic resources and a long-term vision for prosperity and happiness. This proposal would help strapped Americans dream big dreams again, and access the resources and tools necessary to make those dreams a reality. "Responsibility-for-All" isn't just rhetoric; putting it into action would not only increase hope and confidence but would also give everyone a stake in their country's future.

Here's how HOPE would work: The federal government would authorize HOPE accounts and action plans that combine improved technology, streamlined case management, and coordinated access to multiple federal, state, city, and nonprofit programs. Participating low-income workers could voluntarily choose to also have their paychecks deposited directly into the accounts, which would be held by private banks and credit unions that volunteered to participate in the program. Families could also use the accounts to increase their savings, which would be matched by government and private sources, incorporating both IDAs and Kids Accounts. Job training and placement services would be modernized to connect real people with real jobs, and the locations of such services would be easily accessed through the accounts online. All these efforts would work together in harmony to better give people in poverty the tools they need to take charge of their futures and to implement long-term plans to climb into—and stay in—the middle class. If the federal government fails to do so, states or localities could step up to the plate with similar programs.

Specifically, HOPE accounts would enable families to use any smartphone, tablet, or computer to learn about the public and philanthropic programs for which they are eligible—including aid to improve

A BETTER ALTERNATIVE:
ONLINE HOPE ACCOUNTS

health, nutrition, job training and placement, housing, income, etc.—
and then apply for all of these programs at once from the convenience
of their device. If supporting documents need to be submitted with
the application, then families could take pictures of those documents

and submit the pictures with the application. A surprising number of low-income people already have smartphones and/or home computers, not because they are luxuries, but because they are essential tools of learning and working in modern America. But families that don't own a smartphone, tablet, or computer could be provided one, along with a subsidized low-cost Internet or cell phone data access plan.* Those who are uncomfortable with or unable to use technology could go to a library, government office, or nonprofit agency to be helped through the system. For the elderly, people who are homebound, or who otherwise who can't access the technology for any reason, government or nonprofit employees and/or AmeriCorps national service participants (or Service Patriots America members) could make home visits to help. As noted previously, our existing national service program should be expanded dramatically to aid these and other vital efforts.

To make it easier to access healthcare, HOPE accounts could also clearly specify medical benefits and any out-of-pocket costs in plain language for each of the user's eligible health plans and empower participants to easily select the plan that works best for them.

The accounts would also enable working families to file for federal EITC refunds, and in states and localities with their own supplemental EITC payments low-income taxpayers could simultaneously file for those as well. Since the accounts will already have posted online all the financial information needed to file for those payments, families could easily do so with this program, thereby saving the time and money they would otherwise have to spend on third-party tax filing services.

Technology has fundamentally revamped the lives of most Americans, usually for the better. Now it's time for technology to also revolutionize the lives of our lowest-income inhabitants.

While HOPE accounts are a new idea, the concept builds upon existing programs, such as the IDA program, and incorporates technological improvements in social services delivery that some forward-thinking states, cities, and counties are already implementing. For example, in New York City, the government is already using updated technologies to allow families to apply online for multiple government

---

* As I previously mentioned, the federal government should do more to ensure high-speed Internet connections throughout the country, but especially in rural areas.

benefits through a portal called "Access NYC",[52] which allows users to pre-screen their eligibility for an array of government programs and provides online applications for some. New York has even started a pilot project to allow people to apply for SNAP and cash assistance (but not other programs) by smartphone. But even in New York, the number of benefits to which someone can actually apply online remains limited, and applicants still must follow different procedures and timelines to access different programs and still must visit or call multiple offices before the various application processes are completed.

Building on such innovations, but moving beyond them, HOPE accounts would enable families to rapidly apply for—and quickly learn if they are accepted into—*all* federal, state, and local government programs, as well as offer users information for a wide variety of services provided by nonprofit groups. HOPE accounts would also include a calculator system to help families understand the financial impact of receiving one benefit upon other possible benefits they may be getting.

All program benefit funds would go into the same system, with health-care, food, housing, and other specific benefits accounted for separately from the cash. Overall funding for these safety net programs should be at the very least maintained, or preferably increased. Federal entitlements, such as SNAP or Medicaid, are benefits that must be given to anyone who qualifies; the programs do not require annual appropriations from Congress and the amount spent by the feds increases when our country goes through tough economic times and shrinks when more people are able to work and support themselves. Under my suggested system, these benefits would continue to be classified as entitlements, which people would still have a legal right to obtain.

Families would also be encouraged to put their own cash savings into the accounts, which could then be matched by the government. Any cash in the account set aside for education, job training, starting a business, or buying a home would be non-taxable. Sure, that's a bit complicated, but it's still a heck of a lot easier for a family than figuring all this out on their own, considering they would be filing their taxes through the program as well. And if they still need help, some government and nonprofit social workers would remain available to help them navigate the system.

HOPE accounts would allow low-income families to easily access and monitor—in one central online account—the status, amounts, and recertification deadlines for all their benefits and savings. They could also use the accounts to pay all bills online, saving outrageous check-cashing fees and enormous amounts of time traveling to pay bills in cash.

The accounts could also include a budgeting function to give families real-time cash flow data and long-term financial planning information, including helping calculate how much they would lose in interest on credit cards versus how much they would gain in interest by saving more. The accounts would offer a calendar and scheduling function, enabling families to keep track of all job search, work, family, and school obligations, as well as any social service filing or appointment dates.*

Instead of a vast army of government and nonprofit caseworkers in charge of micromanaging the lives of poor people, low-income adults would become, in effect, their *own* case managers. With this newfound power, people would be able spread their wings and take flight.

But to intrude on this love fest just as bit, America, I have to admit that these new apps and social service computer systems will be extraordinarily challenging to build and even more challenging to integrate with each other, especially given the current, antiquated state of government social service computer systems, as well as how much the feds botched the launch of the Obamacare web site. To further complicate matters, these new systems must combine ease of client access with very strict protections against fraud and theft, not easy considerations to balance. That's why the nation's top tech leaders and companies would need to challenge themselves to work together with government to make this a reality. Dear Mr. Gates, Zuckerberg, or Bezos: if you successfully accomplish this, we'll add you to Mt. Rushmore—or if you prefer, we'll carve a new monument near Silicon Valley on one of the Santa Cruz Mountains.** Alternatively, the White House could direct a competition—with input from the Departments of Health and Human Services, Housing and Urban Development, and Agriculture—that

---

* Careful security and privacy protections would need to be put in place, so that only the family, and not the government, nonprofit, or banking partners, would be able to see the private financial and appointment information.

** Dear environmentalists: just kidding about the Santa Cruz Mountains part. Please don't send protesters in rafts to surround my apartment.

would provide an additional monetary reward for the company that built the best app to fuse all these programs.

ACTION PLANS TO RECLAIM THE FUTURE

Helping struggling families save time and money is a good start, America, but that's not enough: they still need clear aspirations for the future. That's why low-income Americans should be given the option of partnering in more depth with government and nonprofit organizations by voluntarily agreeing to long-term HOPE action plans that will specify exactly how all parties will work together to help the families earn, learn, and save better in order to ensure greater economic opportunity for themselves and their children. The idea behind the action plans is to ensure that all the programs and people involved are working together in a long-term, positive relationship for the purpose of ensuing upward mobility.

How might a HOPE action plan work in real life? In direct contrast to plans proposed by Paul Ryan that would force families to sign contracts to take actions that would waste their time and sap their dignity while giving them no additional resources to solve their concrete problems, HOPE action plans would be voluntary and could empower families who agree to them to better organize their time and focus their activities on productive endeavors while providing them extra resources to do so. Some plans could be short-term, over just a year or two, aimed at helping families achieve very basic goals, such as avoiding homelessness and hunger. But they could be long-term as well, with far more ambitious goals for upward mobility.

For example, a single mother of two young children could voluntarily enter into a 10-year plan jointly with her city government's social service agency and with a local United Way. The plan would include yearly benchmarks of how the mother would use increased resources provided by the plan to boost her jobs skills, increase her earnings, improve the housing situation for her family, obtain more nutritious food, and begin to put money aside to help her children pay for college. Once the specific goals are set, the specific actions each entity would be required to take in order for the mother to meet her goals—as well as the money and other resources that would need to be allocated for these actions from the family, the government, and the nonprofit partners—would all be spelled out in the plan. Yes, the mother would need to work hard and sacrifice by saving more, but knowing that government and charities also had a stake and belief in her success, and knowing that she would ultimately advance herself and her family, she'd be glad to do it. It's that hope thing at work again.

This approach may *sound* like traditional social work case management, which often is based on the patronizing belief that social workers—who a little too frequently sit in condescending judgment of other people's life choices—know what's better for low-income people than low-income people themselves. Yet the HOPE approach is entirely different than traditional casework, and is more in line with the kind of guidance a wealthy person gets from a financial advisor who simply works clients through all the available options to boost their economic well-being.

Unlike the mandatory, one-sided contracts proposed by Paul Ryan, under which only the low-income people would be held accountable, under the HOPE proposal, *all* the entities involved—government agencies, nonprofit organizations, and low-income participants—would be *equally* accountable. Unlike Ryan's plan to strip struggling families of agency, the HOPE plan would instead empower them by ensuring that the contract included enforceable language making government and nonprofit agencies accountable to participants for keeping up their part of the bargain.

As I'll say over and over again, *everyone* who receives government help—which means *everyone* in America, from bankers who get government bailouts, to truckers who ride over government roads, to defense contractors, to students who obtain Pell Grants or Stafford Loans, to farmers who obtain federal subsidies, to recipients of anti-poverty benefits—should be required to exercise certain responsibilities in exchange for their government aid.

In the case of HOPE, this new civic compact of mutual responsibility would be a boon to both people in poverty and middle-class taxpayers, restoring each side's faith in the other. America, if you believe in families again, they will believe in you again.

Now, isn't the HOPE approach much better than the social services status quo? Low-income Americans will be happier because they can, all by themselves, receive help in one centralized location instead of dozens of places. They can plan their own futures. They can collect their own feathers, wear them however they like, then fly wherever they want, however they want—reducing depression as they begin exercising their newfound freedom.

Government and nonprofit agency workers will be happier because they are more effective. Taxpayers will be happier because their dollars are used more wisely.[*]

Moreover, HOPE would empower families by giving them the necessary tools to take charge of their own futures—allowing them to obtain concrete tools to "pull themselves up by the bootstraps." By promoting personal responsibility and a more efficient government, as well as increased economic opportunity and easier ways to get government aid, HOPE advances both conservative and liberal priorities. By superseding today's stultified ideological debate, HOPE would actually be radically centrist, prompting massive progressive changes in American society, but would do so based on mainstream values widely embraced by the public. It should be a model for all our governmental policies and a ladder to achieve the American dream, bringing the entire populace together again.

It's finally time to sing "Kumbaya."[**]

NOT SO FAST: OBJECTIONS FROM THOSE WHO HATE ICE CREAM AND HOT FUDGE

America, your joyful celebration won't last long. As common-sense as these reforms are, and as likely as they are to be warmly embraced by the vast majority of the American people, some traditional conservatives as well as some traditional liberals will oppose them, albeit for very different reasons.

---

[*] That's more happiness than Pharrell Williams, unicorns, and rainbows, combined with cute puppies romping in a field of flowers, can bring to you, America.

[**]

Some conservatives fear that an approach like HOPE would make it easier for low-income people to get government assistance, thereby increasing government spending. But HOPE would reduce government bureaucracy and paperwork and ensure that more of the money spent goes to helping families instead of bureaucracies, all of which are professed conservative goals.

Other conservatives will argue getting government help *should* be a difficult, shameful process, and making it less so would only increase dependency on government. But it's inconsistent for the Right to argue for government to be less intrusive in the lives of most people but more intrusive in the lives of low-income Americans. Plus, by freeing up more time for parents to work, study, and spend time with their families, HOPE is "pro-family," "pro-work," and "pro-education"—and thus would *reduce* long-term dependency.

Some liberals will be wary because, at first blush, these accounts and plans *appear* to be similar to the punitive contracts and safety net–slashing block grant proposals advanced by Paul Ryan and other conservatives. But God is in the details, and in reality, the HOPE accounts and action plans would be 180 degrees different in both intention and implementation from the conservative schemes.

Ryan has used his anti-poverty plans as a cover for trying to decimate existing government benefits for low-income families. In contrast, HOPE would provide anti-poverty benefits far above the current levels, so true self-sufficiency could be achieved. Unlike the Ryan and other GOP proposals that would replace existing federal programs, the HOPE accounts and plans would be *in addition to* existing government efforts. Unlike Ryan's proposal, which assumes that his proposed opportunity grants can somehow succeed even if the rest of the safety net is slashed and the economy is still failing, this proposal assumes that HOPE accounts and plans can only be effective in tandem with a strong safety net and the broad-based economic growth that creates jobs and raises wages. HOPE would also end the arbitrary benefits cliffs that kick in when families marginally increase their incomes as they struggle to enter—and remain in—the middle class. Ideally, the HOPE initiative would be funded robustly enough by the government and the philanthropic sectors so that *all* those ends could be achieved.

Liberals may also worry that HOPE might undercut public employees and their unions, which provide liberal candidates with vital troops, votes, and donations. Given that the Scott Walkers and John Kasichs of the world have used "reforms" to try to slash government jobs and destroy public sector unions, and given that mass layoffs of public employees only further decimate the middle class and increase poverty, such concerns are understandable. That is why it is vital to make it crystal clear that the HOPE proposal is based on the assumption that most public employees are dedicated, underpaid, and have a right to unions that bargain collectively on their behalf. Under this proposal, some social workers would keep jobs similar to their existing ones, in order to answer questions about HOPE over the phone or from clients who still prefer face-to-face meetings. While HOPE would indeed eliminate most other government positions that currently exist to handle paperwork and interview clients, this proposal recommends that virtually all the employees holding those positions continue to hold public sector jobs—at the same pay levels at the very least—but over time be transitioned into more useful functions, such as training and placing low-income adults into living-wage jobs, staffing universal Pre-K programs, or aiding homebound seniors. I would argue that public employees themselves would be happier if they spent less time filling out paperwork and more time directly aiding the public.

Some liberals might worry that merely suggesting that government programs can be improved or that low-income Americans have personal responsibility for their own futures reinforces conservative messages, effectively giving "aid and comfort to the enemy." Some might argue that it's inconsistent for anti-poverty advocates like Mariana Chilton and Joel Berg to, on the one hand, effusively praise safety net programs like SNAP, but on the other hand, point out their significant flaws. Those arguments are also reasonable, but ultimately they are not convincing. There's nothing inconsistent in pointing out that programs significantly improve the lives of recipients but could help beneficiaries even more if they were modernized. Just as even generally solid relationships can always be improved by both sides thoroughly addressing life realities (including painful ones), so too social services can be further improved through an unflinching examination of their current defects.

Some progressives might worry that funneling all anti-poverty funding into one program might make it easier in the future for conservatives to cut them. Yet the recent trend of omnibus budget deals has *already* allowed conservatives to cut all anti-poverty programs at once with tools such as the sequestration process (which was, I am obligated to point out, suggested—though as a last resort and a threat, that later blew up in their faces—by the Obama administration).

Taking no action because you are afraid things could get even worse makes little sense. That's sort of like when two people are in front of a firing squad about to be executed, and one asks the other if they should ask for a cigarette, only to hear the response, "Nah, I don't want to make them mad."

Taking the ostrich approach by ignoring both public concerns and real-life problems is a losing strategy, both substantively and politically. In contrast, FDR, the most successful progressive leader in US history, called for "bold, persistent experimentation" because he understood that continually modernizing liberal programs was the best way to save them.

The most effective political defense is an offense. The best way to push back against possible cuts is to fight for *more* funding, which is why progressives should be clear that the HOPE system would need *more* money than the current system.

Because it would build public confidence in government safety net programs, HOPE could actually *increase* the public's willingness to pay for them. While voters tend to give conflicting answers to pollsters as to whether they support increased funding on anti-poverty programs, when they get into the privacy of the polling booth, they tend to vote (especially in lower turnout, off-year, elections) for Senate, House, and gubernatorial candidates who demonize the safety net and promise lower taxes and smaller government. But if the public believed that more up-front expenditures would actually ensure long-term self-sufficiency for families, and thereby reduce the need for the programs and spending over time, they would be far more likely to embrace them. In the end, though, the question that is most important is whether HOPE would make life better or worse—in both the short-term and the long-term—for the people the programs are intended to help.

So let's ask low-income Americans a basic question:

DO YOU WANT TO REPLACE THIS...

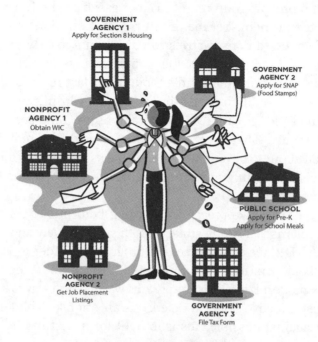

...WITH THIS?

The overwhelming answer from low-income Americans would be a resounding "yes."

YOUR CHANGE IS GONNA COME

Hope is not necessarily about having all the feathers in your possession at once. It is also about dreaming how you will someday get them. Hope is a mixture of exaltation and expectation. It doesn't mean you ignore past setbacks and the pain they brought, but it means that— deep down—you believe you can eventually overcome their legacy and fly away. America, you can hear all of that in Sam Cooke's "A Change is Gonna Come," our national anthem of hope.

The song begins with sorrowful strings and a slow, loping bass line, leading to the howling tale of a man born homeless by a river, who has been on the run his whole life. We can only imagine the realities from which he's been running. He says living is too difficult but he is scared of death, unsure of whether there's a heaven that will offer redemption. Haunting horns and a martial beat kick in, as Jim Crow laws prevent him from so much as spending time in public in his hometown. He then pleads for help from his brother, who responds by whacking him down.* He contemplates early death, a fate for so many men of color. But then, in a marked shift in lyrical and musical tones—he finds some previously buried storehouse of hope—and he concludes, in a soaring voice that he is confident that he will be able to persevere became he knows that change is coming.

In just a few lines, he goes from believing he may die soon, to believing his life might improve, to knowing he would prevail. What changed was that the narrator decided to take matters into his own hands and move from passive suffering or begging into taking concrete, assertive actions that would enable him and his brothers to fly away to build a better life for themselves. He moved from depression to exhilaration by determining his own flight path.

America, you too can come to understand that when even the most

---

* It is unclear whether "brother" refers to an actual sibling or merely to a fellow African American, but there is no question that his "brother" letting him down is a metaphor for all of society letting us all down.

marginalized people demand that government and society enable them to empower themselves, hope and positive change are not only possible, but inevitable. When people have power over their *own* lives and agency to use their feathers however they please, progress will come. My *yes*, it certainly will.

Step Nine:

Beyond Foodies
Ensuring a Cornucopia
for All of Us

"It doesn't matter what side you are on—everybody's gotta eat."
—Frank Underwood, *House of Cards*

I love living in Brooklyn, especially when it comes to food. My apartment is just three blocks away from the Grand Army Plaza Greenmarket, one of the best in the country, where you can shop for seasonal heirloom tomatoes, squash blossoms, and garlic scapes just harvested from upstate New York and New Jersey farms; wild-caught Long Island scallops; and crisper than crisp Hudson Valley apples. My neighborhood has it all, including fake local maple syrup. Elsewhere in Brooklyn, I can go to any number of weekly food festivals and gorge on homemade sausages, artisanal grilled cheese sandwiches, hand-crafted cold sesame noodles, and neighborhood-fermented kombucha. I can get Polish pierogies in Greenpoint, Salvadoran pupusas in Red Hook, Bosnian burgers in Bushwick, or Chinese dumplings in Sunset Park—all of which are world-class in quality.*

Today's Brooklyn is indeed "Foodie Heaven." I—and many others of my middle- and upper-income neighbors—can obtain all those tidbits because we have enough money and time to do so. Yet many of our fellow Brooklynites aren't so fortunate. In the years 2012 to 2014, an average of 569,659 Brooklyn residents (about the combined populations of Des Moines and Wichita) were living on the brink of hunger, unable to afford enough food. One-quarter of Brooklyn children lived in these food-insecure homes. For them, Brooklyn is a food hell.

America, the rest of the nation is equally populated by food "haves"

---

* When I go overboard, I become the fat anti-hunger guy. [No picture available].

and food "have nots." I won't give you a complete plan to end hunger here (because I'm running out of pages in this book and I want to force you to buy my first volume, which does have such a strategy), but beyond just the hunger issue, here is a basic outline of what we need to do to ensure that all Americans—of all income levels—are able to access a cornucopia of affordable, nutritious, sustainably-grown food:

▶ Decrease poverty and increase wages, so everyone can afford to buy the food they need and want for their own families. (Yes, I've made that point zillions of times in this book, but who ever said subtlety was my strong suit—or any suit of mine, for that matter.)

▶ Increase and expand the SNAP program—in particular, make the benefits more available to low-income working families. Make it easier to use SNAP benefits at farmers markets and Community Supported Agriculture (CSA) projects.

▶ Ensure sufficient federal reimbursements to provide all students of all family incomes in all elementary, middle, and high schools nationwide with tasty, nutritious breakfasts, lunches, afterschool suppers, and summer meals—locally and regionally sourced and sustainably produced whenever possible—free of charge, with no required paperwork. Defeat attempts by the big food industry to water down the improved nutritional standards that First Lady Michelle Obama fought for in school meals.

▶ Make the federal Women, Infants, and Children Program (WIC)—which provides nutritional supplements to low-income pregnant woman and children under five—an entitlement program so it will always have sufficient funding to ensure that everyone who qualifies for the help can get it. Make it easier for women to use WIC benefits to obtain fresh produce at farmers markets and CSAs.

▶ Provide start-up and operating subsidies for CSAs that serve low-income neighborhoods, such as the pioneering ones started in New York City by Hunger Free America.*

---

* I'll be waiting by Hunger Free America's mailbox to receive that mammoth new federal grant to expand our CSAs in low-income neighborhoods.

▸ Create a Food Jobs Program by providing targeted seed money and technical assistance to food-related businesses (see details below).

▸ Overhaul food labeling to ensure that all labels are large, clear, and accurate and base their serving sizes on what real people actually eat. The US government has made some progress on this front recently, but we need to do more. The government should also adopt a national food point system—tied to an easy-to-use smartphone app—to simplify and personalize daily nutritional choices for consumers. Any ingredients that include Genetically Modified Organisms (GMOs) should be labeled as such, but not in a way that gives the false impression that GMOs have been proven to harm humans (which they haven't).*

▸ Merge the Food and Drug Administration with the US Department of Agriculture's Food Safety and Inspection Service and make them a single, independent federal agency in charge of food safety. Staff it with impartial experts with unimpeachable expertise, and stop the revolving doors through which so many former regulators head straight to food corporations and trade associations after leaving federal service. It is imperative that consumers have and can count on a government food safety "referee" they truly trust. You wouldn't depend on your mother-in-law for couples counseling, so we shouldn't have to depend upon biased agencies to make food safety rulings.

▸ Build nutrition science fully into the curricula of medical schools, where it's mostly invisible. Reorient the medical profession so it moves beyond a default preference for drugs and surgery to instead focus on wellness, including good nutrition. Force pharmaceutical advertisements to include this line: "Ask your doctor if eating better and exercising more is right for you."

---

* The way GMO monopolies have been used by massive multinational corporations has certainly harmed small farmers worldwide. GMOs may—or may not—be harmful to the environment. But there is not one iota of proof that they harm human health. None. Sorry foodies, that's scientific truth. Your term "Frankenfoods" is an irresponsible scare tactic. If you believe in Frankenfoods, next you'll be taking your vaccine advice from a former actress from *Three's Company*.

▸ Eliminate the billions of dollars the US now spends on subsidies to massive corporate agribusinesses. Of that money
saved, use a third of it to support the anti-hunger programs
mentioned above, a third of it to aid true small- and medium-sized farms (especially fruit and vegetable producers)
with conservation efforts to protect soil and water quality,
and use the remaining third of the money to reduce the federal deficit.

▸ Expand the availability and nutritional quality of meals for
older Americans through Meals on Wheels and aggregate
(senior center) meals programs.

▸ Ensure that all who pick, process, and serve America's food
have safe working conditions and earn a living wage.

Whew! I hope you got all that. Good thing it's written down.

A BETTER WAY TO FIGHT OBESITY

Let's also move beyond the counterproductive, class-biased efforts
to micromanage what low-income people can eat or drink, America.
Let's reset the obesity and hunger debate in order to develop a more
comprehensive plan for enabling Americans in poverty to obtain more
nutritious food.

Even though I believe that all of us, low-income or not, should be able
to occasionally choose a sweetened beverage or have other snack foods as
a small part of an overall balanced diet, there is no question that Americans of all socioeconomic backgrounds drink far too much soda. The
over-consumption of unhealthy foods is surely one of many contributors
to the nation's high obesity, heart disease, and diabetes rates and the
accompanying skyrocketing healthcare costs. I hold special contempt for
food industry efforts that target its unhealthiest products to low-income
neighborhoods, children, and communities of color.

The reason I opposed attempts by then-New York City Mayor
Michael Bloomberg and others since then to ban the ability to purchase
of soda with SNAP benefits is that it was based on a false diagnosis of
the problem, which then resulted in a misguided treatment. Supporters

of the ban, as well as the numerous (mostly unsuccessful) proposals to levy additional taxes on certain foods (including soda), thought that the root of the problem was that low-income people always choose to eat junk food because of ignorance or apathy, thereby requiring coercive or even punitive measures.

In reality, the main reason that low-income people don't eat more healthfully is that nutritious food often doesn't exist in their neighborhoods, and when it does it is frequently too expensive or too time-consuming to obtain and prepare. When those barriers are overcome, low-income people flock to consume better food. Low-income families, for instance, heavily utilize subsidized farmers markets and CSAs when they are available in their neighborhoods.

That is why we should accelerate efforts to increase the availability of healthier food choices in low-income areas. The Obama administration, as well as many state and city governments, have worked with the private and nonprofit sectors in recent years to provide incentives to open more supermarkets, CSAs, and farmers markets in underserved rural and urban communities. For example, New York City has launched a pioneering program to place "Green Cart" fresh produce vendors in food deserts (areas where there is a dearth of healthy, fresh foods). Such efforts should be accelerated and expanded and should ensure that all vendors accept SNAP and WIC benefits.

We should also increase the purchasing power of low-income Americans to buy nutritious foods. As of 2016, SNAP benefits provided, on average, only a little more than $31 per person per week. According to the USDA, non-hungry American families spend about $50 per week per person on food, $12.50 more than food-insecure families. Studies prove that when families have more money for food they will use it to buy healthier, fresher food. Thus the simplest way to increase such food purchasing is to increase the average monthly SNAP allotment and expand the number of low-income people eligible.

Given that struggling workers are so often strapped for time, food that is better for you should also be made more convenient. I challenge entrepreneurs to open truly nutritious, affordable fast food shops and food trucks in low-income neighborhoods and towns across the country.

TURN FOOD DESERTS INTO JOBS OASES

Tens of millions of Americans need more nutritious, more affordable food. Tens of millions need better jobs. Just as the federal government gave some support to "green jobs" initiatives to simultaneously fight unemployment and protect the environment, they should also launch a "Good Food, Good Jobs" project.

Low-income areas across America that lack access to nutritious foods at affordable prices—the so-called "food deserts"—tend to be the same communities and neighborhoods that, even in better economic times, are also "job deserts" that lack sufficient living-wage employment. A concurrent problem has been the growing concentration of our food supply in a handful of food companies that are now "too big to fail." A Good Food, Good Jobs program can address these intertwined economic and social problems.

In partnership with state, local, and tribal governments, nonprofit organizations, and the private sector, a federal food jobs initiative would bolster employment, foster economic growth, fight hunger, cut obesity, cut poverty, improve nutrition, and reduce spending on diet-related health problems.

In the best-case scenario, such a program could create large numbers of living-wage jobs in self-sustaining businesses even as it addresses our food, health, and nutrition problems. But even in a worst-case scenario, the plan would create short-term subsidized jobs that would provide an economic stimulus, and at least offer low-income consumers the choice of more nutritious foods in the areas where they live—a choice so often denied to them.

A Good Food, Good Jobs program could provide the first serious national test of the effectiveness of using food partnerships to boost the economy and improve public health. The new initiative should:

▶ Provide more and better-targeted seed money to food jobs projects: The federal government should expand and more carefully target its existing grants and loans to start new, and expand existing, community food projects, such as city and rooftop gardens; urban farms; food co-ops; farm stands; CSAs; farmers markets; community kitchens; and projects that hire unemployed youth to grow, market, sell, and deliver nutritious foods while teaching them entrepreneurial skills.

▶ Bolster food processing: Since there is far more profit in processing food than in simply growing it (and since farming is only a seasonal occupation), the initiative should focus on supporting food businesses that add value year-round, such as neighborhood food processing/freezing/canning plants; businesses that turn raw produce into ready-to-eat salads, salad dressings, sandwiches, and other products; healthy vending-machine companies; and affordable and nutritious restaurants and catering businesses.

▶ Expand community-based technical assistance and procurement: Federal, state, and local governments should dramatically expand technical assistance to these community food efforts and support them by buying their products for school meals and other government nutrition assistance programs, as well as for jails, military facilities, hospitals, and concession stands in public parks, among other venues.

▶ Invest in urban fish farming: Given that fish is the category of food most likely to be imported, and given the growing environmental concerns over both wild and farm-raised fish, the initiative should provide significant investment into the research and development of environmentally sustainable, urban fish-production facilities.*

▶ Develop a better way of measuring success: the USDA should develop a "food access index," a measure that would take into account both the physical availability and economic affordability of nutritious foods and use this measure as another tool to judge the success of food jobs projects. All such efforts should be subject to strict performance-based

---

* Believe it or not, in the heart of urban Brooklyn, in the basement of a Brooklyn College building, resides the Aquatic Research and Environmental Assessment Center, which has experimented in breeding tilapia. Yes, a fish grows in Brooklyn, in that deep, dark tank, and it's edible.

outcome measures; programs should not receive continued funding unless they can prove their worth.

▶ Implement a focused food jobs research agenda: We should eventually be able to answer the following questions: Can community food enterprises that pay their workers sufficient wages also make products that are affordable? Can these projects become economically self-sufficient over the long run, particularly if they are ramped up to benefit from economies of scale? Would government revenues increase as a result of economic growth and, likewise, spending on healthcare and social services decrease as a result of such efforts? Would the money generated or saved offset the cost of long-term project subsidies? How would the cost and benefits of government spending on community food security compare to the cost and benefits of tens of billions of dollars that the US government now spends on traditional farm programs?

For a community to benefit from good nutrition, three conditions must be present: food must be affordable; food must be physically available and convenient; and individuals and families must have sufficient knowledge about good nutrition with time and ability to act on that knowledge by obtaining, preparing, and eating healthier foods. These comprehensive proposals, when enacted at once, would accomplish all those objectives.*

A NEW FARM BILL COALITION

Starting in the 1930's, anti-poverty advocates backed farm subsidies in exchange for agriculture interests backing food support for people in poverty.

In the first few decades of the coalition's existence, it served a useful purpose. True family farmers were aided by such policies, and in exchange, low-income Americans received increasing food aid. But

---

* Too many well-intentioned, but class-biased people—usually upper-middle-class, and white— think the one and only answer to hunger is better nutrition and shopping education. But unless healthier food is more affordable, convenient, and physically available nearby, all such education efforts will fail.

over time, pushed by campaign donations, Congress gave increasingly large portions of assistance to massive agricultural enterprises that fouled the environment and harmed public health, and less of it went to small family farmers.

Still, anti-hunger advocacy organizations remained tied at the hip to the interests of massive agribusiness. We had an implicit deal: the corporations, most of which were run by conservatives, would hold their noses about all the funding going to poor people, and the anti-hunger groups, usually headed by progressives, would continue to acquiesce to ever-larger corporate welfare. As long as there was enough money for both sides, the deals rolled on.

Yet with each passing year, as concerns over both public health and deficits increased, the pork-laden farm bills became harder to defend as policy, and more difficult to sustain politically. When there was no longer enough money for both hungry Americans and enormous corporate agribusinesses, each lobbying camp of the coalition started whispering to Congress behind closed doors that cuts should come from the others, not from them. At the same time, Congress started losing its willingness to accept, without serious amendment, massive pieces of costly legislation written by a handful of agriculture committee members, who were mostly white men from a few states and districts (and who were the largest recipients of the agriculture campaign donations).

When, in 2013, the House of Representatives tried to pass a farm bill that took SNAP out of the bill entirely, it put a final nail in the coffin of the old-school coalition. Good riddance.

The collapse of the old coalition should prompt us, when next a farm bill is considered by Congress (around 2019 or so) to truly go back to the drawing board to craft an entirely different kind of measure—a comprehensive food bill that reduces hunger, bolsters nutrition, aids family farmers, protects the environment, boosts rural economic development, strengthens food safety, and cuts down on unnecessary spending. To pass it, we'll need an entirely different farm bill coalition, one which forces anti-hunger campaigners and food systems advocates to team up with other activists on all those issues. Recent farm bills have represented the worst of American politics. It's time to build the movement necessary to pass a food bill that represents the best.

Once we make food a right, a joy, and a reality for all Americans, I can go back to happily stuffing my face in Brooklyn's never-ending food jamboree with no remorse.

Step Ten:

Outfoxing Fox
How to Make News, Social Media, and All Society Accountable

After Fox News (otherwise known as Sexual Harassment Central) misleadingly made me the face of welfare-loving, fraud-coddling, liberalism in their prime time "exposé" of food stamps, I received this charming e-mail:

> Dear Mr. Berg,
>   Just like president Obama, you are a liar.
>   I have worked all my life, I am a Vietnam veteran, I pay taxes, and I resent your recruiting able but lazy people to apply for food stamps they do not need or deserve. If you want to be a socialist, move to Europe. Don't try to socialize America.
>   Shame on you.
>
> [Name omitted to respect privacy, as well as to protect my safety.]*
> Mineral Bluff, Georgia

Here was my response:

> Thank you for taking the time to write to me. Thank you for your service to our country.
>   You should be aware that the Fox News report selectively

---

* I figured that leaving out his name will make it marginally less likely that he will track and hunt me down with his *Duck Dynasty*–brand assault weapons, which I assume he owns:

edited my comments and was full of inaccuracies, half-truths, and distortions. You can see the facts here: [Link to a fact sheet produced by my group, rebutting the report point-by-point.]

The reason we conduct SNAP/food stamps outreach is that while 48 million Americans suffer from food insecurity, unable to afford a sufficient supply of food, more than a quarter of the people eligible for benefits do not receive them. The people most likely to be eligible for benefits who fail to receive them are working parents, seniors, and fellow veterans—and our outreach efforts particularly target those populations.

Georgia has a particularly high level of hunger, spread out throughout the rural, suburban, and urban parts of your state. Please see this fact sheet from the Georgia Food Bank Association. [Link to food bank's fact sheet.]

If you still don't believe that hunger is a serious problem in Georgia and America, I would urge you to visit local soup kitchens or food pantries, most of which are run by churches. The people who work and volunteer at these agencies would all tell you that hunger in indeed a serious problem, and most would agree that one of the best ways to fight the problem is to make full use of existing federal programs.

The Fox News report left out these key facts, which I provided them:

[I then explain, in detail, how most SNAP recipients are children, seniors, working parents, and people with disabilities, and how most of the adults who obtain SNAP are hard-working taxpayers]. . .

I have dedicated my whole career to reducing the need of families for such assistance by fighting for more jobs and higher wages. Most able bodied people who are forced to receive SNAP would far prefer to have a living-wage job.

If you agree with me that working families should earn enough to feed their families through their wages, I would suggest that you immediately contact Senator Isakson, Senator Chambliss, and Congressman Collins to request that they support President Obama's call to raise the federal minimum wage, which would reduce the need for government benefits without costing federal taxpayers a penny.

Also, you should be aware that about 900,000 fellow veterans receive SNAP. Even many active duty military families receive SNAP.

Furthermore, the SNAP program is not socialism—it is a voucher program that enables struggling families to shop at private sector businesses, thereby boosting the economy. In India and Brazil, the government food programs send hungry people to government-run food warehouses; in contrast, SNAP enables people to shop at free market, private stores such as those owned by Walmart, Publix, Food Lion, Piggly Wiggly, etc.

I was frankly taken aback by your implication, that I— or anyone else who happens to disagree with your personal views—should leave the country. My late father was a decorated combat veteran of World War II, and he made it crystal clear to me throughout his life that the freedom for which he fought was the freedom to live in a country in which people of different political views could live peacefully side-by-side. I love my country deeply—and one of the ways that I live out my patriotism is to work very hard to make the country even stronger. Massive evidence demonstrates that reducing hunger will make America stronger both militarily and economically.

Given your seeming objection to government spending on social programs, I wonder if you have refused—or will refuse— to accept federal Medicare health benefits when you are eligible for them.

Additionally, I note that your town is near federal park and forest facilities. Do you refuse to use any of their recreational areas?

I have no doubt that you have happily benefited from federally funded roads, air traffic controllers, and food safety inspectors.

My obvious point is that all Americans—including the most conservative, anti-government Americans—benefit repeatedly from government services. Even Congressman Ted Yoho, a hero of the Tea Party movement who has harshly criticized food stamps, once received food stamp benefits for himself and his family.

I would hope we could all understand that we all need temporary help from government—in one form or another—sometimes. Therefore, we shouldn't demonize others who also sometimes need help.

In any case, thanks again for writing.

Sincerely,
Joel Berg

I very much doubt I convinced him, but I am reprinting this exchange to provide an example of how to provide rejoinders to the Far Right that are both respectful but also hold your ground. I also posted the exchange on my organization's website and tweeted it. The public needs to see both what we are up against and that there are effective, well-mannered ways to respond. Note that I try to connect with him on what I assume are our mutual values, citing the importance of work, military service, the free market, freedom, and churches. I love using conservative terms to advance progressive causes, such as when I called SNAP benefits "vouchers" (which they actually are).

If we are to build a progressive America, we are all going to need to find ways to counter the right-wing media machine. Every one of us can do our part to beat back Fox-like propaganda, whether you see right-wing fabrications posted on social media or are yelled at by your most un-PC uncle at Thanksgiving dinner. So here are a few tips for fighting back, America:

▶ Try to be outraged, not angry. That seems like a difference without distinction, but it's not. Outrage expresses healthy opposition to injustice in the world around you. Anger, the default mode of Bill O'Reilly, usually is a sign of self-loathing.*

▶ Stick to the facts, without resorting to name-calling. Don't sink to their level. No matter how personally nasty they get toward you, try to keep it civil and try to keep bringing the

---

* I do wonder what horrible things his parents must have done to him.

discussion back to the issues. No matter how many times they call you something juvenile like "Lib-tard," remember my first point about outrage versus anger.

▶ Think before you re-post. Please don't be a weasel and claim that merely re-posting something doesn't mean you endorse it. If you re-post or forward something nasty or untrue, some of that nastiness and untruth surely rubs off on you. And please check your own facts, or the facts of what you re-post. Plenty of left-wing memes make stuff up, too. If something seems too unbelievable to be true, it likely is, so you should check Snopes.com for hoaxes, or check FactCheck.org or PolitiFact.com for some independent fact-checking. These sites aren't always 100 percent unbiased themselves, but you should at least know what they found before you repeat a sharp charge yourself.

▶ Check out MediaMatters.org and publicize their excellent posts that debunk the right-wing media.

▶ When you see something false or troubling in any media, including on Fox, send them a complaint, either by e-mail, through comments on their website, or through Twitter.

▶ Try to connect with opponents' values. Explain why your positions bolster community, faith, work, opportunity, and freedom—assuming they do.

▶ Press opponents to cite specific sources, then check the validity of their sources.

▶ Whenever possible, link to the most authoritative, hardest-to-debunk sources. If you are trying to prove that climate change exists, link to a NASA report. If you are demonstrating the extent of gun violence, cite FBI statistics. Even better, if you can find something on a right-wing website that proves your point (either intentionally or unintentionally), cite that—it will drive the other side nuts.

▶ Try to proofread your posts or tweets. Now I am the worst at this recommendation, so do as I say, not as I do. I am the king of typos, often leaving the "r" out of the phrase "food pantries." ~~Yolks~~ I mean, yikes. But just a bit of proofreading

can prevent a whole lot of humiliation (trust me on this).
[Note from Joel's copyeditor: trust him on this.]

▶ Know when to let it go. At some point, your time and sanity
matter. If you are getting no traction at all from the other
side, or if the level of personal invective against you is
just getting too enormous, or if your trolling tormentor is
spewing out nothing but racist, misogynist, homophobic,
Islamophobic garbage, etc., that's what the "unfriend" and
"unfollow" buttons were designed for.

Knowledge *is* power, America. The more we can demonstrate that the
facts are on our side, the more sway we will have in the nation's debates.
Please do keep plugging away for the truth. Sure, lots of the most extreme
Americans, including your father-in-law who would scare you to death
even if he didn't always look over at his gun cabinet whenever you walk
through the door, won't let themselves be swayed by the facts, no matter
how incontrovertible, but don't let that deter you.

Intolerant ignoramuses have always sought to impose their worldviews on others. In 1633, the Italian scientist Galileo was put on trial by
the Catholic Church because leaders of the Inquisition were infuriated
by his finding that the Earth moved around the Sun. The church was
adamant that the Earth stayed in one place and made it clear to Galileo
he would face ghastly punishment unless he publicly recanted, which
he did. But right after he recanted, Galileo reportedly said, "*E pur si
muove.*" (And yet it moves).

Always remember, regardless of whether the forces of intolerance
want to obfuscate the facts, that truth, science, and reality will *always*
matter.

Step Eleven:

We *Still* Can Overcome
Movement-Building for the
Twenty-First Century

Lost causes are for *losers*. That's bit harsh, and perhaps a bit too Trumpian, but true. If you are an activist and you relish your perpetual *lack of success* because you think that it reinforces your ideological purity, then you are a poser putting your own self-regard ahead of the cause you claim you want to advance.

Unless you win, at least sometimes, you can't help anyone or change anything. Unless you advance your cause, what's the point of being an activist? Sure, meaningful change sometimes takes a *long* time, but unless you have a game plan for eventually getting there, you're just kidding yourself, and worse, kidding the people you claim to represent.

On the other hand, it's also problematic to settle for microscopic, easy victories that do little to solve vast, structural problems.

Ah, the dilemmas faced by activists.

Here's another tough one: do you accept (and try to deal with)—or do you reject (and try to change)—the political environment in which you currently live?

To me, that's a false choice. In most cases, you should take the best deal you can get *while simultaneously* trying to change the political environment to make it more favorable to your cause.

But too often activists forget the second part and merely settle for crumbs, accepting the false conventional wisdom that society's opposition to their cause is permanent. The truth is that *nothing* in politics is permanent and effective political movements can turn conventional wisdom on its head. The first step to achieving progress is *not accepting* the status quo (for example, we should never accept the justification "there will always be poor people because there have always been poor people," which ignores the fact that poverty rates climb and sink depending on the public policies put in place). The second is *believing* you can change things. The third is creating and implementing *a plan* that is visionary and bold, but also concrete and realistic, in order to achieve your goals.

Progress *is* possible, America, although it is by no means inevitable. Let's learn from the Marriage Equality and Fight for $15 movements about how best to achieve our goals.

Both started with a rejection of the status quo that was visceral, intellectual, and moral all at all once. LGBTQ rights supporters simply refused to accept the notion that LGBTQ people could be classified as subhuman and therefore barred—due to both social convention and US law—from choosing whether to participate in the institution of marriage or to avoid it at all costs (hey, it's a choice!). Likewise, wage activists simply refused to accept the notion that people who work full time should earn so little that they could not afford to feed and house their families.

Both movements envisioned better futures and then implemented point-by-point game plans to get there.

And both won.

Their victories seem inevitable only in retrospect. In 2001, when Evan Wolfson formed the group Freedom to Marry, the first major entity to fight for marriage equality, most of the country, including many in the LGBTQ rights community, thought he was off his rocker. At that time, same-sex marriage was illegal in all 50 states. But now it's legal in all 50.

Likewise right after Thanksgiving 2012, when a few hundred fast-food workers in New York City went on strike to call for a $15 minimum wage, that number seemed liked a pipe dream. After all, the minimum wage at the time was only $7.25 per hour in New York and nationwide.*

They were calling for *doubling* it. They were on Mars, or so the "experts" thought. Yet by

---

* Fight for $15 workers have marched and gone on strike in all sorts of weather, all sort of conditions, demonstrating immense bravery and grit.

June 2016, the entire state of California, much of New York State, and the cities of Seattle and Washington, DC had agreed to raise the wage floor to $15 per hour, and other states and localities started following suit. It is amazing how things that we first think are unthinkable seem, just a few years later, to have always been inevitable.

HOW MOVEMENTS WIN

Some advocates wistfully dream that the key problems they face will mostly remedy themselves over time. They hope that the continued weaknesses in wages and the conservative direction in our politics, for instance, are cyclical and will eventually correct themselves. But that's wishful thinking. The reality is that our social problems, if unaddressed, will only get worse. As the great abolitionist leader Frederick Douglass said, "Without a struggle, there can be no progress . . . Power concedes nothing without a demand. It never did and it never will." History proves that the one and only way to solve our major problems is to create a powerful political movement to force our governmental leaders to solve them.

Those who argue over whether political leaders or social movements are more decisive—such as in the debate over whether Martin Luther King, Jr. or President Lyndon Johnson played the most influential role in passing great pieces of civil rights legislation of the 1960s—are missing the point: that *both* are needed to alternatively push, pull, and aid the other.

So how do political and social movements succeed? Like winning political campaigns, triumphant social movements have simultaneously accomplished these three basic things:

▶ They mobilized their base: Ensured that the people most affected by the issue were energized and heavily engaged in the fight, preferably as leaders.
▶ They won over the "middle": Convinced average people and the masses to support the cause.
▶ They isolated the opposition: Rebutted their arguments and prevented them from winning the media narrative or convincing the masses.

Marc Solomon, one of the key political architects of the successful marriage equality movement, has explained the top lessons learned from that movement.[53] (His points are in italics and my commentary follows each point.)

1. Convey a bold, inspirational vision.

Great movements set clear, transformational goals that would, if achieved, transform the lives of the people in it. Guarantee all women the right to vote. Double our wages. End a war. Give everyone the right to marry. End domestic hunger. A compelling movement goal should need little explanation or equivocation.

2. Have an overarching strategy.

Even if you are seeking transformational changes, you usually need an incremental strategy to get there, often starting with shorter-term goals that you believe you can most realistically achieve. Marriage equality supporters fought for wins in Massachusetts and California before they focused on Utah and Mississippi.

Likewise, labor organizers started with wage targets below $15 and focused first on some of the most liberal, union-oriented cities. Roxana Tina, a top wage activist in Los Angeles, said, "Given the dysfunction of the federal government, our sense is, in a country as huge and complex as ours, cities should serve as the laboratories for change." In 1997, her group, the Los Angeles Alliance for a New Economy, persuaded the Los Angeles City Council to enact one of the nation's first living-wage ordinances, which eventually required the city to pay $12.28 an hour for workers employed by city contractors or companies receiving city tax breaks. Subsequently, they pressured Los Angeles to enact a new minimum wage of $15.37 per hour for hotel workers; it first went into effect for hotels with at least 300 rooms, and a year later for hotels with at least 150 rooms.[54] Great organizers are both fierce and patient, putting in place one building block at a time, choosing each block carefully.

Even when it seems like a particular victory is a quantum leap forward—such as the Supreme Court decision ensuring marriage equality nationwide—a deeper look at the history proves that that huge leap was actually built on years of incremental progress.

3. Focus on values and emotions.

Solomon learned that when marriage equality supporters argued about the legal and financial benefits of marriage or theoretical constitutional principles, they lost the public. It was only after they made the debate about love, commitment, and family that they won. This doesn't mean that any movement should be disconnected from facts, but merely that you need to connect your facts to human emotions.

When fast-food workers testified before the New York State Wage Board in favor of a $15 wage, they didn't offer long, academic explanations of how and why higher wages aided the economy. Instead, they spoke from the heart. Workers after worker who testified focused on two major points: they couldn't afford food for their own families and they just wanted a small bit of human dignity. Worker Chantelle Walker put it this way: "If you work, you should eat." Amen.

4. Meet people where they are.

As Solomon explained,

> To make lasting change in America, it's crucial to make the case—and give time—to people who are conflicted about your cause. On marriage, we knew that pretty much everyone grew up in a society where they were taught that marriage was between a man and a woman, and in a faith tradition where they were taught that homosexuality was wrong. Many good people were conflicted, and we were asking them to take a journey, challenging some of their deep understandings about marriage, family, and religion. . . . To get them to yes, we had to encourage people to open their minds and hearts, to listen, question, and reconsider. That meant starting early and staying with it, making the case in multiple ways. A shift like that is much less likely to happen if you write someone off or call those who aren't with you yet a bigot or bad person.

This same dictum applies to other issues as well. Let's say, for instance, that you are trying to convince someone to support more funding for SNAP but they are opposed because they don't think able-bodied adults should get "free stuff." If you try to convince them that food should be a right for everyone—including healthy adults who don't want to work—then you will likely fail, but if you help them understand how most people on SNAP use the program to supplement meager wages, you might have a chance to sway them.

5. Find the right messengers.

Ever heard of Claudette Colvin? No? Well, she was a young African American woman who refused to abide by bus segregation in Montgomery, Alabama *before* Rosa Parks famously refused to give up her seat. But Colvin was a teenager pregnant with the child of a married man, and civil rights leaders did not think she presented a good image to the public. So when Rosa Parks—who, by conventional standards of the time, was an upstanding community member—refused to stand up, leaders highlighted her instead of Colvin.

Solomon discovered that it was parents of gay people who often made the most effective media spokespersons because more of the public could identify with them.

I am, and have always been, very conflicted about this strategy. I never want to give the impression that there are worthy versus unworthy hungry people, for example, but I do admit that when the media asks our organization to recommend hungry family members to interview, we prefer to suggest people who are working or who are married. Misgivings aside, it is vital to ensure that your messengers are people who favorably reinforce your message to the public.

6. Build state campaigns designed to win.

As Solomon said, "Winning at the state level requires an experienced campaign manager running a professional campaign, with field organizers, communications professionals, and lobbyists reporting to the manager and a tight board managing the campaign and helping raise sufficient resources to carry out the campaign plan." In other words, big, systematic change isn't kid stuff for dilettantes.

7. Invest heavily in local organizing.

There's an old and true political adage: "Message beats money."

Grassroots organizing is one of the most cost-effective ways to deliver a message. Solomon agrees: "On challenging issues, too often advocates think they can win in a legislature with top-notch lobbyists or at the ballot exclusively with good television ads. That's simply not the case. Lawmakers and citizens are most often persuaded because they hear from people locally—from regular citizens, same-sex couples, and influential leaders living in their own communities."

Similarly, Richard Kirsch, a leading organizer for healthcare reform, has found that

> [g]rassroots organizing is essential to overcome the power that big corporations and wealthy elites wield. . . . Where we had a potential advantage over our opponents was outside the Beltway, where members of Congress and their staffs still meet face-to-face with their constituents, and local press corps still report on civic action. If we organized people to raise their voices together, to tell their stories, to build relationships with Congress, and if we kept doing this over and over again and did it all over the country as part of a concerted strategic effort, we could accomplish what had been impossible for the past century. And we understood that doing so required investing money in organizers to do the day-to-day work of identifying, building relationships with, and empowering people.[55]

8. Accept this political reality: Politicians care about reelection above almost everything else.

My general rule is that organizers should try to get elected officials to take actions that are more progressive than they would have taken on their own had they not been pressured by activists, but not to take positions so "out there" that they could lose their seat if they follow your advice. If taking your position means someone loses their seat, that generally means that your movement hasn't done a good enough job of selling the public on the righteousness of your cause.

9. Be serious about reaching across the aisle.

The marriage equality movement worked darn hard to get people to switch from opposing to supporting them. They then fiercely defended those officials who did switch, even if the officials had previously taken horrendous positions against LGBTQ people. Likewise, as cynical as I am about the modern Republican Party, I still work overtime to try to convince any Republicans who even hint at having a secret moderate side that they should support anti-hunger and anti-poverty efforts.

10. Build momentum every day.

It's important to have victories, big or small, as often as possible. Even if you can't declare any real victories on a given day, you must also give your supporters some signs of hope.

It's also important to gird your troops for a long, slow grind. A lot of people have the facile impression that the Civil Rights movement succeeded mostly because it had inspirational leaders who delivered amazing speeches. That certainly helped, but the biggest reason that that movement succeeded is that it had the support of millions of Americans who made sacrifices—both incalculably large and relatively small—over the course of many years, and who worked tirelessly on painstakingly detailed on-the-ground organizing efforts. After all, it was in-the-trenches organizing that *built* the crowds for those amazing speeches.

Meaningful change requires persistent hard work. A few tweets don't cut it.

UNDERSTAND WHAT YOU ARE UP AGAINST

Activists better have a clear-headed idea of what they are really up against and cannot afford to be lulled into complacency by some early victories. In 1966 Martin Luther King, Jr. warned that the future Civil Rights movement, beyond the then-recent victories on segregation and voting rights, would be far "more complex," explaining,

> Slums with hundreds of thousands of living units are not erad-
> icated as easily as lunch counters or buses are integrated. Jobs
> are harder to create than voting rolls. . . .
>   Long-established cultural privileges are threatened in the next

phase. We have seen in the effort to integrate schools, even in the more tolerant Northern urban centers, that many reasonably unbigoted persons assume a new posture . . . in school systems where they have a personal interest. In the quest for genuinely integrated housing, the intensity of opposition from many who considered themselves free of prejudice has made it clear that this struggle will be attended by tenacious difficulties. . . .

As they move forward for fundamental alteration of their lives, a more bitter opposition grows even within groups that were hospitable to earlier superficial amelioration. Conflicts are unavoidable because a stage has been reached in which the reality of equality will require extensive adjustments in the way of life of some of the white majority.

All profound social movements reach a plateau of this sort, short of the summit, and the presence of new opposition should not dismay us. Because we have accumulated substantial successes we have been able to reach the inner walls of resistance. That was our goal. The new obstacles should not be deplored but welcomed because their presence proves we are closer to the ultimate decision. These walls will yield to the same pressures that left the outer battlements in fragments behind us.[56]

MOBILIZING YOUR BASE

Imagine if the US women's suffragette movement had been led entirely by men and its rank-and-file had been mostly male. The movement would surely have been far less galvanizing and assertive. American women might *still* be denied the vote.

While some white activists made the ultimate sacrifice—giving their lives—on behalf of equal rights for African Americans, had the Civil Rights movement been led and populated primarily by whites, that campaign would also have been far less passionate, insistent, and effective, and the Voting Rights and Civil Rights Acts might *still* be languishing in Congress.

Likewise, if the LGBTQ rights crusade had merely waited for straight

Americans to voluntarily grant them the right to marry, they would prob-ably not be able to obtain a marriage license in any state, no less 50.

In fact, no social movement in history has been won entirely by one people on behalf of another.

Let's analyze the example of the anti-hunger movement, a cause that I've worked on for more than two decades.

Even though it is absurd to believe that any attempt to finally end hunger or poverty in the US can succeed without the significant involvement and leadership of low-income Americans, that is exactly the strategy that many anti-hunger groups have followed for years (quite unsuccessfully), although this is beginning to change.

For decades, many of the upper-middle-class white activists who have led and populated the national anti-hunger movement have essen-tially taken the position that if they merely "put a face on hunger"—i.e., tell the stories of struggling Americans and display photos or videos of hungry Americans on their behalf—then average Americans would be so moved and outraged that they would instantaneously support the public policies necessary to end the problem. While I am thankful that some organizations do give scholarships to allow some low-income individuals to attend anti-hunger conferences, most attendees are still upper-middle-class and white; relatively few hungry people—or even formerly hungry people—participate in these meetings, much less lead them. Can you image an American Federation of Teachers convention without educators, or an American Legion convention without vet-erans? The failure of anti-hunger organizations to more fully include the people we represent has made us so weak that we have mostly failed to counteract right-wing policies that increase hunger.

While we certainly still have more work to do to help middle-class Americans understand that it is in their self-interest to decrease pov-erty and hunger, our greatest single challenge is to mobilize our base, ensuring leadership and activism by many of the 48 million Americans who suffered from food insecurity in 2014.

Imagine the political power behind 48 million Americans acting in unison to fight on their own behalf. After all, if you combined the five million members of the NRA, the 11 million members of the AFL-CIO unions, the 1.5 million members of the Human Rights Campaign, the nearly one million members of the Sierra Club, and the seven million members of the National Right to Life Committee, that's still less than half the number of Americans who struggle against hunger.

We should have no illusions about the challenges in building any movement with strong leadership and engagement of the affected Americans. Our entire society and our political system reinforce the cycles of empowerment for the wealthy and disempowerment for the impoverished.

For the nation's elite, any activism on their part is consistently rewarded. They vote regularly and donate to candidates. As a result, elected officials tend to respond to their needs, which reinforces their perception that political activity matters—and is an investment that pays off—so they continue their political activism.

But the nation's poor can't afford to donate to campaigns and generally vote less frequently, so they get less attention from elected officials, which reinforces their original negative perception that politics doesn't matter and their participation won't make a difference anyway. Even in Democratic Party primaries, wealthy people vote more frequently than low-income citizens.

Another challenge is that Americans who are struggling to get by and are wondering if they will have enough food for the month don't want to think of themselves as poor and hungry. In contrast, a top goal of other movements was to make African Americans, women, and the LGBTQ individuals proud of their identities. Yet the greatest goal of poor and hungry people is usually to escape their condition. It's darn hard to organize individuals whose strongest ambition is to no longer be a part of the group being organized. But just because it is difficult doesn't mean it isn't both crucial and possible.

Philadelphia's Witnesses to Hunger, started in 2008 by Dr. Mariana Chilton, is a research and advocacy project partnering with what they call the "real experts on hunger—mothers and caregivers of young children who have experienced hunger and poverty." Through their photographs and testimonials, the Witnesses advocate locally and in Washington, DC for their own families and others and seek to create lasting changes on a local, state, and national level.

In New York City, the group I manage, Hunger Free America, coordinates a Food Action Board (FAB) program to train low-income New Yorkers to lead advocacy efforts. FAB members lobby elected officials in both New York and Washington, testify at public meetings, and communicate through local and national media. Our FAB members are diverse. Darrel Bristow is a father of four who previously served in the Marines. Mariluz Brito is a single mother of three who is unemployed and struggles against hunger and, even though she immigrated legally, she has not been in the US long enough to qualify for SNAP benefits. Soraya Diaz, a part-time student at Lehman College in the Bronx, lives with her elderly grandmother and mother. Ann Jenkins retired from her job as a receptionist at Albert Einstein Hospital and now needs SNAP to feed her family. Oralia Morand, the widow of a veteran, is a longtime volunteer in various soup kitchens and pantries. Jackie Williams is also an active volunteer, a single woman with breast cancer, and a SNAP recipient, who performs freelance work when she can.

When these courageous fighters speak with elected officials or the media, the conversation is entirely different than when I do the same thing. They speak with an urgency and poignancy that no advocate who is not poor can even approximate. They transform policy requests from abstract notions that can be negotiated away over time into flesh-and-blood demands that must be met immediately. It's much harder for members of Congress to explain to a SNAP recipient who is standing right in front of them why they are proposing SNAP cuts than it is to explain it to a mere advocate like me.

While the above section is specific to hunger, those lessons can be applied to any fight on behalf of low-income or otherwise marginalized people.

Both current events and history prove that direct advocacy by low-income Americans fighting for their own interests can have a massive impact.

That is why every poverty and hunger group in the country should begin or expand their efforts to better engage low-income people, whether such activities are modeled on the Witnesses to Hunger, our FABs, or other proven models. Foundations and private donors should also encourage these endeavors by funding them.

The time is long overdue for another, true Poor People's Campaign.

As is the case with every successful movement, the people with the most to gain will always be the activists who make the biggest difference.

HOW TO MOTIVATE THE MASSES

Let's face it, America—most people are *not* actively involved in political or social movements.

Why not? I don't agree with the charge that they simply don't care or are too lazy to do so. I don't even fully agree with the other explanation—that most are too busy to get involved. As busy as people are, most find the time to do the things that *really* matter to them.

Social movements often fail to convince people to get involved because a) they are divided by class, race, gender, sexual orientation and identification, ethnicity, etc., b) they fail to assure people that they can really make a difference, and c) they do not convincingly communicate how their efforts will directly benefit the targeted people and their families.

If progressives want to win, we absolutely need to move beyond mere identity politics, which pit one group's grievances against those of other groups. Of course, we should specifically combat racism, sexism, homophobia, and xenophobia, but we also need to build a broad-based movement that unites *all* causes. Over and over again, we need to remind ourselves that what unites us—being shafted by forces of greed and hatred—is far, far greater than what divides us.

To combat the common belief that average folks can't make a difference, we need to retell the stories—over and over again—of movement victories, continually reminding supporters that people power *has* prevailed, that rank-and-file Americans *can* empower themselves, and that mass movements *do* achieve meaningful, lasting progress.

Most importantly, a new progressive movement must plainly explain to low-income and middle-class Americans in very concrete terms how it will make *their* families more financially secure, healthier, freer, and safer. If people truly believed that they would benefit, they'd leap out of their armchairs and into the streets and voting booths. No force is more powerful than collective self-interest. See, America, this benefits *you*!

Working together, we can *all* be *winners*.

Step Twelve:

The Activist Patriot
It's Up to *You*

"The essence of tragedy is not the doing of evil by evil men but the doing of evil by good men, out of weakness, indecision, sloth, inability to act in accordance with what they know to be right."
—I. F. Stone, 1944[57]

Some progressives run away from overt displays of patriotism. I think we should *run toward* them. Let's remind the country (over and over—and over—again) that the values we progressives and radical centrists cherish—love, work, freedom, community, family, empathy, and neighborliness—are both universal values and the most *American* of values. We should proudly proclaim that we, the people who constantly push America to live up to its best ideals, are the ultimate patriots. America, it is progressives who have your back.

That's why I challenge each and every person reading this book to proudly think of yourself as an "Activist Patriot."

So what, specifically, do I think that you should *do* as an Activist Patriot? I'm glad you asked.

First, I want you to accept that you don't have to be a professional, full-time advocate to make a difference. It is true, as I explained in the last chapter, that most successful movements do need some professional organizers, but please don't take that to mean that part-time, volunteer activists can't—or shouldn't—make a huge difference.

If you do want to make a career out of being an activist or an organizer, go for it. While there is a stereotype that everyone who does so is a 20-something earning dirt wages and living off ramen noodles, that's not always the case. For instance, I have been doing this for a few decades now (sigh)* and I've actually managed to make a decent living of it, earning more than enough to get all the food I need, take some cool trips, and even pay a mortgage. (Yes, I'm damn fortunate.) So, if you do want to work for a social movement, political campaign, or a progressive government agency, do it. I obviously agree that full-time public service can be an excellent way to serve the nation.

But the life of a professional activist or public servant isn't—and shouldn't be—for everyone. That's why my main message in this chapter is for everybody else. Whether you are a physician, store clerk, lawyer, academic, daycare worker, professional alligator wrestler, reality show extra, auto worker, full-time parent, student, trapeze artist, or a corporate titan—or even if you are consistently unemployed—I challenge you to be an Activist Patriot your whole life. All of us, no matter what we do for a living, have a responsibility to make our country better.

If you just take one thing away from this book, it is that, rather than being a lame-ass and blaming "politicians" or the "system" for our country's problems, if you ever want your relationship with America mended, *you* must take personal responsibility to help fix it.

You must also move beyond the mistaken belief that you need to choose between direct community service and political activism.

In a 2015 speech to Tuskegee University, First Lady Michelle Obama said, "You don't have to be president of the United States to start addressing things like poverty, and education, and lack of opportunity. Graduates, today you can mentor a young person and make sure he or she takes the right path. Today, you can volunteer at an after-school program or food pantry."[58] I am a big fan of Michelle Obama, and the historic work she performed battling obesity will save many lives, but the options she gave the graduates for helping was wrongly narrow. She made it seem that the only person in the country who can enact major policy change is the president of the United States—perhaps along with some other top political leaders, so the only thing left for everyone else to do is a little direct, one-on-one community service.

The First Lady *should* have said that if you want to improve education or end hunger, the most important and useful thing that anyone

---

* I know I am old when I am in the office playing some of the hippest music I have and some younger colleague walks by and says, "I know that song—my *parents* used to listen to it." Ouch.

can do is to fight for *policy change* to make those things happen. If your advocacy helps expand government funding for pre-kindergarten, even slightly, that would do more far more to improve education than would spending 10 lifetimes tutoring. The same goes for contacting your senator to ask her or him to oppose SNAP cuts—if you play even a marginal role in getting them to vote your way, that would do far more to limit hunger than 10 lifetimes of packing pantry bags.

But the great news is that you don't have to choose between direct service and policy advocacy. Activist Patriots can—*and should*—do both.

HOW TO BEST FIGHT HUNGER

Yes, I'm back on the hunger issue again, not only because it's what I know best, but because it offers lessons for every other type of social problem. When you do perform direct volunteer service, please try to make it as effective as possible. For instance, many Americans already pack food pantry bags or volunteer at soup kitchens, often on the holidays. But seasonal and charitable work can't end US hunger. That's why Hunger Free America has launched an initiative to make it possible for all Americans to make an even bigger difference, and feel even more gratified, through strategic anti-hunger volunteerism.

What is strategic anti-hunger volunteerism? Simply put, it mobilizes the unique talents and skills of each individual volunteer in order to take the biggest bite out of hunger by:

- Helping a struggling family access SNAP benefits.
- Aiding a small food pantry with accounting, grant writing, IT, graphic design, volunteer management, or legal or strategic planning assistance.
- Raising funds for an anti-hunger advocacy organization.
- Conducting community outreach to increase the number of hungry kids getting school breakfasts or summer meals.
- Contacting your elected officials to get them to raise the minimum wage or increase funding for safety net programs.

Through such strategic volunteerism activities, you can help countless more people eat. If you help a struggling family with two kids access school breakfasts, given that most schools are in session 180 days out of the year, you will have provided 360 meals to low-income kids, many of whom would have otherwise gone without breakfast. If you help just 10 families, that's 3,600 meals going to kids who need it.

Helping in the most effective way means you get the most personal satisfaction too. Not only that, you can also develop valuable professional skills, and build your resume. Go to www.HungerVolunteer.org to sign up to help. Do it now.

ACTIVIST PATRIOT CHECKLIST

Even if you are not a professional activist, here's a handy-dandy list of other things you—yes *you*—can do to make a difference:

- ✓ Learn who all your elected officials are and what they stand for. If you are reading this massive screed on politics, you may already know who they are, but in case you don't, make it your business to know. You obviously know who the president is (assuming that, by the time you read this, Trump hasn't turned himself into an emperor and eliminated the presidency), but also learn about your two US senators and your one member of the House of Representatives. Learn about your governor and the people who represent you in both houses of your state legislature.* Learn about your county executive, county legislators, mayor, city or town councilman or alderman, and your elected school board members (if you still have any).

- ✓ Vote in each and every election, in both primaries and general elections—from president to dog catcher. Don't let any excuse stop you. If you are homebound or expect to be traveling on Election Day, arrange to vote by absentee ballot.

---

* In Nebraska, due to a reform of the Progressive Era, the state legislature only has one house. I guess they spent all that extra money they saved on football.

✓ Call, e-mail, and send snail mail, or visit, your elected officials to lobby them on an issue that matters to you.

✓ Place a bumper sticker on your car, a button on your backpack, a sign on your lawn, and a post on your social media. (But just remember that these tiny acts do not let you off the hook from taking more impactful action.)

✓ Read publications, blogs, books, and posts by people who disagree with you. You might even change your mind on something. At bare minimum, you'll understand the opposition better, which can often help you defeat them.

✓ Join with a civic, political, business, professional, or political group to ask for a direct meeting with each of your elected officials.

✓ Volunteer on political campaigns.

✓ Sponsor or attend meet-ups with other people who are active on an issue.

✓ Attend town meetings held by your elected officials and give them a piece—or a bunch of pieces—of your mind.

✓ Call into talk radio shows (even right-wing ones) or C-SPAN call-in programs.

✓ Send letters to the editor of your local newspaper.

✓ When an article appears online about an issue that matters, and there is a reader comments section, post your own comments. (Such sections overwhelmingly are filled with posts from far-right-wingers and haters, so somewhat sensible ideas would stand out.)

✓ Attend peaceful, productive protests.

✓ Donate to, or volunteer with, excellent, proven advocacy organizations (such as Hunger Free America, hint, hint).

✓ Tweet (or re-tweet) or post (or re-post) your opinions and those of people you agree with, in a fact-based, respectful manner.

✓ Suggest that your book club read a book or two on politics. (Hint, hint.)

You should do one or more—or all—of these things because, if you don't, you must stop friggin' whining about the country. But more importantly, if you do any of these things, they *will* make a difference.

One of the most frequent questions I get is, "Joel, you keep saying that you think the top thing we need to do is influence public policy, but our system is so broken that I just don't think average people like me have any power, so how can we improve things *without* influencing public policy?" That's like asking how we can end drought without water. Let me say this one last time: we simply *can't* solve any major problem facing America or the world unless we change governmental policies.

Believing that your voice doesn't matter is nothing short of a cop-out. Your voice *does* matter. Even if elected officials don't personally read all their own mail or e-mails (and most of the ones in higher office don't), they usually have staff that does, and that staff gives them reports as to what the letters say and how many letters, e-mails, and calls are coming down on each side of an issue. Many elected officials absolutely take positions based on what they are hearing from their constituents who are, after all, their bosses. So, yes, contacting elected officials makes a big difference. This country's overall apathy sucks, and as I've argued throughout this book, has devastating consequences for the nation. There is only one upside to the reality that most people never contact their election officials: those who *do* contact their elected officials have a disproportionate impact on policy. So write or call them, right now.

What are you waiting for? (Don't worry, the book will be over soon if that's what you're waiting for . . .)

The public tends to nurse the warped idea that a super patriot looks like Captain America.* But I think that actual patriots look more like someone writing a letter to a congressman.** Someone like you.

Every American can be a superhero—you don't need a super power. You don't even need a costume or a shield. All you need is your own voice and the guts to use it.

---

*

**

Note to my younger readers: those odd things he is using are called a "pen" and "paper."

Part III.
"Finding Closure"

AMERICA, IF YOU READ ALL THE WAY TO THIS point in the book, I know you've been through a lot. (If you just skipped ahead to this section however, go back to the start, you lazy bum!)

I know that reading parts of this book may have been stressful (but certainly not as aggravating as the 2016 presidential campaign that you survived, barely.)

America, I hereby give you permission to take a short break. Relax a bit. Take a breath. Wind down. Reflect.

(Pause.)

Ah, feel better?

Good, now let me give you one last pep talk.

Let me remind you that we've gotten through times far darker than these—slavery, moves to crush the suffragette movement, the internment of Japanese Americans, state-sponsored violence against unions, World War II, rampant child labor, segregation, the Depression, the McCarthy Era, and on and on. But our nation collectively overcame those stains on our history by banding together to fight for justice.

Also remember that basic human hope can never be fully extinguished. When I am blue on a particularly cold and dark morning in January, I always remind myself that, while the next day may or may not be any warmer, I am guaranteed (in the northern hemisphere) that the next day's sunrise will be just a bit earlier and the sunset just a bit later. That's hope. We can always find some bright side, somewhere.

But if that bit of encouragement doesn't help you—if you are *still* despondent about the human condition—then do what I do when I'm particularly down on the human race: I listen to some of the finest music ever produced. Two suggestions: Miles Davis's *The Complete Live at the*

Plugged Nickel 1965[*] and Johannes Brahms's *The Two Cello Sonatas* performed by Jacqueline du Pré and Daniel Barenboim. Angels, on their best days, wish they could sound this heavenly.

Those classics should immediately comfort you because they just sound so damn good. (If you can't smile listening to them, then I don't know what to tell you, except perhaps try some laughing gas.) But beyond the immediate pleasure of experiencing such timeless classics, think about what those albums represent: that human beings are capable of making works of art that are not only otherworldly in their beauty but reflective of supreme humanity. Always remember that the same human race that is capable of writing *Mein Kampf* is also capable of creating one of Monet's water lily paintings.

For every Hitler, there is a Sophie Scholl, who, as a German dissident opposing him, knowingly gave her life for other people's freedom. Even when some humans show the world their darkest side, we can always find some inspiring, heroic behavior elsewhere.

What makes the difference between a government that, facing a Depression, chooses to create concentration camps to execute its citizens quickly and efficiently, versus a different government that, facing a similar economic meltdown, chooses to create Civilian Conservation Corps (CCC) camps that gave the most destitute citizens food, clothing, shelter, and life-affirming, productive work?

The difference between those two governments is *you*. The difference is *us*. The difference is the character of our nation and its people.

When most regular Germans voted, spoke up, and marched, they did so for Nazism. When most Americans did, we did so for the New Deal.

Don't look for someone else to be your villain or savior. You, I, and everyone around us are America, and *we* make the difference, for good or bad. We can either ignore America's problems, blame them on others, and then take false comfort in claiming we're powerless—or we

---

[*] *The Complete Live at the Plugged Nickel 1965* features Miles Davis on trumpet, Wayne Shorter on tenor sax, Herbie Hancock on piano, Ron Carter on bass, and Tony Williams on drums—musical geniuses all. That's an even greater line-up than the 1927 Yankees. (I threw in that last Yankees reference for my friend, the great Jonathan Eig—brilliant author of the definitive bios of Lou Gehrig, Al Capone, Jackie Robinson, Muhammad Ali, and—for variety—Gregory Goodwin Pincus, the inventor of the birth control pill.)

can take some action, big or small, to get our government and society back on track in a humane, sensible direction.

Auschwitz or a CCC camp? The choice is *ours*.

Those are the stakes.

We must always remember that there is never a right time to do the wrong thing, and never a wrong time to do the right thing. We must know that good citizenship can never be outsourced. When people ask me why I am so passionate about social change, I have a simple response: "Why isn't *everybody*?"

When I suggest to fellow Americans, as I am doing now, that they have a responsibility to take some or all of the steps necessary to be an Activist Patriot, they often demur, saying that it's just too much work, that it's just too futile, that it's just too *hard* to influence elected officials. Give me a friggin' break. Whoever says that just doesn't *know* hard.

Hard is landing at a Normandy Beach under ferocious machine gun and mortar fire. Hard is marching for civil rights over the Edmund Pettus Bridge in Selma while being viciously clubbed.* Hard is looking into your daughter's eyes and having to tell her you don't have any food that night for dinner.

Get over yourself, America, and get to work fixing our country and world. Taking five minutes to contact your elected officials *isn't* hard— it's damn easy, as are most of the other steps I've suggested.

Now, America: you know, deep in your heart, that the way the right wing defines "American exceptionalism"—that each and every facet of America is simply better than each and every aspect of every other country and that God personally wants America to rule the world—is just bunk. But you also know, America, that we *are* an exceptional country.

Yeah, a lot is wrong with us, America, about which I've spent a few hundred pages complaining. But a lot is still *right* with us, too. Let's all of us, our nation and each resident, build upon our greatest strengths— diversity; freedom of speech, press, and religion; openness; free elections; and idealism—in order to build a more perfect union.

---

* Next time you whine that it's just too hard for you to take the time to vote, remember Selma.

In other world capitals, citizens worship at the tombs of dead leaders. In Moscow, residents line up to view the burial place of Lenin. In Beijing, many pay tribute at the mausoleum of Chairman Mao. Even in Paris, in the heart of a democracy, the French pay their respects to the coffins (there are many, nestled within each other) of Emperor Napoleon. Yet while Washington, DC is filled with monuments to presidents, not a single president is actually buried there. Rather, when people wait in a line to worship our civic culture in our nation's capital, they go to the National Archives to see the original Declaration of Independence, the Constitution, and Bill of Rights, documents that proclaim the *ideal* of American freedom. We don't always live up to that ideal, but we still celebrate it, and remembering that ideal occasionally jolts us to try harder to reach it. *That's* what's exceptional about us, America, and don't you forget it.

I once met a Somali refugee in Sweden who had a brother living in Washington, DC. I asked him in which country he'd prefer to live and he said, "America, of course." I pressed him: "Don't you get more government support in Sweden than your brother gets in America?" "Yes," he responded, "but I never feel like I am at home in Sweden—my brother feels like he *belongs* in the United States." America, let's be proud that we are still one of the most welcoming countries on the globe. No matter how the Trumps and Cruzes angrily rant and rave, most of us still want to fully embrace those who still need a safe place to stay.

America, let's remember that day on February 25, 1923, when New York's harbor was clogged with ice, when my mother, Bejla, two months old, was carried off the *S.S. Minnekahda* and into Ellis Island, to freedom, and eventually, to a good life for her family.

Of course you remember that, America. We were all there. Don't we want that freedom, don't we want that good life, for *everybody*? Of course we do.

Let's stay together and let's make this work—for everyone, America.
Are you on board? Are you all in?
(America exuberantly nods.)
Excellent, I'm relieved and overjoyed.
Yes, I *am* still in love with you, America.
You don't have to sleep on the couch anymore.
Come give me—and all 523 million Americans—a big hug.

Appendix

Organizations that Fight Back . . . and Make a Difference!

Below are some of the most effective organizations working on a few of the issues raised in this book. It is by no means an exhaustive list of the thousands of national and international organizations doing great things. but it's a good start. Donate to them, volunteer for them, advocate with them, and discover other ways to help.

DOMESTIC US ORGANIZATIONS

Hunger Free America is headed by Joel Berg, yours truly, the very delightful author of this book (but don't blame the organization if you didn't like it). Founded in 1983 and formerly named the New York City Coalition Against Hunger, it is a nonprofit group building a bold, grassroots, and nonpartisan membership movement in all 50 states to enact the policies and programs necessary to end domestic hunger and ensure that all Americans have sufficient access to nutritious food. Go to www.HungerFreeAmerica.org to learn how you can best advocate and donate to end hunger. Do it now, I'll wait. You can also use our groundbreaking web portal, www.HungerVolunteer.org, to volunteer across the country for high-impact, skills-based anti-hunger projects. This portal is a state-of-the-art tool enabling Americans anywhere to be more effective when they volunteer. So, go sign up now, yes now.

Hunger Free America
50 Broad Street, Suite 1103
New York NY 10004
(212) 825-0028
www.HungerFreeAmerica.org

Appleseed is a nonprofit network of seventeen public interest justice centers in the United States and Mexico working to break down barriers to equal opportunity. Appleseed Centers work with pro bono attorneys and other professionals to research problems, recommend practical and systemic solutions, and engage in targeted and passionate advocacy to win reforms that will mean better lives for people around the country and in Mexico.

Appleseed
727 15th Street NW, 12th Floor
Washington, DC 20005
(202) 347-7960
www.appleseednetwork.org

Center for Financial Services Innovation (CFSI) works to improve the financial health of Americans, especially the underserved, by shaping a robust and innovative financial services marketplace with increased access to higher quality products and practices. They believe finance can be a force for good in people's lives and that serving the needs of consumers responsibly is ultimately more profitable for the financial services industry.

Center for Financial Services Innovation
135 S. LaSalle, Suite 2125
Chicago, IL 60603
(312) 881-5856
www.cfsinnovation.com

United for a Fair Economy raises awareness that concentrated wealth and power undermine the economy, corrupt democracy, deepen the racial divide, and tear communities apart. They support and help build social movements for greater equality through participatory education; media outreach; research; the Responsible Wealth project; and cross-class, cross-race networking opportunities.

United for a Fair Economy
62 Summer Street
Boston, MA 02110
(617) 423-2148
www.faireconomy.org

City Year is a national service program upon which President Bill Clinton modeled the AmeriCorps program. City Year engages idealistic, diverse Americans ages 18–25 in a year of full-time service, working to bridge the gap in high-poverty communities between the support that students in communities actually need and what their schools are designed to provide. In doing so, they're helping to increase graduation rates across the country, and making an impact in the lives of the students they serve.

City Year
287 Columbus Avenue
Boston, MA 02116
(617) 927-2500
www.cityyear.org

INTERNATIONAL ORGANIZATIONS

World Food Program USA works to solve global hunger, building a world where everyone has the food and nutrition needed to lead healthy, productive lives. This group fundraises, advocates, educates, and otherwise builds support for the United Nations World Food Programme, which is the world's largest humanitarian agency fighting hunger worldwide, reaching more than 80 million people in 82 countries with food assistance last year.

World Food Program USA
1725 I Street NW, Suite 510
Washington, DC 20006
(202) 627-3737
www.wfpusa.org

Oxfam is an international confederation of 17 organizations working together with partners and local communities in more than 90 countries. Around the globe, Oxfam works to find practical, innovative ways for people to lift themselves out of poverty and thrive. They save lives and help rebuild livelihoods when crisis strikes. And they campaign so that the voices of people in poverty influence the local and global decisions that affect them.

Oxfam America
226 Causeway Street, 5th Floor
Boston, MA 02114
(800) 776-9326
https://www.oxfamamerica.org/

Acknowledgments

Lots of people with serious jobs ~~to do~~ are funny, although most are unintentionally* so I'll let the reader decide if I succeeded in my aim for this book to be both thoughtful and humorous, but if you think I did, please join me in thanking all those who aided and inspired me in this task. If not, it's [entirely] my ~~entire~~ fault.

Immeasurable appreciation goes to Lori Azim, a world-class researcher, proofreader, fact-checker, and BS-detector. The forcefulness of her vendetta against extraneous commas is exceeded only by the passion of her quest to ~~her~~ get [her] beloved America to practice common sense and open-heartedness again.** Plus, she provided the excellent photo of the Skee-Ball game. She even edited this acknowledgments section, so, to show you all the work she did, I left her editing notes in here.

I can't tell you how [much I appreciate] ~~appreciative I am that~~ [renowned author] Jonathan Eig['s] ~~renowned author, for his~~ clear-eyed editing and sage advice throughout this project. Considering that he was also working on what will surely become the definitive biography of the late ~~Mohamad~~ [Muhammad] Ali and that he was co-parenting three children, the fact that he gave massive amounts of time to help me in such an expert manner—despite the fact that I beat him ~~out~~

---

*

** I previously had a ~~common~~ [comma] between "heartedness" and "again," but Lori took it ~~oot~~ out.

for Spring Valley Senior High School Student-Faculty Council by three votes in 1981—is a gesture of mountainous kindness. (Exactly the kind of phrase Jonathan would note as over-the-top and would delete.) I urge everyone to run out to your nearest bookstore, or to make four clicks in your Amazon account, to buy ~~Eig~~ Jonathan's masterpieces: *Luckiest Man, Opening Day, Get Capone, The Birth of the Pill,* and whatever the heck the Muhammad Ali book is going to be called.

Full disclosure: a few of the best lines in this book were actually suggested by ~~Azim~~ [Lori] or ~~Eig~~ [Jonathan] [—including Lori's idea to show the original draft of this acknowledgment section, edited, although I think she was joking].

A boatload of superlatives goes to graphic designer Cynthia Herrli for designing the original charts and graphs in this book and making them clear and interesting enough that they don't put readers to sleep. Equally huge thanks to Rob Ruiz for his compelling original illustrations for the cover and section dividers. Big thanks also goes to Erin Johnson and Britt Boyd for conceptualizing and designing earlier version[s] of some of the graphs. I thank Barry Wilson for proposing early design ideas for the book and for his photo of the DC restaurant Bullfeathers. I can't thank Sarah Azim enough for her additional design help.

I also want to heap mounds of praise on Seven Stories Press and its publisher, Dan Simon, for unfailingly taking on the "lost causes," both literary and financial. Infinite thanks go to the wise and patient V. Liu for editing this book. More thanks go to Michael Tencer for copy editing it. Still more thanks to Jon Gilbert for the book design and Stewart Cauley for the cover layout. I greatly appreciate all the hardworking staff at Seven Stories who devote countless hours to their jobs for the love of books and progressive causes, not the big bucks. And kudos also to Crystal Yakacki, my former Seven Stories editor, for originally championing this project.

Enormous appreciation goes to the staff, board members, AmeriCorps*VISTA national service members, donors, and volunteers of Hunger Free America, who have so strongly ~~have~~ undergirded the social justice work that makes this book possible.

I also want to thank numerous bloggers (most of whom are underpaid or entirely unpaid) for inspiring, informing, and infuriating me.

A debt of gratitude goes to Al Franken, wh~~om~~ I've only met [twice], very briefly, ~~twice,~~ for writing books that pioneered the intermingling of public policy facts with humor and for generally becoming an excellent US senator, although I am still pissed at him for voting [in favor of] ~~for~~ SNAP cuts, despite the fact that, ~~throughoput~~ [throughout] the rest of his career, he has been a champion of the anti-hunger movement. Unless Franken wants to become "a big fat idiot,"* he should never again vote to take food away from hungry families.

I also want to thank Jennifer Tescher, Will Marshall, Melissa Boteach, and Bert Brandenburg for providing invaluable input on select chapters of this book.

If you are enthralled by this book, it's because of everyone else's excellent help. If you hate it, it's only because I'm a ~~dumb ass~~ [dumbass or dumb-ass].**

---

*

** Lori found ~~eleven~~ 11 other typos (including seven erroneous commas) that she graciously did not show above.

Notes

Introduction: "The Talk"

1   Paul Krugman, "Varieties of Voodoo," *New York Times*, February 19, 2016, http://www.nytimes.com/2016/02/19/opinion/varieties-of-voodoo.html (accessed June 7, 2016).

2   "Sanders: 'We will crush and destroy' ISIS," *MSNBC*, March 23, 2016, http://www.msnbc.com/msnbc-quick-cuts/watch/sanders-we-will-crush-and-destroy-isis-650496067881 (accessed June 7, 2016).

3   Neil Irwin, "After Mass Shootings, It's Often Easier to Buy a Gun," *New York Times*, June 14, 2016, http://www.nytimes.com/2016/06/15/upshot/policy-changes-after-mass-shootings-tend-to-make-guns-easier-to-buy.html (accessed June 22, 2016).

4   "Guns in the U.S.: The Statistics Behind the Violence," *BBC*, January 5, 2016, http://www.bbc.com/news/world-us-canada-34996604 (accessed June 7, 2016).

5   Peter Schroeder and Kevin Cirilli, "Warren, Left Fume over Deal," *Hill*, December 10, 2014, http://thehill.com/regulation/finance/226638-democrats-balking-at-dodd-frank-changes-in-cromnibus (accessed June 21, 2016).

6   Jordan Weissmann, "America May Have the Worst Hunger Problem of Any Rich Nation," *Slate*, September 14, 2014, http://www.slate.com/blogs/moneybox/2014/09/04/american_hunger_it_s_embarrassing_by_rich_country_standards.html (accessed December 27, 2014).

7   Carmen DeNavas-Walt and Bernadette D. Proctor, "Income and Poverty in the United States: 2014," Current Population Reports, US Census Bureau, September 2015, https://www.census.gov/content/dam/Census/library/publications/2015/demo/p60-252.pdf (accessed June 21, 2016).

8   Ibid.

9   Lydia Saad, "The '40-Hour' Workweek is Actually Longer—by Seven Hours," Gallup, August 29, 2014, http://www.gallup.com/poll/175286/hour-workweek-actually-longer-seven-hours.aspx (accessed June 21, 2016).

10 Ashley N. Edwards, "Dynamics of Economic Well-Being: Poverty, 2009–2011," Tables 3 and 4, US Census Bureau, January 2014, https://www.census.gov/library/publications/2014/demo/p70-137.html (accessed September 21, 2016).

11 National Low-Income Housing Coalition, Housing Wage Calculator, http://nlihc.org/library/wagecalc (accessed June 21, 2016).

12 Ariel Kaminer and Sean O'Driscoll, "Workers at N.Y.U.'s Abu Dhabi Site Faced Harsh Conditions," *New York Times*, May 18, 2014, http://www.nytimes.com/2014/05/19/nyregion/workers-at-nyus-abu-dhabi-site-face-harsh-conditions.html (accessed December 28, 2015).

13 "Migrant Workers' Rights on Saadiyat Island in the United Arab Emirates: 2015 Progress Report," Human Rights Watch, February 10, 2015, https://www.hrw.org/report/2015/02/10/migrant-workers-rights-saadiyat-island-united-arab-emirates/2015-progress-report (accessed December 28, 2015).

14 Ariel Kaminer and Alain Delaquérière, "N.Y.U. Gives Its Stars Loans for Summer Homes," *New York Times*, June 17, 2013, http://www.nytimes.com/2013/06/18/nyregion/nyu-gives-stars-loans-for-summer-homes.html (access January 16, 2016).

15 Stephanie Saul, "N.Y.U. President's Penthouse Gets a Face-Lift Worth $1.1 Million (or More)," *New York Times*, December 21, 2015, http://www.nytimes.com/2015/12/22/us/nyu-presidents-penthouse-gets-a-1-1-million-face-lift.html (accessed December 28, 2015).

16 Carina Storrs, "U.S. Suicide Rates Up, Especially among Women, but Down for Black Males," *CNN*, April 22, 2016, http://www.cnn.com/2016/04/22/health/suicide-rates-rise/ (accessed June 7, 2016).

17   Miranda Leitsinger, "Hungry Heroes: 25 Percent of Military Families Seek Food Aid," *NBC News*, August 17, 2014, http://www.nbcnews.com/feature/in-plain-sight/hungry-heroes-25-percent-military-families-seek-food-aid-n180236 (accessed February 13, 2016).

Part I: "The Intervention"

CHAPTER ONE: NO WE CAN'T

1   I am recalling quotes from the pastor more than seven years after they occurred, without having taken notes or recorded that night, so each of the words may not be exact, but I am certain I'm retelling his main points correctly.

2   The Asian-American vote was pushed away from the GOP by that party's anti-immigrant and pro-Christian rhetoric, and pulled to the Democrats by their inclusive economic policies and targeted outreach. See: Karthick Ramakrishnan, "How Asian Americans Became Democrats," *American Prospect*, July 26, 2016, http://prospect.org/article/how-asian-americans-became-democrats-0 (accessed August 1, 2016)

3   Drew DeSilver, "US Voter Turnout Trails Most Developed Countries," Pew Research Center, August 2, 2016, http://www.pewresearch.org/fact-tank/2015/05/06/u-s-voter-turnout-trails-most-developed-countries/ (accessed September 21, 2016).

4   Frequently Asked Questions, "What is an Abandoner?" Abandonment.net, http://www.abandonment.net/abandonment-frequently-asked-questions#a5 (accessed June 22, 2016).

5   Sam Roberts, "2008 Surge in Black Voters Nearly Erased Racial Gap," *New York Times*, July 20, 2009, http://www.nytimes.com/2009/07/21/us/politics/21vote.html (accessed January 23, 2016).

6   Ibid.

7   Angie Drobnic Holan, "Obama Campaign Financed by Large Donors, Too," PolitiFact, April 22, 2010, http://www.politifact.com/truth-o-meter/statements/2010/apr/22/barack-obama/obama-campaign-financed-large-donors-too/ (accessed January 24, 2016).

8   "The Obameter: Tracking Obama's Campaign Promises," PolitiFact, http://www.politifact.com/truth-o-meter/promises/obameter/ (accessed January 24, 2016).

9   Sophia Tesfaye, "A Staggering Number of Republicans Believe President Obama is a Muslim," *Salon*, September 14, 2015, http://www.salon.com/2015/09/14/a_staggering_number_of_republicans_believe_president_obama_is_a_muslim/ (accessed February 12, 2016).

10   Kurt Eichenwald, "Obama's Invasion of Texas: When Partisanship Becomes an Extreme Sport," *Newsweek*, May 12, 2015, http://www.newsweek.com/2015/05/22/obamas-invasion-texas-when-partisanship-becomes-extreme-sport-330947.html (accessed August 1, 2016).

11   Andrew Kaczynski, "A Republican Congressman is Actually Upset about Obama's Tan Suit," *BuzzFeed News*, August, 29, 2014, http://www.buzzfeed.com/andrewkaczynski/beige#.kuWnqMLjy (accessed February 12, 2016).

12   Sara R. Collins, Munira Z. Gunja, and Sophie Beutel, "New U.S. Census Data Show the Number of Uninsured Americans Dropped by 8.8 Million," *To The Point*, a Blog of the Commonwealth Fund, September 16, 2015, http://www.commonwealthfund.org/publications/blog/2015/sept/us-census-data-shows-uninsured-americans-drop (accessed June 22, 2016).

13   Julie Hirschfeld Davis, "The White House Holiday Photo Line: A Tradition of Awkwardness," *New York Times*, December 13, 2015, http://www.nytimes.com/2015/12/14/us/politics/the-white-house-holiday-photo-line-a-tradition-of-awkwardness.html (accessed January 22, 2016).

14   Ron Fournier, "Analysis: Obama and the Perils of Being Aloof," *National Journal*, January 8, 2013, http://www.govexec.com/excellence/promising-practices/2013/01/analysis-obama-and-perils-being-aloof/60534/ (accessed June 22, 2016).

15   Jamelle Bouie, "Is Obama Aloof? Sure. Does it Matter? No.," *American Prospect*, January 8, 2013, http://prospect.org/article/obama-aloof-sure-does-it-matter-no (accessed January 24, 2016).

16   Elias Isquith, "Secretary of Schmoozing: How New Hillary Emails Reveal What Friendliness in Washington Really Means," *Salon*, January 7, 2016, http://www.salon.com/2016/01/07/secretary_of_schmoozing_how_new_hillary_emails_reveal_what_friendliness_in_washington_really_means/ (accessed January 24, 2016).

17   "Michelle Obama Jokes White House Like 'Nice Prison'," *Washington Wire* blog, *Wall Street Journal*, July 2, 2013, http://blogs.wsj.com/washwire/2013/07/02/michelle-obama-jokes-white-house-like-nice-prison/ (Accessed March 8, 2016).

18   WTF with Marc Maron, podcast, "Episode 613 - President Barack Obama," June 22, 2015, http://www.wtfpod.com/podcast/episodes/episode_613_-_president_barack_obama (accessed January 24, 2016).

19   Charles Homans, "All the Presidents' Tailor," *New York Times Magazine*, December 27, 2015, http://www.nytimes.com/interactive/2015/12/16/magazine/the-lives-they-lived.html?_r=0#id-56718d5571fdd40001000069 (accessed December 27, 2015).

20   Nancy Pelosi, "We Must Pass Health Care Reform," *YouTube* video, posted January 28, 2010, https://www.youtube.com/watch?v=Se--vFCx-fs (accessed September 21, 2016).

21   Sam Youngman, "White House Unloads Anger over Criticism from 'Professional Left'," *Hill*, August 10, 2010, http://thehill.com/homenews/administration/113431-white-house-unloads-on-professional-left (accessed January 22, 2016).

22   Alexander Bolton, "Schumer: Dems Erred with ObamaCare," *Hill*, November 25, 2014, http://thehill.com/policy/healthcare/225300-schumer-dems-erred-with-obamacare (accessed January 24, 2016).

23   "Key Facts about the Uninsured Population," Fact Sheet, the Henry J. Kaiser Family Foundation, October 5, 2015, http://kff.org/uninsured/fact-sheet/key-facts-about-the-uninsured-population/ (accessed February 12, 2016).

24   Roger Fisher and William L. Ury, *Getting to Yes: Negotiating Agreement Without Giving In* (New York: Penguin Group, 1981).

25   Alan Rappeport and Jess Bidgood, "Overflow Crowd for Donald Trump in Bernie Sanders's Backyard," *New York Times*, January 7, 2016, http://www.nytimes.com/2016/01/08/us/politics/overflow-crowd-for-donald-trump-in-bernie-sanderss-backyard.html (accessed January 22, 2016).

26   Jeremy Diamond, "Trump: I Could 'shoot somebody and I wouldn't lose voters'," *CNN*, January 23, 2016, http://www.cnn.com/2016/01/23/politics/donald-trump-shoot-somebody-support/index.html (accessed January 23, 2016).

27   Steven Bilakovics, *Democracy without Politics* (Cambridge, Massachusetts: Harvard University Press, 2013), 4-5.

28   Jennifer Epstein, "Obama on Poverty: Few Mentions," *Politico*, September 16, 2012, http://www.politico.com/story/2012/09/obama-leaves-out-most-mentions-of-poverty-081253#ixzz3y14vvoD5 (accessed January 22, 2016).

29   "Remarks by the President in Eulogy for the Honorable Reverend Clementa Pinckney," The White House, June 26, 2015, https://www.whitehouse.gov/the-press-office/2015/06/26/remarks-president-eulogy-honorable-reverend-clementa-pinckney (accessed June 22, 2016).

30   I want to give a particular shout-out to USDA Under Secretary for Food and Nutrition Services, Kevin Concannon, and USDA Food and Nutrition Service Administrator Audrey Rowe, two Obama appointees who oversaw the federal nutrition assistance programs. Both demonstrated a rare combination of phenomenal competence and extraordinary kind-heartedness and used every tool at their disposal to fight hunger.

31   Alfred Lubrano of the *Philadelphia Inquirer* was one of the few journalists to consistently follow up on Obama's pledge to end child hunger.

32   Blake Zeff, "DC Celebrates Itself for Letting Poor Americans Go Hungry," *Salon*, January 31,
      2014, http://www.salon.com/2014/01/31/washington_celebrates_itself_for_helping_poor_
      americans_go_hungry/ (accessed January 24, 2016).

CHAPTER TWO: MONEY CAN'T BUY HAPPINESS

33   Arthur C. Brooks, "A Formula for Happiness," Opinion, *New York Times*, December 14,
      2013, http://www.nytimes.com/2013/12/15/opinion/sunday/a-formula-for-happiness.html
      (accessed January 31, 2016).
34   Derek Thompson, "A World Without Work," *Atlantic*, July/August 2015, http://www.theat-
      lantic.com/magazine/archive/2015/07/world-without-work/395294/ (accessed February 27,
      2016).
35   Life evaluation ratings in the study were determined by answers to questions such as
      "How satisfied are you with your life as a whole these days?" The authors define emotional
      well-being as "emotional quality of an individual's everyday experience—the frequency and
      intensity of experiences of joy, stress, sadness, anger, and affection that make one's life
      pleasant or unpleasant." Daniel Kahneman and Angus Deaton, "High Income Improves
      Evaluation of Life but Not Emotional Well-being," Proceedings of the National Academy of
      Sciences, 38, no. 38 (2010): 16489-16493, http://www.pnas.org/content/107/38/16489.full.
      pdf (accessed January 31, 2016).
36   Carmen DeNavas-Walt, Bernadette D. Proctor, Jessica C. Smith, "Income, Poverty, and
      Health Insurance Coverage in the United States: 2009," US Census Bureau, September
      2010, https://www.census.gov/prod/2010pubs/p60-238.pdf (accessed January 31, 2016).
37   Emily Badger and Christopher Ingraham, "The Remarkably High Odds You'll be Poor at
      Some Point in Your Life," *Washington Post*, July 24, 2015, https://www.washingtonpost.com/
      news/wonk/wp/2015/07/24/the-remarkably-high-odds-youll-be-poor-at-some-point-in-your-
      life/ (accessed February 5, 2016).
38   Sam Fleming and Shawn Donnan, "America's Middle-Class Meltdown: Core Shrinks to Half
      of US Homes," *Financial Times*, December 9, 2015, http://www.ft.com/cms/s/2/98ce14ee-
      99a6-11e5-95c7-d47aa298f769.html#ixzz3zKNCDw1O (accessed February 5, 2016).
39   Keith Miller and David Madland, "As Income Inequality Rises, America's Middle Class
      Shrinks," Center for American Progress, December 18, 2014, https://www.americanprogress.
      org/issues/economy/news/2014/12/18/101790/as-income-inequality-rises-americas-mid-
      dle-class-shrinks/ (accessed February 12, 2016).
40   Carmen DeNavas-Walt and Bernadette D. Proctor, *Income and Poverty in the United States:
      2014*, Current Population Reports, US Census Bureau, September 2015, P60-252, https://
      www.census.gov/content/dam/Census/library/publications/2015/demo/p60-252.pdf
      (accessed June 22, 2016).
41   Median income in 2014 was $42,491 for Hispanics; $35,398 for African Americans; $45,482
      in rural areas. Native-born Americans earned $74,678, more than the $40,795 earned by for-
      eign-born noncitizens, but less than the $59,261 earned by foreign-born naturalized citizens.
      Ibid.
42   John M. Glionna, "Too Poor to Retire and Too Young to Die," *Los Angeles Times*, January 29,
      2016, http://graphics.latimes.com/retirement-nomads/ (accessed February 22, 2016).
43   John W. Schoen, "State Budget Balancing is Putting Pensions at Risk," *CNBC*, June 25,
      2015, http://www.cnbc.com/2015/06/25/t-balancing-inflicts-pension-pain.html (accessed
      September 21, 2016).
44   Mary Williams Walsh, "Teamsters' Pension Fund Warns 400,000 of Cuts," *New York Times*,
      October 6, 2015, http://www.nytimes.com/2015/10/07/business/teamsters-pension-fund-
      warns-400000-of-cuts.html (accessed February 5, 2016).

45 Jennifer Bjorhus and Jim Spencer, "Treasury Rejects Teamster Pension Cuts," *StarTribune*, May 9, 2016, http://www.startribune.com/treasury-to-announce-teamster-pension-cut-decision/378416931/ (accessed June 10, 2016).

46 John M. Glionna, "Too Poor to Retire and Too Young to Die."

47 Ashley N. Edwards, "Dynamics of Economic Well-Being: Poverty, 2009–2011."

48 Carmen DeNavas-Walt and Bernadette D. Proctor, *Income and Poverty in the United States: 2014.*.

49 "The 2016 Distressed Communities Index: An Analysis of Community Well-Being Across the United States," Economic Innovation Group, February 2016, http://eig.org/wp-content/uploads/2016/02/2016-Distressed-Communities-Index-Report.pdf (accessed February 25, 2016).

50 Ibid. The 2014 poverty rate was 10.1 percent for white non-Hispanics, 26.2 percent for blacks, 23.6 for Hispanics of any race. The rate was 18.9 percent in principal cities, 16.5 percent in rural areas, and 11.8 percent in suburbs. 28.5 percent of people with disabilities lived in poverty. 30.6 percent of female householders with no husband were poor, but it is likely that single-led households are caused *by* poverty much more than they are a cause *of* poverty.

51 Ibid.

52 Ibid.

53 H. Luke Shaefer and Kathryn Edin, "The Rise of Extreme Poverty in the United States," *Pathways*, Summer 2014, http://web.stanford.edu/group/scspi/_media/pdf/pathways/summer_2014/Pathways_Summer_2014_ShaeferEdin.pdf (accessed February 1, 2016).

54 Ellen L. Bassuk, Carmela J. DeCandia, Corey Anne Beach and Fred Berman, "America's Youngest Outcasts: A Report Card on Child Homelessness," American Institute for Research, National Center for Family and Homelessness, November 2014, http://www.homelesschildrenamerica.org/mediadocs/282.pdf (accessed February 12, 2016).

55 Kathryn J Edin and H. Luke Shaefer, *$2.00 a Day: Living on Almost Nothing in America* (Boston: Houghton Mifflin Harcourt, 2015).

56 Sarah Maslin Nir, "The Price of Nice Nails," *New York Times*, May 7, 2015, http://www.nytimes.com/2015/05/10/nyregion/at-nail-salons-in-nyc-manicurists-are-underpaid-and-unprotected.html (accessed September 21, 2016).

57 Mark Arsenault and Dan Adams, "Globe, Distributor Trade Blame as Delivery Woes Persist," *Boston Globe*, January 4, 2016, (accessed February 5, 2016)31/ https://www.bostonglobe.com/business/2016/01/03/deliveries/wrEYnoz9F6XFEZeIkTzMQL/story.html (accessed February 5, 2016).

58 Sandro Galea, Melissa Tracy, Katherine J. Hoggatt, Charles DiMaggio, and Adam Karpati, "Estimated Deaths Attributable to Social Factors in the United States," *American Journal of Public Health*, 101, no. 8 (August 2011): 1456–1465, doi: 10.2105/AJPH.2010.300086, http://ajph.aphapublications.org/doi/abs/10.2105/AJPH.2010.300086 (accessed February 3, 2016).

59 Emily Badger and Christopher Ingraham, "The Hidden Inequality of Who Dies in Car Crashes," *Wonkblog, Washington Post*, October 1, 2015, https://www.washingtonpost.com/news/wonk/wp/2015/10/01/the-hidden-inequality-of-who-dies-in-car-crashes/ (accessed February 3, 2016).

60 Olga Khazan, "The Poorest Americans Die Younger Than the Poorest Costa Ricans," *Atlantic*, January 4, 2016, http://www.theatlantic.com/health/archive/2016/01/the-poorest-americans-die-younger-than-the-poorest-costa-ricans/422319/ (accessed January 10, 2016).

61 Sabrina Tavernise, "Disparity in Life Spans of the Rich and the Poor is Growing," *New York Times*, February 13, 2016, http://www.nytimes.com/2016/02/13/health/disparity-in-life-spans-of-the-rich-and-the-poor-is-growing.html (accessed February 13, 2016).

62 Madeline Ostrander, "What Poverty Does to the Young Brain," *New Yorker*, June 4, 2015, http://www.newyorker.com/tech/elements/what-poverty-does-to-the-young-brain (accessed June 22, 2016).

63   "The Long-Term Benefits of the Supplemental Nutritional Assistance Program," White House Council of Economic Advisors, December 2015, https://www.whitehouse.gov/sites/whitehouse.gov/files/documents/SNAP_report_final_nonembargo.pdf (accessed February 3, 2016).

64   "Hunger in America 2014," Feeding America fact sheet, August 2014, http://www.feedingamerica.org/hunger-in-america/our-research/hunger-in-america/ (accessed February 5, 2016). [I don't see a Feeding America Fact Sheet. There's a "Facts and Faces of Hunger" and an Executive Summary to the report, but I can't tell what's being referenced here.]

65   Sara Goldrick-Rab and Katharine M. Broton, "Hungry, Homeless and in College," Opinion, *New York Times*, December 4, 2015, http://www.nytimes.com/2015/12/04/opinion/hungry-homeless-and-in-college.html (accessed December 27, 2015).

66   Eric Levitz, "Trump University Told Recruiters to Target Single Parents with Hungry Kids," *New York Magazine*, June 1, 2016, http://nymag.com/daily/intelligencer/2016/05/trump-u-targeted-single-parents-with-hungry-kids.html (accessed June 10, 2016).

67   Paul Weinstein Jr, and Bethany Patten, "The Price of Paying Taxes II: How Paid Tax Preparer Fees are Diminishing the Earned Income Tax Credit (EITC)," Progressive Policy Institute, April 2016, http://www.progressivepolicy.org/wp-content/uploads/2016/04/2016.04-Weinstein_Patten_The-Price-of-Paying-Takes-II.pdf (accessed June 10, 2016).

68   Dave Sherwood, "Maine's Lottery Amounts to a Multimillion-Dollar Tax on Poor, University Study Shows," Maine Center for Public Interest Reporting, *Portland Press Herald,* October 21, 2015 (updated December 15, 2015),

69   http://www.pressherald.com/2015/10/21/maines-lottery-amounts-to-a-multimillion-dollar-tax-on-poor-university-study-shows/ (accessed June 23, 2016). Mike Tipping, "Anti-Welfare Hysteria Clouds Bigger Lottery Issue of Preying on Poor," *Portland Press Herald*, December 26, 2015, http://www.pressherald.com/2015/12/26/mike-tipping-anti-welfare-hysteria-clouds-bigger-lottery-issue-of-preying-on-poor/ (accessed February 13, 2016).

70   Joseph E. Stiglitz. *The Price of Inequality: How Today's Divided Society Endangers Our Future* (New York: W.W. Norton & Company, 2012), xi–xii.

71   Alan Feurer, "Life on $7.25 an Hour," *New York Times*, February 28, 2013, http://www.nytimes.com/2013/12/01/nyregion/older-workers-are-increasingly-entering-fast-food-industry.html (accessed February 2, 2016).

72   Leslie Patton, "McDonald's $8.25 Man and $8.75 Million CEO Shows Pay Gap," *Bloomberg Business*, December 12, 2012, http://www.bloomberg.com/news/articles/2012-12-12/mcdonald-s-8-25-man-and-8-75-million-ceo-shows-pay-gap (accessed February 5, 2016).

73   John Schmitt and Janelle Jones, "Slow Progress for Fast-Food Workers," *Center for Economic and Policy Research Blog*, August 6, 2013, http://cepr.net/blogs/cepr-blog/slow-progress-for-fast-food-workers (accessed February 5, 2016).

74   Ben Jacobs, "Bertrand Olotara: the US Senate Cook Struggling to Get Off Food Stamps," *Guardian*, April 23, 2015, http://www.theguardian.com/us-news/2015/apr/23/us-senate-cook-bertrand-olotara-public-assistance (accessed February 5, 2016).

75   Mark Nord, "Food Insecurity in Households with Children: Prevalence, Severity, and Household Characteristics," EIB-56, US Department of Agriculture, Economic Research Service, September 2009, http://www.ers.usda.gov/media/155368/eib56_1_.pdf (accessed June 11, 2016).

76   Neil Irwin, "A Big Safety Net and Strong Job Market Can Coexist. Just Ask Scandinavia," *The Upshot, New York Times*, December 17, 2014, http://www.nytimes.com/2014/12/18/upshot/nordic-nations-show-that-big-safety-net-can-allow-for-leap-in-employment-rate-.html (accessed March 3, 2016).

77   "Expanding Opportunity in America: A Discussion Draft from the House Budget Committee," US House of Representatives, July 24, 2014, http://budget.house.gov/uploadedfiles/expanding_opportunity_in_america.pdf (accessed June 22, 2016).

78 Robert Greenstein, "Merging Safety Net Programs Could Increase Poverty, Not Reduce It," Center for Budget and Policy Priorities, January 6, 2016, http://www.cbpp.org/poverty-and-inequality/commentary-merging-safety-net-programs-could-increase-poverty-not-reduce-it (accessed February 3, 2016).

79 "Marco Rubio and the Safety Net," *Economist*, July 12, 2014, http://www.economist.com/news/united-states/21606852-republican-party-should-take-florida-senators-ideas-seriously-marco-rubio-and (accessed June 22, 2016).

80 Tom LoBianco, "Rubio, Dems Trade Shots over Minimum Wage, 'Free Stuff'," *CNN*, October 14, 2015, http://www.cnn.com/2015/10/14/politics/marco-rubio-democratic-debate-free-stuff/ (accessed June 22, 2016).

81 Zack Beauchamp, "Senator: Food Stamps are Just Like Slavery," ThinkProgress, August 26, 2013, http://thinkprogress.org/justice/2013/08/26/2525961/rand-paul-food-health-libertarianism-hayek/ (accessed March 4, 2016).

82 Cary Spivak, "Paul Ryan's Net Worth has Increased 75 Percent in Past Decade," *Seattle Times*, August 12, 2012, http://www.seattletimes.com/nation-world/paul-ryans-net-worth-has-increased-75-percent-in-past-decade/ (accessed February 13, 2016).

83 Juana Summers, "Ryan's Mom a Face in Medicare Wars," *Politico*, August 12, 2012, http://www.politico.com/story/2012/08/ryans-mom-is-new-face-in-medicare-wars-079853 (accessed February 13, 2016).

84 Tony Lee, "Scott Walker: America Exceptional Because 'We Celebrate Independence from Government, Not Our Dependence On It'," *Breitbart*, February 26, 2015, http://www.breitbart.com/big-government/2015/02/26/scott-walker-america-exceptional-because-we-celebrate-independence-from-government-not-our-dependence-on-it/ (accessed June 22, 2016).

85 Mary Spicuzza, Jason Stein, and Crocker Stephenson, "Scott Walker Signs Bill Clearing Public Funds for New Bucks Arena," *Journal Sentinel*, August 12, 2015, http://www.jsonline.com/news/statepolitics/scott-walker-to-sign-bucks-arena-funding-bill-at-wisconsin-state-fair-b99555622z1-321544131.html (accessed June 22, 2016).

86 Onan Coca, "Dr. Ben Carson Speaks Out on the America MLK Jr. Would Want to See," Eaglesharing.com, January 22, 2015, http://eaglerising.com/14189/dr-ben-carson-speaks-america-mlk-jr-want-see/#FMMdqyl80855EF1u.99. As I documented in my first book, *All You Can Eat: How Hungry is America?*, one of the main demands of the Poor People's Movement, launched by Dr. King, was for the federal government to create a nutrition assistance safety net.

87 Kira Lerner, "7 Ridiculous Things Ben Carson Believes," ThinkProgress, May 4, 2015, http://thinkprogress.org/politics/2015/05/04/3646780/ben-carson-announcement/ (accessed June 22, 2016).

88 Katie Sanders, "Does Ben Carson Want to 'Eliminate Dependency on Government' Despite Benefiting from Welfare?," PolitiFact, May 11, 2015, http://www.politifact.com/truth-o-meter/statements/2015/may/11/occupy-democrats/does-ben-carson-want-eliminate-dependency-governme/ (accessed June 22, 2016).

89 Aviva Shen, "Congressman Who Gets Millions in Farm Subsidies Denounces Food Stamps as Stealing 'Other People's Money,'" ThinkProgress, May 21, 2013, http://thinkprogress.org/economy/2013/05/21/2042831/congressman-who-gets-millions-in-farm-subsidies-denounces-food-stamps-as-stealing-other-peoples-money/ (accessed June 22, 2016).

90 Raj Chetty, Nathaniel Hendren, and Lawrence F. Katz, "The Effects of Exposure to Better Neighborhoods on Children: New Evidence from the Moving to Opportunity Experiment," *American Economic Review*, 106, no. 4 (2016): 855–902, http://www.equality-of-opportunity.org/images/mto_paper.pdf (accessed June 22, 2016).

91 "Eligible households do spend more on food and particularly on healthy foods in those months when most (EITC) benefits are paid." Leslie McGranahan and Diane Whitmore Schanzenbach, "The Earned Income Tax Credit and Food Consumption Patterns," Federal

Reserve Bank of Chicago, November 2013, https://www.chicagofed.org/publications/working-papers/2013/wp-14 (accessed June 22, 2016).

92   As quoted in the movie, *Best of Enemies*, 2015.

93   John Tierney, "Which States are Givers and Which are Takers?," *Atlantic*, May 5, 2014, http://www.theatlantic.com/business/archive/2014/05/which-states-are-givers-and-which-are-takers/361668/ (accessed June 11, 2016).

94   Calculations by the author based on public voting data and SNAP caseload data obtained from the US Department of Agriculture: http://www.fns.usda.gov/pd/supplemental-nutrition-assistance-program-snap.

95   Bryce Covert and Josh Israel, "What 7 States Discovered After Spending More Than $1 Million Drug Testing Welfare Recipients," ThinkProgress, February 26, 2015, http://thinkprogress.org/economy/2015/02/26/3624447/tanf-drug-testing-states/ (accessed June 22, 2016).

96   Arthur Delaney, "Food Stamp Drug Testing Could Become a Thing," *Huffington Post*, February 12, 2016, http://www.huffingtonpost.com/entry/snap-drug-test_us_56bdf149e4b-0c3c55050d8b2?section=politics (accessed February 13, 2016).

97   Max Ehrenfreund, "Kansas Has Found the Ultimate Way to Punish the Poor," *Wonkblog, Washington Post*, May 21, 2015, http://www.washingtonpost.com/news/wonkblog/wp/2015/05/21/kansas-has-found-the-ultimate-way-to-punish-the-poor/ (accessed June 22, 2016).

98   Shelley K. Irving and Tracy A. Loveless, "Dynamics of Economic Well-Being: Participation in Government Programs, 2009–2012: Who Gets Assistance?," US Census Bureau, Report Number: P70-141, May 2015, http://www.census.gov/content/dam/Census/library/publications/2015/demo/p70-141.pdf (accessed June 22, 2016).

CHAPTER THREE: EAT, PRAY, LOVE . . .

99   Ariane Hegewisch, Emily Ellis, and Heidi Hartmann, "The Gender Wage Gap: 2014; Earnings Differences by Race and Ethnicity," Institute for Women's Policy Research, March 2015, http://www.iwpr.org/publications/pubs/the-gender-wage-gap-2014-earnings-differences-by-race-and-ethnicity#sthash.peajrx9C.dpuf (accessed February 15, 2016).

100   Elise Gould, "Millions of Working People Don't Get Paid Time Off for Holidays or Vacation," Economic Policy Institute, September 1, 2015, http://www.epi.org/publication/millions-of-working-people-dont-get-paid-time-off-for-holidays-or-vacation/ (accessed February 15, 2016).

101   Mary Clare Jalonick and Erica Werner, "In Speaker Bid, Rep. Ryan Sparks Debate on Work-Life Balance," *Associated Press*, Oct. 22, 2015, http://bigstory.ap.org/article/fe614d-1951954ae7a5c3994f0a3c8db1/ryan-speaker-bid-sparks-debate-work-life-balance (accessed February 15, 2016).

102   "The Need for Paid Family Leave," Fact Sheet, A Better Balance, http://www.abetterbalance.org/web/ourissues/familyleave (accessed February 14, 2016). [I don't know what's being referenced here. The title is for the webpage, but there are two different links for fact sheets . . .]

103   "Collective Bargaining," *The State of Working America*, Economic Policy Institute, http://stateofworkingamerica.org/fact-sheets/collective-bargaining/#sthash.31piMF1r.dpuf (accessed March 4, 2016).

104   David Madland and Keith Miller, "Latest Census Data Underscore How Important Unions are for the Middle Class," Center for American Progress Action Fund, September 17, 2013, https://www.americanprogressaction.org/issues/labor/news/2013/09/17/74363/latest-census-data-underscore-how-important-unions-are-for-the-middle-class/ (accessed February 13, 2016).

105   Kathryn J. Edin and H. Luke Shaefer, *$2.00 a Day*, 47.

106   Calculations made by Hunger Free America based on USDA food security data.

107 David Cooper, "Balancing Paychecks and Public Assistance," Economic Policy Institute, Briefing Paper #418, February 3, 2016, http://www.epi.org/publication/wages-and-transfers/ (accessed February 15, 2016).

108 Helene York, "Do Children Harvest Your Food?," *Atlantic*, March 26, 2012, http://www.theatlantic.com/health/archive/2012/03/do-children-harvest-your-food/254853/ (accessed February 15, 2016).

109 Steven Greenhouse, "Just 13, and Working Risky 12-Hour Shifts in the Tobacco Fields," *New York Times*, September 6, 2014, http://www.nytimes.com/2014/09/07/business/just-13-and-working-risky-12-hour-shifts-in-the-tobacco-fields.html (accessed February 14, 2016).

110 Ibid.

111 José R. Padilla and David Bacon, "Protect Female Farmworkers," Opinion, *New York Times*, January 19, 2016, http://www.nytimes.com/2016/01/19/opinion/how-to-protect-female-farmworkers.html?ref=opinion (accessed February 14, 2016).

112 "Census of Fatal Occupational Injuries Summary, 2014," US Bureau of Labor Statistics, September 17, 2015, http://www.bls.gov/news.release/cfoi.nro.htm (accessed February 14, 2016).

113 Note that Javier's name has been changed to protect him. Nadia Hewka and Michael Hollander, "Wage Theft is an Epidemic. Here's How We Can Help Fix It," TalkPoverty, February 2, 2016, http://talkpoverty.org/2016/02/02/wage-theft-is-epidemic-how-we-can-fix/ (accessed February 14, 2016).

114 "Empty Judgments: The Wage Collection Crises in New York," Community Development Project at the Urban Justice Center Employment Law Unit at The Legal Aid Society, National Center for Law and Economic Justice, February 20, 2015, https://cdp.urbanjustice.org/sites/default/files/CDP.WEB.doc_Empty_Judgments_The_Wage_Collection_Crisis_In_New_York_2015220.pdf (accessed February 14, 2016).

115 Geoff Williams, "3 Strategies for Surviving a Long Commute," *U.S. News & World Report*, March 14, 2014, http://money.usnews.com/money/personal-finance/articles/2014/03/14/3-strategies-for-surviving-a-long-commute (accessed February 14, 2016).

116 Lydia Saad, "The '40-Hour' Workweek is Actually Longer—by Seven Hours," Gallup, August 29, 2014, http://www.gallup.com/poll/175286/hour-workweek-actually-longer-seven-hours.aspx (accessed June 23, 2016).

117 "Economic Report of the President, Together with the Annual Report of the Council of Economic Advisers," Transmitted to the Congress February 2015, https://www.whitehouse.gov/sites/default/files/docs/cea_2015_erp.pdf (accessed June 23, 2016).

118 Kathryn J. Edin and H. Luke Shaefer, *$2.00 a Day*, 27.

119 Arthur Delaney, "What It's Like to be on Food Stamps and Prove You're Looking for Work," *Huffington Post*, January 9, 2016, http://www.huffingtonpost.com/entry/food-stamps-work-requirements_us_568ecde1e4b0cad15e640e5e?utm_hp_ref=politicstics+podcast (accessed February 14, 2016).

120 Robert Pear, "Makeover Coming for HealthCare.gov," *New York Times*, October 12, 2015, http://www.nytimes.com/2015/10/13/us/healthcaregov-to-get-major-changes-to-ease-shopping-for-coverage.html (accessed June 23, 2016).

121 Abby Goodnough, "Insurance Dropouts Present a Challenge for Health Law," *New York Times*, October 11, 2015, http://www.nytimes.com/2015/10/12/us/insurance-dropouts-present-a-challenge-for-health-law.html (accessed June 23, 2016).

122 Given that Alabama now requires an ID to vote, this is another way to limit voting by low-income, nonwhite people. Campbell Robertson, "For Alabama's Poor, the Budget Cuts Trickle Down, Limiting Access to Driver's Licenses," *New York Times*, October 9, 2015, http://www.nytimes.com/2015/10/10/us/alabama-budget-cuts-raise-concern-over-voting-rights.html (accessed June 23, 2016).

CHAPTER FOUR: CHICKEN SOUP FOR THE SOUL
BROTHERS AND SOUL SISTERS

123   Ta-Nehisi Coates, *Between the World and Me* (New York: Spiegel & Grau, 2015), 6–7.
124   Shelby County v. Holder, 133 S. Ct. 2612, 186 L. Ed. 2d 651, 81 U.S.L.W. 4572 (2013) [2013
      BL 167707], http://www2.bloomberglaw.com/public/desktop/document/Shelby_Cnty_v_
      Holder_No_1296_2013_BL_167707_US_June_25_2013_Court (accessed February 18, 2016).
      [I could not open this link because it was down. Here's a link to the ruling (I think?), but I
      don't know if this is the reference needed because the name is a bit different: https://www.
      supremecourt.gov/opinions/12pdf/12-96_6k47.pdf]
125   Carmen DeNavas-Walt and Bernadette D. Proctor, *Income and Poverty in the United States:
      2014.*
126   Amy Traub and Catherine Ruetschlin, "The Racial Wealth Gap: Why Policy Matters," Demos,
      March 10, 2015, http://www.demos.org/publication/racial-wealth-gap-why-policy-matters
      (accessed February 17, 2016). [Note: I could not find a date anywhere on this page]
127   Rakesh Kochhar and Richard Fry, "Wealth Inequality Has Widened Along Racial, Ethnic
      Lines since End of Great Recession," Pew Research Center, December 12, 2014, http://www.
      pewresearch.org/fact-tank/2014/12/12/racial-wealth-gaps-great-recession/ (accessed February
      15, 2016).
128   Paul Kiel, "Debt and the Racial Wealth Gap," *New York Times*, December 31, 2015, http://
      www.nytimes.com/2016/01/03/opinion/debt-and-the-racial-wealth-gap.html (accessed
      January 3, 2016).
129   Chuck Collins and Josh Hoxie, "Billionaire Bonanza: The Forbes 400 and the Rest of Us,"
      Institute for Policy Studies, December 1, 2015, http://www.ips-dc.org/billionaire-bonanza/
      (accessed February 18, 2016).
130   Halley Potter and Kimberly Quick, "The Secret to School Integration," Opinion, *New
      York Times*, February 23, 2016, http://www.nytimes.com/2016/02/23/opinion/the-se-
      cret-to-school-integration.html?ref=opinion (accessed February 23, 2016).
131   S. Jay Olshansky, et al., "Differences in Life Expectancy Due to Race and Educational Differ-
      ences are Widening, and Many May Not Catch Up," *Health Affairs*, 31, no. 8 (August 2012),
      1803–1813, http://content.healthaffairs.org/content/31/8/1803.full (accessed February 14,
      2016).
132   Paul Kiel, "Debt and the Racial Wealth Gap," *New York Times*, December 31, 2015, http://
      www.nytimes.com/2016/01/03/opinion/debt-and-the-racial-wealth-gap.html (accessed
      January 3, 2016).
133   Marianne Bertrand and Sendhil Mullainathan, "Are Emily and Greg More Employable than
      Lakisha and Jamal?: A Field Experiment on Labor Market Discrimination," National Bureau
      of Economic Research, July 2003, http://www.nber.org/papers/w9873.pdf (accessed Feb-
      ruary 18, 2016).
134   Haeyoun Park, Josh Keller, and Josh Williams, "The Faces of American Power, Nearly as
      White as the Oscar Nominees," *New York Times*, February 28, 2016, http://www.nytimes.
      com/interactive/2016/02/26/us/race-of-american-power.html (accessed March 3, 2016).
135   "Fox's Hume: Obama 'Never Talks about the Behaviors by Young African-American Men
      That May Lead Police to be Afraid of Them'," Video (clip from *The O'Reilly Factor*), Media
      Matters for America, December 8, 2014, http://mediamatters.org/video/2014/12/08/foxs-
      hume-obama-never-talks-about-the-behaviors/201803 (accessed June 12, 2016).
136   Jenée Desmond-Harris, "Study: We Love a Good Personal Responsibility Message—When
      the Audience is Black," *Vox*, July 14, 2015, http://www.vox.com/2015/7/14/8949481/race-
      systemic-blame-black (accessed February 16, 2016).
137   N.D.B. Connolly, "'The Black Presidency: Barack Obama and the Politics of Race in America,'
      by Michael Eric Dyson," *New York Times Book Review*, February 2, 2016, http://www.nytimes.

com/2016/02/07/books/review/the-black-presidency-barack-obama-and-the-politics-of-race-in-america-by-michael-eric-dyson.html (accessed February 15, 2016).

138 Emily Alpert Reyes, "Survey Finds Dads Defy Stereotypes about Black Fatherhood," *Los Angeles Times*, December 20, 2013, http://articles.latimes.com/2013/dec/20/local/la-me-black-dads-20131221 (accessed February 18, 2016).

139 Van Jones, "Black People 'Loot' Food . . .White People 'Find' Food," *Huffington Post*, September 1, 2005, updated May 25, 2011, http://www.huffingtonpost.com/van-jones/black-people-loot-food-wh_b_6614.html (accessed June 23, 2016).

140 David Edwards, "Fox Pundit: Oregon Militia are Not 'Thugs' Like Black Protesters Because They Fight 'Government Gone Wild,'" *Raw Story*, January 4, 2016, http://www.rawstory.com/2016/01/fox-pundit-oregon-militia-are-not-thugs-like-black-protesters-because-they-fight-government-gone-wild/ (accessed February 16, 2016).

141 Janell Ross, "Two Decades Later, Black and White Americans Finally Agree on O.J. Simpson's Guilt," *Washington Post*, March 4, 2016, https://www.washingtonpost.com/news/the-fix/wp/2015/09/25/black-and-white-americans-can-now-agree-o-j-was-guilty/ (accessed August 2, 2014).

142 Megan Thee-Brenan, "More Americans Say Race Relations are Bad, and a Survey Explores Why," *New York Times*, June 27, 2016, http://www.nytimes.com/2016/06/28/us/more-americans-say-race-relations-are-bad-and-a-survey-explores-why.html (accessed August 2, 2016).

143 "Race Relations," Poll, Gallup, http://www.gallup.com/poll/1687/race-relations.aspx (accessed February 15, 2016).

144 Pew Research Center, "How Blacks and Whites View the State of Race in America," June 24, 2016, http://www.pewsocialtrends.org/interactives/state-of-race-in-america/ (accessed August 2, 2016).

145 Michael Henderson, Belinda Davis, and Michael Climek, "Views of Recovery Ten Years after Katrina and Rita: A Survey of Residents of the City of New Orleans and Residents throughout Louisiana," Public Policy Research Lab, Louisiana State University, August 24, 2015, http://lsureillycenter.com/wp-content/uploads/2015/12/Views-of-Recovery-August-2015.pdf (accessed June 23, 2016).

146 "In Louisiana, Clinton Keeps Up, Governor Falls," Poll Results, Public Policy Polling, August 21, 2013, http://www.publicpolicypolling.com/main/2013/08/in-louisiana-clinton-keeps-up-governor-falls.html (accessed June 23, 2016).

147 German Lopez, "Chris Rock: It's Not Black People Who Have Progressed. It's White People," *Vox*, February 16, 2016, http://www.vox.com/xpress/2014/12/1/7313467/chris-rock-interview (accessed February 18, 2016).

148 Luke Kerr-Dineen, "Tiger Woods' Former Caddie Says He was Treated like a 'Slave' in New Book," *MSN*, November 1, 2015, http://www.msn.com/en-us/sports/golf/tiger-woods-former-caddie-says-he-was-treated-like-a-slave-in-new-book/ar-BBmGRh8?li=BBgzzfc (accessed February 20, 2016). Also Cork Gaines, "Here's How Many Millions Steve Williams Made as Tiger Woods's Caddy," *Business Insider*, July 21, 2011, http://www.businessinsider.com/tiger-woods-steve-williams-millions-of-reasons-to-be-grateful-2011-7 (accessed February 20, 2016).

149 "Finding a Slave Ship, Uncovering History," Editorial, *New York Times*, June 2, 2015, http://www.nytimes.com/2015/06/02/opinion/finding-a-slave-ship-uncovering-history.html (accessed February 20, 2016).

150 Thomas Piketty, *Capital in the Twenty-First Century*, translated by Arthur Goldhammer (Cambridge: The Belknap Press of the Harvard University Press, 2014),159.

151 Francie Latour, "New England's Hidden History," *Boston Globe*, September 26, 2010, http://www.boston.com/bostonglobe/ideas/articles/2010/09/26/new_englands_hidden_history/ (accessed February 19, 2016).

152 James W. Loewen, "Five Myths about Why the South Seceded," *Washington Post*, February 26, 2011, https://www.washingtonpost.com/outlook/five-myths-about-why-the-south-seceded/2011/01/03/ABHr6jD_story.html (accessed February 19, 2016).

153 Ibid.

154 Kevin Sack and Megan Thee-Brenan, "Poll Finds Most in US Hold Dim View of Race Relations," *New York Times*, July 23, 2015, http://www.nytimes.com/2015/07/24/us/poll-shows-most-americans-think-race-relations-are-bad.html (accessed February 20, 2016).

155 Scott Eric Kaufman, "Jeb Bush: 'The problem with the Confederate flag is what it began to represent later and that's what we have to avoid to heal the wounds,'" *Salon*, December 24, 2015, http://www.salon.com/2015/12/24/jeb_bush_the_problem_with_the_confederate_flag_is_what_it_began_to_represent_later_we_have_to_avoid_to_heal_those_wounds/ (accessed February 15, 2016).

156 I heard Jones make that comment on a panel at the 2015 Brooklyn Book Festival.

157 Jenée Desmond-Harris, "Here's Where 'White' Americans Have the Highest Percentage of African Ancestry," *Vox*, February 20, 2015, http://www.vox.com/2014/12/22/7431391/guess-where-white-americans-have-the-most-african-ancestry (accessed February 15, 2016).

158 "SPLC's Intelligence Report: Amid Year of Lethal Violence, Extremist Groups Expanded Ranks in 2015," Southern Poverty Law Center, February 17, 2016, https://www.splcenter.org/news/2016/02/17/splcs-intelligence-report-amid-year-lethal-violence-extremist-groups-expanded-ranks-2015 (accessed February 20, 2016).

159 Robert Costa and Ed O'Keefe, "House Majority Whip Scalise Confirms He Spoke to White Supremacists in 2002," *Washington Post*, December 29, 2014, https://www.washingtonpost.com/politics/house-majority-whip-scalise-confirms-he-spoke-to-white-nationalists-in-2002/2014/12/29/7f80dc14-8fa3-11e4-a900-9960214d4cd7_story.html (accessed February 20, 2016).

160 Isabel Wilkerson, "Emmett Till and Tamir Rice, Sons of the Great Migration," Opinion, *New York Times*, February 12, 2016, http://www.nytimes.com/2016/02/14/opinion/sunday/emmett-till-and-tamir-rice-sons-of-the-great-migration.html (accessed February 14, 2016).

161 Juliana Menasce Horowitz and Gretchen Livingston, "How Americans View the Black Lives Matter Movement," Pew Research Center, July 8, 2016, http://www.pewresearch.org/fact-tank/2016/07/08/how-americans-view-the-black-lives-matter-movement/ (accessed August 1, 2016).

162 Anna C. Merritt, Daniel A. Effron, and Benoît Monin, "Moral Self-Licensing: When Being Good Frees Us to be Bad," *Social and Personality Psychology Compass*, 4/5 (2010), 344–357, doi:10.1111/j.1751-9004.2010.00263, http://www-psych.stanford.edu/~monin/papers/Merritt,%20Effron%20&%20Monin%202010%20Compass%20on%20Moral%20Licensing.pdf (accessed February 20, 2016).

163 Jonah Goldberg, "Ben Carson, Black Conservative," *Real Clear Politics*, October 31, 2015, http://www.msn.com/en-us/news/opinion/ben-carson-black-conservative/ar-BBmEG70?li=AA54u (accessed February 16, 2016).

164 George Yancy, "Dear White America," Opinion, *New York Times*, December 24, 2015, http://opinionator.blogs.nytimes.com/2015/12/24/dear-white-america/ (accessed February 19, 2016).

165 Peggy McIntosh, "White Privilege: Unpacking the Invisible Knapsack," 1988, excerpted from Working Paper 189, "White Privilege and Male Privilege: A Personal Account of Coming to See Correspondences through Work in Women's Studies," https://www.deanza.edu/faculty/lewisjulie/White%20Priviledge%20Unpacking%20the%20Invisible%20Knapsack.pdf (accessed February 20, 2016).

166 Zeba Blay, "4 'Reverse Racism' Myths That Need To Stop," *Huffington Post*, August 26, 2015, updated July 11, 2016,, http://www.huffingtonpost.com/entry/reverse-racism-isnt-a-thing_us_55d60a91e4b07addcb45da97 (accessed September 21, 2016)

167 Moni Basu, "Census: More People Identify as Mixed Race, " *CNN*, September 27, 2012, http://inamerica.blogs.cnn.com/2012/09/27/census-more-people-identify-as-mixed-race/ (accessed June 12, 2016).

168 Evelyn De Wolfe, "A Chinese Town Underground," *Los Angeles Times*, July 7, 1985, http://articles.latimes.com/1985-07-07/realestate/re-9652_1_chinese-village (accessed March 2, 2016).

169 Ira Berliner, "'The Slave's Cause: A History of Abolition,' by Manisha Sinha," Book Review, *New York Times*, February 26, 2016, http://www.nytimes.com/2016/02/28/books/review/the-slaves-cause-a-history-of-abolition-by-manisha-sinha.html (accessed June 12, 2016).

170 James Baldwin, "A Report from Occupied Territory," *Nation*, July 11, 1966, http://www.thenation.com/article/report-occupied-territory/ (accessed March 1, 2016).

171 Rocco Parascandola and Joseph Stepansky, "NYPD Charges Sergeant in Eric Garner Death Investigation," *New York Daily News*, January 8, 2016, http://www.nydailynews.com/new-york/nypd-charges-sergeant-eric-garner-death-investigation-article-1.2489975 (accessed September 21, 2016).

172 Justin Fenton and Kevin Rector, "Freddie Gray Case: Officer Porter Testifies in Trial of Officer Goodson," *Baltimore Sun*, June 13, 2016, http://www.baltimoresun.com/news/maryland/freddie-gray/bs-md-ci-goodson-trial-day3-20160613-story.html (accessed June 16, 2016).

173 Kevin Johnson, Meghan Hoyer, and Brad Heath, "Local Police Involved in 400 Killings per Year," *USA Today*, August 15, 2014, http://www.usatoday.com/story/news/nation/2014/08/14/police-killings-data/14060357/# (accessed February 14, 2016).

174 Jon Swaine, Oliver Laughland, Jamiles Lartey, and Ciara McCarthy, "Young Black Men Killed by US Police at Highest Rate in Year of 1,134 Deaths," *Guardian*, December 31, 2015, http://www.theguardian.com/us-news/2015/dec/31/the-counted-police-killings-2015-young-black-men (accessed June 12, 2016).

175 Keith L. Alexander, with reporting by Steven Rich, Amy Brittain, Wesley Lowery, and Sandhya Somashekhar, "For 55 Officers Involved in Fatal Shootings This Year, It wasn't Their First Time," *Washington Post*, December 22, 2015, https://www.washingtonpost.com/local/public-safety/for-55-officers-involved-in-fatal-shootings-this-year-it-wasnt-their-first-time/2015/12/22/435cb680-9d04-11e5-a3c5-c77f2cc5a43c_story.html (accessed February 16, 2016).

176 Michael Walsh, "The Myth of the Killer-Cop 'Epidemic,'" *New York Post*, January 2, 2016, http://nypost.com/2016/01/02/myth-of-the-cop-killing-epidemic/ (accessed February 16, 2016).

177 Nate Silver, "Most Police Don't Live in the Cities They Serve," *Five Thirty Eight*, August 20, 2014, http://fivethirtyeight.com/datalab/most-police-dont-live-in-the-cities-they-serve/ (accessed February 14, 2016).

178 "Stop-and-Frisk Data," New York Civil Liberties Union, http://www.nyclu.org/content/stop-and-frisk-data (accessed February 20, 2016).

179 J. David Grossman and Al Baker, "Anxiety Aside, New York Sees Drop in Crime," *New York Times*, December 27, 2015, http://www.nytimes.com/2015/12/27/nyregion/anxiety-aside-new-york-sees-drop-in-crime.html (accessed December 28, 2015).

180 "Respect for NYPD Squandered in Attacks on Bill de Blasio," Editorial, *New York Times*, December 29, 2014, http://www.nytimes.com/2014/12/30/opinion/police-respect-squandered-in-attacks-on-de-blasio.html (accessed February 15, 2016).

181 Michael Javen Fortner, "The Real Roots of '70s Drug Laws," Opinion, *New York Times*, September 28, 2015, http://www.nytimes.com/2015/09/28/opinion/the-real-roots-of-70s-drug-laws.html?ref=opinion (accessed June 23, 2016).

182 "Crime in the United States by Volume and Rate per 100,000 Inhabitants, 1993–2012," Federal Bureau of Investigation, https://www.fbi.gov/about-us/cjis/ucr/crime-in-the-u.s/2012/crime-in-the-u.s.-2012/tables/1tabledatadecoverviewpdf/table_1_crime_in_the_united_states_by_volume_and_rate_per_100000_inhabitants_1993-2012.xls (accessed February 20, 2016).

183   Anthony Conwright, "Black Progressives, It's Time to Unite Against Establishment Politics,"
      Huffington Post, February 15, 2016, http://www.huffingtonpost.com/anthony-conwright/
      black-progressives-its-ti_b_9232920.html (accessed February 20, 2016).

184   Leon Neyfakh, "Black Americans Supported the 1994 Crime Bill, Too," *Slate*, February 12,
      2016, http://www.slate.com/articles/news_and_politics/crime/2016/02/why_many_black_
      politicians_backed_the_1994_crime_bill_championed_by_the.html (accessed February 15,
      2016).

185   Melinda D. Anderson, "When Schooling Meets Policing," *Atlantic*, September 21, 2015,
      http://www.theatlantic.com/education/archive/2015/09/when-schooling-meets-po-
      licing/406348/ (accessed February 21, 2016).

186   Edward J. Smith and Shaun R. Harper, "Disproportionate Impact of K–12 School Suspen-
      sion and Expulsion on Black Students in Southern States," Center for the Study of Race and
      Equity in Education, University of Pennsylvania, 2015, http://www.gse.upenn.edu/equity/
      SouthernStates (accessed June 23, 2016).

187   Edward J. Smith and Shaun R. Harper, "Disproportionate Impact of K-12 School Suspen-
      sion and Expulsion on Black Students in Southern States," Center for Race and Equality in
      Education, University of Pennsylvania, August 2015, accessed June 23, 2016, http://www.gse.
      upenn.edu/equity/SouthernStates.

188   Ta-Nehisi Coates, *Between the World and Me*, 32-33.

189   Rich Juzwiak and Aleksander Chan, "Unarmed People of Color Killed by Police, 1999–2014,"
      Gawker, December 8, 2014, http://gawker.com/unarmed-people-of-color-killed-by-po-
      lice-1999-2014-1666672349 (accessed February 16, 2016).

190   Edward Wyckoff Williams, "Don't White People Kill Each Other, Too?" *Root*, April 10, 2012,
      http://www.theroot.com/articles/culture/2012/04/whiteonwhite_crime_it_goes_against_
      the_false_media_narrative/ (accessed September 21, 2016).

191   "Leading Causes of Death by Age Group, White Males–United States 2013," Centers for
      Disease Control and Prevention, http://www.cdc.gov/men/lcod/2013/whitemen2013.pdf
      (accessed June 22, 2016).

192   "Spike Lee on Chicago's Gun Violence Crisis," Video (clip from *Anderson Cooper 360*),
      CNN, November 12, 2016, http://www.cnn.com/videos/us/2015/11/13/chicago-vio-
      lence-spike-lee-father-pfleger-intv-ac.cnn/video/playlists/violence-in-chicago/ (accessed
      November 12, 2015).

193   Richard Berkow, "Black Journalist Shuts Up NBC Panel: Let's Not Pretend Cops Killing
      Blacks is the Problem," *BPR Bizpac Review*, August 18, 2014, http://www.bizpacreview.
      com/2014/08/18/black-journalist-shuts-up-nbc-panel-lets-not-pretend-cops-killing-blacks-is-
      the-problem-139646 (accessed February 15, 2016).

194   Shaun King, "Don't You Ever Say 'Black on Black Crime' Again," *Daily Kos*, August 14, 2015,
      http://www.dailykos.com/story/2015/8/14/1412131/-Don-t-you-ever-say-black-on-black-crime-
      again (accessed February 21, 2016).

195   Derwyn Bunton, "When the Public Defender Says, 'I Can't Help'," *New York Times*, February
      19, 2016, http://www.nytimes.com/2016/02/19/opinion/when-the-public-defender-says-i-
      cant-help.html?ref=opinion (accessed February 19, 2016).

196   Campbell Robertson, "Suit Alleges 'Scheme' in Criminal Costs Borne by New Orleans's
      Poor," *New York Times*, September 17, 2015, http://www.nytimes.com/2015/09/18/us/suit-
      alleges-scheme-in-criminal-costs-borne-by-new-orleanss-poor.html (accessed February 16,
      2016).

197   SpearIt, "Shackles Beyond the Sentence: How Legal Financial Obligations Create a Perma-
      nent Underclass," *1 Impact 46*, New York Law School, July 9, 2015, http://papers.ssrn.com/
      sol3/papers.cfm?abstract_id=2628977 (accessed December 27, 2015).

198   "Exonerations in 2015," The National Registry of Exonerations, February 3, 2016, http://
      www.law.umich.edu/special/exoneration/Documents/Exonerations_in_2015.pdf (accessed
      February 4, 2016).

199 "Report to the Chief Judge of the State of New York," The Task Force to Expand Access to Civil Legal Services in New York, November 2010, https://www.nycourts.gov/accesstojustice-commission/PDF/CLS-TaskForceREPORT.pdf (accessed June 23, 2016).

200 "Literacy Statistics," Begin to Read, http://www.begintoread.com/research/literacystatistics. html (accessed June 24, 2016).

201 Daniel Strauss, "Read the Full Text of Hillary Clinton's Prison Reform Speech," *LiveWire, Talking Points Memo*, April 29, 2015, http://talkingpointsmemo.com/livewire/hillary-clinton-remarks-prison-reform-speech (accessed June 23, 2016).

202 Lauren-Brooke Eisen and Inimai M. Chettiar, "The Reverse Mass Incarceration Act," The Brennan Center for Justice, October 12, 2015, https://www.brennancenter.org/publication/reverse-mass-incarceration-act#Introduction (accessed February 16, 2016).

203 "Criminal Justice Fact Sheet," NAACP, http://www.naacp.org/pages/criminal-justice-fact-sheet (accessed February 16, 2016).

204 Michelle Alexander, *The New Jim Crow: Mass Incarceration in the Age of Colorblindness* (New York: The New Press, 2010).

205 Saki Knafo, "1 In 3 Black Males will Go to Prison in Their Lifetime, Report Warns," *Huffington Post*, October 4, 2013, http://www.huffingtonpost.com/2013/10/04/racial-disparities-criminal-justice_n_4045144.html (accessed February 21, 2016).

206 "Myth That There are More Black Men in Prison than College is Debunked," *Louisiana Weekly*, February 16, 2015, http://www.louisianaweekly.com/myth-that-there-are-more-black-men-in-prison-than-college-is-debunked/ (accessed February 21, 2016).

207 Ibid.

208 Department of Corrections, Facts and Figures FY 2014, accessed June 23, 2016, http://www. doc.state.vt.us/about/reports/ff-archive/facts-figures-fy2014/view.

209 "Private Prisons," American Civil Liberties Union, https://www.aclu.org/issues/mass-incarceration/privatization-criminal-justice/private-prisons (accessed February 19, 2016).

210 "Criminal: How Lockup Quotas and 'Low Crime Taxes' Guarantee Profits for Private Prison Corporations," In the Public Interest, September 19, 2013, http://www.inthepublicinterest. org/criminal-how-lockup-quotas-and-low-crime-taxes-guarantee-profits-for-private-prison-corporations/ (accessed February 19, 2016).

211 "Deaths in Local Jails and State Prisons Increased for the Third Consecutive Year," Press Release, Bureau of Justice Statistics, August 4, 2015, http://www.bjs.gov/content/pub/press/mljsp0013stpr.cfm (accessed June 12, 2016).

212 Christopher Uggen, Sarah Shannon, and Jeff Manza, "State-Level Estimates of Felon Disenfranchisement in the United States, 2010," The Sentencing Project, July 2012, http://sentencingproject.org/doc/publications/fd_State_Level_Estimates_of_Felon_Disen_2010. pdf (accessed February 16, 2016).

213 Cassie Spodak and Jeff Simon, "2016 Candidates on the Front Lines of N.H. Drug Epidemic," *CNN*, December 25, 2015, http://www.cnn.com/2015/12/22/politics/new-hampshire-2016-addiction/ (accessed June 23, 2016).

214 Ekow N. Yankah, "When Addiction Has a White Face," Opinion, *New York Times*, February 9, 2016, http://www.nytimes.com/2016/02/09/opinion/when-addiction-has-a-white-face.html (accessed February 15, 2016).

215 Jeff Smith, "In Ferguson, Black Town, White Power," *New York Times*, August 17, 2014, http://www.nytimes.com/2014/08/18/opinion/in-ferguson-black-town-white-power.html (accessed December 28, 2015).

216 Sean McElwee, "Black People, White Government," *Al Jazeera*, October 30, 2014, http://america.aljazeera.com/opinions/2014/10/ferguson-africanamericanspoliticalrepresentation. html (accessed December 28, 2015).

217 "Investigation of the Ferguson Police Department," US Department of Justice, Civil Rights Division, March 4, 2015, http://www.justice.gov/sites/default/files/opa/press-releases/attachments/2015/03/04/ferguson_police_department_report.pdf (accessed December 27, 2015).

218   Dr. Marthin Luther King, Jr.. Letter from a Birmingham Jail, April 16, 1963, https://www.
        africa.upenn.edu/Articles_Gen/Letter_Birmingham.html (accessed September 25, 2016)

219   Martin Luther King Response to "You Can't Legislate Morality; You Have to Change Hearts
        First", December 18, 2963, https://blogs.thegospelcoalition.org/justintaylor/2008/09/20/
        martin-luther-king-response-to-you-cant/ (accessed September 25, 2016)

220   Rodolfo Mendoza-Denton and Jason Marsh, "What Leaders Must Do to Battle Bigotry,"
        January 18, 2016, http://greatergood.berkeley.edu/article/item/what_leaders_must_do_to_
        battle_bigotry (accessed February 15, 2016).

221   Rodolfo Mendoza-Denton, "The Top 10 Strategies for Reducing Prejudice," January 3, 2011,
        http://greatergood.berkeley.edu/article/item/top_10_strategies_for_reducing_prejudice
        (accessed February 15, 2016).

222   Douglas S. Massey, Jonathan Rothwell, and Thurston Domina, "The Changing Bases of
        Segregation in the United States," ANNALS of the American Academy of Political and Social
        Science, 626 no. 1 (November 2009), 74–90, http://ann.sagepub.com/content/626/1/74.
        abstract (accessed February 16, 2016).

223   Ta-Nehisi Coates, Between the World and Me, 9.

224   Ibid, 16–18.

225   David Brooks, "Listening to Ta-Nehisi Coates While White," New York Times, July 17, 2015,
        http://www.nytimes.com/2015/07/17/opinion/listening-to-ta-nehisi-coates-while-white.html
        (accessed September 21, 2016).

CHAPTER FIVE: THEY'RE JUST NOT THAT INTO YOU

226   Greg Behrendt and Amiira Ruotola-Behrendt, It's Called a Breakup Because It's Broken: The
        Smart Girl's Break-Up Buddy (New York: Broadway Books, 2005), 6.

227   Domenico Montanaro, Rachel Wellford, and Simone Pathe, "2014 Midterm Election Turnout
        Lowest in 70 Years," PBS NewsHour, November 10, 2014, http://www.pbs.org/newshour/
        updates/2014-midterm-election-turnout-lowest-in-70-years/ (accessed February 23, 2016).

228   Matthew Yglesias, "Democrats are in Denial. Their Party is Actually in Deep Trouble.," Vox,
        October 19, 2015, http://www.vox.com/2015/10/19/9565119/democrats-in-deep-trouble
        (accessed February 23, 2016).

229   Matt Viser, "Unions Look to Weaken Support for Brown," Boston Globe, March 23, 2011,
        http://archive.boston.com/news/politics/articles/2011/03/23/unions_look_to_weaken_sup-
        port_for_brown/ (accessed June 12, 2016).

230   Patrick Healy and Jonathan Martinjan, "For Republicans, Mounting Fears of Lasting Split,"
        New York Times, January 9, 2016, http://www.nytimes.com/2016/01/10/us/politics/for-re-
        publicans-mounting-fears-of-lasting-split.html (accessed February 22, 2016).

231   Domenico Montanaro, "Obama Performance with White Voters on Par with
        Other Democrats," NBC News, November 19, 2012, http://firstread.nbcnews.
        com/_news/2012/11/19/15282553-obama-performance-with-white-voters-on-par-with-other-
        democrats?lite (accessed February 24, 2016).

232   Alec MacGillis, "Who Turned My Blue State Red?," New York Times, November 22, 2015,
        http://www.nytimes.com/2015/11/22/opinion/sunday/who-turned-my-blue-state-red.html
        (accessed February 24, 2016).

233   Bill Bishop, The Big Sort: Why the Clustering of Like-Minded America is Tearing Us Apart (New
        York: Houghton Mifflin Harcourt Publishing Company, 2008): 5–6.

234   "Presidential Tracker 2012," FairVote, http://www.fairvote.org/presidential_
        tracker_2012#2012_campaign_events (accessed June 14, 2016).

235   Thomas Fitzgerald, "Cruz Barnstorms the South, Lining Up Support," Philadelphia Inquirer,
        December 24, 2015, http://articles.philly.com/2015-12-24/news/69263770_1_ted-cruz-immi-
        gration-laws-campaign-logo (accessed February 22, 2016).

236 Lynn Vavreck, "Measuring Donald Trump's Supporters for Intolerance," *New York Times*, February 23, 2016, http://www.nytimes.com/2016/02/25/upshot/measuring-donald-trumps-supporters-for-intolerance.html (accessed September 21, 2016).

237 Scott Wong, "Ryan: Trump's Comments about Judge are 'Textbook' Racism," *Hill*, June 7, 2016, http://thehill.com/homenews/house/282463-ryan-trump-comments-textbook-racism (accessed June 24, 2016).

238 Philip Klinkner, "The Easiest Way to Guess If Someone Supports Trump? Ask if Obama is a Muslim," *Vox*, June 2, 2016, http://www.vox.com/2016/6/2/11833548/donald-trump-support-race-religion-economy (accessed June 15, 2016).

239 Max Ehrenfreund and Scott Clement, "Economic and Racial Anxiety: Two Separate Forces Driving Support for Donald Trump," *Washington Post*, March 22, 2016, https://www.washingtonpost.com/news/wonk/wp/2016/03/22/economic-anxiety-and-racial-anxiety-two-separate-forces-driving-support-for-donald-trump/?tid=a_inl (accessed June 15, 2016).

240 Steven Ertelt, "Donald Trump Defends Planned Parenthood Abortion Biz: 'My Friends Know It Better Than You,'" *LifeNews*, February 21, 2016, http://www.lifenews.com/2016/02/21/donald-trump-defends-planned-parenthood-abortion-biz-my-friends-know-it-better-than-you/ (accessed February 25, 2016).

241 Zaid Jilani, "Donald Trump in 2000: 'I Support the Ban on Assault Weapons,'" *Intercept*, January 27, 2016, https://theintercept.com/2016/01/27/donald-trump-in-2000-i-support-the-ban-on-assault-weapons/ (accessed February 25, 2016).

242 Author's calculation's based on US Census data and US Department of Health and Human Services caseload data, "TANF: Average Monthly Number of Recipients, Fiscal and Calendar Year 2015 as of June 15, 2016," Administration for Children and Families, US Department of Health and Human Services, https://www.acf.hhs.gov/sites/default/files/ofa/2015_recipient_tan.pdf (accessed June 23, 2016).

243 Tom LoBianco, "Jeb Bush Says Dems Lure Black Voters with 'Free Stuff,'" *CNN*, September 25, 2015, http://www.cnn.com/2015/09/25/politics/jeb-bush-free-stuff-black-voters/ (accessed February 22, 2016).

244 Eduardo Porter, "Racial Identity, and Its Hostilities, Are on the Rise in American Politics," *New York Times*, January 6, 2016, http://www.nytimes.com/2016/01/06/business/economy/racial-identity-and-its-hostilities-return-to-american-politics.html (accessed February 16, 2016).

245 Alberto Alesina, Edward Glaeser, and Bruce Sacerdote, "Why Doesn't the US Have a European-Style Welfare System?" National Bureau of Economic Research, Working Paper No. 8524, October 2001, http://www.nber.org/papers/w8524 (accessed February 22, 2016).

246 Abby Goodnough, "Kentucky, Beacon for Health Law, Now a Lab for Its Retreat," *New York Times*, November 27, 2015, http://www.nytimes.com/2015/11/28/us/kentucky-beacon-for-health-law-now-a-lab-for-its-retreat.html (accessed February 22, 2016).

247 Thomas Frank, *What's the Matter with Kansas?: How Conservatives Won the Heart of America* (New York: Henry Holt and Company, 2004), 1, 2, 5, 6.

248 This quote is attributed to Steinbeck in Ronald Wright, *A Short History of Progress* (New York: Carroll and Graf Publishers, 2005), but others have questioned whether Steinbeck really wrote it or said it. Whether he did or not, it's still a great quote.

249 James Swift, "Hipsters and the Co-Option of White Poverty Culture," *Thought Catalog*, May 31, 2014, http://thoughtcatalog.com/james-swift/2014/05/hipsters-and-the-co-option-of-white-poverty-culture/ (accessed June 24, 2016).

250 Rod Dreher, "Trump: Tribune of Poor White People," *American Conservative*, July 22, 2016, http://www.theamericanconservative.com/dreher/trump-us-politics-poor-whites/ (accessed July 30, 2016).

CHAPTER SIX: YOUR BEST LIFE IS ACTUALLY SOMEONE ELSE'S

251 Joel Osteen, *Your Best Life Now: 7 Steps to Living at Your Full Potential* (Nashville: FaithWords, 2004), 232.

252 Michael Young, "Down with Meritocracy," *Guardian*, June 28, 2001, http://www. theguardian.com/politics/2001/jun/29/comment (accessed March 4, 2016).

253 Peter Coy, "The Richest Rich re in a Class by Themselves," *Bloomberg Business*, April 3, 2014, http://www.bloomberg.com/bw/articles/2014-04-03/top-tenth-of-1-percenters-reaps-all-the-riches (accessed March 5, 2016).

254 Chuck Collins and Josh Hoxie, "Billionaire Bonanza: The Forbes 400 and the Rest of Us," Institute for Policy Studies, December 1, 2015, http://www.ips-dc.org/billionaire-bonanza/ (accessed February 18, 2016).

255 Robert Reich, "The Rise of the Non-Working Rich," *Huffington Post*, September 15, 2014, http://www.huffingtonpost.com/robert-reich/the-rise-of-the-non-working-rich_b_5589684. html (accessed March 4, 2016).

256 Matt O'Brien, "Poor Kids Who Do Everything Right Don't Do Better Than Rich Kids Who Do Everything Wrong," *Wonkblog, Washington Post*, November 27, 2014, www.washingtonpost. com/news/wonk/wp/2014/11/27/poor-kids-who-do-everything-right-dont-do-better-than-rich-kids-who-do-everything-wrong/ (accessed March 4, 2016).

257 "Alumni Sons and Daughters," *Columbia College Today*, Fall 2014, https://www.college. columbia.edu/cct/fall14/alumni_profiles1 (accessed June 16, 2016).

258 Alexandra Stevenson, "Chicago's Odd Couple: Mayor Rahm Emanuel and a Billionaire Republican Investor," *New York Times*, April 2, 2015, http://www.nytimes.com/2015/04/03/ business/chicagos-odd-couple-mayor-emanuel-and-billionaire-republican-investor.html (accessed March 4, 2016).

259 Christopher Hayes, *The Twilight of the Elites: America After Meritocracy* (New York: Crown Publishers, 2012), 22.

260 Thomas Piketty, *Capital in the Twenty-First Century*, 85.

261 John Steinbeck, "John Steinbeck on the Violent Repression of the Fight for Migrant Workers' Rights," *Nation*, September 12, 1936, http://www.thenation.com/article/dubious-battle-california/ (accessed March 4, 2016).

262 Joseph Hines, "It Takes Nearly $8 Million to Join the Wealthiest One Percent," Demos, September 19, 2014, http://www.demos.org/blog/9/19/14/it-takes-nearly-8-million-join-wealthiest-one-percent (accessed March 5, 2016); and Luisa Kroll, "Inside the 2013 Forbes 400: Facts and Figures on America's Richest," *Forbes*, September 16, 2013, http://www. forbes.com/sites/luisakroll/2013/09/16/inside-the-2013-forbes-400-facts-and-figures-on-americas-richest/#ee2912a3af52 (accessed March 5, 2016).

263 Ginia Bellafante, "Never Rich Enough," *New York Times*, August 29, 2014, http://www. nytimes.com/2014/08/31/nyregion/never-rich-enough.html (accessed March 5, 2016).

264 Ginia Bellafonte, "Rooting for the Robber Barons, at Least on the Screen," *New York Times*, March 18, 2016, http://www.nytimes.com/2016/03/20/nyregion/rooting-for-the-robber-barons-at-least-on-the-screen.html (accessed March 19, 2016).

265 Peter Haldeman, "In Los Angeles, a Nimby Battle Pits Millionaires vs. Billionaires," *New York Times*, December 5, 2014, http://www.nytimes.com/2014/12/07/style/in-los-angeles-a-nimby-battle-pits-millionaires-vs-billionaires.html (accessed March 4, 2016).

266 Josh Rosenblat, "The Wealthier You Get, the Less Social You Are. Here's Why It Matters," *Vox*, May 5, 2015, http://www.vox.com/2016/5/5/11578994/income-friends-family (accessed June 16, 2016).

267 Jennifer E. Stellar, Vida M. Manzo, Michael W. Kraus, and Dacher Keltner, "Class and Compassion: Socioeconomic Factors Predict Responses to Suffering," American Psychological Association, 2001, http://www.krauslab.com/Stellaretal.Emotion.2012.pdf (accessed June 16, 2016).

268 Joe Coscarelli, "Mayor Bloomberg Says People Stay Homeless Because the Shelters are So Damn Nice," *New York Magazine*, August 24, 2012, http://nymag.com/daily/intelligencer/2012/08/ (accessed March 5, 2016).

269 Kate Taylor, "A Mayor Who Never Slept Here (Gracie Mansion) Says No Successor Should," *New York Times*, March 27, 2012, http://cityroom.blogs.nytimes.com/2012/03/27/mayors-shouldnt-live-in-gracie-mansion-bloomberg-says/ (accessed March 14, 2016).

270 Howard Schultz, "America Deserves a Servant Leader," Opinion, *New York Times*, August 6, 2015, http://www.nytimes.com/2015/08/06/opinion/america-deserves-a-servant-leader.html (accessed March 6, 2016).

271 Burgess Everett and John Bresnahan, "McConnell's Fall Mandate: Keep Calm, Avert Catastrophe," *Politico*, September 14, 2015, http://www.politico.com/story/2015/09/mitch-mcconnell-agenda-2015-shutdown-213582#ixzz3lnv65BDt (accessed February 24, 2016).

272 Robert Reich, "The Rise of the Non-Working Rich," *Huffington Post*, September 14, 2014, http://www.huffingtonpost.com/robert-reich/the-rise-of-the-non-working-rich_b_5589684.html (accessed March 4, 2016).

273 Kathryn J. Edin and H. Luke Shaefer, *$2.00 a Day*, 47.

274 Robert George, "NYC's 'Stealth' Shelters; How to Fight a Sneaky Push for a Homeless Hotel," *New York Post*, July 28, 2002, http://nypost.com/2002/07/28/nycs-stealth-shelters-how-to-fight-a-sneaky-push-for-a-homeless-hotel/ (accessed March 14, 2016).

275 Melissa Russo, "Former Mayor Rudy Giuliani Complains About Homeless Man on Upper East Side Street, Takes Shot at de Blasio," *NBC-4 New York*, August 24, 2015, http://www.nbcnewyork.com/news/local/Rudy-Giuliani-Complains-Homeless-Man-Upper-East-Side-Street-NYPD-322734141.html (accessed March 14, 2016).

276 Emily Green, "Homeless Phone-Charging 'Thief' Wanted Security," *Street Roots News*, March 6, 2015, http://news.streetroots.org/2015/03/06/homeless-phone-charging-thief-wanted-security (accessed March 4, 2016).

277 Both the homeless man and the officer happened to be white. Lee Williams, "Exclusive: Officers Investigated after Inmate is Treated like Animal," *Sarasota Herald-Tribune*, July 27, 2015, http://www.heraldtribune.com/article/20150727/ARTICLE/150729737?p=1&tc=pg&tc=ar (accessed March 4, 2016).

278 Ben Railton, "No, Your Ancestors Didn't Come Here Legally," *Talking Points Memo*, November 20, 2014, http://talkingpointsmemo.com/cafe/no-your-ancestors-didn-t-come-here-legally (accessed March 4, 2016).

279 Jeremy W. Peters, "Marco Rubio's Policies Might Shut the Door to People like His Grandfather," *New York Times*, March 5, 2016, http://www.nytimes.com/2016/03/06/us/politics/marco-rubio-immigration-grandfather.html (accessed March 6, 2016).

280 Gavin Aronsen, "Steve King and Immigration: His 8 Greatest Hits," *Mother Jones*, July 12, 2013, http://www.motherjones.com/mojo/2013/07/steve-king-most-outrageous-immigration-rhetoric (accessed March 6, 2016).

281 Mary C. Waters and Marisa Gerstein Pineau, eds., *The Integration of Immigrants into American Society, Panel on the Integration of Immigrants into American Society* (Washington, DC: The National Academies Press, 2015), 7, https://www.nap.edu/catalog/21746/the-integration-of-immigrants-into-american-society [NOTE: This has instructions for republishing text under "Rights" here: https://www.nap.edu/catalog/21746/the-integration-of-immigrants-into-american-society]

282 Ibid., 49–50; 10.

283 Julia Preston, "Pink Slips at Disney, But First, Training Foreign Replacements.," *New York Times*, June 3, 2015, http://www.nytimes.com/2015/06/04/us/last-task-after-layoff-at-disney-train-foreign-replacements.html (accessed March 4, 2016).

284 Jean-Paul Sartre, "Americans and Their Myths," *Nation*, October 18, 1947, https://www.thenation.com/article/americans-and-their-myths/ (accessed March 4, 2016).

285   Richard Kirsch, *Fighting for Our Health: The Epic Battle to Make Health Care a Right in the United States* (Albany: Rockefeller Institute Press, 2011), 198.

286   Ibid., 199.

287   Rick Perlstein, "Outlook: In America, Crazy is a Pre-existing Condition," *Washington Post*, August 18, 2009, http://www.washingtonpost.com/wp-dyn/content/discussion/2009/08/14/DI2009081402554.html (accessed March 5, 2016).

288   Ibid.

289   "GOP Rep. Trent Franks Calls Obama 'An Enemy of Humanity'," *Huffington Post*, November 29, 2009, updated May 25, 2011, http://www.huffingtonpost.com/2009/09/29/gop-rep-trent-franks-call_n_302713.html (accessed March 15, 2016).

290   Brian Montopoli, "Delaware GOP Candidate: Ask Liberals Why They're Nazis," *CBS News*, September 17, 2010, http://www.cbsnews.com/news/delaware-gop-candidate-ask-liberals-why-theyre-nazis/ (March 15, 2016).

291   I heard Simon say this live at a panel at the 2015 Brooklyn Book Festival.

292   Rachel Brody, "Views You Can Use: Too Much Government in the Toilet," *U.S. News & World Report*, February 4, 2015, http://www.usnews.com/opinion/articles/2015/02/04/sen-thom-tillis-wants-government-to-deregulate-hand-washing-pundits-react (accessed March 4, 2016).

293   John S. Kiernan, "2016's States Most & Least Federally Dependent States," *WalletHub*, https://wallethub.com/edu/states-most-least-dependent-on-the-federal-government/2700 (accessed March 6, 2016).

294   Christopher G. Faricy, *Welfare for the Wealthy: Parties, Social Spending, and Inequality in the United States* (New York: Cambridge University Press, 2015), 5.

295   Jonathan Weisman and Ron Nixon, "House Republicans Push through Farm Bill, Without Food Stamps," *New York Times*, July 11, 2013, http://www.nytimes.com/2013/07/12/us/politics/house-bill-would-split-farm-and-food-stamp-programs.html (accessed March 4, 2016).

296   "Final Vote Results for Roll Call 353," Accounting of the Federal Agriculture Reform and Risk Management Act, H.R. 2642, July 11, 2013, http://clerk.house.gov/evs/2013/roll353.xml#N (accessed March 4, 2016).

297   Jason Easley, "Ted Cruz Demands Federal Money for Texas Floods after Blocking Hurricane Sandy Relief," *Politicus USA*, March 27, 2015, http://www.politicususa.com/2015/05/27/ted-cruz-demands-federal-money-texas-floods-blocking-hurricane-sandy-relief.html (accessed December 29, 2015).

298   Robert Pear, "State-Level Brawls Over Medicaid Reflect Divide in G.O.P.," *New York Times*, December 27, 2015, http://www.nytimes.com/2015/12/28/us/politics/state-level-brawls-over-medicaid-reflect-wider-war-in-gop.html (accessed December 28, 2015).

299   Joe Nocera, "Corporate Welfare for the Kochs," Opinion, *New York Times*, October 10, 2015, http://www.nytimes.com/2015/10/11/opinion/sunday/corporate-welfare-for-the-kochs.html (accessed March 4, 2016).

300   Robert B. Reich, *Saving Capitalism: For the Many, Not the Few* (New York: Alfred A. Knopf, 2015), xiii.

301   Joseph E. Stiglitz, *The Price of Inequality*, 29, 31.

302   Sam Wilkin, *Wealth Secrets of the One Percent: A Modern Manual to Getting Marvelously, Obscenely Rich* (Boston: Little Brown and Company, 2015), 6.

303   "The Growth of Corporate and Decline of Governmental Power," Editorial, *Nation*, May 15, 1873, Number 411, https://books.google.com/books?id=Fvo4AQAAMAA-J&pg=PA328&dq=the+growth+of+corporate+and+decline+of+governmental+power+the+nation&hl=en&sa=X&ved=oahUKEwji-peluMDLAhUHpB4KHcloABoQ6AEIH-DAA#v=onepage&q=the%20growth%20of%20corporate%20and%20decline%20of%20governmental%20power%20the%20nation&f=false (accessed March 14, 2016).

304   Elizabeth Lopatto, "Self-Interest Spurs Society's 'Elite' to Lie, Cheat, Study Finds," *Bloomberg Business*, February 28, 2012, http://www.bloomberg.com/news/articles/2012-02-27/wealthier-people-more-likely-than-poorer-to-lie-or-cheat-researchers-find (accessed March 4, 2016).

305 Andrew Pollack, "Drug Goes from $13.50 a Tablet to $750, Overnight," *New York Times*, September 20, 2015, http://www.nytimes.com/2015/09/21/business/a-huge-overnight-increase-in-a-drugs-price-raises-protests.html?ref=business (accessed March 4, 2016).

306 "Despite Clear Dangers, DuPont Kept Using a Toxic Chemical," Editorial, *New York Times*, January 12, 2016, http://www.nytimes.com/2016/01/12/opinion/despite-clear-dangers-dupont-kept-using-a-toxic-chemical.html (accessed March 6, 2016).

307 Bill Vlasic, "Fiat Chrysler Concedes Violating Rule on Reporting Death and Injury Claims," *New York Times*, September 29, 2015, http://www.nytimes.com/2015/09/30/business/fiat-chrysler-concedes-violating-rule-on-reporting-death-and-injury-claims.html (accessed March 4, 2016).

308 Manny Fernandez, "Many Fertilizer Plants are Poorly Located and Regulated, Says Report on 2013 Blast," *New York Times*, January 28, 2016, http://www.nytimes.com/2016/01/29/us/many-fertilizer-plants-are-poorly-located-and-regulated-says-report-on-2013-blast.html (accessed March 4, 2016).

309 "Death on the Job: The Toll of Neglect, A National and State-by-State Profile of Worker Safety and Health in the United States," 25th Edition, AFL-CIO, April 2016, http://www.aflcio.org/content/download/174867/4158803/1647_DOTJ2016.pdf (accessed June 11, 2016).

310 Andrew Rice, "Stash Pad," *New York Magazine*, June 29, 2014, http://nymag.com/news/features/foreigners-hiding-money-new-york-real-estate-2014-6/ (accessed March 4, 2016).

311 Louise Story and Stephanie Saul, "Stream of Foreign Wealth Flows to Elite New York Real Estate," *New York Times*, February 7, 2015, http://www.nytimes.com/2015/02/08/nyregion/stream-of-foreign-wealth-flows-to-time-warner-condos.html (accessed March 4, 2016).

312 David Gelles, "The Logic of an Empty $100 Million Pad," Wealth, *New York Times*, February 9, 2015, http://www.nytimes.com/2015/02/10/business/the-logic-of-an-empty-dollar100-million-pad.html (accessed March 6, 2016).

313 Hamilton Nolan, "Don't Let Rich People Own Apartments They Don't Live In," *Gawker*, August 14, 2014, http://gawker.com/dont-let-rich-people-own-apartments-they-dont-live-in-1621527767 (accessed August 6, 2016).

314 The New York Times International Luxury Conference website: http://luxurybeyondproduct.com/ (accessed March 4, 2016).

315 Taylor Berman, "Golden Globe Nominees to Eat Dessert Made of Actual Gold, Activists Mad About It," *Gawker*, January 14, 2012, http://gawker.com/5876160/golden-glove-nominees-to-eat-dessert-made-of-actual-gold-activists-mad-about-it (accessed March 4, 2016).

316 James Ford, "Home of the World's Priciest Holiday Meal Says It Understands NYC Residents Struggle with Hunger," *WPIX-11 News*, November 25, 2014, http://pix11.com/2014/11/25/home-of-the-worlds-priciest-holiday-meal-says-it-understands-nyc-residents-struggle-with-hunger/ (accessed February 24, 2016).

317 Helaine Olen, "Swag Reflex," *Slate*, February 26, 2016, http://www.slate.com/articles/business/the_bills/2016/02/the_oscars_swag_bag_is_more_decadent_than_ever_how_did_we_get_here.html (accessed February 28, 2016).

318 Matthew Dalton, "A Banker's Plaintive Wail," *Wall Street Journal*, January 27, 2011, http://blogs.wsj.com/davos/2011/01/27/a-bankers-plaintive-wail/ (accessed February 28, 2016).

319 Charles Murray, *Coming Apart: The State of White America, 1960-2010* (New York: Crown Forum, 2012), 12.

320 Brittany Bronson, "Do We Value Low-Skilled Work?" Opinion, *New York Times*, October 2, 2015, http://www.nytimes.com/2015/10/01/opinion/do-we-value-low-skilled-work.html?ref=opinion (accessed March 4, 2016).

321 Robert B. Reich, *Saving Capitalism*, 61.

322 Franklin D. Roosevelt, "81—Address Before the American Retail Federation, Washington, D.C.," Speech Transcript, May 22, 1939, American Presidency Project, http://www.presidency.ucsb.edu/ws/?pid=15763.

323 Sarah Anderson, "Off the Deep End: The Wall Street Bonus Pool and Low Wage Workers," Institute for Policy Studies, March 11, 2015, http://www.ips-dc.org/wp-content/uploads/2015/03/IPS-Wall-St-Bonuses-Min-Wage-2015.pdf (accessed March 4, 2016).

324 Matt Bewig, "39% of New York Bank Tellers Need Public Assistance," *AllGov*, December 09, 2013, http://www.allgov.com/news/top-stories/39-percent-of-new-york-bank-tellers-need-public-assistance-131209?news=851862 (accessed March 6, 2016).

325 Nick Hanauer, interview with Robin Young, "The Super-Wealthy VC Behind the Fight for a \$15 Minimum Wage," Partial Transcript, *Here and Now*, February 2, 2016, http://here-andnow.wbur.org/2016/02/02/nick-hanauer-minimum-wage (accessed March 4, 2016).

326 Robert Reich, "The Outrageous Ascent of CEO Pay," Blog, August 9, 2015, http://robertreich.org/post/126288944750 (accessed December 26, 2015).

327 Drew Harwell and Danielle Paquette, "Fiorina's Record at HP Defines Her Candidacy—Which Could be a Problem," *Washington Post*, September 26, 2015, https://www.washingtonpost.com/business/economy/fiorinas-record-at-hp-defines-her-candidacy—which-could-be-a-problem/2015/09/26/5a5b5e16-6174-11e5-8e9e-dce8a2a2a679_story.html (accessed March 4, 2016).

328 Robert Reich, "Harvard Business School's Role in Widening Inequality," *LinkedIn*, September 16, 2014, https://www.linkedin.com/pulse/20140916173926-244341831-harvard-business-school-s-role-in-widening-inequality (accessed March 4, 2016).

329 Patricia Cohen, "A Company Copes with Backlash against the Raise That Roared," *New York Times*, July 31, 2015, http://www.nytimes.com/2015/08/02/business/a-company-copes-with-backlash-against-the-raise-that-roared.html (accessed March 4, 2016).

330 Tyler Cowen, "It's Not the Inequality; It's the Immobility," *Upshot*, *New York Times*, April 2, 2015, http://www.nytimes.com/2015/04/05/upshot/its-not-the-inequality-its-the-immobility.html (accessed March 4, 2016).

331 Angus Deaton, *The Great Escape: Health, Wealth, and the Origins of Inequality* (Princeton: Princeton University Press, 2013), xi, xiii, 1.

332 Ibid., 8.

333 William Watson, *The Inequality Trap: Fighting Capitalism Instead of Poverty* (Toronto: University of Toronto Press, 2015), xi–xii.

334 Robert Reich, "The Rise of the Non-Working Rich," *Huffington Post*, July 14, 2014, updated September 14, 2014, http://www.huffingtonpost.com/robert-reich/the-rise-of-the-non-working-rich_b_5589684.html (accessed March 4, 2016).

335 Michael Bloomberg, interview with Chris Smith, "In Conversation: Michael Bloomberg," *New York Magazine*, September 7, 2013, http://nymag.com/news/politics/bloomberg/in-conversation-2013-9/index1.html (accessed March 4, 2016).

336 Paul Krugman, "Voodoo Never Dies," Opinion, *New York Times*, October 2, 2015, http://www.nytimes.com/2015/10/02/opinion/voodoo-never-dies.html?ref=opinion (accessed March 4, 2016).

337 David A. Stockman, "Paul Ryan's Fairy-Tale Budget Plan," Opinion, *New York Times*, August 13, 2012, http://www.nytimes.com/2012/08/14/opinion/paul-ryans-fairy-tale-budget-plan.html?ref=opinion (accessed March 4, 2016).

338 Laura Nahmias, "Budget Includes Sales-Tax Carve Out for Yachts," *Politico New York*, March 30, 2015, http://www.capitalnewyork.com/article/albany/2015/03/8565085/budget-includes-sales-tax-carveout-yachts?news-image (accessed March 4, 2016). [NOTE: I actually cannot find this article, either at this website or anywhere online].

339 Andrew Ross Sorkin, "A Tidal Wave of Corporate Migrants Seeking (Tax) Shelter," *Dealbook*, *New York Times*, January 25, 2016, http://www.nytimes.com/2016/01/26/business/dealbook/a-tidal-wave-of-corporate-migrants-seeking-tax-shelter.html (accessed March 4, 2016).

340 Nicholas Kristof, "The Real Welfare Cheats," Opinion, *New York Times*, April 14, 2016, http://www.nytimes.com/2016/04/14/opinion/the-real-welfare-cheats.html?ref=opinion (accessed June 11, 2016).

341 Noam Scheiber and Patricia Cohen, "For the Wealthiest, a Private Tax System That Saves Them Billions," *New York Times*, December 29, 2015, http://www.nytimes.com/2015/12/30/business/economy/for-the-wealthiest-private-tax-system-saves-them-billions.html (accessed March 4, 2016).

342 Thomas B. Edsal, "America Out of Whack," Opinion, *New York Times*, September 23, 2014, http://www.nytimes.com/2014/09/24/opinion/america-out-of-whack.html (accessed January 3, 2016).

343 Robert Frank, "Billionaires Get 'Low Income' Tax Breaks in NYC Condo Tower," *NBC News*, October 11, 2012, http://business.nbcnews.com/_news/2012/10/11/14368724-billionaires-get-low-income-tax-breaks-in-nyc-condo-tower (accessed March 4, 2016).

CHAPTER SEVEN: THE RULES

344 Ellen Fein and Sherrie Schneider, *The Rules: Time-Tested Secrets for Capturing the Heart of Mr. Right* (New York: Grand Central Publishing, 1995).

345 E.J. Dionne, Jr., *Why the Right Went Wrong: Conservatism—From Goldwater to the Tea Part and Beyond* (New York: Simon & Schuster, 2016), 2.

346 Richard Hofstadter, *The Paranoid Style in American Politics* (New York: Vintage Books, 2008). Originally published by Alfred A. Knopf, 1965.

347 Ibid., 20.

348 David Leonhardt, "Opposition to Health Law is Steeped in Tradition," *Economic Scene, New York Times*, December 14, 2010, http://www.nytimes.com/2010/12/15/business/economy/15leonhardt.html (accessed March 4, 2016).

349 E.J. Dionne, Jr., *Why the Right Went Wrong*, 39.

350 Rick Perlstein, "Birthers, Health Care Hecklers and the Rise of Right-Wing Rage," *Washington Post*, August 16, 2009, http://www.washingtonpost.com/wp-dyn/content/article/2009/08/14/AR2009081401495.html (accessed March 4, 2016).

351 Sean Wilentz, forward to Hofstadter, *The Paranoid Style in American Politics*, xvii.

352 Daniel Bell, ed., *The Radical Right: The New American Right* (Garden City, NY: Doubleday, 1963), 2.

353 Richard Hofstadter, *The Paranoid Style in American Politics*, xxxvi, 3, 53, and 54.

354 Richard Bottoms, "Liddy's Lethal Advice: Red Meat for Republican Voters?" *Fairness and Accuracy In Reporting*, July 1, 1995, http://fair.org/extra-online-articles/liddys-lethal-advice/ (accessed March 4, 2016).

355 E.J. Dionne, Jr., *Why the Right Went Wrong*, 3.

356 Jacob Weisberg, "What Today's Republicans Don't Get About Reagan," *New York Times*, February 24, 2016, http://www.nytimes.com/2016/02/24/opinion/what-todays-republicans-dont-get-about-reagan.html (accessed March 7, 2016).

357 Esther Yu Hsi Lee, "You will Not Believe How Reagan Talked about Immigration During the 1980 GOP Presidential Debate," ThinkProgress, August 6, 2015, http://thinkprogress.org/immigration/2015/08/06/3688656/republican-presidential-primary-debate-immigration-rhetoric/ (accessed March 8, 2016).

358 Richard Hofstadter, *The Paranoid Style in American Politics*, xxv–xxvi.

359 Dan Amira, "AIDS was Hilarious to the Reagan White House, Press Corps," *New York Magazine*, December 2, 2013, http://nymag.com/daily/intelligencer/2013/12/aids-white-house-larry-speakes-joke-press-briefing-1982.html# (accessed March 8, 2016).

360 Peter Baker, "Blunt Political Assessments in Bill Clinton Transcripts," *New York Times*, January 7, 2016, http://www.nytimes.com/2016/01/08/us/politics/bluntness-and-an-r-rating-in-bill-clinton-transcripts.html (accessed March 3, 2016).

361 Felicia Sonmez, "Charity President Unhappy about Paul Ryan Soup Kitchen 'Photo Op'," *Washington Post*, October 15, 2012, https://www.washingtonpost.com/blogs/election-2012/

wp/2012/10/15/charity-president-unhappy-about-paul-ryan-soup-kitchen-photo-op/ (accessed March 2, 2016).

362 Valerie Edwards, "How Ronald Reagan Based His Foreign Policy on Tom Clancy Books: President Told Margaret Thatcher to Read Red Storm Rising Thriller to Understand Russia," *Daily Mail*, December 30, 2015, updated January 4, 2016, http://www.dailymail.co.uk/news/ article-3378683/Ronald-Reagan-advised-Margaret-Thatcher-read-Tom-Clancy-s-thriller-Cold-War-strategy.html (accessed June 16, 2016).

363 Paul Krugman, "The Donald and the Decider," Opinion, *New York Times*, December 21, 2015, http://www.nytimes.com/2015/12/21/opinion/the-donald-and-the-decider.html (accessed March 4, 2016).

364 Christian Avard, "Ambassador Claims Shortly before Invasion, Bush Didn't Know There were Two Sects of Islam," *Raw Story*, August 4, 2006, http://www.rawstory.com/ news/2006/Ambassador_claims_shortly_before_invasion_Bush_0804.html (accessed March 3, 2016).

365 Peter Wehner, "Why I will Never Vote for Donald Trump," Opinion, *New York Times*, January 14, 2016, http://www.nytimes.com/2016/01/14/opinion/campaign-stops/why-i-will-never-vote-for-donald-trump.html (accessed March 2, 2016).

366 Paul Krugman, "The Donald and the Decider."

367 Kerwin Swint, "Founding Fathers' Dirty Campaign," *CNN*, August 22, 2008, http://www. cnn.com/2008/LIVING/wayoflife/08/22/mf.campaign.slurs.slogans/ (accessed March 8, 2016).

368 Greg Mitchell, *The Campaign of the Century: Upton Sinclair's Race for Governor of California and the Birth of Media Politics* (New York: Random House, 1992).

369 Dana Stevens, "Mr. Wedge Issue," *Slate*, September 26, 2008, http://www.slate.com/articles/arts/movies/2008/09/mr_wedge_issue.html (accessed March 8, 2016).

370 Richard Gooding, "The Trashing of John McCain," *Vanity Fair*, September 24, 2008, http:// www.vanityfair.com/news/2004/11/mccain200411 (accessed March 8, 2016).

371 Clark Bensen, "Presidential Results by Congressional District: Obama is Reelected but Romney Carries a Majority of Districts," *Polidata*, April 4, 2013, http://cookpolitical.com/ file/2013-04-50.pdf (accessed March 7, 2016).

372 Greg Giroux, "Republicans Win Congress as Democrats Get Most Votes," *Bloomberg*, March 18, 2013, http://www.bloomberg.com/news/articles/2013-03-19/republicans-win-congress-as-democrats-get-most-votes (accessed March 6, 2016).

373 William Kristol to Republican Leaders, "Defeating President Clinton's Health Care Proposal," Memorandum, December 2, 1993, https://www.scribd.com/document/12926608/ William-Kristol-s-1993-Memo-Defeating-President-Clinton-s-Health-Care-Proposal (accessed September 21, 2016). [NOTE: I changed this to the original source; I hope that's okay . . .]

374 Alan Cooperman, "DeLay Criticized for 'Only Christianity' Remarks," *Washington Post*, April 20, 2002, https://www.washingtonpost.com/archive/politics/2002/04/20/delay-criticized-for-only-christianity-remarks/21016a6c-9733-4518-961b-1c4df9312fc6/ (accessed March 4, 2016).

375 Brianna Ehley, "Cheney: Forget Food Stamps and Highways. Spend More on Military.," *Fiscal Times*, July 14, 2014, http://www.thefiscaltimes.com/Articles/2014/07/14/Cheney-Give-Military-More-Money-Not-Highways (accessed March 7, 2016).

376 Richard Hofstadter, *The Paranoid Style in American Politics*, 5.

377 Christopher Ingraham, "People are Getting Shot by Toddlers on a Weekly Basis This Year," *Wonkblog*, *Washington Post*, October 14, 2015, https://www.washingtonpost.com/news/wonk/ wp/2015/10/14/people-are-getting-shot-by-toddlers-on-a-weekly-basis-this-year/ (accessed February 26, 2016).

378 Christopher Ingraham, "Most Gun Owners Don't Belong to the NRA—and They Don't Agree with It Either," *Wonkblog*, *Washington Post*, October 15, 2015, https://www.washingtonpost.

com/news/wonk/wp/2015/10/15/most-gun-owners-dont-belong-to-the-nra-and-they-dont-agree-with-it-either/ (accessed March 8, 2016).

379 Erick Erickson, "I Shot Holes in the New York Times Editorial," *RedState*, December 5, 2015, http://www.redstate.com/2015/12/05/i-shot-holes-in-the-new-york-times-editorial/ (accessed March 20, 2016).

380 Bruce Drake, "5 Facts about the NRA and Guns in America", Pew Research Center, April 24, 2014, http://www.pewresearch.org/fact-tank/2014/04/24/5-facts-about-the-nra-and-guns-in-america/ (accessed August 7, 2016).

381 Richard Hofstadter, *The Paranoid Style in American Politics*, 49.

382 E.J. Dionne, Jr., *Why the Right Went Wrong*, 1.

CHAPTER EIGHT: FRIENDS WITHOUT BENEFITS

383 Author calculated per-vote spending based on funding totals in this article: Nicholas Confessore and Sarah Cohen, "How Jeb Bush Spent $130 Million Running for President with Nothing to Show for It," *New York Times*, February 22, 2016, http://www.nytimes.com/2016/02/23/us/politics/jeb-bush-campaign.html (accessed March 11, 2016).

384 Lindsay Young, "Outside Spenders' Return on Investment," Sunlight Foundation, December 17, 2012, http://sunlightfoundation.com/blog/2012/12/17/return_on_investment/ (accessed March 14, 2016).

385 Jaime Fuller, "Attention Rich People: You Still Can't Buy Elected Office (for Yourself)," *Washington Post*, July 31, 2014, https://www.washingtonpost.com/news/the-fix/wp/2014/07/31/attention-rich-people-you-still-cant-always-buy-elected-office/ (accessed March 14, 2016).

386 Russell Mokhiber, "Alaska's Lesson for the Left," *Nation*, April 3, 2013, http://www.thenation.com/article/alaskas-lesson-left/ (accessed March 13, 2016).

387 Russ Choma, "One Member of Congress = 18 American Households: Lawmakers' Personal Finances Far from Average," Center for Responsive Politics, January 12, 2015, http://www.opensecrets.org/news/2015/01/one-member-of-congress-18-american-households-lawmakers-personal-finances-far-from-average/ (accessed March 13, 2016).

388 "Personal Finances," Center for Responsive Politics, https://www.opensecrets.org/pfds/ (accessed March 13, 2016).

389 "Media CEOs Dominate Ranks of Top-Paid Executives," *Chicago Tribune*, May 26, 2015, http://www.chicagotribune.com/business/ct-media-ceo-salaries-20150526-story.html (accessed March 3, 2016).

390 "Most Popular Congressional Investments, 2014," Center for Responsive Politics, https://www.opensecrets.org/pfds/overview.php?type=P&year=2014 (accessed March 13, 2016).

391 "Proper Use of Campaign Funds and Resources," House Committee on Ethics, https://ethics.house.gov/campaign-activity/proper-use-campaign-funds-and-resources (accessed March 13, 2016).

392 "Campaign Guide for Congressional Candidates and Committees," Federal Election Commission, June 2014, http://www.fec.gov/pdf/candgui.pdf (accessed March 13, 2016)

393 All campaign spending data is from the Federal Election Commission online database: http://www.fec.gov/.

394 From the database of the Center for Responsive Politics, Opensecrets.org.

395 "Aderholt Bill will Make It Easier for States to Drug Test SNAP Recipients," Press Release, Congressman Robert Aderholt, February 12, 2016, https://aderholt.house.gov/media-center/press-releases/aderholt-bill-will-make-it-easier-states-drug-test-snap-recipients (accessed March 14, 2016).

396 "Money Wins Presidency and 9 of 10 Congressional Races in Priciest U.S. Election Ever," Center for Responsive Politics, November 5, 2008, http://www.opensecrets.org/news/2008/11/money-wins-white-house-and/ (accessed March 13, 2016).

397 Jacob Weisberg, "What Today's Republicans Don't Get about Reagan," Opinion, *New York Times*, February 24, 2016, http://www.nytimes.com/2016/02/24/opinion/what-todays-republicans-dont-get-about-reagan.html?ref=opinion (accessed February 24, 2016).

398 Colby Itkowitz, "Money Pours In for Unopposed Member of Congress," *Washington Post*, July 11, 2014, https://www.washingtonpost.com/blogs/in-the-loop/wp/2014/07/11/money-pours-in-for-unopposed-member-of-congress/ (accessed March 13, 2016).

399 Walter Shapiro, "The Greedy Truth about Media Consultants," *Salon*, May 9, 2016, http://www.salon.com/2006/05/09/campaign_consultants/ (accessed March 13, 2016).

400 Howard Fineman and Paul Blumenthal, "Political Consultants Rake It In, $466 Million and Counting in 2012 Cycle," *Huffington Post*, June 5, 2012, updated June 8, 2012, http://www.huffingtonpost.com/2012/06/05/political-consultants-2012-campaign-big-money_n_1570157.html (accessed March 13, 2016).

401 Steve Israel, "Confessions of a Congressman," Opinion, *New York Times*, January 8, 2016, http://www.nytimes.com/2016/01/09/opinion/steve-israel-confessions-of-a-congressman.html (accessed March 12, 2016).

402 Georgia Logothetis, "Call Time," *Daily Kos*, January 9, 2011, http://www.dailykos.com/story/2011/1/9/934645/- (accessed March 13, 2016).

403 Ibid.

404 Ryan Grim and Sabrina Siddiqui, "Call Time For Congress Shows How Fundraising Dominates Bleak Work Life," *Huffington Post*, January 8, 2013, http://www.huffingtonpost.com/2013/01/08/call-time-congressional-fundraising_n_2427291.html (accessed March 13, 2016).

405 Brian M. Riedl, "Farm Subsidies Ripe for Reform," The Heritage Foundation, March 29, 2011, http://www.heritage.org/research/commentary/2011/03/farm-subsidies-ripe-for-reform (accessed March 14, 2016); Chris Edwards, "Five Reasons to Repeal Farm Subsidies," Cato Institute, May 31, 2013, http://www.cato.org/blog/five-reasons-repeal-farm-subsidies (accessed March 14, 2016).

406 Eric Pianin, "Farm Subsidies are on the Chopping Block," *Fiscal Times*, June 2, 2011, http://www.thefiscaltimes.com/Articles/2011/06/02/Farm-Subsidies-Are-on-the-Chopping-Block (March 14, 2016).

407 "Farm Bills Mock Cost Cutting: Our View," Editorial Board, *USA Today*, July 28, 2013, http://www.usatoday.com/story/opinion/2013/07/28/farm-bills-subsidies-food-stamps-editorials-debates/2594453/ (accessed March 14, 2016).

408 "Agribusiness: Long-Term Contribution Trends," Center for Responsive Politics, http://www.opensecrets.org/industries/totals.php?cycle=2012&ind=A (accessed March 2, 2016).

409 Jackie Calmes, "Crop Insurance Subsidies Prove Cutting Budget is Easier Said Than Done," *New York Times*, November 26, 2015, http://www.nytimes.com/2015/11/27/us/politics/crop-insurance-subsidies-prove-cutting-budget-is-easier-said-than-done.html (accessed March 13, 2016).

410 "Lobbying: Ranked Sectors, 2015," Center for Responsive Politics, https://www.opensecrets.org/lobby/top.php?indexType=c&showYear=2015 (accessed March 14, 2016).

411 "Election Overview: Totals by Sector, 2016" Center for Responsive Politics, https://www.opensecrets.org/bigpicture/sectors.php?cycle=All&bkdn=DemRep&sortBy=Rank (accessed March 14, 2016).

412 Maggie Haberman, "Gay Businessman Who Hosted Ted Cruz Event Apologizes," *First Draft*, *New York Times*, April 26, 2015, http://www.nytimes.com/politics/first-draft/2015/04/26/gay-businessman-who-hosted-cruz-event-apologizes/ (accessed March 12, 2016).

413 "When States Fight Good Local Labor Laws," Editorial, *New York Times*, February 19, 2016, http://www.nytimes.com/2016/02/19/opinion/when-states-fight-to-overturn-good-local-labor-laws.html?ref=opinion (accessed February 19, 2016).

414 Brian Lyman, "Bentley Signs Bill Blocking Birmingham Minimum Wage," *Montgomery Advertiser*, February 26, 2016, http://www.montgomeryadvertiser.com/story/news/

politics/southunionstreet/2016/02/25/alabama-legislature-blocks-birmingham-mini-mum-wage/80941854/ (accessed March 14, 2016).

415 Robert B. Reich, *Saving Capitalism: For the Many, Not the Few*, 33.

416 David Cole, "How Corrupt are Our Politics?" *New York Review of Books*, September 25, 2014, http://www.nybooks.com/articles/2014/09/25/how-corrupt-are-our-politics/ (accessed December 28, 2015).

417 Nicholas Nehamas, "Florida Congressional Delegation Criticizes Proposed Rules on Payday Lending," *Miami Herald*, May 1, 2015, http://www.miamiherald.com/news/business/article20038134.html (accessed March 3, 2016).

418 "National Vaccine Injury Compensation Program," Health Resources and Services Adminis-tration, US Department of Health and Human Services, last reviewed February 2016, http://www.hrsa.gov/vaccinecompensation/ (accessed March 4, 2016).

419 "Pharmaceutical Manufacturing, 2015," Center for Responsive Politics, http://www.opense-crets.org/lobby/induscode.php?id=H4300&year=2015 (accessed March 12, 2016).

420 Noam Scheiber and Patricia Cohen, "For the Wealthiest, a Private Tax System That Saves Them Billions," *New York Times*, December 29, 2015, http://www.nytimes.com/2015/12/30/business/economy/for-the-wealthiest-private-tax-system-saves-them-billions.html (accessed March 4, 2016).

421 Nicholas Confessore, Sarah Cohen, and Karen Yourish, "Buying Power: The Families Funding the 2016 Presidential Election," *New York Times*, October 10, 2015, http://www.nytimes.com/interactive/2015/10/11/us/politics/2016-presidential-election-super-pac-donors.html (accessed March 12, 2016).

422 Nicholas Confessore, "Father of Koch Brothers Helped Build Nazi Oil Refinery, Book Says," *New York Times*, January 11, 2016, http://www.nytimes.com/2016/01/12/us/politics/father-of-koch-brothers-helped-build-nazi-oil-refinery-book-says.html (accessed March 3, 2016).

423 Nicholas Confessore, "Koch Brothers' Budget of $889 Million for 2016 is on Par with Both Parties' Spending," *New York Times*, January 26, 2015, http://www.nytimes.com/2015/01/27/us/politics/kochs-plan-to-spend-900-million-on-2016-campaign.html?_r=0 (accessed March 14, 2016).

424 Nicholas Confessore, "Father of Koch Brothers Helped Build Nazi Oil Refinery, Book Says."

425 Kenneth P. Vogel, "The Kochs' War on Poverty," *Politico*, December 14, 2015, http://www.politico.com/story/2015/12/charles-david-koch-poverty-charity-216631,(accessed January 4, 2016).

426 "Koch Brothers Get Each Other Same Election for Christmas," *The Onion*, 51, no. 49 (December 9, 2015), http://www.theonion.com/article/koch-brothers-get-each-other-same-election-christm-52012 (accessed March 12, 2016).

427 Noam Scheiber and Dalia Sussman, "Inequality Troubles Americans Across Party Lines, Times/CBS Poll Finds," *New York Times*, June 3, 2015, http://www.nytimes.com/2015/06/04/business/inequality-a-major-issue-for-americans-times-cbs-poll-finds.html (accessed March 4, 2016).

428 Martin Gilens and Benjamin I. Page, "Testing Theories of American Politics: Elites, Interest Groups, and Average Citizens," *Perspectives on Politics*, 12, no. 3 (September 2014), 564–81 [576], https://scholar.princeton.edu/sites/default/files/mgilens/files/gilens_and_page_2014_-testing_theories_of_american_politics.doc.pdf (accessed March 12, 2016).

429 Thomas B. Edsall, "How Did the Democrats Become Favorites of the Rich?" Opinion, *New York Times*, October 7, 2015, http://www.nytimes.com/2015/10/07/opinion/how-did-the-democrats-become-favorites-of-the-rich.html (accessed March 12, 2016).

CHAPTER NINE: HOW TO LOSE FRIENDS AND DE-INFLUENCE PEOPLE

430 Robert L. Borosage, "The Populist Moment Has Finally Arrived," *Nation*, March 23, 2015,
     http://www.thenation.com/article/occupy-and-organize/ (accessed March 5, 2016).
431 Kenyon Farrow, "Occupy Wall Street's Race Problem," *American Prospect*, October 24, 2011,
     http://prospect.org/article/occupy-wall-streets-race-problem (accessed March 11, 2016).
432 Nina Mandell, "Occupy Atlanta Denies Lewis Chance to Speak," *New York Daily News*,
     October 10, 2011, http://www.nydailynews.com/news/national/occupy-atlanta-offshoot-
     wall-street-protest-denies-rep-john-lewis-chance-speak-gathering-article-1.960844 (accessed
     March 12, 2016).
433 Quoted from the Occupy Wall Street homepage, http://occupywallst.org/ (accessed March 10,
     2016).
434 "Principles of Solidarity," *#Occupy Wall Street NYC General Assembly*, September 23, 2011,
     http://www.nycga.net/resources/documents/principles-of-solidarity/ (accessed March 10,
     2016).
435 "Declaration of the Occupation of New York City," *#Occupy Wall Street NYC General
     Assembly*, September 29, 2011, http://www.nycga.net/resources/documents/declaration/
     (accessed March 10, 2016).
436 I watched this live, but I don't have a link or site. Just trust me, it really happened!
437 Robert L. Borosage, "The Populist Moment Has Finally Arrived," *Nation*, March 23, 2015,
     http://www.thenation.com/article/occupy-and-organize/ (accessed March 5, 2016).
438 Jillian Berman, "Occupy Wall Street Actually Not at All Representative of the 99 Per-
     cent, Report Finds," *Huffington Post*, January 29, 2013, http://www.huffingtonpost.
     com/2013/01/29/occupy-wall-street-report_n_2574788.html (accessed August 6, 2016).
439 Christopher Hayes, *Twilight of the Elites: America After Meritocracy*, 23.
440 "The Story Continues, Make Your Voice Heard," *Occupy Sandy Recovery*, http://occupysandy.
     net/updates/ (accessed June 14, 2016).
441 Christopher Hayes, *Twilight of the Elites: America After Meritocracy*, 22 and 154.
442 Robert Frank, "More Millionaires Than Ever are Living in the US," *CNBC*, March 10, 2015,
     http://www.cnbc.com/2015/03/09/more-millionaires-than-ever-are-living-in-the-us.html
     (accessed March 12, 2016).
443 Joseph E. Stiglitz, *The Price of Inequality: How Today's Divided Society Endangers Our Future*,
     xxii.
444 Carmen DeNavas-Walt and Bernadette D. Proctor, *Income and Poverty in the United States:
     2014*.
445 "Bernie Sanders (D), Candidate Summary, 2016 Cycle," Center for Responsive Politics,
     https://www.opensecrets.org/pres16/candidate.php?id=N00000528 (accessed June 14,
     2016).
446 Matea Gold and Anu Narayanswamy, "Sanders is Biggest Spender of 2016 So Far—
     Generating Millions for Consultants," *Washington Post*, April 29, 2016, https://www.
     washingtonpost.com/politics/sanders-is-biggest-spender-of-2016-so-far--generating-millions-
     for-consultants/2016/04/28/600170ce-0cf2-11e6-a6b6-2e6de3695b0e_story.html (accessed
     June 14, 2016).
447 "Bernie Sanders (D), Top Contributors, Federal Election Data, Election Cycles Covered:
     2016," Center for Responsive Politics, https://www.opensecrets.org/pres16/contrib.php?cy-
     cle=2016&id=N00000528&type=f (accessed June 17, 2016).
448 Jeanine Skowronski, "More Millennials Say 'no' to Credit Cards," Bankrate, September 8,
     2014, http://www.bankrate.com/finance/credit-cards/more-millennials-say-no-to-credit-
     cards-1.aspx (accessed August 8, 2016).
449 Yes, Sanders often did well with the relatively small sub-group of minority voters under 30,
     but the actual vote totals prove he got creamed in the overall minority vote. For example,
     in the New York primary, here are three very low-income and overwhelmingly nonwhite

election districts and the margins by which Sanders lost to Hillary: Washington Heights, Manhattan ED #11 (44 points); East Concourse, Bronx, ED #56 (52 points); East New York, Brooklyn, ED #77 (67 points). When you are losing by 44 to 67 points in such neighborhoods, you simply must admit that your message is failing to connect.

450 Kirsten West Savali, "Bernie Sanders' 'Ghetto' Gaffe Gave Clinton Supporters the Ammunition They Needed," *Root*, March 8, 2016, http://www.theroot.com/articles/politics/2016/03/bernie_sanders_ghetto_gaffe_gave_clinton_supporters_the_ammunition_they.html (accessed March 19, 2016).

451 "Spotlight on Statistics: Automobiles," Bureau of Labor Statistics, October 2011, http://www.bls.gov/spotlight/2011/auto/ (accessed March 5, 2016).

452 Walker Bragman, "Hillary Clinton is Just Republican Lite: Sorry, Boomers, but This Millennial is Still Only Voting Bernie Sanders," *Salon*, December 22, 2015, http://www.salon.com/2015/12/22/hillary_clinton_is_just_republican_lite_sorry_boomers_but_this_millennial_is_still_only_voting_bernie_sanders/ (accessed March 5, 2016).

453 Thomas Frank, *What's the Matter with Kansas?: How Conservatives Won the Heart of America*, 243.

454 Bill Curry, "Let's Abandon the Democrats: Stop Blaming Fox News and Stop Hoping Elizabeth Warren will Save Us," *Salon*, December 23, 2014, http://www.salon.com/2014/12/23/lets_abandon_loser_democrats_stop_blaming_fox_news_and_hoping_elizabeth_warren_saves_us/ (accessed March 5, 2016).

455 Emma Goldman, "The Tragedy of the Political Exiles," *Nation*, October 10, 1934, http://theanarchistlibrary.org/library/emma-goldman-the-tragedy-of-the-political-exiles (accessed March 11, 2016).

CHAPTER TEN: REPUBLICANS ARE FROM MARS

456 Adam Waytza, Liane L. Young, and Jeremy Ginges, "Motive Attribution Asymmetry for Love vs. Hate Drives Intractable Conflict," *Proceedings of the National Academy of Sciences of the United States of America*, 111, no. 44 (2014), 15687–15692, http://www.pnas.org/content/111/44/15687.full (accessed December 27, 2015).

457 Martha Azzi, "Ex-Convict, Self-Made Millionaire or Psychic? Six Photographers are Told Different Backstories about One Man—and Take Remarkably Different Portraits," *Daily Mail*, November 9, 2015, http://www.dailymail.co.uk/news/article-3311311/Ex-convict-self-millionaire-psychic-Six-photographers-told-different-backstories-one-man-remarkably-different-portraits.html#ixzz3wsPfjSRR (accessed March 17, 2016).

458 Christopher Hayes, *Twilight of the Elites* (New York: Crown Publishing, 2012), 108.

459 Angie Drobnic Holan, "All Politicians Lie. Some Lie More Than Others," Opinion, *New York Times*, December 11, 2015, http://www.nytimes.com/2015/12/13/opinion/campaign-stops/all-politicians-lie-some-lie-more-than-others.html (accessed December 26, 2015).

460 Sean Wilentz, forward to Richard Hofstadter, *The Paranoid Style in American Politics* (New York: Vintage Books, [reprint] 2008), xxxvii–xxxviii.

461 Rick Perlstein, "Outlook: In America, Crazy is a Pre-existing Condition," *Washington Post*, August 18, 2009, http://www.washingtonpost.com/wp-dyn/content/discussion/2009/08/14/DI2009081402554.html (accessed March 17, 2016).

462 "FOX's File," *PunditFact* blog, PolitiFact, http://www.politifact.com/punditfact/tv/fox/ (accessed March 15, 2016).

463 Kevin D. Williamson, "How Stupid Happens," *National Review*, July 16, 2014, http://www.nationalreview.com/article/382851/how-stupid-happens-kevin-d-williamson (accessed July 16, 2014 and March 15, 2016).

464 Ben Dreyfuss, "Obama Just Called Out Fox News for Making the Poor out to be 'Leeches,'"
     Mother Jones, May 12, 2015, http://www.motherjones.com/mojo/2015/05/fox-news-probably-
     never-even-read-the-grapes-of-wrath (accessed March 17, 2016).

465 Charles M. Blow, "The President, Fox News, and the Poor," Opinion, *New York Times*, May
     14, 2015, http://www.nytimes.com/2015/05/14/opinion/charles-blow-the-president-fox-news-
     the-poor.html (accessed March 15, 2016).

466 Tyler Hansen, "Fox Continues Promoting Food Stamp Report Criticized as 'Tour De Force
     of Half-Truths, Distortions, and Outright Lies,'" *Media Matters for America*, August 12, 2013,
     http://mediamatters.org/blog/2013/08/12/fox-continues-promoting-food-stamp-report-
     criti/195363 (accessed March 17, 2016).

467 Peter Boyer, interview by Lauren Green, "A look at 'Fox News Reporting: The Great
     Food Stamp Binge,'" Video, Fox News, August 9, 2013, http://video.foxnews.com/
     v/2595939475001/a-look-at-fox-news-reporting-the-great-food-stamp-binge/?#sp=show-clips
     (accessed March 15, 2016).

468 Kirsten Powers, interview by Bill O'Reilly, "Bill O'Reilly Denies the Existence of Child
     Hunger: 'It's a Total Lie,'" Transcript and Video of Fox News's *The O'Reilly Factor*, *Media
     Matters for America*, October 6, 2015, http://mediamatters.org/video/2015/10/06/bill-oreilly-
     denies-the-existance-of-child-hung/205998 (accessed March 15, 2016).

469 Michael Wines, "Climate Change Threatens to Strip the Identity of Glacier National Park,"
     New York Times, November 22, 2014, http://www.nytimes.com/2014/11/23/us/climate-
     change-threatens-to-strip-the-identity-of-glacier-national-park.html (accessed March 15, 2016).

470 Hadas Gold, "Erick Erickson to Leave RedState," *Politico*, October 5, 2015, http://www.
     politico.com/blogs/on-media/2015/10/erik-erickson-to-leave-redstate-214444#ixzz43C-
     ToW4Pq (accessed March 17, 2016).

471 Erick Erickson, "The Watermelon in the Room: The Paris Climate Accord's Commu-
     nist-Like Approach to Weather," *RedState*, December 13, 2015, http://www.redstate.com/
     erick/2015/12/13/the-watermelon-in-the-room-the-paris-climate-accords-communist-like-ap-
     proach-to-weather/ (accessed March 17, 2016).

472 James Delingpole, "NASA Chief: Global Warming is Real Because I Have Cancer," *Breitbart*,
     January 18, 2016, http://www.breitbart.com/big-government/2016/01/18/nasa-chief-global-
     warming-is-real-because-i-have-cancer/ (accessed March 15, 2016).

473 Carl Hulse, "President Obama to Focus on American Potential in 2016," *New York Times*,
     January 11, 2016, http://www.nytimes.com/2016/01/12/us/politics/president-obama-to-fo-
     cus-on-american-potential-in-2016.html?ref=topics (accessed March 15, 2016).

474 David A. Fahrenthold, "27% of Communication by Members of Congress is Taunting,
     Professor Concludes," *Washington Post*, April 6, 2011, https://www.washingtonpost.com/
     politics/27percent-of-communication-by-members-of-congress-is-taunting-professor-con-
     cludes/2011/04/06/AFIn02qC_story.html (accessed March 17, 2016).

475 Josh Barro, "Marco Rubio and Other Republicans Paved the Way for Donald Trump's 'Narra-
     tive of Bitterness and Anger,'" *Business Insider*, March 12, 2016, http://www.businessinsider.
     com/marco-rubio-donald-trump-obama-2016-3 (accessed March 13, 2016).

476 David Auerbach, "The Bernie Bubble," *Slate*, February 17, 2016, http://www.slate.com/
     articles/technology/future_tense/2016/02/the_bernie_sanders_campaign_owes_a_lot_to_
     social_media.html (accessed March 5, 2016).

477 Emma Roller, "Donald Trump's Unstoppable Virality," Opinion, *New York Times*, December
     29, 2015, http://www.nytimes.com/2015/12/29/opinion/campaign-stops/donald-trumps-un-
     stoppable-virality.html?ref=opinion (accessed December 29, 2015).

478 Katy Waldman, "Yale Students Erupt in Anger Over Administrators Caring More about
     Free Speech Than Safe Spaces," *Slate*, November 7, 2015, http://www.slate.com/blogs/
     the_slatest/2015/11/07/yale_students_protest_over_racial_insensitivity_and_free_speech.
     html (accessed June 17, 2016).

479 "Information Technology Acceptable Use Policy," *Fordham University*, http://www.fordham. edu/info/21366/policies/2792/information_technology_acceptable_use_policy/2 (accessed March 17, 2016).

480 Dahlia Lithwick, "Free Speech or Safe Spaces?" *Slate*, November 25, 2015, http://www.slate. com/articles/news_and_politics/jurisprudence/2015/11/campus_protests_need_dialogue_ not_safe_spaces_and_offense.html (accessed March 17, 2016).

481 Suzanne Nossel, "Who is Entitled to Be Heard?" Opinion, *New York Times*, November 12, 2015, http://www.nytimes.com/2015/11/12/opinion/who-is-entitled-to-be-heard.html (accessed March 17, 2016).

482 "A Letter of Clarification for Amherst Alumni, Family, and Friends," *Amherst Uprising*, http://amherstuprising.com/demands.html (accessed March 15, 2016).

483 John Gray, Men are from Mars, Women are from Venus: The Classic Guide to Understanding the Opposite Sex (New York: HarperCollins Publishers, 1993), 10.

484 Letter from President George H.W. Bush to President-Elect Bill Clinton, according to writer Brad Meltzer. Natasha Lennard, "Bush's Letter to Clinton Revealed," *Politico*, January 11, 2011, http://www.politico.com/click/stories/1101/bushs_letter_to_clinton_revealed.html (accessed March 30, 2016).

485 Thomas E. Mann and Norman J. Ornstein, "Let's Just Say It: The Republicans are the Problem," *Washington Post*, April 27, 2012, https://www.washingtonpost.com/opinions/lets-just-say-it-the-republicans-are-the-problem/2012/04/27/gIQAxCVUlT_story.html (accessed March 18 2016).

486 Mark Sumner, "Why Democrats Should Climb onto the No Labels Stage with Joe Lieberman," *Daily Kos*, January 10, 2016, http://www.dailykos.com/ stories/2016/1/10/1466313/-Why-Democrats-should-climb-onto-the-No-Labels-stage-with-Joe-Lieberman (accessed March 16, 2016).

487 "Strategy and Philosophy," No Labels, http://www.nolabels.org/philosophy/ (accessed March 16, 2016).

488 I wonder if anyone at the American Enterprise Institute ever expected to see something positive written about the institution's points of view by me. Arthur C. Brooks, "We Need Optimists," Opinion, *New York Times*, July 25, 2015, http://www.nytimes.com/2015/07/26/ opinion/sunday/arthur-c-brooks-we-need-optimists.html?ref=opinion (accessed March 16, 2016).

CHAPTER ELEVEN: THREE CUPS OF CRIME SPREE

489 Steve Kroft, "Questions over Greg Mortenson's Stories," Transcript of *60 Minutes* segment, *CBS News*, aired April 17, 2011, http://www.cbsnews.com/news/questions-over-greg-mortensons-stories-19-04-2011/ (accessed March 16, 2016).

490 Carolyn Kellogg, "Greg Mortenson of 'Three Cups of Tea' Returns to Explain His Actions," *Los Angeles Times*, January 20, 2014, http://www.latimes.com/books/jacketcopy/la-et-jc-greg-mortenson-of-three-cups-of-tea-returns-to-explain-his-actions-20140120-story.html (accessed March 19, 2016).

491 Jewish Telegraph Agency, "Ex-FEGS Chief Sues Bankrupt Charity for $1.3M," *Forward*, May 5, 2015, http://forward.com/news/breaking-news/307520/ex-fegs-chief-sues-bankrupt-charity-for-13m/#ixzz43RRrP5Vk (accessed March 19, 2016).

492 Dave Philipps, "Wounded Warrior Project Spends Lavishly on Itself, Insiders Say," *New York Times*, January 27, 2016, http://www.nytimes.com/2016/01/28/us/wounded-warrior-project-spends-lavishly-on-itself-ex-employees-say.html (accessed March 18, 2016).

493 Sharyl Attkisson, "'Feed the Children' Charity Under Fire," *CBS News*, February 18, 2010, https://sharylattkisson.com/feed-the-children-scandal-follow-the-money/ (accessed March 30, 2016).

494 Nolan Clay, "Feed The Children Paid $800,000 to Founder Larry Jones after Firing Him" *Oklahoman*, May 29, 2013, http://newsok.com/article/3835655 (accessed March 20, 2016).

495 David Callahan, "Who will Watch the Charities?" Opinion, *New York Times*, May 30, 2015, http://www.nytimes.com/2015/05/31/opinion/sunday/who-will-watch-the-charities.html (accessed March 18, 2016).

496 Ibid.

497 Joe Stephens and Mary Pat Flaherty, "Inside the Hidden World of Thefts, Scams and Phantom Purchases at the Nation's Nonprofits," *Washington Post*, October 26, 2013, https://www.washingtonpost.com/investigations/inside-the-hidden-world-of-thefts-scams-and-phantom-purchases-at-the-nations-nonprofits/2013/10/26/825a82ca-0c26-11e3-9941-6711ed662e71_story.html (accessed March 20, 2016).

498 Ibid.

499 Suzanne Perry, "1 in 3 Americans Lacks Faith in Charities, Chronicle Poll Finds," *Chronicle of Philanthropy*, October 5, 2015, https://philanthropy.com/article/1-in-3-Americans-Lacks-Faith/233613 (accessed March 19, 2016).

500 Amy S. Blackwood, Katie L. Roeger, and Sarah L. Pettijohn, "The Nonprofit Sector in Brief: Public Charities, Giving, and Volunteering, 2012," Urban Institute, October 5, 2012, http://www.urban.org/sites/default/files/alfresco/publication-pdfs/412674-The-Nonprofit-Sector-in-Brief-Public-Charities-Giving-and-Volunteering-.PDF (accessed March 20, 2016).

501 David Callahan, "Who will Watch the Charities?"

502 The 990-tax form for WNET-TV, filed with the IRS, is available for free at Guidestar.org. See http://www.guidestar.org/profile/26-2810489.

503 The 990-tax forms for Quality Services for the Autism Community, filed with the IRS, are available for free at Guidestar.org. See http://www.guidestar.org/profile/11-2482974.

504 Jennifer O'Neill, "When a Family of 7 Can't Afford Dinner, a Cop Steps In," *Yahoo News*, May 5, 2015, https://www.yahoo.com/parenting/when-a-family-of-six-cant-afford-dinner-a-cop-118224107142.html (accessed March 19, 2016).

505 Matthew Yglesias, "Can the Cans: Why Food Drives are a Terrible Idea," *Slate*, December 7, 2011, http://www.slate.com/articles/business/moneybox/2011/12/food_drives_charities_need_your_money_not_your_random_old_food_.html (accessed March 18, 2016).

506 Kelley Holland, "Teaching Kids Charity? Skip the Soup Kitchen Trip," *CNBC*, October 18, 2013, http://www.cnbc.com/2013/10/17/teaching-kids-charity-skip-the-soup-kitchen-trip.html (accessed March 19, 2016).

507 Ariel Kaminer, "Warm Intentions, Meet Cold Reality," *New York Times*, November 20, 2009, http://www.nytimes.com/2009/11/22/nyregion/22critic.html (accessed March 19, 2016).

508 Anna C. Merritt, Daniel A. Effron, and Benoît Monin, "Moral Self-Licensing: When Being Good Frees Us to be Bad."

509 Alex Daniels, "As Wealthy Give Smaller Share of Income to Charity, Middle Class Digs Deeper," *Chronicle of Philanthropy*, October 5, 2014, https://philanthropy.com/article/As-Wealthy-Give-Smaller-Share/152481#note (accessed March 18, 2016).

510 Daniel M. Hungerman, "Race and Charitable Church Activity," *National Bureau of Economic Research*, August 2007, http://www.nber.org/papers/w13323 (accessed March 18, 2016).

511 And don't forget the Joan and Sanford I. Weill Center for Metabolic Health. Oh, why go on. "Weill Cornell Names Its Department of Medicine for Joan and Sanford I. Weill," Weill Cornell Medical College, February 11, 2014, http://weill.cornell.edu/news/news/2014/02/weill-cornell-names-its-department-of-medicine-for-joan-and-sanford-i-weill.html (accessed March 29, 2016).

512 Pete Farley, "$185M Gift Launches UCSF Weill Institute for Neurosciences," University of California, San Francisco, April 25, 2016, https://www.ucsf.edu/news/2016/04/402471/185m-gift-launches-ucsf-weill-institute-neurosciences (accessed June 25, 2016).

513 Kristin Hussey, "After Ruling, Paul Smith's College Won't Get Weills' $20 Million Renaming Gift," *New York Times*, October 22, 2015, http://www.nytimes.com/2015/10/23/

nyregion/weills-20-million-renaming-gift-to-paul-smiths-college-is-withdrawn.html (accessed March 20, 2016).

514 Peter Buffett, "The Charitable-Industrial Complex," Opinion, *New York Times*, July 26, 2013, http://www.nytimes.com/2013/07/27/opinion/the-charitable-industrial-complex.html (March 18, 2016).

515 Kentaro Toyama, Geek Heresy: Rescuing Social Change from the Cult of Technology (New York: Public Affairs, 2015): 84-87.

516 Ibid., 22.

517 "Update on Central Asia Institute: The Concerns Continue to Support a '?' Rating," *Charity Watch*, January 22, 2015, https://www.charitywatch.org/charitywatch-articles/update-on-central-asia-institute-the-concerns-continue-to-support-a-34-34-rating/149 (accessed March 20, 2016).

518 David Callahan, "Who will Watch the Charities?"

519 Andrew Ross Sorkin, "When Restless Billionaires Trip on Their Toys," *New York Times*, January 11, 2016, http://www.nytimes.com/2016/01/12/business/billionaires-who-trip-on-their-toys.html (accessed March 19, 2016).

CHAPTER TWELVE: SEVEN HABITS OF A HIGHLY UNSUCCESSFUL NATION

520 Andrew Mayeda, "Blissfully Unaware, or Just Blissful? Canadians are a Happy Bunch," *Postmedia News*, November 24, 2010, http://www.canada.com/health/blissfully+unaware+-just+blissful+canadians+happy+bunch/3871940/story.html (accessed March 21, 2016).

521 "State of the Union: The Poverty and Inequality Report, 2016," *Pathways Magazine*, Stanford Center on Poverty and Inequality, Special Issue 2016, http://inequality.stanford.edu/sites/default/files/Pathways-SOTU-2016-2.pdf (accessed March 31, 2016).

522 Stephen R. Covey, *The 7 Habits of Highly Effective People* (New York: Free Press, 1989), 36.

523 Katie Lobosco, "11 States Spend More on Prisons Than on Higher Education," *CNN*, October 1, 2015, http://money.cnn.com/2015/10/01/pf/college/higher-education-prison-state-spending/ (accessed June 17, 2016).

524 Donald S. Shepard, Elizabeth Setren, and Donna Cooper, "Hunger in America: Suffering We All Pay For," Center for American Progress, October 2011, https://www.americanprogress.org/wp-content/uploads/issues/2011/10/pdf/hunger_paper.pdf (accessed June 17, 2016).

525 United Health Foundation, American Public Health Association, and Partnership for Prevention, "The Future Costs of Obesity: National and State Estimates of the Impact of Obesity on Direct Health Care Expenses," updated November 2009, http://www.fightchronicdisease.org/sites/default/files/docs/CostofObesityReport-FINAL.pdf (accessed June 17, 2016).

526 Emma G. Fitzsimmons and David W. Chen, "Aging Infrastructure Plagues Nation's Busiest Rail Corridor," *New York Times*, July 26, 2015, http://www.nytimes.com/2015/07/27/nyregion/aging-infrastructure-plagues-nations-busiest-rail-corridor.html (accessed March 21, 2016).

527 Carl Schurz, "A Special Foreign Policy," *Nation*, 1882. [NOTE: I can't find this anywhere to confirm this citation. Considering that the Spanish-American War was fought in 1898, neither the 1888 date in the text (which I've since changed to 1898, but it may be later) nor this 1882 date here can be correct. But I'm not sure that the article title or journal is either]

528 Bernard Fall and Frances FitzGerald, "The Reporter Who Warned Us Not to Invade Vietnam 10 Years Before the Gulf of Tonkin," *Nation*, March 23, 2015, http://www.thenation.com/article/encounter-bernard-fall-and-frances-fitzgerald/ (accessed March 21, 2016).

529 Joshua Keating, "Destroying Towns to Save Them from ISIS," *Slate*, January 8, 2016, http://www.slate.com/blogs/the_slatest/2016/01/08/the_only_way_we_ve_been_able_to_liberate_cities_from_isis_is_to_demolish.html (accessed March 21, 2016).

530 "World Report 2015: Saudi Arabia, Events of 2014," *Human Rights Watch*, https://www.hrw. org/world-report/2015/country-chapters/saudi-arabia (accessed March 16, 2016).

531 "How Much Petroleum Does the United States Import and Export?" *US Energy Information Administration*, updated April 1, 2016, http://www.eia.gov/tools/faqs/faq.cfm?id=727&t=6 (accessed March 20, 2016).

532 Michael B. Kelley and Geoffrey Ingersoll, "The Staggering Cost of the Last Decade's US War in Iraq—In Numbers," *Business Insider*, June 20, 2014, http://www.businessinsider.com/ the-iraq-war-by-numbers-2014-6 (accessed March 21, 2016).

533 Nicholas Fandos, "US Foreign Arms Deals Increased Nearly $10 Billion in 2014," *New York Times*, December 25, 2015, http://www.nytimes.com/2015/12/26/world/middleeast/us-for-eign-arms-deals-increased-nearly-10-billion-in-2014.html (accessed March 4, 2016).

534 Liz Alderman and Steven Greenhouse, "Living Wages, Rarity for US Fast-Food Workers, Served Up in Denmark," *New York Times*, October 27, 2014, http://www.nytimes. com/2014/10/28/business/international/living-wages-served-in-denmark-fast-food-restau-rants.html (accessed March 4, 2016).

535 Ibid.

536 Hardeep Matharu, "Employers in Sweden Introduce Six-Hour Work Day," *Independent, c.* September 2015 (no date given), updated September 17, 2016, http://www.independent. co.uk/news/world/europe/sweden-introduces-six-hour-work-day-a6674646.html (accessed March 20, 2016 and September 23, 2016).

537 Charles Murray, *Coming Apart: The State of White America 1960–2010* (New York: Crown Forum, 2012), 282.

538 Deborah Hardoon, Sophia Ayele, and Ricardo Fuentes-Nieva, "An Economy for the 1%: How Privilege and Power in the Economy Drive the Extreme Inequality and How This Can be Stopped," *Oxfam International*, January 18, 2016, https://www.oxfam.org/sites/www. oxfam.org/files/file_attachments/bp210-economy-one-percent-tax-havens-180116-en_0.pdf (accessed January 18, 2016).

539 Charles Riley, "China Now Has More Billionaires Than US," *CNN*, October 15, 2015, http:// money.cnn.com/2015/10/15/investing/china-us-billionaires/ (accessed March 21, 2016).

540 Joel Rogers, "Productive Democracy: It's Time to Embrace a New Egalitarian Politics," *Nation*, March 23, 2015, http://www.thenation.com/article/productive-democracy/ (accessed March 12, 2016).

541 Liz Alderman, "Smart Car Standoff Pits Social Progress Against Global Competition," *New York Times*, December 12, 2015, http://www.nytimes.com/2015/12/13/business/interna-tional/smart-car-standoff-pits-social-progress-against-global-competition.html (accessed December 26, 2015).

542 Landon Thomas, Jr., "With Money Drying Up, Greece is All but Bankrupt," *New York Times*, May 25, 2015, http://www.nytimes.com/2015/05/26/business/dealbook/with-money-drying-up-greece-is-all-but-bankrupt.html (accessed March 21, 2016).

543 Pauline Fron, Herwig Immervoll, Maxime Ladaique, and Hilde Olsen, "Society at a Glance: OECD Social Indicators," *Organization of Economic Co-operation and Development*, March 18, 2014, http://www.oecd-ilibrary.org/docserver/download/8113171e.pdf?expires=1451772 025&id=id&accname=guest&checksum=92A8BD52343F781E476AF28936685C44, 11–12 (accessed January 2, 2016).

544 Ibid.

545 Gonzalo Faniul, "Children of the Recession: The Impact of the Economic Crisis on Child Well-Being in Rich Countries," Innocenti Report Card 12, *UNICEF Office of Research*, 2014, http://www.unicef-irc.org/publications/pdf/rc12-eng-web.pdf (accessed March 31, 2016).

546 Jim Yardley, "Has Europe Reached the Breaking Point?" *New York Times Magazine*, December 15, 2015, http://www.nytimes.com/2015/12/20/magazine/has-europe-reached-the-breaking-point.html (accessed March 21, 2016).

547   David Crouch, "Sweden Takes a Left Turn after 8 Years of Rightist Rule," *New York Times*, September 14, 2014, http://www.nytimes.com/2014/09/15/world/europe/sweden-takes-a-left-turn-after-8-years-of-rightist-rule.html?ref=world (accessed March 20, 2016).

548   "India Export Statistics," Agricultural and Processed Food Products Export Development Authority, Ministry of Commerce and Industry, Government of India), http://www.agriex-change.apeda.gov.in/indexp/reportlist.aspx (accessed March 21, 2016).

549   Sharad Tandon and Maurice Landes, "India Continues to Grapple with Food Insecurity," Economic Research Service, United States Department of Agriculture, February 3, 2014, http://www.ers.usda.gov/amber-waves/2014-januaryfebruary/india-continues-to-grap-ple-with-food-insecurity.aspx#.VvAWcXrUoxI (accessed March 31, 2016).

550   "The World's Billionaires," *Forbes*, http://www.forbes.com/billionaires/list/ (accessed March 31, 2016).

551   Ellen Barry, "Desperate for Slumber in Delhi, Homeless Encounter a 'Sleep Mafia,'" *New York Times*, January 18, 2016, http://www.nytimes.com/2016/01/19/world/asia/delhi-sleep-economy.html (accessed March 20, 2016).

552   "Agricultural Trade Multipliers: Effects of Trade on the US Economy—2014," Economic Research Service, United States Department of Agriculture, c. 2014, updated May 5, 2016, http://www.ers.usda.gov/data-products/agricultural-trade-multipliers/effects-of-trade-on-the-us-economy.aspx (accessed March 31, 2016 and September 23, 2016).

553   *French National Institute of Statistics and Economic Studies*, http://www.insee.fr/en/ [NOTE: This is just a website homepage; you seem to be citing a specific report or page, so you'll need to fill in more information here]

554   Tami Luhby, "America's Poor are 'Envy of the World,' Says Richest Congressman," *CNN*, May 7, 2015, http://money.cnn.com/2015/05/07/news/economy/issa-poor/index.html (accessed March 4, 2016).

555   Timothy A. Wise and Biraj Patnaik, "Destruction of US Credibility at WTO," *Livemint*, September 8, 2015, http://www.livemint.com/Opinion/JPi4o78XnwziAnsbzTHgrJ/Destruc-tion-of-US-credibility-at-WTO.html (accessed March 21, 2016).

556   Al Jazeera and Agence France-Presse, "Report: World Grows Less Hungry, but Food Insecurity Remains High," *Al Jazeera America*, May 27, 2015, http://america.aljazeera.com/articles/2015/5/27/un-targets-zero-hunger-in-a-generation-as-numbers-fall.html (accessed March 21, 2016).

557   Nicholas Kristof, "The Most Important Thing, and It's Almost a Secret," Opinion, *New York Times*, October 1, 2015, http://www.nytimes.com/2015/10/01/opinion/nicholas-kristof-the-most-important-thing-and-its-almost-a-secret.html?ref=opinion (accessed March 21, 2016).

558   "World's 2030 Goals Put Hunger and Agriculture at the Center of Global Policy," *Food and Agriculture Organization of the United Nations*, September 25, 2015, http://www.fao.org/news/story/en/item/331906/icode/ (accessed March 21, 2016).

559   Nelson Mandela, "In Full: Mandela's Poverty Speech," Launch of the Make Poverty History Campaign, Trafalgar Square, London, February 3, 2015, *BBC News*, http://news.bbc.co.uk/2/hi/uk_news/politics/4232603.stm (accessed March 21, 2016).

560   Michael B. Kelley and Geoffrey Ingersoll, "The Staggering Cost of the Last Decade's US War in Iraq—In Numbers,"

561   Azam Ahmed, "Tasked with Combating Opium, Afghan Officials Profit from It," *New York Times*, February 15, 2016, http://www.nytimes.com/2016/02/16/world/asia/afghanistan-opi-um-heroin-taliban-helmand.html?ref=world (accessed February 16, 2016).

562   Daniel P. Bolger, "The Truth About Wars," Opinion, *New York Times*, November 10, 2014, http://www.nytimes.com/2014/11/11/opinion/the-truth-about-the-wars-in-iraq-and-afghani-stan.html?ref=opinion (accessed March 20, 2016).

563   "Ammar Al Shamary, "Iraq Starts Operation to Rid Ramadi of Islamic State," *USA Today*, May 27, 2015, http://www.usatoday.com/story/news/world/2015/05/26/iraq-islamic-state-anbar/27947521/ (accessed March 31, 2016).

564   Mustafa al-Kadhimi, "Will Sistani be Able to Control Popular Mobilization Forces?" trans. Joelle El-Khouri, *Al-Monitor*, March 12, 2015, http://www.al-monitor.com/pulse/origi-nals/2015/03/iraq-sistani-righteous-jihad-fatwa-popular-mobilization.html# (accessed March 21, 2016).

CHAPTER THIRTEEN: THE GRANIVORE'S DILEMMA

565   Ben Worthen, "A Dozen Eggs for $8? Michael Pollan Explains the Math of Buying Local," *Wall Street Journal*, August 5, 2010, http://www.wsj.com/articles/SB10001424052748704271 804575405521469248574 (accessed March 20, 2016).

566   Philip B. Stark, "Salad from the Sidewalk," Opinion, *New York Times*, July 9, 2015, http://www.nytimes.com/interactive/2015/07/09/opinion/09bittman.html (accessed March 23, 2016).

567   "Locally Grown, Raised and Produced," *Whole Foods Market*, http://www.wholefoodsmarket.com/local (accessed December 26, 2015).

568   Corinne Ramey, "Baldor will Expand New York City Operations," *Wall Street Journal*, August 4, 2015, http://www.wsj.com/articles/baldor-will-expand-new-york-city-opera-tions-1438736019 (accessed March 23, 2016).

569   Amanda Cohen, "Winter Tomatoes are Deliciously Out of Season," Food, *New York Times*, February 9, 2016, http://www.nytimes.com/2016/02/10/dining/winter-tomato-recipes.html (accessed March 21, 2016).

570   Dong D. Wang, et al., "Trends in Dietary Quality among Adults in the United States, 1999 through 2010," *JAMA Internal Medicine* 174, no. 10 (2014), 1587–1595, http://archinte.jama-network.com/article.aspx?articleid=1899558 (accessed March 23, 2016).

571   James Hamblin, "The Food Gap is Widening," *Atlantic*, September 2, 2014, http://www.theatlantic.com/health/archive/2014/09/access-to-real-food-as-privilege/379482/ (accessed March 23, 2016).

572   Joel Salatin, "Rebel with a Cause: Foodie Elitism," *Handpicked Nation*, March 4, 2012, http://handpickednation.com/rebel-with-a-cause-foodie-elitism/ (accessed March 20, 2016).

573   Jason Mark, "Workers on Organic Farms are Treated as Poorly as Their Conventional Coun-terparts," *Grist*, August 2, 2006, http://grist.org/article/mark/ (accessed March 22, 2016).

574   "It's Dinnertime: A Report on Low-Income Families' Efforts to Plan, Shop for and Cook Healthy Meals," PowerPoint Presentation, Share Our Strength, January 2012, https://www.nokidhungry.org/images/cm-study/report-full.pdf (accessed March 24, 2016).

575   Anna North, "Should You Pack Your Child's Lunch?" Op-Talk, *New York Times*, November 18, 2014, http://op-talk.blogs.nytimes.com/2014/11/18/should-you-pack-your-childs-lunch/ (accessed March 21, 2016).

576   Christine Gilbert, "I Get Food Stamps, and I'm Not Ashamed—I'm Angry," *Vox*, September 16, 2015, http://www.vox.com/2015/6/26/8845881/food-stamps (accessed March 21, 2016).

577   Mark Bittman, "Bad Food? Tax It, and Subsidize Vegetables," Opinion, *New York Times*, July 23, 2011, http://www.nytimes.com/2011/07/24/opinion/sunday/24bittman.html (accessed March 26, 2016).

578   Mark Bittman, "Time to Make the Doughnuts," *New York Times Magazine*, December 11, 2014, http://www.nytimes.com/2014/12/07/magazine/time-to-make-the-doughnuts.html (accessed March 24, 2016).

579   Tamar Haspel, "10 Things We Should Do to Fix Our Broken Food System," *Washington Post*, December 28, 2015, https://www.washingtonpost.com/lifestyle/food/10-things-we-should-do-to-fix-our-broken-food-system/2015/12/28/ea720336-a8f7-11e5-9b92-dea7cd4b1a4d_story.html (accessed December 29, 2015).

580   Marion Nestle, *Soda Politics: Taking on Big Soda (And Winning)* (London: Oxford University Press, 2015), 2.

581 Bryce Covert, "Why Do Americans Feel Entitled to Tell Poor People What to Eat?" *Nation*, February 18, 2015, http://www.thenation.com/article/why-do-americans-feel-entitled-tell-poor-what-eat/ (accessed March 24, 2016).

582 Jessica E. Todd and Michele Ver Ploeg, "Restricting Sugar-Sweetened Beverages from SNAP Purchases Not Likely to Lower Consumption," Economic Research Service, United States Department of Agriculture, March 2, 2015, http://www.ers.usda.gov/ amber-waves/2015-march/restricting-sugar-sweetened-beverages-from-snap-purchas-es-not-likely-to-lower-consumption.aspx#.VvP1h2f2apq (accessed March 24, 2016).

CHAPTER FOURTEEN: AMERICA'S VIRGIN/WHORE COMPLEX

583 Ami Angelowicz, "A Newspaper's Really Bad Advice for A 35-Year-Old Virgin," *Frisky*, December 17, 2009, http://www.thefrisky.com/2009-12-17/really-bad-advice-for-a-35-year-old-virgin (accessed March 24, 2016). The original column has been taken off the website of both the *Chicago Sun-Times* and the creator's syndicate. For another reference to the article, see *Aaroncynic*, "What's an Almost 40-Year-Old Virgin to Do?" *Chicagoist*, December 17, 2009, http://chicagoist.com/2009/12/17/whats_a_40_year_old_virgin_to_do.php (accessed March 30, 2016). Just proving that even if you delete something posted on the Internet, it never completely goes away.

584 Zack Ford, "Kansas Bill Would Pay Students a $2,500 Bounty to Hunt for Trans People in Bathrooms," ThinkProgress, March 22, 2016, http://thinkprogress.org/ lgbt/2016/03/22/3762490/kansas-transgender-ransom-bathrooms/ (accessed March 30, 2016).

585 Peggy Orenstein, "When Did Porn Become Sex Ed?" Opinion, *New York Times*, March 19, 2016, http://www.nytimes.com/2016/03/20/opinion/sunday/when-did-porn-become-sex-ed. html (accessed March 20, 2016).

586 Caitlin MacNeal, "WATCH: Rich Lowry Claims 'Forced Kissing' isn't Sexual Assault," *Talking Points Memo*, December 7, 2014, http://talkingpointsmemo.com/livewire/rich-lowry-forced-kissing-uva (accessed March 23, 2016).

587 Amanda Robb, "Abortion Witch Hunt," Opinion, *New York Times*, March 4, 2016, http:// www.nytimes.com/2016/03/05/opinion/abortion-witch-hunt.html (accessed March 5, 2016).

588 Seth Stephens-Davidowitz, "The Return of the D.I.Y. Abortion," Opinion, *New York Times*, March 5, 2016, http://www.nytimes.com/2016/03/06/opinion/sunday/the-return-of-the-diy-abortion.html (accessed March 7, 2016).

589 Ibid.

590 Emily Bazelon, "Do Women Need Legislative 'Protection'?" *New York Times Magazine*, February 17, 2016, http://www.nytimes.com/2016/02/21/magazine/do-women-need-legisla-tive-protection.html (accessed March 24, 2016).

591 Tracy Clark-Flory and Leigh Cuen, "The Vile Language Hurled at Hillary Clinton on Social Media," *Vocativ*, July 23, 2015, http://www.vocativ.com/news/214710/your-guide-to-anti-hil-lary-clinton-sexism (accessed March 23, 2016).

592 Sady Doyle, "More Than Likable Enough: I Like Hillary Clinton. And I'm Convinced That Saying So Can be a Subversive Act," *Slate*, December 23, 2015, http://www.slate.com/articles/ double_x/doublex/2015/12/saying_nice_things_about_hillary_clinton_has_become_a_sub-versive_act.html (accessed March 23, 2016).

593 Emily Crockett, "The 'Trump That Bitch!' T-Shirt is Emblematic of Trump's Entire Campaign," *Vox*, June 17, 2016, http://www.vox.com/2016/6/17/11953388/trump-that-bitch-t-shirt-hillary-clinton (accessed June 18, 2016).

594 Jamie Self, "Sparring Over Remark Hits SC Senate Floor," *State*, February 17, 2015, http://www.thestate.com/news/politics-government/politics-columns-blogs/the-buzz/ article13956770.html (accessed March 23, 2016). Also see the original story, "SC Senator:

Women are 'A Lesser Cut of Meat,'" *FITSNews*, February 11, 2015, http://www.fitsnews.com/2015/02/11/sc-senator-women-lesser-cut-meat/#2S6pKBDO07C4plRP.99 (accessed March 23, 2016).

595 Anna Gunn, "I Have a Character Issue," Opinion, *New York Times*, August 23, 2013, http://www.nytimes.com/2013/08/24/opinion/i-have-a-character-issue.html (accessed March 23, 2016).

596 Amanda Taub, "Control and Fear: What Mass Killings and Domestic Violence Have in Common," *New York Times*, June 15, 2016, http://www.nytimes.com/2016/06/16/world/americas/control-and-fear-what-mass-killings-and-domestic-violence-have-in-common.html (accessed June 16, 2016).

597 Samantha Allen, "Marital Rape is Semi-Legal in 8 States," *Daily Beast*, June 9, 2015, http://www.thedailybeast.com/articles/2015/06/09/marital-rape-is-semi-legal-in-8-states.html (accessed June 26, 2016).

598 Claire Cain Miller, "As Women Take Over a Male-Dominated Field, the Pay Drops," *New York Times*, March 18, 2016, http://www.nytimes.com/2016/03/20/upshot/as-women-take-over-a-male-dominated-field-the-pay-drops.html?ref=business (accessed March 20, 2016).

599 Mandy Oaklander, "Women Doctors are Paid $20,000 Less Than Male Doctors," *Time*, July 11, 2016, http://time.com/4398888/doctors-gender-wage-gap/ (accessed August 7, 2016).

600 Laura Clawson, "Kasich: New Mothers Should Work at Home Online, Not Get Paid Family Leave," *Daily Kos*, January 11, 2016, http://www.dailykos.com/story/2016/01/11/1468407/-Kasich-New-mothers-should-work-at-home-online-not-get-paid-family-leave (accessed March 4, 2016).

601 Ivana Kottasova, "U.S. is 65th in World on Gender Pay Gap," Money, *CNN*, October 28, 2014, http://money.cnn.com/2014/10/27/news/economy/global-gender-pay-gap/ (accessed June 16, 2016).

602 Patrick Goodenough, "UN Identifies 'Extremism and Conservatism'—Not Islam—As Impediments to Gender Equality," *CNS News*, March 10, 2015, http://www.cnsnews.com/news/article/patrick-goodenough/un-identifies-extremism-and-conservatism-not-islam-impediments (accessed March 30, 2016).

603 Gardiner Harris, "Study Says Pregnant Women in India are Gravely Underweight," *The New York Times*, March 2, 2015, http://www.nytimes.com/2015/03/03/world/asia/-pregnant-women-india-dangerously-underweight-study.html (accessed March 30, 2016).

604 "Saudi Woman to Get 200 Lashes after being Raped," *Middle East Monitor*, March 6, 2015, https://www.middleeastmonitor.com/20150306-saudi-woman-to-get-200-lashes-after-being-raped/ (accessed June 16, 2016).

CHAPTER FIFTEEN: A NON–PURPOSE DRIVEN LIFE

605 Rick Warren, *The Purpose Driven Life: What on Earth Am I Here For?* (Grand Rapids: Zondervan Publishing, 2002), 148.

606 Peter Haldeman, "The Return of Werner Erhard, Father of Self-Help," *New York Times*, November 28, 2015, http://www.nytimes.com/2015/11/29/fashion/the-return-of-werner-erhard-father-of-self-help.html (accessed March 22, 2016).

607 Ronald W. Dworkin, "Psychotherapy and the Pursuit of Happiness," *New Atlantis*, no. 35 (2012), 69–83, http://www.thenewatlantis.com/publications/psychotherapy-and-the-pursuit-of-happiness (accessed March 30, 2016).

608 Jennifer Aaker and Emily Esfahani Smith, "Not Everyone Wants to Be Happy: Americans are Obsessed with Happiness, but Other Cultures See Things Differently," *Scientific American*, October 28, 2014, http://www.scientificamerican.com/article/not-everyone-wants-to-be-happy/ (accessed March 25, 2016).

609 Evgeny Morozov, *The Net Delusion: The Dark Side of Internet Freedom* (New York: Public Affairs, 2011), 187.

610 Taylor and Francis Group, "Does Facebook Affect Our Self-Esteem, Sense of Belonging?" *Science Daily*, May 8, 2014, https://www.sciencedaily.com/releases/2014/05/140508095456. htm (accessed March 30, 2016). See also the original study: Stephanie J. Tobin, Eric J. Vanman, Marnize Verreynne, and Alexander K. Saeri, "Threats to Belonging on Facebook: Lurking and Ostracism," *Social Influence*, 10, no. 1 (2015; published online March 7, 2014), 31–42; doi: 10.1080/15534510.2014.893924, http://www.tandfonline.com/doi/abs/10.1080/1 5534510.2014.893924 (accessed March 30, 2016).

611 Helen Thomas and Craig Crawford, Listen Up, Mr. President: Everything You Always Wanted Your President to Know and Do (New York: Simon and Schuster, 2009), 148.

612 Craig Fehrman, "The Incredible Shrinking Sound Bite," *Boston Globe*, January 2, 2011, http://archive.boston.com/bostonglobe/ideas/articles/2011/01/02/the_incredible_shrinking_sound_bite/ (accessed March 25, 2016).

613 Margaret Sullivan, "Waiter, Where's Our (Political) Spinach?" *New York Times*, March 5, 2016, http://www.nytimes.com/2016/03/06/public-editor/new-york-times-public-editor-presidential-campaign.html (accessed March 30, 2016).

614 Patrick Healy and Amy Chozick, "In Democratic Debate, Hillary Clinton Challenges Bernie Sanders on Policy Shifts," *New York Times*, January 17, 2016, http://www.nytimes.com/2016/01/18/us/politics/democratic-debate.html?ref=politics (accessed January 18, 2016).

615 Jeremy W. Peters, "Marco Rubio Reacts to Those Boots That were Made for Talking," *New York Times*, January 7, 2016, http://www.nytimes.com/politics/first-draft/2016/01/07/marco-rubio-reacts-to-those-boots-that-were-made-for-talking/ (accessed March 25, 2016).

616 "Do You Make $400,000 a Year but Still Feel Broke," Video, *Wall Street Journal*, September 5, 2014, http://www.wsj.com/video/do-you-make-400000-a-year-but-feel-broke/387CA8E8-2C0F-449B-8F8F-7BBCF70EE954.html (accessed December 26, 2015).

617 Stephanie Rosenbloom, "Private Flying for (Some of) the Rest of Us," *New York Times*, August 22, 2013, http://www.nytimes.com/2013/08/25/travel/private-flying-for-some-of-the-rest-of-us.html (accessed March 24, 2016).

618 Amanda Terkel, "Eric Hovde, GOP Senate Candidate: Press Should Stop Writing Sob Stories about Poor People," *Huffington Post*, June 18, 2012, http://www.huffingtonpost.com/2012/06/18/eric-hovde-sob-stories-poor-people_n_1605343.html (accessed March 4, 2016).

619 Ibid.

620 Margaret Sullivan, "Too Little for So Many, Even in The Times," *New York Times*, June 1, 2013, http://www.nytimes.com/2013/06/02/public-editor/those-in-poverty-go-wanting-even-in-the-times.html (accessed March 24, 2016).

621 Jeremy Slevin, "Nightly Newscasts Have Virtually Ignored Poverty in 2016. Here's Why.," Talk Poverty, June 9, 2016, https://talkpoverty.org/2016/06/09/nightly-newscasts-virtually-ignored-poverty-2016-heres/ (accessed June 19, 2016).

622 Evgeny Morozov, The Net Delusion: The Dark Side of Internet Freedom, 4.

623 Ibid., 180, 186, 190, and 191.

624 Mike Elgan, "Software That Lies (So You Don't Have To!)," *Computerworld*, September 1, 2012, http://www.computerworld.com/article/2491931/social-media/software-that-lies—so-you-don-t-have-to—.html (accessed March 23, 2016).

Part II: "The Counseling Session"

STEP TWO: BREAKING GOOD

1   Franklin D. Roosevelt, "Annual Message to Congress," Speech, Washington, DC, January 4, 1935, American Presidency Project, http://www.presidency.ucsb.edu/ws/?pid=14890 (accessed March 25, 2016).

2   Rebecca Vallas, Melissa Boteach, Rachel West, and Jackie Odum, "Removing Barriers to Opportunity for Parents with Criminal Records and Their Children: A Two-Generation Approach," Center for American Progress, December 10, 2015, https://www.americanprogress.org/issues/criminal-justice/report/2015/12/10/126902/removing-barriers-to-opportunity-for-parents-with-criminal-records-and-their-children/ (accessed March 27, 2016).

3   "Connecticut's Second-Chance Society," Editorial, *New York Times*, January 4, 2016, http://www.nytimes.com/2016/01/04/opinion/connecticuts-second-chance-society.html (accessed January 4, 2016).

4   Michael Hiltzik, "Aiming to Bring Smart Guns to U.S. Market," *Los Angeles Times*, December 11, 2015, http://www.latimes.com/business/hiltzik/la-fi-hiltzik-20151213-column.html (accessed March 25, 2016).

5   Patricia Cohen, "What Could Raising Taxes on the 1% Do? Surprising Amounts," *New York Times*, October 16, 2015, http://www.nytimes.com/2015/10/17/business/putting-numbers-to-a-tax-increase-for-the-rich.html (accessed March 26, 2016).

6   Ibid.

7   Donald S. Shepard, Elizabeth Setren, and Donna Cooper, "Hunger in America: Suffering We All Pay For," Center for America Progress, October 2011, https://www.americanprogress.org/wp-content/uploads/issues/2011/10/pdf/hunger_paper.pdf (accessed March 26, 2016).

8   Author calculation for the cost of ending hunger in America. In 2014, according to the USDA, there were 48.135 million people who were food-insecure and they each spent an average of $12.50 per week less on food than non-hungry Americans. If you multiple 48.135 million by $12.50 by 52 (for the number of weeks in the year), the sum is $31.2 billion, the rough annual cost of ending US hunger.

9   Author calculation for the costs of the Service Patriots America plan. This plan assumes that the active duty military would stay about the same size as today and benefits would remain the same for them, thereby requiring no new costs. Additional spending would therefore be required only for the Peace Corps and AmeriCorps portions of this program. The annual Peace Corps budget is currently $418 million, costing about $65,000 per year for every participant, including a "readjustment" allowance of more than $8,000 (pre-tax) upon completion of service. About 6,800 people now serve in the Peace Corps. If each existing participant received an additional $20,000 post-service education award for each year of duty, the extra post-service awards for existing members would total $136 million. If the Peace Corps increased to 30,000 participants per year (an added 23,200 participants) and the cost for each member would be $85,000 per year ($65,000 for the position itself, plus $20,000 for a post-service award), it would equal $1.9 billion. Thus, the total cost of 6,800 additional post-service awards for existing Peace Corps members plus the total costs for 23,200 new Peace Corps volunteers with the new awards—for a new total of 30,000 members—would be roughly $2.1 billion. The annual AmeriCorps budget is currently $782 million, costing the federal government roughly $10,000 for every AmeriCorps member. (Each slot costs about $20,000 overall, but partner nonprofit organizations pick up the difference, which is why most AmeriCorps members work for very well-funded, large nonprofit groups.) To dramatically expand AmeriCorps, and ensure high-quality placements, the program would need to place more members at smaller, less-well-endowed grassroots nonprofit groups or at

local, state, or federal government agencies, which would likely require more federal money, perhaps $5,000 per slot—meaning the cost to the federal government (not including the additional post-service award), would increase to $15,000 per slot. If the current AmeriCorps education award, worth $5,730, were increased to a post-service award of $20,000, this would mean that each AmeriCorps slot would cost the federal government about $30,000 annually. Thus, the extra costs for the higher post-service awards would add an additional $1.5 billion to the existing AmeriCorps program. In order to add another 1.7 million new slots for AmeriCorps (including the higher post-service awards), an additional $51 billion would be needed. Coupled with the larger post-service awards for existing slots, the vastly expanded, 1.8 million-member AmeriCorps program would cost $53 billion. The combined costs of the expanded Peace Corps and expanded AmeriCorps—and thus the total costs for Service Patriots America—would be approximately $55 billion annually. Note that this calculation includes the current annual spending on Peace Corps and AmeriCorps members, but does not include current annual spending on active duty military

STEP THREE: WE THE VOTERS

10 "The 2016 Presidential Money Race," *Economist*, March 7, 2016, http://www.economist.com/blogs/graphicdetail/2016/03/daily-chart-1 (accessed June 21, 2016).

11 Christina A. Cassidy, "Campaign Cash in State Judicial Elections Grows," *Associated Press*, December 28, 2015, http://bigstory.ap.org/article/a8b9c2e0085f459d9f743d8bb375f2de/campaign-cash-state-judicial-elections-grows (accessed March 27, 2016).

12 "Lobbying Database," Center for Responsive Politics, https://www.opensecrets.org/lobby/ (accessed March 27, 2016).

13 "The Politics of Financial Insecurity: A Democratic Tilt, Undercut by Low Participation," Pew Research Center, January 8, 2015, http://www.people-press.org/2015/01/08/the-politics-of-financial-insecurity-a-democratic-tilt-undercut-by-low-participation/ (accessed March 22, 2016).

14 Richard W. Painter, "The Conservative Case for Campaign-Finance Reform," Opinion, *New York Times*, February 3, 2016, http://www.nytimes.com/2016/02/03/opinion/the-conservative-case-forcampaign-finance-reform.html?ref=opinion (accessed March 12, 2016).

15 Eric Black, "Why is Turnout So Low in U.S. Elections? We Make It More Difficult to Vote Than Other Democracies," *MinnPost*, October 1, 2014, https://www.minnpost.com/eric-black-ink/2014/10/why-turnout-so-low-us-elections-we-make-it-more-difficult-vote-other-democrac (accessed March 12, 2016).

STEP FOUR: MR. SMITH, MS. SANCHEZ, MISS PATEL, MS. JONES, AND MR. WANG GO TO WASHINGTON

16 Adam Nagourney, "Similarities Aside, Bernie Sanders isn't Rerunning Howard Dean's 2004 Race," *New York Times*, August 9, 2015, http://www.nytimes.com/2015/08/10/us/politics/similarities-aside-bernie-sanders-isnt-rerunning-howard-deans-2004-race.html?ref=politics (accessed March 13, 2016).

17 Hunter Schwarz, "A Lot of the Celebrities Who Appeared in the Midterm Rock the Vote PSA Didn't Actually Vote in the Last Midterm," *Washington Post*, November 2, 2014, https://www.washingtonpost.com/news/post-politics/wp/2014/11/02/a-lot-of-the-celebrities-who-appeared-in-the-midterm-rock-the-vote-psa-didnt-actually-vote-in-the-last-midterm/ (accessed March 25, 2016).

18 Robert D Putnam, *Bowling Alone: The Collapse and Revival of American Community* (New York: Simon and Schuster, 2000).

19   Robert Wuthnow, *Loose Connections: Joining Together in America's Fragmented Communities* (New York: Harvard University Press, 2002), 20.

STEP FIVE: IF CORPORATIONS ARE PEOPLE, MAKE THEM *GOOD* PEOPLE

20   "Most-Overpaid/Underpaid CEOs," *Bloomberg Markets*, May 30, 2013.
21   Harold Meyerson, "California's Bid to Tax CEOs Who Don't Share the Wealth," Opinion, *Washington Post*, April 30, 2014, https://www.washingtonpost.com/opinions/ harold-meyerson-californias-bid-to-tax-ceos-who-dont-share-the-wealth/2014/04/30/ fc08619c-d07e-11e3-a6b1-45c4dffb85a6_story.html (accessed March 27, 2016).
22   Robert B. Reich, "Raising Taxes on Corporations That Pay Their CEOs Royally and Treat Their Workers Like Serfs," *Robert Reich Blog*, April 21, 2014, http://robertreich.org/ post/83456610643 (accessed March 27, 2016).
23   "To Prevent Corporate 'Inversions,' the American Tax Code Needs to be Fixed," Editorial, *Washington Post*, November 24, 2015, https://www.washingtonpost.com/opinions/ to-prevent-corporate-inversions-the-american-tax-code-needs-to-be-fixed/2015/11/24/ 0c3a7b56-92c3-11e5-a2d6-f57908580b1f_story.html (accessed March 27, 2016).
24   Joseph R. Blasi, Richard B. Freeman, and Douglas L. Kruse, *The Citizen's Share: Putting Ownership Back into Democracy* (New Haven: Yale University Press, 2013).
25   Paul Davidson, "More Worker-Owned Businesses are Sprouting," *USA Today*, May 13, 2016, http://www.usatoday.com/story/money/2016/05/12/more-worker-owned-businesses-sprouting/84245844/ (accessed June 21, 2016).

STEP SIX: WE ARE THE WORLD

26   Martin Luther King, Jr., "Domestic Impact of the War," Speech, National Labor Leadership Assembly for Peace, November 1967, http://www.aavw.org/special_features/speeches_ speech_king03.html (accessed March 26, 2016).
27   Thomas Piketty, *Capital in the Twenty-First Century*, 471 and 515.
28   Jeff Goodell, "John Kerry on Climate Change: The Fight of Our Time," *Rolling Stone*, December 1, 2015, http://www.rollingstone.com/politics/news/john-kerry-on-climate-change-the-fight-of-our-time-20151201 (accessed March 26, 2016).

STEP SEVEN: FROM THE MIDDLE OUT

29   Josh Barro, "What is 'Middle-Class Economics?'" *New York Times*, February 26, 2015, http:// www.nytimes.com/2015/02/26/upshot/what-is-middle-class-economics.html (accessed March 27, 2016).
30   Joseph E. Stiglitz, *The Price of Inequality: How Today's Divided Society Endangers Our Future*, [page numbers?].
31   Chico Harlan, "The 25-Cent Raise: What Life is Like After a Minimum Wage Increase," *Washington Post*, February 17, 2015, https://www.washingtonpost.com/news/wonk/ wp/2015/02/17/the-25-cent-raise-what-life-is-like-after-a-minimum-wage-increase/ (accessed March 6, 2016).
32   David Cooper, "How We Can Save $17 billion in Public Assistance—Annually," *Talk Poverty*, February 18, 2016, https://talkpoverty.org/2016/02/18/can-save-17-billion-public-assistance-annually-minimum-wage/ (accessed February 26, 2016). See also, David Cooper, "Raising the Minimum Wage to $12 by 2020 Would Lift Wages for 35 Million American Workers," Briefing Paper #405, Economic Policy Institute, July 14, 2015, http://www.epi.org/

publication/raising-the-minimum-wage-to-12-by-2020-would-lift-wages-for-35-million-american-workers/ (accessed March 26, 2016).

33   Kaitlin DeWulf, "Clinton Says Most Minimum-Wage Workers are Women," PolitiFact, November 13, 2015, http://www.politifact.com/iowa/statements/2015/nov/13/hillary-clinton/clinton-says-most-minimum-wage-workers-are-women/ (accessed June 23, 2016).

34   Franklin D. Roosevelt, "Address before the American Retail Federation," Speech, Washington, DC, May 22, 1939, American Presidency Project, http://www.presidency.ucsb.edu/ws/?pid=15763 (accessed March 29, 2016).

35   "The Need for Paid Family Leave," Fact sheet, *A Better Balance*, http://www.abetterbalance.org/web/images/stories/Documents/familyleave/fact_sheets/At_a_Glance_FAMILYAct.pdf (accessed February 14, 2016).

36   Mehrsa Baradaran, "If the U.S. Government Treated Poor People as Well as It Treats Banks," *Atlantic*, October 15, 2015, http://www.theatlantic.com/business/archive/2015/10/if-the-us-government-treated-poor-people-as-well-as-it-treats-banks/410614/ (accessed March 26, 2016).

37   Jared Bernstein, "A Final Fiscal Reflection on 2015," *Washington Post*, December 31, 2015, https://www.washingtonpost.com/posteverything/wp/2015/12/31/a-final-fiscal-reflection-on-2015/ (accessed January 3, 2016).

38   Robert Reich, "The Rise of the Non-Working Rich," *Huffington Post*, July 15, 2014, updated September 14, 2014, http://www.huffingtonpost.com/robert-reich/the-rise-of-the-non-working-rich_b_5589684.html (accessed March 4, 2016).

39   Joseph E. Stiglitz, *The Price of Inequality: How Today's Divided Society Endangers Our Future*, 269–270.

40   Associated Press, "Robots Replacing Human Factory Workers at Faster Pace," *Los Angeles Times*, February 10, 2015, http://www.latimes.com/business/la-fi-robots-jobs-20150211-story.html (accessed March 29, 2016).

41   Derek Thompson, "A World Without Work," *Atlantic*, July/August 2015, http://www.theatlantic.com/magazine/archive/2015/07/world-without-work/395294/ (accessed June 30, 2016).

42   Jason Furman, Sandra Black, and Jay Shambaugh, "The 2016 Economic Report of the President," White House, February 22, 2016, https://www.whitehouse.gov/blog/2016/02/22/2016-economic-report-president (accessed February 22, 2016).

43   Derek Thompson, "A World Without Work."

44   Farhad Manjoo, "A Plan in Case Robots Take the Jobs: Give Everyone a Paycheck," *New York Times*, March 2, 2016, http://www.nytimes.com/2016/03/03/technology/plan-to-fight-robot-invasion-at-work-give-everyone-a-paycheck.html?ref=business (accessed March 3, 2016).

45   Angela Hanks and Ethan Gurwitz, "How States are Expanding Apprenticeship," Center for American Progress, February 9, 2016, https://www.americanprogress.org/issues/labor/report/2016/02/09/130750/how-states-are-expanding-apprenticeship/ (accessed February 26, 2016).

STEP EIGHT: HOW TO OVERCOME DEPRESSION WITH FEATHERS

46   Robert L. Woodson, Sr., "Transcending the Poverty Industry," *American Interest*, 8, no. 1 (2012), http://www.the-american-interest.com/2012/08/10/transcending-the-poverty-industry/ (accessed June 30, 2016).

47   Mariana Chilton, interview with the editor of *DrexelNow*, "What I'm Reading: Mariana Chilton," *DrexelNow*, October 11, 2012, http://drexel.edu/now/archive/2012/October/What-Im-Reading-Mariana-Chilton/ (accessed June 30, 2016).

48   Richard Fry and Rakesh Kochhar, "America's Wealth Gap between Middle-Income and Upper-Income Families is Widest on Record," Pew Research Center, December 17, 2014,

http://www.pewresearch.org/fact-tank/2014/12/17/wealth-gap-upper-middle-income/ (accessed June 30, 2016).

49 *American Community Survey*, US Census Bureau, 2011.

50 Laura Sullivan, et al., "The Racial Wealth Gap: Why Policy Matters," Demos and the Institute on Assets and Social Policy at Brandeis University, 2015, http://www.demos.org/sites/default/files/publications/RacialWealthGap_1.pdf (accessed March 26, 2016).

51 James Poterba and Todd Sinai, "Tax Expenditures for Owner-Occupied Housing: Deductions for Property Taxes and Mortgage Interest and the Exclusion of Imputed Rental Income," http://realestate.wharton.upenn.edu/research/papers/full/611.pdf (accessed June 30, 2016).

STEP ELEVEN: WE STILL CAN OVERCOME

52 Go here to check out Access NYC: https://a069-access.nyc.gov.

53 Marc Solomon, "How We Won Marriage: 10 Lessons Learned," *Huffington Post*, June 26, 2015, http://www.huffingtonpost.com/marc-solomon/how-we-won-marriage-10-lessons-learned_b_7666660.html (accessed December 26, 2015).

54 Steven Greenhouse, "The Fight for $15.37 an Hour. How a Coalition Pushed for a Hotel Workers' Minimum Wage.," *New York Times*, November 22, 2014, http://www.nytimes.com/2014/11/23/business/how-a-coalition-pushed-for-a-hotel-workers-minimum-wage.html (accessed March 29, 2016).

55 Richard Kirsch, *Fighting for Our Health: The Epic Battle to Make Health Care a Right in the United States* (Albany: Rockefeller Institute Press, 2011), 358.

56 Martin Luther King, Jr., "The Last Steep Ascent," *Nation*, March 14, 1966, http://www.thenation.com/article/last-steep-ascent/ (accessed March 27, 2016).

STEP TWELVE: THE ACTIVIST PATRIOT

57 I.F. Stone, "For the Jews—Life or Death?" *Nation*, June 10, 1944, http://www.thenation.com/article/jews-life-or-death-2/ (accessed March 27, 2016).

58 Michelle Obama, "Remarks by the First Lady at Tuskegee University Commencement Address," Speech, March 9, 2015, https://www.whitehouse.gov/the-press-office/2015/05/09/remarks-first-lady-tuskegee-university-commencement-address (accessed March 29, 2016).

Index

ABOUT THE AUTHOR

Labeled "Mister Frowny Pants" by *The Daily Show with Jon Stewart* (on which he once appeared), Joel Berg is the CEO of Hunger Free America, which the *Nation* called "one of the leading direct service and advocacy organizations on hunger and poverty in the nation."

Berg wrote the decade's definitive book on US hunger, *All You Can Eat: How Hungry Is America?* (Seven Stories Press, 2008). *Playboy* (which Berg reads only for the reviews) called the book "refreshing" for its "optimism . . . rationality and passion." Berg has also published numerous op-eds, poems, and policy papers and was a Senior Fellow at the Center for American Progress and a Policy Analyst at the Progressive Policy Institute, two DC-based think tanks.

Berg has delivered hundreds of keynote speeches on four continents and in thirty-seven states, from Maine to Alaska, while surviving moose attacks and volcanic eruptions. One audience member wrote, "Seeing Joel Berg speak in person is like watching the History Channel, C-Span, and Comedy Central all at once."

Noted by *City Limits* magazine for his "trademark good-natured snarkiness," Berg has been covered extensively by national and international media, appearing on *Hardball with Chris Matthews*, Fox News, CNN, National Public Radio, *The Kudlow Report*, *All In with Chris Hayes*, and the *NBC Evening News*, and quoted by the *New York Times*, the *Wall Street Journal*, the *Washington Post*, and tons of obscure blogs. Berg has also been featured in three documentary films.

Prior to joining Hunger Free America, Berg worked for eight years in senior executive service positions in Bill Clinton's presidential administration, served on the Clinton/Gore Presidential Transition Team, and staffed the 1992 Bill Clinton for President campaign. While working for 13 years as a political campaign professional, Berg lived in Kansas, Alaska, New Jersey, Maine, Arkansas, and New York.

He now resides in Brooklyn, New York but has yet to overdose on local, artisanal kale chips.